finance 2e

Marcia Millon Cornett
Bentley University

Troy A. Adair, Jr.
Berkeley College

John Nofsinger
Washington State University

McGraw-Hill
Irwin

McGraw-Hill
Irwin

finance

SENIOR VICE PRESIDENT, PRODUCTS & MARKETS: **KURT L. STRAND**

VICE PRESIDENT, CONTENT PRODUCTION & TECHNOLOGY SERVICES: **KIMBERLY MERIWETHER DAVID**

MANAGING DIRECTOR: **DOUGLAS REINER**

EXECUTIVE BRAND MANAGER: **MICHELE JANICEK**

EXECUTIVE BRAND MANAGER: **CHUCK SYNOVEC**

EXECUTIVE DIRECTOR OF DEVELOPMENT: **ANN TORBERT**

DEVELOPMENT EDITOR: **NOELLE BATHURST**

EXECUTIVE MARKETING MANAGER: **MELISSA CAUGHLIN**

DIRECTOR OF DIGITAL CONTENT: **DOUG RUBY**

DIGITAL DEVELOPMENT EDITOR: **MEG M. MALONEY**

LEAD PROJECT MANAGER: **CHRISTINE A. VAUGHAN**

SENIOR BUYER: **CAROL BIELSKI**

SENIOR DESIGNER: **MATT DIAMOND**

COVER/INTERIOR DESIGNER: **© GETTY IMAGES**

CONTENT LICENSING SPECIALIST: **JOANNE MENNEMEIER**

LEAD MEDIA PROJECT MANAGER: **DARRYL HORROCKS**

TYPEFACE: **10/12 MINION PRO REGULAR**

COMPOSITOR: **LASERWORDS PRIVATE LIMITED**

PRINTER: **QUAD/GRAPHICS DUBUQUE**

M: FINANCE, SECOND EDITION

Published by McGraw-Hill/Irwin, a business unit of The McGraw-Hill Companies, Inc., 1221 Avenue of the Americas, New York, NY, 10020. Copyright © 2014 by The McGraw-Hill Companies, Inc. All rights reserved. Printed in the United States of America. Previous edition © 2012. No part of this publication may be reproduced or distributed in any form or by any means, or stored in a database or retrieval system, without the prior written consent of The McGraw-Hill Companies, Inc., including, but not limited to, in any network or other electronic storage or transmission, or broadcast for distance learning.

Some ancillaries, including electronic and print components, may not be available to customers outside the United States.

This book is printed on acid-free paper.

1 2 3 4 5 6 7 8 9 0 QDB/QDB 1 0 9 8 7 6 5 4 3 2

ISBN 978-0-07-803481-7
MHID 0-07-803481-7

All credits appearing on page or at the end of the book are considered to be an extension of the copyright page.

Library of Congress Control Number: 2012946886

The Internet addresses listed in the text were accurate at the time of publication. The inclusion of a website does not indicate an endorsement by the authors or McGraw-Hill, and McGraw-Hill does not guarantee the accuracy of the information presented at these sites.

www.mhhe.com

Guided Examples

4/(1-.31)
        5.797101449

Imagine a time when you have a high income, placing you in the 31 percent marginal tax bracket. You are interested in investing some money in a bond issue and have three alternatives. The first is a corporate bond with a 6.4 percent yield to maturity. The second bond is a Treasury that offers a 5.7 percent yield. The third choice is a municipal bond priced at a yield to maturity of 4.0 percent. Which bond gives you the highest after-tax yield?

Guided Examples provide students with narrated and animated video tutorials and step-by-step walkthroughs of exercises and examples from the text. Students appreciate the Guided Examples because they can learn to solve a problem when they get stuck doing their homework. There are multiple tutorials for each example, including a tutorial with decision points and walkthroughs using different calculators and Excel.

Detailed Feedback

Connect Finance helps students learn by providing complete step-by-step solutions for every problem, and instructors decide when students receive the solutions. These solutions can then be accessed before an exam so students can use them as study tools for their tests.

Explanation:

Step 1: Capital intensity ratio = 2.10 = Total assets / $8.8m => Total assets = 2.1 × $8.8m = $18.48m and Total liabilities and equity = $18.48m

Step 2: Debt ratio = 0.55 = Total debt / $18.48m => Total debt = 0.55 × $18.48m = $10.164m

Step 3: Total equity = $18.48m – $10.164m = $8.316m

Step 4: Fixed asset turnover = 1.2 = $8.8m / Fixed assets => Fixed assets = $8.8m / 1.2 = $7.333m

Step 5: Current assets = $18.48m – $7.333m = $11.147m

Get Engaged.

eBooks

Connect Plus includes a media rich eBook that allows you to share your notes with your students. Your students can insert and review their own notes, highlight the text, search for specific information, and interact with media resources. Using an eBook with *Connect Plus* gives your students a complete digital solution that allows them to access their materials from any computer.

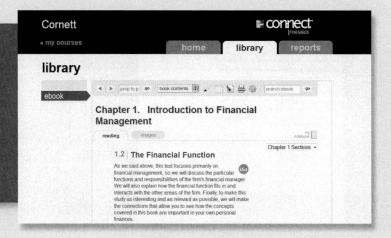

End-of-Chapter and Test Bank Content

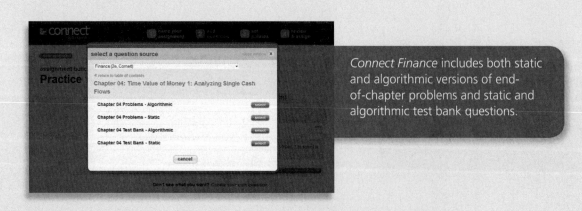

Connect Finance includes both static and algorithmic versions of end-of-chapter problems and static and algorithmic test bank questions.

brief
contents

contents

changes in the
second edition

Based on feedback from users and reviewers, we undertook an ambitious revision in order to make the book follow your teaching strategy even more closely. Below are the changes we made for this second edition, broken out by chapter.

OVERALL

- Simplified figures where appropriate and added captions to emphasize the main "takeaways"
- Updated all data, company names, and scenarios to reflect latest available data and real-world changes
- Added "word" forms of selected formulas before the "number" form to provide an intuitive bridge for a variety of learning styles
- Cross-referenced numbered examples with similar end-of-chapter problems so students can easily model their homework
- Updated the numbers in more than half the end-of-chapter problems to provide variety and limit the transfer of answers from previous classes

chapter one
INTRODUCTION TO FINANCIAL MANAGEMENT

- Revised figures—simplified text within the graphs and collected the figures in sequential order to better illustrate series relationships
- Added captions to graphs/figures to discuss the inputs and highlights
- Added an explicit distinction between finance and accounting as disciplines in the section "What Is Finance?"
- Added a section that deals with the financial crisis and how the events of the crisis pertain to students

chapter two
REVIEWING FINANCIAL STATEMENTS

- Added "other operating expenses" as an income statement item
- Added "net working capital" as a formula

- Added discussion of MACRS versus straight-line depreciation
- Reworked statement of cash flows section to separate GAAP accounting principles and noncash income statement entries
- Revised and updated free cash flow equation and discussion

chapter three
ANALYZING FINANCIAL STATEMENTS

- Placed the discussion of each ratio immediately after the ratio
- Used numbered ratios in examples, with the industry ratio placed alongside each ratio
- Added "other operating expenses" as an income statement item

chapter four
TIME VALUE OF MONEY 1: ANALYZING SINGLE CASH FLOWS

- Expanded the introductory discussion to highlight the relevance of the topic to individual students
- Expanded Example 4.1 to include more explanation
- Included new TVM "Caveat Emptor" box
- Added a new Math Coach box for spreadsheet TVM functions

chapter five
TIME VALUE OF MONEY 2: ANALYZING ANNUITY CASH FLOWS

- Updated the Finance at Work box on retirement to include recent trends
- Added a new Math Coach box on the cash flow registers in the TVM calculator
- Added a new Math Coach to cover annuity computations in spreadsheets
- Added a discussion and end-of-chapter problems about add-on interest

chapter six
(previously chapter 8)
UNDERSTANDING FINANCIAL MARKETS AND INSTITUTIONS

- Moved from Chapter 8 to precede the discussion of stocks and bonds
- Examines how changes in the way financial institutions deliver services played a major part in the events leading up to the severe financial crisis starting in 2008
- Added an online appendix that provides a more detailed discussion of the financial crisis
- Expanded on the previous discussion of a private placement
- Included a discussion of the role of mortgage and derivative securities markets in the financial crisis
- Added a discussion of commercial banks' shift from a risk measurement and management role to an originate and distribute role in financial markets
- Added a discussion of the Federal Reserve's efforts to address the severe financial crisis
- Added a Finance at Work box that discusses the Fed's actions during the crisis

chapter seven
(previously chapter 6)
VALUING BONDS

- Updated to include all real data, companies, and scenarios in the body of the chapter, figures, and tables
- Defined indenture as a new key term
- Added a Math Coach as a reminder on decimal point conversion
- Added mortgage-backed securities discussion and a new Financial Crisis box

chapter eight
(previously chapter 7)
VALUING STOCKS

- Updated to include all real data, companies, and scenarios in the body of the chapter, figures, and tables

- Updated NYSE merger status to reflect its current situation
- Added a discussion on the effects of the financial crisis
- Updated the investor psychology box
- Added additional constant growth rate model analysis

chapter nine
CHARACTERIZING RISK AND RETURN

- Added geometric mean return as a key concept and a key term
- Discussed emotionally based decisions during stock market plunges
- Expanded discussion of portfolio domination
- Expanded diversification discussion to include international markets

chapter ten
ESTIMATING RISK AND RETURN

- Revised introduction to add clarity
- Added a Finance at Work box on "Risk: Theory and Behavior"
- Added behavioral finance concept of overconfidence and highlighted it as a key term

chapter eleven
CALCULATING THE COST OF CAPITAL

- Revised explanation of WACC to add more intuition concerning the explicit meaning of the weights
- Enhanced figure captions and revised figure flow to better explain divisional WACC

chapter twelve
ESTIMATING CASH FLOWS ON CAPITAL BUDGETING PROJECTS

- Enhanced introduction to the topic of pro forma statement analysis to better explain the goal of the chapter
- Simplified discussion of opportunity costs, sunk costs, substitutionary and complementary effects
- Expanded discussion of tax effects of negative EBIT
- Expanded and simplified discussion of inclusion of changes in NWC

chapter thirteen
WEIGHING NET PRESENT VALUE AND OTHER CAPITAL BUDGETING CRITERIA

- Added introductory table comparing and contrasting relevant attributes of all capital budgeting techniques covered in the chapter
- Refined discussion concerning the manager's choice of decision statistic format
- Moved discussion of payback and discounted payback to precede that of NPV to begin discussing capital budgeting techniques with those intuitively easiest to understand
- Added enhanced explanation of relationship between NPV and IRR

- Refined explanation of the superiority of NPV's implicit assumption concerning reinvestment rate
- Enhanced discussion flow of decision processes for choosing between mutually exclusive projects

chapter fourteen
WORKING CAPITAL MANAGEMENT AND POLICIES

- Revised captions and diagrams to simplify discussion of short-term financial policy

finance 2e

introduction to
financial management

chapter one

D o you know: What finance entails? How financial management functions within the business world? Why you might benefit from studying financial principles? This chapter is the ideal place to get answers to those questions. **Finance** is the study of *applying specific value* to things we own, services we use, and decisions we make. Examples are as varied as shares of stock in a company, payments on a home mortgage, the purchase of an entire firm, and the personal decision to retire early. In this text, we focus primarily on one area of finance, financial management, which concentrates on valuing things from the perspective of a company, or firm.

Financial management is critically important to the success of any business organization, and throughout the text we concentrate on describing the key financial concepts in corporate finance. As a bonus, you will find that many tools and techniques for handling the financial management of a firm also apply to broader types of financial problems, such as personal finance decisions.

In finance, *cash flow* is the term that describes the process of paying and receiving money. It makes sense to start our discussion of finance with an illustration of various financial cash flows. We use simple graphics to help explain the nature of finance and to demonstrate the different *subareas* of the field of finance.

After we have an overall picture of finance, we will discuss four important

continued on p. 4

LEARNING GOALS

LG1-1 Define the major areas of finance as they apply to corporate financial management.

LG1-2 Show how finance is at the heart of sound business decisions.

LG1-3 Learn the financial principles that govern your personal decisions.

LG1-4 Examine the three most common forms of business organization in the United States today.

LG1-5 Distinguish among appropriate and inappropriate goals for financial managers.

LG1-6 Identify a firm's primary agency relationship and discuss the possible conflicts that may arise.

LG1-7 Discuss how ethical decision making is part of the study of financial management.

LG1-8 Describe the complex, necessary relationships among firms, financial institutions, and financial markets.

LG1-9 Explain the fundamental causes of the financial crisis that started in 2006.

continued from p. 3

variables in the business environment that can and do have significant impact on the firm's financial decisions. These are (1) the organizational form of the business, (2) the agency relationship between the managers and owners of a firm, (3) ethical considerations as finance is applied in the real world, and (4) the source and implications of the current financial crisis. ■

FINANCE IN BUSINESS AND IN LIFE LG1-1

As you begin this course, what is your first impression of the world of finance? No doubt you've experienced the current economic recession firsthand and read, perhaps in detail, about the financial crisis that peaked in the fall of 2008. An understanding of cause, effect, and future impact will be important as we go forward, so please see the nearby Finance at Work reading and the last section of this chapter for brief background information and some analyses to set the stage for more complete explanations to come. But setting aside thoughts of recession and indulging in a quick look at popular culture, you'll recognize that other influences have been at work for some time. Your opinions already may have been negatively skewed by entertainment. Many movies have portrayed finance professionals as greedy and unethical (see, for example, *Wall Street,* 1987; *Barbarians at the Gate,* 1993; *Boiler Room,* 2000; and *Wall Street: Money Never Sleeps,* 2010). While colorful characters make for good entertainment, fictional depictions do not reflect reality when it comes to what finance professionals actually do and how they contribute to society. The more you study managerial finance, the more you'll appreciate this discipline's broad potential to power the managerial decision making that moves our economy forward.

And what exactly makes up this engine of financial decision making? Successful application of *financial theories* helps money flow from individuals who want to improve their financial future to businesses that want to expand the scale or scope of their operations. These exchanges lead to a growing economy and more employment opportunities for people at all income levels. So, two important things result from this simple exchange: the economy will be more productive as a result, and individuals' wealth will grow into the future.

In this first section, we develop a comprehensive description of finance and its subareas, and we look at the specific decisions that professionals in each subarea must

Caleb has worked very hard to create and expand his juice stand at the mall. He has finally perfected his products and feels that he is offering the right combination of juice and food. As a result, the stand is making a nice profit. Caleb would like to open more stands at malls all over his state and eventually all over the country.

Caleb knows he needs more money to expand. He needs money to buy more equipment, buy more inventory, and hire and train more people. How can Caleb get the capital he needs to expand?

make. As you will see, all areas of finance share a common set of ideas and application tools.

What is Finance?

To get the clearest possible picture of how finance works, let's begin by grouping all of an economy's participants along two dimensions. The first dimension is made up of those who may have "extra" money (i.e., money above and beyond their current spending needs) for investment. The second dimension is made up of those who have an ability to develop viable business ideas, a sense of business creativity. Both money and ideas are fuel for the financial engine. In our simple model, these two dimensions result in four groups representing economic roles in society, as shown in Figure 1.1. Of course, people can move from one group to another over time.

Type 1 people in our model do not lend significant sums of money (*capital*) or spend much money in a business context, so they play no direct role in **financial markets,** the mechanisms by which capital is exchanged. Although these people probably play indirect roles by providing labor to economic

▼FIGURE 1.1 Participants in Our Hypothetical Economy

	No Extra Money	Extra Money
No Economically Viable Business Ideas	Type 1: No money and no ideas	Type 2: Money, but no ideas
Economically Viable Business Ideas	Type 3: No money, but ideas	Type 4: Both money and ideas

Four groups form according to the availability of money and ideas.

enterprises or by consuming their products, for simplicity we focus on those who play direct roles. Therefore, type 1 participants will be asked to step aside.

Type 4 people use financial tools to evaluate their own business concepts and then choose the ideas with the most potential. From there, they create their own enterprises to implement their best ideas efficiently and effectively. Type 4 individuals, however, are self-funded and do not need financial markets. The financial tools they use and the types of decisions they make are narrowly focused or specific to their own purposes. For our discussion, then, type 4 individuals also are asked to move to the sidelines.

Now for our financial role players, the type 2 and type 3 people. Financial markets and financial institutions allow these people to participate in a mutually advantageous exchange. Type 2 people temporarily lend their money to type 3 people, who put that money to use with their good business ideas.

In most developed economies, type 2 participants are usually individual **investors.** *You* will likely be an individual investor for most of your life. Each of us separately may not have a lot of extra money at any one time, but by aggregating our available funds, we can provide sizable amounts for investment.

Type 3 participants, the idea generators, may be individuals, but they are more commonly corporations or other types of companies with research and development (R&D) departments dedicated to developing innovative ideas. It's easy to see that investors and companies can help one another. If investors lend their "extra" capital to companies, as shown in Figure 1.2, then companies can use this capital to fund expansion projects.

Economically successful projects will eventually be able to repay the money (plus profit) to investors, as Figure 1.3 shows.

Of course, not all of the cash will return to the investors. In reality, sources of friction arise in this system, and the amount of capital returned to investors is reduced. Two primary sources of friction are **retained earnings,** which are basically funds the firm keeps for its ongoing operations, and *taxes,* which the government imposes on the company and individuals to help fund public services. Figure 1.4 shows an analysis of cash flows with the associated retained earnings and tax payments. In a very simple way, this figure provides an intuitive overall explanation of finance and of its major subareas. For example, individuals must

finance The study of applying specific value to things we own, services we use, and decisions we make.

financial markets The places and processes that facilitate the trading of financial assets between investors.

investors Those who buy securities or other assets in hopes of earning a return and getting more money back in the future.

retained earnings The portion of company profits that are kept by the company rather than distributed to the stockholders as cash dividends.

▼**FIGURE 1.2** Capital Flow from Investors to Companies

Investors are people or groups who need ideas to make more money, and companies are groups who need money to develop the ideas they do have.

▼**FIGURE 1.3** Return of Capital to Investors

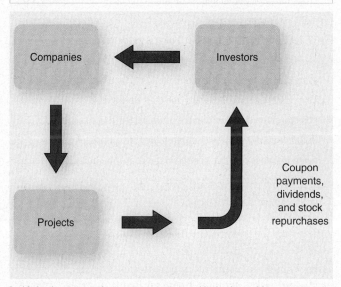

In this basic process, the company can expand its business, hire more employees, and create a promising future for its own growth. Meanwhile, the investor can increase wealth for the future.

finance at work //: markets

At the time of this writing, the world economy has been reeling for over four years from the effects of the worst financial crisis since the Great Depression of the 1930s. By mid-March 2009, the Dow Jones Industrial Average (DJIA) had fallen in value 53.8 percent in less than 1½ years' time, larger than the decline during the market crash of 1937–1938 when it fell 49 percent. Though the Dow has since recovered much of those losses, the markets continue to be very volatile and unsettled: on May 6, 2010, just after 2:30 pm EST, the Dow plunged by 998.50 points, a loss of 9.2 percent and the biggest one-day fall ever.

The commonly accepted cause of the crisis was the collapse of U.S. home prices in late 2006 and early 2007, but the problem has since spread to affect every part of the economy: The investment banking industry saw the failure or acquisition of all but two of its major firms (Goldman Sachs and Morgan Stanley), and these two firms converted to commercial bank holding companies (i.e., banks much like your neighborhood bank that tend to be safer and less profitable than investment banks). AIG, one of the largest insurance companies in the United States, survived only because of a federal government bailout. Commercial banking giant Citigroup required a massive government guarantee against losses and an injection of cash to prevent failure. The crisis spread internationally too. Real estate markets fell in many countries across the world. The crisis had a profound impact on the financial health of banks, especially in Europe. In 2010, the unemployment rate had risen to over 10 percent. By 2012, it was still over 8 percent.

The exact mechanisms by which falling home prices led to such dramatic changes in the economic landscape are complicated and have yet to be covered in this book, so we will delay an in-depth discussion of the crisis until later, but we did feel that this is a good place to touch upon the ways that the fallout from the financial crisis are going to affect you, the student, in the years and decades to come.

First, those of you who hoped to fund your education with student loans may be finding it difficult to obtain such loans, especially at favorable rates. If so, thank the financial crisis: Lenders are much more leery about lending money due to the uncertain economic future they (and you, in your hopeful future employment) face. (And we won't even get into the whole idea of your parents taking out a home equity loan to help you through . . .)

Second, as you've no doubt noticed, jobs are scarce, primarily due to companies' uncertainty about the future. We expect it to stay this way for a while, though the impending retirement of the baby boomers will eventually benefit you.

Third, once you do make it through school and start your career, you may want to hold off on buying a home for a while. Most of the reasons are probably obvious, but compounding the uncertainty about being able to eventually unload any house you buy is the fact that lenders have greatly cut back on the availability of credit, asking for substantial down payments and loan servicing fees when they *do* lend.

By now, you're probably starting to wonder if you missed the part about Eeyore (the gloomy donkey in the Winnie-the-Pooh books) being one of the coauthors of this book. Don't despair: The current financial crisis *does* have potential silver linings to offer to those who are prepared and educated enough to take advantage of them.

After the extent of the crisis had started to become evident to everyone, one of the authors of this book was asked by a television reporter, "Why would anyone want to study finance *now?!?!*" Well, on the one hand, and in the words of the Spanish-born American philosopher and poet George Santayana, "Those who do not learn from history are doomed to repeat it." You *really* don't want to go through this type of thing again, do you?

Another reason to study finance is that some of those silver linings we referred to are beginning to peek through the clouds: for example, in the aftermath of the crisis, more firms in general (and financial institutions in particular) are much more focused on the concepts of measuring and managing risks than ever before, and to effectively do so they need a trained and informed workforce.

Want to know more?

Key Words to Search for Updates: **housing bubble, subprime lending, mortgage-backed securities, AIG, Countrywide Financial**

---

assess which investment opportunities are right for their needs and risk tolerance; financial institutions and markets must efficiently distribute the capital; and companies must evaluate their potential projects and wisely decide which projects to fund, what kind of capital to use, and how much capital to return to investors. All of these types of decisions deal with the basic cash flows of finance shown in Figure 1.4, but from different perspectives.

▼**FIGURE 1.4** The Complete Cash Flows of Finance

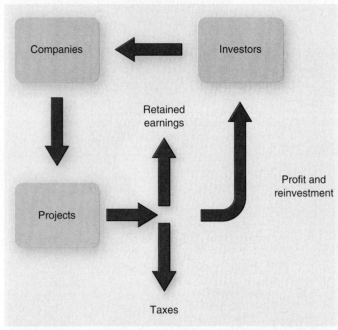

All the subareas of the financial system interact, with retained earnings and taxes playing a role in the flows.

Subareas of Finance

Investments is the subarea of finance that involves methods and techniques for making decisions about what kinds of *securities* to own (e.g., bonds or stocks), which firms' securities to buy, and how to pay the investor back in the form that the investor wishes (e.g., the timing and certainty of the promised

cash flows). Figure 1.5 models cash flows from the investor's perspective. The concerns of the investments subarea of finance are shown (with the movement of red arrows) from the investor's viewpoint (seen as the blue box).

Financial management is the subarea that deals with a firm's decisions in acquiring and using the cash that is received from investors or from retained earnings. Figure 1.6 depicts the financial management process very simply. As we know, this text focuses primarily on financial management. We'll see that this critical area of finance involves decisions about:

- How to organize the firm in a manner that will attract capital.
- How to raise capital (e.g., bonds versus stocks).
- Which projects to fund.
- How much capital to retain for ongoing operations and new projects.
- How to minimize taxation.
- How to pay back capital providers.

All of these decisions are quite involved, and we will discuss them throughout later chapters.

Financial institutions and markets make up another major subarea of finance. These two dynamic entities work in different ways to facilitate capital flows between investors and companies. Figure 1.7 illustrates the process in which the firm acquires capital and investors take part in ongoing securities

investment The analysis and process of choosing securities and other assets to purchase.

financial management The process for and the analysis of making financial decisions in the business context.

▼**FIGURE 1.5** Investments

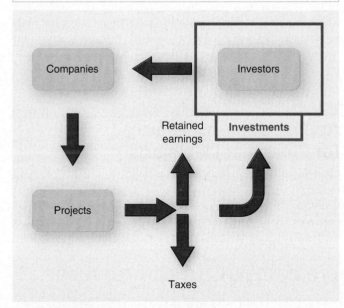

Investors mark the start and end of the financial process; they put money in and reap the rewards (or take the risk).

▼**FIGURE 1.6** Financial Management

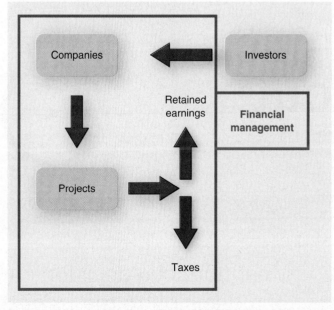

Financial managers make decisions that should benefit both the company and the investor.

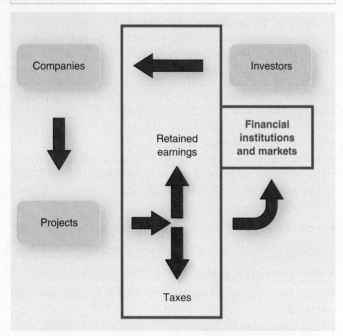

Financial institutions and markets facilitate the flows of money between investors and companies.

trading to increase that capital. Financial institutions, such as banks and pension administrators, are vital players that contribute to the dynamics of interest rates.

International finance is the final major subarea of finance we will study. As the world has transformed into a global economy, finance has had to become much more innovative and sensitive to changes in other countries. Investors, companies,

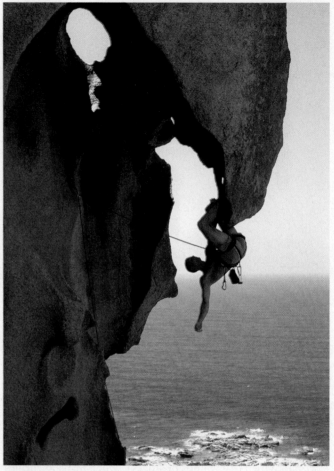

Risk tolerance varies among individuals.

business operations, and capital markets may all be located in different countries. Adapting to this environment requires understanding of international dynamics, as Figure 1.8 shows. In the past, international financial decisions were considered to be a straightforward application of the other three financial subareas. But experience has shown that the uncertainty about future exchange rates, political risk, and changing business laws across the globe adds enough complexity to these decisions to classify international finance as a subarea of finance in its own right.

Application and Theory for Financial Decisions

Cash flows are neither instantaneous nor guaranteed. We need to keep this in mind as we begin to apply finance theory to real decisions. Future cash flows are uncertain in terms of both timing and size, and we refer to this uncertainty as **risk.** Investors

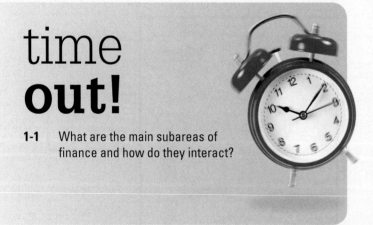

time out!

1-1 What are the main subareas of finance and how do they interact?

"Most financial decisions involve comparing the rewards of a decision to the risks that decision may generate."

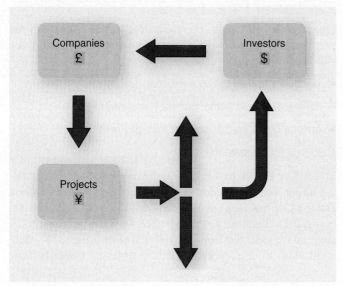

Laws, risks, and business relationships are variable across different countries, but can interact profitably.

experience risk about the return of their capital. Companies experience risk in funding and operating their business projects. Most financial decisions involve comparing the rewards of a decision to the risks that decision may generate.

Comparing rewards with risks frequently involves assessing the value today of cash flows that we expect to receive in the future. For example, the price of a **financial asset,** something worth money, such as a stock or a bond, should depend on the cash flows you expect to receive from that asset in the future. A stock that's expected to deliver high cash flows in the future will be more valuable today than a stock with low expected future cash flows. Of course, investors would like to buy stocks whose market prices are currently lower than their actual values. They want to get stocks on sale! Similarly, a firm's goal is to fund projects that will give them more value than their costs.

Despite the large number of stories about investors who've struck it rich in the stock market, it's actually more likely that a firm will find "bargain" projects, projects that may yield profit for a reasonable investment, than investors will find under-priced stocks. Firms can find bargains because business projects involve **real assets** trading in **real markets** (markets in tangible assets). In the real environment, some level of monopoly power, special knowledge, and expertise possibly can make such projects worth more than they cost. Investors, however, are trading financial assets in financial markets, where the assets are more likely to be worth, on average, exactly what they cost.

The method for relating expected or future cash flows to today's value, called *present value,* is known as **time value of money (TVM).** Chapters 4 and 5 cover this critical financial concept in detail and apply it to the financial world (as well as daily life). Since the expected cash flows of either a business

project or an investment are likely to be uncertain, any TVM analysis must account for both the timing and the risk level of the cash flows.

Finance versus Accounting

In most companies, the financial function is usually closely associated with the accounting function. In a very rough sense, the accountant's job is to keep track of what happened *in the past* to the firm's money, while the finance job uses these historical figures with current information to determine what should happen *now and in the future* with the firm's money. The results of financial decisions will eventually appear in accounting statements, so this close association makes sense. Nevertheless, accounting tends to focus on and characterize the past, while finance focuses on the present and future.

THE FINANCIAL FUNCTION LG1-2

As we said above, this text focuses primarily on financial management, so we will discuss the particular functions and responsibilities of the firm's financial manager. We will also explain how the financial function fits in and interacts with the other areas of the firm. Finally, to make this study as interesting and as relevant as possible, we will make the connections that allow you to see how the concepts covered in this book are important in your own personal finances.

The Financial Manager

The firm's highest-level financial manager is usually the chief financial officer, or CFO. Both the company treasurer and the controller report to the CFO. The treasurer is typically responsible for:

- Managing cash and credit.

- Issuing and repurchasing financial securities such as stocks and bonds.

- Deciding how and when to spend capital for new and existing projects.

- Hedging (reducing the firm's potential risk) against changes in foreign exchange and interest rates.

financial institutions and markets The organizations that facilitate the flow of capital between investors and companies.

international finance The use of finance theory in a global business environment.

risk A potential future negative impact to value and/or cash flows. It is often discussed in terms of the probability of loss and the expected magnitude of the loss.

financial asset A general term for securities like stocks, bonds, and other assets that represent ownership in a cash flow.

real assets Physical property like gold, machinery, equipment, or real estate.

real markets The places and processes that facilitate the trading of real assets.

time value of money (TVM) The theory and application of valuing cash flows at various points in time.

In larger corporations, the treasurer may also oversee other areas, such as purchasing insurance or managing the firm's pension fund investments. The controller oversees the accounting function, usually managing the tax, cost accounting, financial accounting, and data processing functions.

Finance in Other Business Functions

Although the CFO and treasurer positions tend to be the firm's most visible finance-related positions, finance affects the firm in many ways and throughout all levels of a company's organizational chart. Finance permeates the entire business organization, providing guidance for both strategic and day-to-day decisions of the firm and collecting information for control and feedback about the firm's financial decisions.

Operational managers use finance daily to determine how much overtime labor to use, or to perform cost/benefit analysis when they consider new production lines or methods. Marketing managers use finance to assess the cost effectiveness of doing follow-up marketing surveys. Human resource managers use finance to evaluate the company's cost for various employee benefit packages. No matter where you work in business, finance can help you do your job better.

Finance in Your Personal Life LG1-3

Finance can help you make good financial decisions in your personal life. Consider these common activities you will probably face in your life:

- Borrowing money to buy a new car.
- Refinancing your home mortgage at a lower rate.
- Making credit card or student loan payments.
- Saving for retirement.

You will be able to perform all of these tasks better after learning about finance. Recent changes throughout our economy and the U.S. business environment make knowledge of finance even more valuable to you than before. For example, most companies have switched from providing **defined benefit** retirement plans to employees to offering **defined contribution**

time out!

1-2 How might the application of finance improve your professional and personal decisions?

Finance Applications LG1-3

Chloe realizes how important finance will be for her future business career. However, some of the ways that she will see financial applications seem way off in the future. She is curious about how the theory applies to her personal life, both in the near term and in the long term.

SOLUTION:

Chloe will quickly find that her financial health now and in the future will depend upon many decisions she makes as she goes through life—starting now! For example, she will learn that the same tools that she applies to a business loan analysis can be applied to her own personal debt. After this course, Chloe will be able to evaluate credit card offers and select one that could save her hundreds of dollars per year. When she buys a new car and the dealership offers her a low-interest-rate loan or a higher-rate loan with cash back, she will be able to pick the option that will truly cost her the least. Also, when Chloe gets her first professional job, she will know how to direct her retirement account so that she can earn millions of dollars for her future. (Of course, inflation between now and when she retires will imply that Chloe's millions won't be worth as much as they would today.)

plans (such as **401k plans**) and self-funded plans like **Individual Retirement Accounts (IRAs).** Tax changes in the early 1980s made this switch more or less inevitable. It appears that each of us will have to ensure adequate funds for our own retirement—much more so than previous generations.

BUSINESS ORGANIZATION LG1-4

In the United States, people can structure businesses in any of several ways; the number of owners is the key to how business structures are classified. Traditionally, single owners, partners, and corporations operate businesses. We can express the advantages and disadvantages of each organizational form through several dimensions:

- Who controls the firm.
- Who owns the firm.
- What are the owners' risks.
- What access to capital exists.
- What are the tax ramifications.

Recently, small businesses have adopted hybrid structures that capture the benefits from multiple organizational forms, and we'll discuss those hybrid structures after we cover the more common, traditional types of business organizations.

Sole Proprietorships

The **sole proprietorship** represents, by far, the most common type of business in the United States.[1] A sole proprietorship

is defined as any unincorporated business owned by a single individual.[2] Perhaps these businesses are so popular because they are relatively easy to start, and they're subject to a much lighter regulatory and paperwork burden than other business forms. The owner, or sole proprietor, of the business has complete control of the firm's activities. The owner also receives all of the firm's profits and is solely responsible for all losses.

> " The owner, or sole proprietor, of the business has complete control of the firm's activities. The owner also receives all of the firm's profits and is solely responsible for all losses. "

The biggest disadvantage that sole proprietorships carry relative to other organizational forms is that they have **unlimited liability** for their companies' debts and actions. The owner's personal assets may be confiscated if the business fails. The law recognizes no distinction between the owner's business assets and personal assets. The income of the business is also added to the owner's personal income and taxed by the government at the appropriate personal tax rate. Finally, sole proprietors have a difficult time obtaining capital to expand their business operations. Banks and other lenders are not typically interested in lending much money to sole proprietors because small firms have only one person liable for paying back the debt. A sole proprietor could raise capital by issuing **equity** to another investor. **Angel investors** and **venture capitalists** exchange capital for ownership in a business. But this requires re-forming the business as a partnership and the sole proprietor must give up some of the ownership (and thus control) of the firm. Table 1.1 summarizes sole proprietorships' characteristics, along with those of the three other business organizations we will study.

Partnerships

A **general partnership,** or as it is more commonly known, a *partnership,* is an organizational form that features multiple

[1]According to the IRS' *SOI Tax Stats—Integrated Business Data* for 2007, 78.21 percent of all businesses in the U.S. were sole proprietorships.

[2]However, if you are the sole member of a domestic limited liability company (LLC, discussed below), you are not a sole proprietor if you elect to treat the LLC as a corporation.

Venture capital helped Starbucks become a success story.

unlimited liability A situation in which a person's personal assets are at risk from a business liability.

equity An ownership interest in a business enterprise.

angel investors Individuals who provide small amounts of capital and expert business advice to small firms in exchange for an ownership stake in the firm.

venture capitalists Similar to angel investors except that they are organized as groups of investors and can provide larger amounts of capital.

general partnership A form of business organization where the partners own the business together and are personally liable for legal actions and debts of the firm.

individual owners. Each partner can own a different percentage of the firm. Firm control is typically determined by the size of partners' ownership stakes. Business profits are split among the partners according to a prearranged agreement, usually by the percentage of firm ownership. Received profits are added to each partner's personal income and taxed at personal income tax rates.

The partners jointly share unlimited personal liability for the debts of the firm and all are obligated for contracts agreed to by any one of the partners. Banks are more willing to lend to partnerships than to sole proprietorships, because all partners are liable for repaying the debt. Partners would have to give up some ownership and control in the firm to raise more equity capital. In order to raise enough capital for substantial growth, a partnership often changes into a public corporation.

Corporations

A **public corporation** is a legally independent entity entirely separate from its owners. This independence dramatically alters the firm's characteristics. Corporations hold many rights and obligations of individual persons, such as the ability to own property, sign binding contracts, and pay taxes. Federal and state governments tax corporate income once at the corporate level. Then shareholders pay taxes again at the personal level when corporate profits are paid out as dividends. This practice is generally known as **double taxation.**

Corporate owners are stockholders, also called *shareholders*. Public corporations typically have thousands of stockholders. The firm must hire managers to direct the firm, since thousands of individual shareholders could not direct day-to-day operations under any sort of consensus. As a result, managers control the company. Strong possibilities of conflicts of interests arise when one group of people owns the business, but another group controls it. We'll discuss conflicts of interest and their resolution later in the chapter.

As individual legal entities, corporations assume liability for their own debts, so the shareholders have only **limited liability.** That is, corporate shareholders cannot lose more money than they originally paid for their shares of stock. This limited liability is one reason that many people feel comfortable owning stock. Corporations are thus able to raise incredible amounts of money by selling stock (equity) and borrowing money. The largest businesses in the world are organized as corporations.

Hybrid Organizations

To promote the growth of small businesses, the U.S. government allows for several types of business organizations that simultaneously offer limited personal liability for the owners *and* provide a pass-through of all firm earnings to the owners, so that the earnings are subject only to single taxation.

Hybrid organizations offer single taxation and limited liability to all owners. Examples are *S corporations, limited liability partnerships (LLPs),* and *limited liability companies (LLCs).* Others, called *limited partnerships (LPs),* offer single taxation and limited liability to the *limited partners,* but also have *general partners,* who benefit from single taxation but also must bear personal liability for the firm's debts.

The U.S. government typically restricts hybrid organization status to relatively small firms. The government limits the

time out!

1-3 Why must an entrepreneur give up some control of the business as it grows into a public corporation?

1-4 What advantages does the corporate form of organization hold over a partnership?

▼ **TABLE 1.1** Characteristics of Business Organization

	Ownership	Control	Ownership Risk	Access to Capital	Taxes
Sole Proprietor	Single individual	Proprietor	Unlimited liability	Very limited	Paid by owner
Partnership	Multiple people	Shared by partners	Unlimited liability	Limited	Paid by partners
Corporation	Public investors who own the stock	Company managers	Stockholders can only lose their investment in the firm	Easy access	Corporation pays income tax and stockholders pay taxes on dividends
Hybrids: S-corp, LLP, LLC, LP	Partners or shareholders	Shared	Mostly limited	Limited by firm size restrictions	Paid by partners or shareholders

maximum number of shareholders or partners involved,[3] the maximum amount of investment capital allowed, and the lines of business permitted. These restrictions are consistent with the government's stated reason for allowing the formation of these forms of business organization—to encourage the formation and growth of small businesses.

FIRM GOALS LG1-5

Tens of thousands of public corporations operate in the United States. Many of them are the largest business organizations in the world. Because U.S. corporations are so large and because there are so many of them, corporations have a tremendous impact on society. Given the power that these huge firms wield, many people question what the corporate goals should be. Two

[3]For example, current federal regulations limit the number of shareholders in an S corporation to no more than 100.

different, well-developed viewpoints have arisen concerning what the goal of the firm should be. The owners' perspective holds that the only appropriate goal is to **maximize shareholder wealth.** The competing viewpoint is from the **stakeholders'** perspective, which emphasizes social responsibility over profitability. This view maintains that managers must maximize the total satisfaction of all stakeholders in a business. These stakeholders include the owners and shareholders, but also include the business's customers, employees, and local communities.

While strong arguments speak in favor of both perspectives, financial practitioners and academics now tend to believe that the manager's primary responsibility should be to maximize shareholder wealth and give only secondary consideration to other stakeholders' welfare. One of the first, and most

maximization of shareholder wealth A view that management should first and foremost consider the interests of shareholders in its business decisions.

stakeholder A person or organization that has a legitimate interest in a corporation.

finance at work //: corporate

Google Buys YouTube

In November 2006, Web search leader Google purchased the online video-sharing phenomenon YouTube for $1.65 billion. Google bought the firm by giving YouTube owners shares of Google stock in exchange for their ownership in YouTube. YouTube was a private corporation owned primarily by cofounders Chad Hurley and Steve Chen, who each received over $300 million of Google stock. Venture capital firm Sequoia Capital had backed YouTube and received $442 million of Google stock. Two dozen YouTube employees also had ownership stakes; some of them became millionaires from the deal.

YouTube was founded in February 2005. Imagine starting a business that was purchased for $1.65 billion less than two years later! Consider how many finance people and applications were needed to organize the buyout. Google's CFO George Reyes and team had to determine the value that YouTube could bring to Google. They also had to convince their own Google stockholders that Google did not overpay for the purchase. To do so, auditors had to evaluate YouTube's cash flows and the riskiness of those cash flows. The CFO, along with investment banker advisors, had to decide how to pay for YouTube. Google swapped its own stock for the firm but could have paid all cash or used a combination of cash and stock.

YouTube owners also had to assess the value of their stock to ensure that they received a fair price. Google's offer had to be

compared to alternatives. For example, YouTube could have waited for a better offer from Google or sought an offer from another firm. Or YouTube owners could have decided to take the company public and sold shares to public investors.

This chapter illustrates the kinds of issues that finance addresses. The rest of the book describes the theories and tools needed to make these judgments. The practice of finance isn't just about numbers—the results of financial analysis are very dynamic and exciting!

Want to know more?

Key Words to Search for Updates: **Google, YouTube**

well-known, proponents of this viewpoint was Adam Smith, an 18th-century economist who argued that, in capitalism, an individual pursuing his own interests tends also to promote the good of his community.[4]

Smith argued that the **invisible hand** of the market, acting through competition and the free price system, would ensure that only those activities most efficient and beneficial to society as a whole would survive in the long run. Thus, those same activities would also profit the individual most. When companies try to implement a goal other than profit maximization, their efforts tend to backfire. Consider the firm that tries to maximize employment. The high number of employees raises costs. Soon the firm will find that its costs are too high to allow it to compete against more efficient firms, especially in a global business environment. When the firm fails, all employees are let go and employment ends up being minimized, not maximized.

Regardless of whether you believe Smith's assertion or not, a more pragmatic reason supports the argument that maximizing owners' wealth is an admirable goal. As we discuss below, the owners of the firm hire managers to work on their behalf, so the manager is morally, ethically, and legally required to act in the owners' best interests. Any relationships between the manager and other firm stakeholders are necessarily secondary to the goal that shareholders give to their hired managers.

Maximizing owners' equity value means carefully considering:

- How best to bring additional funds into the firm.
- Which projects to invest in.
- How best to return the profits from those projects to the owners over time.

For corporations, maximizing the value of owners' equity can also be stated as *maximizing the current value per share, or* **stock price,** *of existing shares.* To the extent that the current stock price can be expected to include the present value of any future expected cash flows accruing to the owners, the goal of maximizing stock price provides us with a single, concrete, measurable gauge of value. You may be tempted to choose several other potential goals over maximizing the value of owners' equity. Common alternatives are:

- Maximizing net income or profit.
- Minimizing costs.
- Maximizing market share.

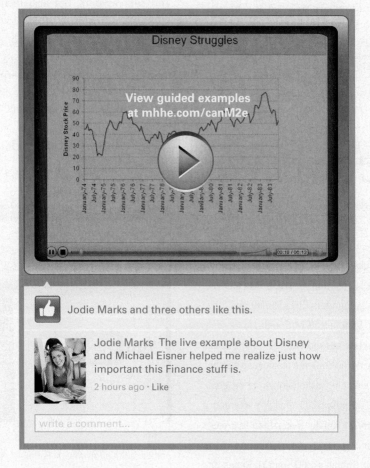

Jodie Marks and three others like this.

Jodie Marks The live example about Disney and Michael Eisner helped me realize just how important this Finance stuff is.
2 hours ago · Like

write a comment...

Although these may look appealing, each of these goals has some potentially serious shortcomings. For example, net income is measured on a year-by-year or quarter-by-quarter basis. When we say that we want to maximize profits, to *which* net income figure are we referring? We can maximize this year's net income in several legitimate ways, but many of these ways impose costs which will reduce future income. Or, current net income can be pushed into future years. Neither of these two extremes will likely encourage the firm's short-term and long-term stability. One more likely goal would be to maximize today's value of *all* future years of net income. Of course, this possible goal is very close to maximizing the current stock price, without the convenient market-oriented measure of the stock price. Another problem with considering maximizing all future profits as the goal is that net income (for reasons we'll go into later) does not really measure how much money the firm is actually earning.

Minimizing costs and *maximizing market share* also have fundamental problems as potential goals. Certainly minimizing costs would not make some stakeholders, such as employees, very happy. In addition, without spending the money on R&D and new product development, many companies would not survive long in the ever-evolving economy without improving their products. A firm can always increase market share by lowering price. But if a firm loses money on every product sold, then selling more products will simply drive the firm into fiscal distress.

[4]See Book IV of Smith's *The Wealth of Nations.*

time out!

1-5 Describe why the primary objective of maximizing shareholder value may actually be the most beneficial for society in the long run.

AGENCY THEORY LG1-6

Whenever one party (the *principal*) hires someone else (the *agent*) to work for him or her, their interaction is called an *agency relationship*. The agent is always supposed to act in the principal's best interests. For example, an apartment complex manager should ensure that tenants aren't doing willful damage to the property, that fire codes are enforced, and that the vacancy rate is kept as low as possible, because these are best for the apartment owner.

Agency Problem

In the context of a public corporation, we have already noted that stockholders hire managers to run the firm. Ideally, managers will operate the firm so that the shareholders realize maximum value for their equity. But managers may be tempted to operate the firm to serve their own best interests. Managers could spend company money to improve their own lifestyle instead of earning more profits for shareholders. Sometimes the manager's best interest does not necessarily align with shareholder goals. This creates a situation that we refer to as the **agency problem.**

For example, suppose it is time to buy a new corporate car for the firm's **chief executive officer (CEO).** Assuming that the CEO has no extraordinary driving requirements, shareholders

Perks can range from extra vacation to private transportation.

might wish for the CEO to buy a nice, conservative domestic sedan. But suppose that the CEO demands the newest, biggest luxury car available. It's tempting to say that the shareholders could just tell the CEO which car to buy. But remember, the CEO has most of the control in a public corporation. Organizational behavior specialists have identified three basic approaches to minimize this conflict of interest. First, ignore it. If the amount of money involved is small enough relative to the firm's cash flows, or if the suitability of the purchase in question is ambiguous enough, shareholders might be best served to simply overlook the problem. A good deal of research literature suggests that allowing the manager a certain amount of such **perks (perquisites)** might actually enhance owner value, in that such items may boost managers' productivity.[5]

The second approach to mitigating this conflict is to monitor managers' actions. Monitoring at too fine a level of detail is probably counterproductive and prohibitively expensive. However, major firm decisions are usually monitored at least roughly through the accounting auditing process. Also, shareholders can benefit indirectly from the fact that current debt holders with a relatively large stake in the firm will usually engage in at least some additional monitoring of their own to ensure their investments.[6]

The final approach for aligning managers' personal interests with those of owners is to make the managers owners—that is, to offer managers an equity stake in the firm so that management participates in any equity value increase. Many corporations take this approach, either through explicitly granting shares to managers, by awarding them **options** on the firm's stock, or by allowing them to purchase shares at a subsidized price through an **employee stock option plan (ESOP).** When firm managers are also firm owners, their incentives are more likely to align with stockholders' best interests.

[5]See, for example, Raghuram Rajan and Julie Wulf, "Are Perks Really Managerial Excess?" *Journal of Financial Economics* 79(1), 2006, 1–33.

[6]Potential acquirers will also often monitor firms for evidence that assets are being under- or misused by current management. To the extent that these acquirers may offer to buy the company when existing management is not doing a good job, current shareholders can benefit from this type of indirect monitoring, too.

invisible hand A metaphor used to illustrate how an individual pursuing his own interests also tends to promote the good of the community.

stock price The price of a share of stock trading on a stock market.

agency problem The difficulties that arise when a principal hires an agent and cannot fully monitor the agent's actions.

chief executive officer (CEO) The highest-ranking corporate manager.

perks/perquisites Nonwage compensation, often in the form of company car, golf club membership, etc.

option The opportunity to buy stock at a fixed price over a specific period of time.

employee stock option plan (ESOP) An incentive program that grants options to employees (typically managers) as compensation.

Corporate Governance

We refer to the process of monitoring managers and aligning their incentives with shareholder goals as **corporate governance.** Theoretically, managers work for shareholders. In reality, because shareholders are usually inactive, the firm actually seems to belong to management. Generally speaking, the investing public does not know what goes on at the firm's operational level. Managers handle day-to-day operations, and they know that their work is mostly unknown to investors. This lack of supervision demonstrates the need for monitors. Figure 1.9 shows the people and organizations that help monitor corporate activities.

The monitors inside a public firm are the **board of directors,** who are appointed to represent shareholders' interests. The board hires the CEO, evaluates management, and can also design compensation contracts to tie management's salaries to firm performance.

The monitors outside the firm include auditors, analysts, investment banks, and credit rating agencies. **Auditors** examine the firm's accounting systems and comment on whether financial statements fairly represent the firm's financial position. **Investment analysts** follow a firm, conduct their own evaluations of the company's business activities, and report to the investment community. **Investment banks,** which help firms access capital markets and advise managers about how to interact with those capital markets, also monitor firm performance. **Credit analysts** examine a firm's financial strength for its debt holders. The government also monitors business activities through the Securities and Exchange Commission (SEC) and the Internal Revenue Service (IRS).

The Role of Ethics LG1-7

Ethics must play a strong role in any practice of finance. Finance professionals commonly manage other people's money. For example, corporate managers control the stockholder's

---

▼**FIGURE 1.9** Corporate Governance Monitors

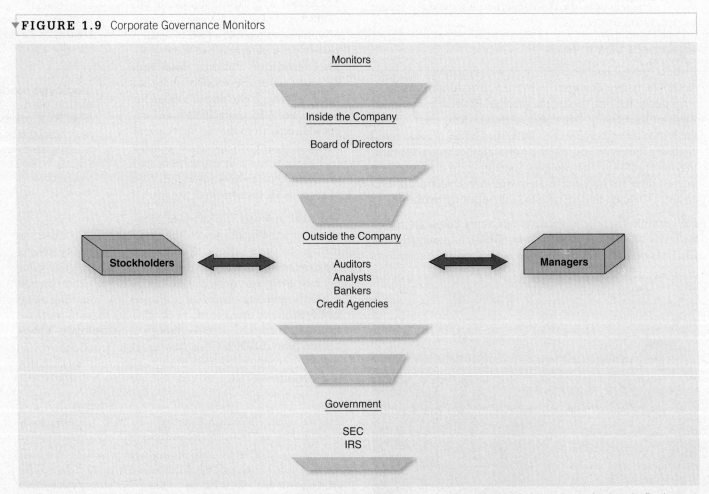

Corporate governance balances the needs of stockholders and managers. Inside the public firm, the members of the board of directors monitor how the firm is run. Outside the firm, auditors, analysts, investment banks, and credit rating agencies act as monitors.

time out!

1-6 What unethical activities might managers engage in because of the agency problem?

1-7 Explain how the corporate governance system reduces the agency problem.

firm, bank employees manage deposits, and investment advisors manage people's investment portfolios. These **fiduciary** relationships create tempting opportunities for finance professionals to make decisions that either benefit the client or benefit the advisors themselves. Professional associations (such as for treasurers, bank executives, investment professionals, etc.) place a strong emphasis on ethical behavior and provide ethics training and standards. Nevertheless, as with any

profession with millions of practitioners, a few are bound to act unethically.

The agency relationship between corporate managers and stockholders can create ethical dilemmas. Sometimes the corporate governance system has failed to prevent unethical managers from stealing from firms, which ultimately means stealing from shareholders. Governments all over the world have passed laws and regulations meant to ensure compliance with ethical codes of behavior.[7] And if professionals don't act appropriately, governments have set up strong punishments for financial malfeasance. In the end, financial managers must realize that they not only owe their shareholders the very best decisions to further shareholder interests, but they also have a broader obligation to society as a whole.

[7]The Sarbanes-Oxley Act of 2002 was passed in response to a number of recent major corporate accounting scandals including those affecting Enron, Tyco International, and WorldCom. The goal of the act was to make the accounting and auditing procedures more transparent and trustworthy.

investment analyst A person who analyzes a company's business prospects and gives opinions about its future success.

investment banks Banks that help companies and governments raise capital.

credit analysts A person who analyzes a company's ability to repay its debts and reports the findings as a grade.

ethics The study of values, morals, and morality.

fiduciary A legal duty between two parties where one party must act in the interest of the other party.

EXAMPLE 1-2

Executive Compensation LG1-6

For interactive versions of this example visit www.mhhe.com/canM2e

In 2005, firms in the Standard & Poor's 500 Index paid their CEOs, on average, $13.51 million, a 16.1 percent increase over the previous year. So the average CEO compensation was 411 times the average employee's compensation. In 2006, the increase in CEO pay was 8.9 percent. Every year, the controversy over CEO pay arises again. What arguments could be made for each side?

SOLUTION:

Many people believe that CEOs are paid too much for the services they provide. They receive compensation that is far higher than workers' pay within their firms. Over the years, executive compensation has also increased at a faster and higher rate than has the value of the stockholders' wealth. For example, the return for stockholders of the S&P 500 Index firms was 15.6 percent in 2006 and 4.9 percent in 2005, compared to CEO pay increases of 8.9 percent and 16.1 percent, respectively. Each firm's board of directors sets CEO compensation. However, CEOs may have undue influence over director selection, tenure, and committee assignments—even over selecting the compensation advisors. This practice creates an unhealthy conflict of interest.

Others believe that a skilled CEO can positively affect company performance and that, therefore, the firm needs to offer high compensation and a bundle of perquisites to attract the best talent. To overcome agency problems, managers must be given incentives that pay very well when the company performs very well. If CEOs create a substantial amount of shareholder wealth, then who is to say that they are overpaid?

finance at work //: corporate

The Amazing Story of Apple Inc. and Steve Jobs

Steven Jobs and Stephen Wozniak started Apple Computer in 1976 as an equal partnership. Together, they built 50 computers in a garage using money borrowed from family, the proceeds from the sale of a VW bus, and credit from the parts distributor.

Jobs and Wozniak then designed the Apple II computer. But a higher production level to make more than 50 computers required more space and employees. They needed much more capital. They could not get a loan until angel investor Mike Markkula (an Intel executive) became a partner in the firm. He invested $92,000 and his personal guarantee induced a bank to loan Apple $250,000. As production ramped up in 1977, Apple Computer incorporated. Most shares were owned by Jobs, Wozniak, and Markkula, but the principals made some shares available to employees. They also hired an experienced manager (Mike Scott) to be the CEO and run the firm. Note that as the firm expanded, Jobs' ownership level and control got diluted. By 1980, Apple Computer had sold a total of 121,000 computers—against a potential demand of millions more. Apple needed even more capital.

At the end of 1980, Apple became a public corporation and sold $65 million worth of stock to public investors. Steve Jobs, cofounder of Apple, still owned more shares than anyone else (7.5 million), but he owned less than half of the firm. He gave up a great deal of ownership to new investors in exchange for the capital to expand the firm. Unhappy with Mike Scott's leadership, Steve Jobs also became CEO of Apple.

After a couple of years, Apple's board of directors felt that Jobs was not experienced enough to steer the firm through its rapid expansion. They hired John Sculley as CEO in 1983. In 1985, a power struggle ensued for control of the firm, and the board backed Sculley over Jobs. Jobs was forced out of Apple and no longer had a say in business operations, even though he was the largest shareholder and an original cofounder of the firm.

So, Steve Jobs bought Pixar in 1986 for $5 million and founded NeXT Computer. Over the next 10 years, Jobs' Pixar produced mega hit movies like *Toy Story, A Bug's Life,* and *Monsters, Inc.* This time, he kept 53 percent ownership of Pixar to ensure keeping full control. In the meantime, Apple Computer began to struggle, with losses of $800 million in 1996 and $1 billion in 1997. To get Steve Jobs back into the firm, Apple bought NeXT for $400 million and hired him as Apple's CEO. Over the next few years, Jobs introduced the iMac, iPod, and iTunes, and Apple became very profitable again! Jobs was given the use of a $90 million Gulfstream jet as a perk. To realign his incentives, he became an Apple owner again via compensation that included options on 10 million shares of stock and 30 million shares of **restricted stock.** Then in 2006, Disney bought Pixar by swapping $7.4 billion worth of Disney stock for Pixar stock. When the deal closed, Steve Jobs became the largest owner of Disney stock (7 percent) and joined Disney's board of directors.

Wow! What a story of accessing capital, business organizational form, company control, and corporate governance.

Want to know more?

Key Words to Search for Updates: **Steve Jobs, Apple Computer, Pixar**

FINANCIAL MARKETS, INTERMEDIARIES, AND THE FIRM LG1-8

Astute readers will note that our emphasis on the role of financial markets and intermediaries grew throughout this chapter.

This emphasis is intentional, as we feel that you must understand the role and impact of these institutions on the firm if you are to grasp the context in which professionals make financial management decisions.

We want to emphasize one other important point about these financial institutions (FI). Very astute readers may wonder how, if financial markets are competitive, investment banks and other financial institutions are able to make such impressive profits. Although FIs assist others with transactions involving financial assets in the financial markets, they do so as paid services. Successful execution of those services takes unique assets and expertise. As shown in Figure 1.10, it's the use of those unique assets and expertise that provides financial institutions with their high profit margins.

time out!

1-8 What is the role of financial institutions in a capitalist economy?

THE FINANCIAL CRISIS LG1-9

It would be impossible to write a new edition of this book without mentioning the 800-pound gorilla in the room that is the financial crisis. We will be discussing aspects of the crisis throughout the book, but we give you a little bit of insight concerning the causes of the crisis here to provide a foundation that we can refer to later.

What Started It

Signs of significant problems in the U.S. economy arose in late 2006 and the first half of 2007, when home prices plummeted and defaults by **subprime mortgage borrowers** (i.e., those borrowers charged higher interest rates because of their higher chance of default) began to affect the mortgage lending industry as a whole, as well as other parts of the economy noticeably. Mortgage delinquencies, particularly on subprime mortgages, surged in the last quarter of 2006 through 2008 as home owners who stretched themselves

financially to buy a home or refinance a mortgage in the early 2000s fell behind on their loan payments. Foreclosure filings jumped 93 percent in July 2007 over July 2006. Between August 2007 and October 2008, an additional 936,439 homes were lost to foreclosure.

These problems arose after one of the largest periods of home-ownership growth in U.S. history, with the seasonally adjusted home ownership rate reaching a peak of 69.2 percent in the first quarter of 2005. To fund this unprecedented growth, mortgage lenders had increasingly started to sell the rights to the payments on the loans they had originated to other financial institutions or investors. This process is called **securitization.**

As a result, when mortgage borrowers started to default on their mortgages in late 2006, it was not just the lenders who had originated the mortgages who were affected, but also the broad variety of individual investors, pension funds, insurance companies, and many others who had invested heavily in such **mortgage-backed securities.**

restricted stock
A special type of stock that is not transferable from the current holder to others until specific conditions are satisfied.

subprime mortgage borrowers Borrowers charged higher interest rates because of their higher chance of default.

securitization
A process where loan originators sell the rights to the payments on the loans to other financial institutions or investors.

mortgage-backed securities Securities that represent a claim against the cash flows from a pool of mortgage loans.

▼**FIGURE 1.10** Financial Institutions' Cash Flows

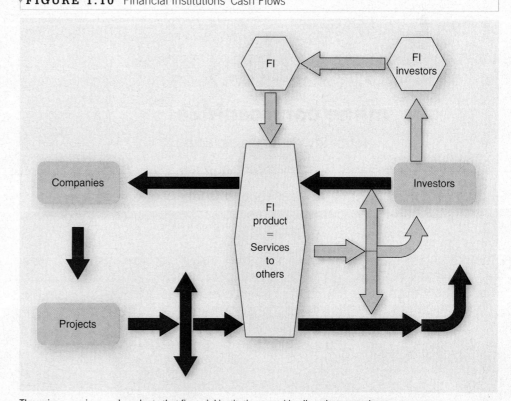

The unique services and products that financial institutions provide allow them to make money.

Why It Got Worse

The widespread effects of the collapse of the housing bubble damaged financial institutions severely, raising questions about solvency even for those institutions which survived the bubble. As a result, the surviving institutions tightened their lending standards, making credit less available for both consumers and businesses in the economy.

This decreased availability of credit, along with damaged investor confidence, led businesses to reduce their forecasted sales and revenue figures. In turn, lower forecasted demand for products in the economy led employers to reduce their workforces, resulting in double-digit unemployment figures and further eroding consumer confidence.

The Effect on the Public Sector

In the aftermath of the housing bubble collapse, the federal government took extensive steps to stimulate the economy to provide for an economic "soft landing." The American Recovery and Reinvestment Act, passed by the U.S. Congress on February 13, 2009, devoted $308.3 billion to appropriations spending, including $120 billion on infrastructure and science and more than $30 billion on energy-related infrastructure projects. Another $267 billion would go for direct spending,

including increased unemployment benefits and food stamps. Finally, $212 billion was set aside for tax breaks for individuals and businesses.

By the summer and fall of 2009, the economy appeared to be slowly beginning to recover. Pending home sales and residential construction both posted significant increases, the unemployment rate dropped below 10 percent, GDP was once again increasing, and consumer spending was once again on the rise. Unfortunately, state and local governments have continued to struggle with the aftermath of the crisis, enduring both reduced income tax revenues and decreasing property tax revenues caused by property reappraisals. So the economy never experienced the typical post-recession high-growth rebound and has been sputtering ever since.

Looking Ahead

At the time of this writing, the financial crisis appears to be starting to get somewhat better. Increasing consumer demand and diminishing unemployment point to better times ahead. However, both lenders' and consumers' tendencies to be more cautious, along with the continuing fiscal problems facing state and local municipalities in the foreseeable future, are likely to make the road to recovery a long and slow one. ■

Get Online

mhhe.com/canM2e

for study materials including
self-test problems with solutions, quizzes,
research projects, minicases, and videos

Your Turn...

Questions

1. Describe the type of people who use the financial markets. *(LG1-1)*

2. What is the purpose of financial management? Describe the kinds of activities that financial management involves. *(LG1-1)*

3. What is the difference in perspective between finance and accounting? *(LG1-2)*

4. What personal decisions can you think of that will benefit from your learning finance? *(LG1-3)*

5. What are the three basic forms of business ownership? What are the advantages and disadvantages to each? *(LG1-4)*

6. Between the three basic forms of business ownership, describe the ability of each form to access capital. *(LG1-4)*

7. Explain how the founder of a business can eventually lose control of the firm. How can the founder ensure this will not happen? *(LG1-4)*

8. Explain the shareholder wealth maximization goal of the firm and how it can be measured. Make an argument for why it is a better goal than maximizing profit. *(LG1-5)*

9. Name and describe as many corporate stakeholders as you can. *(LG1-5)*

10. What conflicts of interest can arise between managers and stockholders? *(LG1-6)*

11. Figure 1.9 shows firm monitors. In your opinion, which group is in the best position to monitor the firm? Explain. Which group has the potential to be the weakest monitor? Explain. *(LG1-6)*

12. In recent years, governments all over the world have passed laws that increased the penalties for executives' crimes. Do you think this will deter unethical corporate managers? Explain. *(LG1-6)*

13. Every year, the media report on the vast amounts of money (sometimes hundreds of millions of dollars) that some CEOs earn from the companies they manage. Are these CEOs worth it? Give examples. *(LG1-6)*

14. Why is ethical behavior so important in the field of finance? *(LG1-7)*

15. Does the goal of shareholder wealth maximization conflict with behaving ethically? Explain. *(LG1-7)*

16. Describe how financial institutions and markets facilitate the expansion of a company's business. *(LG1-8)*

orporate managers must issue many reports to the public. Most stockholders, analysts, government entities, and other interested parties pay particular attention to annual reports. An annual report provides four basic *financial statements:* the balance sheet, the income statement, the statement of cash flows, and the statement of retained earnings.

A **financial statement** provides an accounting-based picture of a firm's financial position.

Whereas accountants use reports to present a picture of what happened in the past, finance professionals use financial statements to draw inferences about the future. The four statements function to provide key information to managers, who make financial

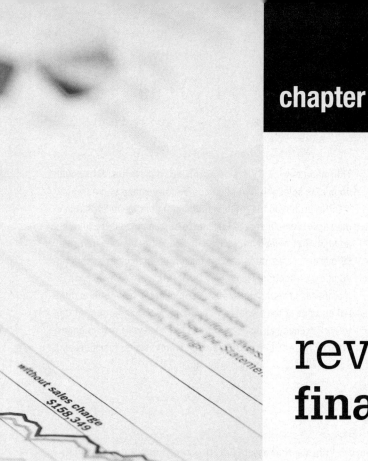

two

reviewing
financial statements

decisions, and to investors, who will accept or reject possible future investments in the firm. When you encountered these four financial statements in accounting classes, you learned how they function to place the right information in the right places. In this chapter, you will see how understanding these statements, which are the "right places"

continued on p. 24

LEARNING GOALS

LG2-1 Recall the major financial statements that firms must prepare and provide.

LG2-2 Differentiate between book (or accounting) value and market value.

LG2-3 Explain how taxes influence corporate managers' and investors' decisions.

LG2-4 Differentiate between accounting income and cash flows.

LG2-5 Demonstrate how to use a firm's financial statements to calculate its cash flows.

LG2-6 Observe cautions that should be taken when examining financial statements.

continued from p. 23

for crucial information, creates a solid base for your understanding of decision-making processes in managerial finance.

This chapter examines each statement to clarify its major features and uses. We highlight the differences between the accounting-based (book) value of a firm (reflected in these statements) and the true market value of a firm, which we will come to understand more fully. We also make a clear distinction between accounting-based income and actual cash flows, a topic further explored in Chapter 3, where we see how important cash flows are to the study of finance.

We open a discussion in this chapter about how firms choose to represent their earnings. We'll see that managers have substantial discretion in preparing their firms' financial statements, depending on strategic plans for the organization's future. This is worth looking into as we keep the discipline of finance grounded in a real-world context. Finally, leading into Chapter 3, we discuss some cautions to bear in mind when reviewing and analyzing financial statements. ■

BALANCE SHEET LG2-1

The **balance sheet** reports a firm's assets, liabilities, and equity at a particular point in time. It is a picture of the assets the firm owns and who has claims on these assets as of a given date, for example, December 31, 2012. A firm's assets must equal (balance) the liabilities and equity used to purchase the assets (hence the term *balance sheet*):

$$\text{Assets} = \text{Liabilities} + \text{Equity} \qquad (2\text{-}1)$$

Figure 2.1 illustrates a basic balance sheet and Table 2.1 presents a simple balance sheet for DPH Tree Farm Inc. as of December 31, 2012 and 2011. The left side of the balance sheet lists assets of the firm and the right side lists liabilities and equity. Both assets and liabilities are listed in descending order of **liquidity**, that is, the time and effort needed to convert the accounts to cash. The most liquid assets—called *current assets*—appear first on the asset side of the balance sheet. The least liquid, called *fixed assets,* appear last. Similarly, current liabilities—those obligations that the firm must pay within a year—appear first on the right side of the balance sheet. Stockholders' equity, which never matures, appears last on the balance sheet.

The managers of DPH Tree Farm Inc. believe the firm could double its sales if it had additional factory space and acreage. If DPH purchased the factory space and acreage in 2013, these new assets would cost $27 million to build and would require an additional $1 million in cash, $5 million in accounts receivable, $6 million in inventory, and $4 million in accounts payable. In addition to accounts payable, DPH Tree Farm would finance the new assets with the sale of a combination of long-term debt (40 percent of the total) and common stock (60 percent of the total). Assuming all else stays constant, what will these changes do to DPH Tree Farm's 2013 balance sheet assets, liabilities, and equity? (See 2012 balance sheet on p. 26)

Assets

Figure 2.1 shows that assets fall into two major categories: current assets and fixed assets. **Current assets** will normally convert to cash within one year. They include cash and **marketable securities** (short-term, low-rate investment securities held by the firm for liquidity purposes), accounts receivable, and inventory. **Fixed assets** have a useful life exceeding one year. This class of assets includes physical (tangible) assets, such as net plant and equipment, and other, less tangible, long-term assets, such as patents and trademarks. We find the value of net plant and equipment by taking the difference between gross plant and equipment (or the fixed assets' original value) and the depreciation accumulated against the fixed assets since their purchase.

Liabilities and Stockholders' Equity

Lenders provide funds, which become **liabilities,** to the firm. Liabilities fall into two categories as well: current or long-term.

▼**FIGURE 2.1** The Basic Balance Sheet

Total Assets	Total Liabilities and Equity
Current assets	Current liabilities
Cash and marketable securities	Accrued wages and taxes
Accounts receivable	Accounts payable
Inventory	Notes payable
Fixed assets	Long-term debt
Gross plant and equipment	
Less: Depreciation	Stockholders' equity
Net plant and equipment	Preferred stock
Other long-term assets	Common stock and paid-in surplus
	Retained earnings

personal APPLICATION

Chris Ryan is looking to invest in DPH Tree Farm Inc. Chris has the most recent set of financial statements from DPH Tree Farm's annual report but is not sure how to read them or what they mean. What are the four financial statements that Chris should pay most attention to? What information will these key financial statements contain?

Thinking of starting your own business? Learn more . . . Scan the QR code for an extended look. Turn to the back of the book for solutions to these applications.

Current liabilities constitute the firm's obligations due within one year, including accrued wages and taxes, accounts payable, and notes payable. **Long-term debt** includes long-term loans and bonds with maturities of more than one year.

The difference between total assets and total liabilities of a firm is the stockholders' (or owners') equity. The firm's preferred and common stock owners provide the funds known as **stockholders' equity. Preferred stock** is a hybrid security that has characteristics of both long-term debt and common stock. Preferred stock is similar to common stock in that it represents an ownership interest in the issuing firm but, like long-term debt, it pays a fixed periodic (dividend) payment. Preferred stock appears on the balance sheet as the cash proceeds when the firm sells preferred stock in a public offering. **Common stock and paid-in surplus** is the fundamental ownership claim in a public or private company. The proceeds from common stock and paid-in surplus appear as the other component of stockholders' equity. If the firm's managers decide to reinvest cumulative earnings rather than pay the dividends to stockholders, the balance sheet will record these funds as **retained earnings.**

Managing the Balance Sheet

Managers must monitor a number of issues underlying items reported on their firms' balance sheets. We examine these issues in detail throughout the text. In this chapter, we briefly introduce them. These issues include:

- The accounting method for fixed asset depreciation.
- The level of net working capital.
- The liquidity position of the firm.
- The method for financing the firm's assets—equity or debt.

- The difference between the book value reported on the balance sheet and the true market value of the firm.

Accounting Method for Fixed Asset Depreciation Managers can choose the accounting method they use to record depreciation against their fixed assets. Recall from accounting that *depreciation* is the charge against income that reflects the estimated dollar cost of the firm's fixed assets. The straight-line method and the MACRS (modified accelerated cost recovery system) are two choices. Companies commonly choose MACRS when computing the firm's taxes and the straight-line method when reporting income to the firm's stockholders. The MACRS method accelerates depreciation, which results in higher depreciation expenses and lower taxable income, thus lower taxes, in the early years of a project's life. Regardless of the depreciation method used, over time both the straight-line and MACRS methods result in the same amount of depreciation and therefore tax (cash) outflows. However, because the MACRS method defers the payment of taxes to later periods, firms often favor it over the straight-line method of depreciation. We discuss this choice further in Chapter 12.

Net Working Capital We arrive at a **net working capital** figure by taking the difference between a firm's current assets and current liabilities.

Net working capital
= Current assets − Current liabilities

(2-2)

So, clearly, net working capital is positive when the firm has more current assets than current liabilities. Table 2.1 shows the 2012 and 2011 year-end balance sheets for DPH Tree Farm Inc. At year-end 2012, the firm had $205 million of current assets and $120 million of current liabilities. So the firm's net working capital was $85 million. A firm needs cash and other liquid assets to pay its bills as expenses come due. As described in more detail in Chapter 14, liability holders monitor net working capital as

▼ **TABLE 2.1** Balance Sheet for DPH Tree Farm Inc.

DPH TREE FARM INC.				
Balance Sheet as of December 31, 2012 and 2011 (in millions of dollars)				
Assets	**2012**	**2011**	**Liabilities and Equity**	**2012**	**2011**
Current assets			Current liabilities		
Cash and marketable securities	$ 24	$ 25	Accrued wages and taxes	$ 20	$ 15
Accounts receivable	70	65	Accounts payable	55	50
Inventory	111	100	Notes payable	45	45
Total	$205	$190	Total	$120	$110
Fixed assets			Long-term debt	195	190
Gross plant and equipment	$368	$300	Total debt	315	300
Less: Depreciation	53	40	Stockholders' equity		
Net plant and equipment	$315	$260	Preferred stock (5 million shares)	$ 5	$ 5
Other long-term assets	50	50	Common stock and paid-in surplus (20 million shares)	40	40
Total	$365	$310	Retained earnings	210	155
			Total	$255	$200
Total assets	$570	$500	Total liabilities and equity	$570	$500

a measure of a firm's ability to pay its obligations. Positive net working capital values are usually a sign of a healthy firm.

Liquidity As we noted above, any firm needs cash and other liquid assets to pay its bills as debts come due. Liquidity actually refers to two dimensions: the ease with which the firm can convert an asset to cash, and the degree to which such a conversion takes place at a fair market value. You can convert any asset to cash quickly if you price the asset low enough. But clearly, you will wish to convert the asset without giving up a great portion of its value. So a highly liquid asset can be sold quickly at its fair market value. An illiquid asset, on the other hand, cannot be sold quickly unless you reduce the price far below fair value.

Current assets, by definition, remain relatively liquid, including cash and assets that will convert to cash within the next year. Inventory is the least liquid of the current assets. Fixed assets, then, remain relatively illiquid. In the normal course of business, the firm would have no plans to liquefy or convert these tangible assets such as buildings and equipment into cash.

Liquidity presents a double-edged sword on a balance sheet. The more liquid assets a firm holds, the less likely the firm will be to experience financial distress. However, liquid assets generate little or no profits for a firm. For example, cash is the most liquid of all assets, but it earns little, if any, for the firm. In contrast, fixed assets are illiquid, but provide the means to generate revenue. Thus, managers must consider

> " *Positive net working capital values are usually a sign of a healthy firm.* "

the trade-off between the advantages of liquidity on the balance sheet and the disadvantages of having money sit idle rather than generating profits.

Debt Versus Equity Financing
Ever since your high school physics class, you have known that levers are very useful and powerful machines—given a long enough lever, you can move almost anything. **Financial leverage** is likewise very powerful. Leverage in the financial sense refers to the extent to which a firm chooses to finance its ventures or assets by issuing debt securities. The more debt a firm issues as a percentage of its total assets, the greater its financial leverage. We discuss in later chapters why financial leverage can greatly magnify the firm's gains *and* losses for the firm's stockholders.

When a firm issues debt securities—usually bonds—to finance its activities and assets, debt holders usually demand first claim to a fixed amount of the firm's cash flows. Their claims are fixed because the firm must only pay the interest owed to bondholders and any principal repayments that come due within any given period. Stockholders—who buy equity securities or stocks—claim any cash flows left after debt holders are paid. When a firm does well, financial leverage increases shareholders' rewards, since the share of the firm's profits promised to debt holders is set and predictable.

However, financial leverage also increases risk. Leverage can create the potential for the firm to experience financial distress and even bankruptcy. If the firm has a bad year and cannot make its scheduled debt payments, debt holders can force the firm into bankruptcy. But managers generally prefer to fund firm activities using debt, precisely because they can calculate the cost of doing business without giving away too much of the firm's value. Managers often walk a fine line as they decide upon the firm's **capital structure**—the amount of debt versus equity financing held on the balance sheet—because it can determine whether the firm stays in business or goes bankrupt.

Book Value versus Market Value LG2-2

Beginning finance students usually have already taken accounting, so they are familiar with the accounting point of view. For example, a firm's balance sheet shows its **book (or historical cost) value** based on generally accepted accounting principles (GAAP). Under GAAP, assets appear on the balance sheet at what the firm paid for them, regardless of what those assets might be worth today if the firm were to sell them. Inflation and market forces make many assets worth more now than they were worth when the firm bought them. So in many cases, book values differ widely from **market values** for the same assets—the amount that the assets would fetch if the firm actually sold them. For the firm's current assets—those that mature within a year—the book value and market value of any particular asset will remain very close. For example, the balance sheet lists cash and marketable securities at their market value. Similarly, firms acquire accounts receivable and inventory and then convert these short-term assets into cash fairly quickly, so the book value of these assets is generally close to their market value.

The "book value versus market value" issue really arises when we try to determine how much a firm's fixed assets are worth. In this case, book value is often very different from market value. For example, if a firm owns land for 100 years, this asset appears on the balance sheet at its historical cost (of 100 years ago). Most likely, the firm would reap a much higher price on the land upon its sale than the historical price would indicate.

Again, accounting tools reflect the past: Balance sheet assets are listed at historical cost. Managers would thus see little relation between the total asset value listed on the balance sheet and the current market value of the firm's assets. Similarly, the stockholders' equity listed on the balance sheet generally differs from the true market value of the equity. In this case, the market value may be higher or lower than the value listed on the firm's accounting books. So financial managers and investors often find that balance sheet values are not always the most relevant numbers. The following example illustrates the difference between the book value and the market value of a firm's assets.

INCOME STATEMENT

You will recall that **income statements** show the total revenues that a firm earns and the total expenses the firm incurs to generate those revenues over a specific period of time, for example, the year 2012. Remember that while the balance sheet reports a firm's position at a point in time, the income statement reports performance over a period of time, for example, over the last year. Figure 2.2 illustrates a basic income statement and Table 2.2 shows a simple income statement for DPH Tree Farm Inc. for the years ended December 31, 2012 and 2011. DPH's revenues

The book value and market value of a classic car can be very different.

net working capital The difference between a firm's current assets and current liabilities.

financial leverage The extent to which debt securities are used by a firm.

capital structure The amount of debt versus equity financing held on the balance sheet.

book (or historical cost) value Assets are listed on the balance sheet at the amount the firm paid for them.

market value Assets are listed at the amount the firm would get if it sold them.

income statement Financial statement that reports the total revenues and expenses over a specific period of time.

time out!

2-1 What is a balance sheet?

2-2 Which are the most liquid assets and liabilities on a balance sheet?

EXAMPLE 2-1

For interactive versions of this example visit www.mhhe.com/canM2e

Calculating Book versus Market Value LG2-2

EZ Toy Inc. lists fixed assets of $25 million on its balance sheet. The firm's fixed assets were recently appraised at $32 million. EZ Toy Inc.'s balance sheet also lists current assets at $10 million. Current assets were appraised at $11 million. Current liabilities' book and market values stand at $6 million and the firm's long-term debt is $15 million. Calculate the book and market values of the firm's stockholders' equity. Construct the book value and market value balance sheets for EZ Toy Inc.

SOLUTION:

Recall the balance sheet identity in equation 2-1: Assets = Liabilities + Equity. Rearranging this equation: Equity = Assets − Liabilities. Thus, the balance sheets would appear as follows:

Assets	Book Value	Market Value	Liabilities and Equity	Book Value	Market Value
Current assets	$10m	$11m	Current liabilities	$ 6m	$ 6m
Fixed assets	25m	32m	Long-term debt	15m	15m
			Stockholders' equity	14m	22m
Total	$35m	$43m	Total	$35m	$43m

Similar to problems 2-15, 2-16

(or net sales) appear at the top of the income statement. The income statement then shows various expenses (cost of goods sold, depreciation, other operating expenses, interest, and taxes) subtracted from revenues to arrive at profit or income measures.

The top part of the income statement reports the firm's operating income. First, we subtract the cost of goods sold (the direct costs of producing the firm's product) from net sales to get **gross profit** (so, DPH Tree Farm enjoyed gross profits of $155 million in 2011 and $182 million in 2012). Next, we deduct depreciation and other operating expenses from gross profits to get operating profit or earnings before interest and taxes (**EBIT**) (so DPH Tree Farm's EBIT was $128 million in 2011 and $152 million in 2012). Other operating expenses include marketing and selling expenses as well as general and administrative expenses. The EBIT figure represents the profit earned from the sale of the product without any financing cost or tax considerations.

▼**FIGURE 2.2** The Basic Income Statement

Net sales
Less: Cost of goods sold
Gross profits
Less: Depreciation
    Other operating expenses
Earnings before interest and taxes (EBIT)
} Operating income

Less: Interest
Earnings before taxes (EBT)
Less: Taxes
} Financing and tax considerations

Net income before preferred dividends
Less: Preferred stock dividends
Net income available to common stockholders

The bottom part of the income statement summarizes the firm's financial and tax structure. First, we subtract interest expense (the cost to service the firm's debt) from EBIT to get earnings before taxes (**EBT**). So, as we follow our sample income statement, DPH Tree Farm had EBT of $110 million in 2011 and $136 million in 2012. Of course, firms differ in their financial structures and tax situations. These differences can cause two firms with identical operating income to report differing levels of net income. For example, one firm may finance its assets with only debt, while another finances with only common equity. The company with no debt would have no interest expense. Thus, even though EBIT for the two firms is identical, the firm with all-equity financing and no debt would report higher net income. We subtract taxes from EBT to get the last item on the income statement (the "bottom line"), or **net income.** DPH Tree Farm Inc. reported net income of $70 million in 2011 and $90 million in 2012.

Below the net income, or bottom line, on the income statement, firms often report additional information summarizing income and firm value. For example, with its $90 million of net income in 2012, DPH Tree Farm Inc. paid its preferred stockholders cash dividends of $10 million and its common stockholders cash dividends of $25 million, and added the remaining $55 million to retained earnings. Table 2.1 shows that retained earnings on the balance sheet increased from $155 million in 2011 to $210 million in 2012. Other items reported below the bottom line include:

$$\text{Earnings per share (EPS)} = \frac{\text{Net income available to common stockholders}}{\text{Total shares of common stock outstanding}} \quad (2\text{-}3)$$

$$\text{Dividends per share (DPS)} = \frac{\text{Common stock dividends paid}}{\text{Number of shares of common stock outstanding}} \quad (2\text{-}4)$$

$$\text{Book value per share (BVPS)} = \frac{\text{Common stock + Paid-in surplus + Retained earnings}}{\text{Number of shares of common stock outstanding}} \quad (2\text{-}5)$$

$$\text{Market value per share (MVPS)} = \frac{\text{Market price of the firm's common stock}}{} \quad (2\text{-}6)$$

We discuss these items further in Chapter 3.

Corporate Income Taxes LG2-3

Firms pay out a large portion of their earnings in taxes. For example, in 2009, Microsoft had EBT of $19.8 billion. Of this amount, Microsoft paid $5.3 billion (over 26 percent of EBT) in taxes. Congress oversees the U.S. tax code, which determines corporate tax obligations. Corporate taxes can thus change with changes of administration or other changes in the business or public environment. As you might expect, the U.S. tax system is extremely complicated, so we do not attempt to cover it in detail here. However, firms recognize taxes as a major expense item and many financial decisions arise from tax considerations. In this section we provide a general overview of the U.S. corporate tax system.

The 2012 corporate tax schedule appears in Table 2.3. Note from this table that the U.S. tax structure is progressive, meaning that the larger the income, the higher the taxes assessed. However, corporate tax rates do not increase in any kind of linear way based on this progressive nature: They rise from a low of 15 percent to a high of 39 percent, then drop to 34 percent, rise to 38 percent, and finally drop to 35 percent.

▼**TABLE 2.2** Income Statement for DPH Tree Farm Inc.

DPH TREE FARM INC. Income Statement for Years Ending December 31, 2012 and 2011 (in millions of dollars)		
	2012	2011
Net sales (all credit)	$ 315	$ 275
Less: Cost of goods sold	133	120
Gross profits	$ 182	$ 155
Less: Depreciation	13	12
Other operating expenses	17	15
Earnings before interest and taxes (EBIT)	$ 152	$ 128
Less: Interest	16	18
Earnings before taxes (EBT)	$ 136	$ 110
Less: Taxes	46	40
Net income	$ 90	$ 70
Less: Preferred stock dividends	$ 10	$ 10
Net income available to common stockholders	$ 80	$ 60
Less: Common stock dividends	25	25
Addition to retained earnings	$ 55	$ 35
Per (common) share data:		
Earnings per share (EPS)	$ 4.00	$ 3.00
Dividends per share (DPS)	$ 1.25	$ 1.25
Book value per share (BVPS)	$12.50	$ 9.75
Market value (price) per share (MVPS)	$17.25	$15.60

▼ TABLE 2.3 Corporate Tax Rates as of 2012

Taxable Income	Pay this Amount on Base Income	Plus This Percentage on Anything Over the Base
$0–$50,000	$ 0	15%
$50,001–$75,000	7,500	25
$75,001–$100,000	13,750	34
$100,001–$335,000	22,250	39
$335,001–$10,000,000	113,900	34
$10,000,001–$15,000,000	3,400,000	35
$15,000,001–$18,333,333	5,150,000	38
Over $18,333,333	6,416,667	35

From your economics classes, you can probably guess that the firm's marginal tax rate is the amount of additional taxes a firm must pay out for every additional dollar of taxable income it earns.

Interest and Dividends Received by Corporations

Any interest that corporations receive is taxable, although a notable exception arises: Interest on state and local government bonds is exempt from federal taxes. The U.S. tax code allows this exception to encourage corporations to be better community citizens by supporting local governments. Another exception of sorts arises when one corporation owns stock in another corporation. Seventy percent of any dividends received from other corporations is tax exempt. Only the remaining 30 percent is taxed at the receiving corporation's tax rate.[1]

In addition to calculating their tax liability, firms also want to know their **average tax rate** and **marginal tax rate.** You can figure the average tax rate as the percentage of each dollar of taxable income that the firm pays in taxes.

$$\text{Average tax rate} = \frac{\text{Tax liability}}{\text{Taxable income}} \qquad (2\text{-}7)$$

[1]This tax code provision prevents or reduces any triple taxation that could occur: income could be taxed at three levels: (1) on the income from the dividend-paying firm, (2) as income for the dividend-receiving firm, and (3) finally, on the personal income of stockholders who receive dividends.

EXAMPLE 2-2

For interactive versions of this example visit www.mhhe.com/canM2e

Calculation of Corporate Taxes LG2-3

Indian Point Kennels Inc. earned $16.5 million taxable income (EBT) in 2012. Use the tax schedule in Table 2.3 to determine the firm's 2012 tax liability, its average tax rate, and its marginal tax rate.

SOLUTION:

From Table 2.3, the $16.5 million of taxable income puts Indian Point Kennels in the 38 percent marginal tax bracket. Thus

Tax liability = Tax on base amount + Tax rate (Amount over base)

= $5,150,000 + 0.38($16,500,000 − $15,000,000) = $5,720,000

Note that the base amount is the maximum dollar value listed in the previous tax bracket. In this example, we take the highest dollar value ($15,000,000) in the preceding tax bracket (35 percent). The additional percentage owed results from multiplying the income above and beyond the $15,000,000 (or $1,500,000) by the marginal tax rate (38 percent). The *average* tax rate for Indian Point Kennels Inc. comes to:

$$\text{Average tax rate} = \frac{\text{Tax liability}}{\text{Taxable income}}$$

$$= \$5,720,000/\$16,500,000 = 34.67\%$$

If Indian Point Kennels earned $1 more of taxable income, it would pay 38 cents (its tax rate of 38 percent) more in taxes. Thus, the firm's marginal tax rate is 38 percent.

Similar to problems 2-5, 2-6, 2-21, 2-22

Interest and Dividends Paid by Corporations

Corporate interest payments appear on the income statement as an expense item, so we deduct interest payments from operating income when the firm calculates taxable income. But any dividends paid by corporations to their shareholders are not tax deductible. This is one factor that encourages managers to finance projects with debt financing rather than to sell more stock. Suppose one firm uses mainly debt financing and another firm, with identical operations, uses mainly equity financing. The equity-financed firm will have very little interest expense to deduct for tax purposes. Thus, it will have higher taxable income and pay more taxes than the debt-financed firm. The debt-financed firm will pay fewer taxes and be able to pay more of its operating income to asset funders, that is, its bondholders and stockholders. So even stockholders prefer that firms finance assets primarily with debt rather than with stock. However, as mentioned earlier, increasing the amount of debt financing of the firm's assets also increases risks. So these affects must be balanced when selecting the optimal capital structure for a firm. The debt-versus-equity financing issue is called *capital structure*, which we address more fully later in the book.

time out!

2-3 What is an income statement?

2-4 When a corporation owns stock in another corporation, what percentage of dividends received on the stock is taxed?

EXAMPLE 2-3

For interactive versions of this example visit www.mhhe.com/canM2e

Corporate Taxes with Interest and Dividend Income LG2-3

In the previous example, suppose that in addition to the $16.5 million of taxable income, Indian Point Kennels Inc. received $250,000 of interest on state-issued bonds and $500,000 of dividends on common stock it owns in DPH Tree Farm Inc. How do these items affect Indian Point Kennel's tax liability, average tax rate, and marginal tax rate?

SOLUTION:

In this case, interest on the state-issued bonds is not taxable and should not be included in taxable income. Further, the first 70 percent of the dividends received from DPH Tree Farm is not taxable. Thus, only 30 percent of the dividends received are taxed, so:

Taxable income = $16,500,000 + (0.3)$500,000 = $16,650,000

Now Indian Point Kennel's tax liability will be:

Tax liability = $5,150,000 + 0.38($16,650,000 − $15,000,000) = $5,777,000

The $500,000 of dividend income increased Indian Point Kennel's tax liability by $57,000. Indian Point Kennels Inc.'s resulting average tax rate is now:

Average tax rate = $5,777,000/$16,650,000 = 34.70%

Finally, if Indian Point Kennels earned $1 more of taxable income, it would still pay 38 cents (based upon its marginal tax rate of 38 percent) more in taxes.

Similar to problems 2-6, 2-21, 2-22

EXAMPLE 2-4

Effect of Debt-versus-Equity Financing on Funders' Returns LG2-1

For interactive versions of this example visit www.mhhe.com/canM2e

Suppose that you are considering a stock investment in one of two firms (AllDebt Inc. and AllEquity Inc.), both of which operate in the same industry and have identical operating incomes of $5 million. AllDebt Inc. finances its $12 million in assets with $11 million in debt (on which it pays 10 percent interest) and $1 million in equity. AllEquity Inc. finances its $12 million in assets with no debt and $12 million in equity. Both firms pay 30 percent tax on their taxable income. Calculate the income that each firm has available to pay its debt and stockholders (the firms' asset funders) and the resulting returns to these asset funders for the two firms.

SOLUTION:

	AllDebt	AllEquity
Operating income	$5.00m	$5.00m
Less: Interest	1.10m	0.00m
Taxable income	$3.90m	$5.00m
Less: Taxes (30%)	1.17m	1.50m
Net income	$2.73m	$3.50m
Income available for asset funders (= Operating income − Taxes)	$3.83m	$3.50m
Return on asset-funders' investment	$3.83m/$12.00m = 31.92%	$3.50m/$12.00m = 29.17%

By financing most of its assets with debt and receiving the associated tax benefits from the interest paid on this debt, AllDebt Inc. is able to pay more of its operating income to the funders of its assets, i.e., its debt holders and stockholders, than AllEquity Inc.

Similar to problems 2-17, 2-18

STATEMENT OF CASH FLOWS LG2-4

Income statements and balance sheets are the most common financial documents available to the public. However, managers who make financial decisions need more than these two statements—reports of past performance—on which to base their decisions for today and into the future. A very important distinction between the accounting point of view and the finance point of view is that financial managers and investors are *far more interested in actual cash flows* than in the backward-looking profit listed on the income statement.

The **statement of cash flows** is a financial statement that shows the firm's cash flows over a given period of time. This statement reports the amounts of cash the firm has generated and distributed during a particular time period. The bottom line on the statement of cash flows—the difference between cash sources and uses—equals the change in cash and marketable securities on the firm's balance sheet from the previous year's balance. That is, the statement of cash flows reconciles noncash balance sheet items and income statement items to show changes in the cash and marketable securities account on the balance sheet over the particular analysis period.

To clarify why this statement is so crucial, it helps to understand that figures on an income statement may not represent the actual cash inflows and outflows for a firm during a given period of time. There are two main issues, GAAP accounting principles and non-cash income statement entries.

GAAP Accounting Principles

Company accountants must prepare firm income statements following GAAP principles. GAAP procedures require that the firm recognize revenue at the time of sale. But sometimes the company receives the cash before or after the time of sale. Likewise, GAAP counsels the firm to show production and other expenses on the balance sheet as the sales of those goods take place. So production and other expenses associated with a particular product's sale appear on the income statement (for example, cost of goods sold and depreciation) only when that product

▼**FIGURE 2.3** Sources and Uses of Cash

Sources of Cash	Uses of Cash
Net income	Net losses
Depreciation	Increase a noncash current asset
Decrease a noncash current asset	Increase a fixed asset
Decrease a fixed asset	Decrease a current liability
Increase a current liability	Decrease long-term debt
Increase long-term debt	Repurchase common or preferred stock
Sell common or preferred stock	Pay dividends

▼**FIGURE 2.4** The Statement of Cash Flows

Section A. Cash flows from operating activities

Net income

Additions (sources of cash):

Depreciation

Decrease in noncash current assets

Increase in accrued wages and taxes

Increase in accounts payable

Subtractions (uses of cash):

Increase in noncash current assets

Decrease in accrued wages and taxes

Decrease in accounts payable

Section B. Cash flows from investing activities

Additions:

Decrease in fixed assets

Decrease in other long-term assets

Subtractions:

Increase in fixed assets

Increase in other long-term assets

Section C. Cash flows from financing activities

Additions:

Increase in notes payable

Increase in long-term debt

Increase in common and preferred stock

Subtraction:

Decrease in notes payable

Decrease in long-term debt

Decrease in common and preferred stock

Dividends paid

Section D. Net change in cash and marketable securities

sells. Of course, just as with revenue recognition, actual cash outflows incurred with production may occur at a very different point in time—usually much earlier than GAAP principles allow the firm to formally recognize the expenses.

Noncash Income Statement Entries

Further, income statements contain several noncash entries, the largest of which is depreciation. Depreciation attempts to capture the noncash expense incurred as fixed assets deteriorate from the time of purchase to the point when those assets must be replaced.

Let's illustrate the effect of depreciation: Suppose a firm purchases a machine for $100,000. The machine has an expected life of five years and at the end of those five years, the machine will have no expected salvage value. The firm incurs a $100,000 cash outflow at the time of purchase. But the entire $100,000 does not appear on the income statement in the year that the firm purchases the machine—in accounting terms, the machine is not expensed in the year of purchase. Rather, if the firm's accounting department uses the straight-line depreciation method, it deducts only $100,000/5, or $20,000, each year as an expense. This $20,000 equipment expense is not a cash outflow for the firm. The person in charge of buying the machine knows that the cash flow occurred at the time of purchase—and it totaled $100,000 rather than $20,000.

In conclusion, finance professionals know that the firm needs cash, not accounting profits, to pay the firm's obligations as they come due, to fund the firm's operations and growth, and to compensate the firm's ultimate owners: its shareholders.

Sources and Uses of Cash LG2-5

In general, some activities increase cash (cash sources) and some decrease cash (cash uses). Figure 2.3 classifies the firm's basic cash sources and uses. Cash sources include decreasing noncash assets or increasing liabilities (or equity). For example, a drop in accounts receivable means that the firm has collected cash from its credit sales—a cash source. Likewise, if a firm sells new common stock, the firm has used primary markets to raise cash. In contrast, a firm uses cash when it increases noncash assets (buying inventory) or decreases a liability (paying off a bank loan). The statement of cash flows separates these cash flows into three categories or sections:

1. Cash flows from operating activities.

2. Cash flows from investing activities.

3. Cash flows from financing activities.

4. Net change in cash and marketable securities.

The basic setup of a statement of cash flows is shown in Figure 2.4 and a more detailed statement of cash flows for DPH Tree Farm Inc. for the year ending December 31, 2012, appears as Table 2.4.

Cash flows from operations (Section A in Figure 2.4 and Table 2.4) are those cash inflows and outflows that result directly from producing and selling the firm's products. These cash flows include:

- Net income.

- Depreciation.

- Working capital accounts other than cash and operations-related short-term debt.

Most finance professionals consider this top section of the statement of cash flows to be the most important. It shows quickly and compactly the firm's cash flows generated by and used for the production process. For example, DPH Tree Farm Inc. generated $97 million in cash flows from its 2012 production. That is, producing and selling the firm's product resulted in a net cash inflow for the firm. Managers and investors look for positive cash flows from operations as a sign of a successful firm—positive cash flows from the firm's operations is precisely what gives the firm value. Unless the firm has a stable, healthy pattern in its cash flows from operations, it is not financially healthy no matter what its level of cash flow from investing activities or cash flows from financing activities.

Cash flows from investing activities (Section B in Figure 2.4 and Table 2.4) are cash flows associated with buying or selling of fixed or other long-term assets. This section of the statement of cash flows shows cash inflows and outflows from long-term investing activities—most significantly the firm's investment in fixed assets. For example, DPH Tree Farm Inc. used $68 million in cash to purchase fixed and other long-term assets in 2012. DPH funded this $68 million cash outflow with the $97 million cash surplus DPH Tree Farm produced from its operations.

Cash flows from financing activities (Section C in Figure 2.4 and Table 2.4) are cash flows that result from debt and equity financing transactions. These include raising cash by:

- Issuing short-term debt.

- Issuing long-term debt.

- Issuing stock.

or using cash to:

- Pay dividends.

- Pay off debt.

- Buy back stock.

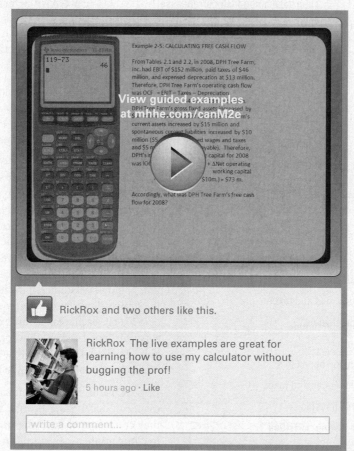

Example 2-5: CALCULATING FREE CASH FLOW

From Tables 2.1 and 2.2, in 2008, DPH Tree Farm, Inc. had EBIT of $152 million, paid taxes of $46 million, and expensed deprecation at $13 million. Therefore, DPH Tree Farm's operating cash flow was OCF = EBIT − Taxes − Depreciation.

View guided examples at mhhe.com/canM2e

DPH Tree Farm's gross fixed assets increased by [...] current assets increased by $15 million and spontaneous current liabilities increased by $10 million ($5 [...] wages and taxes and $5 m[...] yable). Therefore, DPH's i[...] capital for 2008 was IO[...] + ΔNet operating working capital [...] $10m.) = $73 m.

Accordingly, what was DPH Tree Farm's free cash flow for 2008?

👍 RickRox and two others like this.

RickRox The live examples are great for learning how to use my calculator without bugging the prof!

5 hours ago · Like

write a comment...

In 2012, DPH Tree Farm Inc.'s financing activities produced a net cash outflow of $30 million. As we saw with cash flows from financing activities, this $30 million cash outflow was funded (at least partially) with the $97 million cash surplus DPH Tree Farm produced from its operations. Managers, investors, and analysts normally expect the cash flows from financing activities to include small amounts of net borrowing along with dividend payments. If, however, a firm is going through a major period of expansion, net borrowing could reasonably be much higher.

Net change in cash and marketable securities (Section D in Figure 2.4 and Table 2.4), the bottom line of the statement of cash flows, shows the sum of cash flows

DPH Tree Farm reported net income of $90 million yet reported a net change in cash and marketable securities of − $1 million on its statement of cash flows.

DPH TREE FARM INC. Statement of Cash Flows for Year Ending December 31, 2012 (in millions of dollars)	
	2012
Section A. Cash flows from operating activities	
Net income	$90
Additions (sources of cash):	
Depreciation	13
Increase in accrued wages and taxes	5
Increase in accounts payable	5
Subtractions (uses of cash):	
Increase in accounts receivable	−5
Increase in inventory	−11
Net cash flow from operating activities	$97
Section B. Cash flows from investing activities	
Subtractions:	
Increase in fixed assets	−$68
Increase in other long-term assets	0
Net cash flow from investing activities	−$68
Section C. Cash flows from financing activities	
Additions:	
Increase in notes payable	$ 0
Increase in long-term debt	5
Increase in common and preferred stock	0
Subtractions:	
Preferred stock dividends paid	−10
Common stock dividends paid	−25
Net cash flow from financing activities	−$30
Section D. Net change in cash and marketable securities	−$ 1

from operations, investing activities, and financing activities. This sum will reconcile to the net change in cash and marketable securities account on the balance sheet over the period of analysis. For example, the bottom line of the statement of cash flows for DPH Tree Farm is −$1 million. This is also the change in the cash and marketable securities account on the balance sheet (in Table 2.1) between 2011 and 2012 ($24 million − $25 million = −$1 million). In this case, the firm's operating, investing, and financing activities combined to produce a net drain on the firm's cash during 2012—cash outflows were greater than cash inflows, largely because of the $68 million investment in long-term and fixed assets. Of course, when the bottom line is positive, a firm's cash inflows exceed cash outflows for the period.

Even though a company may report a large amount of net income on its income statement during a year, the firm may actually receive a positive, negative, or zero amount of cash. For example, DPH Tree Farm Inc. reported net income of $90 million on its income statement (in Table 2.2), yet reported a net change in cash and marketable securities of −$1 million on its statement of cash flows (in Table 2.4). Accounting rules under GAAP create this sense of discord: Net income is the result of accounting rules, or GAAP, that do not necessarily reflect the firm's cash flows. While the income statement shows a firm's accounting-based income, the statement of cash flows more often reflects reality today and is thus more important to managers and investors as they seek to answer such important questions as:

- Does the firm generate sufficient cash to pay its obligations, thus avoiding financial distress?

- Does the firm generate sufficient cash to purchase assets needed for sustained growth?

- Does the firm generate sufficient cash to pay down its outstanding debt obligations?

cash flows from operations Cash flows that are the direct result of the production and sale of the firm's products.

cash flows from investing activities Cash flows associated with the purchase or sale of fixed or other long-term assets.

cash flows from financing activities Cash flows that result from debt and equity financing transactions.

net change in cash and marketable securities The sum of the cash flows from operations, investing activities, and financing activities.

free cash flows The cash that is actually available for distribution to the investors in the firm after the investments that are necessary to sustain the firm's ongoing operations are made.

FREE CASH FLOW

The statement of cash flows measures net cash flow as net income plus noncash adjustments. However, to maintain cash flows over time, firms must continually replace working capital and fixed assets and develop new products. Thus, firm managers cannot use the available cash flows any way they please. Specifically, the value of a firm's operations depends on the future expected **free cash flows,** defined as after-tax operating profit minus the amount of new investment in working capital, fixed assets, and the development of new products. Thus, free cash flow represents the cash that is actually available for distribution to the investors in the firm—the firm's debt holders and stockholders—after the investments that are necessary to sustain the firm's ongoing operations are made.

To calculate free cash flow (FCF), we use the mathematical equation that appears below:

$$\begin{aligned} FCF &= [EBIT(1 - Tax\ rate) + Depreciation] \\ &\quad - [\Delta\ Gross\ fixed\ assets \\ &\quad + \Delta Net\ operating\ working\ capital] \\ &= Operating\ cash\ flow \\ &\quad - Investment\ in\ operating\ capital \quad (2\text{-}8) \end{aligned}$$

To calculate free cash flow, we start with operating cash flow. Firms generate operating cash flow (OCF) after they have paid necessary operating expenses and taxes. Depreciation, a noncash charge, is added back to after-tax operating profit to determine total OCF. We add other relevant noncash charges, such as amortization and depletion, back as well. Firms either buy physical assets or earmark funds for eventual equipment replacement to sustain firm operations; this is called *investment in operating capital (IOC)*. In accounting terms, IOC includes the firm's gross investments (or changes) in fixed assets, current assets, and spontaneous current liabilities (such as accounts payable and accrued wages).

Like the bottom line shown on the statement of cash flows, the level of free cash flow can be positive, zero, or negative. A positive free cash flow value means that the firm may distribute funds to its investors (debt holders and stockholders.) When the firm's free cash flows come in as zero or negative, however, the firm's operations produce no cash flows available for investors. Of course, if free cash flow is negative because operating cash flow is negative, investors are likely to take up the issue with the firm's management. Negative free cash flows as a result of negative operating cash flows generally indicate that the firm is experiencing operating or managerial problems.

A firm with positive operating cash flows, but negative free cash flows, however, is not necessarily a poorly managed firm. Firms that invest heavily in operating capital to support growth often have positive operating cash flows but negative free cash flows, but in this case, the negative free cash flow will likely result in growing future profits.

time out!

2-5 What is a statement of cash flows?

2-6 What do the three main sections on the statement of cash flows measure?

EXAMPLE 2-5

For interactive versions of this example visit www.mhhe.com/canM2e

Calculating Free Cash Flow LG2-5

From Tables 2.1 and 2.2, in 2012, DPH Tree Farm Inc. had EBIT of $152 million, a tax rate of 33.82 percent ($46m/$136m), and depreciation expense of $13 million. Therefore, DPH Tree Farm's operating cash flow was:

OCF = EBIT (1 − Tax rate) + Depreciation

= $152m (1 − 0.3382) + $13m = $114m

DPH Tree Farm's gross fixed assets increased by $68 million between 2011 and 2012. The firm's current assets increased by $15 million and spontaneous current liabilities increased by $10 million ($5 million in accrued wages and taxes and $5 million in accounts payable). Therefore, DPH's investment in operating capital for 2012 was:

IOC = Δ Gross fixed assets + Δ Net operating working capital

= $68m + ($15m − $10m) = $73m

Accordingly, what was DPH Tree Farm's free cash flow for 2012?

SOLUTION:

FCF = Operating cash flow − Investment in operating capital

= $114m − $73m = $41m

In other words, in 2012, DPH Tree Farm Inc. had cash flows of $41 million available to pay its stockholders and debt holders.

Similar to problems 2-9, 2-10

STATEMENT OF RETAINED EARNINGS

The **statement of retained earnings** provides additional details about changes in retained earnings during a reporting period. This financial statement reconciles net income earned during a given period and any cash dividends paid within that period on one side with the change in retained earnings between the beginning and ending of the period on the other. Table 2.5 presents DPH Tree Farm Inc.'s statement of retained earnings as of December 31, 2012. The statement shows that DPH Tree Farms brought in a net income of $90 million during 2012. The firm paid out $10 million in dividends to preferred stockholders and another $25 million to common stockholders. The firm then had $55 million to reinvest back into the firm, which shows as an increase in retained earnings. Thus, the retained earnings account on the balance sheet (Table 2.1) increased from $155 million at year-end 2011 to $210 million at year-end 2012.

Increases in retained earnings occur not just because a firm has net income, but also because the firm's common stockholders agree to let management reinvest net income back into the firm rather than pay it out as dividends. Reinvesting net income into retained earnings allows the firm to grow by providing additional funds that can be spent on plant and equipment, inventory, and other assets needed to generate even more profit. So, retained earnings represent a claim against all of the firm's assets and not against a particular asset.

statement of retained earnings Financial statement that reconciles net income earned during a given period and any cash dividends paid with the change in retained earnings over the period.

▼ **TABLE 2.5** Statement of Retained Earnings for DPH Tree Farm Inc.

DPH TREE FARM INC. Statement of Retained Earnings as of December 31, 2012 (in millions of dollars)		
		2012
Balance of retained earnings, December 31, 2011		$155
Plus: Net income for 2012		90
Less: Cash dividends paid		
Preferred stock	$10	
Common stock	25	
Total cash dividends paid		35
Balance of retained earnings, December 31, 2012		$210

EXAMPLE 2-6

Statement of Retained Earnings LG2-1

For interactive versions of this example visit www.mhhe.com/canM2e

Indian Point Kennels Inc. earned net income in 2012 of $10.78 million. The firm paid out $1 million in cash dividends to its preferred stockholders and $2.5 million in cash dividends to its common stockholders. The firm ended 2011 with $135.75 million in retained earnings. Construct a statement of retained earnings to calculate the year-end 2012 balance of retained earnings.

SOLUTION:

The statement of retained earnings for 2012 is as follows:

INDIAN POINT KENNELS INC. Statement of Retained Earnings as of December 31, 2012 (in millions of dollars)		
Balance of retained earnings, December 31, 2011		$135.75
Plus: Net income for 2012		10.78
Less: Cash dividends paid		
Preferred stock	$1.0	
Common stock	2.5	
Total cash dividends paid		3.50
Balance of retained earnings, December 31, 2012		$143.03

Similar to problems 2-11, 2-12

2-7 What is a statement of retained earnings?

2-8 If, during a given period, a firm pays out more in dividends than it has net income, what happens to the firm's retained earnings?

CAUTIONS IN INTERPRETING FINANCIAL STATEMENTS LG2-6

As we mentioned earlier in the chapter, firms must prepare their financial statements according to GAAP. GAAP provides a common set of standards intended to produce objective and precise financial statements. But recall also that managers have significant discretion over their reported earnings. Managers and financial analysts have recognized for years that firms use considerable latitude in using accounting rules to manage their reported

finance at work //: markets

Coldwater Creek Receives Automatic Delisting Notice from Nasdaq as a Result of Incomplete 10-Q Filing

Coldwater Creek Inc. announced today that it received a Nasdaq Staff Determination on June 14, 2006, stating that Coldwater Creek (the "Company") failed to comply with Marketplace Rule 4310(c)(14) because its Quarterly Report on Form 10-Q for the quarter ended April 29, 2006 (the "Form 10-Q") filed on June 8, 2006, was incomplete. NASDAQ Staff Determination notices are generated automatically in these circumstances and indicate that, due to such noncompliance, Coldwater Creek's common stock will be subject to delisting.

As indicated in the Form 10-Q, the Company's independently registered public accounting firm had not completed its review of the financial information included in the Form 10-Q when it made the filing due to the Company's pending restatement of certain historical financial information. As a result, the Company was unable to provide the officer certifications required by . . . the Sarbanes-Oxley Act of 2002 with the Form 10-Q.

In the interim, the Company is working diligently to complete the amendment to its Form 10-K for the fiscal year ended January 28, 2006 to reflect the restated financial information so that the Company's independently registered public accounting firm can complete its review of the financial information in the Form 10-Q. Once this review is completed, the Company intends to file as soon as possible a fully compliant amended Form 10-Q/A, including the certifications required under . . . the Sarbanes-Oxley Act. It is currently expected that the Company's amended Form 10-K filing will be finalized prior to the Nasdaq hearing date, which will enable the Company to file its amended Form 10-Q and return to compliance with Nasdaq's Marketplace Rules.

Stories like these are not all that rare. In 2010 and 2011, tech company Quantum and retailer American Apparel also faced similar problems.

Want to know more?

Key Words to Search For Updates: **Sarbanes-Oxley Act of 2002, financial statements, 10Q filing, 10K filing**

Source: *The Wall Street Journal,* June 20, 2006, p. A3.

earnings in a wide variety of contexts. Indeed, within the GAAP framework, firms can "smooth" earnings. That is, firms often take steps to over- or understate earnings at various times. Managers may choose to smooth earnings to show investors that firm assets are growing steadily. Similarly, one firm may be using straight-line depreciation for its fixed assets, while another is using a modified accelerated cost recovery method (MACRS), which causes depreciation to accrue quickly. If the firm uses MACRS accounting methods, its managers write fixed asset values down quickly; assets will thus have lower book values than if the firm used straight-line depreciation methods.

This process of controlling a firm's earnings is called **earnings management.** At the extreme, earnings management has resulted in some widely reported accounting scandals involving Enron, Merck, WorldCom, and other major U.S. corporations that tried to artificially influence their earnings by manipulating accounting rules. Congress responded to the spate of corporate scandals that emerged after 2001 with the **Sarbanes-Oxley Act,** passed in June 2002. Sarbanes-Oxley requires public companies to ensure that their corporate boards' audit committees have considerable experience applying generally accepted accounting principles (GAAP) for financial statements. The act also requires that a firm's senior management must sign off on the financial statements of the firm, certifying the statements as accurate and representative of the firm's financial condition during the period covered. If a firm's board of directors or senior managers fail to comply with Sarbanes-Oxley (SOX), the firm may be delisted from stock exchanges.

As illustrated in the Finance at Work reading, Quantum Technologies failed to file quarterly reports for July and October 2009 in a timely manner. As a result, the firm's common stock became subject to delisting. Congress's goal in passing SOX was to prevent deceptive accounting and management practices and to bring stability to jittery stock markets battered in 2002 by accounting and managerial scandals that cost employees their life savings and harmed many innocent shareholders as well. ■

time **out!**

2-9 What is earnings management?

Get Online

mhhe.com/canM2e

for study materials including self-test problems with solutions, quizzes, research projects, minicases, and videos

Your Turn...

Questions

1. List and describe the four major financial statements. *(LG2-1)*

2. On which of the four major financial statements *(balance sheet, income statement, statement of cash flows, or statement of retained earnings)* would you find the following items? *(LG2-1)*

   a. Earnings before taxes.

   b. Net plant and equipment.

   c. Increase in fixed assets.

   d. Gross profits.

   e. Balance of retained earnings, December 31, 20xx.

   f. Common stock and paid-in surplus.

   g. Net cash flow from investing activities.

   h. Accrued wages and taxes.

   i. Increase in inventory.

3. What is the difference between current liabilities and long-term debt? *(LG2-1)*

4. How does the choice of accounting method used to record fixed asset depreciation affect management of the balance sheet? *(LG2-1)*

5. What are the costs and benefits of holding liquid securities on a firm's balance sheet? *(LG2-1)*

6. Why can the book value and market value of a firm differ? *(LG2-2)*

7. From a firm manager's or investor's point of view, which is more important—the book value of a firm or the market value of the firm? *(LG2-2)*

8. What do we mean by a progressive tax structure? *(LG2-3)*

9. What is the difference between an average tax rate and a marginal tax rate? *(LG2-3)*

10. How does the payment of interest on debt affect the amount of taxes the firm must pay? *(LG2-3)*

11. The income statement is prepared using GAAP. How does this affect the reported revenue and expense measures listed on the balance sheet? *(LG2-4)*

12. Why do financial managers and investors find cash flow to be more important than accounting profit? *(LG2-4)*

13. Which of the following activities result in an increase (decrease) in a firm's cash? *(LG2-5)*

    a. Decrease fixed assets.

    b. Decrease accounts payable.

    c. Pay dividends.

    d. Sell common stock.

    e. Decrease accounts receivable.

    f. Increase notes payable.

14. What is the difference between net cash flow from operating activities, net cash flow from investing activities, and net cash flow from financing activities? *(LG2-5)*

15. What are free cash flows for a firm? What does it mean when a firm's free cash flow is negative? *(LG2-5)*

16. What is earnings management? *(LG2-6)*

17. What does the Sarbanes-Oxley Act require of firm managers? *(LG2-6)*

Problems

BASIC PROBLEMS

2-1 **Balance Sheet** You are evaluating the balance sheet for Goodman's Bees Corporation. From the balance sheet you find the following balances: cash and marketable securities $=$ $100,000; accounts receivable $=$ $1,200,000; inventory $=$ $2,100,000; accrued wages and taxes $=$ $500,000; accounts payable $=$ $800,000; and notes payable $=$ $600,000. Calculate Goodman Bees' net working capital. *(LG2-1)*

2-2 **Balance Sheet** Zoeckler Mowing & Landscaping's year-end 2012 balance sheet lists current assets of $435,200; fixed assets of $550,800; current liabilities of $416,600; and long-term debt of $314,500. Calculate Zoeckler's total stockholders' equity. *(LG2-1)*

2-3 **Income Statement** The Fitness Studio Inc.'s 2012 income statement lists the following income and expenses: EBIT $=$ $538,000; interest expense $=$ $63,000; and net income $=$ $435,000. Calculate the 2012 taxes reported on the income statement. *(LG2-1)*

2-4 **Income Statement** The Fitness Studio Inc.'s 2012 income statement lists the following income and expenses: EBIT $=$ $773,500; interest expense $=$ $100,000; and taxes = $234,500. The firm has no preferred stock outstanding and 100,000 shares of common stock outstanding. Calculate the 2012 earnings per share. *(LG2-1)*

2-5 **Corporate Taxes** Oakdale Fashions Inc. had $245,000 in 2012 taxable income. Using the tax schedule in Table 2.3, calculate the company's 2012 income taxes. What is the average tax rate? What is the marginal tax rate? *(LG2-3)*

2-6 **Corporate Taxes** Hunt Taxidermy Inc. is concerned about the taxes paid by the company in 2012. In addition to $42.4 million of taxable income, the firm received $2,975,000 of interest on state-issued bonds and $1,000,000 of dividends on common stock it owns in Oakdale Fashions Inc. Calculate Hunt Taxidermy's tax liability, average tax rate, and marginal tax rate. *(LG2-3)*

2-7 **Statement of Cash Flows** Ramakrishnan Inc. reported 2012 net income of $15 million and depreciation of $2,650,000. The top part of Ramakrishnan Inc.'s 2012 and 2011 balance sheets is reproduced below (in millions of dollars).

	2012	2011		2012	2011
Current assets:			Current liabilities:		
Cash and marketable securities	$ 20	$ 15	Accrued wages and taxes	$ 19	$ 18
Accounts receivable	84	75	Accounts payable	51	45
Inventory	121	110	Notes payable	45	40
Total	$225	$200	Total	$115	$103

Calculate the 2012 net cash flow from operating activities for Ramakrishnan Inc. *(LG2-4)*

2-8 **Statement of Cash Flows** In 2012, Usher Sports Shop had cash flows from investing activities of −$4,364,000 and cash flows from financing activities of −$5,880,000. The balance in the firm's cash account was $1,615,000 at the beginning of 2012 and $1,742,000 at the end of the year. Calculate Usher Sports Shop's cash flow from operations for 2012. *(LG2-4)*

2-9 **Free Cash Flow** You are considering an investment in Fields and Struthers Inc. and want to evaluate the firm's free cash flow. From the income statement, you see that Fields and Struthers earned an EBIT of $62 million, had a tax rate of 30 percent, and its depreciation expense was $5 million. Fields and Struthers' gross fixed assets increased by $32 million from 2011 to 2012. The firm's current assets increased by $20 million and spontaneous current liabilities increased by $12 million. Calculate Fields and Struthers' operating cash flow, investment in operating capital, and free cash flow for 2012. *(LG2-5)*

2-10 **Free Cash Flow** Tater and Pepper Corp. reported free cash flows for 2012 of $39.1 million and investment in operating capital of $22.1 million. Tater and Pepper incurred $13.6 million in depreciation expense and paid $28.9 million in taxes on EBIT in 2012. Calculate Tater and Pepper's 2012 EBIT. *(LG2-5)*

2-11 **Statement of Retained Earnings** Mr. Husker's Tuxedos Corp. began the year 2012 with $256 million in retained earnings. The firm earned net income of $33 million in 2012 and paid dividends of $5 million to its preferred stockholders and $10 million to its common stockholders. What is the year-end 2012 balance in retained earnings for Mr. Husker's Tuxedos? *(LG2-1)*

2-12 **Statement of Retained Earnings** Use the following information to find dividends paid to common stockholders during 2012. *(LG2-1)*

Balance of retained earnings, December 31, 2011		$462m
Plus: Net income for 2012		15m
Less: Cash dividends paid		
Preferred stock	$ 1m	
Common stock	☐	
Total cash dividends paid		☐
Balance of retained earnings, December 31, 2012		$470m

2-13 Balance Sheet Brenda's Bar and Grill has total assets of $15 million, of which $5 million are current assets. Cash makes up 10 percent of the current assets and accounts receivable makes up another 40 percent of current assets. Brenda's gross plant and equipment has a book value of $11.5 million and other long-term assets have a book value of $500,000. Using this information, what is the balance of inventory and the balance of depreciation on Bennda's Bar and Grill's balance sheet? *(LG2-1)*

2-14 Balance Sheet Glen's Tobacco Shop has total assets of $91.8 million. Fifty percent of these assets are financed with debt of which $28.9 million is current liabilities. The firm has no preferred stock but the balance in common stock and paid-in surplus is $20.4 million. Using this information, what is the balance for long-term debt and retained earnings on Glen's Tobacco Shop's balance sheet? *(LG2-1)*

2-15 Market Value versus Book Value Muffin's Masonry Inc.'s balance sheet lists net fixed assets as $14 million. The fixed assets could currently be sold for $19 million. Muffin's current balance sheet shows current liabilities of $5.5 million and net working capital of $4.5 million. If all the current accounts were liquidated today, the company would receive $7.25 million cash after paying the $5.5 million in current liabilities. What is the book value of Muffin's Masonry's assets today? What is the market value of these assets? *(LG2-2)*

2-16 Market Value versus Book Value Ava's SpinBall Corp. lists fixed assets of $12 million on its balance sheet. The firm's fixed assets have recently been appraised at $16 million. Ava's SpinBall Corp.'s balance sheet also lists current assets at $5 million. Current assets were appraised at $6 million. Current liabilities' book and market values stand at $3 million and the firm's book and market values of long-term debt are $7 million. Calculate the book and market values of the firm's stockholders' equity. Construct the book value and market value balance sheets for Ava's SpinBall Corp. *(LG2-2)*

2-17 Debt versus Equity Financing You are considering a stock investment in one of two firms (NoEquity Inc. and NoDebt Inc.), both of which operate in the same industry and have identical operating income of $32.5 million. NoEquity Inc. finances its $65 million in assets with $64 million in debt (on which it pays 10 percent interest annually) and $1 million in equity. NoDebt Inc. finances its $65 million in assets with no debt and $65 million in equity. Both firms pay a tax rate of 30 percent on their taxable income. Calculate the net income and return on assets for the two firms. *(LG2-1)*

2-18 Debt versus Equity Financing You are considering a stock investment in one of two firms (AllDebt Inc. and AllEquity Inc.), both of which operate in the same industry and have identical operating income of $12.5 million. AllDebt Inc. finances its $25 million in assets with $24 million in debt (on which it pays 10 percent interest annually) and $1 million in equity. AllEquity Inc. finances its $25 million in assets with no debt and $25 million in equity. Both firms pay a tax rate of 30 percent on their taxable income. Calculate the income available to pay the asset funders (the debt holders and stockholders) and resulting return on assets for the two firms. *(LG2-1)*

2-19 Income Statement You have been given the following information for Corky's Bedding Corp.:

    a. Net sales = $11,250,000.

    b. Cost of goods sold = $7,500,000.

    c. Other operating expenses = $250,000.

    d. Addition to retained earnings = $1,000,000.

    e. Dividends paid to preferred and common stockholders = $495,000.

    f. Interest expense = $850,000.

The firm's tax rate is 35 percent. Calculate the depreciation expense for Corky's Bedding Corp. *(LG2-1)*

2-20 Income Statement You have been given the following information for Moore's HoneyBee Corp.:

a. Net sales = $32,000,000.

b. Gross profit = $18,700,000.

c. Other operating expenses = $2,500,000.

d. Addition to retained earnings = $4,700,000.

e. Dividends paid to preferred and common stockholders = $2,900,000.

f. Depreciation expense = $2,800,000.

The firm's tax rate is 35 percent. Calculate the cost of goods sold and the interest expense for Moore's HoneyBee Corp. *(LG2-1)*

2-21 Corporate Taxes The Dakota Corporation had a 2012 taxable income of $33,365,000 from operations after all operating costs but before (1) interest charges of $8,500,000; (2) dividends received of $750,000; (3) dividends paid of $5,250,000; and (4) income taxes. *(LG2-3)*

a. Use the tax schedule in Table 2.3 to calculate Dakota's income tax liability.

b. What are Dakota's average and marginal tax rates on taxable income?

2-22 Corporate Taxes Suppose that in addition to $17.85 million of taxable income, Texas Taco Inc. received $1,105,000 of interest on state-issued bonds and $760,000 of dividends on common stock it owns in Arizona Taco Inc. *(LG2-3)*

a. Use the tax schedule in Table 2.3 to calculate Texas Taco's income tax liability.

b. What are Texas Taco's average and marginal tax rates on taxable income?

2-23 Statement of Cash Flows Use the balance sheet and income statement below to construct a statement of cash flows for Clancy's Dog Biscuit Corporation. *(LG2-5)*

CLANCY'S DOG BISCUIT CORPORATION Balance Sheet as of December 31, 2012 and 2011 (in millions of dollars)					
Assets	2012	2011	**Liabilities and Equity**	2012	2011
Current assets:			Current liabilities:		
Cash and marketable securities	$ 5	$ 5	Accrued wages and taxes	$ 10	$ 6
Accounts receivable	20	19	Accounts payable	16	15
Inventory	36	29	Notes payable	14	13
Total	$ 61	$ 53	Total	$ 40	$ 34
Fixed assets:			Long-term debt:	$ 57	$ 53
Gross plant and equipment	$106	$ 88	Stockholders' equity:		
Less: Depreciation	15	11	Preferred stock (2 million shares)	$ 2	$ 2
Net plant and equipment	$ 91	$ 77	Common stock and paid-in surplus (5 million shares)	11	11
Other long-term assets	15	15	Retained earnings	57	45
Total	$106	$ 92	Total	$ 70	$ 58
Total assets	$167	$145	Total liabilities and equity	$167	$145

CLANCY'S DOG BISCUIT CORPORATION
Income Statement for Years Ending December 31, 2012 and 2011
(in millions of dollars)

	2012	2011
Net sales	$76	$80
Less: Cost of goods sold	38	34
Gross profits	$38	$46
Less: Depreciation	4	4
Other operating expenses	6	5
Earnings before interest and taxes (EBIT)	$28	$37
Less: Interest	5	5
Earnings before taxes (EBT)	$23	$32
Less: Taxes	7	10
Net income	$16	$22
Less: Preferred stock dividends	$ 1	$ 1
Net income available to common stockholders	$15	$21
Less: Common stock dividends	3	3
Addition to retained earnings	$12	$18
Per (common) share data:		
Earnings per share (EPS)	$ 3.00	$ 4.20
Dividends per share (DPS)	$ 0.60	$ 0.60
Book value per share (BVPS)	$13.60	$11.20
Market value (price) per share (MVPS)	$14.25	$14.60

2-24 Statement of Cash Flows Use the balance sheet and income statement below to construct a statement of cash flows for Valium's Medical Supply Corporation. *(LG2-5)*

VALIUM'S MEDICAL SUPPLY CORPORATION
Balance Sheet as of December 31, 2012 and 2011
(in thousands of dollars)

Assets	2012	2011	Liabilities and Equity	2012	2012
Current assets:			Current liabilities:		
Cash and marketable securities	$ 74	$ 73	Accrued wages and taxes	$ 58	$ 45
Accounts receivable	199	189	Accounts payable	159	145
Inventory	322	291	Notes payable	131	131
Total	$ 595	$ 553	Total	$ 348	$ 321
Fixed assets:			Long-term debt:	$ 565	$ 549
Gross plant and equipment	$1,084	$ 886	Stockholders' equity:		
Less: Depreciation	153	116	Preferred stock (6 thousand shares)	$ 6	$ 6
Net plant and equipment	$ 931	$ 770	Common stock and paid-in surplus (100 thousand shares)	120	120
Other long-term assets	130	130	Retained earnings	617	457
Total	$1,061	$ 900	Total	$ 743	$ 583
Total assets	$1,656	$1,453	Total liabilities and equity	$1,656	$1,453

VALIUM'S MEDICAL SUPPLY CORPORATION Income Statement for Years Ending December 31, 2012 and 2011 (in thousands of dollars)		
	2012	2011
Net sales	$888	$798
Less: Cost of goods sold	387	350
Gross profits	$501	$448
Less: Depreciation	37	35
Other operating expenses	48	42
Earnings before interest and taxes (EBIT)	$416	$371
Less: Interest	46	40
Earnings before taxes (EBT)	$370	$331
Less: Taxes	129	112
Net income	$241	$219
Less: Preferred stock dividends	$ 6	$ 6
Net income available to common stockholders	$235	$213
Less: Common stock dividends	75	75
Addition to retained earnings	$160	$138
Per (common) share data:		
Earnings per share (EPS)	$ 2.35	$ 2.13
Dividends per share (DPS)	$ 0.75	$ 0.75
Book value per share (BVPS)	$ 7.37	$ 5.77
Market value (price) per share (MVPS)	$ 8.40	$ 6.25

2-25 **Statement of Cash Flows** Chris's Outdoor Furniture Inc. has net cash flows from operating activities for the last year of $340 million. The income statement shows that net income is $315 million and depreciation expense is $46 million. During the year, the change in inventory on the balance sheet was $38 million, change in accrued wages and taxes was $15 million, and change in accounts payable was $20 million. At the beginning of the year, the balance of accounts receivable was $50 million. Calculate the end-of-year balance for accounts receivable. *(LG2-5)*

2-26 **Statement of Cash Flows** Dogs 4 U Corporation has net cash flow from financing activities for the last year of $34 million. The company paid $178 million in dividends last year. During the year, the change in notes payable on the balance sheet was $39 million and change in common and preferred stock was $0. The end-of-year balance for long-term debt was $315 million. Calculate the beginning-of-year balance for long-term debt. *(LG2-5)*

2-27 **Free Cash Flow** The 2012 income statement for Duffy's Pest Control shows that depreciation expense was $197 million, EBIT was $494 million, and the tax rate was 30 percent. At the beginning of the year, the balance of gross fixed assets was $1,562 million and net operating working capital was $417 million. At the end of the year, gross fixed assets was $1,803 million. Duffy's free cash flow for the year was $424 million. Calculate the end-of-year balance for net operating working capital. *(LG2-5)*

2-28 **Free Cash Flow** The 2012 income statement for Egyptian Noise Blasters shows that depreciation expense is $85 million, EBIT is $365 million, and taxes paid on EBIT are $119 million. At the end of the year, the balance of gross fixed assets was $655 million. The change in net operating working capital during the year was $73 million. Egyptian's free cash flow for the year was $190 million. Calculate the beginning-of-year balance for gross fixed assets. *(LG2-5)*

2-29 Statement of Retained Earnings Thelma and Louie Inc. started the year with a balance of retained earnings of $543 million and ended the year with retained earnings of $589 million. The company paid dividends of $35 million to the preferred stockholders and $88 million to common stockholders. Calculate Thelma and Louie's net income for the year. *(LG2-1)*

2-30 Statement of Retained Earnings Jamaica Tours Inc. started the year with a balance of retained earnings of $1,780 million. The company reported net income for the year of $284 million and paid dividends of $17 million to the preferred stockholders and $59 million to common stockholders. Calculate Jamaica Tour's end-of-year balance in retained earnings. *(LG2-1)*

ADVANCED PROBLEMS

2-31 Income Statement Listed below is the 2012 income statement for Tom and Sue Travels Inc.

TOM AND SUE TRAVELS INC. Income Statement for Year Ending December 31, 2012 (in millions of dollars)	
Net sales	$16.500
Less: Cost of goods sold	7.100
Gross profits	$ 9.400
Less: Depreciation	2.900
Other operating expenses	3.200
Earnings before interest and taxes (EBIT)	$ 3.300
Less: Interest	0.950
Earnings before taxes (EBT)	$ 2.350
Less: Taxes	0.705
Net income	$ 1.645

The CEO of Tom and Sue's wants the company to earn a net income of $2.25 million in 2013. Cost of goods sold is expected to be 60 percent of net sales, depreciation and other operating expenses are not expected to change, interest expense is expected to increase to $1.05 million, and the firm's tax rate will be 30 percent. Calculate the net sales needed to produce net income of $2.25 million. *(LG2-1)*

2-32 Income Statement You have been given the following information for Kellygirl's Athletic Wear Corp. for the year 2012:

 a. Net sales = $38,250,000.

 b. Cost of goods sold = $22,070,000.

 c. Other operating expenses = $5,300,000.

 d. Addition to retained earnings = $1,195,500.

 e. Dividends paid to preferred and common stockholders = $1,912,000.

 f. Interest expense = $1,785,000.

 g. The firm's tax rate is 30 percent.

 h. In 2013, net sales are expected to increase by $9.75 million.

 i. Cost of goods sold is expected to be 60 percent of net sales.

 j. Depreciation and other operating expenses are expected to be the same as in 2012.

 k. Interest expense is expected to be $2,004,286.

l. The tax rate is expected to be 30 percent of EBT.

m. Dividends paid to preferred and common stockholders will not change.

Calculate the addition to retained earnings expected in 2013. *(LG2-1)*

2-33 **Free Cash Flow** Rebecky's Flowers 4U Inc. had free cash flows during 2012 of $43 million, EBIT of $110 million, tax expense paid on its EBIT of $25 million, and depreciation of $14 million. Using this information, fill in the blanks on Rebecky's balance sheet below. *(LG2-5)*

REBECKY'S FLOWERS 4U INC. Balance Sheet as of December 31, 2012 and 2011 (in millions of dollars)					
Assets	2012	2011	**Liabilities and Equity**	2012	2011
Current assets:			Current liabilities:		
Cash and marketable securities	$ 28	$ 25	Accrued wages and taxes	$ 17	$ 15
Accounts receivable	75	65	Accounts payable		50
Inventory	118	100	Notes payable	45	45
Total	$221	$190	Total	$	$110
Fixed assets:			Long-term debt:	$	$190
Gross plant and equipment	$333	$300	Stockholders' equity:		
Less: Depreciation	54	40	Preferred stock (5 million shares)	$ 5	$ 5
Net plant and equipment	$279	$260	Common stock and paid-in surplus (20 million shares)	40	40
Other long-term assets	50	50	Retained earnings	192	155
Total	$329	$310	Total	$237	$200
Total assets	$550	$500	Total liabilities and equity	$550	$500

2-34 **Free Cash Flow** Vinny's Overhead Construction had free cash flow during 2012 of $25.4 million. The change in gross fixed assets on Vinny's balance sheet during 2012 was $7.0 million and the change in net operating working capital was $8.4 million. Using this information, fill in the blanks on Vinny's income statement below. *(LG2-5)*

VINNY'S OVERHEAD CONSTRUCTION CORP. Income Statement for Year Ending December 31, 2012 (in millions of dollars)	
Net sales	$
Less: Cost of goods sold	116.10
Gross profits	$66.00
Less: Depreciation	10.20
Other operating expenses	$12.40
Earnings before interest and taxes (EBIT)	
Less: Interest	
Earnings before taxes (EBT)	$
Less: Taxes	
Net income	$27.64

analyzing
financial statements

We reviewed the major financial statements in Chapter 2. These financial statements provide information on a firm's financial position at a point in time or its operations over some past period of time. But these financial statements' real value lies in the fact that managers, investors, and analysts can use the information the statements contain to analyze the current financial performance or condition of the firm. More importantly, managers can use this information to plan changes that will improve the firm's future performance and, ultimately, its market value.

Managers, investors, and analysts universally use ratios to evaluate financial statements. **Ratio analysis** involves calculating and analyzing financial ratios to assess a firm's performance and to identify actions that could improve firm performance. The most frequently used ratios fall into five groups: (1) liquidity ratios, (2) asset management ratios, (3) debt management ratios, (4) profitability ratios, and (5) market value ratios. Each of the five groups focuses on a specific area of the financial statements that managers, investors, and analysts assess. ■

ratio analysis
The process of calculating and analyzing financial ratios to assess the firm's performance and to identify actions needed to improve firm performance.

liquidity ratios
Measure the relation between a firm's liquid (or current) assets and its current liabilities.

In this chapter, we review these ratios, describe what each ratio means, and identify the general trend (higher or lower) that managers and investment analysts look for in each ratio. Note as we review the ratios that the number calculated for a ratio is not always good or bad and that extreme values (either high or low) can be a bad sign for a firm. We will discuss how a ratio that seems too good can actually be bad for a company. We will also see how ratios interrelate—how a change in one ratio may affect the value of several ratios. It is often hard to make sense of a set of performance ratios. Thus, when managers or investors review a firm's financial position through ratio analysis, they often start by evaluating trends in the firm's financial ratios over time and by comparing their firm's ratios with that of other firms in the same industry. Finally, we discuss cautions that you should take when using ratio analysis to evaluate firm performance. As we go through the chapter, we show sample ratio analysis using the financial statements for DPH Tree Farm Inc. listed in Tables 2.1 and 2.2.

LIQUIDITY RATIOS LG3-1

As we stated in Chapter 2, firms need cash and other liquid assets (or current assets) to pay their bills (or current liabilities) as they come due. **Liquidity ratios** measure the relationship between a firm's liquid (or current) assets and its current liabilities. The three most commonly used liquidity ratios are the current ratio, the quick (or acid-test) ratio, and the cash ratio.

$$\text{Current ratio} = \frac{\text{Current assets}}{\text{Current liabilities}} \quad (3\text{-}1)$$

The broadest liquidity measure, the current ratio, measures the dollars of current assets available to pay each dollar of current liabilities.

$$\begin{matrix}\text{Quick ratio} \\ (\text{acid-test ratio})\end{matrix} = \frac{\text{Current assets} - \text{Inventory}}{\text{Current liabilities}} \quad (3\text{-}2)$$

Inventories are generally the least liquid of a firm's current assets. Further, inventory is the current asset for which book values are the least reliable measures of market value. In practical terms, what this means is that if the firm must sell inventory to pay upcoming bills, the firm will most likely have to discount inventory items in order to liquidate them, and therefore, they are the current assets on which losses are most likely to occur. Therefore, the quick (or acid-test) ratio measures a firm's ability to pay off short-term obligations without relying on inventory sales. The quick ratio measures the dollars of more liquid assets (cash and marketable securities and accounts receivable) available to pay each dollar of current liabilities.

$$\text{Cash ratio} = \frac{\text{Cash and marketable securities}}{\text{Current liabilities}} \quad (3\text{-}3)$$

If the firm sells accounts receivable to pay upcoming bills, the firm must often discount the accounts receivable to sell them—the assets once again bring less than their book value. Therefore, the cash ratio measures a firm's ability to pay short-term obligations with its available cash and marketable securities.

Of course, liquidity on the balance sheet is important. The more liquid assets a firm holds, the less likely the firm is to experience financial distress. Thus, the higher the liquidity ratios, the less liquidity risk a firm has. But as with everything else in business, high liquidity represents a painful trade-off for the firm. Liquid assets generate little, if any, profits for the firm. In contrast,

time out!

3-1 What are the three major liquidity ratios used in evaluating financial statements?

3-2 How do the three major liquidity ratios used in evaluating financial statements differ?

3-3 Does a firm generally want to have high or low liquidity ratios? Why?

fixed assets are illiquid, but generate revenue for the firm. Thus, extremely high levels of liquidity guard against liquidity crises, but at the cost of lower returns on assets. High liquidity levels may actually show bad or indecisive firm management. Thus, in deciding the appropriate level of current assets to hold on the balance sheet, managers must consider the trade-off between

the advantages of being liquid versus the disadvantages of reduced profits. Note that a company with very predictable cash flows can maintain low levels of liquidity without incurring much liquidity risk.

asset management ratios Measure how efficiently a firm uses its assets (inventory, accounts receivable, and fixed assets), as well as its accounts payable.

ASSET MANAGEMENT RATIOS LG3-2

Asset management ratios measure how efficiently a firm uses its assets (inventory, accounts receivable, and fixed assets), as well as how efficiently the firm manages its accounts payable. The specific ratios allow managers and investors to evaluate whether a firm is holding a reasonable amount of each type of asset and whether management uses each type of asset to effectively generate sales. The most frequently used asset management ratios are listed below, grouped by type of asset.

Inventory Management

As they decide the optimal inventory level to hold on the balance sheet, managers must consider the trade-off between the advantages of holding sufficient levels of inventory to keep the production process going versus the costs of holding large

---

Calculating Liquidity Ratios LG3-1

Use the balance sheet (Table 2.1) and income statement (Table 2.2) for DPH Tree Farm Inc. to calculate the firm's 2012 values for the liquidity ratios.

SOLUTION:

The liquidity ratios for DPH Tree Farm Inc. are calculated as follows. The industry average is reported alongside each ratio.

$$\text{Current ratio} = \frac{\$205m}{\$120m} = 1.71 \text{ times} \qquad \text{Industry average} = 1.50 \text{ times}$$

$$\text{Quick ratio (acid-test ratio)} = \frac{\$205m - \$111m}{\$120m} = 0.78 \text{ times} \qquad \text{Industry average} = 0.50 \text{ times}$$

$$\text{Cash ratio} = \frac{\$24m}{\$120m} = 0.20 \text{ times} \qquad \text{Industry average} = 0.15 \text{ times}$$

All three liquidity ratios show that DPH Tree Farm Inc. has more liquidity on its balance sheet than the industry average (we discuss the process used to develop an industry average below). Thus, DPH Tree Farm has more cash and other liquid assets (or current assets) available to pay its bills (or current liabilities) as they come due than does the average firm in the tree farm industry.

Similar to Problems 3-1, 3-2

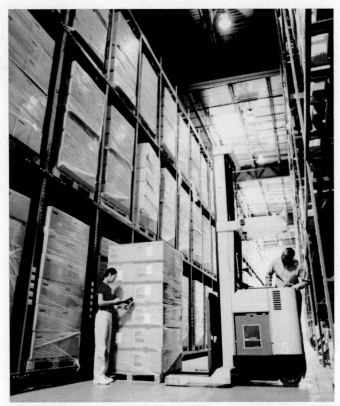

The inventory turnover ratio measures the number of dollars of sales produced per dollar of inventory.

reduced warehousing, monitoring, insurance, and any other costs of servicing the inventory. So, a high inventory turnover ratio or a low days' sales in inventory is generally a sign of good management.

However, if the inventory turnover ratio is extremely high and the days' sales in inventory is extremely low, the firm may not be holding sufficient inventory to prevent running out (or stocking out) of the raw materials needed to keep the production process going. Thus, production and sales stop, which wastes the firm's fixed resources. So, extremely high levels for the inventory turnover ratio and low levels for the days' sales in inventory ratio may actually be a sign of bad firm or production management. Note that companies with very good supply chain relations can maintain lower levels of inventory without incurring as much risk of stockouts.

Accounts Receivable Management

As they decide what level of accounts receivable to hold on the firm's balance sheet, managers must consider the trade-off between the advantages of increased sales by offering customers better terms versus the disadvantages of financing large amounts of accounts receivable. Two ratios used here are the average collection period and accounts receivable turnover.

$$\text{Average collection period (ACP)} = \frac{\text{Accounts receivable} \times 365 \text{ days}}{\text{Credit sales}} \quad (3\text{-}6)$$

The average collection period (ACP) measures the number of days accounts receivable are held before the firm collects cash from the sale.

amounts of inventory. Two frequently used ratios are the inventory turnover and days' sales in inventory.

$$\text{Inventory turnover} = \frac{\text{Sales or cost of goods sold}}{\text{Inventory}} \quad (3\text{-}4)$$

The inventory turnover measures the number of dollars of sales produced per dollar of inventory. Cost of goods sold is used in the numerator when managers want to emphasize that inventory is listed on the balance sheet at cost, that is, the cost of sales generated per dollar of inventory.

$$\text{Days' sales in inventory} = \frac{\text{Inventory} \times 365 \text{ days}}{\text{Sales or cost of goods sold}} \quad (3\text{-}5)$$

The days' sales in inventory ratio measures the number of days that inventory is held before the final product is sold.

$$\text{Accounts receivable turnover} = \frac{\text{Credit sales}}{\text{Accounts receivable}} \quad (3\text{-}7)$$

The accounts receivable turnover measures the number of dollars of sales produced per dollar of accounts receivable.

In general, a firm wants to produce a high level of sales per dollar of accounts receivable; that is, it wants to collect its accounts receivable as quickly as possible to reduce any cost of financing accounts receivable, including interest expense on liabilities used to finance accounts receivable and defaults

> "Firms offer accounts receivable terms as an incentive to get customers to buy products from their firm rather than a competing firm."

In general, a firm wants to produce a high level of sales per dollar of inventory; that is, it wants to turn inventory over (from raw materials to finished goods to sold goods) as quickly as possible. A high level of sales per dollar of inventory implies

associated with accounts receivable. In general, a high accounts receivable turnover or a low ACP is a sign of good management, which is well aware of financing costs and customer remittance habits.

However, if the accounts receivable turnover is extremely high and the ACP is extremely low, the firm's accounts receivable policy may be so strict that customers prefer to do business with competing firms. Firms offer accounts receivable terms as an incentive to get customers to buy products from their firm rather than a competing firm. By offering customers the accounts receivable privilege, management allows them to buy (more) now and pay later. Without this incentive, customers may choose to buy the goods from the firm's competitors who offer better credit terms. So extremely high accounts receivable turnover levels and low ACP levels may be a sign of bad firm management.

Accounts Payable Management

As they decide the accounts payable level to hold on the balance sheet, managers must consider the trade-off between maximizing the use of free financing that raw material suppliers offer versus the risk of losing the opportunity to buy on account. Two ratios commonly used are the average payment period and accounts payable turnover.

$$\text{Average payment} \atop \text{period (APP)} = \frac{\text{Accounts payable} \times 365 \text{ days}}{\text{Cost of goods sold}} \qquad (3\text{-}8)$$

The average payment period (APP) measures the number of days that the firm holds accounts payable before it has to extend cash to pay for its purchases.

$$\text{Accounts payable turnover} = \frac{\text{Cost of goods sold}}{\text{Accounts payable}} \qquad (3\text{-}9)$$

The accounts payable turnover ratio measures the dollar cost of goods sold per dollar of accounts payable.

In general, a firm wants to pay for its purchases as slowly as possible. The slower the firm pays for its supply purchases, the

If this situation is developing, extremely high levels for the APP and low levels for the accounts receivable turnover may point to bad firm management.

Fixed Asset and Working Capital Management

Two ratios that summarize the efficiency in a firm's overall asset management are the fixed asset turnover and sales to working capital ratios.

$$\text{Fixed asset turnover} = \frac{\text{Sales}}{\text{Fixed assets}} \qquad (3\text{-}10)$$

The fixed asset turnover ratio measures the number of dollars of sales produced per dollar of fixed assets.

$$\text{Sales to working capital} = \frac{\text{Sales}}{\text{Working capital}} \qquad (3\text{-}11)$$

Similarly, the sales to working capital ratio measures the number of dollars of sales produced per dollar of net working capital (current assets minus current liabilities).

In general, the higher the level of sales per dollar of fixed assets and working capital, the more efficiently the firm is being run. Thus, high fixed asset turnover and sales to working capital ratios are generally signs of good management. However, if either the fixed asset turnover or sales to working capital ratio is extremely high, the firm may be close to its maximum production capacity. If capacity is hit, the firm cannot increase production or sales. Accordingly, extremely high fixed asset turnover and sales to working capital ratio levels may actually indicate bad firm management if managers have allowed the company to approach maximum capacity without making any accommodations for growth.

Note a word of caution here. The age of a firm's fixed assets will affect the fixed asset turnover ratio level. A firm with older fixed

> ## In general, the higher the level of sales per dollar of fixed assets and working capital, the more efficiently the firm is being run.

longer it can avoid obtaining other costly sources of financing such as notes payable or long-term debt. Thus, a high APP or a low accounts payable turnover is generally a sign of good management.

However, if the APP is extremely high and the accounts payable turnover is extremely low, the firm may be abusing the credit terms that its raw materials suppliers offer. At some point, the firm's suppliers may revoke its ability to buy raw materials on account and the firm will lose this source of free financing.

assets, listed on its balance sheet at historical cost, will tend to have a higher fixed asset turnover ratio than will a firm that has just replaced its fixed assets and lists them on its balance sheet at a (most likely) higher value. Accordingly, the firm with newer fixed assets would have a lower fixed asset turnover ratio. But this is because it has updated its fixed assets, while the other firm has not. It is *not* correct to conclude that the firm with new assets is underperforming relative to the firm with older fixed assets listed on its balance sheet.

EXAMPLE 3-2

Calculating Asset Management Ratios LG3-2

Use the balance sheet (Table 2.1) and income statement (Table 2.2) for DPH Tree Farm Inc. to calculate the firm's 2012 values for the asset management ratios.

SOLUTION:

We calculate the asset management ratios for DPH Tree Farm Inc. as follows. The industry average is reported alongside each ratio.

i. Inventory turnover $= \dfrac{\$315m}{\$111m} = 2.84$ times   Industry average = 2.15 times

ii. Days' sales in inventory $= \dfrac{\$111m \times 365 \text{ days}}{\$315m} = 129$ days   Industry average = 170 days

iii. Average collection period $= \dfrac{\$70m \times 365 \text{ days}}{\$315m} = 81$ days   Industry average = 95 days

iv. Accounts receivable turnover $= \dfrac{\$315m}{\$70m} = 4.50$ times   Industry average = 3.84 times

v. Average payment period $= \dfrac{\$55m \times 365 \text{ days}}{\$133m} = 151$ days   Industry average = 102 days

vi. Accounts payable turnover $= \dfrac{\$133m}{\$55m} = 2.42$ times   Industry average = 3.55 times

vii. Fixed asset turnover $= \dfrac{\$315m}{\$315m} = 1.00$ times   Industry average = 0.85 times

viii. Sales to working capital $= \dfrac{\$315m}{\$205m - \$120m} = 3.71$ times   Industry average = 3.20 times

ix. Total assets turnover $= \dfrac{\$315m}{\$570m} = 0.55$ times   Industry average = 0.40 times

x. Capital intensity $= \dfrac{\$570m}{\$315m} = 1.81$ times   Industry average = 2.50 times

In all cases, asset management ratios show that DPH Tree Farm Inc. is outperforming the industry average. The firm is turning over its inventory faster than the average firm in the tree farm industry, thus producing more dollars of sales per dollar of inventory. It is also collecting its accounts receivable faster and paying its accounts payable slower than the average firm. Further, DPH Tree Farm is producing more sales per dollar of fixed assets, working capital, and total assets than the average firm in the industry.

Similar to Problems 3-3, 3-4

Total Asset Management

The final two asset management ratios put it all together. They are the total asset turnover and capital intensity ratios.

$$\text{Total asset turnover} = \frac{\text{Sales}}{\text{Total assets}} \qquad (3\text{-}12)$$

The total asset turnover ratio measures the number of dollars of sales produced per dollar of total assets.

$$\text{Capital intensity} = \frac{\text{Total assets}}{\text{Sales}} \qquad (3\text{-}13)$$

Similarly, the capital intensity ratio measures the dollars of total assets needed to produce a dollar of sales.

In general, a well-managed firm produces many dollars of sales per dollar of total assets, or uses few dollars of assets per dollar of sales. Thus, in general, the higher the total asset turnover and lower the capital intensity ratio, the more efficient the overall asset management of the firm will be. However, if the total asset turnover is extremely high and the capital intensity ratio is extremely low, the firm may actually have an asset management problem. As described above, inventory stockouts, capacity problems, or tight account receivables policies can all lead to a high total asset turnover and may actually be signs of poor firm management.

time out!

3-4 What are the major asset management ratios?

3-5 Does a firm generally want to have high or low values for each of these ratios?

3-6 Explain why many of these ratios are mirror images of one another.

DEBT MANAGEMENT RATIOS LG3-3

As we discussed in Chapter 2, financial leverage refers to the extent to which the firm uses debt securities in its capital structure. The more debt a firm uses as a percentage of its total assets, the greater is its financial leverage. **Debt management ratios** measure the extent to which the firm uses debt (or financial leverage) versus equity to finance its assets. The specific ratios allow managers and investors to evaluate whether a firm is financing its assets with a reasonable amount of debt versus equity financing, as well as whether the firm is generating sufficient earnings or cash to make the promised payments on its debt. The most commonly used debt management ratios are listed below.

Debt versus Equity Financing

Managers' choice of **capital structure**—the amount of debt versus equity to issue—affects the firm's viability as a long-term entity. In deciding the level of debt versus equity financing to hold on the balance sheet, managers must consider the trade-off between maximizing cash flows to the firm's stockholders

> When a firm issues debt to finance its assets, it gives the debt holders first claim to a fixed amount of its cash flows.

versus the risk of being unable to make promised debt payments. Ratios that are commonly used are the debt ratio, the debt-to-equity, and the equity multiplier.

$$\text{Debt ratio} = \frac{\text{Total debt}}{\text{Total assets}} \quad (3\text{-}14)$$

The debt ratio measures the percentage of total assets financed with debt.

$$\text{Debt-to-equity} = \frac{\text{Total debt}}{\text{Total equity}} \quad (3\text{-}15)$$

The debt-to-equity ratio measures the dollars of debt financing used for every dollar of equity financing.

$$\frac{\text{Equity}}{\text{multiplier}} = \frac{\text{Total assets}}{\text{Total equity}} \text{ or } \frac{\text{Total assets}}{\text{Common stockholders' equity}} \quad (3\text{-}16)$$

The equity multiplier ratio measures the dollars of assets on the balance sheet for every dollar of equity (or just common stockholders' equity) financing.

As you might suspect, all three measures are related.[1] Specifically,

$$\text{Debt-to-equity} = \frac{1}{(1/\text{Debt ratio}) - 1} = \text{Equity multiplier} - 1$$

$$\text{Equity multiplier} = \frac{1}{1 - \text{Debt ratio}} = \text{Debt-to-equity} + 1$$

So, the lower the debt, debt-to-equity, or equity multiplier, the less debt and more equity the firm uses to finance its assets (i.e., the bigger the firm's equity cushion).

When a firm issues debt to finance its assets, it gives the debt holders first claim to a fixed amount of its cash flows. Stockholders are entitled to any residual cash flows—those left after debt holders are paid. When a firm does well, financial leverage increases the reward to shareholders since the amount of cash flows promised to debt holders is constant and capped. So when firms do well, financial leverage creates more cash flows to share with stockholders—it magnifies the return to the stockholders of the firm (recall Example 2-4). This magnification is one reason that stockholders encourage the use of debt financing.

However, financial leverage also increases the firm's potential for financial distress and even failure. If the firm has a bad

[1]To see this remember the balance sheet identity is Assets (A) = Debt (D) + Equity (E). Dividing each side of this equation by equity, we get A/E = D/E + E/E, or A/E = D/E + 1. Also, rearranging this equation, D/E = A/E − 1.

debt management ratios Measure the extent to which the firm uses debt (or financial leverage) versus equity to finance its assets.

capital structure The amount of debt versus equity held on the balance sheet.

year and cannot make promised debt payments, debt holders can force the firm into bankruptcy. Thus, a firm's current and potential debt holders (and even stockholders) look at equity financing as a safety cushion that can absorb fluctuations in the firm's earnings and asset values and guarantee debt service payments. Clearly, the larger the fluctuations or variability of a firm's cash flows, the greater the need for an equity cushion.

Coverage Ratios

Three additional debt management ratios are the times interest earned, fixed-charge coverage, and cash coverage ratios. These ratios are different measures of a firm's ability to meet its debt obligations.

$$\text{Times interest earned} = \frac{\text{EBIT}}{\text{Interest}} \qquad (3\text{-}17)$$

The times interest earned ratio measures the number of dollars of operating earnings available to meet each dollar of interest obligations on the firm's debt.

$$\frac{\text{Fixed-charge}}{\text{coverage}} = \frac{\text{Earnings available to meet fixed charges}}{\text{Fixed charges}}$$
$$(3\text{-}18)$$

The fixed-charge coverage ratio measures the number of dollars of operating *earnings* available to meet the firm's interest obligations and other fixed charges.

EXAMPLE 3-3

For interactive versions of this example visit www.mhhe.com/canM2e

Calculating Debt Management Ratios LG3-3

Use the balance sheet (Table 2.1) and income statement (Table 2.2) for DPH Tree Farm Inc. to calculate the firm's 2012 values for the debt management ratios.

SOLUTION:

The debt management ratios for DPH Tree Farm Inc. are calculated as follows. The industry average is reported alongside each ratio.

i. Debt ratio $= \dfrac{\$120m + \$195m}{\$570m} = 55.26\%$ Industry average = 68.50%

ii. Debt-to-equity $= \dfrac{\$120m + \$195m}{\$255m} = 1.24$ times   Industry average = 2.17 times

iii. Equity multiplier $= \dfrac{\$570m}{\$255m} = 2.24$ times   Industry average = 4.10 times

or $\dfrac{\$570m}{\$255m - \$5m} = 2.28$ times   Industry average = 4.14 times

iv. Times interest earned $= \dfrac{\$152m}{\$16m} = 9.50$ times   Industry average = 5.15 times

v. Fixed-charge coverage $= \dfrac{\$152m}{\$16m} = 9.50$ times   Industry average = 5.70 times

vi. Cash coverage $= \dfrac{\$152m + \$13m}{\$16m} = 10.31$ times   Industry average = 7.78 times

In all cases, debt management ratios show that DPH Tree Farm Inc. holds less debt on its balance sheet than the average firm in the tree farm industry. Further, the firm has more dollars of operating earnings and cash available to meet each dollar of interest obligations (there are no other fixed charges listed on DPH Tree Farm's income statement) on the firm's debt. This lack of financial leverage decreases the firm's potential for financial distress and even failure, but may also decrease equity shareholders' chance for magnified earnings. If the firm has a bad year, it has promised relatively few payments to debt holders. Thus, the risk of bankruptcy is small. However, when DPH Tree Farm Inc. does well, the low level of financial leverage dilutes the return to the stockholders of the firm. This dilution of profit is likely to upset common stockholders of the firm.

Similar to Problems 3-5, 3-6

$$\text{Cash coverage} = \frac{\text{EBIT} + \text{Depreciation}}{\text{Fixed charges}} \qquad (3\text{-}19)$$

The cash coverage ratio measures the number of dollars of operating *cash* available to meet each dollar of interest and other fixed charges that the firm owes.

With the help of the times interest earned, fixed-charge coverage, and cash coverage ratios, managers, investors, and analysts can determine whether a firm has taken on a debt burden that is too large. These ratios measure the dollars available to meet debt and other fixed-charge obligations. A value of one for these ratios means that $1 of earnings or cash is available to meet each dollar of interest or fixed-charge obligations. A value of less (greater) than one means that the firm has less (more) than $1 of earnings or cash available to pay each dollar of interest or fixed-charge obligations.[2] Further, the higher the times interest earned, fixed-charge coverage, and cash coverage ratios, the more equity and less debt the firm uses to finance its assets. Thus, low levels of debt will lead to a dilution of the return to stockholders due to increased use of equity as well as to not taking advantage of the tax deductibility of interest expense.

time out!

3-7 What are the major debt management ratios?

3-8 Does a firm generally want to have high or low values for each of these ratios?

3-9 What is the trade-off between using too much financial leverage and not using enough leverage? Who is likely to complain the most in each case?

PROFITABILITY RATIOS LG3-4

The liquidity, asset management, and debt management ratios examined so far allow for an isolated or narrow look at a firm's performance. **Profitability ratios** show the combined effects of liquidity, asset management, and debt management on the

[2]The fixed-charge and cash coverage ratios can be tailored to a particular firm's situation, depending on what really constitutes fixed charges that must be paid. One version of it follows: (EBIT + Lease payments)/[Interest + Lease payments + Sinking fund/$(1 - t)$], where t is the firm's marginal tax rate. Here, it is assumed that sinking fund payments must be made. They are adjusted by the division of $(1 - t)$ into a before-tax cash outflow so they can be added to other before-tax cash outflows.

overall operating results of the firm. Profitability ratios are among the most watched and best known of the financial ratios. Indeed, firm values (or stock prices) react quickly to unexpected changes in these ratios. The most commonly used profitability ratios are listed below.

profitability ratios Ratios that show the combined effect of liquidity, asset management, and debt management on the firm's overall operating results.

$$\frac{\text{Profit}}{\text{margin}} = \frac{\text{Net income available to common stockholders}}{\text{Sales}} \qquad (3\text{-}20)$$

The profit margin is the percentage of sales left after all firm expenses are deducted.

$$\text{Basic earnings power (BEP)} = \frac{\text{EBIT}}{\text{Total assets}} \qquad (3\text{-}21)$$

The basic earnings power ratio measures the operating return on the firm's assets, regardless of financial leverage and taxes. This ratio measures the operating profit (EBIT) earned per dollar of assets on the firm's balance sheet.

$$\text{Return on assets (ROA)} = \frac{\text{Net income available to common stockholders}}{\text{Total assets}} \qquad (3\text{-}22)$$

Return on assets (ROA) measures the overall return on the firm's assets, including financial leverage and taxes. This ratio is the net income earned per dollar of assets on the firm's balance sheet.

$$\frac{\text{Return on}}{\text{equity (ROE)}} = \frac{\text{Net income available to common stockholders}}{\text{Common stockholders' equity}} \qquad (3\text{-}23)$$

Return on equity (ROE) measures the return on the common stockholders' investment in the assets of the firm. ROE is the net income earned per dollar of common stockholders' equity. The value of a firm's ROE is affected not only by net income, but also by the amount of financial leverage or debt that firm uses. As stated above, financial leverage magnifies the return to the stockholders of the firm. However, financial leverage also

A company's profit margin is inversely related to its sales.

increases the firm's potential for financial distress and even failure. Generally, a high ROE is considered to be a positive sign of firm performance. However, if performance comes from a high degree of financial leverage, a high ROE can indicate a firm with an unacceptably high level of bankruptcy risk as well.

$$\text{Dividend payout} = \frac{\text{Common stock dividends}}{\substack{\text{Net income available} \\ \text{to common stockholders}}} \quad (3\text{-}24)$$

Finally, the dividend payout ratio is the percentage of net income available to common stockholders that the firm actually pays as cash to these investors.

For all but the dividend payout, the higher the value of the ratio, the higher the profitability of the firm. But just as has been the case previously in this chapter, high profitability ratio levels may result from poor management in other areas of the firm as much as superior financial management. A high profit margin means that the firm has low expenses relative to sales. The BEP reflects how much the firm's assets earn from operations, regardless of financial leverage and taxes. It follows logically that managers, investors, and analysts find BEP a useful ratio when they compare firms that differ in financial leverage and taxes. In contrast, ROA measures the firm's overall performance. It shows how the firm's assets generate a return that includes financial leverage and tax decisions made by management.

ROE measures the return on common stockholders' investment. Since managers seek to maximize common stock price, managers, investors, and analysts monitor ROE above all other ratios. The dividend payout ratio measures how much of the profit the firm retains versus how much it pays out to common stockholders as dividends. The lower the dividend payout ratio, the more profits the firm retains for future growth or other projects. A profitable firm that retains its earnings increases its level of equity capital as well as its own value.

EXAMPLE 3-4

For interactive versions of this example visit www.mhhe.com/canM2e

Calculating Profitability Ratios LG3-4

Use the balance sheet (Table 2.1) and income statement (Table 2.2) for DPH Tree Farm Inc. to calculate the firm's 2012 values for the profitability ratios.

SOLUTION:

The profitability ratios for DPH Tree Farm Inc. are calculated as follows. The industry average is reported alongside each ratio.

i. $\text{Profit margin} = \dfrac{\$80m}{\$315m} = 25.40\%$ Industry average = 23.25%

ii. $\text{Basic earnings power (BEP)} = \dfrac{\$152m}{\$570m} = 26.67\%$ Industry average = 22.85%

iii. $\text{Return on assets (ROA)} = \dfrac{\$80m}{\$570m} = 14.04\%$ Industry average = 9.30%

iv. $\text{Return on equity (ROE)} = \dfrac{\$80m}{\$40m + \$210m} = 32.00\%$ Industry average = 38.00%

v. $\text{Dividend payout} = \dfrac{\$25m}{\$80m} = 31.25\%$ Industry average = 30.90%

These ratios show that DPH Tree Farm Inc. is more profitable than the average firm in the tree farm industry. The profit margin, BEP, and ROA are all higher than industry figures. Despite this, the ROE for DPH Tree Farm is much lower than the industry average. DPH's low debt level and high equity level relative to the industry is the main reason for DPH's strong figures relative to the industry. As we mentioned above, DPH's managerial decisions about capital structure dilute its returns, which will likely upset its common stockholders. To counteract common stockholders' discontent, DPH Tree Farm pays out a slightly larger percentage of its income to its common stockholders as cash dividends. Of course, this slightly high dividend payout ratio means that DPH Tree Farm retains less of its profits to reinvest into the business. A profitable firm that retains its earnings increases its equity capital level as well as its own value.

Similar to Problems 3-7, 3-8

time out!

3-10 What are the major profitability ratios?

3-11 Does a firm generally want to have high or low values for each of these ratios?

3-12 What are the trade-offs to having especially high or low values for ROE?

MARKET VALUE RATIOS LG3-5

As we note above, ROE is a most important financial statement ratio for managers and investors to monitor. Generally, a high ROE is considered to be a positive sign of firm performance. However, if a high ROE results from a highly leveraged position, it can signal a firm with a high level of bankruptcy risk. While ROE does not directly incorporate this risk, for publicly traded firms, market prices of the firm's stock do. (We look at stock valuation in Chapter 8.) Since the firm's stockholders earn their returns primarily from the firm's stock market value, ratios

that incorporate stock market values are equally (arguably more) important than other financial statement ratios.

The final group of ratios is market value ratios. **Market value ratios** relate a firm's stock price to its earnings and its book value. For publicly traded firms, market value ratios measure what investors think of the company's future performance and risk.

$$\text{Market-to-book ratio} = \frac{\text{Market price per share}}{\text{Book value per share}} \quad (3\text{-}25)$$

The market-to-book ratio measures the amount that investors will pay for the firm's stock per dollar of equity used to finance the firm's assets. Book value per share is an accounting-based number reflecting the firm's assets' historical costs, and hence historical value. The market-to-book ratio compares the market (current) value of the firm's equity to its historical cost. In general, the higher the market-to-book ratio, the better the firm. If liquidity, asset management, debt management, and accounting profitability are good for a firm, then the market-to-book ratio will be high. A market-to-book ratio greater than one (or 100 percent) means that stockholders will pay a premium over book value for their equity investment in the firm.

$$\text{Price-earnings (PE) ratio} = \frac{\text{Market price per share}}{\text{Earnings per share}} \quad (3\text{-}26)$$

Probably the best known and most often quoted figure, the price-earnings (or PE) ratio measures how much investors are

---

EXAMPLE 3-5

Calculating Market Value Ratios LG3-4

For interactive versions of this example visit www.mhhe.com/canM2e

Use the balance sheet (Table 2.1) and income statement (Table 2.2) for DPH Tree Farm Inc. to calculate the firm's 2012 values for the market value ratios.

SOLUTION:

The market value ratios for DPH Tree Farm Inc. are calculated as follows. The industry average is reported alongside each ratio.

i. Market-to-book ratio $= \dfrac{\$17.25}{\$12.50} = 1.38$ times   Industry average = 2.15 times

ii. Price-earnings (PE) ratio $= \dfrac{\$17.25}{\$1.00} = 4.31$ times   Industry average = 6.25 times

These ratios show that DPH Tree Farm's investors will not pay as much for a share of DPH's stock per dollar of book value and earnings as the average for the industry. DPH's low leverage level and high reliance on equity relative to the industry are likely the main reason for investors' disinterest. As mentioned above, DPH's seemingly intentional return dilution will likely upset the firm's common stockholders. Accordingly, stockholders lower the amount they are willing to invest per dollar of book value and EPS.

Similar to Problems 3-9, 3-10

DuPont system of analysis An analytical method that uses the balance sheet and income statement to break the ROA and ROE ratios into component pieces.

willing to pay for each dollar the firm earns per share of its stock. PE ratios are often quoted in multiples—the number of dollars per share—that fund managers, investors, and analysts compare within industry classes. Managers and investors often use PE ratios to evaluate the relative financial performance of the firm's stock. Generally, the higher the PE ratio, the better the firm's performance. Analysts and investors, as well as managers, expect companies with high PE ratios to experience future growth, to have rapid future

dividend increases, or both, because retained earnings will support the company's goals. However, for value-seeking investors, high-PE firms indicate expensive companies. Further, higher PE ratios carry greater risk because investors are willing to pay higher prices today for a stock in anticipation of higher earnings in the future. These earnings may or may not materialize. Low-PE firms are generally companies with little expected growth or low earnings. However, note that earnings depend on many factors (such as financial leverage or taxes) that have nothing to do directly with firm operations.

time out!

3-13 What are the major market value ratios?

3-14 Does a firm generally want to have high or low values for each of these ratios?

3-15 Discuss the price-earnings ratio and explain why it assumes particular importance among all of the other ratios we have presented.

DUPONT ANALYSIS LG3-6

Table 3.1 lists the ratios we discuss, their values for DPH Tree Farm Inc. as of 2012, and the corresponding values for the tree farm industry. The value of each ratio for DPH Tree Farm is highlighted in green if it is generally stronger than the industry and is highlighted in red if it is generally a negative sign for the firm. As we noted in this chapter's introduction, many of the ratios we have discussed thus far are interrelated. So a change in one ratio may well affect the value of several ratios. Often these interrelations can help evaluate firm performance. Managers and investors often perform a detailed analysis of ROA (return on assets) and ROE (return on equity) using the **DuPont system of analysis.** Popularized by the DuPont Corporation, the DuPont system of analysis uses the balance sheet and income statement to break the ROA and ROE ratios into component pieces.

▼**TABLE 3.1** Summary of Ratios and Their Values for DPH Tree Farm Inc. and the Tree Farm Industry

Ratio	Value for DPH Tree Farm Inc.	Value for the Tree Farm Industry
Liquidity ratios:		
Current ratio $= \dfrac{\text{Current assets}}{\text{Current liabilities}}$	1.71 times	1.50 times
Quick ratio (acid-test ratio) $= \dfrac{\text{Current assets} - \text{Inventory}}{\text{Current liabilities}}$	0.78 times	0.50 times
Cash ratio $= \dfrac{\text{Cash and marketable securities}}{\text{Current liabilities}}$	0.20 times	0.15 times
Asset management ratios:		
Inventory turnover $= \dfrac{\text{Sales or cost of goods sold}}{\text{Inventory}}$	2.84 times	2.15 times
Days' sales in inventory $= \dfrac{\text{Inventory} \times 365 \text{ days}}{\text{Sales or cost of goods sold}}$	129 days	170 days
Average collection period $= \dfrac{\text{Accounts receivable} \times 365 \text{ days}}{\text{Credit sales}}$	81 days	95 days
Accounts receivable turnover $= \dfrac{\text{Credit sales}}{\text{Accounts receivable}}$	4.50 times	3.84 times
Average payment period (APP) $= \dfrac{\text{Accounts payable} \times 365 \text{ days}}{\text{Cost of goods sold}}$	151 days	102 days

Ratio	Value for DPH Tree Farm Inc.	Value for the Tree Farm Industry
Accounts payable turnover $= \dfrac{\text{Cost of goods sold}}{\text{Accounts payable}}$	2.42 times	3.55 times
Fixed asset turnover $= \dfrac{\text{Sales}}{\text{Fixed assets}}$	1.00 times	0.85 times
Sales to working capital $= \dfrac{\text{Sales}}{\text{Working capital}}$	3.71 times	3.20 times
Total assets turnover $= \dfrac{\text{Sales}}{\text{Total assets}}$	0.55 times	0.40 times
Capital intensity $= \dfrac{\text{Total assets}}{\text{Sales}}$	1.81 times	2.50 times
Debt management ratios:		
Debt ratio $= \dfrac{\text{Total debt}}{\text{Total assets}}$	55.26%	68.50%
Debt-to-equity $= \dfrac{\text{Total debt}}{\text{Total equity}}$	1.24 times	2.17 times
Equity multiplier $= \dfrac{\text{Total assets}}{\text{Total equity}}$	2.24 times	4.10 times
$\text{or} \dfrac{\text{Total assets}}{\text{Common stockholders' equity}}$	2.28 times	4.14 times
Times interest earned $= \dfrac{\text{EBIT}}{\text{Interest}}$	9.50 times	5.15 times
Fixed-charge coverage $= \dfrac{\text{Earnings available to meet fixed charges}}{\text{Fixed charges}}$	9.50 times	5.70 times
Cash coverage $= \dfrac{\text{EBIT} + \text{Depreciation}}{\text{Fixed charges}}$	10.31 times	7.78 times
Profitability ratios:		
Profit margin $= \dfrac{\text{Net income available to common stockholders}}{\text{Sales}}$	25.40%	23.25%
Basic earnings power $= \dfrac{\text{EBIT}}{\text{Total assets}}$	26.67%	22.85%
Return on assets $= \dfrac{\text{Net income available to common stockholders}}{\text{Total assets}}$	14.04%	9.30%
Return on equity $= \dfrac{\text{Net income available to common stockholders}}{\text{Common stockholders' equity}}$	32.00%	38.00%
Dividend payout $= \dfrac{\text{Common stock dividends}}{\text{Net income available to common stockholders}}$	31.25%	30.90%
Market value ratios:		
Market-to-book ratio $= \dfrac{\text{Market price per share}}{\text{Book value per share}}$	1.38 times	2.15 times
Price-earnings ratio $= \dfrac{\text{Market price per share}}{\text{Earnings per share}}$	4.31 times	6.25 times

The basic DuPont equation looks at ROA as the product of the profit margin and the total asset turnover ratios:

$$\text{ROA} = \text{Profit margin} \times \text{Total asset turnover}$$

$$\frac{\text{Net income available to common stockholders}}{\text{Total assets}} = \frac{\text{Net income available to common stockholders}}{\text{Sales}} \times \frac{\text{Sales}}{\text{Total assets}} \quad (3\text{-}27)$$

The basic DuPont equation looks at the firm's overall profitability as a function of the profit the firm earns per dollar of sales (operating efficiency) and the dollar of sales produced per dollar of assets on the balance sheet (efficiency in asset use). With this tool, managers can see the reason for any changes in ROA in more detail. For example, if ROA increases, the DuPont equation may show

that the net profit margin was constant, but the total asset turnover (efficiency in using assets) increased, or that total asset turnover remained constant, but profit margins (operating efficiency) increased. Managers can more specifically identify the reasons for an ROA change by using the ratios described above to further break down operating efficiency and efficiency in asset use.

Next, the DuPont system looks at ROE as the product of ROA and the equity multiplier.

$$\text{ROE} = \text{ROA} \times \text{Equity multiplier}$$

$$\frac{\text{Net income available to common stockholders}}{\text{Common stockholders' equity}} = \text{ROA} \times \frac{\text{Total assets}}{\text{Common stockholders' equity}} \quad (3\text{-}28)$$

EXAMPLE 3-6

For interactive versions of this example visit
www.mhhe.com/canM2e

Application of DuPont Analysis LG3-6

Use the balance sheet (Table 2.1) and income statement (Table 2.2) for DPH Tree Farm Inc. to calculate the firm's 2012 values for the ROA and ROE DuPont equations.

SOLUTION:

The ROA and ROE DuPont equations for DPH Tree Farm Inc. are calculated as follows. The industry average is reported below each ratio.

i. | ROA | = | Profit margin | × | Total asset turnover |
    | 14.04% | = | 25.39683% | × | 0.55263 times |
    | Industry average: 9.30% | = | 23.25% | × | 0.40 times |

$$\frac{\text{Net income available to common stockholders}}{\text{Total assets}} = \frac{\text{Net income available to common stockholders}}{\text{Sales}} \times \frac{\text{Sales}}{\text{Total assets}}$$

$$\frac{\$80m}{\$570m} = \frac{\$80m}{\$315m} \times \frac{\$315m}{\$570m}$$

ii. | ROE | = Profit margin × Total asset turnover × Equity multiplier |
    | 32.00% | = 25.39683% × 0.55263 times × 2.28 times |
    | Industry average: 38.50% = | 23.25% × 0.40 times × 4.13978 times |

$$\frac{\text{Net income available to common stockholders}}{\text{Common stockholders' equity}} = \frac{\text{Net income available to common stockholders}}{\text{Sales}} \times \frac{\text{Sales}}{\text{Total assets}} \times \frac{\text{Total assets}}{\text{Common stockholders' equity}}$$

$$\frac{\$80m}{\$40m + \$210m} = \frac{\$80m}{\$315m} \times \frac{\$315m}{\$570m} \times \frac{\$570m}{\$40m + \$210m}$$

As we saw with profitability ratios, DPH Tree Farm Inc. is more profitable than the average firm in the tree farm industry when it comes to overall efficiency expressed as return on assets, or ROA. The DuPont equation highlights that this superior performance comes from both profit margin (operating efficiency) and total asset turnover (efficiency in asset use). Despite this, the ROE for DPH Tree Farm lags the average industry ROE. The DuPont equation highlights that this inferior performance is due solely to the low level of debt and high level of equity used by DPH Tree Farm relative to the industry.

Similar to Problems 3-11, 3-12

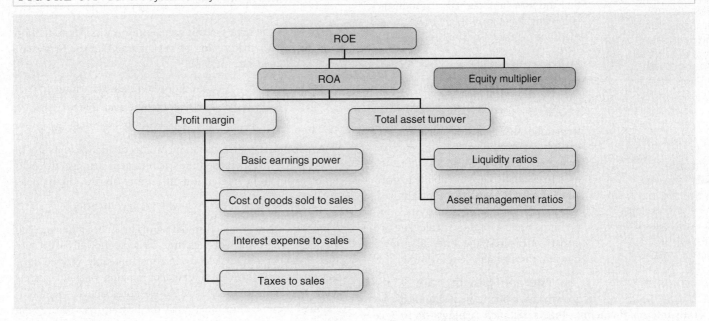

Notice that this version of the equity multiplier uses the return to common stockholders (the firm's owners) only. So the DuPont equity multiplier uses common stockholders' equity only, rather than total equity (which includes preferred stock).

Taking this breakdown one step further, the DuPont system breaks ROE into the product of the profit margin, the total asset turnover, and the equity multiplier.

$$
\begin{aligned}
\text{ROE} &= \text{Profit margin} \\
&\quad \times \text{Total asset turnover} \\
&\quad \times \text{Equity multiplier}
\end{aligned}
$$

$$
\frac{\text{Net income available to common stockholders}}{\text{Common stockholders' equity}} = \frac{\text{Net income available to common stockholders}}{\text{Sales}}
$$

$$
\times \frac{\text{Sales}}{\text{Total assets}}
$$

$$
\times \frac{\text{Total assets}}{\text{Common stockholders' equity}} \quad (3\text{-}29)
$$

This presentation of ROE allows managers, analysts, and investors to look at the return on equity as a function of the net profit margin (profit per dollar of sales from the income statement), the total asset turnover (efficiency in the use of assets from the balance sheet), and the equity multiplier (financial leverage from the balance sheet). Again, we can break these components down to more specifically identify possible causes for a ROE change. Figure 3.1 illustrates the DuPont system of analysis breakdown of ROA and ROE. The figure highlights how many of the ratios discussed in this chapter are linked.

time **out!**

3-16 What are the DuPont ROA and ROE equations?

3-17 How do each of these equations help to explain firm performance and pinpoint areas for improvement?

OTHER RATIOS LG3-6

Spreading the Financial Statements

In addition to the many ratios listed above, managers, analysts, and investors can also compute additional ratios by dividing all balance sheet amounts by total assets and all income statement amounts by net sales. These calculations, sometimes called *spreading the financial statements,* yield what we call **common-size financial statements** that correct for sizes. Using common-size financial statements, interested parties can identify changes in corporate performance. Year-to-year growth rates in common-size balance sheets and income statement balances also provide useful ratios for identifying trends. They also allow for an easy comparison of balance sheets and income statements across firms in the industry. Common-size financial statements may provide

common-size financial statements Dividing all balance sheet amounts by total assets and all income statement amounts by net sales.

internal growth rate The growth rate a firm can sustain if it finances growth using only internal financing, that is, retained earnings growth.

sustainable growth rate The growth rate a firm can sustain if it finances growth using both debt and internal financing such that the debt ratio remains constant.

quantitative clues about the direction that the firm (and perhaps the industry) is moving. They may thus provide roadmaps for managers' next moves.

Internal and Sustainable Growth Rates

Remember again that any firm manager's job is to maximize the firm's market value. The firm's ROA and ROE can be used to evaluate the firm's ability to grow and its market value to be maximized. Specifically, managers, analysts, and investors use these ratios to calculate two growth measures: the internal growth rate and the sustainable growth rate.

The **internal growth rate** is the growth rate a firm can sustain if it uses only internal financing—that is, retained earnings—to finance future growth. Mathematically, the internal growth rate is:

$$\text{Internal growth rate} = \frac{\text{ROA} \times \text{RR}}{1 - (\text{ROA} \times \text{RR})} \quad (3\text{-}30)$$

where RR is the firm's earnings retention ratio. The retention ratio represents the portion of net income that the firm reinvests as retained earnings:

$$\text{Retention ratio (RR)} = \frac{\text{Addition to retained earnings}}{\text{Net income available to common stockholders}} \quad (3\text{-}31)$$

Since a firm either pays its net income as dividends to its stockholders or reinvests those funds as retained earnings, the dividend payout and the retention ratios must always add to one:

$$\text{Retention ratio} = 1 - \text{Dividend payout ratio} \quad (3\text{-}32)$$

A problem arises when a firm relies only on internal financing to support asset growth: Through time, its debt ratio will fall because as asset values grow, total debt stays constant—only retained earnings finance asset growth. If total debt remains constant as assets grow, the debt ratio decreases. As we noted above, shareholders often become disgruntled if, as the firm grows, a decreasing debt ratio (increasing equity financing) dilutes their return. So as firms grow, managers must often try to maintain a debt ratio that

---

EXAMPLE 3-7

For interactive versions of this example visit www.mhhe.com/canM2e

Calculating Internal and Sustainable Growth Rates LG3-6

Use the balance sheet (Table 2.1) and income statement (Table 2.2) for DPH Tree Farm Inc. to calculate the firm's 2012 internal and sustainable growth rates.

SOLUTION:

The internal and sustainable growth rates for DPH Tree Farm Inc. are calculated as follows. The industry average is reported alongside each ratio.

$$\text{Retention rate (RR)} = \frac{\$210m - \$155m}{\$80m}$$
$$= 0.6875 \text{ or } 68.75\%$$

$$\text{Industry RR} = 1 - \frac{\text{Industry dividend payout ratio}}{}$$
$$= 1 - 0.3090 = 0.6910$$

i. $$\text{Internal growth rate} = \frac{0.1404 \times 0.6875}{1 - (0.1404 \times 0.6875)}$$
$$= 0.1068 \text{ or } 10.68\%$$

$$\text{Industry average internal growth rate} = \frac{0.0930 \times 0.6910}{1 - (0.0930 \times 0.6910)}$$
$$= 0.0687 \text{ or } 6.87\%$$

ii. $$\text{Sustainable growth rate} = \frac{0.3200 \times 0.6875}{1 - (0.3200 \times 0.6875)}$$
$$= 0.2821 \text{ or } 28.21\%$$

$$\text{Industry average sustainable growth rate} = \frac{0.3800 \times 0.6910}{1 - (0.3800 \times 0.6910)}$$
$$= 0.3561 \text{ or } 35.61\%$$

These ratios show that DPH Tree Farm Inc. can grow faster than the industry if the firm uses only retained earnings to finance the growth. However, if DPH grows while keeping the debt *ratio* constant (e.g., both debt and retained earnings are used to finance the growth), industry firms can grow much faster than DPH Tree Farm. Once again, DPH's low debt level and high equity level relative to the industry creates this disparity. Therefore, DPH Tree Farm limits its growth as a result of its managerial decisions.

Similar to Problems 3-13, 3-14

the Math Coach on...

Equations

❝ When putting values into the equation, enter them in decimal format, not percentage format

CORRECT 1 − (0.1404 × 0.6875)

NOT CORRECT 1 − (14.04 × 68.75) ❞

time series analysis Analyzing firm performance by monitoring ratio trends.

cross-sectional analysis Analyzing the performance of a firm against one or more companies in the same industry.

they view as optimal. In this case, managers finance asset growth with new debt *and* retained earnings. The maximum growth rate that can be achieved this way is the **sustainable growth rate.** Mathematically, the sustainable growth rate is:

$$\text{Sustainable growth rate} = \frac{\text{ROE} \times \text{RR}}{1 - (\text{ROE} \times \text{RR})} \qquad (3\text{-}33)$$

Maximizing the sustainable growth rate helps firm managers maximize firm value. When applying the DuPont ROE equation (3-29) here (i.e., ROE = Profit margin × Total asset turnover × Equity multiplier), notice that a firm's sustainable growth depends on four factors:

1. The profit margin (operating efficiency).

2. The total asset turnover (efficiency in asset use).

3. Financial leverage (the use of debt versus equity to finance assets).

4. Profit retention (reinvestment of net income into the firm rather than paying it out as dividends).

Increasing any of these factors increases the firm's sustainable growth rate and hence helps to maximize firm value. Managers, analysts, and investors will want to focus on these areas as they evaluate firm performance and market value.

time out!

3-18 What does "spreading the financial statements" mean?

3-19 What are retention rates and internal and sustainable growth rates?

3-20 What factors enter into sustainable growth rates?

TIME SERIES AND CROSS-SECTIONAL ANALYSIS LG3-7

We have explored many ratios that allow managers and investors to examine firm performance. But to really analyze performance in a meaningful way, we must interpret our ratio results against some kind of standard or benchmark. To interpret financial ratios, managers, analysts, and investors use two major types of benchmarks: (1) performance of the firm over time (**time series analysis**) and (2) performance of the firm against one or more companies in the same industry (**cross-sectional analysis**).

Analyzing ratio trends over time, along with absolute ratio levels, gives managers, analysts, and investors information about whether a firm's financial condition is improving or deteriorating. For example, ratio analysis may reveal that the days' sales in inventory is increasing. This suggests that inventories, relative to the sales they support, are not being used as well as they were in the past. If this increase is the result of a deliberate policy to increase inventories to offer customers a wider choice and if it results in higher future sales volumes or increased margins that more than compensate for increased capital tied up in inventory, the increased relative size of the inventories is good for the firm. Managers and investors should be concerned, on the other hand, if increased inventories result from declining sales but steady purchases of supplies and production.

Looking at one firm's financial ratios, even through time, gives managers, analysts, and investors only a limited picture of firm performance. Ratio analysis almost always includes a comparison of one firm's ratios relative to the ratios of other firms in the industry, or cross-sectional analysis. The key to cross-sectional analysis is identifying similar firms that compete in the same markets, have similar asset sizes, and operate in a similar manner to the firm being analyzed. Since no two firms are identical, obtaining such a comparison group is no easy task. Thus, the choice of companies to use in cross-sectional analysis is at best subjective. Note that as we calculated the financial ratios for DPH Tree Farm Inc. throughout the chapter, we compared them to the industry average. Comparative ratios that can be used in cross-sectional analysis are available from many sources. For example, Value Line Investment Surveys, Robert Morris Associates, Hoover's Online (at **www.hoovers.com**), and MSN

Money website (at **moneycentral.msn.com**) are examples of four major sources of financial ratios for numerous industries that operate within the U.S. and worldwide.

time out!

3-21 What is time series analysis of a firm's operations?

3-22 What is cross-sectional analysis of a firm's operations?

3-23 How do time series and cross-sectional analyses differ, and what information would you expect to gain from each?

CAUTIONS IN USING RATIOS TO EVALUATE FIRM PERFORMANCE LG3-8

Financial statement analysis allows managers, analysts, and investors to better understand a firm's performance. However, data from financial statements should not be received without certain cautions. These include:

1. Financial statement data are historical. Historical data may not reflect future performance. While we can make projections using historical data, we must also remember that projections may be inaccurate if historical performance does not persist.

2. As we discussed in Chapter 2, firms use different accounting procedures. For example, inventory methods can vary. One firm may use FIFO (first-in, first-out), transferring inventory at the first purchase price, while another uses LIFO (last-in, first-out), transferring inventory at the last purchase price. Likewise, the depreciation method used to value a firm's fixed assets over time may vary across firms. One firm may use straight-line depreciation, while another may use an accelerated depreciation method (e.g., MACRS). Particularly, when reviewing cross-sectional ratios, differences in accounting rules can affect balance sheet values and financial ratios. It is important to know which accounting rules the firms under consideration are using before making any conclusions about their performance from ratio analysis.

3. Similarly, a firm's cross-sectional competitors may often be located around the world. Financial statements for firms based outside the United States do not necessarily conform to GAAP. Even beyond inventory pricing and depreciation methods, different accounting standards and procedures make it hard to compare financial statements and ratios of firms based in different countries.

4. Sales and expenses vary throughout the year. Managers, analysts, and investors need to note the timing of these fund flows when performing cross-sectional analysis. Otherwise they may draw conclusions from comparisons that are actually the result of seasonal cash flow differences. Similarly, firms end their fiscal years at different dates. For cross-sectional analysis, this complicates any comparison of balance sheets during the year. Likewise, one-time events, such as a merger, may affect a firm's financial performance. Cross-sectional analysis involving these events can result in misleading conclusions.

5. Large firms often have multiple divisions or business units engaged in different lines of business. In this case, it is difficult to truly compare a set of firms with which managers and investors can perform cross-sectional analysis.

6. Firms often window dress their financial statements to make annual results look better. For example, to improve liquidity ratios calculated with year-end balance sheets, firms often delay payments for raw materials, equipment, loans, and so on to build up their liquid accounts and thus their liquidity ratios. If possible, it is often more accurate to use something other than year-end financial statements to conduct ratio analysis.

7. Individual analysts may calculate ratios in modified forms. For example, one analyst may calculate ratios using year-end balance sheet data, while another

ROE DuPont equations

View guided examples at mhhe.com/canM2e

The ROE DuPont equation is calculated as follows:

ROE = Profit Margin x Total asset turnover x Equity multiplier

ROE = 25.39683% x 0.55262... 8 times = 32.00%

ROE = $\frac{NI}{Sales}$ x ... A... = ...quity

Catt Riley and eight others like this.

Catt Riley Seeing the book example discussed in real-time was a HUGE help to getting the concept. Thanks!

3 hours ago · Like

write a comment...

may use the average of the beginning- and end-of-year balance sheet data. If the firm's balance sheet has changed significantly during the year, this difference in the way the ratio is calculated can cause large variations in ratio values for a given period of analysis and large variations in any conclusions drawn from these ratios regarding the financial health of the firm.

Financial statement ratio analysis is a major part of evaluating a firm's performance. If managers, analysts, or investors ignore the issues noted here, they may well draw faulty conclusions from their analysis. However, used intelligently and with good judgment, ratio analysis can provide useful information on a firm's current position and hint at future performance. ■

time **out!**

3-24 What cautions should managers and investors take when using ratio analysis to evaluate a firm?

Your Turn...

Questions

1. Classify each of the following ratios according to a ratio category (liquidity ratio, asset management ratio, debt management ratio, profitability ratio, or market value ratio). *(LG3-1–LG3-5)*

   a. Current ratio

   b. Inventory turnover

   c. Return on assets

   d. Average payment period

   e. Times interest earned

   f. Capital intensity

   g. Equity multiplier

   h. Basic earnings power

2. For each of the actions listed below, determine what would happen to the current ratio. Assume nothing else on the balance sheet changes and that net working capital is positive. *(LG3-1)*

   a. Accounts receivable are paid in cash

   b. Notes payable are paid off with cash

   c. Inventory is sold on account

   d. Inventory is purchased on account

   e. Accrued wages and taxes increase

   f. Long-term debt is paid with cash

   g. Cash from a short-term bank loan is received

3. Explain the meaning and significance of the following ratios. *(LG3-1–LG3-5)*

   a. Quick ratio

   b. Average collection period

   c. Return on equity

   d. Days' sales in inventory

   e. Debt ratio

   f. Profit margin

   g. Accounts payable turnover

   h. Market-to-book ratio

4. A firm has an average collection period of 10 days. The industry average ACP is 25 days. Is this a good or poor sign about the management of the firm's accounts receivable? *(LG3-2)*

5. A firm has a debt ratio of 20 percent. The industry average debt ratio is 65 percent. Is this a good or poor sign about the management of the firm's financial leverage? *(LG3-3)*

6. A firm has an ROE of 20 percent. The industry average ROE is 12 percent. Is this a good or poor sign about the management of the firm? *(LG3-4)*

7. Why is the DuPont system of analysis an important tool when evaluating firm performance? *(LG3-6)*

8. A firm has an ROE of 10 percent. The industry average ROE is 15 percent. How can the DuPont system of analysis help the firm's managers identify the reasons for this difference? *(LG3-6)*

9. What is the difference between the internal growth rate and the sustainable growth rate? *(LG3-6)*

10. What is the difference between time series analysis and cross-sectional analysis? *(LG3-7)*

11. What information does time series and cross-sectional analysis provide for firm managers, analysts, and investors? *(LG3-7)*

12. Why is it important to know a firm's accounting rules before making any conclusions about its performance from ratios analysis? *(LG3-8)*

13. What does it mean when a firm window dresses its financial statements? *(LG3-8)*

Problems

BASIC PROBLEMS

3-1 **Liquidity Ratios** You are evaluating the balance sheet for Goodman's Bees Corporation. From the balance sheet you find the following balances: cash and marketable securities = $400,000; accounts receivable = $1,200,000; inventory = $2,100,000; accrued wages and taxes = $500,000; accounts payable = $800,000; and notes payable = $600,000. Calculate Goodman Bees' current ratio, quick ratio, and cash ratio. *(LG3-1)*

3-2 **Liquidity Ratios** The top part of Ramakrishnan Inc.'s 2012 and 2011 balance sheets is listed below (in millions of dollars).

	2012	2011		2012	2011
Current assets:			Current liabilities:		
Cash and marketable securities	$ 34	$ 25	Accrued wages and taxes	$ 32	$ 31
Accounts receivable	143	128	Accounts payable	87	76
Inventory	206	187	Notes payable	76	68
Total	$383	$340	Total	$195	$175

Calculate Ramakrishnan Inc.'s current ratio, quick ratio, and cash ratio for 2012 and 2011. *(LG3-1)*

3-3   Asset Management Ratios Tater and Pepper Corp. reported sales for 2012 of $23 million. Tater and Pepper listed $5.6 million of inventory on its balance sheet. Using a 365-day year, how many days did Tater and Pepper's inventory stay on the premises? How many times per year did Tater and Pepper's inventory turnover? *(LG3-2)*

3-4   Asset Management Ratios Mr. Husker's Tuxedos Corp. ended the year 2012 with an average collection period of 32 days. The firm's credit sales for 2012 were $56.1 million. What is the year-end 2012 balance in accounts receivable for Mr. Husker's Tuxedos? *(LG3-2)*

3-5   Debt Management Ratios Tiggie's Dog Toys Inc. reported a debt-to-equity ratio of 1.75 times at the end of 2012. If the firm's total debt at year-end was $25 million, how much equity does Tiggie's have on its balance sheet? *(LG3-3)*

3-6   Debt Management Ratios You are considering a stock investment in one of two firms (LotsofDebt Inc. and LotsofEquity Inc.), both of which operate in the same industry. LotsofDebt Inc. finances its $30 million in assets with $29 million in debt and $1 million in equity. LotsofEquity Inc. finances its $30 million in assets with $1 million in debt and $29 million in equity. Calculate the debt ratio, equity multiplier, and debt-to-equity ratio for the two firms. *(LG3-3)*

3-7   Profitability Ratios Maggie's Skunk Removal Corp.'s 2012 income statement listed net sales of $12.5 million, EBIT of $5.6 million, net income available to common stockholders of $3.2 million, and common stock dividends of $1.2 million. The 2012 year-end balance sheet listed total assets of $52.5 million and common stockholders' equity of $21 million with 2 million shares outstanding. Calculate the profit margin, basic earnings power, ROA, ROE, and dividend payout. *(LG3-4)*

3-8   Profitability Ratios In 2012, Jake's Jamming Music Inc. announced an ROA of 8.56 percent, ROE of 14.5 percent, and a profit margin of 20.5 percent. The firm had total assets of $9.5 million at year-end 2012. Calculate the 2012 values of net income available to common stockholders, common stockholders' equity, and net sales for Jake's Jamming Music Inc. *(LG3-4)*

3-9   Market Value Ratios You are considering an investment in Roxie's Bed & Breakfast Corp. During the last year, the firm's income statement listed an addition to retained earnings of $4.8 million and common stock dividends of $2.2 million. Roxie's year-end balance sheet shows common stockholders' equity of $35 million with 10 million shares of common stock outstanding. The common stock's market price per share was $9.00. What is Roxie's Bed & Breakfast's book value per share and earnings per share? Calculate the market-to-book ratio and PE ratio. *(LG3-5)*

3-10   Market Value Ratios Dudley Hill Golf Club's market-to-book ratio is currently 2.5 times and the PE ratio is 6.75 times. If Dudley Hill Golf Club's common stock is currently selling at $22.50 per share, what is the book value per share and earnings per share? *(LG3-5)*

3-11   DuPont Analysis If Silas 4-Wheeler Inc. has an ROE of 18 percent, equity multiplier of 2, and a profit margin of 18.75 percent, what is the total asset turnover and the capital intensity? *(LG3-6)*

3-12 DuPont Analysis Last year, Hassan's Madhatter Inc. had an ROA of 7.5 percent, a profit margin of 12 percent, and sales of $25 million. Calculate Hassan's Madhatter's total assets. *(LG3-6)*

3-13 Internal Growth Rate Last year, Lakesha's Lounge Furniture Corporation had an ROA of 7.5 percent and a dividend payout ratio of 25 percent. What is the internal growth rate? *(LG3-6)*

3-14 Sustainable Growth Rate Last year Lakesha's Lounge Furniture Corporation had an ROE of 17.5 percent and a dividend payout ratio of 20 percent. What is the sustainable growth rate? *(LG3-6)*

INTERMEDIATE PROBLEMS

3-15 Liquidity Ratios Brenda's Bar and Grill has current liabilities of $15 million. Cash makes up 10 percent of the current assets and accounts receivable makes up another 40 percent of current assets. Brenda's current ratio is 2.1 times. Calculate the value of inventory listed on the firm's balance sheet. *(LG3-1)*

3-16 Liquidity and Asset Management Ratios Mandesa Inc. has current liabilities of $8 million, current ratio of 2 times, inventory turnover of 12 times, average collection period of 30 days, and credit sales of $64 million. Calculate the value of cash and marketable securities. *(LG3-1, LG3-2)*

3-17 Asset Management and Profitability Ratios You have the following information on Els' Putters Inc.: sales to working capital is 4.6 times, profit margin is 20 percent, net income available to common stockholders is $5 million, and current liabilities are $6 million. What is the firm's balance of current assets? *(LG3-2, LG3-4)*

3-18 Asset Management and Debt Management Ratios Use the following information to complete the balance sheet below: Sales are $8.8 million, capital intensity ratio is 2.10 times, debt ratio is 55 percent, and fixed asset turnover is 1.2 times. *(LG3-2, LG3-3)*

Assets		Liabilities and Equity	
Current assets	$_____	Total liabilities	$_____
Fixed assets	_____	Total equity	_____
Total assets	$_____	Total liabilities and equity	$_____

3-19 Debt Management Ratios Tiggie's Dog Toys Inc. reported a debt-to-equity ratio of 1.75 times at the end of 2012. If the firm's total assets at year-end were $25 million, how much of their assets are financed with debt and how much with equity? *(LG3-3)*

3-20 Debt Management Ratios Calculate the times interest earned ratio for LaTonya's Flop Shops Inc. using the following information. Sales are $1.5 million, cost of goods sold is $600,000, depreciation expense is $150,000, other operating expenses is $300,000, addition to retained earnings is $146,250, dividends per share is $1, tax rate is 30 percent, and number of shares of common stock outstanding is 90,000. LaTonya's Flop Shops has no preferred stock outstanding. *(LG3-3)*

3-21 Profitability and Asset Management Ratios You are thinking of investing in Nikki T's Inc. You have only the following information on the firm at year-end 2012: net income is $250,000, total debt is $2.5 million, and debt ratio is 55 percent. What is Nikki T's ROE for 2012? *(LG3-2, LG3-4)*

3-22 Profitability Ratios Rick's Travel Service has asked you to help piece together financial information on the firm for the most current year. Managers give you the following information: Sales are $8.2 million, total debt is $2.1 million, debt ratio is 40 percent, and ROE is 18 percent. Using this information, calculate Rick's ROA. *(LG3-4)*

3-23 **Market Value Ratios** Leonatti Labs' year-end price on its common stock is $35. The firm has total assets of $50 million, debt ratio of 65 percent, no preferred stock, and 3 million shares of common stock outstanding. Calculate the market-to-book ratio for Leonatti Labs. *(LG3-5)*

3-24 **Market Value Ratios** Leonatti Labs' year-end price on its common stock is $15. The firm has a profit margin of 8 percent, total assets of $42 million, a total asset turnover of 0.75, no preferred stock, and 3 million shares of common stock outstanding. Calculate the PE ratio for Leonatti Labs. *(LG3-5)*

3-25 **DuPont Analysis** Last year, Stumble-on-Inn Inc. reported an ROE of 18 percent. The firm's debt ratio was 55 percent, sales were $15 million, and the capital intensity was 1.25 times. Calculate the net income for Stumble-on-Inn last year. *(LG3-6)*

3-26 **DuPont Analysis** You are considering investing in Nuran Security Services. You have been able to locate the following information on the firm: total assets are $24 million, accounts receivable are $3.3 million, ACP is 25 days, net income is $3.5 million, and debt-to-equity is 1.2 times. Calculate the ROE for the firm. *(LG3-6)*

3-27 **Internal Growth Rate** Dogs R Us reported a profit margin of 10.5 percent, total asset turnover of 0.75 times, debt-to-equity of 0.80 times, net income of $500,000, and dividends paid to common stockholders of $200,000. The firm has no preferred stock outstanding. What is Dogs R Us's internal growth rate? *(LG3-6)*

3-28 **Sustainable Growth Rate** You have located the following information on Webb's Heating & Air Conditioning: Debt ratio is 54 percent, capital intensity is 1.10 times, profit margin is 12.5 percent, and the dividend payout is 25 percent. Calculate the sustainable growth rate for Webb. *(LG3-6)*

Use the following financial statements for Lake of Egypt Marina Inc. to answer Problems 3-29 through 3-33.

LAKE OF EGYPT MARINA INC. Balance Sheet as of December 31, 2012 and 2011 (in millions of dollars)					
Assets	2012	2011	**Liabilities and Equity**	2012	2011
Current assets:			Current liabilities:		
Cash and marketable securities	$ 75	$ 65	Accrued wages and taxes	$ 40	$ 43
Accounts receivable	115	110	Accounts payable	90	80
Inventory	200	190	Notes payable	80	70
Total	$390	$365	Total	$210	$193
Fixed assets:			Long term debt:	$300	$280
Gross plant and equipment	$580	$471	Stockholders' equity:		
Less: Depreciation	110	100	Preferred stock (5 million shares)	$ 5	$ 5
Net plant and equipment	$470	$371	Common stock and paid in surplus (65 million shares)	65	65
Other long term assets	50	49	Retained earnings	330	242
Total	$520	$420	Total	$400	$312
Total assets	$910	$785	Total liabilities and equity	$910	$785

LAKE OF EGYPT MARINA INC. Income Statement for Years Ending December 31, 2012 and 2011 (in millions of dollars)		
	2012	2011
Net sales (all credit)	$ 515	$ 432
Less: Cost of goods sold	230	175
Gross profits	$ 285	$ 257
Less: Depreciation	22	20
Other operating expenses	30	25
Earnings before interest and taxes (EBIT)	$ 233	$ 212
Less: Interest	33	30
Earnings before taxes (EBT)	$ 200	$ 182
Less: Taxes	57	55
Net income	$ 143	$ 127
Less: Preferred stock dividends	$ 5	$ 5
Net income available to common stockholders	$ 138	$ 122
Less: Common stock dividends	65	65
Addition to retained earnings	$ 73	$ 57
Per (common) share data:		
Earnings per share (EPS)	$ 2.123	$ 1.877
Dividends per share (DPS)	$ 1.000	$ 1.000
Book value per share (BVPS)	$ 6.077	$ 4.723
Market value (price) per share (MVPS)	$14.750	$12.550

3-29 Spreading the Financial Statements Spread the balance sheets and income statements of Lake of Egypt Marina Inc. for 2012 and 2011. *(LG3-6)*

3-30 Calculating Ratios Calculate the following ratios for Lake of Egypt Marina Inc. as of year-end 2012. *(LG3-1–LG3-5)*

Lake of Egypt Marina Inc.	Industry	Lake of Egypt Marina Inc.	Industry
a. Current ratio	2.00 times	m. Debt-to-equity	1.67 times
b. Quick ratio	1.20 times	n. Equity multiplier	2.67 times
c. Cash ratio	0.25 times	o. Times interest earned	8.50 times
d. Inventory turnover	3.60 times	p. Cash coverage	8.75 times
e. Days' sales in inventory	101.39 days	q. Profit margin	28.75%
f. Average collection period	32.50 days	r. Basic earnings power	32.50%
g. Average payment period	45.00 days	s. ROA	19.75%
h. Fixed asset turnover	1.25 times	t. ROE	36.88%
i. Sales to working capital	4.25 times	u. Dividend payout	35.00%
j. Total asset turnover	0.85 times	v. Market-to-book ratio	2.55 times
k. Capital intensity	1.18 times	w. PE ratio	15.60 times
l. Debt ratio	62.50%		

3-31 DuPont Analysis Construct the DuPont ROA and ROE breakdowns for Lake of Egypt Marina Inc. *(LG3-6)*

3-32 Internal and Sustainable Growth Rates Calculate the internal and sustainable growth rate for Lake of Egypt Marina Inc. *(LG3-6)*

3-33 Cross-Sectional Analysis Using the ratios from Problem 3-30 for Lake of Egypt Marina Inc. and the industry, what can you conclude about Lake of Egypt Marina's financial performance for 2012? *(LG3-7)*

ADVANCED PROBLEMS

3-34 Ratio Analysis Use the following information to complete the balance sheet below. *(LG3-1–LG3-5)*

> Current ratio = 2.5 times
> Profit margin = 10%
> Sales = $1,200m
> ROE = 20%
> Long-term debt to Long-term debt and equity = 55%

Current assets	$_____	Current liabilities	$210m
Fixed assets	_____	Long-term debt	_____
		Stockholders' equity	_____
Total assets	$_____	Total liabilities and equity	$_____

3-35 Ratio Analysis Use the following information to complete the balance sheet below. *(LG3-1–LG3-5)*

> Current ratio = 2.20 times
> Credit sales = $1,200m
> Average collection period = 60 days
> Inventory turnover = 1.50 times
> Total asset turnover = 0.75 times
> Debt ratio = 60%

Cash	$_____		
Accounts receivable	_____	Current liabilities	$500m
Inventory	_____	Long-term debt	_____
Current assets	$_____	Total debt	$_____
Fixed assets	_____	Stockholders' equity	_____
Total assets	$_____	Total liabilities and equity	$_____

time value of money 1:
analyzing single cash flows

Both this chapter and the next illustrate time value of money (TVM) calculations, which we will use throughout the rest of this book. We hope you will see what powerful tools they are for making financial decisions. Whether you're managing the financial or other functional area of a business or making decisions in your personal life, being able to make TVM calculations will help you make financially sound decisions.

This background will also allow you to understand why CEOs, CFOs, and other professionals make the decisions that they do. Together, this chapter and the next will present all aspects of TVM. Since some students find this topic intimidating, we split the topic into two chapters as a way of providing more examples and practice opportunities.

As you see the examples and work the practice problems, we believe that you will find that TVM is not difficult.

Factors to consider when making time value of money decisions include:

- Size of the cash flows.
- Time between the cash flows.
- Rate of return we can earn.

The title of this chapter refers to the time value of money. But why might money change values, and why does it depend on time? Consider that $100 can buy you an assortment of food and drinks today. Will you be able to buy those same items in five years with the same $100? Probably not. Inflation might cause these items to cost $120. If so, in terms of buying "stuff," the dollar would have lost value over the five years. If you don't need to spend your money today,

continued on p. 76

LEARNING GOALS

LG4-1 Create a cash flow time line.

LG4-2 Compute the future value of money.

LG4-3 Show how the power of compound interest increases wealth.

LG4-4 Calculate the present value of a payment made in the future.

LG4-5 Move cash flows from one year to another.

LG4-6 Apply the Rule of 72.

LG4-7 Compute the rate of return realized on selling an investment.

LG4-8 Calculate the number of years needed to grow an investment.

continued from p. 75

putting it in your mattress will only cause it to lose value over time. Instead, there are banks that would like to use your money and pay you back later, with interest. This interest is your compensation to offset the money's decline in value. Each dollar will be worth less in the future, but you'll get more dollars. So you'll be able to buy the same items as before.

The basic idea behind the time value of money is that $1 today is worth more than $1 promised next year. But how much more? Is $1 today worth $1.05 next year? $1.08? $1.12? The answer varies depending on current interest rates. This chapter describes the time value of money concept and provides the tools needed to analyze single cash flows at different points in time. ■

ORGANIZING CASH FLOWS LG4-1

Managing cash flow timing is one of the most important tasks in successfully operating a business. A helpful tool for organizing our analysis is the **time line,** which shows the magnitude of cash flows at different points in time, such as monthly, quarterly, semiannually, or yearly. Cash we receive is called an **inflow,** and we denote it with a positive number. Cash that leaves us, such as a payment or contribution to a deposit, is an **outflow** designated with a negative number.

The time line below illustrates a $100 deposit you made at a bank that pays 5 percent interest. In one year, the $100 has become $105. *Given that interest rate,* having $100 now (in year 0) has the same value as having $105 in one year.

Here's a simple example: suppose you allowed the bank to rent your $100 for a year at a cost of 5 percent, or $5. This cost is known as the **interest rate.**

Period	0	5%	1	2 years
Cash flow	−100		105	

Interest rates will affect you throughout your life, both in business and in your personal life. Companies borrow money to build factories and expand into new locations and markets. They expect the future revenues generated by these activities to more than cover the interest payments and repay the loan. People borrow money on credit cards and obtain loans for cars and home mortgages. They expect their purchases to give them the satisfaction in the future that compensates them for the interest payments charged on the loan. Understanding the dynamics between interest rates and cash inflows and outflows over time

is key to financial success. The best place to start learning these concepts lies in understanding how money grows over time.

time out!

4-1 Why is a dollar worth more today than a dollar received one year from now?

4-2 Drawing on your past classes in accounting, explain why time lines must show one negative cash flow and one positive cash flow.

4-3 Set up a time line, given a 6 percent interest rate, with a cash inflow of $200 today and a cash outflow of $212 in one year.

FUTURE VALUE

The $105 payment that your bank credits to your account in one year is known as a **future value (FV)** of $100 in one year at a 5 percent annual interest rate. If interest rates were higher than 5 percent, then the future value of your $100 would also be higher. If you left your money in the bank for more than one year, then its future value would continue to grow over time. Let's see why.

Payday lending has become a multibillion-dollar industry across the United States in just a few years. It provides people with short-term loans and gets its name from the fact that the loan is to be paid back at the borrower's next payday. Anthony is short a few hundred dollars and his next paycheck is two weeks away. For a $300 loan, Anthony must pay a $50 "fee" in advance and repay the $300 loan in two weeks. What implied interest rate would Anthony pay for this two-week period? Is this a good deal?

But what if Anthony can't pay the loan back on time? Scan the QR code for an extended look. Turn to the back of the book for solutions to these applications.

Single-Period Future Value LG4-2

Computing the future value of a sum of money one year from today is straightforward: add the interest earned to today's cash flow. In this case:

Value in 1 year = Today's cash flow + Interest earned

$105 = $100 + $5

We computed the $5 interest figure by multiplying the interest rate by today's cash flow ($100 × 5%). Note that in equations, interest rates appear in decimal format. So we use 0.05 for 5 percent:

$100 + ($100 × 0.05) = $105

Note that this is the same as:

$100 × (1 + 0.05) = $105

We need the 1 in the parentheses to recapture the original deposit and the 0.05 is for the interest earned. We can generalize this computation to any amount of today's cash flow. In the general form of the future value equation, we call cash today **present value,** or **PV.** We compute the future value one year from now, called FV_1, using the interest rate, i:

$$\text{Value in 1 year} = \text{Today's value} \times \left(1 + \text{Interest rate}\right)$$

$$FV_1 = PV \times (1 + i) \qquad (4\text{-}1)$$

Notice that this is the same equation we used to figure the future value of your $100. We've simply made it generic so we can use it over and over again. The 1 subscript means that we are calculating for only one period—in this case, one year. If interest rates were 6 percent instead of 5 percent per year, for instance, we could use equation 4-1 to find that the future value of $100 in one year is $106 [=$100 × (1 + 0.06)].

Of course, the higher the interest rate, the larger the future value will be. Table 4.1 shows the interest cost and future value for a sample of different cash flows and interest rates. Notice from the first two lines of the table that, while the difference in interest earned between 5 percent and 6 percent ($1) doesn't seem like much on a $100 deposit, the difference on a $15,000 deposit (the following two lines) is substantial ($150).

Compounding and Future Value LG4-1, LG4-3

After depositing $100 for one year, you must decide whether to take the $105 or leave the money at the bank for another year to earn another 5 percent (or whatever interest rate the bank currently pays). In the second year at the bank, the deposit earns 5 percent on the $105 value, which is $5.25 (= $105 × 0.05). Importantly, you get more than the $5 earned the first year, which would be a simple total of $110. The extra 25 cents earned in the second year is interest *on interest that was earned in the first year.* We call this process of earning interest both on the original deposit and on the earlier interest payments **compounding.**

So, let's illustrate a $100 deposit made for two years at 5 percent in the time line on the next page.

▼ **TABLE 4.1** Higher Interest Rates and Cash Flows Lead to Higher Future Value

Higher Interest Rates Lead to Higher Future Value

Today's Cash Flow	Interest Rate	Interest Cost	Next Year's Future Value
$ 100.00	5%	$ 5.00	$ 105.00
$ 100.00	6%	$ 6.00	$ 106.00
$15,000.00	5%	$ 750.00	$ 15,750.00
$15,000.00	6%	$ 900.00	$ 15,900.00

Higher Cash Flows Today Lead to Higher Future Values

Today's Cash Flow	Interest Rate	Interest Cost	Next Year's Future Value
$500.00	7.50	$37.50	$537.50
$750.00	7.50	$56.25	$806.25

Period	0	5%	1	5%	2 years
Cash flow	−100				?

The question mark denotes the amount we want to solve for. As with all TVM problems, we simply have to identify what element we're solving for; in this case, we're looking for the FV. To compute the two-year compounded future value, simply use the 1-year equation (4-1) twice.

$$\$100 \times (1 + 0.05) \times (1 + 0.05) = \$110.25$$

So the future value of $100 deposited today at 5 percent interest is $110.25 in period 2. You can see that this represents $10 of interest payments generated from the original $100 ($5 each year) and $0.25 of interest earned in the second year on previously earned interest payments. The $5 of interest earned every year on the original deposit is called **simple interest**. Any amount of interest earned above the $5 in any given year comes from compounding. Over time, the new interest payments earned from compounding can become substantial. The multiyear form of equation 4-1 is the future value in year N, shown as:

$$\frac{\text{Future value}}{\text{in } N \text{ years}} = \frac{\text{Present}}{\text{value}} \times \frac{N \text{ years of}}{\text{compounding}}$$

$$FV_N = PV \times (1 + i)^N \qquad (4\text{-}2)$$

We can solve the 2-year deposit problem more directly using equation 4-2 as $110.25 = \$100 \times (1.05)^2$. Here, solving for FV in the equation requires solving for only one unknown. In fact, all TVM equations that you will encounter only require figuring out what is unknown in the situation and solving for that one unknown factor.

We can easily adapt equation 4-2 to many different future value problems. What is the future value in 30 years of that $100 earning 5 percent per year? Using equation 4-2, we see that the future value is $100 × (1.05)^{30} = \$432.19$. The money has increased substantially! You have made a profit of $332.19 over and above your original $100. Of this profit, only $150 (= $5 × 30 years) came from simple interest earned on the original deposit. The rest, $182.19 (= $332.19 − $150), is from the compounding effect of earning interest on previously earned interest.

Remember that the difference between earning 5 percent and 6 percent in interest on the $100 was only $1 the first year. So what is the future value difference after 15 years? Is it $15? No, as Figure 4.1 shows, the difference in future value substantially increases over time. The difference is $31.76 in year 15 and $142.15 in year 30.

The Power of Compounding Compound interest is indeed a powerful tool for building wealth. Albert Einstein, the German-born American physicist who developed the special and general theories of relativity and won the Nobel Prize for Physics in 1921, is supposed to have said, "The most powerful force in the universe is compound interest."[1] Figure 4.2 illustrates this point. It shows the original $100 deposited, the cumulative interest earned on that deposit, and the cumulative interest-on-interest earned. By the 27th year, the money from the interest-on-interest exceeds the interest earned on the original deposit. By the 40th year, interest-on-interest contributes more than double the interest on the deposit. The longer money can earn interest, the greater the compounding effect.

Earning higher interest rates on the investment for additional time periods magnifies compounding power. Consider the future value of $100 deposited at different interest rates and over different time periods as shown in Table 4.2. The future value of $100 earning 5 percent per year for five years is $127.63, for a profit of $27.63. Would you double your profit by simply investing that same $100 at double the interest rate, 10 percent? No, because compounding changes the nature of the investment so that your money grows exponentially, not in a simple linear relationship. The future value of $100 in five years at 10 percent is $161.05. The $61.05 profit is *more* than double the profit of $27.63 earned at 5 percent. Tripling the interest rate to 15 percent shows a profit of $201.14 that is nearly *quadruple* the profit earned at 5 percent.

[1] No one seems to know exactly what he said, when he said it, or to whom. Similar statements commonly attributed to Einstein are: (1) compound interest is the greatest wonder of the universe, (2) compound interest is the ninth wonder of the world, and (3) it is the greatest mathematical discovery of all time. If he did not say any of these things, he (or someone else) should have!

▼ **FIGURE 4.1** The Future Value of $100

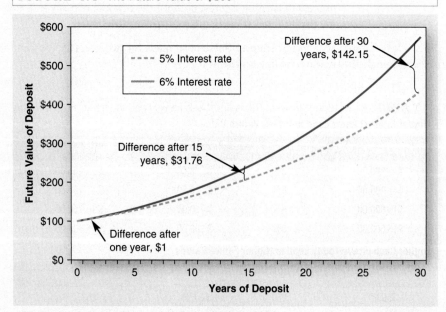

Small differences in interest rates can really add up over time!

▼**FIGURE 4.2** Interest Earned on Prior Interest at a 5 Percent Rate

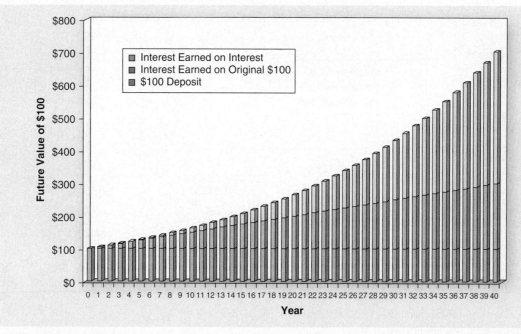

The money from interest-on-interest will eventually exceed the interest from the original deposit.

The same effect occurs when we increase the time. When the deposit earns 10 percent per year for five years, it makes a profit of $61.05. When we double the amount of time to 10 years, the profit more than doubles to $159.37. If we double the time again to 20 years, the profit increases not to just $318.74 (= $159.37 × 2) but to $572.75. At 10 percent for 30 years, the profit on $100 is a whopping $1,644.94. Interest rates and time *are both* important factors in compounding! These relationships are illustrated in Figure 4.3.

▼**TABLE 4.2** Compounding Builds Wealth Over Time

Future Value of $100 Deposited at 5%, 10%, and 15% Interest Rates				
	Future Value			
Interest Rate Earned	5 years	10 years	20 years	30 years
5%	$127.63	$162.89	$ 265.33	$ 432.19
10	161.05	259.37	672.75	1,744.94
15	201.14	404.56	1,636.65	6,621.18

time out!

4-4 How does compounding help build wealth (or increase debt) over time?

4-5 Why does doubling the interest rate or time quickly cause more than a doubling of the future value?

Compounding at Different Interest Rates Over Time

Interest rates have varied over time. In the past half-century, banks have offered depositors rates lower than

1 percent and as high as double digits. They've also charged interest from about 5.5 percent to 21.6 percent to consumers for various kinds of loans. Let's look at how to compute future value when rates change, so that money earns interest at multiple interest rates over time. In our first example in this chapter, your deposit of $100 earned 5 percent interest. Now consider the future value when the bank announces it will pay 6 percent interest in the second year. How much will you earn now? We can illustrate the question with this time line:

We already know that the $100 deposit will grow to $105 at the end of the first year. This $105 will then earn 6 percent in the second year and have a value of $111.30 (= $105 × 1.06). If we put the two steps together into one equation, the solution appears as $111.30 = $100 × 1.05 × 1.06. From this you should

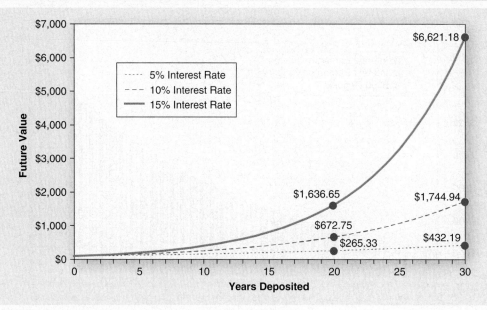

The future value differences between compounding interest rates expand exponentially over time.

(Future value of $100 deposited at 5%, 10%, and 15% interest rates)

EXAMPLE 4-1

For interactive versions of this example visit www.mhhe.com/canM2e

CALCULATOR HINTS

$N = 3$
$I = 7$
$PV = 1500$
$PMT = 0$
$CPT\ FV = -1837.56$

Graduation Celebration Loan LG4-3

Dominic is a fourth-year business student who wants to go on a graduation celebration/vacation in Mexico but he has no money to pay for the trip. After the vacation, Dominic will start his career. His job will require moving to a new town and buying professional clothes. He asked his parents to lend him $1,500, which he figures he will be able to pay back in three years. His parents agree to lend him the money, but they will charge 7 percent interest per year. What amount will Dominic need to pay back? How much interest will he pay? How much of what he pays is interest-on-interest?

SOLUTION:

Dominic will have to pay:

$$FV_3 = \$1,500 \times (1.07)^3 = \$1,500 \times 1.225 = \$1,837.56$$

Of the $1,837.56 he owes his parents, $337.56 (= $1,837.56 − $1,500) is interest. We can illustrate this time-value problem in the following time line.

Period	0	7%	1	7%	2	7%	3 years
Cash flow	1,500						−1,837.56

Compare this compound interest with simple interest. Simple interest would be 7 percent of $1,500 (which is $105) per year. The 3-year cost would then be $315 (= 3 × $105). The difference between the compound interest of $337.56 and the total simple interest of $315 is the interest-on-interest of $22.56.

Similar to Problems 4-3, 4-4, 4-5, 4-6, 4-21, 4-22, 4-33, 4-34

EXAMPLE 4-2

For interactive versions of this example visit www.mhhe.com/canM2e

Celebration Loan with Payback Incentive LG4-3

Reexamine the loan Dominic was seeking from his parents in the previous example. His parents want to give him an incentive to pay off the loan as quickly as possible. They structure the loan so they charge 7 percent interest the first year and increase the rate 1 percent each year until the loan is paid. How much will Dominic owe if he waits three years to pay off the loan? Say that in the third year he considers whether to pay off the loan or wait one more year. How much more will he pay if he waits one more year?

SOLUTION:

For a payment in the third year, Dominic will pay interest of 7 percent the first year, 8 percent the second year, and 9 percent the third year. He will have to pay:

$$FV_3 = \$1,500 \times 1.07 \times 1.08 \times 1.09 = \$1,500 \times 1.2596 = \$1,889.41$$

The cash flow time line is:

Period	0	7%	1	8%	2	9%	3 years
Cash flow	1,500						−1,889.41

Even worse, if he waits until the fourth year, he will pay one year of interest at 10 percent. The total payment will be

$$FV_4 = \$1,889.41 \times 1.10 = \$2,078.35$$

Because of both the escalating interest rate and the compounding effect, Dominic must make timely and increasing payments the longer he delays in paying off the loan. Deciding in the third year to put off the payment an extra year would cost him an additional $188.94 (= $2,078.35 − $1,889.41).

Similar to Problems 4-7, 4-8

---

not be surprised that a general equation for future value of multiple interest rates is:

$$\frac{\text{Future value in}}{N \text{ periods}} = \frac{\text{Today's}}{\text{value}} \times \frac{\text{Each period's}}{\text{compounding}}$$

$$\begin{aligned} FV_N = PV &\times (1 + i_{\text{period 1}}) \\ &\times (1 + i_{\text{period 2}}) \\ &\times (1 + i_{\text{period 3}}) \times \cdots \\ &\times (1 + i_{\text{period } N}) \end{aligned} \qquad (4\text{-}3)$$

Note that the future value equation 4-2 is a special case of the more general equation 4-3. If the interest rate every period is the same, we can write equation 4-3 as equation 4-2.

PRESENT VALUE LG4-4

We asked earlier what happens when you deposit $100 of cash in the bank to earn 5 percent interest for one year—the bank pays you a $105 future value. However, we could have asked the question in reverse. That is, if the bank will pay $105 in one year and interest rates are 5 percent, how much would you be willing to deposit now, to receive that payment in a year? Here, we start with a future value and must find the present value—a different kind of calculation called discounting.

Discounting

While the process of a present value growing over time into the future is called *compounding*, the process of figuring out how much an amount that you expect to receive in the future is worth today is **discounting.** Just as compounding significantly increases the present value into the future, discounting significantly decreases the value of a future amount to the present. Since discounting is the reverse of compounding, we can rearrange equation 4-1 to solve for the present value of a cash flow received one year in the future.

$$\frac{\text{Present value of next}}{\text{period's cash flow}} = \frac{\text{Next period's}}{\text{value}} \div \frac{\text{One period of}}{\text{discounting}}$$

$$PV = \frac{FV_1}{(1 + i)} \qquad (4\text{-}4)$$

the
Math Coach on...

Using a Financial Calculator

Financial, or business, calculators are programmed to perform the time value of money equations we develop in this chapter and the next. The two most common types of inexpensive financial calculators that can perform such functions are the Hewlett-Packard 10B II Business Calculator and the Texas Instruments BA II (Plus or Professional). Among many useful financial shortcuts these calculators have five specific financial buttons. The relevant financial buttons for time value of money (TVM) calculations are listed below. The HP10BII calculator buttons look like this:

1. N (for the number of periods),
2. I/YR (for the interest rate),
3. PV (for present value),
4. PMT (for a constant payment every period), and
5. FV (for future value).

Notice that the TI BA II Plus financial calculator buttons appear to be very similar:

A common, more sophisticated and expensive calculator is the TI-83. This calculator has a menu system that includes the financial functions as shown:

To get to the TVM menu, select APPLICATIONS and then choose FINANCE, and finally 1 TVM SOLVER on the previous screens.

Setting Up Your Calculator: Both of these calculators come from the factory with specific settings. You will find it useful to change two of them. The first is to set the number of digits shown after the decimal point on the calculator display. The factory setting is for two digits. However, consider a problem in which we use a 5.6 percent interest rate. The decimal version of this percentage is 0.056, which a two-digit display would round to 0.06. It's less worrisome to set the calculator to display the number of digits necessary to show the right number; this is called a *floating point display.* To set a floating point display for the HP calculator, press the color button, then the DISP button, and finally the decimal (.) button. To set the display for a floating point decimal on the TI calculator, push the 2ND button, followed by the FORMAT button, followed by the 9 button, and finally the ENTER button.

The second change you'll want to make is to set the number of times the calculator compounds each period. The settings may be preset to 12 times per period. Reset this to one time per period. To change the HP calculator to compound once per period, push the 1 button, then the color button, and finally the P/YR button. On the TI calculator, simply push the 2ND button, the P/Y button, the number one, and the ENTER button. These new settings will remain in the calculator until you either change them or remove the calculator's batteries.

Using Your Calculator: The calculators compute time-value problems in similar ways. Enter the cash flows into the time-value buttons (PV, PMT, and FV) consistent with the way they are shown in a time line. In other words, cash inflows should be positive and cash outflows negative. Thus, PV and FV cash flows are nearly always opposite in sign. Enter interest rates (I) in the percentage form, not the decimal form. Also enter the number of periods in the problem (N).

Consider our earlier example of the $100 deposit for two years earning a 5 percent interest rate.

1. To set the number of years, press 2 and then the N button.
2. To set the interest rate, press 5 and then the I button. (*Note* that interest rates are in percentage format for using a financial calculator and in decimal format for using the equations.)
3. To enter the current cash flow: press 100, then make it negative by pressing the $+/-$ button, then press the PV button.
4. We won't use the PMT button, so enter 0 and then the PMT button.
5. To solve for future value, press the compute button (CPT) [for the TI] and then the FV button [press the FV button only for the HP].
6. Solution: the display should show FV = 110.25

How much would you be willing to deposit now to receive a certain payment in a year?

Suppose the bank is going to pay $105 in one year and interest rates are 5 percent. Then the present value of the payment is $105/1.05 = $100. Present values are always smaller than future values (as long as interest rates are greater than zero!), and the difference between what an investment is worth today and what it's worth when you're supposed to redeem it gets larger as the interest rate increases. Likewise, if the amount of time until the expected payment date increases, the difference will also increase in value.

Discounting over Multiple Periods LG4-1

Discounting over multiple periods is the reverse process of compounding over multiple periods. If we know that, we can find the general equation for present value by rearranging the terms in equation 4-2 to form:

$$\frac{\text{PV of cash flow}}{\text{made in } N \text{ years}} = \frac{\text{Cash flow}}{\text{in year } N} \div \frac{N \text{ years}}{\text{of discounting}}$$

$$PV = \frac{FV_N}{(1+i)^N} \tag{4-5}$$

The interest rate, i, which we use to calculate present value, is often referred to as the **discount rate.** How much is a $100 payment to be made in the future worth today? Of course, it depends on how far into the future you expect to receive the payment and the discount rate used. If you receive a $100 cash flow in five years, then its present value is $78.35, discounted at 5 percent:

CALCULATOR HINTS

N = 5
I = 5
PMT = 0
FV = 100
$CPT\ PV$ = −78.35

$$PV = \$100/(1.05)^5 = \$100/1.2763 = \$78.35$$

The time line looks like this:

Period	0	5%	1	5%	2	5%	3	5%	4	5%	5 years
Cash flow	−78.35										100

If the discount rate rises to 10 percent, the present value of our $100 to be paid to us in five years is only $62.09 today. At a 15 percent interest rate, the present value declines to less than half the future cash flow: $49.72. Higher interest rates discount future cash flows more quickly and dramatically. You can see this principle illustrated in Figure 4.4.

the Math Coach on...

Entering TVM

❝ When using a financial calculator, be sure to either clear the time value of money buttons or enter a zero for the factors that you won't use to solve the problem. ❞

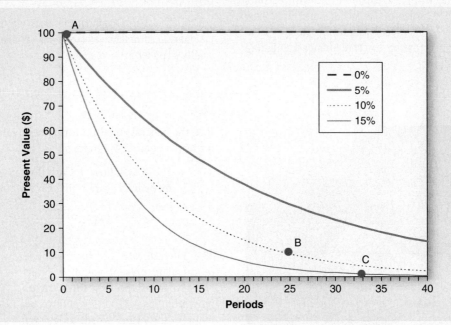

The higher the discount rate, the more quickly the cash flow value falls.

EXAMPLE 4-3

For interactive versions
of this example visit
www.mhhe.com/canM2e

CALCULATOR HINTS

N = 2
I = 7.5
PMT = 0
FV = 1000
CPT PV = −865.33

Buy Now and Don't Pay for Two Years LG4-4

Suppose that a marketing manager for a retail furniture company proposes a sale. Customers can buy now but don't have to pay for their furniture purchases for two years. From a time value of money perspective, selling furniture at full price with payment in two years is equivalent to selling furniture at a sale, or discounted, price with immediate payment. If interest rates are 7.5 percent per year, what is the equivalent sale price of a $1,000 sleeper-sofa when the customer takes the full two years to pay for it?

SOLUTION:

The time line for this problem is:

Period	0	7.5%	1	2 years
Cash flow	?			1,000

Using equation 4-5, the present value computation is

$$PV = \frac{FV_N}{(1+i)^N} = \frac{\$1,000}{1.075^2} = \frac{\$1,000}{1.1556} = \$865.33$$

In this case, the marketing proposal for delaying payment for two years is equivalent to selling the $1,000 sleeper-sofa for a sale price of $865.33, or a 13.5 percent discount. When stores promote such sales, they often believe that customers will not be able to pay the full amount at the end of the two years and then must pay high interest rate charges and late fees. Customers who do pay on time are getting a good deal.

Similar to Problems 4-9, 4-10, 4-11, 4-12

time **out!**

4-6 How are interest rates in the economy related to the way people value future cash payments?

4-7 Explain how discounting is the reverse of compounding.

8.5 percent in the third year. In this environment, how would we work out the present value of a future $2,500 cash flow in year 3? The time line for this problem is

Period	0	7%	1	8%	2	8.5%	3 years
Cash flow	?						2,500

Using equation 4-6 shows that the present value is $1,993.90:

$$PV = \frac{\$2,500}{1.07 \times 1.08 \times 1.085} = \frac{\$2,500}{1.2538} = \$1,993.90$$

Moving right from point A in the figure, notice that if interest rates are 0 percent, the present value will equal the future value. Also note from the curved lines that when the discount rate is greater than zero, the discounting to present value is not linear through time. The higher the discount rate, the more quickly the cash flow value falls. If the discount rate is 10 percent, a $100 cash flow that you would receive in 25 years is worth less than $10 today, as shown at point B in the figure. With a 15 percent discount rate, the $100 payment to be received in 33 years, at point C, is worth less than $1 today.

Discounting with Multiple Rates LG4-4

We can also discount a future cash flow at different interest rates per period. We find the general form of the equation for present value with multiple discount rates by rearranging equation 4-3:

$$\text{Present value with different discount rates} = \text{Future cash flow} \div \text{Each period's discounting}$$

$$PV = \frac{FV_N}{(1 + i_{\text{period 1}}) \times (1 + i_{\text{period 2}}) \times (1 + i_{\text{period 3}}) \times \cdots \times (1 + i_{\text{period } N})} \quad (4\text{-}6)$$

Suppose that we expect interest rates to increase over the next few years, from 7 percent this year, to 8 percent next year, to

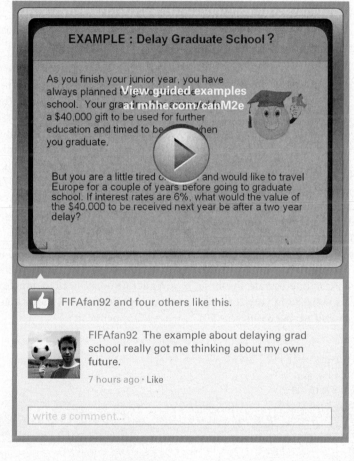

EXAMPLE : Delay Graduate School ?

As you finish your junior year, you have always planned to go to graduate school. Your grandmother has a $40,000 gift to be used for further education and timed to be given when you graduate.

But you are a little tired of school and would like to travel Europe for a couple of years before going to graduate school. If interest rates are 6%, what would the value of the $40,000 to be received next year be after a two year delay?

FIFAfan92 and four others like this.

FIFAfan92 The example about delaying grad school really got me thinking about my own future.

7 hours ago · Like

write a comment...

USING PRESENT VALUE AND FUTURE VALUE

Moving Cash Flows LG4-1, LG4-5

As managers analyze investment projects, debt management, and cash flow, they frequently find it useful to move cash flows to different points in time. While you may be planning to keep money deposited in the bank for three years when you will buy a car, life often has a way of altering plans. What type of car might you purchase if the money earns interest for only two years, or for four years? How is a corporate financial forecast affected if the firm needs to remodel a factory two years sooner than planned? Moving cash flows around in time is important to businesses and individuals alike for sound financial planning and decision making.

Moving cash flows from one point in time to another requires us to use both present value and future value equations. Specifically, we use the present value equation for moving cash flows *earlier* in time, and the future value cash flows for moving cash flows *later* in time. For example, what's the value in year 2 of a $200 cash flow to be received in three years, when interest rates are 6 percent? This problem requires moving the $200 payment in the third year to a value in the second year, as shown in the time line:

Period	0	1	2	6%	3 years
Cash flow			?		200

Since the cash flow is to be moved one year *earlier* in time, we use the present value equation:

$$PV_2 = FV_3/(1 + i)^1$$
$$= \$200/(1.06)^1 = \$188.68$$

CALCULATOR HINTS

N = 1
I = 6
PMT = 0
FV = 200
CPT PV = −188.68

When interest rates are 6 percent, a $188.68 payment in year 2 equates to a $200 payment in year 3.

What about moving the $200 cash flow to year 5? Since this requires moving the cash flow later in time by two years, we use the future value equation. In this case, the equivalent of $200 in the third year is a fifth-year payment of:

$$FV_5 = PV_3 \times (1 + i)^2 = \$200 \times (1.06)^2$$
$$= \$200 \times 1.1236 = \$224.72$$

CALCULATOR HINTS

N = 2
I = 6
PV = 200
PMT = 0
CPT FV = −224.72

Table 4.3 illustrates how we might move several cash flows. At an 8 percent interest rate, a $1,000 cash flow due in year 5 compounded to year 10 equals $1,469.33. We could also discount that same $1,000 cash flow to a value of $793.83 in year 2. At an 8 percent interest rate, the three cash flows ($793.83 in year 2, $1,000 in year 5, and $1,469.33 in year 10)

become equivalent. Table 4.3 illustrates the movement of other cash flows given different interest rates and time periods.

Moving cash flows from one year to another creates an easy way to compare or combine two cash flows. Would you rather receive $150 in year 2 or $160 in year 2? Since both cash flows occur in the same year, the comparison is straightforward. But we can't directly add or compare cash flows in different years until we consider their time value. We can compare cash flows in different years by moving one cash flow to the same time as the other using the present value or future value equations. Once you have the value of each cash flow in the same year, you can directly compare or combine them.

Rule of 72 Albert Einstein is also credited with popularizing compound interest by introducing a simple mathematical approximation for the number of years required to double an investment. It's called the **Rule of 72.**

$$\frac{\text{Approximate number of years to}}{\text{double an investment}} = \frac{72}{\text{Interest rate}} \quad (4\text{-}7)$$

The Rule of 72 illustrates the power of compound interest. How many years will it take to double money deposited at 6 percent per year? Using the Rule of 72, we find the answer is 12 years (= 72/6). A higher interest rate causes faster increases in future value. A 9 percent interest rate allows money to double in just eight years. Remember that this rule provides only a mathematical approximation. It's more accurate with lower interest rates. After all, with a 72 percent interest rate, the rule predicts that it will take one year to double the money. However, we know that it actually takes a 100 percent rate to double money in one year.

We can also use the Rule of 72 to approximate the interest rate needed to double an investment in a specific amount of time. What rate do we need to double an investment in 5 years? Rearranging equation 4-7 shows that the rate needed is 14.4 percent (= 72/5) per year.

▼ **TABLE 4.3** Equivalent Cash Flows in Time

When Interest Rates Are	A Cash Flow of	In Year	Can be Moved to Year	With Equation	Equivalent Cash Flow
Moving Later versus Moving Earlier					
8%	$1,000	5	10	$FV_{10} = PV_5 \times (1 + i)^5 = \$1,000 \times (1.08)^5 =$	$1,469.33
8	1,000	5	2	$PV_2 = FV_5/(1 + i)^3 = \$1,000/(1.08)^3 =$	793.83
Moving Earlier					
10	500	9	8	$PV_8 = FV_9/(1 + i)^1 = \$500/(1.10)^1 =$	454.55
10	500	9	0	$PV_0 = FV_9/(1 + i)^9 = \$500/(1.10)^9 =$	212.05
Moving Later					
12	100	4	20	$FV_{20} = PV_4 \times (1 + i)^{16} = \$100 \times (1.12)^{16} =$	613.04
12	100	4	30	$FV_{30} = PV_4 \times (1 + i)^{26} = \$100 \times (1.12)^{26} =$	1,904.01

EXAMPLE 4-4

Pay Damages or Appeal? LG4-5

For interactive versions of this example visit www.mhhe.com/canM2e

Timber Inc. lost a lawsuit in a business dispute. The judge ordered the company to pay the plaintiff $175,000 in one year. Timber's attorney advises Timber to appeal the ruling. If so, Timber will likely lose again and will still have to pay the $175,000. But by appealing, Timber moves the $175,000 payment to year 2, along with the attorney's fee of $20,000 for the extra work. The interest rate is 7 percent. What decision should Timber make?

SOLUTION:

Timber executives must decide whether to pay $175,000 in one year or $195,000 in two years. To compare the two choices more directly, move the payment in year 2 to year 1 and then compare it to $175,000. Timber should choose to make the smaller payment. The computation is:

$$PV_1 = FV_2/(1 + i)^1 = \$195,000/(1.07)^1 = \$182,242.99$$

The value in year 1 of a year 2 payment of $195,000 is $182,242.99, which is clearly more than the $175,000 year 1 payment. So Timber should *not* appeal and should pay the plaintiff $175,000 in one year (and may want to look for another attorney).

Similar to Problems 4-23, 4-24, 4-25, 4-26, 4-27, 4-28, 4-40

CALCULATOR HINTS

$N = 1$
$I = 7$
$PMT = 0$
$FV = 195000$
$CPT\ PV = -182,242.99$

time out!

4-8 In Example 4-4, could Timber Inc. have performed its analysis by moving the $175,000 to year 2 and comparing? Would the firm then have made the same decision?

4-9 At what interest rate (and number of years) does the Rule of 72 become too inaccurate to use?

COMPUTING INTEREST RATES LG4-1, LG4-7

Time value of money calculations come in handy when we know two cash flows and need to find the interest rate. The investment industry often uses this analysis. Solving for the interest rate, or rate of return,[2] can answer questions like, "If

you bought a gold coin for $350 three years ago and sell it now for $475, what rate of return have you earned?" The time line for this problem looks like this:

Period	0	1	?%	2		3 years
Cash flow	−350					475

In general, computing interest rates is easiest with a financial calculator. To compute the answer using the time-value equations, consider how the cash flows fit into the future value equation 4-2:

$$FV_N = PV \times (1 + i)^N$$

$$\$475 = \$350 \times (1 + i)^3$$

CALCULATOR HINTS

$N = 3$
$PV = -350$
$PMT = 0$
$FV = 475$
$CPT\ I = 10.716$

Rearranging gives:

$$\$475/\$350 = (1 + i)^3, \quad \text{or} \quad 1.357 = (1 + i)^3$$

To solve for the interest rate, i, take the third root of both sides of the equation. To do this, take 1.357 to the 1/3 power using the y^x button on your calculator.[3] Doing this leads to:

$$1.107 = (1 + i), \text{or } i = 0.107 = 10.7\%$$

If you buy a gold coin for $350 and sell it three years later for $475, you earn a 10.7 percent return per year.

---

[2]The terms *interest rate* and *rate of return* are referring to the same thing. However, it is a common convention to refer to interest rate when you are the one paying the cash flows and refer to rate of return when you are the one receiving the cash flows.

[3]The general equation for computing the interest rate is $i = \left({FV_N}/{PV} \right)^{\frac{1}{N}} - 1$.

finance at work //: investments

TVM Caveat Emptor

Not making your payments on time can get very expensive. Reconsider the furniture selling experience in Example 4-3. The store has given customers the opportunity to buy the sleeper-sofa today and not pay the $1,000 price for two years. But what happens if you forget to pay on time? Indeed, many people do forget. Others simply haven't saved $1,000 and can't make the payment. The fine print in these deals provides the penalties for late payment. For example, the late clause might require a 10 percent annually compounded interest rate to apply to any late payment—retroactive to the sale date. Thus, being one day late with the payment will automatically incur an interest charge for the entire two years of $210 (= $1,000 × 1.1^2 − $1,000), which is in addition to the original $1,000 still owed, of course.

The impact of making late payments can also show up later when you apply for credit cards, auto loans, and other credit. Credit rating agencies gather information on us from companies, banks, and landlords to grade our payment history. If you consistently make late payments on your apartment, credit card, or electric bill, these agencies will give you a poor grade. The higher your grade, called a credit score, the more likely you are to be able to get a loan and pay a lower interest rate on that loan. People with lower credit scores may not be able to borrow money and when they can, they will pay higher interest rates on their credit cards and auto loans. Paying a higher interest rate can really cost you a lot of money. Remember the future value differences between interest rates illustrated in Table 4.2 and Figure 4.3. Those people

who have really bad credit scores can't get loans from banks and merchants and have to rely on payday lending places that charge enormously high rates, as highlighted in this chapter's Personal Application Viewpoint.

Making a late payment might not seem like a big deal at the time, but it can really cost you!

Want to know more?

Key Words to Search for Updates: **Credit report, credit ratings, credit score**

the Math Coach on...
Cash Flows

" When using a financial calculator to compute an interest rate between two cash flows, you must enter one cash flow as a negative number. This is because you must inform the calculator which payments are cash inflows and which are cash outflows. If you input all the cash flows as the same sign, the calculator will show an error when asked to compute the interest rate. "

Time is an important factor in computing the return that you're earning per year. Turning a $100 investment into $200 is a 100 percent return. If your investments earn this much in two years, then they earned a 41.42 percent rate of return per year [$100 × $(1.4142)^2$ = $200]. Table 4.4 shows the annual interest rate earned for doubling an investment over various time periods. Notice how compounding complicates the solution: It's not as simple as just dividing by the number of years. Getting a 100 percent return in two years means earning

41.42 percent per year, not 50 percent per year. Table 4.4 also shows the Rule of 72 interest rate estimate.

Return Asymmetries LG4-6

Suppose you bought a gold coin for $700 last year and now the market will pay you only $350. Clearly, the investment earned a negative rate of return. Use a financial calculator or a time-value equation to verify that this is a return of −50 percent. You lost half your money! So, in order to break even and get back to $700, you need to earn a positive 50 percent, right? Wrong. Note that to get from $350 to $700, your money needs to double! You need a 100 percent return to make up for a 50 percent decline. Similarly, you need a gain of 33.33 percent to make up for a 25 percent decline. If your investment declines by 10 percent, you'll need an 11.11 percent gain to offset the loss. In general, only a higher positive return can offset any given negative return.

▼ **TABLE 4.4** Interest Rate per Year to Double an Investment

Number of Years to Double Investment	Precise Annual Interest Rate	Rule of 72 Interest Rate Estimate
1	100.00%	72.00%
2	41.42	36.00
3	25.99	24.00
4	18.92	18.00
5	14.87	14.40
6	12.25	12.00
7	10.41	10.29
8	9.05	9.00
9	8.01	8.00
10	7.18	7.20
15	4.73	4.80
20	3.53	3.60
25	2.81	2.88
30	2.34	2.40

the
Math Coach on...

Simple TVM Spreadsheet Functions

Common spreadsheet programs include time value of money functions. The functions are:

Compute a future value = FV(rate,nper,pmt,pv,type)

Compute a present value = PV(rate,nper,pmt,fv,type)

Compute the number of periods = NPER(rate,pmt,pv,fv,type)

Compute an interest rate = RATE(nper,pmt,pv,fv,type)

Compute a repeating payment = PMT(rate,nper,pv,fv,type)

The five input/outputs (FV, PV, NPER, RATE, PMT) work similarly to the five TVM buttons on a business calculator. The *type* input defaults to 0 for normal situations, but can be set to 1 for computing annuity due problems (see Chapter 5). Different spreadsheet programs might have slightly different notations for these five functions.

Consider the future value problem of Example 4-1. The spreadsheet solution is the same as the TVM calculator solution. Note that since the PV is listed as a positive number, the FV output is a negative number.

	A	B	C	D
1				
2	Present Value =	$1,500		
3	Future Cash Flow =	-$1,837.56	=FV(B4,B5,0,B2,0)	
4	Interest Rate =	7%		
5	# of Periods =	3		

The inputs to the function can be directed to other cells, like the *rate*, *nper*, and *py* in the this illustration. Or the input can be the actual number, like *pmt* and *type*.

	A	B	C	D
1				
2	Present Value =	-$350		
3	Future Cash Flow =	$475		
4	Interest Rate =	10.72%	=RATE(B5,0,B2,B3,0)	
5	# of Periods =	3		

This spreadsheet solves for the interest rate in the preceding example in the text. Just like using the TVM calculator, the PV and FV must be of opposite signs to avoid getting an error message.

See this textbook's online student center to watch instructional videos on using spreadsheets. Also note that the solution for all the examples in the book are illustrated using spreadsheets in videos that are also available on the textbook website.

EXAMPLE 4-5

Growth in Staffing Needs LG4-8

CALCULATOR HINTS

I = 7
PV = −350
PMT = 0
FV = 500
CPT N = 5.27

Say that you are the sales manager of a company that produces software for human resource departments. You are planning your staffing needs, which depend on the volume of sales over time. Your company currently sells $350 million of merchandise per year and has grown 7 percent per year in the past. If this growth rate continues, how long will it be before the firm reaches $500 million in sales? How long before it reaches $600 million?

SOLUTION:

You could set up the following time line to illustrate the problem:

Period	0		1	7%	2	? years
				...		
Cash flow	−350					500

As shown in the margin, $350 million of sales growing at 7 percent per year will reach $500 million in five years and three months. To reach $600 million will take just two weeks short of eight years.

Similar to Problems 4-31, 4-32

SOLVING FOR TIME

LG4-7, LG4-8

Sometimes you may need to determine the time period needed to accumulate a specific amount of money. If you know the starting cash flow, the interest rate, and the future cash flow (the sum you will need), you can solve the time value equations for the number of years that you will need to accumulate that money. Just as with solving for different interest rates, solving for the number of periods is complicated and requires using natural logarithms.[4] Many people prefer to use a financial calculator to solve for the number of periods.

When interest rates are 9 percent, how long will it take for a $5,000 investment to double? Finding the solution with a financial calculator entails entering the following:

- I = 9
- PV = −5,000
- PMT = 0
- FV = 10,000

[4]The equation for solving for the number of periods is $N = \dfrac{\ln\left(^{FV_N}/_{PV}\right)}{\ln(1 + i)}$.

The answer is 8.04 years, or eight years and two weeks. The Rule of 72 closely approximates the answer, which predicts eight years (= 72/9). ∎

time out!

4-10 Say you double your money in three years. Explain why the rate of return is NOT 33.3 percent per year.

4-11 Show that you must earn a 25 percent return to offset a 20 percent loss.

4-12 In Example 4-5, how long will it take your company to double its sales?

4-13 In what other areas of business can these time-value concepts be used?

Get Online

mhhe.com/canM2e

for study materials including self-test problems with solutions, quizzes, research projects, minicases, and videos

Your Turn...

Questions

1. List and describe the purpose of each part of a time line with an initial cash inflow and a future cash outflow. Which cash flows should be negative and which positive? Why? *(LG4-1)*

2. How are the present value and future value related? *(LG4-2)*

3. Would you prefer to have an investment earning 5 percent for 40 years or an investment earning 10 percent for 20 years? Explain. *(LG4-3)*

4. How are present values affected by changes in interest rates? *(LG4-4)*

5. What do you think about the following statement? "I am going to receive $100 two years from now and $200 three years from now, so I am getting a $300 future value." How could the two cash flows be compared or combined? *(LG4-5)*

6. Show how the Rule of 72 can be used to approximate the number of years to quadruple an investment. *(LG4-6)*

7. Without making any computations, indicate which of each pair has a higher interest rate: *(LG4-7)*

   a. $100 doubles to $200 in five years *or* seven years.

   b. $500 increases in four years to $750 *or* to $800.

   c. $300 increases to $450 in two years *or* increases to $500 in three years.

8. A $1,000 investment has doubled to $2,000 in eight years because of a 9 percent rate of return. How much longer will it take for the investment to reach $4,000 if it continues to earn a 9 percent rate? *(LG4-8)*

Problems

4-1 **Time Line** Show the time line for a $600 cash inflow today, a $726 cash outflow in year 2, and a 10 percent interest rate. *(LG4-1)*

4-2 **Time Line** Show the time line for a $400 cash outflow today, a $518 cash inflow in year 3, and a 9 percent interest rate. *(LG4-1)*

4-3 **One Year Future Value** What is the future value of $500 deposited for one year earning a 9 percent interest rate annually? *(LG4-2)*

4-4 **One Year Future Value** What is the future value of $400 deposited for one year earning an interest rate of 9 percent per year? *(LG4-2)*

4-5 **Multiyear Future Value** How much would be in your savings account in eight years after depositing $150 today if the bank pays 8 percent per year? *(LG4-3)*

4-6 **Multiyear Future Value** Compute the value in 25 years of a $1,000 deposit earning 10 percent per year. *(LG4-3)*

4-7 **Compounding with Different Interest Rates** A deposit of $350 earns the following interest rates:

   a. 8 percent in the first year.

   b. 6 percent in the second year.

   c. 5 percent in the third year.

   What would be the third year future value? *(LG4-3)*

4-8 **Compounding with Different Interest Rates** A deposit of $750 earns interest rates of 9 percent in the first year and 12 percent in the second year. What would be the second year future value? *(LG4-3)*

4-9 **Discounting One Year** What is the present value of a $250 payment in one year when the discount rate is 10 percent? *(LG4-4)*

4-10 **Discounting One Year** What is the present value of a $200 payment in one year when the discount rate is 7 percent? *(LG4-4)*

4-11 **Present Value** What is the present value of a $1,500 payment made in six years when the discount rate is 8 percent? *(LG4-4)*

4-12 **Present Value** Compute the present value of an $850 payment made in ten years when the discount rate is 12 percent. *(LG4-4)*

4-13 **Present Value with Different Discount Rates** Compute the present value of $1,000 paid in three years using the following discount rates: 6 percent in the first year, 7 percent in the second year, and 8 percent in the third year. *(LG4-4)*

4-14 **Present Value with Different Discount Rates** Compute the present value of $5,000 paid in two years using the following discount rates: 8 percent in the first year and 7 percent in the second year. *(LG4-4)*

4-15 **Rule of 72** Approximately how many years are needed to double a $100 investment when interest rates are 7 percent per year? *(LG4-6)*

4-16 **Rule of 72** Approximately how many years are needed to double a $500 investment when interest rates are 10 percent per year? *(LG4-6)*

4-17 **Rule of 72** Approximately what interest rate is needed to double an investment over five years? *(LG4-6)*

4-18 **Rule of 72** Approximately what interest rate is earned when an investment doubles over 12 years? *(LG4-6)*

4-19 **Rates over One Year** Determine the interest rate earned on a $1,400 deposit when $1,700 is paid back in one year. *(LG4-7)*

4-20 Rates over One Year Determine the interest rate earned on a $2,300 deposit when $2,900 is paid back in one year. *(LG4-7)*

4-21 Interest-on-Interest Consider a $2,000 deposit earning 8 percent interest per year for five years. What is the future value, and how much total interest is earned on the original deposit versus how much is interest earned on interest due to compounding? *(LG4-3)*

4-22 Interest-on-Interest Consider a $5,000 deposit earning 10 percent interest per year for ten years. What is the future value, how much total interest is earned on the original deposit, and how much is interest earned on interest due to compounding? *(LG4-3)*

4-23 Comparing Cash Flows What would be more valuable, receiving $500 today or receiving $625 in three years if interest rates are 8 percent? Why? *(LG4-5)*

4-24 Comparing Cash Flows Which cash flow would you rather pay, $425 today or $500 in two years if interest rates are 10 percent? Why? *(LG4-5)*

4-25 Moving Cash Flows What is the value in year 3 of a $700 cash flow made in year 6 if interest rates are 10 percent? *(LG4-5)*

4-26 Moving Cash Flows What is the value in year 4 of a $1,000 cash flow made in year 6 if interest rates are 8 percent? *(LG4-5)*

4-27 Moving Cash Flows What is the value in year 10 of a $1,000 cash flow made in year 4 if interest rates are 9 percent? *(LG4-5)*

4-28 Moving Cash Flows What is the value in year 15 of a $250 cash flow made in year 3 if interest rates are 11 percent? *(LG4-5)*

4-29 Solving for Rates What annual rate of return is earned on a $1,000 investment when it grows to $2,500 in six years? *(LG4-7)*

4-30 Solving for Rates What annual rate of return is earned on a $5,000 investment when it grows to $9,500 in five years? *(LG4-7)*

4-31 Solving for Time How many years (and months) will it take $2 million to grow to $5 million with an annual interest rate of 7 percent? *(LG4-8)*

4-32 Solving for Time How long will it take $2,000 to reach $5,000 when it grows at 10 percent per year? *(LG4-8)*

4-33 Future Value At age 30 you invest $1,000 that earns 8 percent each year. At age 40 you invest $1,000 that earns 11 percent per year. In which case would you have more money at age 60? *(LG4-2)*

4-34 Future Value At age 25 you invest $1,500 that earns 8 percent each year. At age 40 you invest $1,500 that earns 11 percent per year. In which case would you have more money at age 65? *(LG4-2)*

4-35 Solving for Rates You invested $2,000 in the stock market one year ago. Today, the investment is valued at $1,500. What return did you earn? What return would you need to get next year to break even overall? *(LG4-7)*

4-36 Solving for Rates You invested $3,000 in the stock market one year ago. Today, the investment is valued at $3,750. What return did you earn? What return would you suffer next year for your investment to be valued at the original $3,000? *(LG4-7)*

4-37 Solving for Rates What annual rate of return is earned on a $4,000 investment made in year 2 when it grows to $7,000 by the end of year 7? *(LG4-7)*

4-38 Solving for Rates What annual rate of return is implied on a $2,500 loan taken next year when $3,500 must be repaid in year 4? *(LG4-7)*

4-39 General TVM Ten years ago, Hailey invested $2,000 and locked in a 9 percent annual interest rate for 30 years (ending 20 years from now). Aidan can make a 20-year investment today and lock in a 10 percent interest rate. How much money should he invest now in order to have the same amount of money in 20 years as Hailey? *(LG4-2, LG4-4)*

4-40 **Moving Cash Flows** You are scheduled to *receive* a $500 cash flow in one year, a $1,000 cash flow in two years, and *pay* an $800 payment in three years. If interest rates are 10 percent per year, what is the combined present value of these cash flows? *(LG4-5)*

4-41 **Spreadsheet Problem** Oil prices have increased a great deal in the last decade. The table below shows the average oil price for each year since 1949. Many companies use oil products as a resource in their own business operations (like airline firms and manufacturers of plastic products). Managers of these firms will keep a close watch on how rising oil prices will impact their costs. The interest rate in the PV/FV equations can also be interpreted as a growth rate in sales, costs, profits, and so on (see Example 4-5).

a. Using the 1949 oil price and the 1969 oil price, compute the annual growth rate in oil prices during those 20 years.

b. Compute the annual growth rate between 1969 and 1989 and between 1989 and 2010.

c. Given the price of oil in 2010 and your computed growth rate between 1989 and 2010, compute the future price of oil in 2015 and 2020.

Average Oil Prices					
Year	Per Barrel	Year	Per Barrel	Year	Per Barrel
1949	$2.54	1970	$ 3.18	1991	$16.54
1950	$2.51	1971	$ 3.39	1992	$15.99
1951	$2.53	1972	$ 3.39	1993	$14.25
1952	$2.53	1973	$ 3.89	1994	$13.19
1953	$2.68	1974	$ 6.87	1995	$14.62
1954	$2.78	1975	$ 7.67	1996	$18.46
1955	$2.77	1976	$ 8.19	1997	$17.23
1956	$2.79	1977	$ 8.57	1998	$10.87
1957	$3.09	1978	$ 9.00	1999	$15.56
1958	$3.01	1979	$12.64	2000	$26.72
1959	$2.90	1980	$21.59	2001	$21.84
1960	$2.88	1981	$31.77	2002	$22.51
1961	$2.89	1982	$28.52	2003	$27.54
1962	$2.90	1983	$26.19	2004	$38.93
1963	$2.89	1984	$25.88	2005	$46.47
1964	$2.88	1985	$24.09	2006	$58.30
1965	$2.86	1986	$12.51	2007	$64.67
1966	$2.88	1987	$15.40	2008	$91.48
1967	$2.92	1988	$12.58	2009	$53.48
1968	$2.94	1989	$15.86	2010	$71.57
1969	$3.09	1990	$20.03		

time value of money 2:
analyzing annuity cash flows

We explained basic time value computations in the previous chapter. Those TVM equations covered moving a single cash flow from one point in time to another. While this circumstance does describe *some* problems that businesses and individuals face, most debt and investment applications of time value of money feature multiple cash flows. In fact, *most* situations require many equal payments over time. Since these situations require a bit more complicated analysis, this chapter continues the TVM topic for applications that require many equal payments over time. For example, car loans and home mortgage loans require the borrower to make the same monthly payment for many months or years. People save for the future through monthly contributions to their pension portfolios. People in retirement must convert their savings into monthly income. Companies also make regular payments. Johnson & Johnson (ticker: JNJ) will pay level semiannual interest payments through 2033 on money it borrowed. General Motors (ticker: GM) paid a $0.50 per share quarterly dividend to stockholders for six straight years until 2006, when it switched to a $0.25 dividend. These examples require payments (and compounding) over different time intervals (monthly for car loans and semiannually for company debt). How are we to value these payments into common or comparable terms? In this chapter, we illustrate how to value multiple cash flows over time, including many equal payments, and how to incorporate different compounding frequencies. ■

LEARNING GOALS

LG5-1 Compound multiple cash flows to the future.

LG5-2 Compute the future value of frequent, level cash flows.

LG5-3 Discount multiple cash flows to the present.

LG5-4 Compute the present value of an annuity.

LG5-5 Figure cash flows and present value of a perpetuity.

LG5-6 Adjust values for beginning-of-period annuity payments.

LG5-7 Explain the impact of compound frequency and the difference between the annual percentage rate and the effective annual rate.

LG5-8 Compute the interest rate of annuity payments.

LG5-9 Compute payments and amortization schedules for car and mortgage loans.

L5-10 Calculate the number of payments on a loan.

FUTURE VALUE OF MULTIPLE CASH FLOWS

Chapter 4 illustrated how to take single payments and compound them into the future. To save enough money for a down payment on a house or for retirement, people typically make many contributions over time to their savings accounts. We can add the future value of each contribution together to see what the total will be worth at some future point in time—such as age 65 for retirement or in two years for a down payment on a house.

Finding the Future Value of Several Cash Flows LG5-1

Consider the following contributions to a savings account over time. You make a $100 deposit today, followed by a $125 deposit next year, and a $150 deposit at the end of the second year. If interest rates are 7 percent, what's the future value of your deposits at the end of the third year? The time line for this problem is illustrated as:

Period	0	1	7%	2	3 years
Cash flow	−100	−125		−150	?

Note that the first deposit will compound for three years. That is, the future value in year 3 of a cash flow in year 0 will compound 3 (= 3 − 0) times. The deposit at the end of the first year will compound twice (= 3 − 1). In general, a deposit in year m will compound $N - m$ times for a future value in year N. We can find the total amount at the end of three years by computing the future value of each deposit and then adding them together. Using the future value equation from Chapter 4, the future value of today's deposit is $100 \times (1 + 0.07)^3 = \$122.50$. Similarly, the future value of the next two deposits are $\$125 \times (1 + 0.07)^2 = \$143.11$ and $\$150 \times (1 + 0.07)^1 = \$160.50$, respectively.

Putting these three individual future value equations together would yield:

$$FV_3 = \$100 \times (1 + 0.07)^3 + \$125 \times (1 + 0.07)^2$$
$$+ \ \$150 \times (1 + 0.07)^1 = \$426.11$$

The general equation for computing the future value of multiple and varying cash flows (or payments) is:

FV_N = Future value of first cash flow
+ Future value of second cash flow
+ $\cdots$ + Future value of last cash flow

$$= PMT_m \times (1 + i)^{N-m}$$
$$+ \ PMT_n \times (1 + i)^{N-n} + \cdots$$
$$+ \ PMT_p \times (1 + i)^{N-p} \qquad (5\text{-}1)$$

In this equation, the letters m, n, and p denote when the cash flows occur in time. Each deposit can be different from the others.

»viewpoints

business APPLICATION

Walkabout Music Inc. issued $20 million in debt ten years ago to finance its factory construction. The debt allows Walkabout to make interest-only payments at a 7 percent coupon rate, paid semiannually for 30 years. Debt issued today would carry only 6 percent interest. The company's CFO is considering whether or not to issue new debt (for 20 years) to pay off the old debt. To pay off the old debt early, Walkabout would have to pay a special "call premium" totaling $1.4 million to its debt holders. To issue new debt, the firm would have to pay investment bankers a fee of $1.2 million. Should the CFO replace the old debt with new debt?

Future Value of Level Cash Flows LG5-2

Now suppose that each cash flow is the same and occurs every year. Level sets of frequent cash flows are common in finance—we call them **annuities.** The first cash flow of an annuity occurs at the end of the first year (or other time period) and continues every year to the last year. We derive the equation for the future value of an annuity from the general equation for future value of multiple cash flows, equation 5-1. Since each cash flow is the same, and the cash flows are every period, the equation appears as:

FVA_N = Future value of first payment
$\times$ Future value of second payment
+ $\cdots$ + Last payment

$$= PMT \times (1 + i)^{N-1} + PMT$$
$$\times (1 + i)^{N-2} + PMT \times (1 + i)^{N-3}$$
$$+ \cdots + PMT(1 + i)^0$$

The term FVA is used to denote that this is the future value of an annuity. Factoring out the common level cash flow, PMT, we can summarize and reduce the equation as:

$$\frac{\text{Future value}}{\text{of an annuity}} = \text{Payment}$$
$$\times \text{Annuity compounding}$$

$$FVA_N = PMT \times \frac{(1 + i)^N - 1}{i} \qquad (5\text{-}2)$$

annuity A stream of level and frequent cash flows paid at the end of each time period—often referred to as an *ordinary annuity*.

personal APPLICATION

Say that you obtained a mortgage for $150,000 three years ago when you purchased your home. You've been paying monthly payments on the 30-year mortgage with a fixed 8 percent interest rate and have $145,920.10 of principal left to pay. Recently, your mortgage broker called to mention that interest rates on new mortgages have declined to 7 percent. He suggested that you could save money every month if you refinanced your mortgage. You could find a 27-year mortgage at the new interest rate for a $1,000 fee. Should you refinance your mortgage?

But what if you want to move in the next few years? Is it still a good idea?
Scan the QR code for an extended look.
Turn to the back of the book for solutions to these applications.

Suppose that $100 deposits are made at the end of each year for five years. If interest rates are 8 percent per year, the future

value of this annuity stream is computed using equation 5-2 as:

$$FVA_5 = \$100 \times \frac{(1 + 0.08)^5 - 1}{0.08}$$
$$= \$100 \times 5.8666 = \$586.66$$

We can show these deposits and future value on a time line as:

Period	0	1	2	8%	3	4	5 years
Cash flow		−100	−100		−100	−100	−100
							586.66

Five deposits of $100 each were made. So, the $586.66 future value represents $86.66 of interest paid. As with almost any TVM problem, the length of time of the annuity and the interest rate for compounding are very important factors in accumulating wealth within the annuity. Consider the examples in Table 5.1. A $50 deposit made every year for 20 years will grow to $1,839.28 with a 6 percent interest rate. Doubling the annual deposits to $100 also doubles the future value to $3,678.56. However, making $100 deposits for *twice* the amount of time, 40 years, more than *quadruples* the future value to $15,476.20! Longer time periods lead to more total compounding and much more wealth. Interest rates also have this effect. Increasing the interest rate from 6 percent to 10 percent on the 40-year annuity results in nearly tripling the future value to $44,259.26.

EXAMPLE 5-1 | Saving for a Car LG5-1

For interactive versions of this example visit www.mhhe.com/canM2e

CALCULATOR HINTS

FV OF 1ST CASH FLOW:
N = 2
I = 5
PV = −2000
PMT = 0
CPT FV = 2,205

FV OF 2ND CASH FLOW:
N = 1
I = 5
PV = −2500
PMT = 0
CPT FV = 2,625

FV TOTAL = 2,205
+ 2,625 + 3,000
= $7,830

Say that as a freshman in college, you will be working as a house painter for each of the next three summers. You intend to set aside some money from each summer's paycheck to buy a car for your senior year. If you can deposit $2,000 from the first summer, $2,500 in the second summer, and $3,000 in the last summer, how much money will you have to buy a car if interest rates are 5 percent?

SOLUTION:

The time line for the forecast is:

Period	0	1	5%	2	3 years
Cash flow	0	−2,000		−2,500	−3,000
					?

The first cash flow, which occurs at the end of the first year, will compound for two years. The second cash flow will be invested for only one year. The last contribution will not have any time to grow before the purchase of the car. Using equation 5-1, the solution is

$$FV_3 = [\$2,000 \times (1 + 0.05)^{3-1}] + [\$2,500 \times (1 + 0.05)^{3-2}] + [\$3,000 \times (1 + 0.05)^{3-3}]$$
$$= (\$2,000 \times 1.1025) + (\$2,500 \times 1.05) + (\$3,000 \times 1) = \$7,830$$

You will have $7,830 in cash to purchase a car for your senior year.

Similar to Problems 5-1, 5-2, 5-17, 5-18, 5-43, 5-44

Annuity Cash Flow	Number of Years	Interest Rate	Future Value
$ 50	20	6%	$ 1,839.28
100	20	6	3,678.56
100	40	6	15,476.20
100	40	10	44,259.26

Think about it: Depositing only $100 per year (about 25 lattes per year) can generate some serious money over time. See Figure 5.1. What would $2,000 annual deposits grow to?

Future Value of Multiple Annuities

At times, multiple annuities can occur in both business and personal life. For example, you may find that you can increase the amount of money you save each year because of a promotion or a new and better job. As an illustration, reconsider the annual $100 deposits made for five years at 8 percent per year. This time, the deposit can be increased to $150 for the fourth and fifth years. How can we use the annuity equation to compute the future value when we have two levels of cash flows? In this case, the cash flow can be categorized as two

the
Math Coach on...

Annuities And the Financial Calculator

" In the previous chapter, the level payment button (PMT) in the financial calculator was always set to zero because no constant payments were made every period. We use the PMT button to input the annuity amount. For calculators, the present value is of the opposite sign (positive versus negative) from the future value. This is also the case with annuities. The level cash flow will be of the opposite sign as the future value, as the previous time line shows.

You would use the financial calculator to solve the above problem of depositing $100 for five years via the following inputs: $N = 5$, $I = 8$, $PV = 0$, $PMT = -100$. In this case, the input for present value is zero because no deposit is made today. The result of computing the future value is 586.66. "

EXAMPLE 5-2

For interactive versions of this example visit www.mhhe.com/canM2e

CALCULATOR HINTS

$N = 40$
$I = 7$
$PV = 0$
$PMT = -4500$
$CPT\ FV = 898,358.00$

NOW CHANGE TO:
$I = 8$
$CPT\ FV = 1,165,754.33$

Saving in the Company Pension Plan LG5-2

You started your first job after graduating from college. Your company offers a retirement plan for which the company contributes 50 percent of what you contribute each year. So, if you contribute $3,000 per year from your salary, the company adds another $1,500. You get to decide how to invest the total annual contribution from several portfolio choices that the plan administrator provides. Suppose that you pick a mixture of stocks and bonds that is expected to earn 7 percent per year. If you plan to retire in 40 years, how big will you expect that retirement account to be? If you could earn 8 percent per year, how much money would be available?

SOLUTION:

Every year, you and your employer will set aside a total of $4,500 for your retirement. Using equation 5-2 shows that the future value of this annuity is:

$$FVA_{40} = \$4,500 \times \frac{(1 + 0.07)^{40} - 1}{0.07} = \$4,500 \times 199.6351 = \$898,358.00$$

Note that you can build a substantial amount of wealth ($898,358) through your pension plan at work. If you can earn just 1 percent more each year, 8 percent total, you could be a millionaire!

$$FVA_{40} = \$4,500 \times \frac{(1 + 0.08)^{40} - 1}{0.08} = \$4,500 \times 259.0565 = \$1,165,754.33$$

Similar to Problems 5-3, 5-4

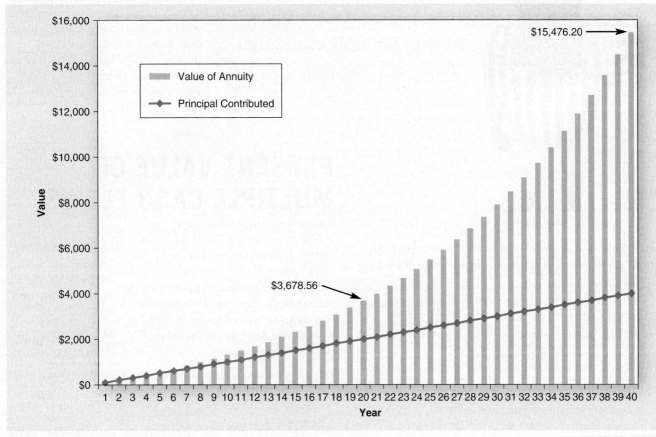

Longer time periods lead to more total compounding and much more wealth.

EXAMPLE 5-3

**For interactive versions
of this example visit
www.mhhe.com/canM2e**

CALCULATOR HINTS

ADD TO PREVIOUS
ANSWER

N = 20
I = 7
PV = 0
PMT = −1500
CPT FV = 61,493.24

Growing Retirement Contributions LG5-2

In the previous example, you are investing a total of $4,500 per year for 40 years in your employer's retirement program. You believe that with raises and promotions, you will eventually be able to contribute more money each year. Consider that halfway through your career, you are able to increase your investment in the retirement program to $6,000 per year (your contribution plus the company match). What would be the future value of your retirement wealth from this program if investments are compounded at 7 percent?

SOLUTION:

You can compute the future value using two annuities. The first annuity is one with payments of $4,500 that lasts 40 years. The second is a $1,500 (= $6,000 − $4,500) annuity that lasts only 20 years. We already computed the future value of the first annuity in the previous example: $898,358. The future value of the second annuity is:

$$FVA_{20} = \$1,500 \times \frac{(1 + 0.07)^{20} - 1}{0.07} = \$1,500 \times 40.9955 = \$61,493.24$$

So, your retirement wealth from this program would be $959,851 (= $898,358 + $61,493).

Similar to Problems 5-19, 5-20

the
Math Coach on...
Solving Multiple Annuities

" The trick to solving multiple annuity problems is to disentangle cash flows into groups of level payments ending in the future value year that we've designated. "

annuities. The first annuity is a $100 cash flow for five years. The second annuity is a $50 cash flow for two years. We demonstrate this as:

Period	0	1	2	8%	3	4	5 years
Cash flow	0	−100	−100	−100		−100	−100
						−50	−50
							?

To determine the future value of these two annuities, compute the future value of each one separately, and then simply add them together. The future value of the $100 annuity is the same as computed before, $586.66. The future value of the $50 annuity, using the TVM equation for the future value of a cash stream, is:

$$FVA_N = \$50 \times \frac{(1 + 0.08)^2 - 1}{0.08}$$

$$= \$50 \times 2.08 = \$104$$

time out!

5-1 Describe how compounding affects the future value computation of an annuity.

5-2 Reconsider your original retirement plan example to invest $4,500 per year for 40 years. Now consider the result if you don't contribute anything for four years (years 19 to 22) while your child goes to college. How many annuity equations will you need to find the future value of your 401(k) in this situation?

So, the future value of both of the annuities is $690.66 (= $586.66 + $104). In the same way, we could easily compute the future value if the last two cash flows are $50 *lower* ($50 each), instead of $50 higher ($150 each). To solve this alternative version, we would simply *subtract* the $104 future value instead of adding it.

PRESENT VALUE OF MULTIPLE CASH FLOWS

The future value concept is very useful to understand how to build wealth for the future. The present value concept will help you most particularly for personal applications such as evaluating loans (like car and mortgage loans) and business applications (like determining the value of business opportunities).

Finding the Present Value of Several Cash Flows LG5-3

Consider the cash flows that we showed at the very beginning of the chapter: you deposit $100 today, followed by a $125 deposit next year, and a $150 deposit at the end of the second year. In the previous situation, we sought the future value when interest rates are 7 percent. Instead of future value, we compute the present value of these three cash flows. The time line for this problem appears as:

Period	0	1	7%	2 years
Cash flow	−100	−125		−150
	?			

The first cash flow is already in year zero, so its value will not change. We will discount the second cash flow one year and the third cash flow two years. Using the present value equation from the previous chapter, the present value of today's payment is simply $100 ÷ (1 + 0.07)^0 = $100. Similarly, the present value of the next two cash flows are $125 ÷ (1 + 0.07)^1 = $116.82 and $150 ÷ (1 + 0.07)^2 = $131.02,

CALCULATOR HINTS

PV OF 1ST CASH FLOW IS $100.

PV OF 2ND CASH FLOW:
N = 1
I = 7
PMT = 0
FV = −125
CPT PV = 116.82

PV OF 3RD CASH FLOW:
N = 2
I = 7
PMT = 0
FV = −150
CPT PV = 131.02

ADD THE 3 PVS.

CALCULATOR HINTS

USE THE CF REGISTERS TO SOLVE:
CF
CF0 = 100
C01 = 125
F01 = 1
C02 = 150
F02 = 1

NPV
I = 7
CPT NPV = 347.84

finance at work //: personal

Who Will Save for Their Future?

Though it seems way too early for you to think about planning for your "golden years," financially wise people realize that it's never too early to start. Unfortunately, most people save little for their retirement years. Of those people over 55 years of age, 49 percent have saved less than $50,000. How far does that get you? Using a 6 percent investment return, $50,000 can generate a monthly income of only $299.78 for 30 years, at which time it is used up. That is less than $3,600 per year! The average Social Security monthly benefit is just over $1,100 per month, or about $13,400 per year. While about half of the U.S. population over 55 has saved *less* than $50,000, another 10 percent has saved between $50,000 and $99,999.

This chapter illustrates that much higher amounts of wealth can be accumulated if you start early! One easy way to do this is through a retirement plan at work. Most company and government employers offer employees defined contribution plans. (The corporate version is called a 401(k) plan; a nonbusiness plan is usually referred to as a 403(b) plan—both named after the legislation that created the plans.) These plans place all of the responsibility on employees to provide for their retirement. Employees contribute from their own paychecks and decide how to invest. Employees' decisions about how much to contribute and how early to start contributing have a dramatic impact on retirement wealth. Consider employees who earn $50,000 annually for 40 years and then retire. Note that if the employees contribute for 40 years, they must start by age 25 or so—starting early is vitally important! Contributing 5 percent of their salaries ($2,500) to the 401(k) plan every year and having it earn a 4 percent return will generate $237,564 for retirement. A 10 percent contribution ($5,000) would create $475,128 for retirement. Finally, investment decisions that yield an 8 percent return would yield

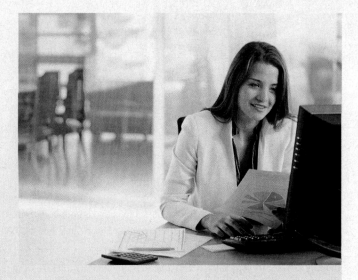

$1.3 million with a 10 percent contribution. This is quite a range of retirement wealth generated from just three important decisions each employee must make—how much to contribute, how to invest the funds, and when to start! Unfortunately, too many people make poor decisions. The average 401(k) account value for people in their 60s is only $136,400—often because people start 401(k) contributions too late to allow the funds to compound much.

Saving and investing money through a defined contribution plan is a good way to build wealth for retirement. But you must follow these rules: Start Early, Save Much, and Don't Touch!

Want to know more?

Key Words to Search for Updates: **Employee Benefit Research Institute (go to www.ebri.org), retirement income**

Sources: "How Much Have American Workers Saved for Retirement?" *Fast Facts from EBRI,* #119, April 16, 2009.

respectively. Therefore, the present value of these cash flows is $347.84 (= $100 + $116.82 + $131.02).

Putting these three individual present value equations together would yield:

$$PV = [\$100 \div (1 + 0.07)^0] + [\$125 \div (1 + 0.07)^1]$$
$$+ [\$150 \div (1 + 0.07)^2]$$
$$= \$347.84$$

The general equation for discounting multiple and varying cash flows is:

PV = Present value of first cash flow
  + Present value of second cash flow
  + · · · + Present value of last cash flow

$$= \frac{PMT_m}{(1 + i)^{N-m}} + \frac{PMT_n}{(1 + i)^{N-n}}$$
$$+ \cdots + \frac{PMT_p}{(1 + i)^{N-p}} \qquad (5\text{-}3)$$

In this equation, the letters m, n, and p denote when the cash flows occur in time. Each deposit can differ from the others in terms of size and timing.

the Math Coach on...

Using a Financial Calculator—Part 2

The five TVM buttons/functions in financial calculators have been fine, so far, for the types of TVM problems we've been solving. Sometimes we had to use them two or three times for a single problem, but that was usually because we needed an intermediate calculation to input into another TVM equation.

Luckily, most financial calculators also have built-in worksheets specifically designed for computing TVM in problems with multiple nonconstant cash flows.

To make calculator worksheets as flexible as possible, they are usually divided into two parts: one for input, which we'll refer to as the CF (cash flow) worksheet, and one or more for calculating decision statistics. We'll go over the conventions concerning the CF worksheet here, and we'll discuss the decision statistics in Chapter 13.

The CF worksheet is usually designed to handle inputting sets of multiple cash flows as quickly as possible. As a result, it normally consists of two sets of variables or cells—one for the cash flows and one to hold a set of frequency counts for the cash flows, so that we can tell it we have seven $1,500 cash flows in a row instead of having to enter $1,500 seven times.

Using the frequency counts to reduce the number of inputs is handy, but you must take care. Frequency counts are only good for embedded annuities of identical cash flows. You have to ensure that you don't mistake another kind of cash flow for an annuity.

Also, using frequency counts will usually affect the way that the calculator counts time periods. As an example, let's talk about how we would put the set of cash flows shown here into a CF worksheet:

Period	0	1	2	3	4	5	6	7	8
Cash flow	−$800	$150	$200		$150	$150	$150	$75	$75

(10%)

To designate which particular value we'll place into each particular cash flow cell in this worksheet, we'll note the value and the cell identifier, such as CF0, CF1, and so forth. We'll do the same for the frequency cells, using F1, F2, etc., to identify which CF cell the frequency cell goes with. (Note that, in most calculators, CF0 is treated as a unique value with an unalterable frequency of 1; we're going to make the same assumption here so you'll never see a listing for F0. For this sample timeline, our inputs would be:

−$800	[CF0]		
$150	[CF1]	1	[F1]
$200	[CF2]	1	[F2]
$0	[CF3]	1	[F3]
$150	[CF4]	3	[F4]
$75	[CF5]	2	[F5]

To compute the present value of these cash flows, use the NPV calculator function. The NPV function computes the present value of all the future cash flows and then adds the year 0 cash flow. Then, on the NPV worksheet, you would simply need to enter the interest rate and solve for the NPV:

10%	[I]
[CPT]	[NPV] = −$144.61

Note a few important things about this example:

1. We had to manually enter a value of $0 for CF3. If we hadn't, the calculator wouldn't have known about it and would have implicitly assumed that CF4 came one period after CF2.

2. Once we use a frequency cell for one cash flow, all numbering on any subsequent cash flows that we enter into the calculator is going to be messed up, at least from our point of view. For instance, the first $75 isn't what we would call "CF5," is it? We'd call it "CF7" because it comes at time period 7; but calculators usually treat CF5 as "the fifth set of cash flows," so we'll just have to try to do the same to be consistent.

3. If we really don't need to use frequency cells, we will usually just leave them out of the guidance instructions in this chapter to save space.

Present Value of Level Cash Flows LG5-4

You will find that this present value of an annuity concept will have many business and personal applications throughout your life. Most loans are set up so that the amount borrowed (the present value) is repaid through level payments made every period (the annuity). Lenders will examine borrowers' budgets and determine how much each borrower can afford as a payment. The maximum loan offered will be the present value of that annuity payment. The equation for the present value of an annuity can be derived from the general equation for the present value of multiple cash flows, equation 5-3. Since each cash flow is the same, and the borrower pays the cash flows every period, the present value of an annuity, PVA, can be written as:

Present value = Payment × Annuity discount

$$PVA_N = PMT \times \left[\frac{1 - \dfrac{1}{(1+i)^N}}{i} \right] \qquad (5\text{-}4)$$

Suppose that someone makes $100 payments at the end of each year for five years. If interest rates are 8 percent per year, the present value of this annuity stream is computed using equation 5-4 as:

$$PVA_5 = \$100 \times \left[\frac{1 - \dfrac{1}{(1+0.08)^5}}{0.08} \right]$$

$$= \$100 \times 3.9927 = \$399.27$$

CALCULATOR HINTS

N = 5
I = 8
PMT = −100
FV = 0
CPT PV = 399.27

▼ **TABLE 5.2** Magnitude of the Annuity, Number of Years Invested, and Interest Rate on PV

Annuity Cash Flow	Number of Years	Interest Rate	Present Value
$ 50	20	6%	$ 573.50
100	20	6	1,146.99
100	40	6	1,504.63
100	40	10	977.91

The time line for these payments and present value appears as:

Period	0	1	2 8% 3	4	5 years
Cash flow		−100	−100 −100	−100	−100

399.27

Notice that although five payments of $100 each were made, $500 total, the present value is only $399.27. As we've noted previously, the span of time over which the borrower pays the annuity and the interest rate for discounting strongly affect present value computations. When you borrow money from the bank, the bank views the amount it lends as the present value of the annuity it receives over time from the borrower. Consider the examples in Table 5.2.

A $50 deposit made every year for 20 years is discounted to $573.50 with a 6 percent discount rate. Doubling the annual cash flow to $100 also doubles the present value to $1,146.99. But extending the time period does not impact the present value as much as you might expect. Making $100 payments for twice the amount of time—40 years—does not double the present value. As you can see in Table 5.2, the present value increases less than 50 percent to only $1,504.63! If the discount rate increases from 6 percent to 10 percent on the 40-year annuity, the present value will shrink to $977.91.

EXAMPLE 5-4

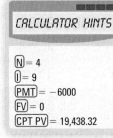

For interactive versions of this example visit www.mhhe.com/canM2e

CALCULATOR HINTS

N = 4
I = 9
PMT = −6000
FV = 0
CPT PV = 19,438.32

Value of Payments LG5-4

Your firm needs to buy additional physical therapy equipment that costs $20,000. The equipment manufacturer will give you the equipment now if you will pay $6,000 per year for the next four years. If your firm can borrow money at a 9 percent interest rate, should you pay the manufacturer the $20,000 now or accept the 4-year annuity offer of $6,000?

SOLUTION:

We can find the cost of the 4-year, $6,000 annuity in present value terms using equation 5-4:

$$PVA_4 = \$6,000 \times \left[\frac{1 - \dfrac{1}{(1+0.09)^4}}{0.09} \right] = \$6,000 \times 3.2397 = \$19,438.32$$

The cost of paying for the equipment over time is $19,438.32. This is less, in present value terms, than paying $20,000 cash. The firm should take the annuity payment plan.

Similar to Problems 5-7, 5-8

The present value of a cash flow made far into the future is not very valuable today, as Figure 5.2 illustrates. That's why doubling the number of years in the table from 20 to 40 only increased the present value by approximately 30 percent. Notice how the present value of $100 annuity payments declines for the cash flows made later in time, especially at higher discount rates. The $100 cash flow in year 20 is worth less than $15 today if we use a 10 percent discount rate; they're worth more than double, at nearly $38 today, if we use a discount rate of 5 percent. The figure also shows how quickly present value declines with a higher discount rate relative to a lower rate. As we showed above, the present values of the annuities in the figure are the sums of the present values shown. Since the present values for the 10 percent discount rate are smaller, the present value of an annuity is smaller as interest rates rise.

Present Value of Multiple Annuities

Just as we can combine annuities to solve various future value problems, we can also combine annuities to solve some present value problems with changing cash flows. Consider Alex Rodriguez's (A-Rod's) baseball contract in 2000 with the Texas Rangers. This contract made A-Rod into the "$252 million man." The contract was structured so that the Rangers paid A-Rod a $10 million signing bonus, $21 million per year in 2001 through 2004, $25 million per year in 2005 and 2006, and $27 million per year in 2007 through 2010.[1] Note that adding the signing bonus to the annual salary equals the $252 million figure. However, Rodriguez would receive the salary in the future. Using an 8 percent discount rate, what is the present value of A-Rod's contract?

[1] The contract actually contains some complications like incentives to play well and salary deferral. We ignore those complicating factors here.

The reported values for many sports contracts may be misleading in present value terms.

▼ **FIGURE 5.2** Present Value of Each Annuity Cash Flow

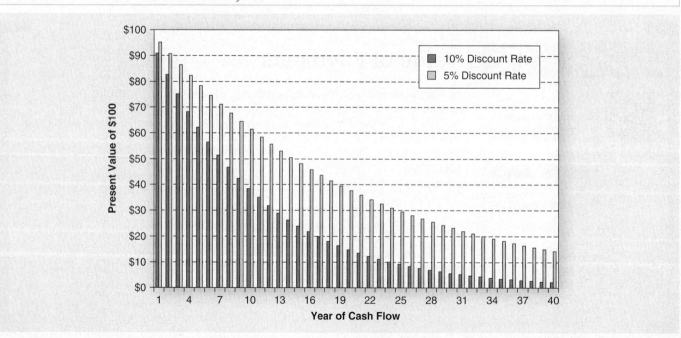

We begin by showing the salary cash flows with the time line:

Period	0	1	2	3	4	5	6	7	8	9	10 years
			8%								
Cash flow	?	21	21	21	21	25	25	27	27	27	27

First create a $27 million, 10-year annuity. Here are the associated cash flows:

Period	0	1	2	3	4	5	6	7	8	9	10 years
			8%								
Cash flow	?	27	27	27	27	27	27	27	27	27	27
			−6	−6	−6	−6	−2	−2			

Now create a −$2 million, six-year annuity:

Period	0	1	2	3	4	5	6	7	8	9	10 years
			8%								
Cash flow	?	27	27	27	27	27	27	27	27	27	27
			−2	−2	−2	−2	−2	−2			
			−4	−4	−4	−4					

Notice that creating the −$2 million annuity also resulted in the third annuity of −$4 million for four years. This time line shows three annuities. If you add the cash flows in any year, the sum is A-Rod's salary for that year. Now we can find the present value of each annuity using equation 5-4 three times.

$$PVA_{10} = \$27m \times \left[\frac{1 - \frac{1}{(1 + 0.08)^{10}}}{0.08} \right]$$

$$= \$27m \times 6.7101 = \$181.17 \text{ million}$$

$$PVA_6 = -\$2m \times \left[\frac{1 - \frac{1}{(1 + 0.08)^6}}{0.08} \right]$$

$$= -\$2m \times 4.6228 = \$-9.25 \text{ million}$$

$$PVA_4 = -\$4m \times \left[\frac{1 - \frac{1}{(1 + 0.08)^4}}{0.08} \right]$$

$$= -\$4m \times 3.3121 = -13.25 \text{ million}$$

CALCULATOR HINTS

N = 10
I = 8
PMT = −27
FV = 0
CPT PV = 181.17

NOW CHANGE TO
N = 6
PMT = 2
CPT PV = −9.25

NOW CHANGE TO
N = 4
PMT = 4
CPT PV = −13.25

Adding the value of the three annuities reveals that the present value of A-Rod's salary was $158.67 million (= $181.17m − $9.25m − $13.25m). Adding in the $10 million signing bonus produces a contract value of $168.67 million. So, the present value of A-Rod's contract turns out to be quite considerable, but you might not call him the $252 million man![2]

[2]Rodriguez opted out of the contract after the 2007 season and then re-signed with the New York Yankees with a new contract.

Perpetuity—A Special Annuity LG5-5

A perpetuity is a special type of annuity with a stream of level cash flows that are paid forever. These arrangements are called **perpetuities** because payments are perpetual. Assets that offer investors perpetual payments are preferred stocks and British 2½% Consolidated Stock, a debt referred to as **consols.**

The value of an investment like this is the present value of all future annuity payments. As the cash flow continues indefinitely, we can't use equation 5-4. Luckily, mathematicians have figured out that when the number of periods, N, in equation 5-4 goes to infinity, the equation reduces to a very simple one:

Present value of a perpetuity = Payment ÷ Interest rate

$$PV \text{ of a perpetuity} = \frac{PMT}{i} \qquad (5\text{-}5)$$

For example, the present value of an annual $100 perpetuity discounted at 10 percent is $1,000 (= $100 ÷ 0.10). Compare this to the present value of a $100 annuity of 40 years as shown in Table 5.2. The 40-year annuity's value is $977.91. You'll see that extending the payments from 40 years to an infinite number of years adds only $22.09 (= $1,000 − $977.91) of value. This demonstrates once again how little value today is placed on cash flows paid many years into the future.

time out!

5-3 How important is the magnitude of the discount rate in present value computations? Do significantly higher interest rates lead to significantly higher present values?

5-4 Reconsider the physical therapy equipment example. If interest rates are only 7 percent, should you pay the up-front fee or the annuity?

ORDINARY ANNUITIES VERSUS ANNUITIES DUE LG5-6

So far, we've assumed that every cash flow comes in at the end of every period. But in many instances, cash flows come in at the beginning of each period. An annuity in which the cash flows

annuity due An annuity in which cash flows are paid at the beginning of each time period.

occur at the beginning of each period is called an **annuity due.**

Consider the 5-year $100 annuity due. The cash flow in the beginning of year 1 looks like it's actually a cash flow today.

Period 0   1   2   8%   3   4   5 years

Cash flow   −100   −100   −100   −100   −100

Note that these five annuity-due cash flows are essentially the same as a payment today and a four-year ordinary annuity.

Future Value of an Annuity Due

So, how do we calculate the future value of the 5-year annuity due shown in the time line? The first cash flow of an ordinary 5-year annuity can compound for four years. The last cash flow does not compound at all. From the time line, you can see that the first cash flow of the annuity due essentially occurs in year zero, or today. So the first cash flow compounds for five years. The last cash flow of an annuity due compounds one year. The main difference between an annuity due and an ordinary annuity is that all the cash flows of the annuity due compound one more year than the ordinary annuity. The future value of the annuity due will simply be the future value of the ordinary annuity multiplied by $(1 + i)$:

$$\text{Future value of an annuity due} = \text{Future value of an annuity} \times \text{One year of compounding}$$

$$FVA_N \text{ due} = FVA_N \times (1 + i) \qquad (5\text{-}6)$$

Earlier in the chapter, the future value of this ordinary annuity was shown to be $586.66. Therefore, the future value of the annuity due is $633.59 (= $586.66 × 1.08).

Present Value of an Annuity Due

What is a five-year annuity due, shown above, worth today? Remember that we discount the first cash flow of an ordinary five-year annuity one year. We discount the last cash flow for the full five years. But since the first cash flow of the annuity due is already paid today, we don't discount it at all. We discount the last cash flow of an annuity due only four years. Indeed, we discount all the cash flows of the annuity due one year less than we would discount the ordinary annuity. Therefore, the present value of the annuity due is simply the present value of the ordinary annuity multiplied by $(1 + i)$:

$$PVA_N \text{ due} = PVA_N \times (1 + i) \qquad (5\text{-}7)$$

Earlier in the chapter, we discovered that the present value of this ordinary annuity was $399.27. So the present value of the annuity due is $431.21 (= $399.27 × 1.08).

Interestingly, we make the same adjustment, $(1 + i)$, to both the ordinary annuity present value and future value to compute the annuity due value.

CALCULATOR HINTS

CHANGE TO BGN
N = 5
I = 8
PMT = −100
FV = 0
CPT PV = 431.21

> ## THE MAIN DIFFERENCE BETWEEN AN ANNUITY DUE AND AN ORDINARY ANNUITY IS THAT ALL THE CASH FLOWS OF THE ANNUITY DUE COMPOUND ONE MORE YEAR THAN THE ORDINARY ANNUITY.

the Math Coach on...

Setting Financial Calculators for Annuity Due

" Financial calculators can be set for beginning-of-period payments. Once set, you compute future and present values of annuities due just as you would the ordinary annuity. To set the HP calculator, press the color button followed by the BEG/END button. To set the TI calculator for an annuity due, push the 2ND button, followed by the BGN button, followed by the 2ND button again, followed by the SET button, and followed by the 2ND button a third time, finally the QUIT button. To set the HP and TI calculators back to end-of-period cash flows, repeat these procedures. "

finance at work //: behavioral

Take Your Lottery Winnings Now or Later?

On February 18, 2006, a group of ConAgra Foods co-workers won a record Powerball jackpot of $365 million. The group had two choices for payment. They could take a much-discounted lump sum cash payment immediately, or take 30 annuity payments (one immediately and then one every year for 29 years, which is a 30-year annuity due). The annuity payment would be $12.17 million (= $365 million ÷ 30). The lump sum payment offered was $177.3 million. One way to decide between the two alternatives would be to use the time value of money concepts. They might have computed the present value of the annuity and compared it to the lump sum cash payment.

At the time, long-term interest rates were 5 percent. The present value of the annuity offered was $196.38 million. (Compute this yourself.) Notice that winning $365 million does not deliver $365 million of value! If the decision was made from this perspective, the group should take the annuity choice because it has more value than the cash alternative. However, this group selected the immediate cash option. Most winners do. Financial advisors tend to recommend that lottery winners take the lump sum because they believe that the money can earn a higher return than the 5 percent interest rate.

Good reasons arise for taking the annuity, however. To earn the higher return on the lump sum, the advisor (and the group of owners) would have to take risks. In addition, most of the lump sum would have to be invested. But most people who take a lump sum end up spending much of it in the first couple of years. Stories abound about lottery winners who declare bankruptcy a few years after receiving their money. Taking the money as an annuity helps instill financial discipline, since the winners can't waste money today that they won't receive for years.

Want to know more?

Key Words to Search for Updates: **Powerball winners (go to www.powerball.com)**

Sources: "8 Win Record U.S. Lottery Jackpot, $365 million," *The New York Times,* February 23, 2006, page A24, and **www.powerball.com**.

time out!

5-5 In what situations might you need to use annuity due analysis instead of an ordinary annuity analysis?

5-6 Reconsider your retirement plan earlier in this chapter. What would your retirement wealth grow to be if you started contributing today?

COMPOUNDING FREQUENCY

So far, all of our examples and illustrations have used annual payments and annual compounding or discounting periods. But many situations that use cash flow time-value-of-money analysis require more frequent or less frequent time periods than simple yearly entries. Bonds make semiannual interest payments; stocks pay quarterly dividends. Most consumer loans require monthly payments. Monthly payments require monthly compounding. In this section, we'll discuss the implications of compounding more than once a year.

Effect of Compounding Frequency LG5-7

Consider a $100 deposit made today with a 12 percent annual interest rate. What's the future value of this deposit in one year? Equation 4-2 from the previous chapter shows that the answer is $112. What would happen if the bank compounded the interest every six months instead of at the end of the year? Halfway through the year, the bank would compute that the deposit has grown 6 percent (half the annual 12 percent rate) to $106. At the end of the year, the bank would compute another 6 percent interest payment. However, this 6 percent is earned on $106, not the original $100 deposit. The end-of-year value is therefore $112.36 (= $106 × 1.06). By compounding twice per year instead of just once, the future value is $0.36 higher. Though

the Math Coach on...

Annuity Computations in Spreadsheets

" The TVM functions in a spreadsheet handle annuity payments similar to financial calculators. The spreadsheet Math Coach in Chapter 4 shows the functions. The functions have an annuity input.

The example illustrated earlier in this chapter asks for the FV of annual $100 deposits earning 8 percent. The spreadsheet solution is the same as the equation and calculator solutions. If you want the FV of an annuity due, just change the *type* from 0 to 1.

	A	B	C	D
1				
2	Present Value =	$0		
3	Future Value =	$586.66	=FV(B5,B6,B4,B2,0)	
4	Annuity Payment =	-$100.00		
5	Interest Rate =	8%		
6	# of Periods =	5		

"

this amount may seem negligible, you might be surprised to see how quickly the difference becomes significant.

Instead of compounding annually or semiannually, what might happen if compounding were quarterly? Since each year contains four quarters, the interest rate per quarter would be 3 percent (= 12 percent ÷ 4 quarters). The future value in one year, compounded quarterly, is $112.55 (= $100 × 1.03⁴). Again, the compounding frequency increased and so did the future value.

Table 5.3 shows the effect of various compounding frequencies. We'd like to draw your attention to two important points in the table. First, the higher the compound frequency, the higher the future value will be. Second, the relative increase in value from increasing compounding frequency seems to diminish with increasing frequencies. For example, increasing frequency from annual to semiannual increased the future value by 36 cents. However, increasing frequency from daily to hourly compounding increases the future value by only 0.1 cent.[3]

[3] It is also possible to continuously compound. The future value of a continuously compounded deposit is $FV_N = PV \times e^{(i \times N)}$, where e has a value of 2.7183.

For interactive versions of this example visit www.mhhe.com/canM2e

EXAMPLE 5-5

Car Loan Debt LG5-4

CALCULATOR HINTS

N = 48
I = 0.75
PMT = −500
FV = 0
CPT PV = 20,092.39

THEN CHANGE N TO 72
CPT PV = 27,738.42

Now you would like to buy a car. You have reviewed your budget and determined that you can afford to pay $500 per month as a car payment. How much can you borrow if interest rates are 9 percent and you pay the loan over four years? How much could you borrow if you agree to pay for six years instead?

SOLUTION:

The loan amount is the present value of the 48-month, $500 annuity. Note that the loan term will be 48 (= 4 × 12) months and the interest rate is 0.75 (= 9 ÷ 12) percent. Using equation 5-4, you discover that you can borrow up to $20,092 to buy a car:

$$PVA_{48} = \$500 \times \left[\frac{1 - \dfrac{1}{(1 + 0.0075)^{48}}}{0.0075} \right] = \$500 \times 40.1848 = \$20,092.39$$

If you are willing to borrow money for six years instead of four, the small change to the equation results in your ability to borrow $27,738. Although this would allow you to buy a more expensive car, it would also require two more years of $500 payments (an additional $12,000 of payments!).

Similar to Problems 5-25, 5-26

When we work with annuity cash flows, the compound frequency used is the same as the timing of the cash flows. When annuity cash flows are paid monthly, then interest is also compounded monthly, as seen in the following two examples.

EARs and APRs

If you borrowed $100 at a 12 percent interest rate, you would expect to pay $112 in one year. If the loan compounded monthly, then you would owe $112.68 at the end of the year, as Table 5.3 shows. So a 12 percent loan compounded monthly means that you really pay more than 12 percent. In fact, you would pay 12.68 percent. In this example, the 12 percent rate is called the **annual percentage rate (APR)**. The higher rate, 12.68 percent, is called the **effective annual rate (EAR)**—a more accurate measurement of what you will actually pay.

Lenders are legally required to show potential borrowers the APR on any loan offered. While the difference in APR and EAR is not that large in this example, it's interesting that the law requires only the less accurate (and lower) one to be shown. Since the EAR is a more accurate measure of what you will pay, it's useful to know how to convert a stated APR to an EAR. Equation 5-8 shows this conversion with a compounding frequency of m times per year:

$$EAR = \left(1 + \frac{APR}{m}\right)^m - 1 \qquad (5\text{-}8)$$

Table 5.4 shows various EAR conversions. If compounding occurs annually, you will see that the EAR and the APR will be the same. If compounding happens more than once a year, then the EAR will be higher than the APR. The table also demonstrates that the compound frequency effect grows substantially for higher interest rates or longer term loans. Compounded quarterly, the EAR is hardly different at all from a 5 percent APR: 5.09 percent versus 5 percent. The difference is larger when the APR is 12 percent. Compounded quarterly, the EAR is higher at 12.55 percent.

> **annual percentage rate (APR)** The interest rate per period times the number of periods in a year.

> **effective annual rate (EAR)** An interest rate that reflects annualizing with compounding figured in.

▼**TABLE 5.3** Future Value in One Year and Compounding Frequency of $100 at 12 percent

Frequency	Period Interest Rate	Future Value Equation	Future Value
Annual	12%	$100 × 1.12^1	$112.00
Semiannual	6	100 × 1.06^2	112.36
Quarterly	3	100 × 1.03^4	112.55
Monthly	1	100 × 1.01^{12}	112.68
Daily	0.032877	100 × 1.00032877^{365}	112.748
Hourly	0.00136986	100 × 1.0000136986^{8760}	112.749

Note: The higher the compound frequency, the higher the future value will be.

EXAMPLE 5-6

For interactive versions of this example visit www.mhhe.com/canM2e

Making Monthly Pension Contributions LG5-7

Reexamine your original plan to contribute to your company retirement plan. Instead of a total contribution of $4,500 per year for 40 years, you are able to contribute monthly. Given your expected 7 percent per year investment return, how much money can you expect in your retirement account?

CALCULATOR HINTS

N = 480
I = 7 ÷ 12
PV = 0
PMT = −375
CPT FV = 984,305.02

SOLUTION:

Now your total monthly contribution will be $375 (= $4,500 ÷ 12), which will continue for 480 months and earn a 0.58333 (= 7 ÷ 12) percent monthly return. The results of equation 5-2 show that the future value of this annuity is:

$$FVA_{40} = \$375 \times \frac{[1 + (0.07/12)]^{480} - 1}{0.07/12} = \$375 \times 2,624.8135 = \$984,305.02$$

When you made contributions annually, the future value was $898,358 (Example 5-2). By changing to monthly contributions, your retirement nest egg increased by nearly $86,000 to $984,305!

Similar to Problems 5-51, 5-52

the Math Coach on...

Common Mistakes

❝ As you figure present and future values of annuity cash flows, check that all terms are consistent: the number of payments, interest rate, and payment size all need to use common terms. If your payments are monthly, then the number of payments must reflect the number of months; the interest rate must be stated as a per-month rate, and the payment register must reflect that monthly payment. ❞

▼ **TABLE 5.4** The EAR Is Higher than the APR

APR	Compounding Periods	Equation	= EAR
Varying the Compounding Periods			
5%	1	$(1 + 0.05/1)^1 - 1$	5.00%
5	4	$(1 + 0.05/4)^4 - 1$	5.09
5	12	$(1 + 0.05/12)^{12} - 1$	5.12
Vary APR and Compounding Periods			
9	4	$(1 + 0.09/4)^4 - 1$	9.31
9	12	$(1 + 0.09/12)^{12} - 1$	9.38
12	4	$(1 + 0.12/4)^4 - 1$	12.55
12	12	$(1 + 0.12/12)^{12} - 1$	12.68

Note: This compound frequency effect grows substantially for higher interest rates or longer term loans.

time **out!**

5-7 Why is EAR a more accurate measure of the rate actually paid than APR?

5-8 What would have a smaller present value: a future sum discounted annually or one discounted monthly?

EXAMPLE 5-7

For interactive versions of this example visit www.mhhe.com/canM2e

Evaluating Credit Card Offers LG5-7

As a college student, you probably receive many credit card offers in the mail. Consider these two offers. The first card charges a 16 percent APR. An examination of the footnotes reveals that this card compounds monthly. The second credit card charges 15.5 percent APR and compounds weekly. Which card has a lower effective annual rate?

SOLUTION:

Compute the EAR of each card to compare them in common (and realistic) terms. The first card has an EAR of:

$$EAR = \left(1 + \frac{0.16}{12}\right)^{12} - 1 = 0.1732, \text{ or } 17.23\%$$

The EAR of the second card is:

$$EAR = \left(1 + \frac{0.155}{52}\right)^{52} - 1 = 0.1674, \text{ or } 16.74\%$$

You should pick the second credit card because it has a lower effective annual rate. But note also that you will always be better off if you pay your credit card balance whenever the bill comes due.

Similar to Problems 5-15, 5-16

ANNUITY LOANS

In this chapter, we've focused on computing the future and present value of annuities. But in many situations, these values are already known and what we really need to compare are the payments or implied interest rate—usually, the highest interest rate offered.

What Is the Interest Rate? LG5-8

Many business and personal applications already state the cost of an investment, as well as the annuity cash flows and time period. We need, then, to solve for the implied interest rate of this investment. Unfortunately, we have no general, easy equation to solve for the interest rate. Even financial calculators use an iterating process, which causes them to "think" a little longer before displaying the estimated interest rate result.

Consider the plight of a manager of a small doctor's office who has the opportunity to buy a piece of imaging equipment for $100,000. The equipment will allow the office to generate $25,000 in profits for six years, at which time the equipment will be worn out and without value in the U.S.[4] What rate of

[4]Some charities are now gathering "obsolete" U.S. medical equipment and sending the materials to less developed countries—a situation in which everybody wins.

the Math Coach on...
More Common Mistakes

" As we noted in Chapter 4, when computing the interest rate, make sure that the present value and the annuity payments are of different signs (positive versus negative). Otherwise, the calculator will show an error. "

return does this purchase offer the doctor's office? The time line for this problem appears as:

Period	0	1	2	3	4	5	6 years
Cash flow	−100,000	25,000	25,000	25,000	25,000	25,000	25,000

For the financial calculator solution, input N = 6, PV = −100,000, PMT = 25000, and FV = 0. The interest rate result is then 12.98 percent. So, if this is a high enough return relative to other uses of the $100,000, the doctor's office should seriously consider purchasing the imaging machine.

Finding Payments on an Amortized Loan LG5-9

Many consumers and small business owners already know how much money they want to borrow and the level of current interest rates. Usually, they need to translate this information into the actual payments to determine if they can really afford the purchase. A loan structured for annuity payments that completely pay off the debt is called an **amortized loan**. To compute the annuity cash flow of an amortized loan, rearrange the

---

Computing Interest Rate Needed LG5-8

After saving diligently your entire career, you and your spouse are finally ready to retire with a nest egg of $800,000. You need to invest this money in a mix of stocks and bonds that will allow you to withdraw $6,000 per month for 30 years. What interest rate do you need to earn?

SOLUTION:

Use a financial calculator and input N = 360, PV = −800,000, PMT = 6000, and FV = 0. The interest rate result is 0.6860 percent. But remember, since the periods and payments are in months, the interest rate is too. It is customary to report this as an APR: 8.23 percent (= 0.6860 percent × 12). However, the EAR more accurately reflects the true interest rate, 8.55 percent (= $1.00686^{12} - 1$). In order for your money to last for 30 years while funding a $6,000 per month income, you must earn at least an 8.23 APR per year return.

If you have uneven cash flows, use the calculator CF worksheet and then solve with the IRR function.

Similar to Problems 5-33, 5-34, 5-35, 5-36

present value of an annuity formula, equation 5-4, to solve for the payment:

Payment = Present value × Amortization

$$PMT_N = PV \times \left[\dfrac{i}{1 - \dfrac{1}{(1+i)^N}} \right] \qquad (5\text{-}9)$$

Most car loans require monthly payments for three to five years. Assume that you need a $10,000 loan to buy a car. The loan is for four years and interest rates are 9 percent per year APR. To implement equation 5-9, use an interest rate of 0.75 percent (= 9 percent / 12) and 48 periods (= 4 × 12) as:

$$PMT_{48} = \$10{,}000 \times \left[\dfrac{0.0075}{1 - \dfrac{1}{(1 + 0.0075)^{48}}} \right]$$

$$= \$10{,}000 \times 0.024885 = \$248.85$$

CALCULATOR HINTS

N = 48
I = 0.75
PV = 10000
FV = 0
CPT PMT = −248.85

So, when interest rates are 9 percent, it takes monthly payments of $248.85 to pay off a $10,000 loan in four years.

Interest rate levels and loan length strongly affect how large your payments will be. Table 5.5 shows the monthly payments needed to pay off a mortgage debt at various interest rates and lengths of time. (Try computing the payments yourself!) Note that as the interest rate declines, the monthly payment also declines. This is why people rush to refinance their mortgages after interest rates fall. A decline of 1 or 2 percent can save a homeowner hundreds of dollars every month. You will also see from the table that paying off a mortgage in only 15 years requires larger payments, but generally saves thousands in interest.

Amortized Loan Schedules When you pay a car loan or home mortgage, you will often find it useful to know how much of the debt, or **loan principal,** you still owe. For

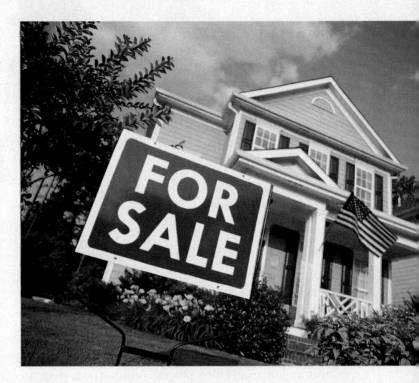

example, consider a case wherein you bought a car two years ago using a 4-year loan. In order to sell the car now, the loan balance will have to be paid off. Being able to compute this principal balance may influence your chances of selling the car.

An interest-only loan allows the borrower to make payments that consist totally of interest payments, so none of the debt is reduced. A $10,000 interest-only loan with a 9 percent APR paid monthly will cost $75 per month (= $10,000 × 0.09 ÷ 12). Amortizing this loan over four years requires monthly payments of $248.85 (see earlier car loan problem). The difference in the first month's payment on the two loans is $173.85 (= $248.85 − $75) and represents the amount of the regular amortized loan's payment that goes to reducing the principal balance. So after the first month's payment, the amortized loan's balance has fallen to $9,826.15, while the interest-only loan still has a balance of $10,000.

In the second month, the interest incurred on the regular amortized loan is $73.70 (= $9,826.15 × 0.09 ÷ 12), so the $248.85 second-month payment represents principal payment of $175.15. These numbers are shown in the **amortization schedule** of Table 5.6. The table will show you that the early payments on a car loan go mostly to paying the interest rather than reducing the principal. That interest component declines over time, and then the principal balance declines.

The amortization schedule shows that if you wish to sell the car after two years, you will have to pay the loan company a car loan (principal) debt of $5,447.13. Of course, if you had an interest-only loan, you would still owe the full principal of $10,000 after two years. Amortization schedules are also useful for determining other things, like the total amount of interest that you will

▼ **TABLE 5.5** Monthly Payments on a $225,000 Loan

Annual Percentage Rate (APR)	Years to Repay Loan	Monthly Payment
30-Year Mortgages		
10%	30	$1,974.54
8	30	1,650.97
7	30	1,496.93
6	30	1,348.99
15-Year Mortgages		
8	15	2,150.22
7	15	2,022.36
6	15	1,898.68

pay over the life of the loan. In this case, if you take a regular loan in which you pay both principal and interest, you pay $10,000 in principal and nearly $1,945 in interest during the four years of the loan. The interest component is an even larger component of longer-term loans, like 30-year mortgages. Depending on the interest rate charged, the first payment in a mortgage consists of 75 percent to 95 percent interest. The home mortgage principal balance falls very slowly in the first years of the loan.

We construct amortization schedules by showing the loan's principal balance at the beginning of the month. This is the same as the balance at the end of the previous month (except

for the very first payment). Then we compute the interest owed on that balance for the month. After paying that interest, what's left of the monthly payment reduces the loan balance for the next month. Because of these repetitive computations, spreadsheets make amortization schedules easy to construct.

Compute the Time Period LG5-10 You might well also find it useful to know how long it will take to pay off a loan

["Depending on the interest rate charged, the first payment in a mortgage consists of 75 percent to 95 percent interest."]

▼ **TABLE 5.6** Amortization Schedule over Four Years (9 percent APR)

Month	Beginning Balance	Total Payment	Interest Paid	Principal Paid	Ending Balance	Month	Beginning Balance	Total Payment	Interest Paid	Principal Paid	Ending Balance
1	$10,000.00	$248.85	$75.00	$173.85	$9,826.15	25	$5,447.13	$248.85	$40.85	$208.00	$5,239.14
2	9,826.15	248.85	73.70	175.15	9,651.00	26	5,239.14	248.85	39.29	209.56	5,029.58
3	9,651.00	248.85	72.38	176.47	9,474.53	27	5,029.58	248.85	37.72	211.13	4,818.45
4	9,474.53	248.85	71.06	177.79	9,296.74	28	4,818.45	248.85	36.14	212.71	4,605.74
5	9,296.74	248.85	69.73	179.12	9,117.61	29	4,605.74	248.85	34.54	214.31	4,391.43
6	9,117.61	248.85	68.38	180.47	8,937.15	30	4,391.43	248.85	32.94	215.91	4,175.52
7	8,937.15	248.85	67.03	181.82	8,755.32	31	4,175.52	248.85	31.32	217.53	3,957.99
8	8,755.32	248.85	65.66	183.19	8,572.14	32	3,957.99	248.85	29.68	219.17	3,738.82
9	8,572.14	248.85	64.29	184.56	8,387.58	33	3,738.82	248.85	28.04	220.81	3,518.01
10	8,387.58	248.85	62.91	185.94	8,201.64	34	3,518.01	248.85	26.39	222.46	3,295.55
11	8,201.64	248.85	61.51	187.34	8,014.30	35	3,295.55	248.85	24.72	224.13	3,071.41
12	8,014.30	248.85	60.11	188.74	7,825.56	36	3,071.41	248.85	23.04	225.81	2,845.60
13	7,825.56	248.85	58.69	190.16	7,635.40	37	2,845.60	248.85	21.34	227.51	2,618.09
14	7,635.40	248.85	57.27	191.58	7,443.81	38	2,618.09	248.85	19.64	229.21	2,388.88
15	7,443.81	248.85	55.83	193.02	7,250.79	39	2,388.88	248.85	17.92	230.93	2,157.94
16	7,250.79	248.85	54.38	194.47	7,056.32	40	2,157.94	248.85	16.18	232.67	1,925.28
17	7,056.32	248.85	52.92	195.93	6,860.40	41	1,925.28	248.85	14.44	234.41	1,690.87
18	6,860.40	248.85	51.45	197.40	6,663.00	42	1,690.87	248.85	12.68	236.17	1,454.70
19	6,663.00	248.85	49.97	198.88	6,464.12	43	1,454.70	248.85	10.91	237.94	1,216.76
20	6,464.12	248.85	48.48	200.37	6,263.75	44	1,216.76	248.85	9.13	239.72	977.04
21	6,263.75	248.85	46.98	201.87	6,061.88	45	977.04	248.85	7.33	241.52	735.51
22	6,061.88	248.85	45.46	203.39	5,858.49	46	735.51	248.85	5.52	243.33	492.18
23	5,858.49	248.85	43.94	204.91	5,653.58	47	492.18	248.85	3.69	245.16	247.02
24	5,653.58	248.85	42.40	206.45	5,447.13	48	247.02	248.87	1.85	247.02	0.00

EXAMPLE 5-9

Monthly Mortgage Payments LG5-9

For interactive versions
of this example visit
www.mhhe.com/canM2e

Say that you have your heart set on purchasing a beautiful, old Tudor-style house for $250,000. A mortgage broker says that you can qualify for a mortgage for 80 percent (or $200,000) of the price. If you get a 15-year mortgage, the interest rate will be 6.1 percent APR. A 30-year mortgage costs 6.4 percent. One of the factors that will help you decide which mortgage to take is the magnitude of the monthly payments. What will they be?[5]

SOLUTION:

To pay off the mortgage in only 15 years, the payments would have to be larger than for the 30-year mortgage. The higher payment will be eased somewhat because the interest rate is lower on the 15-year mortgage. The payment for the 15-year mortgage is:

$$PMT_{180} = \$200,000 \times \left[\frac{0.0050833}{1 - \dfrac{1}{(1 + 0.0050833)^{180}}} \right] = \$200,000 \times 0.0084927 = \$1,698.54$$

The payment for the 30-year mortgage would be:

$$PMT_{360} = \$200,000 \times \left[\frac{0.0053333}{1 - \dfrac{1}{(1 + 0.0053333)^{360}}} \right] = \$200,000 \times 0.00625506 = \$1,251.01$$

So, the payments on the 15-year mortgage are nearly $450 more each month than the 30-year mortgage payments. You must decide whether the cost of paying the extra $450 each month is worth it to own the house with no debt 15 years sooner. The decision would depend on your financial budget and the strength of your desire to be debt free.

Similar to Problems 5-39, 5-40

[5]Most homeowners are actually most interested in their total payment, which will include hazard insurance for the home and property taxes. Such payments are referred to as PITI—principal, interest, taxes, and insurance. For simplicity, we use only PI payments here—principal and interest only.

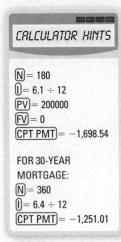

CALCULATOR HINTS

N = 180
I = 6.1 ÷ 12
PV = 200000
FV = 0
CPT PMT = −1,698.54

FOR 30-YEAR
MORTGAGE:
N = 360
I = 6.4 ÷ 12
CPT PMT = −1,251.01

---

with specific annuity payments. To find the number of periods, you can solve equation 5-9 for *N*—the number of payments—but the equation becomes quite complicated.[6] Many people just use a financial calculator or spreadsheet. We can check to see if the $248.85 monthly payment would indeed pay off the $10,000, 9 percent car loan in four years. Finding the solution with a financial calculator entails entering I = 0.75, PV = 10000, PMT = −248.85, and FV = 0. The answer is 48 months.

Add-On Interest One method of calculating payments of a loan that is popular in payday lending is called **add-on interest.** This method computes the amount of the interest payable at the beginning of the loan, which is then added to the principal of the loan. This total is then divided into the number of payments to be made. Consider a loan of $1,000 to be paid with 9 percent add-on interest and repaid in six monthly payments.

[6]The equation for solving for the number of periods in an annuity is:

$$N = \frac{\ln\left(\dfrac{PMT}{(PMT - PVA_N \times i)}\right)}{\ln(1 + i)}$$

time out!

5-9 How might credit card companies keep their cardholders in debt for a long time? What payment do the credit card companies expect your friend to make so that he never pays down the debt?

5-10 Can you find the interest rate if you know the annuity payments and a future value? Under what circumstances might you want to solve this kind of problem? Which equation would you use?

The total interest for this loan is computed as 9 percent of $1,000 for 6 months, or $45 (= 0.09 × $1,000 × ½). This is added to the principal for a total of $1,045. Each of the six monthly payments is then $1,045 ÷ 6 = $174.17. Be alert that the add-on interest method seriously understates the real interest rate that is being paid! If you borrow $1,000 and repay a $174.17 monthly annuity for six months, the monthly interest rate is 1.27 percent. This is a 15.27 percent APR (= 1.27% × 12) and a 16.39 percent EAR (= $1.0127^{12} - 1$)—both much higher than the advertised 9 percent interest rate of this loan.

CALCULATOR HINTS

N = 6
PV = 1,000
PMT = −174.17
FV = 0
CPT I = 1.27

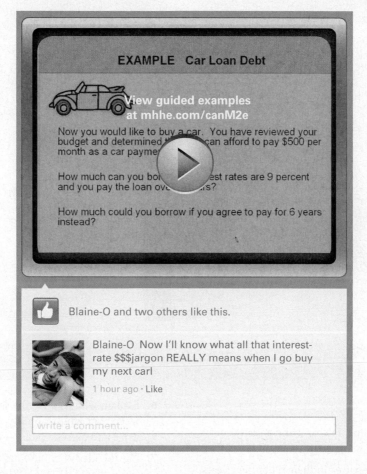

EXAMPLE   Car Loan Debt

View guided examples at mhhe.com/canM2e

Now you would like to buy a car. You have reviewed your budget and determined that you can afford to pay $500 per month as a car payment.

How much can you borrow if interest rates are 9 percent and you pay the loan over 5 years?

How much could you borrow if you agree to pay for 6 years instead?

👍 Blaine-O and two others like this.

Blaine-O Now I'll know what all that interest-rate $$$jargon REALLY means when I go buy my next car!
1 hour ago · Like

write a comment...

EXAMPLE 5-10

For interactive versions of this example visit www.mhhe.com/canM2e

Time to Pay Off a Credit Card Balance LG5-10

Through poor financial management, your friend has racked up $5,000 in debt on his credit card. The card charges a 19 percent APR and compounds monthly. His latest bill shows that he must pay a minimum of $150 this month. At this rate, how long will it take your friend to pay off his credit card debt?

SOLUTION:

Using the financial calculator, input I = 1.58333 (= 19/12), PV = 5000, PMT = 2150, FV = 0. The answer is 48 months, or 4 years. If the friend pays the minimum payment, then it will be a long time before he will be out of debt. The credit card company is very content to continue to earn the high return for many years—essentially, the interest on the loan and a very small portion of the principal. Your friend should pay more than the minimum charge to reduce his debt quicker.

Similar to Problems 5-41, 5-42

Get Online

mhhe.com/canM2e

for study materials including self-test
problems with solutions, quizzes, research
projects, minicases, and videos

Your Turn...

Questions

1. How can you add a cash flow in year 2 and a cash flow in year 4 in year 7? *(LG5-1)*

2. People can become millionaires in their retirement years quite easily if they start saving early in employer 401(k) or 403(b) programs (or even if their employers don't offer such programs). Demonstrate the growth of a $250 monthly contribution for 40 years earning 9 percent APR. *(LG5-2)*

3. When you discount multiple cash flows, how does the future period that a cash flow is paid affect its present value and its contribution to the value of all the cash flows? *(LG5-3)*

4. How can you use the present value of an annuity concept to determine the price of a house you can afford? *(LG5-4)*

5. Since perpetuity payments continue forever, how can a present value be computed? Why isn't the present value infinite? *(LG5-5)*

6. Explain why you use the same adjustment factor, $(1 + i)$, when you adjust annuity due payments for both future value and present value. *(LG5-6)*

7. Use the idea of compound interest to explain why EAR is larger than APR. *(LG5-7)*

8. Would you rather pay $10,000 for a 5-year, $2,500 annuity or a 10-year, $1,250 annuity? Why? *(LG5-8)*

9. The interest on your home mortgage is tax deductible. Why are the early years of the mortgage more helpful in reducing taxes than in the later years? *(LG5-9)*

10. How can you use the concepts illustrated in computing the number of payments in an annuity to figure how to pay off a credit card balance? How does the magnitude of the payment impact the number of months? *(LG5-10)*

Problems

5-1 **Future Value** Compute the future value in year 8 of a $2,000 deposit in year 1 and another $1,500 deposit at the end of year 3 using a 10 percent interest rate. *(LG5-1)*

5-2 **Future Value** Compute the future value in year 7 of a $2,000 deposit in year 1 and another $2,500 deposit at the end of year 4 using an 8 percent interest rate. *(LG5-1)*

5-3 **Future Value of an Annuity** What is the future value of a $900 annuity payment over five years if interest rates are 9 percent? *(LG5-2)*

5-4 **Future Value of an Annuity** What is the future value of a $700 annuity payment over six years if interest rates are 10 percent? *(LG5-2)*

5-5 **Present Value** Compute the present value of a $2,000 deposit in year 1 and another $1,500 deposit at the end of year 3 if interest rates are 10 percent. *(LG5-3)*

5-6 **Present Value** Compute the present value of a $2,000 deposit in year 1 and another $2,500 deposit at the end of year 4 using an 8 percent interest rate. *(LG5-3)*

5-7 **Present Value of an Annuity** What's the present value of a $900 annuity payment over five years if interest rates are 9 percent? *(LG5-4)*

5-8 **Present Value of an Annuity** What's the present value of a $700 annuity payment over six years if interest rates are 10 percent? *(LG5-4)*

5-9 **Present Value of a Perpetuity** What's the present value, when interest rates are 7.5 percent, of a $50 payment made every year forever? *(LG5-5)*

5-10 **Present Value of a Perpetuity** What's the present value, when interest rates are 8.5 percent, of a $75 payment made every year forever? *(LG5-5)*

5-11 **Present Value of an Annuity Due** If the present value of an ordinary, 7-year annuity is $6,500 and interest rates are 8.5 percent, what's the present value of the same annuity due? *(LG5-6)*

5-12 **Present Value of an Annuity Due** If the present value of an ordinary, 6-year annuity is $8,500 and interest rates are 9.5 percent, what's the present value of the same annuity due? *(LG5-6)*

5-13 **Future Value of an Annuity Due** If the future value of an ordinary, 7-year annuity is $6,500 and interest rates are 8.5 percent, what is the future value of the same annuity due? *(LG5-6)*

5-14 **Future Value of an Annuity Due** If the future value of an ordinary, 6-year annuity is $8,500 and interest rates are 9.5 percent, what's the future value of the same annuity due? *(LG5-6)*

5-15 **Effective Annual Rate** A loan is offered with monthly payments and a 10 percent APR. What's the loan's effective annual rate (EAR)? *(LG5-7)*

5-16 **Effective Annual Rate** A loan is offered with monthly payments and a 13 percent APR. What's the loan's effective annual rate (EAR)? *(LG5-7)*

5-17 **Future Value** Given a 4 percent interest rate, compute the year 6 future value of deposits made in years 1, 2, 3, and 4 of $1,000, $1,200, $1,200, and $1,500. *(LG5-1)*

5-18 **Future Value** Given a 5 percent interest rate, compute the year 6 future value of deposits made in years 1, 2, 3, and 4 of $1,000, $1,300, $1,300, and $1,400. *(LG5-1)*

5-19 **Future Value of Multiple Annuities** Assume that you contribute $200 per month to a retirement plan for 20 years. Then you are able to increase the contribution to $400 per month for another 30 years. Given a 7 percent interest rate, what is the value of your retirement plan after the 50 years? *(LG5-2)*

5-20 **Future Value of Multiple Annuities** Assume that you contribute $150 per month to a retirement plan for 15 years. Then you are able to increase the contribution to $350 per month for the next 25 years. Given an 8 percent interest rate, what is the value of your retirement plan after the 40 years? *(LG5-2)*

5-21 **Present Value** Given a 6 percent interest rate, compute the present value of payments made in years 1, 2, 3, and 4 of $1,000, $1,200, $1,200, and $1,500. *(LG5-3)*

5-22 **Present Value** Given a 7 percent interest rate, compute the present value of payments made in years 1, 2, 3, and 4 of $1,000, $1,300, $1,300, and $1,400. *(LG5-3)*

5-23 **Present Value of Multiple Annuities** A small business owner visits her bank to ask for a loan. The owner states that she can repay a loan at $1,000 per month for the next three years and then $2,000 per month for two years after that. If the bank is charging customers 7.5 percent APR, how much would it be willing to lend the business owner? *(LG5-4)*

5-24 **Present Value of Multiple Annuities** A small business owner visits his bank to ask for a loan. The owner states that he can repay a loan at $1,500 per month for the next three years and then $500 per month for two years after that. If the bank is charging customers 8.5 percent APR, how much would it be willing to lend the business owner? *(LG5-4)*

5-25 **Present Value** You are looking to buy a car. You can afford $450 in monthly payments for four years. In addition to the loan, you can make a $1,000 down payment. If interest rates are 7 percent APR, what price of car can you afford? *(LG5-4)*

5-26 **Present Value** You are looking to buy a car. You can afford $650 in monthly payments for five years. In addition to the loan, you can make a $750 down payment. If interest rates are 8 percent APR, what price of car can you afford? *(LG5-4)*

5-27 **Present Value of a Perpetuity** A perpetuity pays $100 per year and interest rates are 7.5 percent. How much would its value change if interest rates increased to 9 percent? Did the value increase or decrease? *(LG5-5)*

5-28 **Present Value of a Perpetuity** A perpetuity pays $50 per year and interest rates are 9 percent. How much would its value change if interest rates decreased to 7.5 percent? Did the value increase or decrease? *(LG5-5)*

5-29 **Future and Present Value of an Annuity Due** If you start making $50 monthly contributions today and continue them for five years, what's their future value if the compounding rate is 10 percent APR? What is the present value of this annuity? *(LG5-6)*

5-30 **Future and Present Value of an Annuity Due** If you start making $75 monthly contributions today and continue them for four years, what is their future value if the compounding rate is 12 percent APR? What is the present value of this annuity? *(LG5-6)*

5-31 **Compound Frequency** Payday loans are very short-term loans that charge very high interest rates. You can borrow $225 today and repay $300 in two weeks. What is the compounded *annual* rate implied by this 33.33 percent rate charged for only two weeks? *(LG5-7)*

5-32 **Compound Frequency** Payday loans are very short-term loans that charge very high interest rates. You can borrow $500 today and repay $590 in two weeks. What is the compounded *annual* rate implied by this 18 percent rate charged for only two weeks? *(LG5-7)*

5-33 **Annuity Interest Rate** What's the interest rate of a 5-year, annual $5,000 annuity with present value of $20,000? *(LG5-8)*

5-34 **Annuity Interest Rate** What's the interest rate of a 7-year, annual $4,000 annuity with present value of $20,000? *(LG5-8)*

5-35 **Annuity Interest Rate** What annual interest rate would you need to earn if you wanted a $1,000 per month contribution to grow to $75,000 in six years? *(LG5-8)*

5-36 **Annuity Interest Rate** What annual interest rate would you need to earn if you wanted a $600 per month contribution to grow to $45,000 in six years? *(LG5-8)*

5-37 **Add-On Interest Payments** To borrow $500, you are offered an add-on interest loan at 8 percent. Two loan payments are to be made, one at six months and the other at the end of the year. Compute the two equal payments. *(LG5-8)*

5-38 **Add-On Interest Payments** To borrow $800, you are offered an add-on interest loan at 7 percent. Three loan payments are to be made, one at four months, another at eight months, and the last one at the end of the year. Compute the three equal payments. *(LG5-8)*

5-39 **Loan Payments** You wish to buy a $25,000 car. The dealer offers you a 4-year loan with a 10 percent APR. What are the monthly payments? How would the payment differ if you paid interest only? What would the consequences of such a decision be? *(LG5-9)*

5-40 **Loan Payments** You wish to buy a $10,000 dining room set. The furniture store offers you a 3-year loan with an 11 percent APR. What are the monthly payments? How would the payment differ if you paid interest only? What would the consequences of such a decision be? *(LG5-9)*

5-41 **Number of Annuity Payments** Joey realizes that he has charged too much on his credit card and has racked up $5,000 in debt. If he can pay $150 each month and the card charges 17 percent APR (compounded monthly), how long will it take him to pay off the debt? *(LG5-10)*

5-42 **Number of Annuity Payments** Phoebe realizes that she has charged too much on her credit card and has racked up $6,000 in debt. If she can pay $200 each month and the card charges 18 percent APR (compounded monthly), how long will it take her to pay off the debt? *(LG5-10)*

ADVANCED PROBLEMS

5-43 **Future Value** Given an 8 percent interest rate, compute the year 7 future value if deposits of $1,000 and $2,000 are made in years 1 and 3, respectively, and a withdrawal of $700 is made in year 4. *(LG5-1)*

5-44 **Future Value** Given a 9 percent interest rate, compute the year 6 future value if deposits of $1,500 and $2,500 are made in years 2 and 3, respectively, and a withdrawal of $600 is made in year 5. *(LG5-1)*

5-45 **EAR of Add-On Interest Loan** To borrow $2,000, you are offered an add-on interest loan at 10 percent with 12 monthly payments. First compute the 12 equal payments and then compute the EAR of the loan. *(LG5-7, LG5-8)*

5-46 **EAR of Add-On Interest Loan** To borrow $700, you are offered an add-on interest loan at 9 percent with 12 monthly payments. First compute the 12 equal payments and then compute the EAR of the loan. *(LG5-7, LG5-8)*

5-47 **Low Financing or Cash Back?** A car company is offering a choice of deals. You can receive $500 cash back on the purchase or a 3 percent APR, 4-year loan. The price of the car is $15,000 and you could obtain a 4-year loan from your credit union, at 7 percent APR. Which deal is cheaper? *(LG5-4, LG5-9)*

5-48 **Low Financing or Cash Back?** A car company is offering a choice of deals. You can receive $1,000 cash back on the purchase, or a 2 percent APR, 5-year loan. The price of the car is $20,000 and you could obtain a 5-year loan from your credit union, at 7 percent APR. Which deal is cheaper? *(LG5-4, LG5-9)*

5-49 **Amortization Schedule** Create the amortization schedule for a loan of $15,000, paid monthly over three years using a 9 percent APR. *(LG5-9)*

5-50 **Amortization Schedule** Create the amortization schedule for a loan of $5,000, paid monthly over two years using an 8 percent APR. *(LG5-9)*

5-51 **Investing for Retirement** Monica has decided that she wants to build enough retirement wealth that, if invested at 8 percent per year, will provide her with $3,500 of monthly income for 25 years. To date, she has saved nothing, but she still has 30 years until she retires. How much money does she need to contribute per month to reach her goal? *(LG5-4, LG5-9)*

5-52 **Investing for Retirement** Ross has decided that he wants to build enough retirement wealth that, if invested at 7 percent per year, will provide him with $3,000 of monthly income for 30 years. To date, he has saved nothing, but he still has 20 years until he retires. How much money does he need to contribute per month to reach his goal? *(LG5-4, LG5-9)*

5-53 **Loan Balance** Rachel purchased a $15,000 car three years ago using an 8 percent, 4-year loan. She has decided that she would sell the car now, if she could get a price that would pay off the balance of her loan. What is the minimum price Rachel would need to receive for her car? *(LG5-9)*

5-54 **Loan Balance** Hank purchased a $20,000 car two years ago using a 9 percent, 5-year loan. He has decided that he would sell the car now, if he could get a price that would pay off the balance of his loan. What's the minimum price Hank would need to receive for his car? *(LG5-9)*

5-55 **Teaser Rate Mortgage** A mortgage broker is offering a $183,900 30-year mortgage with a teaser rate. In the first two years of the mortgage, the borrower makes monthly payments on only a 4 percent APR interest rate. After the second year, the mortgage interest rate charged increases to 7 percent APR. What are the monthly payments in the first two years? What are the monthly payments after the second year? *(LG5-9)*

5-56 **Teaser Rate Mortgage** A mortgage broker is offering a $279,000 30-year mortgage with a teaser rate. In the first two years of the mortgage, the borrower makes monthly payments on only a 4.5 percent APR interest rate. After the second year, the mortgage interest rate charged increases to 7.5 percent APR. What are the monthly payments in the first two years? What are the monthly payments after the second year? *(LG5-9)*

  5-57 **Spreadsheet Problem** Consider a person who begins contributing to a retirement plan at age 25 and contributes for 40 years until retirement at age 65. For the first ten years, she contributes $3,000 per year. She increases the contribution rate to $5,000 per year in years 11 through 20. This is followed by increases to $10,000 per year in years 21 through 30 and to $15,000 per year for the last ten years. This money earns a 9 percent return. First compute the value of the retirement plan when she turns age 65. Then compute the annual payment she would receive over the next 40 years if the wealth was converted to an annuity payment at 8 percent. *(LG5-2, LG5-9)*

Combined Chapter 4 and Chapter 5 Problems

4&5-1 **Future Value** Consider that you are 35 years old and have just changed to a new job. You have $80,000 in the retirement plan from your former employer. You can roll that money into the retirement plan of the new employer. You will also contribute $3,600 each year into your new employer's plan. If the rolled-over money and the new contributions both earn a 7 percent return, how much should you expect to have when you retire in 30 years?

4&5-2 **Future Value** Consider that you are 45 years old and have just changed to a new job. You have $150,000 in the retirement plan from your former employer. You can roll that money into the retirement plan of the new employer. You will also contribute $7,200 each year into your new employer's plan. If the rolled-over money and the new contributions both earn an 8 percent return, how much should you expect to have when you retire in 20 years?

4&5-3 **Future Value and Number of Annuity Payments** Your client has been given a trust fund valued at $1 million. He cannot access the money until he turns 65 years old, which is in 25 years. At that time, he can withdraw $25,000 per month. If the trust fund is invested at a 5.5 percent rate, how many months will it last your client once he starts to withdraw the money?

4&5-4 **Future Value and Number of Annuity Payments** Your client has been given a trust fund valued at $1.5 million. She cannot access the money until she turns 65 years old, which is in 15 years. At that time, she can withdraw $20,000 per month. If the trust fund is invested at a 5 percent rate, how many months will it last your client once she starts to withdraw the money?

4&5-5 **Present Value and Annuity Payments** A local furniture store is advertising a deal in which you buy a $3,000 dining room set and do not need to pay for two years (no interest cost is incurred). How much money would you have to deposit now in a savings account earning 5 percent APR, compounded monthly, to pay the $3,000 bill in two years? Alternatively, how much would you have to deposit in the savings account each month to be able to pay the bill?

4&5-6 **Present Value and Annuity Payments** A local furniture store is advertising a deal in which you buy a $5,000 living room set with three years before you need to make any payments (no interest cost is incurred). How much money would you have to deposit now in a savings account earning 4 percent APR, compounded monthly, to pay the $5,000 bill in three years? Alternatively, how much would you have to deposit in the savings account each month to be able to pay the bill?

4&5-7 **House Appreciation and Mortgage Payments** Say that you purchase a house for $200,000 by getting a mortgage for $180,000 and paying a $20,000 down payment. If you get a 30-year mortgage with a 7 percent interest rate, what are the monthly payments? What would the loan balance be in ten years? If the house appreciates at 3 percent per year, what will be the value of the house in ten years? How much of this value is your equity?

4&5-8 **House Appreciation and Mortgage Payments** Say that you purchase a house for $150,000 by getting a mortgage for $135,000 and paying a $15,000 down payment. If you get a 15-year mortgage with a 7 percent interest rate, what are the monthly payments? What would the loan balance be in five years? If the house appreciates at 4 percent per year, what will be the value of the house in five years? How much of this value is your equity?

4&5-9 **Construction Loan** You have secured a loan from your bank for two years to build your home. The terms of the loan are that you will borrow $200,000 now and an additional $100,000 in one year. Interest of 10 percent APR will be charged on the balance monthly. Since no payments will be made during the 2-year loan, the balance will grow at the 10 percent compounded rate. At the end of the two years, the balance will be converted to a traditional 30-year mortgage at a 6 percent interest rate. What will you be paying as monthly mortgage payments (principal and interest only)?

4&5-10 **Construction Loan** You have secured a loan from your bank for two years to build your home. The terms of the loan are that you will borrow $100,000 now and an additional $50,000 in one year. Interest of 9 percent APR will be charged on the balance monthly. Since no payments will be made during the 2-year loan, the balance will grow. At the end of the two years, the balance will be converted to a traditional 15-year mortgage at a 7 percent interest rate. What will you pay as monthly mortgage payments (principal and interest only)?

chapter SIX

How do funds flow through-out the economy? How do financial markets operate and relate to one another? As an individual investor or a financial manager you need to know. Your future decision-making skills depend on it. Investors' funds flow through financial markets such as the New York Stock Exchange and mortgage markets. Financial institutions—commercial banks (e.g., Bank of America), investment banks (e.g., Morgan Stanley), and mutual funds (e.g., Fidelity)—act as intermediaries to channel funds from individual savers or investors through financial markets. This chapter looks at the nature and opera-tions of financial markets and discusses the financial institutions (FIs) that par-ticipate in those markets. Bonds, stocks, and other securities that trade in the markets are covered in Chapters 7 and 8.

In this chapter we also examine how significant changes in the way financial institutions deliver services played a major role in forming the

continued on p. 126

understanding financial
markets + institutions*

LEARNING GOALS

LG6-1 Differentiate between primary and secondary markets and between money and capital markets.

LG6-2 List the types of securities traded in money and capital markets.

LG6-3 Identify different types of finan-cial institutions and the services that each provides.

LG6-4 Analyze specific factors that influence interest rates.

LG6-5 Offer different theories that explain the shape of the term structure of interest rates.

LG6-6 Demonstrate how forward interest rates derive from the term struc-ture of interest rates.

*See Appendix 6A: The Financial Crisis: The Failure of Financial Institution Specialness online at **www.mhhe.com/canM2e**.

continued from p. 125

severe financial crisis that began in late 2008. We examine some of the crisis's underlying causes, review some of the major events that occurred during that time, and discuss some resulting regulatory and industry changes that are in effect today in Appendix 6A, which is located on the book's website (www.mhhe.com/canM2e). ■

FINANCIAL MARKETS

Financial markets exist to manage the flow of funds from investors to borrowers as well as from one investor to another. We generally differentiate financial markets by their primary financial instruments' characteristics (such as bond maturities) or the market's location. Specifically, we can distinguish markets along two major dimensions:

- Primary versus secondary markets.

- Money versus capital markets.

Primary Markets versus Secondary Markets LG6-1

Primary markets provide a forum in which demanders of funds (e.g., corporations or government entities such as IBM or the U.S. Treasury) raise funds by issuing new financial instruments, such as stocks and bonds. Corporations or government entities continually have new projects or expanded production needs, but do not have sufficient internally generated funds (such as retained earnings) to support their capital needs. Thus, corporations and governments issue securities in external primary markets to raise additional funds. These entities sell the new financial instrument issues to initial fund suppliers (e.g., households) in exchange for the funds (money) that the issuer requires.

In the U.S., financial institutions called **investment banks** arrange most primary market transactions for businesses. Some of the best-known examples of U.S. investment banks include Morgan Stanley, Goldman Sachs, or Merrill Lynch (owned by Bank of America, a commercial bank). These firms intermediate between issuing parties (fund demanders) and investors (fund suppliers). Investment banks provide fund demanders with a number of services, including advising the company or government agency about the securities issue (such as an appropriate offer price and number of securities to issue) and attracting initial public purchasers of the customer's securities offerings. Firms that need funds are seldom expert at raising capital themselves, so they avert risk and lower their costs by turning to experts at investment banks to issue their primary market securities.

DPH Corporation needs to issue new bonds either this year or in two years. DPH Corp. is a profitable firm, but if the U.S. economy were to experience a downturn, the company would see a big drop in sales over the next two years as its products are very sensitive to changes in the overall economy. DPH Corp. currently has $10 million in public debt outstanding, but its bonds are not actively traded. What questions must DPH Corp. consider as its managers decide whether to issue bonds today or in two years? How can DPH Corp. get these bonds to potential buyers and thus raise the needed capital?

The initial (or primary market) sale of securities occurs either through a public offering or as a private placement to a small group of investors. An investment bank serves as a security underwriter in a public offering. In a private placement, the security issuer engages the group of buyers (usually fewer than 10) to purchase the whole issue. Buyers are typically financial institutions. To protect smaller individual investors against a lack of disclosure, publicly traded securities must be registered with the Securities and Exchange Commission (SEC). Private placements, on the other hand, can be unregistered and resold to large, financially sophisticated investors only. Large investors supposedly possess the resources and expertise to analyze a security's risk. Privately placed bonds and stocks traditionally have been among the most illiquid securities in the securities markets; only the very largest financial institutions or institutional investors are able or willing to buy and hold them in the absence of an active secondary market. Issuers of privately placed securities tend to be less well known (e.g., medium-sized municipalities and corporations). Because of this lack of information and its associated higher risk, returns paid to holders of privately placed securities tend to be higher than those on publicly placed securities issues.

Figure 6.1 illustrates a time line for the primary market exchange of funds for a new issue of corporate bonds or equity. We will further discuss how companies, the U.S. Treasury, and government agencies that market primary government securities, such as Ginnie Mae and Freddie Mac, go about selling primary market securities in Chapter 8. Throughout this text, we focus on government securities from the *buyer's,* rather than the seller's, point of view. You can find in-depth discussions of government securities from the sellers' point of view in a public finance text.

Primary market financial instruments include stock issues from firms initially going public (e.g., allowing their equity shares to

personal APPLICATION

John Adams wants to invest in one of two corporate bonds issued by separate firms. One bond yields 8.00 percent with a 10-year maturity; the other offers a 10.00 percent yield and a 9-year maturity. The second bond *seems* to be the better deal. Is it necessarily the bond in which John should invest? Once he decides which bond represents the better investment, how can John go about buying the bond?

Should John consider bonds from other countries? **Scan the QR code for an extended look. Turn to the back of the book for solutions to these applications.**

be publicly traded on stock markets for the first time). We usually refer to these first-time issues as **initial public offerings (IPOs).** For example, on May 28, 2010, Toys 'R' Us announced an $800 million IPO of its common stock. Toys 'R' Us used several investment banks, including Goldman Sachs, to underwrite the company's stock. Publicly traded firms may issue additional bonds or stocks as primary market securities. For example, in March 18, 2010, Genpact Limited announced that it would sell an additional 38,640,000 shares of common stock (at $15.00 per share) underwritten by investment banks such as Morgan Stanley, Goldman Sachs, Citigroup Global Markets, Credit Suisse, and UBS Securities. These funds augmented Genpact Limited's existing capital (equity) of $1,313 million.

Secondary Markets Once firms issue financial instruments in primary markets, these same stocks and bonds are then traded—that is, bought and resold—in **secondary markets.**

The New York Stock Exchange (NYSE) and the NASDAQ are two well-known examples of secondary markets for trading stocks (see Chapters 7 and 8). In addition to stocks and bonds, secondary markets also exist for financial instruments backed by mortgages and other assets, foreign exchange, and futures and options (i.e., derivative securities, discussed later in the chapter).

Buyers find sellers of secondary market securities in economic agents that need funds (fund demanders). Secondary markets provide a centralized marketplace where economic agents know that they can buy or sell most securities quickly and efficiently. Secondary markets, therefore, save economic agents the search costs of finding buyers or sellers on their own. Figure 6.2 illustrates a secondary market transfer of funds. Secondary market buyers often use securities brokers such as Charles Schwab or other brokerage firms to act as intermediaries as they exchange funds for securities (see Chapter 8). An important note: the firm that originally issued the stock or bond is not involved in secondary market transactions in any way—no money accrues to the company itself when its stock trades in a secondary market.

Secondary markets offer benefits to both investors (fund suppliers) and issuers (fund demanders). Investors gain liquidity and diversification benefits (see Chapter 10). Although corporate security issuers are not directly involved in secondary market transactions, issuers do gain information about their securities' current market value. Publicly traded firms can thus observe how investors perceive their corporate value and their corporate decisions by tracking their firms' securities' secondary market prices. Such price information allows issuers to evaluate how well they are using internal funds as well as the funds generated from previously issued stocks and bonds and provides indications about how well any subsequent bond or stock offerings might be received—and at what price.

Secondary market **trading volume** can be quite large. Trading volume is defined as the number of shares of a security that are simultaneously bought and sold during a given period. Each seller and each buyer actually

financial markets
The arenas through which funds flow.

primary markets
Markets in which corporations raise funds through new issues of securities.

investment banks Financial institutions that arrange primary market transactions for businesses.

initial public offerings (IPOs) The first public issue of financial instruments by a firm.

secondary markets Markets that trade financial instruments once they are issued.

trading volume
The number of shares of a security that are simultaneously bought and sold during a period.

▼**FIGURE 6.1** Primary Market Transfer of Funds

Primary Markets
(Where new issues of financial instruments are offered for sale)

Demanders of funds (corporations issuing debt/equity instruments)	Securities →→→→→ Cash ←←←←	Underwriting with investment bank	Securities →→→→→ Cash ←←←←	Initial suppliers of funds (investors)

→→→→ Financial instrument flow
←←←← Funds flow

▼FIGURE 6.2 Secondary Market Transfer of Funds

Secondary Markets
(Where financial instruments, once issued, are traded)

Financial markets → Securities →→→→→ Securities brokers → Securities →→→→→→→→ Other suppliers of funds
← Cash ←←←←← ← Cash ←←←←←←←←←

→→→→→→→ Financial instruments flow
←←←←←← Funds flow

▼FIGURE 6.3 Money versus Capital Market Maturities

	Capital Market Securities			
Money market securities	Notes and bonds	Stocks (equities)		Maturity
0	1 year to maturity	30 years to maturity	No specified maturity	

contract with the exchange's clearinghouse, which then matches sell and buy orders for each transaction. The clearinghouse is a company whose stock trades on the exchange, and the clearinghouse runs on a for-profit basis.

The exchange and the clearinghouse can process many transactions in a single day. For example, on October 28, 1997, NYSE trading volume exceeded 1 billion shares for the first time ever. On October 10, 2008 (at the height of the financial crisis), NYSE trading volume topped 7.3 billion shares, the highest level to date. In contrast, during the mid-1980s, a NYSE trading day during which 250 million shares traded was considered a high-volume day.

Money Markets versus Capital Markets LG6-1

We noted above that financial markets are differentiated in part by the maturity dates of the instruments traded. This distinction becomes important when we differentiate money markets from capital markets. Both of these markets deal in debt securities (capital markets also deal in equity securities); the question becomes one of when the securities come due.

Money Markets **Money markets**

feature debt securities or instruments with maturities of one year or less (see Figure 6.3). In money markets, agents with excess short-term funds can lend (or supply) to economic agents who need (or demand) short-term funds. The suppliers of funds buy money market instruments and the demanders of funds sell money market instruments. Because money market instruments trade for only short periods of time, fluctuations in secondary-market prices are usually quite small. With less volatility, money market securities are thus less risky than longer-term instruments. In the United States, many money market securities do not trade in a specific location; rather, transactions occur via telephones, wire transfers, and computer trading. Thus, most U.S. money markets are said to be **over-the-counter** (OTC) **markets.**

Money Market Instruments LG6-2 Corporations

and government entities issue a variety of money market securities to obtain short-term funds. These securities include:

- Treasury bills.
- Federal funds and repurchase agreements.
- Commercial paper.
- Negotiable certificates of deposit.
- Banker's acceptances.

Table 6.1 lists and defines each money market security. Figure 6.4 graphically depicts the proportion of U.S. money market instruments outstanding across three decades. Notice that, in 2011, negotiable CDs commanded the highest dollar value of all money market instruments, followed by Treasury bills, commercial paper, and federal funds and repurchase agreements.

▼TABLE 6.1 Money Market Instruments

Treasury bills: short-term U.S. government obligations.

Federal funds: short-term funds transferred between financial institutions, usually for no more than one day.

Repurchase agreements (repos): agreements involving security sales by one party to another, with the promise to reverse the transaction at a specified date and price, usually at a discounted price.

Commercial paper: short-term unsecured promissory notes that companies issue to raise short-term cash (sometimes called Paper).

Negotiable certificates of deposit: bank-issued time deposits that specify an interest rate and maturity date and are negotiable—that is, traded on an exchange. Their face value is usually at least $100,000.

Banker acceptances (BAs): bank-guaranteed time drafts payable to a vendor of goods.

Capital Markets LG6-1 Capital markets

Capital markets are markets in which parties trade equity (stocks) and debt (bonds) instruments that mature in more than one year (see Figure 6.3). Given their longer maturities, capital market instruments are subject to wider price fluctuations than are money market instruments (see the term structure discussion below and in Chapter 7).

Capital Market Instruments LG6-2

Capital market securities include:

- U.S. Treasury notes and bonds.
- State and local government bonds.
- U.S government agency bonds.
- Mortgages and mortgage-backed securities.
- Corporate bonds.
- Corporate stocks.

Table 6.2 lists and defines each capital market security. Figure 6.5 graphically depicts U.S. capital market instruments outstanding over three decades. Note that corporate stocks (equities) represent the largest capital market instrument, followed by mortgages and mortgage-backed securities and then corporate bonds. The relative size of capital markets depends on two factors: the number of securities issued and their market prices. The 1990s saw consistently rising bull markets; hence the sharp increase in equities'

money markets	over-the-counter market	capital markets
Markets that trade debt securities or instruments with maturities of less than one year.	Markets that do not operate in a specific fixed location—rather, transactions occur via telephones, wire transfers, and computer trading.	Markets that trade debt (bonds) and equity (stock) instruments with maturities of more than one year.

▼**TABLE 6.2** Capital Market Instruments

Treasury notes and bonds: U.S. Treasury long-term obligations issued to finance the national debt and pay for other federal government expenditures.

State and local government bonds: debt securities issued by state and local (e.g., county, city, school) governments, usually to cover capital (long-term) improvements.

Mortgages: long-term loans issued to individuals or businesses to purchase homes, pieces of land, or other real property.

Mortgage-backed securities: long-term debt securities that offer expected principal and interest payments as collateral. These securities, made up of many mortgages, are gathered into a pool and are thus "backed" by promised principal and interest cash flows.

Corporate bonds: long-term debt securities issued by corporations.

Corporate stocks: long-term equity securities issued by public corporations; stock shares represent fundamental corporate ownership claims.

dollar value outstanding. Stock values fell in the early 2000s as the U.S. economy experienced a downturn—partly because of 9/11 and partly because interest rates began to rise—and stock prices fell. Stock prices in most sectors subsequently recovered

▼**FIGURE 6.4** Money Market Instruments Outstanding

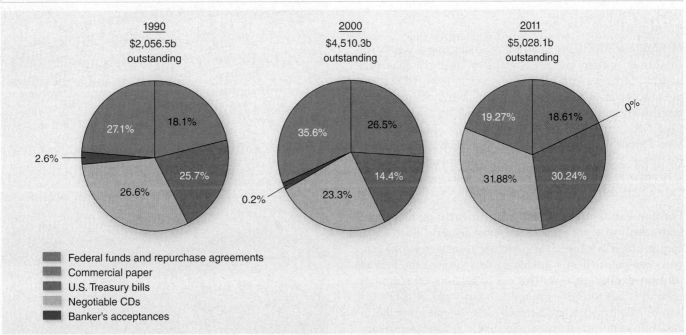

Here we see how the percentage of each money market instrument traded changes across three decades.

Source: Federal Reserve Board, "Flow of Fund Accounts," *Statistical Releases,* Washington, DC, various issues. **www.federalreserve.gov**

▼FIGURE 6.5 Capital Market Instruments Outstanding

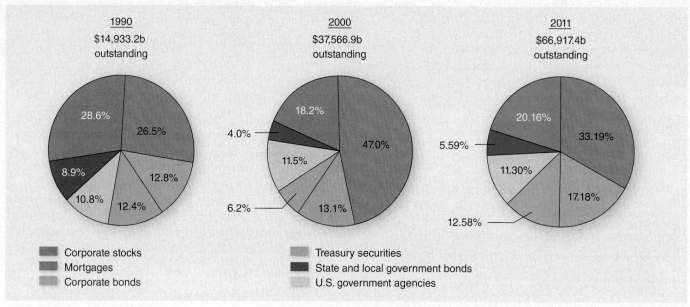

1990	**2000**	**2011**
$14,933.2b outstanding	$37,566.9b outstanding	$66,917.4b outstanding

Legend:
- Corporate stocks
- Mortgages
- Corporate bonds
- Treasury securities
- State and local government bonds
- U.S. government agencies

Source: Federal Reserve Board, "Flow of Fund Accounts," *Statistical Releases,* Washington, DC, various issues. **www.federalreserve.gov**

and, by 2007, even surpassed their 1999 levels. Stock prices fell precipitously during the financial crisis of 2008–2009. As of mid-March 2009, the Dow Jones Industrial Average (DJIA) had fallen in value 53.8 percent in less than 1½ year's time. This was greater than the decline during the market crash of 1937–1938, when it fell 49 percent. However, stock prices recovered along with the economy in the last half of 2009 and first half of 2010, rising 71.1 percent between March 2009 and April 2010.

Other Markets

Foreign Exchange Markets Today, most U.S.-based companies operate globally. Competent financial managers understand how events and movements in financial markets in other countries can potentially affect their own companies' profitability and performance. For example, in the late 2000s, Coca-Cola received some 31 percent of its operating profit from Europe. Despite increasing volume share in Europe by 4 percent in 2009, unfavorable currency movements between the U.S. dollar and the euro contributed to an 11 percent drop in Coca-Cola's consolidated operating income.

Foreign exchange markets trade currencies for immediate (also called "spot") or some future stated delivery. When a U.S. corporation sells securities or goods overseas, the resulting cash flows denominated in a foreign currency expose the firm to **foreign exchange risk.** This risk arises from the unknown value at which foreign currency cash flows can be converted into U.S. dollars. Foreign currency exchange rates vary day to day with worldwide demand and supply of foreign currency and U.S. dollars. Investors who deal in foreign-denominated securities face the same risk.

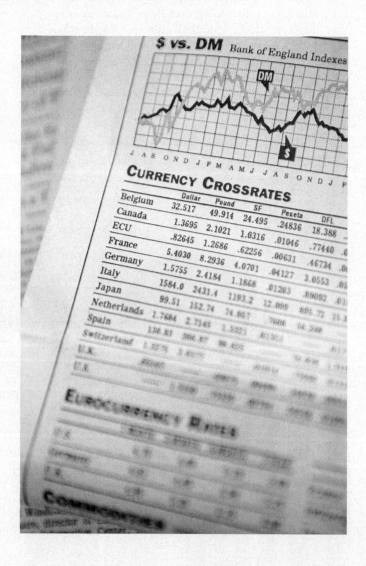

The actual number of U.S. dollars that a firm receives on a foreign investment depends on the exchange rate between the U.S. dollar and the foreign currency just as much as it does on the investment's performance. Firms will have to convert the foreign currency into U.S. dollars at the prevailing exchange rate. If the foreign currency depreciates (falls in value) relative to the U.S. dollar (say from 0.1679 dollar per unit of foreign currency to 0.1550 dollar per unit of foreign currency) over the investment period (i.e., the period between when a foreign investment is made and the time it comes to fruition), the dollar value of cash flows received will fall. If the foreign currency appreciates, or rises in value, relative to the U.S. dollar, the dollar value of cash flows received from the foreign investment will increase.

Foreign currency exchange rates are variable. They vary day to day with demand for and supply of foreign currency and with demand for and supply of dollars worldwide. Central governments sometimes intervene in foreign exchange markets directly—such as China's recent valuing of the yuan at artificially high rates relative to the dollar. Governments also affect foreign exchange rates indirectly by altering prevailing interest rates within their own countries.

Derivative Securities Markets

A **derivative security** is a financial security (such as a futures contract, option contract, or mortgage-backed security) that is linked to another, underlying security, such as a stock traded in capital markets or British pounds traded in foreign exchange (forex) markets. Derivative securities generally involve an agreement between two parties to exchange a standard quantity of an asset or cash flow at a predetermined price and at a specified date in the future. As the value of the underlying security changes, the value of the derivative security changes.

While derivative security contracts, especially for physical commodities like corn or gold, have existed for centuries, derivative securities markets grew increasingly popular in the 1970s, 1980s, and 1990s as traders, firms, and academics figured out how to spread risk for more and more underlying commodities and securities by using derivative contracts. Derivative contracts generally feature a high degree of leverage; that is, the investor only has to put up a very small portion of the underlying commodity or security's value to affect or control the underlying commodity or security.

Derivative securities traders can be either users of derivative contracts (for hedging and other purposes) or dealers (such as banks) that act as counterparties in customer trades for fees. An example of hedging involves commodities such as corn, wheat, or soybeans. For example, suppose you run a flour mill and will need to buy either soft wheat (Chicago) or hard red winter wheat (Kansas City) in the future. If you are concerned that the price of wheat will rise, you might lock in a price today to meet your needs six months from now by buying wheat futures on a commodities exchange. If you are correct and wheat prices rise over the six months, you may purchase the wheat by closing out your futures positions, buying the wheat at the futures price rather than the higher market price. Likewise, if you know that you will be delivering a large shipment to, say, Europe, in three months, you might take an offsetting position in euro futures contracts to lock in the exchange rate between the dollar and the euro as it stands today—and (you hope) eliminate foreign exchange risk from the transaction.

Derivative securities markets are the newest—and potentially the riskiest—of the financial security markets. Losses associated with off-balance-sheet mortgage-backed securities created and held by FIs were at the very heart of the financial crisis. Signs of significant problems in the U.S. economy first appeared in late 2006 and early 2007 when home prices plummeted and defaults began to affect the mortgage lending industry as a whole, as well as other parts of the economy noticeably. Mortgage delinquencies, particularly on subprime mortgages, surged in the last quarter of 2006 through 2008 as homeowners who had stretched themselves to buy or refinance a home in the early 2000s fell behind on their loan payments. As mortgage borrowers defaulted, the financial institutions that held their mortgages and credit derivative securities (in the form of mortgage-backed securities) started announcing huge losses on them. These losses reached $700 billion worldwide by early 2009. The situation resulted in the failure, acquisition, or bailout of some of the largest FIs and a near meltdown of the world's financial and economic systems.

time out!

6-1 How do primary and secondary markets differ?

6-2 What are foreign exchange markets?

6-3 What are derivatives securities?

FINANCIAL INSTITUTIONS LG6-3

Financial institutions (e.g., banks, thrifts, insurance companies, mutual funds) perform vital functions to securities markets of all sorts. Institutions channel funds from those with surplus funds (suppliers of funds) to those with shortages of funds (demanders of funds). In other words, FIs operate financial markets. FIs allow financial markets to function by providing the least costly and most efficient way to channel funds to and from these markets. FIs play a second crucial role by spreading risk among market participants. This risk-spreading function is vital to entrepreneurial efforts, for few firms or individuals could afford the risk of launching an expensive new product or process by themselves. Individual investors take on pieces of the risk by buying shares in risky enterprises. Investors then mitigate their own risks by diversifying their holdings into appropriate portfolios, which we cover in Chapters 9 and 10. Table 6.3 lists and summarizes the various types of FIs. The Finance at Work box highlights Walmart's ultimately unsuccessful attempts to operate as a financial institution.

To understand just how important FIs are to the efficient operation of financial markets, imagine a simple world in which FIs did not exist. In such a world, suppliers of funds (e.g., households), generating excess savings by consuming less than they earn, would have a basic choice. They could either hold cash as an asset or invest that cash in the securities issued by users of funds (e.g., corporations, governments, or retail borrowers). In general, demanders (users) of funds issue financial claims (e.g., equity and debt securities) to finance the gap between their investment expenditures and their internally generated savings, such as retained earnings or tax funds. As shown in Figure 6.6, in a world without financial institutions, we would have **direct transfers** of funds from fund suppliers to fund users. In return, financial claims would flow directly from fund users to fund suppliers.

In this economy without FIs, the amount of funds flowing between fund suppliers and fund users through financial markets would likely be quite low for several reasons:

- Once they have lent money in exchange for financial claims, fund suppliers would need to continually monitor the use of their funds. Fund suppliers must ensure that fund users neither steal the funds outright nor waste the funds on projects that have low or negative returns, since either theft or waste would lower fund suppliers' chances of being repaid and/or earning a positive return on their investments (such as through the receipt of dividends or interest). Monitoring against theft, misuse, or underuse of their funds would cost any given fund supplier a lot of time and effort, and of course each fund supplier, regardless

▼FIGURE 6.6 Flow of Funds in a World without FIs

Financial claims
(equity and debt instruments)

Securities

| Users of funds (corporations) | →→→→→→→→→→→→→→
 ←←←←←←←←←←←← | Suppliers of funds (household) |

Cash

▼TABLE 6.3 Types of Financial Institutions

Commercial banks: depository institutions whose major assets are loans and whose major liabilities are deposits. Commercial bank loans cover a broader range, including consumer, commercial, and real estate loans, than do loans from other depository institutions. Because they are larger and more likely to have access to public securities markets, commercial bank liabilities generally include more nondeposit sources of funds than do those of other depository institutions.

Thrifts: depository institutions including savings associations, savings banks, and credit unions. Thrifts generally perform services similar to commercial banks, but they tend to concentrate their loans in one segment, such as real estate loans or consumer loans. Credit unions operate on a not-for-profit basis for particular groups of individuals, such as a labor union or a particular company's employees.

Insurance companies: protect individuals and corporations (policyholders) from financially adverse events. Life insurance companies provide protection in the event of untimely death or illness, and help in planning retirement. Property casualty insurance protects against personal injury and liability due to accidents, theft, fire, and so on.

Securities firms and investment banks: underwrite securities and engage in related activities such as securities brokerage, securities trading, and making markets in which securities trade.

Finance companies: make loans to both individuals and businesses. Unlike depository institutions, finance companies do not accept deposits, but instead rely on short- and long-term debt for funding, and many of their loans are collateralized with some kind of durable good, such as washer/dryers, furniture, carpets, and the like.

Mutual funds: pool many individuals' and companies' financial resources and invest those resources in diversified asset portfolios.

Pension funds: offer savings plans through which fund participants accumulate savings during their working years. Participants then withdraw their pension resources (which have presumably earned additional returns in the interim) during their retirement years. Funds originally invested in and accumulated in a pension fund are exempt from current taxation. Participants pay taxes on distributions taken after age 55, when their tax brackets are (presumably) lower.

of the dollar value of the investment, would have to carry out the same costly and time-consuming process. Further, many investors do not have the financial training to understand the necessary business information to assess whether a securities issuer is making the best use of their funds. In fact, so many investment opportunities are available to fund suppliers, that even those trained in financial analysis rarely have the time to monitor how their funds are used in all of their investments. The resulting lack of monitoring increases the risk of directly investing in financial claims. Given these challenges, fund suppliers would likely prefer to delegate the task of monitoring fund borrowers to ensure good performance to others.

- Many financial claims feature a long-term commitment (e.g., mortgages, corporate stock, and bonds) for fund suppliers, but suppliers may not wish to hold these instruments directly. Specifically, given the choice between holding cash or long-term securities, fund suppliers may choose to hold cash for its **liquidity.** This is especially true if the suppliers plan to use their savings to finance consumption expenditures before their creditors expect to repay them. Fund suppliers may also fear that they will not find anyone to purchase their financial claim and free up their funds. When financial markets are not very developed, or deep, in terms of the number of active buyers and sellers in the market, such liquidity concerns arise.

- Even though real-world financial markets provide some liquidity services by allowing fund suppliers to trade financial securities among themselves, fund suppliers face **price risk** when they buy securities—fund suppliers may not get their principal back, let alone any return on their investment. Trading securities on secondary markets involves various transaction costs. The price at which investors can sell a security on secondary markets such as the New York Stock Exchange (NYSE) or NASDAQ may well differ from the price they initially paid for the security. The investment community as a whole may change the security's valuation between the time the fund supplier bought it and the time the fund supplier sold it. Also, dealers, acting as intermediaries between buyers and sellers, charge transaction costs for completing a trade. So even if an investor bought a security and then sold it the next day, the investor would likely lose money from transaction and other costs.

Unique Economic Functions Performed by Financial Institutions

Because of (1) monitoring costs, (2) liquidity costs, and (3) price risk, most average investors may well view direct investment in financial claims and markets as an unattractive proposition and, as fund suppliers, they will likely prefer to hold cash. As a result, financial market activity (and therefore savings and investment) would likely remain quite low. However, the financial system has developed an alternative, indirect way for investors (or fund suppliers) to channel funds to users of funds: financial intermediaries **indirectly transfer** funds to ultimate fund

users. Because of monitoring, liquidity risk, and price risk costs, fund suppliers often prefer to hold financial intermediaries' financial claims rather than those directly issued by the ultimate fund users. Consider Figure 6.7, which more closely represents the way that funds flow in the U.S. financial system than does Figure 6.6. Notice how financial institutions stand—or intermediate—between fund suppliers and fund users. That is, FIs channel funds from ultimate suppliers to ultimate fund users. Fund suppliers and users use these FIs to channel funds because of financial intermediaries' unique ability to measure and manage risk, and thus reduce monitoring costs, liquidity costs, and price risk.

Monitoring Costs As we noted above, a fund suppler who directly invests in a fund user's financial claims faces a high cost of comprehensively monitoring the fund user's actions in a timely way. One solution to this problem is that a large number of small investors can group their funds together by holding claims issued by an FI. In turn, the FI will invest in direct financial claims that fund users issue. Financial institutions' aggregation of funds from fund suppliers resolves a number of problems:

- First, large FIs now have much greater incentive to collect information and monitor the ultimate fund user's actions, because the FI has far more at stake than any small individual fund supplier would have.

- Second, the FI performs the necessary monitoring function via its own internal experts. In an economic sense, fund suppliers appoint the FI as a **delegated monitor** to act on their behalf. For example, full-service securities firms such as Merrill Lynch carry out investment research on new issues and make investment recommendations for their retail clients (investors), while commercial banks collect deposits from fund suppliers and lend these funds to ultimate users, such as corporations. An important part of these FIs' functions is their ability and incentive to monitor ultimate fund users.

liquidity The ease with which an asset can be converted into cash.

price risk The risk that an asset's sale price will be lower than its purchase price.

indirect transfer A transfer of funds between suppliers and users of funds through a financial institution.

delegated monitor An economic agent appointed to act on behalf of smaller investors in collecting information and/or investing funds on their behalf.

▼**FIGURE 6.7** Flow of Funds in a World with FIs

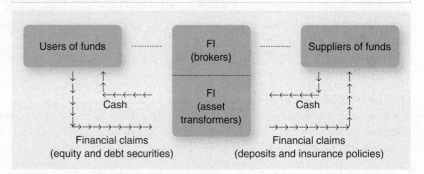

Financial institutions stand between fund suppliers and users.

finance at work //: markets

Retail Giant to Battle over Bank Plans

Walmart, ever looking for ways to expand its already huge empire, has asked the government for permission to move into an entirely different industry: running its own in-house bank. The world's largest retailer asked the Federal Deposit Insurance Corp. for permission to open a bank that can process millions of checks and credit card payments each month, operating out of its many stores. The company says it's not interested in running a consumer bank as well, but some of its opponents still fear that allowing Walmart into the banking industry in any way could hurt local banks in much the same way that Walmart decimated mom-and-pop stores during [its] rapid—some would even say ruthless—expansion.

This is Walmart's fourth bid at establishing its own bank—and its previous requests unleashed an unprecedented flood of comments to the FDIC. . . . "It's a landmark battle in both U.S. business and financial services history," said Jerry Comizio, a financial services lawyer for Thacher, Proffitt & Wood LLP in Washington D.C., and former senior attorney with the Securities and Exchange Commission and deputy general counsel of the U.S. Department of the Treasury's Office of Thrift Supervision.

Walmart says consumers and retail banks have nothing to fear. The retail giant pledges to stay out of branch banking and says it will not provide consumer lending, but for opponents, those assurances ring hollow. "There is reason to believe that these (Walmart's) plans could be expansive. Walmart has attempted on several occasions to enter the full-service banking business," said American Bankers Association's head of government relations Art Johnson, in testimony prepared for the FDIC hearing. "The ABA believes that banking is too important to the nation to try such a risky experiment."

Walmart says that it can save money if allowed to operate an in-house bank to handle the 140 million credit, debit card, and electronic check payments it handles each year. Concerns are twofold. One is the mixing of banking and commerce—parts of the economy that have traditionally been kept separate until the repeal of the Glass-Steagall Act in 1999. The other worry stems from the fact that

a Walmart bank could swallow local banks with its national presence and deep pockets, outcompeting even large institutions such as Bank of America, Chase, and Wachovia that have also grown at the expense of local ownership.

Want to know more?

Key Words to Search for Updates: **Walmart, banking; FDIC; ABA; Glass-Steagall repeal; electronic check payments**

Source: Adapted from *The Wall Street Journal*, April 8, 2006, p. A3.

Liquidity and Price Risk In addition to providing more and better information about fund users' activities, financial intermediaries provide additional liquidity to fund suppliers, acting as **asset transformers** as follows: FIs purchase the financial claims that fund users issue—primary securities such as mortgages, bonds, and stocks—and finance these purchases by selling financial claims to household investors and other fund suppliers

as deposits, insurance policies, or other **secondary securities.** The secondary securities—packages or pools of primary claims—that FIs collect and then issue are often more liquid than are the primary securities themselves. For example, banks and thrift institutions (e.g., savings associations) offer draft deposit accounts with fixed principal values and (often) guaranteed interest rates. Fund suppliers can generally access the funds in those accounts on demand. Money market mutual funds issue shares to household savers that allow the savers to maintain almost fixed principal amounts while earning somewhat higher interest rates than on bank deposits. Further, savers can also withdraw these funds on demand whenever the saver writes a check on the account. Even life insurance companies allow policyholders to borrow against their company-held policy balances with very short notice.

The Shift Away from Risk Measurement and Management and the Financial Crisis

Certainly, a major event that changed and reshaped the financial services industry was the financial crisis of the late 2000s. As FIs adjusted to regulatory changes brought about in the 1980s and 1990s, one result was a dramatic increase in systemic risk of the financial system, caused in large part by a shift in the banking model from that of "originate and hold" to "originate to distribute." In the traditional model, banks take short-term deposits and other sources of funds and use them to fund longer term loans to businesses and consumers. Banks typically hold these loans to maturity, and thus have an incentive to screen and monitor borrower activities even after a loan is made. However, the traditional banking model exposes the institution to potential liquidity, interest rate, and credit risk. In attempts to avoid these risk exposures and generate improved return-risk trade-offs, banks shifted to an underwriting model in which they originated or warehoused loans, and then quickly sold them. Indeed, most large banks organized as financial service holding companies to facilitate these new activities. These innovations removed risk from the balance sheet of financial institutions and shifted risk off the balance sheet and to other parts of the financial system. Since the FIs, acting as underwriters, were not exposed to the credit, liquidity, and interest rate risks of traditional banking, they had little incentive to screen and monitor activities of borrowers to whom they originated loans. Thus, FIs failed to act as specialists in risk measurement and management as described above.

Adding to FIs' move away from risk measurement and management was the boom ("bubble") in the housing markets, which began building in 2001, particularly after the terrorist attacks of 9/11. The immediate response by regulators to the terrorist attacks was to create stability in the financial markets by providing liquidity to FIs. For example, the Federal Reserve lowered the short-term money market rate that banks and other financial institutions pay in the federal funds market and even made lender of last resort funds available to nonbank FIs such as investment banks. Perhaps not surprisingly, low interest rates and the increased liquidity provided by central banks resulted in a rapid expansion in consumer, mortgage, and corporate debt financing. Demand for residential mortgages and credit card debt rose dramatically. As the demand for mortgage debt grew, especially among those who had previously been excluded from participating in the market because of their poor credit ratings, FIs began lowering their credit quality cutoff points. Moreover, to boost their earnings, in the market now popularly known as the "subprime market," banks and other mortgage-supplying institutions often offered relatively low "teaser" rates

on adjustable rate mortgages (ARMs) at exceptionally low initial interest rates, but with substantial step-up in rates after the initial rate period expired two or three years later and if market rates rose in the future. Under the traditional banking structure, banks might have been reluctant to so aggressively pursue low credit quality borrowers for fear that the loans would default. However, under the originate-to-distribute model of banking, asset securitization and loan syndication allowed banks to retain little or no part of the loans, and hence the default risk on loans that they originated. Thus, as long as the borrower did not default within the first few months after a loan's issuance and the loans were sold or securitized without recourse back to the bank, the issuing bank could ignore longer term credit risk concerns. The result was deterioration in credit quality, at the same time as there was a dramatic increase in consumer and corporate leverage.

Eventually, in 2006, housing prices started to fall. At the same time, the Federal Reserve started to raise interest rates in the

asset transformer Service provided by financial institutions in which financial claims issued by an FI are more attractive to investors than are the claims directly issued by corporations.

secondary securities Packages or pools of primary claims.

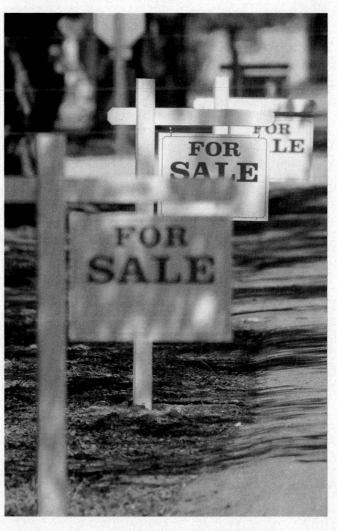

money market as it began to fear inflation. Since many subprime mortgages originated in the 2001–2005 period had floating rates, the cost of meeting mortgage commitments rose to unsustainable levels for many low-income households. The confluence of falling house prices, rising interest rates, and rising mortgage costs led to a wave of mortgage defaults in the subprime market and foreclosures that only reinforced the downward trend in house prices. As this happened, the poor quality of the collateral and credit quality underlying subprime mortgage pools became apparent, with default rates far exceeding those apparently anticipated by the rating agencies in setting their initial subprime mortgage securitizations ratings. These effects built throughout 2006 and through the middle of 2007. By February 2007, the percentage of subprime mortgage-backed securities delinquent by 90 days or more was 10.09 percent, substantially higher than the 5.37 percent rate in May 2005. The number of subprime mortgages that were more than 60 days behind on their payments was 17.1 percent in June 2007 and over 20 percent in August 2007. As borrowers had difficulty repaying their existing mortgages, they found it impossible to refinance their existing loans prior to the higher step-up interest rates kicking in. By the fall of 2007, the National Association of Realtors was projecting a decline of 24 percent in new home sales and 8.6 percent in existing home sales. The financial crisis began. Appendix 6A to this chapter provides a detailed discussion of the causes of, major events during, and regulatory and industry changes resulting from the financial crisis.

The economy relies on financial institutions to act as specialists in risk measurement and management. The importance of this was demonstrated in the aftermath of the FIs' failure to perform this critical function during the global financial crisis, which resulted in the worldwide breakdown in credit markets, as well as an enhanced level of equity market volatility. When FIs failed to perform their critical risk measurement and management functions, the result was a crisis of confidence that disrupted financial markets.

time out!

6-4 List the major types of financial institutions.

6-5 What three main issues would deter fund suppliers from directly purchasing securities?

6-6 What events resulted in banks' shift from the traditional banking model of "originate and hold" to a model of "originate and distribute"?

INTEREST RATES

We often speak of "the interest rate" as if only one rate applies to all financial situations or transactions. In fact, we can list tens or hundreds of interest rates that are appropriate in various conditions or situations within the U.S. economy on any particular day. Let's explore a bit how the financial sector sets these rates and how the rates relate to one another. We actually observe **nominal interest rates** in financial markets—these are the rates most often quoted by financial news services. As we will see in Chapters 7 and 8, nominal interest rates (or, simply, interest rates) directly affect most tradable securities' value or price. Since any change in nominal interest rates has such profound effects on security prices, financial managers and individual investors spend a lot of time and effort trying to identify factors that may influence future interest rate levels.

Of course, interest rate changes influence investment performance and trigger buy or sell decisions for individual investors, businesses, and governmental units alike. For example, in 2008–2009, the Federal Reserve, in an effort to address the severe financial crisis, unexpectedly announced that it would drop its target fed funds rate to a range between 0 and 0.25 percent and lowered its discount window rate to 0.5 percent, the lowest level since the 1940s. The Finance at Work box discusses the decision behind this decrease in interest rates.

Figure 6.8 illustrates the movement of several key U.S. interest rates over the past 38 years:

- The prime commercial loan rate.
- The 3-month T-bill rate.
- The high-grade corporate bond rate.
- The home mortgage rate.

Figure 6.8 shows how interest rates vary over time. For example, the prime rate hit highs of over 20 percent in the early 1980s, yet fell as low as 4.75 percent in the early 1970s. The prime rate stayed below 10 percent throughout much of the 1990s, fell back further to 4.00 percent in the early 2000s, then rose to as high as 8.25 percent in the mid-2000s. During the financial crisis of 2008–2009, the Fed took aggressive actions to stimulate the economy, including dropping interest rates to historic lows. As a result, the prime rate fell to 3.25 percent and stayed there through 2010.

Factors That Influence Interest Rates for Individual Securities LG6-4

Specific factors that affect nominal interest rates for any particular security include:

- Inflation.
- The real interest rate.

- Default risk.

- Liquidity risk.

- Special provisions regarding the use of funds raised by a particular security issuer.

- The security's term to maturity.

We will discuss each of these factors after summarizing them in Table 6.4.

Inflation The first factor that influences interest rates is the economywide *actual or expected inflation rate*. Specifically, the higher the level of actual or expected inflation, the higher will be the level of interest rates. We define **inflation** of the general price index of goods and services (or the inflation premium, IP) as the (percentage) increase in the price of a standardized basket of goods and services over a given period of time. The U.S. Department of Commerce measures inflation using indexes such as the consumer price index (CPI) and the producer price index (PPI). For example, the annual inflation rate using the CPI index between years t and $t + 1$ would be equal to:

$$IP = \frac{CPI_{t+1} - CPI_t}{CPI_t} \times 100 \qquad (6\text{-}1)$$

The positive relationship between interest rates and inflation rates is fairly intuitive: When inflation raises the general price level, investors who buy financial assets must earn a higher interest rate (or inflation premium) to compensate for continuing to hold the investment. Holding on to their investments means that they incur higher costs of forgoing consumption of real goods and services today, only to have to buy these same goods and services at higher prices in the future. In other words, the higher the rate of inflation, the more expensive the same basket of goods and services will be in the future.

Real Interest Rates A **real interest rate** is the rate that a security would pay if no inflation were expected over its holding period (e.g., a year). As such, it measures only society's

▼FIGURE 6.8 Key U.S. Interest Rates, 1972–2010

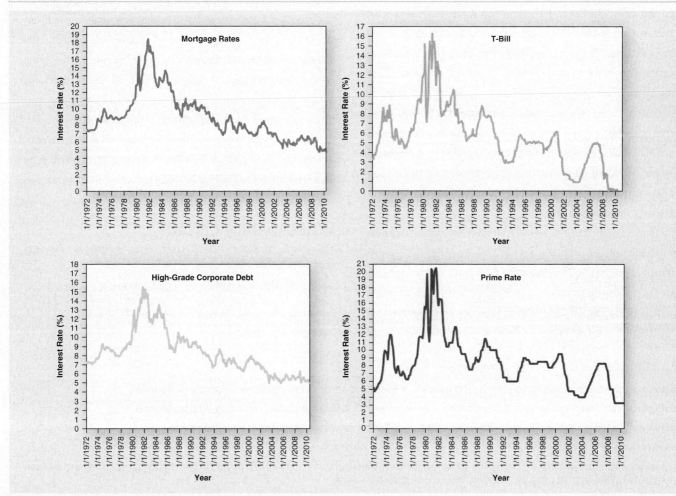

Source: Federal Reserve Board, website, various dates. **www.federalreserve.gov**

finance at work //: markets

Fed Cuts Rates Near Zero to Battle Slump

The Federal Reserve cut its target interest rate Tuesday to historic lows between zero and a quarter percentage point and said it could expand a program of unorthodox lending and securities purchases. After two days of discussion among Fed officials, the central bank said it would use every weapon from its arsenal to lift the U.S. from recession. It began by reducing its target interest rate—an overnight bank-lending rate called the federal-funds rate—from 1%. Another Fed lending rate, the discount rate, will go to half a percentage point, a level last seen in the 1940s. The cut was more than many economists expected, and the statement that came with it marked the latest signal by the Fed and its chairman, Ben Bernanke, that the central bank was prepared to take aggressive steps to revive the economy.

"The Federal Reserve will employ all available tools to promote the resumption of sustainable economic growth and to preserve price stability," the Fed said in a statement. It added that it expected interest rates to remain "exceptionally" low for some time, a subtle commitment to the current policy that could help bring down longer-term interest rates. In normal times, lower rates reduce the cost of borrowing for households, businesses and financial institutions, which spurs borrowing and economic activity. Those effects are being muted now, however, because many businesses and households are weighed down by heavy debts . . . A number of official borrowing rates—such as rates on three-month Treasury bills—have tumbled to near zero, a level they haven't been near since the Great Depression.

Officials spent much of two days of meetings deliberating over what other rescue steps the central bank could take as interest rates approach zero. Mr. Bernanke spent much of his academic career studying that and other questions related to financial crises, and the Fed is now employing almost every prescription he laid out

in the past. The approach carries several risks. It could eventually lead to the opposite of the current problem: higher inflation. It also exposes the independent central bank to political meddling and to losses on loans. Then there's the risk that it won't work. The Fed has already started a campaign to lend directly to damaged financial markets and companies—nearly anyone with collateral. Its statement Tuesday said those efforts could "sustain the size of the Federal Reserve's balance sheet at a high level." By such lending, officials have effectively concluded that if banks and financial markets won't extend credit, it will do part of the job for them.

Mortgage rates have been one of the few areas in financial markets where credit costs have fallen in the past few weeks. In its statement, the Fed said it stood ready to expand the program "as conditions warrant."

Want to know more?

Key Words to Search for Updates: **Federal Reserve, discount window, fed funds rate**

Source: *The Wall Street Journal,* December 17, 2008, p. AI, by Jon Hilsenrath. Reprinted by permission of *The Wall Street Journal.* © 2008 Dow Jones & Company, Inc. All Rights Reserved Worldwide.

▼ **TABLE 6.4** Factors Affecting Nominal Interest Rates

Inflation: a continual increase in the price level of a basket of goods and services throughout the economy as a whole.

Real interest rate: interest rate adjusted for inflation; generally lower than nominal interest rates at any particular time.

Default risk: risk that a security issuer will miss an interest or principal payment or continue to miss such payments.

Liquidity risk: risk that a security cannot be sold at a price relatively close to its value with low transaction costs on short notice.

Special provisions: provisions (e.g., taxability, convertibility, and callability) that impact a security holder beneficially or adversely and as such are reflected in the interest rates on securities that contain such provisions.

Time to maturity: length of time until a security is repaid; used in debt securities as the date upon which the security holders get their principal back.

relative time preference for consuming today rather than tomorrow. The higher society's preference to consume today (i.e., the higher its time value of money or rate of time preference), the higher the real interest rate (RIR) will be.

Fisher Effect Economists often refer to the relationship among real interest rates (RIR), expected inflation (expected IP), and nominal interest rates (*i*), described above, as the Fisher effect, named for Irving Fisher, who identified these economic relationships early last century. The Fisher effect theorizes that nominal interest rates that we observe in financial markets (e.g., the 1-year Treasury bill rate) must compensate investors for:

- Any inflation-related reduction in purchasing power lost on funds lent or principal due.

- An additional premium above the expected rate of inflation for forgoing present consumption (which reflects the real interest rate issue discussed above).

$$i = \text{Expected } IP + RIR \qquad (6\text{-}2)$$

Thus, the nominal interest rate will equal the real interest rate only when market participants expect inflation to be zero: Expected *IP* = 0. Similarly, the nominal interest rate will equal the expected inflation rate only when the real interest rate is zero. We can rearrange the nominal interest rate equation to show what determines the real interest rate:[1]

$$RIR = i - \text{Expected } IP \qquad (6\text{-}3)$$

It needs to be noted that the expected inflation rate is difficult to estimate accurately; therefore, the real interest rate can be difficult to measure accurately. Investors' expectations are not always realized either.

[1]Often the Fisher effect formula is written as $(1 + i) = (1 + IP) \times (1 + RIR)$, which, when solved for *i*, becomes: $i = \text{Expected } IP + RIR + (\text{Expected } IP \times RIR)$, where Expected $IP \times RIR$ is the inflation premium for the loss of purchasing power on the promised nominal interest rate payments due to inflation. For small values of Expected IP and RIR this term is negligible. The approximation formula used here assumes these values are small.

The 1-year T-bill rate in 2009 was 0.47 percent, while the CPI for the year was 2.70 percent, which implies a real interest rate of −2.23 percent—that is, the real interest rate was actually negative. Thus, the real value of investments actually decreased in that year.

Figure 6.9 shows the nominal interest rate (1-year T-bill rate) versus the change in the CPI from 1962 through 2010. Note that generally the T-bill rate is greater than the CPI, that is, the real interest rate earned on securities is positive. It is during periods of economic slowdowns that the T-bill rate is less than the CPI, that is, real interest rates are negative.

Default or Credit Risk **Default risk** is the risk that a security issuer may fail to make its promised interest and principal payments to its bondholders (or its dividend in the case of preferred stockholders). The higher the default risk, the higher the interest rate that security buyers will demand to compensate them for this default (or credit) risk relative to default-risk-free U.S. Treasury securities. Since the U.S. government has taxation powers and can print currency, the risk of its defaulting on debt payments is practically zero. But some borrowers, such as corporations or individuals, have less predictable cash flows (and no powers to tax anyone to raise funds immediately). So investors must charge issuers other than the U.S. government a premium for any perceived probability of default and the cost of potentially recovering the amount loaned built into their regular interest rate premium. The difference between a quoted interest rate on a security (security *j*) and a Treasury security with similar maturity, liquidity, tax, and other features is called a *default* or *credit risk premium* (DRP_j). That is:

$$DRP_j = i_{jt} - i_{Tt} \qquad (6\text{-}4)$$

where i_{jt} = Interest rate on a security issued by a non-Treasury issuer (issuer *j*) of maturity *m* at time *t*.

      i_{Tt} = Interest rate on a security issued by the U.S. Treasury of maturity *m* at time *t*.

default risk **default risk** The risk that a security issuer will default on that security by being late on or missing an interest or principal payment.

EXAMPLE 6-1   Calculating Real Interest Rates LG6-4

For interactive versions of this example visit www.mhhe.com/canM2e

One-year Treasury bill rates in 2007 averaged 4.53 percent and inflation (measured by the consumer price index) for the year was 4.10 percent. If investors had expected the same inflation rate as that actually realized, calculate the real interest rate for 2007 according to the Fisher effect.

SOLUTION:

$$4.53\% - 4.10\% = 0.43\%$$

Similar to Problems 6-1, 6-2

▼ FIGURE 6.9 Nominal Interest Rates versus Inflation

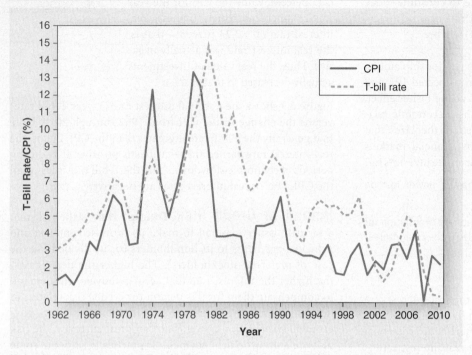

Notice the difference between the nominal interest rate and the change in CPI over the last several decades.

Source: Federal Reserve Board and U.S. Department of Labor websites, various dates. **www.federalreserve. gov** and **www.states.bls.gov/cpi/home.htm**

The interest rate on a security reflects its relative liquidity, with highly liquid assets carrying the lowest interest rates (all other characteristics remaining the same). Likewise, if a security is illiquid, investors add a **liquidity risk** premium (LRP) to the interest rate on the security. In the United States, most government securities sell in liquid markets, as do large corporations' stocks and bonds. Securities issued by smaller companies trade in relatively less liquid markets.

A different type of liquidity risk premium may also exist if investors dislike long-term securities because their prices (present values, as discussed below and in Chapters 4 and 7) react more to interest rate changes than short-term securities do. In this case, a higher liquidity risk premium may be added to a security with a longer maturity because of its greater exposure to price risk (loss of capital value) on the longer-term security as interest rates change.

Various rating agencies, including Moody's and Standard & Poor's, evaluate and categorize the potential default risk on many corporate bonds, some state and municipal bonds, and some stocks. We cover these ratings in more detail in Chapter 8. For example, in 2010, the 10-year Treasury rate was 3.31 percent. Moody's Aaa-rated and Baa-rated corporate debt carried interest rates of 4.98 percent and 6.23 percent, respectively. Thus, the average default risk premiums on the Aaa-rated and Baa-rated corporate debt were:

$$DRP_{Aaa} = 4.98\% - 3.31\% = 1.67\%$$

$$DRP_{Baa} = 6.23\% - 3.31\% = 2.92\%$$

Figure 6.10 presents these risk premiums for the stated creditworthiness categories of bonds from 1977 through 2010. Notice from this figure and Figure 6.9 that default risk premiums tend to increase when the economy is contracting and decrease when the economy is expanding. For example, from 2007 to 2008, real interest rates (T-bills − CPI in Figure 6.9) increased from 0.43 percent to 1.73 percent. Over the same period, default risk premiums on Aaa-rated bonds increased from 1.39 percent to 1.97 percent. Baa-rated bonds showed a default risk premium increase from 2.55 percent to 3.78 percent.

Liquidity Risk
A highly liquid asset can be sold at a predictable price with low transaction costs. That is, the holder can convert the asset at its fair market value on short notice.

Special Provisions or Covenants
Sometimes a security's issuing party attaches special provisions or covenants to the security issued. Such provisions affect the interest rates on these securities relative to securities without such provisions attached to them. Some of these special provisions include the security's taxability, convertibility, and callability. For example,

▼ FIGURE 6.10 Default Risk Premiums on Corporate Bonds

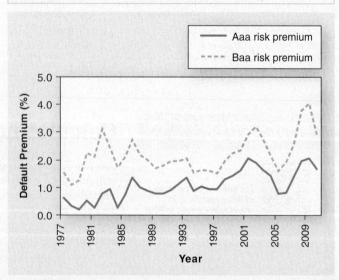

Source: Federal Reserve Board website, various dates. **www.federalreserve.gov**

investors pay no federal taxes on interest payments received from municipal securities. So a municipal bond holder may demand a lower interest rate than that demanded on a comparable taxable bond—such as a Treasury bond (which is taxable at the federal level but not at the state or local levels) or a corporate bond (the interest on which is taxable at the state, local, and federal levels).

Another special covenant is convertibility: A convertible bond offers the holder the opportunity to exchange the bond for another type of the issuer's securities—usually preferred or common stock—at a preset price (see Chapter 7). This conversion option can be valuable to purchasers, so convertible security buyers require lower interest rates than a comparable nonconvertible security holder would require (all else equal). In general, special provisions that benefit security holders (e.g., tax-free status and convertibility) bring with them lower interest rates, and special provisions that benefit security issuers (e.g., callability, by which an issuer has the option to retire, or call, the security prior to maturity at a preset price) require higher interest rates to encourage purchase.

Term to Maturity

Interest rates also change—sometimes daily—because of a bond's term to maturity. Financial professionals refer to this daily or even hourly changeability in interest rates as the **term structure of interest rates,** or the yield curve. The shape of the yield curve derives directly from time value of money principles. The term structure of interest rates compares interest rates on debt securities based on their time to maturity, assuming that all characteristics (i.e., default risk, liquidity risk) are equal. Interest rates change as the maturity of a debt security changes; in general, the longer the term to maturity, the higher the required interest rate buyers will demand. This addition to the required interest rate is the maturity premium (MP). The MP, which is the difference between the required yield on long- versus short-term securities of the same characteristics except maturity, can be positive, negative, or zero.

The financial industry most often reports and analyzes

the yield curve for U.S. Treasury securities. The yield curve for U.S. Treasury securities has taken many shapes over the years, but the three most common shapes appear in Figure 6.11. In graph (a), the yield curve on June 8, 2010, yields rise steadily with maturity when the yield curve slopes upward. This is the most common yield curve. On average, the MP is positive, as you might expect. Graph (b) shows an inverted, or downward-sloping, yield curve, reported on November 24, 2000, in which yields decline as maturity increases. Inverted yield curves do not generally last very long. In this case, the yield curve inverted as the U.S. Treasury began retiring long-term (30-year) bonds as the country began to pay off the national debt. Finally, graph (c) shows a flat yield curve, reported on June 4, 2007, when the yield to maturity is virtually unaffected by the term to maturity.

Note that yield curves may reflect factors other than investors' preferences for the maturity of a security. In reality, liquidity differences may arise among the securities traded at different points along the yield curve. For example, newly issued 20-year Treasury bonds offer a lower rate of return than previously issued Treasury bonds (so-called seasoned issues), all else being equal. Ten-year Treasury bonds may be more liquid if investors prefer new ("on the run") securities to previously issued ("off the run") securities. Specifically, since the U.S. Treasury has historically issued new 10-year notes and 20-year bonds only at the long end of the maturity spectrum, a seasoned 10-year Treasury bond would have to have been issued 10 years previously (i.e., it was originally a 20-year bond when it was issued 10 years previously). Increased demand for previously issued (and thus more liquid) 20-year Treasury bonds relative to the newly issued but less liquid 10-year Treasury bonds can be large enough to push the equilibrium interest rate on the 20-year Treasury bonds below that for the 10-year Treasury bonds and even below short-term rates. In the next section,

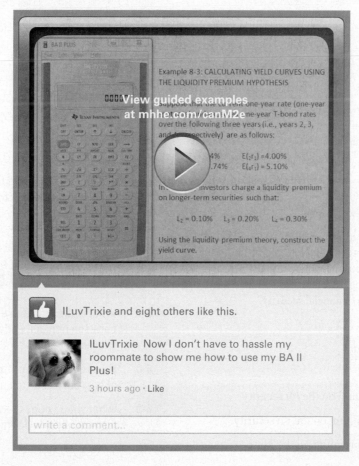

Example 8-3: CALCULATING YIELD CURVES USING THE LIQUIDITY PREMIUM HYPOTHESIS

one-year rate (one-year one-year T-bond rates over the following three years (i.e., years 2, 3, and ...respectively) are as follows:

4% $E(_2r_1)$ = 4.00%
.74% $E(_4r_1)$ = 5.10%

In... investors charge a liquidity premium on longer-term securities such that:

L_2 = 0.10% L_3 = 0.20% L_4 = 0.30%

Using the liquidity premium theory, construct the yield curve.

View guided examples at mhhe.com/canM2e

👍 ILuvTrixie and eight others like this.

ILuvTrixie Now I don't have to hassle my roommate to show me how to use my BA II Plus!

3 hours ago · Like

write a comment...

liquidity risk The risk that a security cannot be sold at a predictable price with low transaction costs on short notice.

term structure of interest rates A comparison of market yields on securities, assuming all characteristics except maturity are the same.

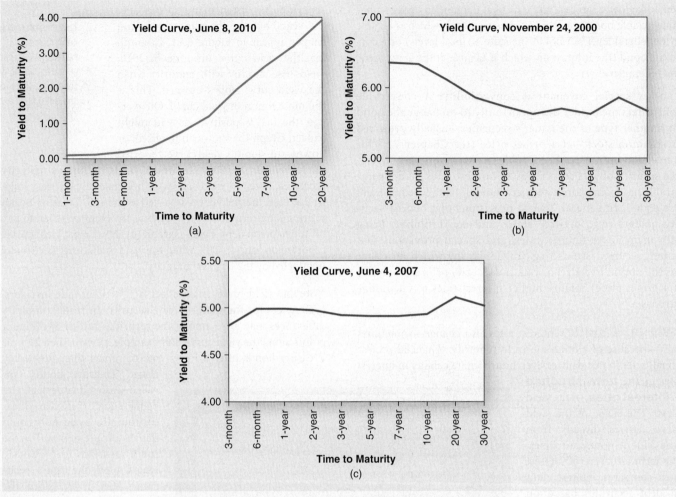

Three common yield curve shapes are (a) upward sloping, (b) downward sloping, and (c) a flat slope.

Source: U.S. Treasury, Office of Debt Management, Daily Treasury Yield Curves, various dates. **www.ustreas.gov**

we will review three major theories that financial analysts often use to explain the shape of the yield-to-maturity curve (or the shape of the term structure of interest rates).

Putting together the factors that affect interest rates in different markets, we can use the following general equation to note the influence of the factors that functionally impact the fair interest rate—the rate necessary to compensate investors for all security risks—(i_j^*) on an individual (jth) financial security.

$$i_j^* = f\,(IP, RIR, DRP_j, LRP_j, SCP_j, MP_j) \qquad (6\text{-}5)$$

where IP = Inflation premium

RIR = Real interest rate

DRP_j = Default risk premium on the jth security

LRP_j = Liquidity risk premium on the jth security

SCP_j = Special covenant premium on the jth security

MP_j = Maturity premium on the jth security

The first two factors, IP and RIR, are common to all financial securities, while the other factors can uniquely influence the price of a single security.

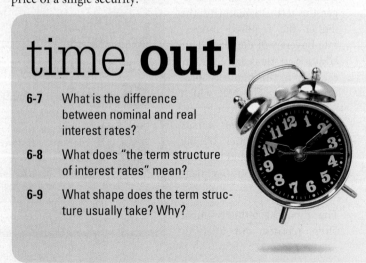

time out!

6-7 What is the difference between nominal and real interest rates?

6-8 What does "the term structure of interest rates" mean?

6-9 What shape does the term structure usually take? Why?

Theories Explaining the Shape of the Term Structure of Interest Rates LG6-5

We just explained the necessity of a maturity premium, the relationship between a security's interest rate and its remaining term to maturity. We can illustrate these issues by showing that the term structure of interest rates can take a number of different shapes. As you might expect, economists and financial theorists with various viewpoints differ among themselves in theorizing why the yield curve takes different shapes. Explanations for the yield curve's shape fall predominantly into three categories:

- The unbiased expectations theory.
- The liquidity premium theory.
- The market segmentation theory.

Look again at Figure 6.11 (a), which presents the Treasury yield curve as of June 8, 2010. We see that the yield curve on this date reflected the normal upward-sloping relationship between yield and maturity. Now let's turn to explanations for this shape based on the three predominant theories noted above.

Unbiased Expectations Theory According to the unbiased expectations theory of the term structure of interest rates, at any given point in time, the yield curve reflects the *market's current expectations of future short-term rates*. As illustrated in Figure 6.12, the intuition behind the unbiased expectations theory is this: If investors have a 4-year investment horizon, they could either buy current 4-year bonds and earn the current (or spot) yield on a 4-year bond ($_1R_4$, if held to maturity) each year, or they could invest in four successive 1-year bonds (of which they know only the current 1-year spot rate ($_1R_1$). But investors also expect what the unknown future 1-year rates [$E(_2r_1)$, $E(_3r_1)$, and $E(_4r_1)$] will be. Note that each interest rate term has two subscripts, e.g., $_1R_4$. The first subscript indicates the period in which the security is bought, so that 1 represents the purchase of a security in period 1. The second subscript indicates the maturity on the security. Thus, 4 represents the purchase of a security with a 4-year life. Similarly, $E(_3r_1)$ is the expected return on a security with a 1-year life purchased in period 3.

According to the unbiased expectations theory, the return for holding a 4-year bond to maturity should equal the expected return for investing in four successive 1-year bonds (as long as the market is in equilibrium). If this equality does not hold, an arbitrage opportunity exists. That is, if investors could earn more on the 1-year bond investments, they could short (or sell) the 4-year bond, use the proceeds to buy the four successive 1-year bonds, and earn a guaranteed profit over the 4-year investment horizon. So, according to the unbiased expectations hypothesis, if the market expects future 1-year rates to rise each successive year into the future, then the yield curve will slope upward. Specifically, the current 4-year T-bond rate or return will exceed the 3-year bond rate, which will exceed the 2-year bond rate, and so on. Similarly, if the market expects future 1-year rates to remain constant each successive year into the future, then the 4-year bond rate will equal the 3-year bond rate. That is, the term structure of interest rates will remain constant (flat) over the relevant time period. Specifically, the unbiased expectation theory states that current long-term interest rates are geometric averages of current and expected *future* short-term interest rates. The mathematical equation representing this relationship is:

$$(1 + {}_1R_N)^N = (1 + {}_1R_1)[1 + E({}_2r_1)] \ldots [1 + E({}_Nr_1)] \quad \text{(6-6)}$$

therefore:

$$_1R_N = \{[1 + {}_1R_1][1 + E({}_2r_1)] \ldots [1 + E({}_Nr_1)]\}^{1/N} - 1 \quad \text{(6-7)}$$

where $_1R_N$ = Actual N-period rate today (i.e., the first day of year 1)

N = Term to maturity

$_1R_1$ = Actual 1-year rate today

$E(_ir_1)$ = Expected 1-year rates for years 2, 3, 4, ..., N in the future

Notice, as above, that uppercase interest rate terms, $_1R_t$, are the actual current interest rates on securities purchased today with a maturity of t years. Lowercase interest rate terms, $_tr_1$, represent estimates of future 1-year interest rates starting t years into the future.

Liquidity Premium Theory The second popular explanation—the liquidity premium theory of the term structure of interest rates—builds on the unbiased expectations theory. The liquidity premium idea is as follows: Investors will hold long-term maturities only if these securities with longer term maturities are offered at a premium to compensate for future uncertainty in the security's value. Of course, uncertainty or risk increases with an asset's maturity. This theory is thus consistent with our discussions of market risk

▼**FIGURE 6.12** Unbiased Expectations Theory of the Term Structure of Interest Rates

Return from buying four 1-year maturity bonds versus buying one 4-year maturity bond.

EXAMPLE 6-2 | Calculating Yield Curves LG6-5

Suppose that the current 1-year rate (1-year spot rate) and expected 1-year T-bond rates over the following three years (i.e., years 2, 3, and 4, respectively) are as follows:

$$_1R_1 = 2.94\% \qquad E(_2r_1) = 4\% \qquad E(_3r_1) = 4.74\% \qquad E(_4r_1) = 5.10\%$$

Construct a yield curve using the unbiased expectations theory.

SOLUTION:

Using the unbiased expectations theory, current (or today's) rates for 1-, 2-, 3-, and 4-year maturity Treasury securities should be:

$$_1R_1 = 2.94\% \qquad \text{(Expected return of security with 1-year life purchased in period 1)}$$

$$_1R_2 = [(1 + 0.0294)(1 + 0.04)]^{1/2} - 1 = 3.47\%$$

$$_1R_3 = [(1 + 0.0294)(1 + 0.04)(1 + 0.0474)]^{1/3} - 1 = 3.89\%$$

$$_1R_4 = [(1 + 0.0294)(1 + 0.04)(1 + 0.0474)(1 + 0.051)]^{1/4} - 1 = 4.19\%$$

and the current yield to maturity curve will be upward sloping as shown:

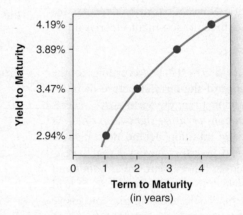

This upward-sloping yield curve reflects the market's expectation of persistently rising 1-year (short-term) interest rates over the future horizon.[2]

Similar to Problems 6-5, 6-6

[2]That is, $E(_4r_1) > E(_3r_1) > E(_2r_1) > {_1R_1}$.

and liquidity risk, above. Specifically, in a world of uncertainty, short-term securities provide greater marketability (due to their more active secondary markets) and have less price risk than long-term securities do. As a result (due to smaller price fluctuations for a given change in interest rates), investors will prefer to hold shorter-term securities because this kind of paper can be converted into cash with little market risk. Said another way, investors face little risk of a capital loss, i.e., a fall in the price of the security below its original purchase price. So, investors must be offered a liquidity premium to buy longer-term securities that carry higher capital loss risk. This difference in market

and liquidity risk can be directly related to the fact that longer-term securities are more sensitive to interest rate changes in the market than are shorter-term securities—Chapter 7 discusses bond interest rate sensitivity and the link to a bond's maturity. Because longer maturities on securities mean greater market and liquidity risk, the liquidity premium increases as maturity increases.

The liquidity premium theory states that long-term rates are equal to geometric averages of current and expected short-term rates (like the unbiased expectations theory), plus liquidity risk

the Math Coach on...

Interest Rates

" When putting interest rates into the equation, enter them in decimal format, not percentage format.

Correct: $(1 + 0.0294)$

Not correct: $(1 + 2.94)$ "

premiums that increase with the security's maturity (this is the extension of the liquidity premium added to the unbiased expectations theory). Figure 6.13 illustrates the differences in the shape of the yield curve under the unbiased expectations hypothesis versus the liquidity premium hypothesis. For example, according to the liquidity premium theory, an upward-sloping yield curve may reflect investors' expectations that future short-term rates will be flat, but because liquidity premiums increase with maturity, the yield curve will nevertheless slope upward. Indeed, an upward-sloping yield curve may reflect expectations that future interest rates will rise, be flat, or even fall as long as the liquidity premium increases with maturity fast enough to produce an upward-sloping yield curve. The liquidity premium theory can be mathematically represented as

$$_1R_N = \{[1 + {}_1R_1][1 + E({}_2r_1) + L_2] \ldots$$
$$[1 + E({}_Nr_1) + L_N]\}^{1/N} - 1 \quad (6\text{-}8)$$

where L_t = Liquidity premium for a period t and $L_2 < L_3 < L_N$.

Let's compare the yield curves in Examples 6.2 (using the unbiased expectations hypothesis) and 6.3. Notice that the liquidity premium in year 2 ($L_2 = 0.10\%$) produces a 0.05 (= 3.52% − 3.47%) percent premium on the yield to maturity on a 2-year T-note, the liquidity premium for year 3 ($L_3 = 0.20\%$) produces a 0.10 (= 3.99% − 3.89%) percent premium on the yield to maturity on the 3-year T-note, and the liquidity premium for year 4 ($L_4 = 0.30\%$) produces a 0.15 (= 4.34% − 4.19%) percent premium on the yield to maturity on the 4-year T-note.

Market Segmentation Theory
The market segmentation theory does not build on the unbiased expectations theory or the liquidity premium hypothesis, but rather argues that individual investors and FIs have specific maturity preferences, and

convincing them to hold securities with maturities other than their most preferred requires a higher interest rate (maturity premium). The main thrust of the market segmentation theory is that investors do not consider securities with different maturities as perfect substitutes. Rather, individual investors and FIs have distinctly preferred investment horizons dictated by the dates when their liabilities will come due. For example, banks might prefer to hold relatively short-term U.S. Treasury bonds because their deposit liabilities also tend to be short-term—recall that bank customers can access their funds on demand. Insurance companies, on the other hand, may prefer to hold long-term U.S. Treasury bonds because life insurance contracts usually expose insurance firms to long-term liabilities. Accordingly, distinct supply and demand conditions within a particular maturity segment—such as the

▼**FIGURE 6.13** Yield Curve Using the Unbiased Expectation Hypothesis (UEH) versus the Liquidity Premium Hypothesis (LPH)

Notice the differences in the shape of the yield curve under the UEH and the LPH.

EXAMPLE 6-3

Calculating Yield Curves Using the Liquidity Premium Hypothesis LG6-5

Suppose that the current 1-year rate (1-year spot rate) and expected 1-year T-bond rates over the following three years (i.e., years 2, 3, and 4, respectively) are as follows:

$$_1R_1 = 2.94\%, \quad E(_2r_1) = 4.00\%, \quad E(_3r_1) = 4.74\% \quad E(_4r_1) = 5.10\%$$

In addition, investors charge a liquidity premium on longer-term securities such that:

$$L_2 = 0.10\% \quad L_3 = 0.20\%, \quad L_4 = 0.30\%$$

Using the liquidity premium theory, construct the yield curve.

SOLUTION:

Using the liquidity premium theory, current rates for 1-, 2-, 3-, and 4-year maturity Treasury securities should be:

$$_1R_1 = 2.94\%$$

$$_1R_2 = [(1 + 0.0294)(1 + 0.04 + 0.001)]^{1/2} - 1 = 3.52\%$$

$$_1R_3 = [(1 + 0.0294)(1 + 0.04 + 0.001)(1 + 0.0474 + 0.002)]^{1/3} - 1 = 3.99\%$$

$$_1R_4 = [(1 + 0.0294)(1 + 0.04 + 0.001)(1 + 0.0474 + 0.002)(1 + 0.051 + 0.003)]^{1/4} - 1 = 4.34\%$$

and the current yield to maturity curve will be upward sloping as shown:

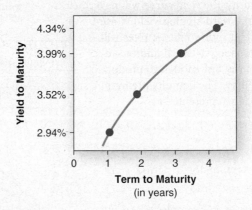

Similar to Problems 6-7, 6-8

short end and long end of the bond market—determine interest rates under the market segmentation theory.

The market segmentation theory assumes that investors and borrowers generally do not want to shift from one maturity sector to another without adequate compensation—that is, an interest rate premium. Figure 6.14 demonstrates how changes in supply for short- versus long-term bond market segments result in changing shapes of the yield to maturity curve. Specifically, as shown in Figure 6.14, the higher the demand for securities, the higher the yield on those securities.[3] Further, as the supply of securities decreases in the short-term market and increases in the long-term market, the slope of the

yield curve becomes steeper. If the supply of short-term securities had increased while the supply of long-term securities had decreased, the yield curve would have a flatter slope and might even have sloped downward. Indeed, the U.S. Treasury's large-scale repurchases of long-term Treasury bonds (i.e., reductions in supply) in early 2000 has been viewed as the major cause of the inverted yield curve that appeared in February 2000.

[3]In general, the price and yield on a bond are inversely related. Thus, as the price of a bond falls (becomes cheaper), the demand for the bond will rise. This is the same as saying that as the yield on a bond rises, it becomes cheaper and the demand for it increases. See Chapter 7.

forward rate An expected rate (quoted today) on a security that originates at some point in the future.

▼**FIGURE 6.14** Market Segmentation and Determination of the Slope of Yield Curve

The higher the demand for securities, the higher the yield on those securities.

time out!

6-10 What three theories explain the shape of the yield curve?

6-11 Explain how arbitrage plays a role in the unbiased expectations explanation of the shape of the yield curve.

Forecasting Interest Rates LG6-6

We noted in the time value of money (TVM) chapters (Chapters 4 and 5) that as interest rates change, so do the values of financial securities. Accordingly, both individual investors and public corporations want to be able to predict or forecast interest rates if they wish to trade profitably. For example, if interest rates rise, the value of investment portfolios of individuals and corporations will fall, resulting in a loss of wealth. So, interest rate forecasts are extremely important for the financial wealth of both public corporations and individuals.

Recall our discussion of the unbiased expectations hypothesis in the previous section of this chapter. That hypothesis indicated that the market's expectation of future short-term interest rates determines the shape of the yield curve. For example, an upward-sloping yield curve implies that the market expects future short-term interest rates to rise. So, we can use the unbiased expectations hypothesis to forecast (short-term) interest rates in the future (i.e., forward 1-year interest rates). A **forward rate** is an expected, or implied, rate on a short-term security that will originate at some point in the future. Using the equations in the unbiased expectations theory, we can directly derive the market's expectation of forward rates from existing or actual rates on spot market securities.

EXAMPLE 6-4

Estimating Forward Rates LG6-6

In the mid-2000s, the existing or current (spot) 1-, 2-, 3-, and 4-year zero coupon Treasury security rates were as follows:

$$_1R_1 = 5.00\%, \quad _1R_2 = 4.95\%, \quad _1R_3 = 4.93\%, \quad _1R_4 = 4.94\%$$

Using the unbiased expectations theory, calculate 1-year forward rates on zero coupon Treasury bonds for years 2, 3, and 4.

SOLUTION:

$$_2f_1 = [(1.0495)^2/(1.0500)] - 1 = 4.90\%$$

$$_3f_1 = [(1.0493)^3/(1.0495)^2] - 1 = 4.89\%$$

$$_4f_1 = [(1.0494)^4/(1.0493)^3] - 1 = 4.97\%$$

Similar to Problems 6-15, 6-16

To find an implied forward rate on a 1-year security to be issued one year from today, we can rewrite the unbiased expectations hypothesis equation as follows:

$$_1R_2 = [(1 + {}_1R_1)(1 + {}_2f_1)]^{1/2} - 1 \qquad (6\text{-}9)$$

where $_2f_1$ = expected 1-year rate for year 2, or the implied forward 1-year rate for next year.

Saying that $_2f_1$ is the expected 1-year rate for year 2 is the same as saying that, once we isolate the $_2f_1$ term, the equation will give us the market's estimate of the expected 1-year rate for year 2. Solving for $_2f_1$ we get:

$$_2f_1 = [(1 + {}_1R_2)^2/(1 + {}_1R_1)] - 1 \qquad (6\text{-}10)$$

In general, we can find the forward rate for any year, N, into the future using the following generalized equation derived from the unbiased expectations hypothesis:

$$_Nf_1 = [(1 + {}_1R_N)^N/(1 + {}_1R_{N-1})^{N-1}] - 1 \qquad (6\text{-}11)$$

View Appendix 6A: The Financial Crisis: The Failure of Financial Institution Specialness at the website for this textbook (www.mhhe.com/canM2e). ∎

time out!

6-12 What is a forward rate?

6-13 How can we obtain an implied forward rate from current short- and long-term interest rates?

6-14 Why is it useful to calculate forward rates?

Get Online

mhhe.com/canM2e

for study materials including self-test problems with solutions, quizzes, research projects, minicases, and videos

Your Turn...

Questions

1. Classify the following transactions as taking place in the primary or secondary markets *(LG6-1)*:

   a. IBM issues $200 million of new common stock.

   b. The New Company issues $50 million of common stock in an IPO.

   c. IBM sells $5 million of GM preferred stock out of its marketable securities portfolio.

   d. The Magellan Fund buys $100 million of previously issued IBM bonds.

   e. Prudential Insurance Co. sells $10 million of GM common stock.

2. Classify the following financial instruments as money market securities or capital market securities *(LG6-2)*:

   a. Federal funds

   b. Common stock

   c. Corporate bonds

   d. Mortgages

   e. Negotiable certificates of deposit

   f. U.S. Treasury bills

   g. U.S. Treasury notes

   h. U.S. Treasury bonds

   i. State and government bonds

3. What are the different types of financial institutions? Include a description of the main services offered by each. *(LG6-3)*

4. How would economic transactions between suppliers of funds (e.g., households) and users of funds (e.g., corporations) occur in a world without FIs? *(LG6-3)*

5. Why would a world limited to the direct transfer of funds from suppliers of funds to users of funds likely result in quite low levels of fund flows? *(LG6-3)*

6. How do FIs reduce monitoring costs associated with the flow of funds from fund suppliers to fund users? *(LG6-3)*

7. How do FIs alleviate the problem of liquidity risk faced by investors wishing to invest in securities of corporations? *(LG6-3)*

8. What are six factors that determine the nominal interest rate on a security? *(LG6-4)*

9. What should happen to a security's equilibrium interest rate as the security's liquidity risk increases? *(LG6-4)*

10. Discuss and compare the three explanations for the shape of the yield curve. *(LG6-5)*

11. Are the unbiased expectations and liquidity premium hypotheses explanations for the shape of the yield curve completely independent theories? Explain why or why not. *(LG6-5)*

12. What is a forward interest rate? *(LG6-6)*

13. If we observe a 1-year Treasury security rate that is higher than the 2-year Treasury security rate, what can we infer about the 1-year rate expected one year from now? *(LG6-6)*

Problems

6-1 **Determinants of Interest Rates for Individual Securities** A particular security's default risk premium is 2 percent. For all securities, the inflation risk premium is 1.75 percent and the real interest rate is 3.5 percent. The security's liquidity risk premium is 0.25 percent and maturity risk premium is 0.85 percent. The security has no special covenants. Calculate the security's equilibrium rate of return. *(LG6-4)*

6-2 **Determinants of Interest Rates for Individual Securities** You are considering an investment in 30-year bonds issued by Moore Corporation. The bonds have no special covenants. *The Wall Street Journal* reports that 1-year T-bills are currently earning 1.25 percent. Your broker has determined the following information about economic activity and Moore Corporation bonds:

Real interest rate = 0.75%

Default risk premium = 1.15%

Liquidity risk premium = 0.50%

Maturity risk premium = 1.75%

a. What is the inflation premium? *(LG6-4)*

b. What is the fair interest rate on Moore Corporation 30-year bonds? *(LG6-4)*

6-3 **Determinants of Interest Rates for Individual Securities** Dakota Corporation 15-year bonds have an equilibrium rate of return of 8 percent. For all securities, the inflation risk premium is 1.75 percent and the real interest rate is 3.50 percent. The security's liquidity risk premium is 0.25 percent and maturity risk premium is 0.85 percent. The security has no special covenants. Calculate the bond's default risk premium. *(LG6-4)*

6-4 **Determinants of Interest Rates for Individual Securities** A 2-year Treasury security currently earns 1.94 percent. Over the next two years, the real interest rate is expected to be 1.00 percent per year and the inflation premium is expected to be 0.50 percent per year. Calculate the maturity risk premium on the 2-year Treasury security. *(LG6-4)*

6-5 **Unbiased Expectations Theory** Suppose that the current 1-year rate (1-year spot rate) and expected 1-year T-bill rates over the following three years (i.e., years 2, 3, and 4, respectively) are as follows:

$$_1R_1 = 6\%, \ E(_2r_1) = 7\%, \ E(_3r_1) = 7.5\%, \ E(_4r_1) = 7.85\%$$

Using the unbiased expectations theory, calculate the current (long-term) rates for 1-, 2-, 3-, and 4-year-maturity Treasury securities. Plot the resulting yield curve. *(LG6-5)*

6-6 **Unbiased Expectations Theory** One-year Treasury bills currently earn 1.45 percent. You expected that one year from now, 1-year Treasury bill rates will increase to 1.65 percent. If the unbiased expectations theory is correct, what should the current rate be on 2-year Treasury securities? *(LG6-5)*

6-7 **Liquidity Premium Hypothesis** One-year Treasury bills currently earn 3.45 percent. You expect that one year from now, 1-year Treasury bill rates will increase to 3.65 percent. The liquidity premium on 2-year securities is 0.05 percent. If the liquidity theory is correct, what should the current rate be on 2-year Treasury securities? *(LG6-5)*

6-8 **Liquidity Premium Hypothesis** Based on economists' forecasts and analysis, 1-year Treasury bill rates and liquidity premiums for the next four years are expected to be as follows:

$$R_1 = 0.65\%$$

$$E(_2r_1) = 1.75\% \qquad L_2 = 0.05\%$$

$$E(_3r_1) = 1.85\% \qquad L_3 = 0.10\%$$

$$E(_4r_1) = 2.15\% \qquad L_4 = 0.12\%$$

Using the liquidity premium hypothesis, plot the current yield curve. Make sure you label the axes on the graph and identify the four annual rates on the curve both on the axes and on the yield curve itself. *(LG6-5)*

INTERMEDIATE PROBLEMS

6-9 **Determinants of Interest Rates for Individual Securities** Tom and Sue's Flowers Inc.'s 15-year bonds are currently yielding a return of 8.25 percent. The expected inflation premium is 2.25 percent annually and the real interest rate is expected to be 3.50 percent annually over the next 15 years. The default risk premium on Tom and Sue's Flowers' bonds is 0.80 percent. The maturity risk premium is 0.75 percent on 5-year securities and increases by 0.04 percent for each additional year to maturity. Calculate the liquidity risk premium on Tom and Sue's Flowers Inc.'s 15-year bonds. *(LG6-4)*

6-10 **Determinants of Interest Rates for Individual Securities** Nikki G's Corporation's 10-year bonds are currently yielding a return of 6.05 percent. The expected inflation premium is 1.00 percent annually and the real interest rate is expected to be 2.10 percent annually over the next ten years. The liquidity risk premium on Nikki G's bonds is 0.25 percent. The maturity risk premium is 0.10 percent on 2-year securities and increases by 0.05 percent for each additional year to maturity. Calculate the default risk premium on Nikki G's 10-year bonds. *(LG6-4)*

6-11 **Unbiased Expectations Theory** Suppose we observe the following rates: $_1R_1 = 8\%$, $_1R_2 = 10\%$. If the unbiased expectations theory of the term structure of interest rates holds, what is the 1-year interest rate expected one year from now, $E(_2r_1)$? *(LG6-5)*

6-12 **Unbiased Expectations Theory** *The Wall Street Journal* reports that the rate on 4-year Treasury securities is 1.60 percent and the rate on 5-year Treasury securities is 2.15 percent. According to the unbiased expectations hypotheses, what does the market expect the 1-year Treasury rate to be four years from today, $E(_5r_1)$? *(LG6-5)*

6-13 **Liquidity Premium Hypothesis** *The Wall Street Journal* reports that the rate on 3-year Treasury securities is 5.25 percent and the rate on 4-year Treasury securities is 5.50 percent. The 1-year interest rate expected in three years is, $E(_4r_1)$, is 6.10 percent. According to the liquidity premium hypotheses, what is the liquidity premium on the 4-year Treasury security, L_4? *(LG6-5)*

6-14 **Liquidity Premium Hypothesis** Suppose we observe the following rates: $_1R_1 = 0.75\%$, $_1R_2 = 1.20\%$, and $E(_2r_1) = 0.907\%$. If the liquidity premium theory of the term structure of interest rates holds, what is the liquidity premium for year 2, L_2? *(LG6-5)*

6-15 **Forecasting Interest Rates** You note the following yield curve in *The Wall Street Journal*. According to the unbiased expectations hypothesis, what is the 1-year forward rate for the period beginning one year from today, $_2f_1$? *(LG6-6)*

Maturity	Yield
One day	2.00%
One year	5.50
Two years	6.50
Three years	9.00

6-16 **Forecasting Interest Rates** On March 11, 20XX, the existing or current (spot) 1-, 2-, 3-, and 4-year zero coupon Treasury security rates were as follows:

$$_1R_1 = 0.75\%, \quad _1R_2 = 1.35\%, \quad _1R_3 = 1.75\%, \quad _1R_4 = 1.90\%$$

Using the unbiased expectations theory, calculate the 1-year forward rates on zero coupon Treasury bonds for years 2, 3, and 4 as of March 11, 20XX. *(LG6-6)*

ADVANCED PROBLEMS

6-17 **Determinants of Interest Rates for Individual Securities** *The Wall Street Journal* reports that the current rate on 10-year Treasury bonds is 7.25 percent, on 20-year Treasury bonds it's 7.85 percent, and on a 20-year corporate bond issued by MHM Corp. it's 8.75 percent. Assume that the maturity risk premium is zero. If the default risk premium and liquidity risk premium on a 10-year corporate bond issued by MHM Corp. are the same as those on the 20-year corporate bond, calculate the current rate on MHM Corp.'s 10-year corporate bond. *(LG6-4)*

6-18 **Determinants of Interest Rates for Individual Securities** *The Wall Street Journal* reports that the current rate on 5-year Treasury bonds is 1.85 percent and on 10-year Treasury bonds it's 3.35 percent. Assume that the maturity risk premium is zero. Calculate the expected rate on a 5-year Treasury bond purchased five years from today, $E(_5r_5)$. *(LG6-4)*

6-19 **Unbiased Expectations Theory** Suppose we observe the 3-year Treasury security rate $(_1R_3)$ to be 8 percent, the expected 1-year rate next year—$E(_2r_1)$—to be 4 percent, and the expected one-year rate the following year—$E(_3r_1)$—to be 6 percent. If the unbiased expectations theory of the term structure of interest rates holds, what is the 1-year Treasury security rate, $_1R_1$? *(LG6-5)*

6-20 **Unbiased Expectations Theory** *The Wall Street Journal* reports that the rate on three-year Treasury securities is 1.20 percent and the rate on 5-year Treasury securities is 2.15 percent. According to the unbiased expectations hypothesis, what does the market expect the 2-year Treasury rate to be three years from today, $E(_3r_2)$? *(LG6-5)*

6-21 **Forecasting Interest Rates** Assume the current interest rate on a 1-year Treasury bond $(_1R_1)$ is 4.50 percent, the current rate on a 2-year Treasury bond $(_1R_2)$ is 5.25 percent, and the current rate on a 3-year Treasury bond $(_1R_3)$ is 6.50 percent. If the unbiased expectations theory of the term structure of interest rates is correct, what is the 1-year forward rate expected on Treasury bills during year 3, $_3f_1$? *(LG6-6)*

6-22 **Forecasting Interest Rates** A recent edition of *The Wall Street Journal* reported interest rates of 1.25 percent, 1.60 percent, 1.98 percent, and 2.25 percent for 3-, 4-, 5-, and 6-year Treasury security yields, respectively. According to the unbiased expectation theory of the term structure of interest rates, what are the expected 1-year forward rates for years 4, 5, and 6? *(LG6-6)*

valuing
bonds

How important are bonds and the bond market to a capitalist economy? Those unfamiliar with the financial markets may have the impression that the stock market dominates capital markets in the United States and in other countries. Stock market performance appears constantly on 24-hour TV news channels and on the evening news. By contrast, we seldom hear any mention of the bond market. While bonds may not generate the same excitement that stocks do, they are an even more important capital source for companies, governments, and other organizations. The bond market is actually larger than the stock market. At the end of 2010, the U.S. bond market represented roughly $36 trillion in outstanding debt obligations. At the same time, the market value of all common stock issues was worth about one-third the value of the bond market, at roughly $13.2 trillion.

Bonds also trade in great volume and frequency. In June 2012, the total average daily trading in all types of U.S. bonds reached over $999 billion. Investors are often attracted to the

continued on p. 156

LEARNING GOALS

LG7-1 Describe bond characteristics.

LG7-2 Identify various bond issuers and their motivation for issuing debt.

LG7-3 Read and interpret bond quotes.

LG7-4 Compute bond prices using present value concepts.

LG7-5 Explain the relationship between bond prices and interest rates.

LG7-6 Compute bond yields.

LG7-7 Find bond ratings and assess credit risk's effects on bond yields.

LG7-8 Assess bond market performance.

continued from p. 155

stock market because it offers the potential for high investor returns—but great risks come with that high potential return. While some bonds offer safer and more stable returns than stocks, other bonds also offer high potential rewards and, consequently, higher risk.

In this chapter, we will explore bond characteristics and their price dynamics. You will see that bond pricing uses many time value of money principles that we've used in the preceding chapters. ■

BOND MARKET OVERVIEW

Bond Characteristics LG7-1

Bonds are debt obligation securities that corporations, the federal government or its agencies, or states and local governments issue to fund various projects or operations. All of these organizations periodically need to raise capital for various reasons, which was formally discussed in Chapter 6. Bonds are also known as **fixed-income securities** because bondholders (investors) know both how much they will receive in interest payments and when their principal will be returned. From the bond issuer's point of view, the bond is a loan that requires regular interest payments and an eventual repayment of the borrowed **principal.** Investors—often pension funds, banks, and mutual funds—buy bonds to earn investment returns. Most bonds follow a relatively standard structure. A legal contract called the **indenture agreement** outlines the precise terms between the issuer and the bondholders. Any bond's main characteristics include:

- The date the principal will be repaid (the **maturity date**).

- The **par value,** or face value, of each bond, which is the principal loan amount that the borrower must repay.

>>viewpoints

business APPLICATION

You are the chief financial officer (CFO) for Beach Sand Resorts. The firm needs $150 million of new capital to renovate a hotel property. As you discuss the firm's plans with a credit rating agency, you learn that if 15-year bonds are used to raise this capital, the bonds will be rated BB and will have to offer a 7 percent return. How many bonds will you have to issue to raise the necessary capital? What semiannual interest payments will Beach Sand have to make?

- The coupon (interest) rate.

- A description of any property to be pledged as collateral.

- Steps that the bondholder can take in the event that the issuer fails to pay the interest or principal.

Table 7.1 describes par value and other bond characteristics. Most bonds have a par value of $1,000. This is the amount of principal the issuer has promised to repay. Bonds have fixed lives. The bond's life ends when the issuer repays the par value to the buyer on the bond's maturity date. Although a bond will mature on a specific calendar date, the bond is usually referenced by its **time to maturity,** that is, 2 years, 5 years, 20 years, and so on. In fact, the market groups bonds together by their time to maturity and classifies them as short-term bonds, medium-term bonds, or long-term bonds, regardless of

▼**TABLE 7.1** Typical Bond Features

Characteristic	Description	Common Values
Par value	The amount of the loan to be repaid. This is often referred to as the *principal* of the bond.	$1,000
Time to maturity	The number of years left until the maturity date.	1 year to 30 years
Call	The opportunity for the issuer to repay the principal before the maturity date, usually because interest rates have fallen or issuer's circumstances have changed. When calling a bond, the issuer commonly pays the principal and one year of interest payments.	Many bonds are not callable. For those that are, a common feature is that the bond can be called any time after 10 years of issuance.
Coupon rate	The interest rate used to compute the bond's interest payment each year. Listed as a percentage of par value, the actual payments usually are paid twice per year.	2 to 10 percent
Bond price	The bond's market price reported as a percentage of par value.	80 to 120 percent of par value

personal APPLICATION

You would like to invest in bonds. Your broker suggests two different bonds. The first, issued by Trust Media, will mature in 2018. Its price is quoted at 96.21 and it pays a 5.7 percent coupon. The second bond suggested, issued by Abalon Inc. also matures in 2018. This bond's price is 101.94 and pays a 5.375 percent coupon. To help you decide between the bonds, you want to know how much money it will cost to buy 10 bonds, what interest payments you will receive, and what return the bonds offer if purchased today. Also, you want to understand the differences between what the two bonds imply about their risk.

How do you even purchase a bond in the first place? Scan the QR code for an extended look. Turn to the back of the book for solutions to these applications.

issuer. Long-term bonds carry 20 or 30 years to maturity. Of course, over time, the 30-year bond becomes a 20-year bond, 10-year bond, and eventually matures. But other time periods to maturity do exist. For example, Ford Motor issued bonds with 100 years to maturity on May 15, 1997. The bonds have a coupon (interest) rate of 7.70 percent and mature in 2097.

When interest rates economywide fall several percentage points (which often takes several years), homeowners everywhere seek to refinance their home mortgages. They want to make lower interest payments (and sometimes want to pay down their mortgage principal) every month. Corporations that have outstanding bond debt will also want to refinance those bonds. Sometimes the indenture contract (the legal contract between a bond issuer and bondholders) allows companies to do so; sometimes the indenture prohibits refinancing. Bonds that can be refinanced have a **call** feature, which means that the issuer can "call" the bonds back and repay the principal before the maturity date. To compensate the bondholders for getting the bond called, the issuer pays the principal and a

call premium. The most common call premium is one year's worth of interest payments. In some indentures, the call premium declines over time.

The bond's **coupon rate** determines the dollar amount of interest paid to bondholders. The coupon rate appears on the bond and is listed as a percentage of the par value. So a 5 percent coupon rate means that the issuer will pay 5 percent of $1,000, or $50, in interest every year, usually divided into two equal semiannual payments. So a 5 percent coupon bond will pay $25 every six months. The name *coupon* is a holdover from the past, when bonds were actually issued with a coupon book. Every six months a bondholder would tear out a coupon and mail it to the issuer, who would then make the interest payment. These are sometimes referred to as *bearer bonds* (often a feature of spy or mystery movies), because whoever held the coupon book could receive the payments. Nowadays, issuers register bond owners and automatically wire interest payments to the owner's bank or brokerage account. Nevertheless, the term *coupon* persists today.

At original issue, bonds typically sell at par value, unless interest rates are very volatile. Bondholders recoup the par value on the bond's maturity date. However, at all times in between these two dates, bonds might trade among investors in the secondary bond market. The **bond's price** as it trades in the secondary market will not likely be the

bond Publicly traded form of debt.

fixed-income securities Any securities that make fixed payments.

principal Face amount, or par value, of debt.

indenture agreement Legal contract describing the bond characteristics and the bondholder and issuer rights.

maturity date The calendar date on which the bond principal comes due.

par value Amount of debt borrowed to be repaid; face value.

time to maturity The length of time (in years) until the bond matures and the issuer repays the par value.

call An issuer redeeming the bond before the scheduled maturity date.

call premium The amount in addition to the par value paid by the issuer when calling a bond.

coupon rate The annual amount of interest paid expressed as a percentage of the bond's par value.

bond price Current price that the bond sells for in the bond market.

the Math Coach on...
Percent-to-Decimal Conversions

❝ When discussing interest rates or using them in calculator or spreadsheet time value of money functions, the value should be in percent (%) form, like 2.5%, 7%, and 11%. When using interest rates in formulas, the value needs to be in decimal form, like 0.025, 0.07, and 0.11.

To convert between the two forms of representing an interest rate, use

$$\text{Decimal} = \frac{\text{Percent (\%)}}{100}$$ ❞

EXAMPLE 7-1

For interactive versions of this example visit www.mhhe.com/canM2e

Bond Characteristics LG7-2

Consider a bond issued 10 years ago with an at-issue time to maturity of 30 years. The bond's coupon rate is 8 percent and it currently trades in the bond market for 109. Assuming a par value of $1,000, what is the bond's current time to maturity, semiannual interest payment, and bond price in dollars?

SOLUTION:

Time to maturity = 30 years −10 years = 20 years
Annual payment = 0.08 × $1,000 = $80, so semiannual payment is $40
Bond price = 1.09 × $1,000 = $1,090

Similar to Problems 7-1, 7-2, 7-3, 7-4

---

par value. Bonds trade for higher and lower prices than their par values. We'll thoroughly demonstrate the reasons for bond pricing in a later section of this chapter. Bond prices are quoted in terms of percent of par value rather than in dollar terms. Sources of trading information list a bond that traded at $1,150 as 115, and a bond that traded for $870 as 87.

Bond Issuers LG7-2

For many years, bonds were considered stodgy, overly conservative investments. Not anymore! The fixed-income industry has seen tremendous innovation in the past couple of decades.

The financial industry has created and issued many new types of bonds and fixed-income securities, some with odd-sounding acronyms, like TIGRs, CATS, COUGRs, and PINEs, all of which are securities based on U.S. Treasuries. Even with all the innovation, the traditional three main bond issuers remain: U.S. Treasury bonds, corporate bonds, and municipal bonds. Figure 7.1 shows the amount of money that these bond issuers have raised each year.

Treasury Bonds Treasury bonds carry the "full-faith-and-credit" backing of the U.S. government and investors have long considered them among the safest fixed-income investments in the world. The federal government sells Treasury securities through public auctions to finance the federal deficit. When the deficit is large, more bonds come to auction. In addition, the Federal Reserve System (the Fed) uses Treasury securities to implement monetary policy. Technically, Treasury securities issued with 1 to 10 years until maturity are Treasury notes. Securities issued with 10 to 30 years until maturity are Treasury bonds. The figure shows that the number of new Treasuries being offered actually declined in the late 1990s as the federal budget deficit declined. However, this dramatically reversed in 2002 when the trend toward issuing more federal debt reversed and accelerated.

FIGURE 7.1 Amount of Capital Raised Yearly from Bonds Issued by Local and Federal Government and Corporations

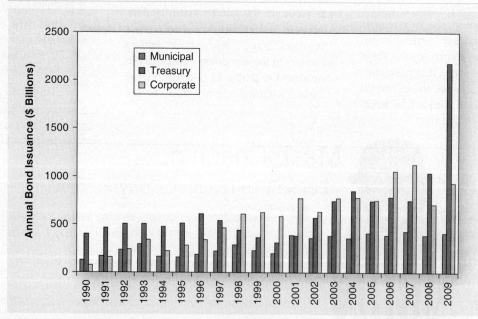

Local or municipal governments, the U.S. Treasury, and corporations have issued many new types of bonds and fixed-income securities over the past two decades.

Data Source: Securities Industry and Financial Markets Association.

Corporate Bonds Corporations raise capital to finance investments in inventory, plant and equipment, research and development, and general business expansion. As managers decide how to raise capital, corporations can issue debt, equity (stocks), or a mixture of both. The driving force behind a corporation's financing strategy is the desire to minimize its total capital costs. Through much of the 1990s, corporations tended to issue equity (stocks) to raise capital. Beginning in 1998 and through 2009, corporations switched to raising capital by issuing bonds to take advantage of low interest rates and issued $9.4 trillion in new bonds. You can see this rise in capital reflected in Figure 7.1.

Municipal Bonds State and local governments borrow money to build, repair, or improve streets, highways, hospitals, schools, sewer systems, and so on. The interest and principal on these municipal bonds are repaid in two ways. Projects that benefit the entire community, such as courthouses, schools, and municipal office buildings, are typically funded by general obligation bonds and repaid using tax revenues. Projects that benefit only certain groups of people, such as toll roads and airports, are typically funded by revenue bonds and repaid from user fees. Interest payments paid to municipal bondholders are not taxed at the federal level, or by the state for which the bond is issued.

Other Bonds and Bond-Based Securities

Treasury Inflation-Protected Securities (TIPS) have proved one of the most successful recent innovations in the bond market. The U.S. Treasury began issuing this new type of Treasury bond, which is indexed to inflation, in 1997. TIPS have fixed coupon rates like traditional Treasuries. The new aspect is that the federal government adjusts the par value of the TIPS bond for inflation. Specifically, it increases at the rate of inflation (measured by the consumer price index, CPI). As the bond's par value changes over time, interest payments also change. At maturity, investors receive an inflation-adjusted principal amount. If inflation has been high, investors will expect that the adjusted principal amount will be substantially higher than the original $1,000. Consider a 10-year TIPS issued on January 15, 2007, that pays a 2⅜ percent coupon. The reference CPI for these bonds is 201.66452. Three years later (on January 15, 2010) the reference CPI was 216.24610. So the par value of the TIPS in early 2010 was $1,072.31 (= $1,000 × 216.24610 ÷ 201.66452). Therefore, the 2⅜ percent coupon (paid semiannually) would be $12.73 (= 0.02375 × $1,072.31 ÷ 2). A TIPS' total return comes from both the interest payments and the inflation adjustment to the par value.

U.S. government agency securities are debt securities issued to provide low-cost financing for desirable private-sector activities such as home ownership, education, and farming. Fannie Mae, Freddie Mac, Student Loan Marketing Association (Sallie Mae), Federal Farm Credit System, Federal Home Loan Banks, and the Small Business Administration, among others, issue

Treasury Inflation-Protected Securities TIPS are U.S. government bonds where the par value changes with inflation.

EXAMPLE 7-2

TIPS Payments LG7-2

For interactive versions of this example visit www.mhhe.com/canM2e

A TIPS bond was issued on July 15, 2006, that pays a 2½ percent coupon. The reference CPI at issue was 201.95. The reference CPI for the following interest payments were:

January 2009	214.70
July 2009	213.52
January 2010	216.25

Given these numbers, what is the par value and interest payment of the TIPS on the three interest-payment dates? What is the total return from January 2009 to January 2010?

SOLUTION:
Compute the TIPS index ratio for each period as current CPI divided by the at-issue CPI: The par value for January 2009 is $1,000 × 214.70 ÷ 201.95 = $1,063.13, so the interest payment is 0.025 × $1,063.13 ÷ 2 = $13.29. The answers for the next two dates are:

| July 2009 | Par value = $1,057.29 | Interest payment = $13.22 |
| January 2010 | Par value = $1,070.81 | Interest payment = $13.39 |

The capital gain between January 2009 and January 2010 is $1,070.81 − $1,063.13 = $7.68. Adding the two interest payments together results in $26.61 (= $13.22 + $13.39). Thus, the total return is 3.23% = ($7.68 + $26.61)/$1,063.13.

Similar to Problems 7-7, 7-8, 7-19, 7-20, 7-33, 7-34

agency bonds Bonds issued by U.S. government agencies.

mortgage-backed securities Debt securities whose interest and par value payments originate from real estate mortgage payments.

these **agency bonds** to support particular sectors of the economy. Agency securities do not carry the federal government's full-faith-and-credit guarantee, but the government has never let one of its agencies fail. Because investors believe that the federal government will continue in this watchdog role, agency bonds are thought to be very safe and may provide a slightly higher return than Treasury securities do.

U.S. government agencies invented one popular type of debt security: **mortgage-backed securities** (MBSs). Fannie Mae and Freddie Mac offer subsidies or mortgage guarantees for people who wouldn't otherwise qualify for mortgages, especially first-time homeowners. Fannie Mae started out as a government-owned enterprise in 1938 and became a publicly held corporation in 1968. Freddie Mac was chartered as a publicly held corporation at its inception in 1970. Since 2008, both

have been in government conservatorship and run by the Federal Housing Finance Agency. To increase the amount of money available (liquidity) for the home mortgage market, Fannie Mae and Freddie Mac purchase home mortgages from banks, credit unions, and other lenders. They combine the mortgages into diversified portfolios of such loans and then issue mortgage-backed securities, which represent a share in the mortgage debt, to investors. As homeowners pay off or refinance the underlying portfolio of mortgage loans, MBS investors receive interest and principal payments. After selling mortgages to Fannie Mae or Freddie Mac, mortgage lenders have "new" cash to provide more mortgage loans. This process worked well for decades until the late 2000s, when subprime mortgages were given to people who couldn't afford them. As you know, defaults on these loans were the underpinnings of the financial crisis.

We could apply the same concept to any type of loan; indeed, the financial markets have already invented many such pooled-debt securities. Typical examples include credit card debt, auto loans, home equity loans, and equipment leases. Like

finance at work //: personal finance

Buy Treasuries Direct!

Treasury bonds are U.S. government-issued debt securities that investors trade on secondary markets. The government also issues nonmarketable debt, called "savings bonds," directly to investors. The common EE savings bonds, introduced in 1980, do not pay regular interest payments. Instead, interest accrues and adds to the bond's value. After a 1-year holding period, they can be redeemed at almost any bank or credit union. You can now purchase savings bonds and other Treasury securities (bills, notes, bonds, and TIPS) electronically through the U.S. Treasury's website, TreasuryDirect. You can set up an account in minutes and buy savings bonds with cash from your bank account. You can also redeem your bonds and transfer the proceeds back to your bank account. Bonds can be purchased 24 hours a day, 7 days a week at no cost.

When bondholders redeem savings bonds, they receive the original value paid plus the accrued interest. Paper bonds sell at half of the face value; if investors hold them for the full 30 years, they receive the par value. Investors buy electronic bonds at face value and earn interest in addition to the par value. Unlike other bonds, savers need not report income from these interest payments to the IRS until they actually redeem the bonds. So savings bonds count as tax-deferred investments.

About one in six Americans owns savings bonds. Savings bonds are used for a variety of purposes, such as personal savings

instruments or gifts from grandparents to grandchildren. After the September 11, 2001, terrorist attacks, many Americans wanted to show support for the government. In December 2001, banks selling government EE savings bonds began printing "Patriot bond" on them. So EE savings bonds are now often called Patriot Bonds.

Want to know more?

Key Words to Search for Updates: **TreasuryDirect (www.treasury direct.gov)** mortgage-backed securities, investors receive interest and principal from **asset-backed securities** as borrowers pay off their consumer loans. The asset-backed securities market is one of the fastest-growing areas in the financial services sector.

Reading Bond Quotes LG7-3

To those familiar with bond terminology, bond quotes provide all of the information needed to make informed investment decisions. The volume of Treasury securities traded each day is substantial. Treasury bonds and notes average more than a half billion dollars in trading daily. Investors exhibit much less enthusiasm for corporate or municipal bonds, perhaps because the markets for each particular bond or bonds with the same maturity, coupon rate, and credit ratings are much thinner and, therefore, less liquid. Most bond quote tables report only a small fraction of the outstanding bonds on any given day. Bond quotes can be found in *The Wall Street Journal* and online at

places like Yahoo! Finance (**yahoo. finance.com**) and BondsOnline (**www. bonds-online.com**). Table 7.2 shows three bond quote examples.

A typical listing for Treasury bonds appears first. Here, this Treasury bond pays bondholders a coupon of 2.75 percent. On a $1,000 par value bond, this interest income would be $27.50 annually, paid as $13.75 every six months per bond. The bond will mature in February of 2014—since this is fairly soon, the bond is considered a short-term bond. The "n" in the quote indicates that this bond was originally issued as a note (1–10 years maturity). Both the bid and the ask quotes for the bond appear, expressed as percentages of the bond's par value of $1,000. The bid price is the price at which investors can sell the bond. Numbers after the colon represent 32nds of 1 percent. A bid of 104:25 means that a buyer paid $1,047.81 (= $1,000 × 104 25/32%).

asset-backed securities Debt securities whose payments originate from other loans, such as credit card debt, auto loans, and home equity loans.

finance at work //: markets

Mortgage-Backed Securities and Financial Crisis

In the old days, a bank with $100,000 to lend would fund a mortgage and charge a fee for originating the loan. The bank would then collect interest on the loan over time. In the past few decades, the process changed to where that bank could sell that mortgage to investment banks and get the $100,000 back. The bank could then originate another mortgage and collect another fee. Bank revenue transitioned from interest earnings to fee earnings. This worked pretty well for several decades because the bank made more profits and more money was funneled into the community for home buyers. It is the securitization of debt that makes this possible. Financial institutions like Fannie Mae and investment banks bought up these mortgages, pooled them, and issued bonds against them (called mortgage-backed securities, or MBSs) to sell to investors. In effect, buyers of the MBSs are the actual lenders of the mortgage and banks simply earned fees for servicing the loans.

Note that this lending model gives banks and mortgage brokers the incentive to initiate as many mortgage loans as they can resell to maximize fee income. Then in 2000 to early 2004, the Federal Reserve kept adjusting interest rates on federal funds downward and kept them low. This both made home ownership more affordable, sparking a housing bubble, and drove investors to look for bonds that paid higher yields. Consequently, many loans were granted to individuals with poor creditworthiness (subprime

borrowers). These subprime borrowers were charged higher interest rates. When these subprime mortgages were packed into the pool of mortgages, the MBSs offered higher yields. Thus, there was a high demand from investors for these MBSs, which fostered more poor credit quality loan originations.

Then from July 2004 to July 2006, the Federal Reserve started increasing interest rates. This placed some downward pressure on housing prices because it made homes less affordable. At the same time, most subprime mortgages originating from 2005 and 2006 were written on adjustable rates, and those interest rates adjusted upward too, making the payments too high for many borrowers. The subprime borrowers soon began to fall behind on their monthly payments leading to foreclosures and additional downward pressure on housing prices. The devaluation of housing prices eroded the home equity of homeowners and led to further foreclosures and further price decreases. The MBSs also devalued quickly.

Who owns MBSs? It turns out that the owners of these securities are financial firms, such as investment banks, commercial banks, insurance companies, mutual funds and pension funds all over the world. Their weakened financial strength led to bank failures, bailouts and a global credit crisis.

Want to know more?

Key Words to Search for Updates: **subprime, MBS, financial crisis**

Source: Yuliya Demyanyk, and Otto Van Hemert, "Understanding the Subprime Mortgage Crisis," *Review of Financial Studies,* 2009.

premium bond
A bond selling for greater than its par value.

discount bond
A bond selling for lower than its par value.

Investors can buy this bond at the ask price of 104:26, or $1,048.13. Since the price is higher than the par value of the bond, the bond is selling at a premium to par because its coupon rate is higher than current rates. Thus, investors call this kind of security a **premium bond.**

Notice that the ask price is higher than the bid price. The difference is known as the bid-ask spread. Investors buy at the higher price and sell at the lower price. The bid-ask spread is thus the cost of actively trading bonds. Investors buy and sell

with a bond dealer. Since the bond dealer takes the opposite side of the transaction, the dealer buys at the low price and

▼**TABLE 7.2** Bond Quote Examples

Treasury Securities COUPON RATE	MO/YR	BID	ASKED	CHG	ASK YLD
2.750	Feb 14n	104:25	104:26	−3	0.898

Corporate Bond COMPANY	COUPON	MATURITY	LAST PRICE	YIELD	
CIT Group	7.00	May 2016	91.735	8.838	

Municipal Bond ISSUE	COUPON	MATURITY	PRICE		BID YLD
NYC Muni Wtr Fin Auth	4.500	06-15-37	97.570		4.66

EXAMPLE 7-3

Bond Quotes LG7-3

For interactive versions of this example visit www.mhhe.com/canM2e

You note the following bond quotes and wish to determine each bond's price, term, and interest payments.

Treasury Securities MATURITY RATE	MO/YR	BID	ASKED	CHG	ASK YLD
9.00	Nov 18	137:19	137:20	−5	4.80

Corporate Bond COMPANY	COUPON	MATURITY	LAST PRICE	LAST YIELD
Kohls Corp	7.375	Oct 15, 2011	110.01	4.991

Municipal Bond ISSUE	COUPON	MATURITY	PRICE	YLD TO MAT
Florida St Aquis & Bridge Constr	5.00	July 1, 2025	106.78	4.458

SOLUTION:

The Treasury bond matures in November of 2018 and pays 9 percent interest. Investors receive a cash interest payment of $45 (= 0.09 × $1,000 ÷ 2) semiannually. Since the bond matures in less than ten years but more than one year, we would consider it a mid-term bond. Since no "n" appears next to the maturity date, we can also tell that the security was issued as a bond that would mature in 30 years. Investors could sell this bond for $1,375.94 (= 137 $\frac{19}{32}$% × $1,000) and buy it for $1,376.25 (= 137 $\frac{20}{32}$% × $1,000 = 1.37625 × $1,000). The price fell on this particular day by $1.56 (= −$\frac{5}{32}$% × $1,000 = −0.0015625 × $1,000). The dealer earned $0.31 (= $1,376.25 − $1,375.94) on each trade of these premium bonds.

The Kohls corporate bond pays a semiannual interest payment of $36.88 (= 0.07375 × $1,000 ÷ 2) and its price is $1,100.10 (= 1.1001 × $1,000). This premium bond's 7.375% rate is likely well above market rates, which is why an investor would be willing to pay a premium for it.

The state of Florida issued the muni bond to fund bridge construction. With a $5,000 par value, the interest payments are $125 (= 0.05 × $5,000 ÷ 2) every six months. The bonds are priced at $5,339.00 (= 1.0678 × $5,000).

Similar to Problems 7-9, 7-10

sells at the higher price. The bid-ask spread is part of the dealer's compensation for taking on risk. An investor who bought this bond and held it to maturity would experience a $48.13 (= $1,048.13 − $1,000) capital loss (−4.59 percent [= −$48.13/$1,048.13]). The bond lost ³⁄₃₂ percent of its value during the day's trading—a change of −$0.94 for a $1,000 par value bond. Last, the bond is offering investors who purchase it at the ask price and hold it to maturity a 0.898 percent annual return.

Corporate bond quotes provide similar information. The table shows the quote for a CIT Group bond that offers bondholders a coupon of 7.00 percent, or $35.00 semiannually (= $1,000 × 0.07 ÷ 2). The bond would be considered a midterm bond (usually 5 years to maturity), since it matures in the year 2016. Corporate bonds are also quoted in percentage of par value, but (thankfully) the 32nds convention is not used. The price quote of 91.735 indicates that the last trade occurred at a price of $917.35 per bond. Since the bond is selling for a price lower than its $1,000 par value, it's called a **discount bond.** An investor who bought this bond would reap an $82.65 (= $1,000 − $917.35) capital gain if the bond were held to maturity. The CIT Group bond represents an annual return of 8.838 percent for the investor who purchases the bond at $917.35. Notice that this corporate bond offers a higher return than does the Treasury bond's 0.898 percent return. This price relationship is no coincidence; it is consistent with financial theory. CIT Group doesn't enjoy the luxury of virtually unlimited resources as the U.S. government does. The company therefore is more likely to have more difficulty paying back its debt than the U.S. government would have in repaying its bond. Since the CIT Group bond represents a riskier investment, it should offer investors a higher rate of return.

Companies set a bond's coupon rate when they originally issue the bond. A number of factors determine that coupon rate:

- The amount of uncertainty about whether the company will be able to make all the payments.

- The term of the loan.

- The level of interest rates in the overall economy at the time.

Bonds from different companies carry different coupon rates because some, or all, of these determining factors differ. Even a single company that has raised capital through bond issues many times may carry very different coupon rates on its various issues, because the bond issues would be offered in different years when the overall economic condition and interest rates differ.

Table 7.2 also shows a quote for a municipal bond issued by the New York City Municipal Water Finance Authority. This city government agency has raised capital by issuing municipal bonds to build reservoir facilities to provide water to New York City. The bond pays a 4.500 percent coupon, and since it matures in 2037, it's considered a long-term

bond. According to Table 7.2, the bond is trading at a price just below par value—97.57 percent. Most municipal bonds, unlike other bonds, feature a $5,000 face value rather than the typical par value of $1,000. So, the 97.57 percent price quote represents a dollar amount of $4,878.50 (= 0.9757 × $5,000). The low rate of return relative to Treasury bonds with similar maturities also has an explanation. Municipal bondholders do not have to pay federal income taxes on the interest payments that they receive from those securities. We explore this (sometimes) substantial advantage further in a later section of this chapter.

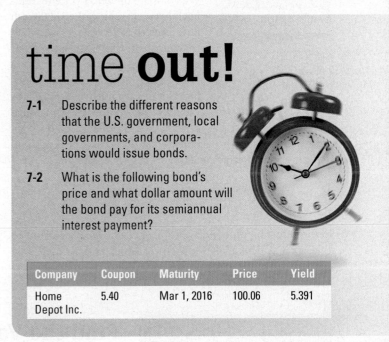

time out!

7-1 Describe the different reasons that the U.S. government, local governments, and corporations would issue bonds.

7-2 What is the following bond's price and what dollar amount will the bond pay for its semiannual interest payment?

Company	Coupon	Maturity	Price	Yield
Home Depot Inc.	5.40	Mar 1, 2016	100.06	5.391

BOND VALUATION

Present Value of Bond Cash Flows LG7-4

Any bond's value computation directly applies time value of money concepts. Bondholders know the interest payments that they are scheduled to receive and the repayment of the par value at maturity. The current price of a bond is, therefore, the *present value of these future cash flows discounted at the prevailing market interest rate.* The prevailing market interest rate will depend on the bond's term to maturity, credit quality, and tax status.

The simplest type of bond for time value of money calculations is a **zero coupon bond.** As you might guess from its name, a zero coupon bond makes no interest payments. Instead, the bond pays only the par value payment at its maturity date. So a zero coupon bond sells at a substantial discount from its par value. For example, a bond with a par value of $1,000, maturing in 20 years, and priced to yield 6 percent, might be purchased for about $306.56. At the end of 20 years, the bond investor will receive $1,000. The difference between $1,000 and $306.56 (which is $693.44) represents the interest income received over the 20 years based upon the discount rate of 6 percent. The time line for this zero coupon bond valuation appears as:

	6%				
Period	0	5	10	15	20 years
Cash flow	?				1,000

CALCULATOR HINTS

$N = 40$
$I = 3$
$PMT = 0$
$FV = 1000$
$CPT\ PV = -306.56$

We compute the zero's price by finding the present value of the $1,000 cash flow received in 20 years. However, to be consistent with regular coupon-paying bonds, zero coupon bonds are priced using semiannual compounding. So the formula and calculator valuation would use 40 semiannual periods at a 3 percent interest rate rather than 20 periods at 6 percent. Using the present value equation of Chapter 4 results in

$$PV = \frac{FV_N}{(1 + i)^N} = \frac{\$1,000}{1.03^{40}} = \frac{\$1,000}{3.262} = \$306.56$$

So the zero coupon bond's price is indeed a steep discount to its par value. This makes sense because investors would only buy a security that pays $1,000 in many years for a price that is much lower in order to make enough profit to make up for the forgone semiannual interest payments. For comparison's sake, instead of the 20-year zero, consider a 20-year bond with a 7 percent coupon. So this 20-year maturity bond pays $35 in interest payments every six months. We can think of these interest payments as an annuity stream. If the market discount rate is 6 percent annually, the time line appears as

						3%		Semiannual periods	
Period	0	1	2	3	4 ...	37	38	39	40
Cash flow	?	35	35	35	35 ···	35	35	35	35 1,000

The time line shows the 40 semiannual payments (with the accompanying semiannual interest rate at 3 percent) of $35 and the par value payment at the bond's maturity. Think through this: When bonds pay semiannual payments, the discount rate must be a semiannual rate. Thus, the 6 percent annual rate becomes a 3 percent semiannual rate. So we then compute the price of this bond by adding the present value of the interest payment annuity cash flow to the present value of the future par value. A combination of the present value equations for the annuity cash flows and the value of the par redemption appear in the bond valuation equation 7-1:

$$\begin{array}{ccc} \text{Present value} \\ \text{of bond} \end{array} = \begin{array}{c} \text{Present value of} \\ \text{interest payments} \end{array} + \begin{array}{c} \text{Present value of} \\ \text{of par value} \end{array}$$

$$= PMT \times \left[\frac{1 - \dfrac{1}{(1 + i)^N}}{i} \right] + \frac{\$1,000}{(1 + i)^N} \quad (7\text{-}1)$$

Similar to Problems 7-21, 7-22, 7-23, 7-24

EXAMPLE 7-4

For interactive versions of this example visit www.mhhe.com/canM2e

CALCULATOR HINTS

$N = 30$
$I = 3.25$
$PMT = 27.50$
$FV = 1000$
$CPT\ PV = -905.09$

Find the Value of a Bond LG7-4

Consider a 15-year bond that has a 5.5 percent coupon, paid semiannually. If the current market interest rate is 6.5 percent, and the bond is priced at $940, should you buy this bond?

SOLUTION:
Compute the value of the bond using equation 7.1. Use semiannual compounding ($N = 2 \times 15 = 30$, $I = 6.5 \div 2 = 3.25$, and $PMT = 0.055 \times \$1,000 \div 2 = \$27.50$) as:

$$\text{Bond value} = \$27.50 \times \left[\frac{1 - \dfrac{1}{(1 + 0.0325)^{30}}}{0.0325} \right] + \frac{\$1,000}{(1 + 0.0325)^{30}}$$

$$= \$522.00 + \$383.09 = \$905.09$$

So this bond's value is $905.09, which is less than the $940 price. The bond is overvalued in the market and you should not buy it.

Similar to Problems 7-21, 7-22, 7-23, 7-24

where *PMT* is the interest payment, *N* is the number of periods until maturity, and *i* is the market interest rate per period on securities with the same bond characteristics. If this bond paid interest annually, then these variables would take yearly period values. Since this bond pays semiannually, *PMT, N,* and *i* are all denoted in semiannual periods. The price of this coupon bond should be:

$$\text{Bond price} = \$35 \times \left[\frac{1 - \dfrac{1}{(1 + 0.03)^{40}}}{0.03} \right] + \frac{\$1,000}{(1 + 0.03)^{40}}$$

$$= \$809.017 + \$306.557 = \$1,115.57$$

Of the $1,115.57 bond price, most of the value comes from the semiannual $35 coupon payments ($809.017) and not the value from the future par value payment ($306.557).

Because equation 7-1 is quite complex, we usually compute bond prices using a financial calculator or computer program. An investor would compute the bond value using a financial calculator by entering $N = 40$, $I = 3$, PMT = 35, FV = 1000, and computing the present value (PV). The calculator solution is $1,115.57.[1]

Bond Prices and Interest Rate Risk LG7-5

At the time of purchase, the bond's interest payments and par value expected at maturity are fixed and known. Over time, economywide interest rates change, but the bond's coupon rate remains fixed. A rise in prevailing interest rates (also called

---

[1]In order to focus on the valuation concepts, we present these examples with the full six months until the bond's next interest payment. However, bonds can be sold anytime between interest payments. When this occurs, we simply add the interest accrued since the last payment to the price.

increasing the discount rate) reduces all bonds' values. If interest rates fall, all bonds will enjoy rising values. Consider that when interest rates rise, newly issued bonds offer to pay higher interest rates than the rates offered on existing bonds. So to sell an existing bond with its lower coupon rate, its market price must fall so that the buyer can expect a profit similar to that offered by newly issued bonds. Similarly, when prevailing interest rates fall, market prices for outstanding bonds rise to bring the offered return on older bonds with higher coupon rates into line with new issues. So market interest rates and bond prices are *inversely* related. That is, they move in opposite directions.

Figure 7.2 demonstrates how the price of a 30-year Treasury bond may change over time. The 11.7 percent coupon exactly matched prevailing interest rates when the bond was issued in 1980. Consequently, the bond sells for its par value of $1,000. Shortly thereafter, interest rates quickly rose to very high levels (over 15 percent) in the economy. As interest rates rose, bond prices had to decline. Then in 1984, interest rates started a prolonged descent to near 0 in 2009. Note that while a bond is issued at $1,000 and returns $1,000 at maturity, its price can vary a great deal in between. Bond investors must be aware that bond prices fluctuate on a day-to-day basis as interest rates fluctuate. Bondholders can incur large capital gains or capital losses.

The fact that, as prevailing interest rates change, the prices of existing bonds will change has a specific name in the financial industry—interest rate risk. **Interest rate risk** means that during periods when interest rates change substantially (and quickly), bondholders experience distinct gains and losses in their bond inventories. But interest rate risk does not affect all bonds exactly the same. Very short-term bonds experience little or no fluctuation in their prices, and thus expose the bondholder to little interest rate risk. Long-term bondholders experience substantial interest rate risk. Table 7.3 illustrates the impact of interest rate risk on bonds with different coupons and times to maturity.

The first four rows show the prices and price changes for 30-year bonds with different coupon rates. Notice that the bonds

the Math Coach on...

Bond Pricing and Periods

❝ Since most bonds have semiannual interest payments, we must use semiannual periods to discount the cash flows. Most errors in computing a bond price occur in the adjustment for semiannual periods. The errors happen whether you are using either the bond pricing equation or a financial calculator. To convert to semiannual periods, be sure to adjust the three variables: number of periods, interest rate, and payments.

The number of years needs to be multiplied by 2 for the number of semiannual periods. The interest rate should be divided by 2 for a 6-month rate. Divide the annual coupon payment by 2 for the 6-month payment. Remember to adjust all three inputs for the semiannual periods.

A coupon-paying bond's price should hover reasonably around the par value of the bond. For a $1,000 par value bond, we could expect a price in the range of $700 to $1,300. If you compute a price outside this range, check to see whether you made the semiannual period adjustments correctly. ❞

with higher coupon rates also have higher prices. Bondholders as a rule find it more valuable to receive the large annuity payments. Also notice that a 1 percent increase in interest rates from 6 percent to 7 percent causes bond prices to fall. Bondholders with higher coupon bonds are not affected as much by interest rate increases because they can take the large coupon payments and reinvest those cash flows in new bonds that offer higher returns.

The price decline is greater for bonds with lower coupons because of **reinvestment rate risk.** When interest rates increase, bondholders' cash flows—both periodic payments and final payoff at maturity—are discounted at a higher rate, decreasing a bond's value. Because the cash flows from low-coupon bonds are smaller, the holder of such bonds will have less money available from interest payments to buy the new, higher coupon bonds. Thus bondholders of lower coupon bonds have their capital tied up in assets that are not making them as much money. They face a bad dilemma: They can sell their lower coupon bonds and take a greater capital loss, using the (smaller) proceeds to buy new bonds with higher coupon rates. Or they can continue to receive the small income payments and hold their lower coupon bonds to maturity to avoid locking in the capital loss. Either way, they lose money relative to those bondholders with higher coupon rates. You can see this illustrated in the 30-year bonds shown in Table 7.3. Reinvestment rates tend to help partially offset changing discount rates for higher coupon paying bonds.

Another factor that influences the amount of reinvestment risk bondholders face is their bonds' time to maturity. The last four bonds in the table all have a 5 percent coupon but have different times to maturity. Note that when interest rates increase, the bond prices of longer-term bonds decline more than shorter-term bonds. This shows that bonds with longer maturities and lower coupons have the highest interest rate risk. Short-term bonds with high coupons have the lowest interest rate risk. High interest rate risk bonds experience considerable price

▼**TABLE 7.3** Interest Rate Risk

Time to Maturity	Coupon	Price at 6%	Price at 7%	Change
THE IMPACT OF THE COUPON RATE ON PRICE				
30 years	0%	$ 169.73	$ 126.93	−25.2%
30 years	5	861.62	750.55	−12.9
30 years	7	1,138.38	1,000.00	−12.2
30 years	10	1,553.51	1,374.17	−11.5
THE IMPACT OF TIME TO MATURITY ON PRICE				
20 years	5	884.43	786.45	−11.1
10 years	5	925.61	857.88	−7.3
5 years	5	957.35	916.83	−4.2
2 years	5	981.41	963.27	−1.8

▼**FIGURE 7.2** A Demonstration of the Price and Market Interest Rate over Time of a 30-Year Treasury Bond Issued in 1980 with a Coupon of 11.7 Percent

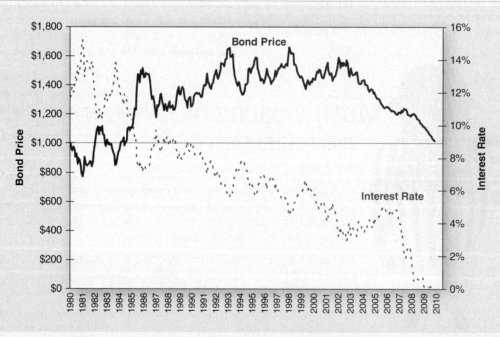

As interest rates rise, bond prices fall. Here you can see great variance in the economy over 30 years. Long-term bondholders experience substantial interest rate risk.

declines when interest rates are rising. However, these bonds also experience dramatic capital gains when interest rates are falling. While a 1 percent change in market interest rates is not commonly seen on a daily or monthly basis, such a change is not unusual over the course of several months or a year.

BOND YIELDS

Current Yield

Although we speak about "the prevailing interest rate," bond relationships reflect many interest rates (also called *yields*). Some rates are difficult to calculate but accurately reflect the return the bond is offering. Others, like the **current yield,** are easy to compute but only approximate the bond's true return. A bond's current yield is defined as the bond's annual coupon rate divided by the bond's current market price. Current yield measures the rate of return a bondholder would earn annually from the coupon interest payments alone if the bond were purchased at a stated price. Current yield does not measure the total expected return because it does not account for any capital gains or losses that will occur from purchasing the bond at a discount or premium to par.

Yield to Maturity LG7-6

Yield to maturity is a more meaningful equation for investors than the simple current yield calculation. The yield to maturity calculation tells bond investors the total rate of return that they

current yield Return from interest payments; computed as the annual interest payment divided by the current bond price.

yield to maturity The total return the bond offers if purchased at the current price and held to maturity.

time out!

7-3 Show the time line and compute the present value for an 8.5 percent coupon bond (paid semiannually) with 12 years left to maturity and a market interest rate of 7.5 percent.

7-4 Describe the relationship between interest rate changes and bond prices.

 EXAMPLE 7-5

Capital Gains in the Bond Market LG7-5

For interactive versions of this example visit www.mhhe.com/canM2e

Say that you anticipate falling long-term interest rates from 6 percent to 5.5 percent during the next year. If this occurs, what will be the total return for a 20-year, 6.5 percent coupon bond through the interest rate decline?

SOLUTION:
To determine the total return, compute the capital gain or loss and the interest paid over the year. The capital gain or loss is determined from the change in price. The current bond price is:

$$\text{Bond price} = \$32.50 \times \left[\frac{1 - \frac{1}{(1 + 0.03)^{40}}}{0.03} \right] + \frac{\$1,000}{(1 + 0.03)^{40}}$$

$$= \$751.230 + \$306.557 = \$1,057.79$$

The price in one year would be:

$$\text{Bond price} = \$32.50 \times \left[\frac{1 - \frac{1}{(1 + 0.0275)^{38}}}{0.0275} \right] + \frac{\$1,000}{(1 + 0.0275)^{38}}$$

$$= \$760.276 + \$356.690 = \$1,116.97$$

So, the capital gain is $59.18 (= $1,116.97 − $1,057.79). The interest payment during the year is $65 (= 0.065 × $1,000). If interest rates fall to 5.5 percent, then this bond should provide a total return of $124.18, which would be an 11.74 percent return (= $124.18 ÷ $1,057.79). Of course, this is only an anticipated interest rate change and it may not occur.

Similar to Problems 7-25, 7-26, 7-35, 7-36

```
■ ■ ■ ■ ■
CALCULATOR HINTS

Ⓝ = 40
Ⓘ = 3
PMT = 32.50
FV = −1,057.79

CPT PV = 21,057.79

THEN CHANGE

Ⓝ = 38
Ⓘ = 2.75

CPT PV = −1,116.97
```

might expect if the bond were bought at a particular price and held to maturity. While the yield to maturity calculation provides more information than the current yield calculation, it's also more difficult to compute, because we must compute the bond's cash flows' internal rate of return. This calculation seeks to equate the bond's current market price with the value of all anticipated future interest and par value payments. In other words, it is the discount rate that equates the present value of all future cash flows with the current price of the bond. To calculate yield to maturity, investors must solve for the interest rate, i, in equation 7-2, or solve for i in:

$$\text{Bond price} = \text{PV of annuity}\,(PMT, i, N) + PV(FV, i, N) \quad (7\text{-}2)$$

Investors commonly compute the yield to maturity using financial calculators. For example, consider a 7 percent coupon bond (paid semiannually) with eight years to maturity and a current price of $1,150. The return that the bond offers investors, the yield to maturity, is computed as $N = 16$, $PV = -1150$, $PMT = 35$, and $FV = 1000$. Computing the interest rate (I) gives us 2.363 percent. We must remember, however, that 2.363 percent is only the return for six months because the bond pays semiannually. Yield to maturity always means an annual return. So, this bond's yield to maturity is 4.73 percent (2×2.363 percent).

Notice the link between a bond's yield to maturity and the prevailing market interest rates used to determine a bond's price as we discussed in the previous section. We use the market interest rate to compute the bond's value. We use the actual bond price to compute its yield to maturity. If the bond is correctly priced at its economic value, then the market interest rate will equal the yield to maturity. Thus, the relationship that we previously identified between bond prices and market interest rates applies to yields as well. This shows the inverse relationship between bond prices and bond yields. As a bond's price falls, its yield to maturity increases and a rising bond price accompanies a falling yield. Look back at Figure 7.2 and you will see this relationship clearly.

Yield to Call

The yield to maturity computation assumes that the bondholder will hold the bond to its maturity. But remember that many bonds have call provisions that allow the issuers to repay the bondholder's par value prior to its scheduled maturity. Issuers often call bonds after large drops in market interest rates. In such cases, issuers commonly pay bondholders the bond's par value plus one year of interest payments. The reasons behind early bond redemptions are obvious. When interest rates fall, issuers can sell new bonds at lower interest rates. Companies want to refinance their debt—just as homeowners do—to reduce their interest payments.

Issuers gain important advantages with call provisions because they allow refinancing opportunities. Of course, the same provisions are disadvantages for bond investors. When bonds are called, investors receive the par value and call premium, but then investors must seek equally profitable bonds to buy with the proceeds. You will recall that investors can face reinvestment risk—the available bonds aren't as profitable because interest rates have declined. Bonds are called away at the worst time for investors. In addition, bond prices will rise as market interest rates fall, which

---

Computing Current Yield and Yield to Maturity LG7-6

You have identified a 3.5 percent Treasury bond with four years left to maturity and a quoted price of 96:09. Calculate the bond's current yield and yield to maturity.

SOLUTION:

(1) First, identify that the bond's price is $962.81 (= 96 09/32% × $1,000 = 0.9628125 × $1,000).
(2) The annual $35 in interest payments is paid in two $17.50 semiannual payments. Therefore, the current yield of the bond is 3.64 percent (= $35 ÷ $962.81).
(3) The yield to maturity is computed using equation 7-2 and the financial calculator as $N = 8$, $PV = -962.81$, $PMT = 17.50$, and $FV = 1,000$. Computing the interest rate (I) results in 2.263 percent and multiplying by 2 gives the yield to maturity of 4.53 percent.
(4) Note that the current yield is less than the yield to maturity because it does not account for the capital gain to be earned if held to maturity.

Similar to Problems 7-13, 7-14, 7-27, 7-28

could provide issuers opportunities to sell the bonds at a profit. But the price increases will be limited by the fact that the bond will likely be called early. The possibility that bonds can be called early dampens their upside price potential. We can even compute the price of a bond that's likely to be called from the equation:

the
Math Coach on...
Bond Yields and Financial Calculators

❝ People computing a bond's yield to maturity make three common mistakes. To avoid the first mistake, ensure that the bond price (PV) is a different sign than the interest and par value cash flows (PMT and FV). The second mistake: People forget to make the number of periods (N) and the per-period interest payment (PMT) consistent. Both should be in semiannual terms if the coupon payment is paid semiannually. Last, many people forget to multiply the resulting calculator interest rate (I) output by 2 to convert the semiannual rate back to an annual rate. ❞

$$\frac{\text{Price of a}}{\text{callable bond}} = \frac{\text{Present value of interest}}{\text{payments to call date}} + \frac{\text{Present value of}}{\text{of call price}}$$

$$= PMT \times \left[\frac{1 - \dfrac{1}{(1+i)^N}}{i}\right] + \frac{\text{Call price}}{(1+i)^N} \qquad (7\text{-}3)$$

In this case, N is the number of periods until the bond can be called and i is the prevailing market rate. The prevailing market interest rate will probably differ from the rate for a noncallable bond. The previous section demonstrated via the yield curve that bonds with different maturities have different yields. A bond that matures in 20 years, but is likely to be called in five years, will carry a yield appropriate for a 5-year bond.

Now, reconsider the 20-year bond with a 7 percent coupon that we discussed previously (see p. 165). If the bond can be called in five years with a call price of $1,070, the appropriate discount rate happens to be 5.75 percent annually at that time (instead of the 6 percent in the original problem). This time line would be

					2.875%			Semiannual periods	
Period	0	1	2	3	4 ... 7	8	9	10	
Cash flow	?	35	35	35	35 ··· 35	35	35	35	
								1,070	

The changes in this time line are only 10 semiannual payments of $35 (rather than 40 such semiannual payments), a 2.875 percent semiannual discount rate, and the call price payment of $1,070. The price of this callable bond would be:

$$\frac{\text{Bond}}{\text{price}} = \$35 \times \left[\frac{1 - \dfrac{1}{(1+0.02875)^{10}}}{0.02875}\right] + \frac{\$1,070}{(1+0.02875)^{10}}$$

$$= \$300.47 + \$805.91 = \$1,106.38$$

In this example, the callable bond would be priced at $1,106.38, which is slightly lower than an identical bond that was not callable, priced at $1,115.57.

If a bond is likely to be called, then the yield to maturity calculation does not give investors a good estimate of their return. Bondholders can use instead a **yield to call** calculation, which differs from the yield to maturity only in that its calculation assumes that the investor will receive the par value and call premium at the earliest call date.

CALCULATOR HINTS

N = 10
I = 2.875
PMT = 35
FV = 1070
CPT PV = −1,106.38

For example, reconsider the 7 percent coupon bond (paid semiannually) with 8 years to maturity, which we examined previously (see p. 168). The current bond price is $1,130 (which is slightly lower than the yield to maturity bond price of $1,150). If the bond can be called in three years at a specific call price of the par value plus one annual coupon, then what is the yield to call? The yield to call is computed as $N = 6$, $PV = -1130$, $PMT = 35$, and $FV = 1070$. The resulting interest rate (I) is 2.26 percent. The yield to call for this bond is thus 4.52 percent ($= 2 \times 2.26\%$).

Municipal Bonds and Yield

Municipal bonds (munis) seem to offer low yields to maturity compared to the return that corporate bonds and Treasury securities offer. Munis offer lower rates because the interest income they generate for investors is tax-exempt—at least at the federal level.[2] Specifically, income from municipal bonds is not subject to taxation by the federal government or the state government where the bonds are issued. As a result, municipal bond investors willingly accept lower yields than

[2]States have differing rules about whether they tax the income from a particular municipal bond—they will generally tax income from munis issued out of state. Further, capital gains arising from municipal bond sales may be taxed, and the income from municipal bonds must be added to overall income when determining the Alternative Minimum Tax consequences.

the Math Coach on...

Spreadsheets and Bond Pricing

Common spreadsheet programs have functions that can compute the price or yield to maturity of a bond. The functions are:

Compute a bond price =

PRICE(settlement,maturity,rate,yld,redemption,frequency,basis)

Compute a yield to maturity =

YIELD(settlement,maturity,rate,pr,redemption,frequency,basis)

Settlement is the bond's settlement date. This is the purchase date of the bond; typically it is today. *Maturity* is the bond's maturity date. *Rate* is the bond's annual coupon rate. *Pr* is the bond's price per $100 face value. Note that the par value of a bond is typically $1,000, so an adjustment is needed for this input. *Redemption* is the bond's redemption value per $100 face value. *Frequency* is the number of coupon payments per year. For semiannual, frequency = 2. *Basis* is the type of day count basis to use.

Consider the bond valuation problem of Example 7-4. The spreadsheet solution is the same as the TVM calculator solution and the pricing equation.

	A	B	C	D	E
1					
2	Settlement date	11/15/2011	=DATE(2011,11,15)		
3	Maturity date	11/15/2026	=DATE(2026,11,15)		
4	Coupon Rate	5.50%			
5	Interest rate (Yld)	6.50%			
6	Redemption	100			
7	Frequency	2			
8					
9	Bond price (per $100 par value) =	$90.51	=PRICE(B2,B3,B4,B5,B6,B7,1)		
10	Bond price (per $1000 par value) =	$905.09	=10*B9		

Also consider the yield to maturity problem in Example 7-6. This spreadsheet solves for the yield to maturity.

	A	B	C	D	E
1					
2	Settlement date	11/15/2011	=DATE(2011,11,15)		
3	Maturity date	11/15/2015	=DATE(2015,11,15)		
4	Coupon Rate	3.50%			
5	Bond Price	96.28			
6	Redemption	100			
7	Frequency	2			
8					
9	Yield to Maturity =	4.53%	=YIELD(B2,B3,B4,B5,B6,B7,1)		

See this textbook's online student center to watch instructional videos on using spreadsheets. Also note that the solutions for all the examples in the book are illustrated using spreadsheets in videos that are also available on the textbook website.

EXAMPLE 7-7

For interactive versions of this example visit www.mhhe.com/canM2e

Which Bond Has a Better After-Tax Yield? LG7-6

Imagine a time when you have a high income, placing you in the 31 percent marginal tax bracket. You are interested in investing some money in a bond issue and have three alternatives. The first is a corporate bond with a 6.4 percent yield to maturity. The second bond is a Treasury that offers a 5.7 percent yield. The third choice is a municipal bond priced at a yield to maturity of 4.0 percent. Which bond gives you the highest after-tax yield?

SOLUTION:

The Treasury and corporate bonds are both taxable, so we can compare them directly with each other. The yield of 6.4 percent on the corporate bond is clearly higher than the 5.7 percent yield offered by the Treasury bond. To include a comparison with the nontaxable municipal bond, compute its equivalent taxable yield as in equation 7-4:

$$\text{Equivalent taxable yield} = \frac{4.0\%}{1 - 0.31} = 5.80\%$$

The municipal bond's equivalent taxable yield of 5.80 percent is higher than the Treasury but lower than the corporate bond.

Similar to Problems 7-15, 7-16, 7-31, 7-32, 7-37, 7-38

those they can obtain from taxable bonds. Generally speaking, investors compare the after-tax interest income earned on taxable bonds against the return earned on municipal bonds. For example, suppose an investor in the 35 percent *marginal* income tax bracket has $100,000 to invest in either corporate or municipal bonds. The $100,000 investment would earn a taxable $7,000 annually from 7 percent corporate bonds or $5,000 from tax-exempt 5 percent municipal bonds. After taxes, the corporate bond leaves the investor with $4,550 [=(1 − 0.35) × $7,000]. Obviously, this is less than the tax-free income of $5,000 generated by the muni bond.

A common way to compare yields from muni bonds versus those from taxable bonds is to convert the yield to maturity of the muni to a **taxable equivalent yield,** as shown in equation 7-4.

$$\text{Equivalent taxable yield} = \frac{\text{Muni yield}}{1 - \text{Tax rate}} \qquad (7\text{-}4)$$

For high-income investors (in the 35 percent marginal tax bracket) a 5 percent muni bond has an equivalent taxable yield of 7.69 percent [= 0.05 ÷ (1 − 0.35)]. The 5 percent muni is more attractive for this investor than a 7 percent corporate bond. However, for an investor with lower income (in the 28 percent marginal tax bracket) the equivalent taxable yield is only 6.94 percent. The corporate bond provides more after-tax profit than the muni for this investor. It's easy to see why muni bonds are popular among high-income investors (those with substantial marginal tax rates).

Summarizing Yields

In this section, we have presented several different types of interest rates, or yields, associated with bonds. See a summary in Table 7.4. Many of these yields relate to one another. Consider the bonds and associated yields reported in Table 7.5. Treasury bonds (1) to (3) show how coupon rates, current yield, and yield to maturity relate. When a bond trades at its par value (usually $1,000), then the coupon rate, current yield, and yield to maturity are all the same. When that bond is priced at a premium (bond 2), then both the current yield and the yield to maturity will be lower than the coupon rate. They are both higher than the coupon rate when the bond trades at a discount. Notice that yield to maturity is higher than current yield for discount bonds, and that yield to maturity is lower than current yield for premium bonds. In other words, the current yield always lies between the coupon rate and the yield to maturity. Both the current yield and the yield to maturity move in the opposite direction to the bond's price.

Bonds (4) to (6) are callable corporate bonds. Recall that all the yields (current yield, yield to maturity, and yield to call) are identical when the bond trades at par value. When interest rates fall and bond prices increase, as with bond (5), the issuing corporation has a strong incentive to call the bond after five years, as allowed in the indenture agreement. So investors should base their purchase decisions on the yield to call. When interest rates increase, bond prices decline (as bond (6) shows). In this case, investors could compute the yield to call (as shown), but the

taxable equivalent yield Modification of a municipal bond's yield to maturity used to compare muni bond yields to taxable bond yields.

▼ **TABLE 7.4** Summary of Interest Rates

Interest Rate	Purpose	Description
Coupon rate	Compute bond cash interest payments	The coupon rate is reported as a bond characteristic. It is reported as a percentage and is multiplied by the par value of the bond to determine the annual cash interest payment. The coupon rate will not change through the life of the bond.
Current yield	Quick assessment of the interest rate a bond is offering	Computed as the annual interest payment divided by the current price of the bond. It measures the return to be expected from just the interest payments if the bond was purchased at the current price. Since the bond price may change daily, the current yield will change daily.
Yield to maturity	Accurate measurement of the interest rate a bond is offering	The return offered by the bond if purchased at the current price. This return includes both the expected income and capital gain/loss if held to the maturity date. The yield to maturity will change daily as the bond price changes.
Yield to call	Interest rate obtained if the bond is called	Same as the yield to maturity except that it is assumed that the bond will be called at the earliest date it can be called.
Taxable equivalent yield	Comparison of nontaxable bond yields to taxable bond yields	Investors must pay taxes on most types of bonds. However, municipal bonds are tax free. To compare the muni's nontaxable yield to maturity to that of taxable bonds, divide the yield by one minus the investor's marginal tax rate.
Market interest rate	Comparison of prices of all bonds	The interest rate determined by the bond prices of actual trades between buyers and sellers. The market interest rate will be different for bonds of different times to maturity and different levels of risk.
Total return	Determine realized performance of an investment	Realized return that includes both income and capital gain/loss profits.

compute the municipal bond's taxable equivalent yield first. Here, we use a marginal tax rate of 35 percent in the calculation. The last column of the table shows that the taxable equivalent yield of the municipal bonds is really quite competitive with corporate bond yields. Any investor with income taxed at the 35 percent marginal tax bracket would prefer the municipal bond over the corporate bond if the muni's taxable equivalent yield is higher than the yield to maturity (or yield to call) of the corporate bond.

The table also shows that Treasury securities offer lower yields than corporate bonds with similar terms to maturity. The difference (or spread) between Treasury and corporate yields gives rise to a discussion of bond credit risk, which follows.

time out!

7-5 Calculate the yield to maturity for a zero coupon bond with a price of $525 and ten years left to maturity.

7-6 Which is higher for a discount bond, the yield to maturity or the coupon rate? Why?

Bonds issued for municipal projects tend to offer lower yields because their income is tax exempt.

information isn't useful because the company will not likely call the bond while interest rates are high.

The last three bonds shown in the table are municipal bonds. Recall that these bonds typically offer lower yields because the income from munis is tax exempt. It is easier to compare municipal bonds with Treasuries and corporate bonds if you

CREDIT RISK

Bond Ratings LG7-7

Will a bond issuer make the promised interest and par value payments over the next 10, 20, or even 30 years? **Credit quality risk** is the chance that the bond issuer will not be able to make timely payments. To assess this risk, independent **bond rating** agencies, such as Moody's and Standard & Poor's, monitor corporate, U.S. agency, or municipal developments during the bond's lifetime and report their findings as a grade or rating. The U.S. government issues the highest credit quality debt, though that consensus has recently come into doubt as the U.S. debt and budget deficit have ballooned.

▼ **TABLE 7.5** Price, Coupon, and Yield Relationships of a 10-Year Bond

	Price	Coupon Rate	Current Yield	Yield to Maturity	Yield to Call (In 5 Years)	Taxable Equivalent Yield (35% Tax Rate)
(1) Treasury	$1,000.00	5%	5%	5%		5%
(2) Treasury	1,100.00	5	4.55	3.79		3.79
(3) Treasury	900.00	5	5.56	6.37		6.37
(4) Corporate	1,000.00	6	6	6	6%	6
(5) Corporate	1,110.00	6	5.41	4.61	4.59	4.61
(6) Corporate	900.00	6	6.67	7.44	9.52	7.44
(7) Muni	1,000.00	4	4	4		6.15
(8) Muni	1,100.00	4	3.64	2.84		4.37
(9) Muni	900.00	4	4.44	5.30		8.16

Call price = Par value + One year's interest

Bond credit rating agencies in the United States include Moody's Investors Service, Standard & Poor's Corporation, Fitch IBCA Inc., Dominion Bond Rating Service, and A.M. Best Co. Each of these credit analysis firms assigns similar ratings based on detailed analyses of issuers' financial condition, general economic and credit market conditions, and the economic value of any underlying collateral. The Standard & Poor's ratings are shown in Table 7.6. Their highest credit-quality rating is AAA. Bonds rated AAA, AA, A, or BBB are considered **investment grade** bonds. The issuers of these securities have the highest chance of making all interest and par value payments promised in the indenture agreement.

The investment community considers bonds rated BB and below to be below-investment grade bonds, and some investors, such as pension funds or other fiduciaries, cannot purchase these securities for their portfolios. These bonds are considered to be speculative because they carry a significant risk that the issuer will not make current or future payments. Speculative bonds are sometimes called **junk bonds** because of this risk. In order to attract buyers, issuers sell these bonds at a considerable discount from par and a high associated yield to maturity. Agencies often enhance ratings from "AA" to "CCC" with the addition of a plus (+) or minus (−) sign to show relative standing within the major rating categories. For example, Black Hills Corporation, an electrical power company, saw its bonds upgraded from BBB− to BBB + by Standard & Poor's on July 14, 2010. On the other hand, on July 13, Moody's downgraded Portugal's government bonds from Aa2 to A1. These rating changes impact not only the current prices of these bonds, but also the interest rate Black Hills and Portugal would have to pay if they issued new bonds.

Standard & Poor's signals that it's considering a rating change by placing an individual bond, or all of a given issuer's bonds, on CreditWatch (S&P). Rating agencies make their ratings information available to the public through their ratings information desks. In addition to published reports, ratings are made available in many public libraries and over the Internet.

Credit rating agencies conduct general economic analyses of companies' business and analyze firms' specific financial situations. A single company may carry several outstanding bond issues. If these issues feature fundamental differences, then they may have different credit level risks. For example, **unsecured corporate bonds,** or **debentures,** are backed only by the reputation

credit quality risk The chance that the issuer will not make timely interest payments or even default.

bond rating A grade of credit quality as reported by credit rating agencies.

investment grade High credit quality corporate bonds.

junk bonds Low credit quality corporate bonds, also called speculative bonds or high-yield bonds.

unsecured corporate bonds Corporate debt not secured by collateral such as land, buildings, or equipment.

debentures Unsecured bonds.

▼ **TABLE 7.6** Standard & Poor's Bond Credit Ratings

Credit Risk	Credit Rating	Description
Investment Grade		
Highest quality	AAA	The obligor's (issuer's) capacity to meet its financial commitment on the obligation is extremely strong.
High quality	AA	The obligor's capacity to meet its financial commitment on the obligation is very strong.
Upper medium grade	A	The obligor's capacity to meet its financial commitment on the obligation is still strong, though somewhat susceptible to the adverse effects of changes in circumstances and economic conditions.
Medium grade	BBB	The obligor exhibits adequate protection. However, adverse economic conditions or changing circumstances are more likely to lead to a weakened capacity to meet its financial commitment.
Below Investment Grade		
Somewhat speculative	BB	Faces major ongoing uncertainties or exposure to adverse business, financial, or economic conditions which could lead to the obligor's inadequate capacity to meet its financial commitment.
Speculative	B	Adverse business, financial, or economic conditions will likely impair the obligor's capacity or willingness to meet its financial commitment.
Highly speculative	CCC	Currently vulnerable to nonpayment, and is dependent upon favorable business, financial, and economic conditions for the obligor to meet its financial commitment.
Most speculative	CC	Currently highly vulnerable to nonpayment.
Imminent default	C	Bankruptcy petition has been filed or similar action taken, but payments on this obligation are being continued.
Default	D	Obligations are in default or the filing of a bankruptcy petition has occurred and payments are jeopardized.

Source: Standard & Poor's Web page.

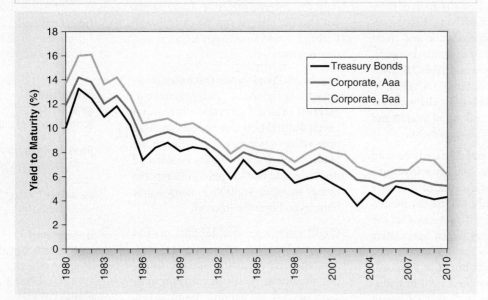

Looking at the historical yields for long-term Treasury and corporate bonds, notice how the yield spread between high- and low-quality bonds varies substantially over time.

Differences in credit risk are a prime source of differences in yields between government and various corporate bonds. Figure 7.3 shows the historical average annual yields for long-term Treasury bonds and corporate bonds with credit ratings of Aaa and Baa since 1980. Riskier low-quality bonds always offer a higher yield than the higher quality bonds. However, the yield spread between high- and low-quality bonds varies substantially over time. The yield difference between Baa bonds and Treasuries was as high as 3.7 percent and 3.3 percent in 1982 and 2003, respectively. The spread has been as narrow as 1.3 percent and 1.4 percent in 1994 and 2006, respectively.

How do some corporations' debt obligations become junk bonds? Some companies that aren't economically sound or those that use a high degree of financial leverage issue junk bonds. In other cases, financially strong companies issue investment grade bonds and then, over time, begin to have trouble. Eventually a company's bonds can be downgraded to junk status. For example, General Motors (GM) bonds were considered of the highest quality from the 1950s through the 1980s and much of the 1990s. On May 9, 2005, Standard & Poor's downgraded GM bonds to junk status. Junk bonds that were originally issued at investment grade status are called *fallen angels*. GM eventually filed for bankruptcy protection in June 2009.

and financial stability of the corporation. A **senior bond** has a priority claim over junior (more recently issued) securities in the event of default or bankruptcy. So, senior bonds carry less credit risk than junior bonds. Some bonds are secured with collateral. When you buy a car using a loan, the car is collateral for that loan. If you don't make the loan payments, the bank will repossess the car. Companies can also offer collateral when issuing bonds. When a firm uses collateral such as real estate or factory equipment, the bonds are called **mortgage bonds** or **equipment trust certificates,** respectively. Bonds issued with no collateral generally carry higher credit risk.

Credit Risk and Yield

Investors will only purchase higher risk bonds if those securities offer higher returns. Therefore, issuers price bonds with high credit risk to offer high yields to maturity. So another common name for junk bonds is **high-yield bonds.**

Bonds that experience credit-rating downgrades must offer a higher yield. As all the future cash flows are fixed, the bond price must fall to create a higher yield to maturity. Alternatively, bonds that are upgraded experience price increases and yield decreases. Bond upgrades often occur during strong economic periods because corporate issuers tend to perform better financially at these times. In a weak economy, high-yield bonds lose their luster because the default risk rises. More credit downgrades occur during economic recessions.

time out!

7-7 Explain why a change in a bond's credit rating will cause its price to change.

7-8 One company has issued two bond classes. One issue is a mortgage bond and the other is a debenture. Which issue will have a higher bond rating and which will offer a higher yield?

BOND MARKETS LG7-8

The majority of trading volume in the bond market occurs in a decentralized, over-the-counter market. Most trades occur between bond dealers and large institutions (like mutual funds, pension funds, and insurance companies). Dealers bid for bonds that investors seek to sell and offer bonds from their own inventory when investors want to buy. This is especially true for the very active Treasury securities market. However, a small number of corporate bonds are listed on centralized exchanges.

The NYSE operates the largest centralized U.S. bond market. The majority of bond volume at the NYSE is in corporate debt. The

senior bonds Older bonds that carry a higher claim to the issuer's assets.

mortgage bonds Bonds secured with real estate as collateral.

equipment trust certificates Bonds secured with factory and equipment as collateral.

high-yield bonds Bonds with low credit quality that offer a high yield to maturity, also called junk bonds.

finance at work //: markets

A Greek Tragedy: Debt Crisis

Greece joined the European monetary union in 2000, which means the euro replaced drachmas as the national currency. The euro was a much stronger currency than the drachma because it was backed by the economic prosperity of the whole European Union. Hence, the Greek government was able to borrow from foreign investors at much lower interest rates. This contributed to the ensuing economic boom and expansion of government spending in Greece.

The Greek government has long been operating on high budget deficits and borrowing. But the problems really began in the Fall of 2009 when the new elected government found that it had inherited a financial burden that was much larger than previously reported. The budget deficit was revised to be larger than 13 percent of the size of the economy. The revelation of these huge government deficits and debts cast enormous doubt on the ability of the Greek government to pay its debts.

This increase in risk was reflected on December 8, 2009, by the downgrade to BBB (lowest in the Euro Zone) of the Sovereign bond of Greece by the Fitch credit rating firm. Standard & Poor's and Moody's both downgraded Greece Sovereigns to junk bond status in May and June of 2010. As a consequence, Greece found that it was difficult to borrow more money and had to offer lenders yields of as much as 12 percent and a financial crisis developed.

In order to restore investor confidence, the Greek government has pledged to an austerity plan that cuts spending and reduces the

budget deficit. However, the success of the plans has been undermined by strong domestic opposition as illustrated by strikes and even riots. As a temporary solution, the European Union and the International Monetary Fund together offered a large loan package to help out Greece. Then in March of 2012, Greece defaulted on part of its debt. The process was termed "restructuring" so as to be less inflammatory. Even so, Greece's debts and budget deficit remain too high. These events are likely to continue to unfold over the next few years and other countries may find themselves in similar trouble.

Want to know more?

Key Words to Search for Updates: **Greek bonds, Greek debt crisis**

Issuer Name	Symbol	Coupon	Maturity	Rating Moody's/S&P/ Fitch	High	Low	Last	Change	Yield %
CITIGROUP FUNDING	C.HTH	1.875%	Nov 2012	Aaa/AAA/AAA	102.148	101.534	102.119	0.165	0.950
KRAFT FOODS	KFT.GZ	6.500%	Feb 2040	Baa2/BBB-/BBB-	112.001	108.559	111.488	1.180	5.692
CITIGROUP	C.HRY	8.500%	May 2019	A3/A/A+	124.101	121.752	122.314	0.182	5.304
BP CAPITAL MARKETS PLC	BP.JM	1.550%	Aug 2011	A2/A/BBB	98.375	96.200	97.719	-0.131	3.762
BP CAPITAL MARKETS PLC	BP.JH	3.875%	Mar 2015	A2/A/BBB	93.774	91.453	93.332	-0.518	5.522
DOW CHEMICAL CO	DOW.TY	8.550%	May 2019	Baa3/BBB-/BBB	123.402	121.500	122.132	-0.191	5.366
JPMORGAN CHASE & CO	JPM.MXL	4.950%	Mar 2020	Aa3/A+/AA-	107.223	104.799	105.504	-1.000	4.250
ALTRIA GP	MO.HC	9.700%	Nov 2018	Baa1/BBB/BBB+	130.380	126.696	128.639	0.194	5.378
PFIZER	PFE.GQ	5.350%	Mar 2015	A1/AA/AA-	113.465	111.682	113.348	0.253	2.309
BANK OF AMERICA CORP	BAC.BP	5.625%	Jul 2020	A2/A/A+	105.051	101.400	102.902	0.379	N/A

This is an example of the most actively traded bonds for a given day on the New York Stock Exchange.
Source: *The Wall Street Journal Online.*

most actively traded bonds for the day are shown in Figure 7.4. Even the most active corporate bonds experience relatively low trading volume. Note that some of the bonds traded are short-term, like Citigroup Funding and one of the BP Capital Markets issues. Other bonds have many years to maturity, like the Kraft Foods bond that matures in February 2040. This Kraft bond is not rated very higly, offers a 6.5 percent coupon rate, and is currently priced for a 5.69 percent yield to maturity.

Following the Bond Market

The entire bond market encompasses a wide variety of securities with varying credit quality from different issuers. Large differences also arise among bonds in terms of their characteristics such as term to maturity and size of the coupon. The biggest factor associated with changes in bond prices is changes in interest rates. So, one common way to describe the direction of bond prices is simply to report the change in interest rates, since we know that interest rate changes will affect all bonds the same way. The interest rate referenced is the yield to maturity and daily yield change for the 10-year Treasury. Knowing how this interest rate changed today gives bond investors a good idea of the general price movement of all types of bonds.

Bond indexes track specific segments of the bond market. Various securities firms, such as Barclays Capital or Merrill Lynch,

maintain these indexes that capture bond price and yield changes in particular segments. You can find information about major bond indexes on the Internet and in publications like *The Wall Street Journal* (both in print and online). Figure 7.5 shows indexes that track bonds by type of issuer (federal government, corporation, local government, etc.) and time to maturity (short, intermediate, and long). ■

time **out!**

7-9 Why can we use various interest rates to describe the performance of the entire bond market?

7-10 What bond segments are measured by which bond indexes?

Index	Close	% Chg	YTD total return	52-wk % Chg	YIELD (%), 52-WEEK RANGE			SPREAD, 52-WEEK RANGE (●) Latest			
					Latest	Low	High	Latest	Low		High
Broad Market Barclays Capital											
U.S. Government/Credit	1735.48	0.39	5.49	8.89	2.570	2.560	3.680	63.00	50.00		112.00
Barclays Aggregate	1524.31	0.29	5.45	8.75	2.810	2.790	4.170	51.00	46.00		103.00
Hourly Treasury Indexes Barclays Capital											
Composite (Price Return)	1416.36	0.36	3.65	2.74	1.860	1.810	2.670	-6.00	-6.00		6.00
Composite (Total Return)	11723.42	0.37	5.38	6.07	1.860	1.810	2.670	-6.00	-6.00		-5.00
Intermediate (Price Return)	1274.80	0.27	2.90	2.07	1.580	1.530	2.320	-6.00	-7.00		-5.00
Intermediate (Total Return)	10025.46	0.28	4.46	5.09	1.580	1.530	2.320	-6.00	-7.00		6.00
Long-Term (Price Return)	1904.60	0.95	8.71	6.84	3.750	3.620	4.600	-5.00	-5.00		-4.00
Long-Term (Total Return)	18446.30	0.96	11.56	12.14	3.750	3.620	4.600	-5.00	-5.00		4.00
U.S. Corporate Indexes Barclays Capital											
U.S. Corporate	1905.84	0.53	6.19	15.30	4.160	4.160	5.910	182.00	139.00		297.00
Intermediate	1925.13	0.38	5.60	13.65	3.590	3.590	5.570	175.00	132.00		308.00
Long-term	2224.92	0.97	7.91	20.46	5.840	5.780	6.990	201.00	159.00		261.00
Double-A-rated (AA)	409.26	0.44	5.27	11.19	3.240	3.240	4.570	122.00	86.60		195.00
Triple-B-rated (Baa)	444.51	0.56	6.41	17.95	4.740	4.680	6.850	228.00	173.00		381.00
High Yield Bonds Merrill Lynch											
High Yield Constrained*	241.66	0.24	6.49	29.04	8.637	7.975	12.984	670.00	542.00		1057.00
Triple-C-rated (CCC)	231.11	0.24	8.31	53.12	12.350	10.849	20.274	1071.00	855.00		1822.00
High Yield 100	1760.45	0.203	5.38	17.42	7.421	6.779	9.253	572.00	454.00		703.00
Europe High Yield Constrained	170.01	0.42	7.11	33.10	9.087	7.981	17.222	724.00	592.00		1397.00
Global High Yield Constrained	214.30	0.27	6.83	30.43	8.739	8.042	13.775	680.00	554.00		1122.00
Mortgage-Backed Merrill Lynch											
Ginnie Mae (GNMA)	595.39	0.26	6.79	9.31	3.330	3.305	4.661	24.00	-10.00		34.00
Fannie Mae (FNMA)	570.54	0.29	6.97	8.34	3.599	3.480	4.671	20.00	-5.00		37.00
Freddie Mae (FHLMC)	352.32	0.29	7.16	8.54	3.643	3.567	4.710	23.00	0.00		39.00
Tax-Exempt Merrill Lynch											
Muni Master	399.43	0.07	4.06	7.80	2.876	2.875	3.451	41.00	34.00		63.00
7-12 years	272.98	0.08	5.48	9.09	2.936	2.893	3.580	53.00	43.00		77.00
12-22 years	284.55	0.06	4.68	9.61	4.130	3.878	4.707	41.00	32.00		66.00
22-plus years	262.16	0.07	4.52	13.79	5.001	4.722	5.771	68.00	57.00		118.00
Bond Buyer 6% Muni	115.72	0.11	3.18	8.66	5.130	4.930	5.600	...	...		...

Here are indexes that track bonds by type of issuer (federal government, corporation, local government, etc.) and time to maturity (short, intermediate, and long).
Source: *The Wall Street Journal Online.* Major Bond Indexes Web page.

Get Online

mhhe.com/canM2e

for study materials including self-test
problems with solutions, quizzes,
research projects, minicases, and videos

Your Turn...

Questions

1. What does a call provision allow issuers to do, and why would they do it? *(LG7-1)*

2. List the differences between the new TIPS and traditional Treasury bonds. *(LG7-2)*

3. Explain how mortgage-backed securities work. *(LG7-2)*

4. Provide the definitions of a discount bond and a premium bond. Give examples. *(LG7-3)*

5. Describe the differences in interest payments and bond price between a 5 percent coupon bond and a zero coupon bond. *(LG7-4)*

6. All else equal, which bond's price is more affected by a change in interest rates, a short-term bond or a longer-term bond? Why? *(LG7-5)*

7. All else equal, which bond's price is more affected by a change in interest rates, a bond with a large coupon or a small coupon? Why? *(LG7-5)*

8. Explain how a bond's interest rate can change over time even if interest rates in the economy do not change. *(LG7-5)*

9. Compare and contrast the advantages and disadvantages of the current yield computation versus yield to maturity calculations. *(LG7-6)*

10. What is the yield to call and why is it important to a bond investor? *(LG7-6)*

11. What is the purpose of computing the equivalent taxable yield of a municipal bond? *(LG7-6)*

12. Explain why high-income and wealthy people are more likely to buy a municipal bond than a corporate bond. *(LG7-6)*

13. Why does a Treasury bond offer a lower yield than a corporate bond with the same time to maturity? Could a corporate bond with a different time to maturity offer a lower yield? Explain. *(LG7-7)*

14. Describe the difference between a bond issued as a high-yield bond and one that has become a "fallen angel." *(LG7-7)*

15. What is the difference in the trading volume between Treasury bonds and corporate bonds? Give examples and/or evidence. *(LG7-8)*

Problems

7-1 Interest Payments Determine the interest payment for the following three bonds: 3½ percent coupon corporate bond (paid semiannually), 4.25 percent coupon Treasury note, and a corporate zero coupon bond maturing in ten years. (Assume a $1,000 par value.) *(LG7-1)*

7-2 Interest Payments Determine the interest payment for the following three bonds: 4½ percent coupon corporate bond (paid semiannually), 5.15 percent coupon Treasury note, and a corporate zero coupon bond maturing in 15 years. (Assume a $1,000 par value.) *(LG7-1)*

7-3 Time to Maturity A bond issued by Ford on May 15, 1997, is scheduled to mature on May 15, 2097. If today is November 16, 2012, what is this bond's time to maturity? *(LG7-1)*

7-4 Time to Maturity A bond issued by IBM on December 1, 1996, is scheduled to mature on December 1, 2096. If today is December 2, 2013, what is this bond's time to maturity? *(LG7-1)*

7-5 Call Premium A 6 percent corporate coupon bond is callable in five years for a call premium of one year of coupon payments. Assuming a par value of $1,000, what is the price paid to the bondholder if the issuer calls the bond? *(LG7-1)*

7-6 Call Premium A 5.5 percent corporate coupon bond is callable in ten years for a call premium of one year of coupon payments. Assuming a par value of $1,000, what is the price paid to the bondholder if the issuer calls the bond? *(LG7-1)*

7-7 TIPS Interest and Par Value A 2¾ percent TIPS has an original reference CPI of 185.4. If the current CPI is 210.7, what is the current interest payment and par value of the TIPS? *(LG7-2)*

7-8 TIPS Interest and Par Value A 3 ⅛ percent TIPS has an original reference CPI of 180.5. If the current CPI is 206.8, what is the current interest payment and par value of the TIPS? *(LG7-2)*

7-9 Bond Quotes Consider the following three bond quotes: a Treasury note quoted at 97:27, a corporate bond quoted at 103.25, and a municipal bond quoted at 101.90. If the Treasury and corporate bonds have a par value of $1,000 and the municipal bond has a par value of $5,000, what is the price of these three bonds in dollars? *(LG7-3)*

7-10 Bond Quotes Consider the following three bond quotes: a Treasury bond quoted at 106:14, a corporate bond quoted at 96.55, and a municipal bond quoted at 100.95. If the Treasury and corporate bonds have a par value of $1,000 and the municipal bond has a par value of $5,000, what is the price of these three bonds in dollars? *(LG7-3)*

7-11 Zero Coupon Bond Price Calculate the price of a zero coupon bond that matures in 20 years if the market interest rate is 4.5 percent. *(LG7-4)*

7-12 Zero Coupon Bond Price Calculate the price of a zero coupon bond that matures in 15 years if the market interest rate is 5.75 percent. *(LG7-4)*

7-13 Current Yield What's the current yield of a 4.5 percent coupon corporate bond quoted at a price of 102.08? *(LG7-6)*

7-14 Current Yield What's the current yield of a 5.2 percent coupon corporate bond quoted at a price of 96.78? *(LG7-6)*

7-15 Taxable Equivalent Yield What's the taxable equivalent yield on a municipal bond with a yield to maturity of 3.5 percent for an investor in the 33 percent marginal tax bracket? *(LG7-6)*

7-16 Taxable Equivalent Yield What's the taxable equivalent yield on a municipal bond with a yield to maturity of 2.9 percent for an investor in the 28 percent marginal tax bracket? *(LG7-6)*

7-17 Credit Risk and Yield Rank from highest credit risk to lowest risk the following bonds, with the same time to maturity, by their yield to maturity: Treasury bond with yield of 5.55 percent, IBM bond with yield of 7.49 percent, Trump Casino bond with yield of 8.76 percent, and Banc One bond with a yield of 5.99 percent. *(LG7-7)*

7-18   **Credit Risk and Yield**   Rank the following bonds in order from lowest credit risk to highest risk all with the same time to maturity, by their yield to maturity: Treasury bond with yield of 4.65 percent, United Airline bond with yield of 9.07 percent, Bank of America bond with a yield of 6.25 percent, and Hewlett-Packard bond with yield of 6.78 percent. *(LG7-7)*

7-19   **TIPS Capital Return**   Consider a 3.5 percent TIPS with an issue CPI reference of 185.6. At the beginning of this year, the CPI was 193.5 and was at 199.6 at the end of the year. What was the capital gain of the TIPS in dollars and in percentage terms? *(LG7-2)*

7-20   **TIPS Capital Return**   Consider a 2.25 percent TIPS with an issue CPI reference of 187.2. At the beginning of this year, the CPI was 197.1 and was at 203.8 at the end of the year. What was the capital gain of the TIPS in dollars and in percentage terms? *(LG7-2)*

7-21   **Compute Bond Price**   Compute the price of a 4.5 percent coupon bond with 15 years left to maturity and a market interest rate of 6.8 percent. (Assume interest payments are semiannual.) Is this a discount or premium bond? *(LG7-4)*

7-22   **Compute Bond Price**   Compute the price of a 5.6 percent coupon bond with ten years left to maturity and a market interest rate of 7.0 percent. (Assume interest payments are semiannual.) Is this a discount or premium bond? *(LG7-4)*

7-23   **Compute Bond Price**   Calculate the price of a 5.2 percent coupon bond with 18 years left to maturity and a market interest rate of 4.6 percent. (Assume interest payments are semiannual.) Is this a discount or premium bond? *(LG7-4)*

7-24   **Compute Bond Price**   Calculate the price of a 5.7 percent coupon bond with 22 years left to maturity and a market interest rate of 6.5 percent. (Assume interest payments are semiannual.) Is this a discount or premium bond? *(LG7-4)*

7-25   **Bond Prices and Interest Rate Changes**   A 5.75 percent coupon bond with ten years left to maturity is priced to offer a 6.5 percent yield to maturity. You believe that in one year, the yield to maturity will be 6.0 percent. What is the change in price the bond will experience in dollars? *(LG7-5)*

7-26   **Bond Prices and Interest Rate Changes**   A 6.5 percent coupon bond with 14 years left to maturity is priced to offer a 7.2 percent yield to maturity. You believe that in one year, the yield to maturity will be 6.8 percent. What is the change in price the bond will experience in dollars? *(LG7-5)*

7-27   **Yield to Maturity**   A 5.65 percent coupon bond with 19 years left to maturity is offered for sale at $1,035.25. What yield to maturity is the bond offering? (Assume interest payments are semiannual.) *(LG7-6)*

7-28   **Yield to Maturity**   A 4.30 percent coupon bond with 14 years left to maturity is offered for sale at $943.22. What yield to maturity is the bond offering? (Assume interest payments are semiannual.) *(LG7-6)*

7-29   **Yield to Call**   A 6.75 percent coupon bond with 26 years left to maturity can be called in six years. The call premium is one year of coupon payments. It is offered for sale at $1,135.25. What is the yield to call of the bond? (Assume interest payments are semiannual.) *(LG7-6)*

7-30   **Yield to Call**   A 5.25 percent coupon bond with 14 years left to maturity can be called in four years. The call premium is one year of coupon payments. It is offered for sale at $1,075.50. What is the yield to call of the bond? (Assume interest payments are semiannual.) *(LG7-6)*

7-31   **Comparing Bond Yields**   A client in the 33 percent marginal tax bracket is comparing a municipal bond that offers a 4.5 percent yield to maturity and a similar-risk corporate bond that offers a 6.45 percent yield. Which bond will give the client more profit after taxes? *(LG7-6)*

7-32   **Comparing Bond Yields**   A client in the 28 percent marginal tax bracket is comparing a municipal bond that offers a 4.5 percent yield to maturity and a similar-risk corporate bond that offers a 6.45 percent yield. Which bond will give the client more profit after taxes? *(LG7-6)*

7-33 **TIPS Total Return** Reconsider the 3.5 percent TIPS discussed in problem 7-19. It was issued with a CPI reference of 185.6. The bond is purchased at the beginning of the year (*after the interest payment*), when the CPI was 193.5. For the interest payment in the middle of the year, the CPI was 195.1. Now, at the end of the year, the CPI is 199.6 and the interest payment has been made. What is the total return of the TIPS in dollars and in percentage terms for the year? *(LG7-2)*

7-34 **TIPS Total Return** Reconsider the 2.25 percent TIPS discussed in problem 7-20. It was issued with a CPI reference of 187.2. The bond is purchased at the beginning of the year (after the interest payment), when the CPI was 197.1. For the interest payment in the middle of the year, the CPI was 200.1. Now, at the end of the year, the CPI is 203.8 and the interest payment has been made. What is the total return of the TIPS in dollars and in percentage terms for the year? *(LG7-2)*

7-35 **Bond Prices and Interest Rate Changes** A 6.25 percent coupon bond with 22 years left to maturity is priced to offer a 5.5 percent yield to maturity. You believe that in one year, the yield to maturity will be 6.0 percent. If this occurs, what would be the total return of the bond in dollars and percent? *(LG7-5)*

7-36 **Bond Prices and Interest Rate Changes** A 7.5 percent coupon bond with 13 years left to maturity is priced to offer a 6.25 percent yield to maturity. You believe that in one year, the yield to maturity will be 7.0 percent. If this occurs, what would be the total return of the bond in dollars and percentage terms? *(LG7-5)*

7-37 **Yields of a Bond** A 2.50 percent coupon municipal bond has 12 years left to maturity and has a price quote of 98.45. The bond can be called in four years. The call premium is one year of coupon payments. Compute and discuss the bond's current yield, yield to maturity, taxable equivalent yield (for an investor in the 35 percent marginal tax bracket), and yield to call. (Assume interest payments are semiannual and a par value of $5,000.) *(LG7-6)*

7-38 **Yields of a Bond** A 3.85 percent coupon municipal bond has 18 years left to maturity and has a price quote of 103.20. The bond can be called in eight years. The call premium is one year of coupon payments. Compute and discuss the bond's current yield, yield to maturity, taxable equivalent yield (for an investor in the 35 percent marginal tax bracket), and yield to call. (Assume interest payments are semiannual and a par value of $5,000.) *(LG7-6)*

7-39 **Bond Ratings and Prices** A corporate bond with a 6.5 percent coupon has 15 years left to maturity. It has had a credit rating of BBB and a yield to maturity of 7.2 percent. The firm has recently gotten into some trouble and the rating agency is downgrading the bonds to BB. The new appropriate discount rate will be 8.5 percent. What will be the change in the bond's price in dollars and percentage terms? (Assume interest payments are semiannual.) *(LG7-7)*

7-40 **Bond Ratings and Prices** A corporate bond with a 6.75 percent coupon has ten years left to maturity. It has had a credit rating of BB and a yield to maturity of 8.2 percent. The firm has recently become more financially stable and the rating agency is upgrading the bonds to BBB. The new appropriate discount rate will be 7.1 percent. What will be the change in the bond's price in dollars and percentage terms? (Assume interest payments are semiannual.) *(LG7-7)*

 7-41 **Spreadsheet Problem** Say that in June of 2012, a company issued bonds that are scheduled to mature in June of 2015. The coupon rate is 5.75 percent and is semiannually. The bond issue was rated AAA.

a. Build a spreadsheet that shows how much money the firm pays for each interest rate payment and when those payments will occur if the bond issue sells 50,000 bonds.

b. If the bond issue rating would have been BBB, then the coupon rate would have been 6.30 percent. Show the interest payments with this rating. Explain why bond ratings are important to firms issuing capital debt.

c. Consider that interest rates in the economy increased in the first half of 2012. If the firm would have issued the bonds in January of 2012, then the coupon rate would have only been 5.40 percent. How much extra money per year is the firm paying because it issued the bonds in June instead of January?

valuing stocks

Businesses need capital to start up operations, expand product lines and services, and serve new markets. In the last chapter, we discussed debt, which is one source of financial capital upon which businesses can draw. Their other source of capital is called equity, or business ownership. Public corporations share business ownership and raise money by issuing stocks to investors. When the company sells this form of equity ownership to raise money, it gives up some ownership—and thus some control—over the business. Investors buy stock to receive the benefits of business ownership. Most citizens do not have the time or expertise to operate their own businesses. Buying stock allows them to participate in the profits of economic activities. Access to equity capital has allowed entrepreneurs like Steve Jobs of Apple and Larry Page of Google to take their companies public so that their businesses can become large corporations. Both the company founders and the new owners (stock investors) have amassed much wealth over the years under this arrangement. One very important reason that investors

continued on p. 184

LEARNING GOALS

LG8-1 Understand the rights and returns that come with common stock ownership.

LG8-2 Know how stock exchanges function.

LG8-3 Track the wider stock market with stock indexes and differentiate among the kinds of information each index provides.

LG8-4 Know the terminology of stock trading.

LG8-5 Compute stock values using dividend discount and constant-growth models.

LG8-6 Calculate the stock value of a variable-growth-rate company.

LG8-7 Assess relative stock values using the P/E ratio model.

continued from p.183

are willing to buy company stock as an investment is that they know that they can sell the stock during any trading day. Investors buy and sell stocks among themselves in stock markets. Well-functioning stock markets are critical to any capitalistic economy. In this chapter, we'll discuss stock market operations and stock valuation. ■

COMMON STOCK LG8-1

Equity securities (stocks) represent ownership shares in a corporation. **Common stock** offers buyers the potential for current income from dividends and capital appreciation from any stock price increases. Over time, some corporate profits are reinvested in the firm, which increases the value of each shareholder's stake in the business. At any point in time, the market value of a firm's common stock depends on many factors, including:

- The company's profitability.
- Growth prospects for the future.
- Current market interest rates.
- Conditions in the overall stock market.

Over periods of 30 to 40 years, stocks have offered investors the best opportunities to increase wealth. Since stocks are also susceptible to price declines and stock price fluctuations can be very volatile over short periods of time, stock investing requires a longer-term outlook.

»viewpoints

business APPLICATION

As CEO of your firm, Dawa Tech, which makes computer components, you have been able to grow its dividends by 8 percent per year to a recent $2 per share. You expect this growth to continue. As a result, the stock price has risen to $65 and has a P/E ratio of 16.25.

Tomorrow, you are scheduled to meet with some stockholders and financial analysts. To prepare for the meeting, you should know what return the shareholders seem to expect and estimate where the Dawa stock price may be in three years. How will you go about preparing for this meeting?

right to claim any cash flows or value after all other claimants have received what they are owed. As a company earns cash flows, it must pay suppliers, employees, expenses, taxes, and debt interest payments. Stockholders claim the leftover (or residual) cash flow. These profits can be used to reinvest in the firm to foster growth, pay dividends to shareholders, or a combination of the two.

Stocks of growing firms are valuable. Stocks in firms that pay dividends to shareholders are also valuable. Stocks issued by firms that have greater amounts of residual cash flow are more

> **STOCKS OF GROWING FIRMS ARE VALUABLE. STOCKS IN FIRMS THAT PAY DIVIDENDS TO SHAREHOLDERS ARE ALSO VALUABLE. STOCKS ISSUED BY FIRMS THAT HAVE GREATER AMOUNTS OF RESIDUAL CASH FLOW ARE MORE VALUABLE.**

Virtually any business firm that is organized as a corporation (see Chapter 1) may choose to issue publicly traded stock. Common stockholders vote to elect the board of directors; they also vote on various other proposals requested by other shareholders or the management team. As owners of the firm, common stockholders are considered to be **residual claimants.** This means that common stockholders have the

valuable. The value is reflected in the stock price. *Therefore, stock price values arise from the company's underlying business success.* Many different investors and analysts may estimate a stock's fundamental value based upon some outlook or theory. But the actual stock price is determined on stock exchanges when investors seek to trade with one another. Let's discuss this trading process and then explore how stocks are valued.

STOCK MARKETS LG8-2

In general, people will invest significant amounts of their wealth in stocks only if they know that they can convert their shares into cash at any time. Stock exchanges provide this liquidity, allowing buyers and sellers the means to transact stock trades with each other. This liquidity gives many people the confidence to invest in the first place and makes stocks (as well as bonds) attractive investments relative to less-liquid assets like real estate or fine collectibles—which can be difficult to sell quickly at full value.

The most well-known stock exchange in the world is the **New York Stock Exchange (NYSE).** The New York Stock Exchange, located in New York City on the corner of Wall Street and Broad Street, is the largest U.S. stock exchange as measured by the value of companies listed and the dollar value of trading activity. The NYSE is the largest equities marketplace in the world and is home to approximately 2,300 companies (many with multiple securities listed). While other exchanges may boast more companies listed, the largest companies in the world tend to list in New York. The holding company that owns the NYSE, NYSE Euronext, also operates Euronext N.V., a Europe-based electronic exchange market. Together, the NYSE and the Euronext list more than 8,000 equity, derivate, fixed-income, and exchanged-traded securities.

Much of the stock buying and selling at the NYSE occurs at 17 stations, called **trading posts,** on the trading floor. Each post is staffed by a **specialist,** who oversees the orderly trading of the specific stocks assigned to that post. **Brokers,** located around the perimeter of the floor, act as agents for those buying and selling stocks. Brokers execute orders by matching buy and sell orders. Once the buy and sell orders match, the transaction is completed and the trade appears on trading screens viewed by people all over the world.

Consider this scenario. You decide to buy shares of McDonald's stock because of new menu items and other initiatives. You place a buy order for 100 shares with your broker—either with a simple phone call or through an online brokerage service. The broker then sends the order to the NYSE electronically via the SuperDOT® System to the trading post assigned for McDonald's stock. At the trading post, the specialist makes sure the transaction is executed in a fair and orderly manner. Your buy order competes with other orders at the point of sale for the best price and an on-floor broker executes your purchase. You will receive a trade confirmation from your broker describing the trade and noting the exact amount you owe for the 100 shares of McDonald's plus any applicable commissions. The NYSE reports the transaction and it appears within seconds on displays across the country and around the world. Note that buy and sell orders are electronically routed from all over the world to the NYSE, which

common stock An ownership stake in a corporation.

residual claimants Ownership of cash flows and value after other claimants are paid.

New York Stock Exchange (NYSE) Large and prestigious stock exchange with a trading floor.

trading posts Trading location on the floor of a stock exchange.

specialist Person charged with managing the trading process for several individual stocks on the trading floor.

brokers Floor traders who execute orders for others and themselves.

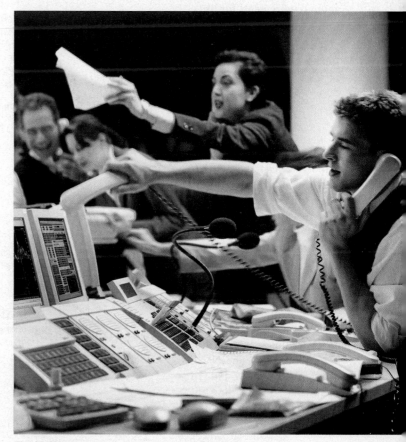

The NYSE trades millions upon millions of stock shares in a given day.

then routes trade results back. Since most of the trade orders are already in electronic form, why not electronically match buy and sell orders and bypass any human intervention in floor trading? Indeed, the NYSE has joined many other exchanges in becoming increasingly electronic. Some floor specialist firms can see a time when no human intervention will be a part of floor trading at the NYSE. Their claim that human intervention can detect and prevent problems with electronic trades has been widely questioned.

The NYSE will trade hundreds of thousands, even millions, of McDonald's stock shares in a given day. An intraday (during trading hours) stock quote for McDonald's stock, **ticker symbol** MCD, is shown in Figure 8.1. On September 27, 2010, more than 3 million McDonald's shares traded by early afternoon. The stock traded at $75.01 per share, which was $0.09 lower than the closing price of the previous day. At this price, McDonald's stock is currently much closer to its 52-week high of $76.26 than to its 52-week low of $56.03.

To list its stock on the NYSE, a company must meet minimum requirements for its:

- Total number of stockholders.
- Level of trading volume.
- Corporate earnings.
- Firm size.

The exchange also charges an initial list fee and an annual fee. Listing standards and fees are higher for the NYSE than for other stock exchanges, so many firms cannot (or choose not to) list their stocks there. An alternative, the **American Stock Exchange (AMEX),** used to exist right down the street. But, in 2008, the NYSE purchased the AMEX and the stock trading was moved to the NYSE floor. The NYSE was mostly interested in acquiring the trading of the exchange-traded fund securities.

Another popular stock trading system is the **NASDAQ Stock Market,** an electronic stock market without a physical trading floor. Today, NASDAQ features many of the big-name high-tech companies investors have come to know, like Apple Computer (ticker: AAPL), Intel (ticker: INTC), Microsoft (ticker: MSFT), and Qualcomm (ticker: QCOM). Many newer high-tech companies like Google (ticker: GOOG), Netflix (ticker: NFLX), and Adobe Systems Inc. (ticker: ADBE), are also listed on NASDAQ. NASDAQ ranks second, behind the NYSE, among the world's equity markets in terms of total dollar volume. NASDAQ lists approximately 2,800 domestic and foreign companies.

Instead of having a trading floor, NASDAQ uses a vast electronic trading system that executes trades via computer rather than in person. Instead of one specialist overseeing the process for an individual stock on a trading floor, Nasdaq's system uses multiple **market makers,** or **dealers.** Market makers use their own stock inventory and capital to compete with other dealers to buy and sell the stocks they represent. When an investor places an order through a stockbroker for a NASDAQ-listed stock, the electronic system routes the order and the investor buys shares from the dealer offering the best (lowest) price. Typical NASDAQ stocks support ten market makers actively competing with one another for investor trades.

FIGURE 8.1 Read a Stock Quote

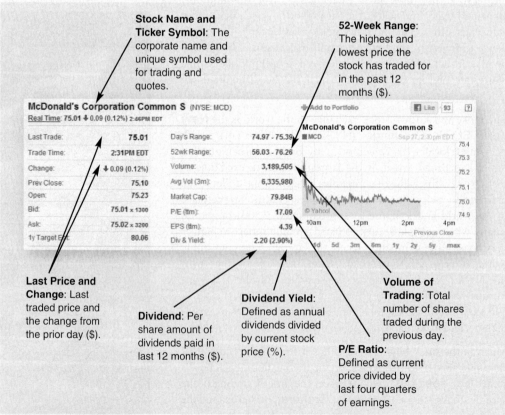

If you know what to look for, reading a stock quote is not as complicated as it first may appear.

Table 8.1 shows trading activity on the three main stock exchanges for one day in September 2010. The NYSE and NASDAQ each show a high amount of trading, with a total volume of over 3 billion for the NYSE and nearly 2 billion for NASDAQ. Trading on the AMEX is much smaller at less than 1 billion shares traded.

The business of providing platforms or forums for investors and speculators to trade stocks and other financial assets has been changing rapidly. Many exchanges that previously used physical floor trading systems with specialists and open outcry to establish stock prices are shifting to electronic systems with no trading floors. Long-standing, traditional exchanges are also merging with other domestic and international exchanges to create fewer, but larger, forums that focus not just on U.S. securities but on many more internationally focused financial assets. The wider range of represented securities allows traders new opportunities to explore trading relationships among securities traded across the world. This worldwide trading will establish economically sound prices and additional financial stability around the world.

▼ **TABLE 8.1** Trading on the NYSE, NASDAQ, and AMEX, September 28, 2010

	NYSE	AMEX	NASDAQ
Total issues	3,192	708	2,756
Advancing issues	2,190	491	1,751
Declining issues	903	178	891
Unchanged issues	99	39	114
New highs	273	40	123
New lows	14	10	21
Total volume	3,787,608,269	819,013,492	1,910,213,309

Source: Yahoo! Finance (http://finance.yahoo.com/advances)

time out!

8-1 What are three primary stock exchanges in the United States and where are they located? For which of the exchanges does physical location matter? Why?

8-2 Describe differences in trading procedures on the NYSE versus the NASDAQ. Which do you think is most fair to investors? Why?

Tracking the Stock Market LG8-3

With thousands of stocks trading every minute, many stock prices rise while others fall. Table 8.1 also shows that, throughout the trading day, 2,190 stocks increased in price on the NYSE while 903 stocks decreased in price. On the AMEX and NASDAQ, too, more stocks increased in price than decreased. In addition to the number of stocks advancing and declining, the table also shows the number of stocks that hit new 52-week price highs (273 listed on the NYSE) and new lows (14 on the NYSE) on that day. So, was this a good day or a bad day in the stock market?

To say anything about the *general* direction of the stock market, **stock indexes** are useful. Dozens of stock indexes are designed to track the overall market; many more track different market segments. The three most recognized indexes are the **Dow Jones Industrial Average (DJIA),** the **Standard & Poor's 500 Index (S&P 500),** and the **NASDAQ Composite Index.**

Charles H. Dow invented the first stock average in 1884. At the turn of the 20th century, railroads were the first major corporations. So he began with 11 stocks, mostly railroads. Dow created a price average by simply adding up 11 stock prices and dividing by the number 11. Two years later, Dow began tracking a 12-stock industrial average. This industrial average would eventually evolve into the modern DJIA, which is a price average of 30 large, industry-leading stocks that together represent roughly 30 percent of the total stock value of all U.S. equities. DJIA level changes describe how the largest companies that participate in the stock market performed over a given period. The DJIA was at 10,858.14, a change of +46.10 (or 0.43 percent), on the day illustrated in Table 8.1.

The Standard & Poor's Corp. introduced its 500-stock index in 1957. Standard & Poor's chooses companies to include in the S&P 500 Index to represent the 10 sectors of the economy:

- Financial
- Information technology
- Health care
- Industrials
- Consumer discretionary
- Consumer staples

- Energy
- Telecom services
- Utilities
- Materials

S&P uses **market capitalization** (a measure of company size using stock price times shares outstanding), not just stock prices, of the largest 500 U.S. firms to compute the index. These 500 firms represent roughly 80 percent of the overall stock market capitalization (number of shares times share price). Although the DJIA is a long-time favorite with the media and individual investors, the S&P 500 is much preferred in the investment industry because of its broader representation of the market as a whole. S&P 500 performance provides a standard against which most U.S. money managers and pension plan sponsors can compare

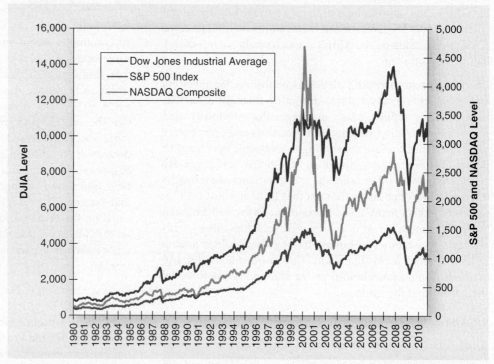

▼FIGURE 8.2 Stock Market Index Levels Since 1980

This graph comparing the DJIA, S&P 500, and NASDAQ Composite indexes gives you a picture of their magnitude, as well as their patterns.

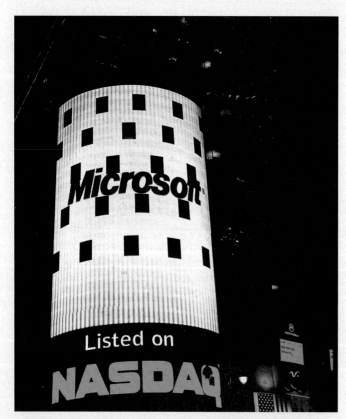

Investors consider the NASDAQ to be a reflection of the tech sector's general performance.

their investment performance. During trading on September 28, 2010, the S&P 500 gained 5.54 (0.49 percent) to close at 1,147.70.

The NASDAQ Composite Index measures the market capitalization of all common stocks listed on the NASDAQ stock exchange. Since the NASDAQ lists so many large, technology-oriented companies, many investors and analysts consider this index to reflect the tech sector performance more than that of the overall stock market. The NASDAQ Composite gained 9.82 to 2,379.59 on September 28, 2010, a gain of 0.41 percent. Because all three popular indexes were up on this day, most reports would reflect a good day for the stock market.

Figure 8.2 shows the levels of all these stock indexes since 1980. The DJIA (maroon line) level appears on the left-hand axis. Both the S&P 500 (green line) and the NASDAQ Composite (orange line) run from the right-hand axis. The rapid price appreciation for NASDAQ stocks during the late 1990s— the tech boom years—is unprecedented for such a large and widely followed market index. The NASDAQ Composite soared from 817 in March 1995 to peak on March 10, 2000, at 5,048.62, for a 518 percent total return in only five years— a 43.9 percent annual rate of share-price appreciation for NASDAQ stocks. The NASDAQ index performed much better than did the DJIA (19.0 percent per year) or the S&P 500 (22.7 percent per year). The NASDAQ "price bubble" set the stage for one of the most dramatic stock price declines in history: The NASDAQ Composite Index plunged to 1,114.11 on October 9, 2002, losing 78 percent of its value. The other index values also fell during this period, albeit not as sharply. Note that the DJIA didn't climb back to its 2000 high until March 2006. The S&P 500 Index finally recovered in May 2007. The NASDAQ Composite still has a long way to go to recover from its fall from pre-2000 levels.

The figure also shows the stock market reaction to the financial crisis that began in 2008. There were sharp declines in all three indexes. After closing at a new high of 14,093.08 on October 12, 2007, the DJIA then fell to close at only 6,547.05 on March 9, 2009. Over three years later, the indexes still have not reached their previous highs.

market capitalization
The size of the firm measured as the current stock price multiplied by the number of shares outstanding.

finance at work //: behavioral

Investor Psychology

To us today, it may seem ludicrous that in the years 1634 to 1636, the people of Holland were in the midst of "Tulip Mania," and the price for a single rare tulip bulb approached the equivalent of $35,000. Then, the bubble burst and tulip prices quickly plunged to less than the equivalent of $1. We may call those people who invested in a $35,000 tulip bulb irrational or even "crazy."

But this type of story seems to repeat itself throughout history. Investors paid extremely high prices for the new computer stocks in the 1960s, the "nifty fifty" companies in the 1970s, Japanese stocks during the 1980s, and Internet stocks during the late 1990s. The mania for stocks like Iomega drove its price from an equivalent of $1 per share in January of 1995 to over $75 in just 16 months. When the bubble burst, the price fell hard. Many years later, in 2008, the company was purchased by EMC Corporation for dollars per share. But that's just one company. A portfolio full of Internet stocks experienced a similar price mania followed by a severe fall. Investors created a stock index (TheStreet.com Internet Index) designed to track Internet stocks in late 1998, but by that time, part-time investors and veterans alike were already well into the craze. The Internet index started at 250, quickly rose to 1,270 by March of 2000, and subsequently fell to a low of 63 in October of 2002. Of course, the tech stock bubble was followed by the real estate bubble. In retrospect, irrational bubble-like prices are not confined to tulips and the 17th century in Holland.

Seemingly irrational behavior may not occur only during highly emotional periods of a price bubble. Recently, a growing recognition has arisen that "normal" investors often behave in a way that might not be described as fully rational. Investors, being human, are subject to cognitive biases and emotions. Studies of investor

behavior have discovered that investors commonly succumb to psychological biases and:

- Trade too much.
- Sell winners too soon.
- Refuse to realize losses.
- Become overconfident—especially when trading online.
- Seek stocks that have already increased in price—perhaps up to their full potential price.
- Consider and react to what's happening with each stock in isolation, rather than remembering the purpose for forming an overall portfolio.

Investors who succeed in the long run are those who learn to avoid these psychological biases.

Want to know more?

Key Words to Search for Updates: **irrational exuberance, price bubble, mania**

8-3 Discuss why the day's market return may be different when measured by the DJIA, S&P 500 Index, and NASDAQ Composite taken separately.

8-4 Why might the "market bubble" phenomenon appear more dramatic because it occurred in the NASDAQ Composite rather than by the DJIA or S&P 500 Index?

8-5 If you followed the market regularly, to which index would you give the most credence? Why?

Trading Stocks LG8-4

People who wish to buy and sell stocks need to open stock brokerage accounts. Traditional, full-service stockbrokers (e.g., Morgan Stanley Smith Barney, Merrill Lynch, UBS, Edward Jones) provide clients with research and advice in addition to executing trades. Their clients pay for this research and advice: Commission fees for these services may run well over $100 per trade. Discount brokerage firms (e.g., Charles Schwab, E-trade, Scottrade, TD Ameritrade) charge a much lower commission, $5 to $30 per trade, but do not provide the additional services. Investors at discount brokerages usually place trades through the brokerage's Internet sites.

Buy and sell orders go through the brokerage firm to a market maker (a dealer or a specialist) at a stock exchange. The quoted **bid** is the highest price at which the market maker offers to pay for the stock. Investors have little choice but to accept this selling price, because regardless of the broker used, the market maker offers the only place to sell the stock. The quoted **ask** price is the lowest price at which a market maker will sell a stock—so investors buy at the ask price. The difference between the bid and the ask price may be only $0.01 for high-volume stocks and can be as high as $0.20 for less-often traded companies. The spread between the bid and the ask price is a cost to the investor and a profit for the market maker. This profit compensates the market maker for providing a market and liquidity for that stock.

> **Bid and ask prices tell investors at what prices the stock can currently be traded in general.**

Investors can place a buy or sell **market order.** A market order to buy stock will be filled immediately at the current ask price when routed to the stock exchange. A sell market order will be filled at the current bid price. The advantage of a market order is that it executes immediately at the best available price. The disadvantage of a market order is that the investor does not know in advance what that fill price will be. Investors can name their own prices by using **limit orders,** in which investors specify the price at which they are willing to execute the buy or sell order. With a buy limit order, a trade is executed if the ask quote is at or below the price target. For a sell limit order, a trade is executed if the bid quote moves through the specified price. If the current quote does not meet the price cited in the limit order, the trade is not executed. The advantage of a limit order is that the investor makes the trade at the desired price; the disadvantage is that the trade might not be executed at all.

Consider a quote of McDonald's stock with a bid price of $75.00 and an ask price of $75.05. An investor placing a market buy order would purchase the stock at $75.05. A market sell order would execute as the price rises through $75.00. Note that an investor who simultaneously bought and sold 100 shares would pay $7,505 and receive $7,500—losing $5. An investor who places a buy limit order at $74.75 will only purchase the shares if the ask price falls to $74.75 or lower. If the ask does not fall, the order will not execute. Bid and ask prices tell investors at what prices the stock can currently be traded in general. But being able to buy at the ask price does not guarantee that the stock should be *valued* at that price. We'll discuss various ways to arrive at reasonable per-share stock values in the next section.

time **out!**

8-6 Explain how the difference in the bid and ask prices might be considered a hidden cost to the investor.

8-7 The bid and ask prices for Amazon.com are $37.79 and $37.85. If these quotes occur when a trade order is made, at what price would a market buy order execute? Would a limit sell order execute with a target price of $37.75?

BASIC STOCK VALUATION

Cash Flows LG8-5

In the previous chapter, we showed how we value bonds by finding the present value of the future interest payments and the future par value. Stock valuation uses the same concept of finding the present value of future dividends and the future selling price. But of course uncertainty about both price appreciation and future dividend payment streams complicate stock valuation. Consider the simple case of valuing a stock to be held for one year shown in the time line.

Period	0	i	1 years
Cash flow	?		$D_1 + P_1$

The value of such a stock today, P_0, is the present value of the dividend to be received in the first year, D_1, plus the present value of the expected sales price in one year, P_1. The interest rate used to discount the cash flows is shown as i. Using the present value equation from Chapter 4 results in:

Today's value = Present value of next year's dividend and price

$$P_0 = \frac{D_1 + P_1}{1 + i} \qquad (8\text{-}1)$$

Whenever investors deal with future stock prices and future dividend payments, they must use expected values, not certain ones. Companies rarely decrease their dividends; most companies' dividends either remain constant or slowly grow. Examining a firm's dividend history over the past few years will give clues to that company's future dividend policy. For example, The Coca-Cola Company (ticker: KO) paid a $0.31 per share dividend for each quarter in 2006. The firm then raised the quarterly dividend to $0.34 for each quarterly dividend in 2007. The company paid quarterly dividends in 2008, 2009, and 2010 of $0.38, $0.41, and $0.44, respectively. This increase of $0.03 in the dividend every year seems fairly stable.

Stock prices, though, show much more volatility than dividend histories do. We face much uncertainty in trying to predict stock prices in the short term. Using a longer holding period to estimate stock value reduces *some*, but by no means all, of the uncertainty. A 2-year holding period appears like this:

Period	0	i	1	2 years
Cash flow	?		D_1	$D_2 + P_2$

The present value of the cash flows in years 1 and 2 is today's stock value:

Today's value = Present value of next year's dividend, the second year's dividend, and the future price

$$P_0 = \frac{D_1}{1 + i} + \frac{D_2 + P_2}{(1 + i)^2} \qquad (8\text{-}2)$$

Notice that the divisor for the second term on the right-hand side of equation 8.2 is raised to the second power. This reflects the two years over which those cash flows must be discounted. You can do this analysis over any holding period. For a holding period of n years, the value of a stock is measured by the present value of dividends over the n years, and the eventual sale price, P_n.

P_0 = Sum of the present value of each payment received

$$P_0 = \frac{D_1}{1 + i} + \frac{D_2}{(1 + i)^2} + \cdots + \frac{D_n + P_n}{(1 + i)^n} \qquad (8\text{-}3)$$

This formula incorporates both dividend income and capital appreciation or capital loss. It fully includes both major components of the investor's total return from investment.

As is often the case in finance, implementing equation 8-3 presents problems for some firms in practical terms. What will the

bid The quoted price investors are likely to receive when they sell stock.

ask The quoted price investors are likely to pay when they buy stock.

market order A stock buy or sell order to be immediately executed at the current market price.

limit order A stock buy or sell order at a specific price. It will only be executed if the market price meets the specified price.

Coca-Cola increased its dividend by 3 cents per year over a five-year span.

EXAMPLE 8-1

Valuing Coca-Cola Stock LG8-5

In January, year 1, you are valuing Coca-Cola stock to compare its value to its market price. The current market price is $65. Given the history of Coca-Cola's dividends, you believe that the company will pay total dividends in year 1 of $1.88 (= 4 × $0.47). Your analysis indicates that the total dividends in year 2 and year 3 will be $2.00 and $2.12, respectively. In addition, you believe that the price of Coca-Cola stock at the end of year 3 will be $85 per share. If the appropriate discount rate is 11.5 percent, what is the value of Coca-Cola stock?

SOLUTION:

To organize your data, you first create the following timeline:

Period	0	11.5%	1	2	3 years
Cash flow	?		$1.88	$2.00	$2.12+$85

Using equation 8-3, you compute the stock value as:

$$P_0 = \frac{\$1.88}{1 + 0.115} + \frac{\$2.00}{(1 + 0.115)^2} + \frac{\$2.12 + \$85}{(1 + 0.115)^3} = \$1.686 + \$1.609 + \$62.848 = \$66.14$$

Since your analysis shows that Coca-Cola's stock should be valued at $66.14 while it's selling for only $65, the stock appears to be slightly undervalued. You believe that this might be a good time to buy some Coca-Cola stock.

Similar to Problems 8-15, 8-16, 8-27, 8-28

CALCULATOR HINTS

1ST CASH FLOW:
N = 1, I = 11.5
PMT = 0, FV = 1.88
CPT PV = −$1.686

2ND CASH FLOW:
N = 2, I = 11.5
PMT = 0, FV = 2.00
CPT PV = −$1.609

3RD CASH FLOW:
N = 3, I = 11.5
PMT = 0, FV = 87.12
CPT PV = −$62.848

VALUE = $1.686
+$1.609 +$62.848
= $66.14

future dividends of the firm be? What will the stock price be in three, five, or ten years? While it seems that the dividend growth of Coca-Cola will be constant, consider the actual dividends and stock price of McDonald's Corp. since 2000 shown in Figure 8.3.

McDonald's paid an annual dividend from 2000 to 2007. Some increases were small, like the $0.01 increase from 2000 to 2001 and again to 2002. Other increases were quite large, like the $0.50 increase between 2006 and 2007. Then McDonald's changed to the more common quarterly dividend in 2008. The figure also shows that McDonald's stock price has been very volatile. The price fell from $37 in 2000 to nearly $12 in 2003 and then rapidly increased to $60 in 2007. The stock went sideways during the financial crisis and then shot up to $73 in 2010. An investor in 2000 would have had a very difficult time accurately forecasting these future dividends and stock prices. Indeed, short-term stock price changes seem almost random. Stock valuation can really only be viewed from a long-term perspective. Because predicting future dividends is uncertain at best, it's better to project valuation as a likely range of prices under reasonable assumptions rather than as a single price.

From 2000 to 2007, McDonald's paid an annual dividend instead of quarterly dividends.

▼**FIGURE 8.3** Dividends and Stock Price of McDonald's since 2000

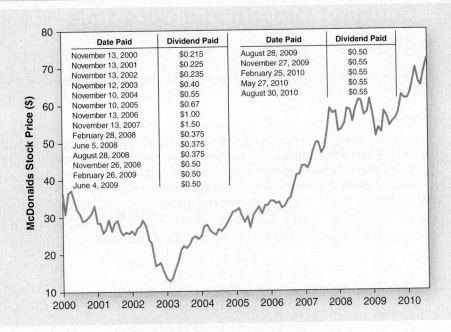

Date Paid	Dividend Paid	Date Paid	Dividend Paid
November 13, 2000	$0.215	August 28, 2009	$0.50
November 13, 2001	$0.225	November 27, 2009	$0.55
November 13, 2002	$0.235	February 25, 2010	$0.55
November 12, 2003	$0.40	May 27, 2010	$0.55
November 10, 2004	$0.55	August 30, 2010	$0.55
November 10, 2005	$0.67		
November 13, 2006	$1.00		
November 13, 2007	$1.50		
February 28, 2008	$0.375		
June 5, 2008	$0.375		
August 28, 2008	$0.375		
November 26, 2008	$0.50		
February 26, 2009	$0.50		
June 4, 2009	$0.50		

Dividends rarely decline, but stock prices often do!

Dividend Discount Models LG8-5

We can extend the discounted cash flow approach in equation 8-3 for an infinite stream of dividends, $n \to \infty$, and no final future selling price. If stockholders receive all future cash flows as future dividends, the stock's value to the investor is the present value of all these future dividends. In other words, embedded in any stock price is the value of all future dividends. We can demonstrate this value as:

$$P_0 = \frac{D_1}{1+i} + \frac{D_2}{(1+i)^2} + \frac{D_3}{(1+i)^3} + \cdots \qquad (8\text{-}4)$$

This equation shows the general case of the **dividend discount model.** The dividend discount model provides a useful theoretical basis because it illustrates the importance of dividends as a fundamental stock price determinant.

But, again, finance professionals find it difficult to apply the dividend discount model because it requires that they estimate an infinite number of future dividends. To use the model in practice, analysts make simplifying assumptions to make the model workable. One common assumption: The firm has a constant dividend growth rate, g. If this is the case, next year's dividend is simply this year's dividend that grew one year at the growth rate, that is, $D_1 = D_0 \times (1 + g)$. In fact, we can express each dividend as a function of D_0 and we can rewrite equation 8-4 as:

$$P_0 = \frac{D_0(1+g)}{1+i} + \frac{D_0(1+g)^2}{(1+i)^2} + \frac{D_0(1+g)^3}{(1+i)^3} + \cdots \qquad (8\text{-}5)$$

So, with this version of the model, we need not forecast an infinite string of dividends; D_0 and g take care of that. However, we must still compute an infinite sum of numbers. Luckily, mathematicians know equations like these; they are known as power series. This power series can be simplified to the **constant-growth model,** and it assumes that the growth rate is smaller than the discount rate (i.e., for $g < i$):

Stock value = Next year's dividend
   ÷ (Discount rate − Growth rate)

$$\text{Constant growth model} = P_0 = \frac{D_0(1+g)}{(i-g)} = \frac{D_1}{(i-g)} \qquad (8\text{-}6)$$

If $g \geq i$, then the denominator would be zero or negative. Economically and mathematically, this is a nonsensical result. In the short run, a firm can grow very quickly. In the long run, no company can grow faster than the overall economic growth rate forever. You may hear the constant-growth model referred to as the *Gordon growth model*, after financial economist Myron J. Gordon.

Investors use several methods to estimate a firm's growth rate for this model. They can project the dividend trend into the future and determine the implied growth rate, compute the past growth rate, or even consider a financial analyst's growth rate predictions. Consider Coca-Cola's dividend behavior. If the 2010 dividend was $1.76 and the projected dividends will grow to $2.24 in 2014, the implied projected dividend growth rate is therefore 6.21 percent (N = 4, PV = −1.76, PMT = 0, FV = 2.24, CPT I = 6.21) annually. The growth rate in dividend changes from 2006 to 2010 was 9.15 percent (N = 4, PV = −1.24, PMT = 0, FV = 1.76, CPT I = 9.15) per year. You can find analyst forecasts many places online. The Yahoo! Finance web page for Coca-Cola has an Analyst Estimates link, which shows the average analysts' forecast for the firm's growth in the next five years at 8.50 percent.

EXAMPLE 8-2

For interactive versions of this example visit www.mhhe.com/canM2e

Constant Growth and Coca-Cola Stock LG8-3

Assume that you are valuing Coca-Cola stock again. This time you are using the constant-growth model, assuming a discount rate of 11.5 percent.

SOLUTION:

You have a choice of three growth rates to use. The implied projected dividend growth rate is 6.21 percent. Past dividend growth has been 9.15 percent and analysts forecast an 8.50 percent growth. Compute the stock value using all three growth rates.

Using a dividend growth rate of 6.21 percent and equation 8-6, the stock value is $35.34:

$$P_0 = \frac{\$1.76 \times (1 + 0.0621)}{0.115 - 0.0621} = \$35.34$$

Using a dividend growth rate of 8.50 percent, the stock value is $63.65:

$$P_0 = \frac{\$1.76 \times (1 + 0.0850)}{0.115 - 0.0850} = \$63.65$$

Using a dividend growth rate of 9.15 percent, the stock value is $81.75:

$$P_0 = \frac{\$1.76 \times (1 + 0.0915)}{0.115 - 0.0915} = \$81.75$$

Notice how a small change in the growth rate has a large impact on the stock value in this model. At a current price of $65 per share, Coca-Cola could be considered undervalued, about right, or overvalued depending on the growth rate used.

Similar to Problems 8-19, 8-20, 8-29, 8-30, 8-31, 8-32

Preferred Stock LG8-5

A special case of the constant-growth model occurs when the dividend does not grow but is the same every year. This zero-growth rate case describes a **preferred stock.** The term *preferred* comes from the fact that this type of stock takes preference over common stock in bankruptcy proceedings. Preferred stockholders have a higher priority for receiving proceeds from bankruptcy proceedings than do common stockholders. Preferred stock is largely owned by other companies, rather than by individual investors, because its dividends are mostly nontaxable income (70 percent of the income is exempt from taxes) to other corporations. Preferred stockholders do not have voting rights like common stockholders, though, which prevents one company from controlling another through preferred stock ownership.

An interesting characteristic of preferred stock is that it pays a constant dividend. Because the dividend does not change, the preferred stock can be valued using the constant-growth-rate model with a zero growth rate expressed as $P = D/i$. What would Coca-Cola's stock be worth if its dividend stayed at $1.76 and never grew? Using the same 11.5 percent discount rate, the stock would be valued at $15.30 (= $1.76 ÷ 0.115). Given Coca-Cola's current stock price of $65,

the
Math Coach on...

Using the Constant-Growth-Rate Model

❝ The distinction between the recent year's dividends, D_0, and next year's dividends, D_1, can be confusing in the constant-growth-rate model. The model's equation presents two different numerators. If you are given information about dividends last year or just paid, use the $D_0(1 + g)$ version of the equation. If you have information about expected dividends or next year's dividend, use the D_1 version of the equation. ❞

over 76.5 percent [= ($65 − $15.30) ÷ $65] of its stock value comes from the expectation that Coca-Cola's dividend will grow. In other words, investors highly value a growing firm.

Most companies issue only common stock, but nearly 1,000 preferred stock issues still exist. Table 8.2 compares the common stock and preferred stock for six firms. Many of the preferred stocks come from the finance, energy, and real estate sectors. Notice that the **dividend yield** for preferred stock is higher than for the common stock, because preferred stock investors should expect a return from dividend payments only. Common stockholders will also expect a return from capital appreciation over time. Common stocks also trade much more frequently than preferred stocks do.

The zero-growth-rate version of the constant-growth valuation model shows that, since dividends are fixed, a preferred stock's price changes because of changes in the discount rate, i. When interest rates throughout the economy change, the discount rate also changes. Preferred stock prices thus tend to act like bond prices. When interest rates rise, preferred stock prices fall. When interest rates decline, preferred stock prices rise. Preferred stock is usually categorized with bonds in the fixed-income security group because it acts so much like debt securities, even though a preferred stock represents equity ownership, like common stock.

Expected Return LG8-5

Stock valuation models require a discount rate, i, in order to compute the present value of the future cash flows. The discount rate used should reflect the investment risk level. Higher risk investments should be evaluated using higher interest rates. For example, the previous chapter on bonds demonstrated that higher risk bonds, such as junk bonds, offer higher rates of return. Similarly, investors demand higher returns from higher risk stocks than they do from lower risk stocks. We discuss stock risk measurement and appropriate expected returns later in this book.

However, one method for determining what return stock investors require from a stock is to use the constant-growth-rate model. If the current stock price fairly reflects its value, then the discount rate, i, in equation 8-6 should be the expected return for the stock. Solving for this expected return results in equation 8-7:

$$\text{Expected return} = i = \frac{D_1}{P_0} + g = \text{Dividend yield} + \text{Capital gain}$$

(8-7)

Note that the expected return comes again from two sources: dividend yield and expected appreciation of the stock price, or capital gain. For example, assume that Coca-Cola's dividend next year, D_1, is expected to be $1.88 per share. At a current price of $65, Coca-Cola offers a dividend yield of 2.89 percent (=$1.88 ÷ $65). Since analysts believe that the firm's stock price will grow at 8.50 percent in the future, investors expect a total return of 11.39 percent (=2.89% + 8.50%). Dividend yield can represent a substantial portion of the profits for an investor. Many people get too enamored of high **growth stocks**

["Many people get too enamored of high growth stocks that do not pay dividends and therefore miss out on an important source of stable returns."]

▼ **TABLE 8.2** Common and Preferred Stock, September 28, 2010

Company	Common Stock				Preferred Stock			
	Ticker	Price	Annual Dividend (Yield%)	Volume	Ticker	Price	Annual Dividend (Yield%)	Volume
Alcoa Inc.	AA	$12.22	$0.12(1.0)	30,122,719	AA.PR	$68.50	$3.75(5.5)	3,100
El Du Pont de Nemours & Co.	DD	45.67	1.64(3.6)	5,777,108	DDPRA	72.00	3.50(4.9)	300
Ford Motor Co.	F	12.52	0.00(0.0)	42,671,766	FPRS	48.18	3.25(6.8)	146,166
National Healthcare	NHC	36.30	1.12(3.1)	30,004	NHCA	13.40	0.80(6.0)	2,456
PG&E Corp.	PCG	45.55	1.82(4.0)	2,565,535	PCG.PRA	27.26	1.50(5.5)	1,311
Public Storage Inc.	PSA	98.36	3.20(3.3)	1,694,942	PSAPRL	25.55	1.68(6.6)	9,324

Source: New York Stock Exchange (www.nyse.com)

that do not pay dividends and therefore miss out on an important source of stable returns.

Corporate managers conduct an important application of the expected return concept to determine the return that their shareholders expect of them. We will discuss this application in detail in later chapters.

ADDITIONAL VALUATION METHODS LG8-6

Variable-Growth Techniques

Some companies grow at such a high rate that we cannot use the constant-growth-rate model to forecast their value. High growth rates might be sustainable for several years, but cannot continue forever. Consider what happens to a high-growth firm. Other companies will surely notice the market potential for high-growth rates and will enter those product markets to compete with the high-growth firm. The competition will soon drive down the growth rates for all companies in that product market. Companies that experience unusually high-growth tend to see that growth become only average in the future unless they possess some kind of entry barrier such as a patent or government regulation due to economies of scale.

Remember that the constant-growth-rate model does not work for companies where $g > i$. And of course, we do not really expect the growth rate for these fast-growing firms to remain constant. To value these firms, we must use a **variable growth rate** technique. The variable-growth-rate method combines the

time **out!**

8-8 Explain how valuable a firm's (and therefore its stock's) growth is. Demonstrate this with growth and no-growth examples.

8-9 What proportion of the 11.39 percent of Coca-Cola's expected return above comes from dividend yield?

finance at work //: investments

Financial Analysts' Predictions and Opinions

Financial analysts examine a firm's business and financial success and assess long-term prospects and management effectiveness. They combine this microeconomic analysis with a macroeconomic view of the conditions of the economy, financial markets, and industry outlooks. Their evaluation results in earnings predictions, stock price targets, and opinions about whether investors should buy the stock. Such recommendations can help investors decide whether to buy, hold, or sell the stock.

Analysts hired by brokerage firms and investment banks are called *sell-side analysts* because their firms make money by selling stocks and bonds. These analysts publicize their predictions and opinions publicly and in company "tip sheets" that are passed along to clients. Keep in mind that sell-side analysts often have incentives to be optimistic. Pension funds and mutual funds often hire analysts to give fund managers private opinions about securities. These analysts are referred to as *buy-side analysts* because they are hired by investment firms looking for advice on what stocks to buy for their portfolios. Because this is private, little buy-side research is made public.

Consider the 15 sell-side analysts' predictions reported for Coca-Cola on the Yahoo! Finance website. The average 5-year share price growth prediction from these analysts is 8.50 percent. This is lower than the growth prediction for the industry (13.58 percent) and sector (13.2 percent). Last, analysts give opinions on whether investors should buy, sell, or hold Coca-Cola stock. Recommendations come in five levels: Strong Buy, Buy, Hold, Sell, and Strong Sell. Of the 15 analysts, five recommend a Strong Buy, eight recommend a Buy, and two recommend a Hold. Note that even though the analysts predict lower than average growth for the industry and sector, and that the analysts provide meager price targets, none of the analysts recommend a Sell or Strong Sell of the stock. This optimism in analysts' opinions is common. Knowledgeable investors know that a "hold" recommendation is as negative as most public or sell-side analysts get, and therefore a "hold" may actually represent a signal to sell.

Want to know more?

Key Words to Search for Updates: **analyst opinion, financial analyst bias** present-value cash flow from equation 8-3 and the constant-growth-rate model from equation 8-6.

First, the investor chooses two different growth rates for two stages of the analysis. The first and higher growth rate, g_1, is the current growth rate, which we expect to last only a few years. A few years from now, we expect the firm to grow at a slower but more sustainable rate of growth, g_2. Figure 8.4 shows the cash flow time line when the first growth rate applies for the first n years, followed by the second growth rate, which applies forever.

When we analyze a variable-growth-rate stock like the one in the figure, we know the recent dividend, D_0, and the two expected growth rates. Therefore, we can calculate each of the dividends shown in general terms (i.e., D_1). For example, the dividend in the first year (D_1) is the year zero dividend that grows at g_1, specifically $D_1 = D_0 \times (1 + g_1)$. The dividend then grows at g_1 again for the second year dividend, $D_2 = D_0 \times (1 + g_1)^2$. The dividend continues to grow through the first stage to year n at $D_n = D_0 \times (1 + g_1)^n$. Figure 8.5 shows the first-stage dividends.

At this point, the company starts to move into stage 2 at the more modest growth rate, g_2, and the dividends reflect that slower growth rate. So D_{n+1} is the dividend D_n that grew at the rate g_2, or $D_{n+1} = D_0 \times (1 + g_1)^n \times (1 + g_2)$. Similarly, the dividend in year $n + 2$ is $D_{n+2} = D_0 \times (1 + g_1)^n \times (1 + g_2)^2$. We can now substitute the known dividends as presented in Figure 8.5 into Figure 8.6.

Once we have calculated all of the dividends, we can begin finding the value of the variable-growth stock by focusing on Stage 2 of the problem. Assume that the dividends in Stage 2 are growing at a modest rate, g_2, forever. As long as $g_2 < i$, Stage 2 can use the constant-growth model, equation 8-6. Remember that the constant-growth model, $P_0 = D_1/(i - g)$,

replaces all future dividends with one value in the previous period. In previous applications, the growth began in year 1, so the value used for all future dividends came from the year 0 dividend. In this case, the change in the dividend rate occurs in year $n + 1$, so we will use the value from year n. So, using the constant-growth model, we can replace all the cash flows in Stage 2 with one value from year n, as:

$$P_n = \frac{D_{n+1}}{i - g_2} = \frac{D_0(1 + g_1)^n(1 + g_2)}{i - g_2}$$

▼**FIGURE 8.4** Variable Dividend Growth

Divide into two stages at the first year of the new growth rate.

▼**FIGURE 8.5** Stage 1 Dividends

Calculate the dividends in the first stage.

▼**FIGURE 8.6** Details of the Variable Growth Dividends

Compute the dividends in the second stage.

The cash flows from Figure 8.6 now appear as shown in Figure 8.7.

By replacing all the Stage 2 cash flows that continued indefinitely with one terminal price in year *n*, we reduce the problem to a fixed number of cash flows. The value of this variable-growth stock is finally computed as the present value of these cash flows, as solved with equation 8-3. Substituting the cash flows shown in Figure 8.7 into equation 8-3 gives us the general formula for finding the value of a variable-growth stock:

▼ **FIGURE 8.7** New Stage 1 of the Variable Growth Dividend Technique

Replace all of the dividends to infinity with the price in year *n*. Stage 2 disappears.

EXAMPLE 8-3

For interactive versions of this example visit www.mhhe.com/canM2e

Variable Growth and McDonald's Stock LG8-6

The dividend has grown from $1.00 per share on November 13, 2006 to $2.20 during 2010. This represents an annual growth rate of 21.8 percent (N = 4, PV = −1.00, PMT = 0, FV = 2.20, C PT I = 21.8). You think this growth rate will continue for three years and then fall to the long-term growth rate of 10.2 percent predicted by analysts. You assume a 14 percent discount rate.

SOLUTION:

Figure 8.3 shows a $2.20 (= 4 × $0.55) per share recent annual dividend. Modify equation 8-8 for a Stage 1 length of three years and then substitute $i = 0.14$, $g_1 = 0.218$, $g_2 = 0.102$, and $D_0 = 2.20. The valuation equation and solution becomes:

Period	0	1	2	3
Dividends	$D_0 = 2.20	$D_1 = 2.20 × (1.218)	$D_2 = 2.20 × (1.218)²	$D_3 = 2.20 × (1.218)³

$$P_3 = \$2.20 \times (1.218)^3 \times (1.102) \div (0.14 - 0.102)$$

$$P_0 = \frac{\$2.20(1+0.218)}{1+0.14} + \frac{\$2.20(1+0.218)^2}{(1+0.14)^2}$$

$$+ \frac{\$2.20(1+0.218)^3 + \dfrac{\$2.20(1+0.218)^3(1+0.102)}{0.14-0.102}}{(1+0.14)^3}$$

$$= \$2.35 + \$2.51 + \frac{\$3.98 + \$115.28}{1.482}$$

$$= \$85.33$$

Given these parameters, McDonald's stock is worth just over $85 per share. Figure 8.3 shows that the stock price at the end of 2010 was around $73. Comparing the stock's value to its market price, the stock is undervalued.

Similar to Problems 8-33, 8-34

General two-stage growth valuation model:

$$\text{Stock value} = \begin{array}{c}\text{Present value of each}\\ \text{dividend during}\\ \text{the first growth stage}\end{array} + \begin{array}{c}\text{Present value of the}\\ \text{second stage}\\ \text{growth}\end{array}$$

$$P_0 = \frac{D_0(1+g_1)}{1+i} + \frac{D_0(1+g_1)^2}{(1+i)^2} + \frac{D_0(1+g_1)^3}{(1+i)^3} + \cdots$$

$$+ \frac{D_0(1+g_1)^n + \dfrac{D_0(1+g_1)^n(1+g_2)}{i-g_2}}{(1+i)^n} \qquad (8\text{-}8)$$

The practical application of the variable-growth valuation technique requires the investor to decide how long the current high-growth rate will last before declining to a more stable rate.

time out!

8-10 Explain how the variable-growth-rate technique could be used for a firm whose dividend is not expected to grow for three years and then will grow at 5 percent indefinitely.

8-11 Set up and solve the McDonald's valuation problem assuming that the first stage growth will last only two years.

The P/E Model LG8-7

The valuation models that we've presented thus far help investors attempt to compute a stock's fundamental value based upon its cash flows to the investor. Another common approach is to assess a stock's **relative value.** This approach compares one company's stock valuation to other firms' stock values to evaluate whether your target company's stock is appropriately priced. The price of a stock taken in isolation doesn't give us a good measure of how expensive it is. Let's use an analogy: At the grocery store, we are less concerned with the total price of a bag of sugar than we are with the price per pound. Similarly, the price of the stock matters less than its price per one dollar of earnings.

Consider one company that earned $5 per share in profits for the year. Its stock sells for $100. Another company earned $2 per share and its

stock price is $50 per share. At first glance, the first stock appears to be more expensive because its price is a high $100 compared to the lower $50 price of the second stock. However, the first company generated higher per-share profits than did the second company. Buying the first stock means that you purchase $5 in earnings. The $100 stock price implies a cost of $20 for every $1 in earnings (= $100 ÷ $5) generated. The $50 price of the second stock implies a cost of $25 for every $1 in earnings (= $50 ÷ $2). So in this regard, the second company becomes more expensive. The **price-earnings (P/E) ratio** represents the most common valuation yardstick in the investment industry; it allows investors to quickly compare the cost of earnings. The P/E ratio is simply the current price of the stock divided by the last four quarters of earnings per share:

$$\text{P/E} = \frac{\text{Current stock price}}{\text{Per-share earnings for last 12 months}} \qquad (8\text{-}9)$$

More accurately, this figure is the **trailing P/E ratio** and it is often denoted as P/E_0, where the 0 subscript denotes the past (or trailing) earnings.

Figure 8.8 shows two companies' trailing P/E ratios: Coca-Cola and McDonald's, as well as the Dow Jones Industrial Average's trailing P/E ratio over a 14-year period. The P/E ratio for the DJIA changes slowly and mostly stays in the 18–27 range until the drop to 15 in 2010. Historically, the DJIA's P/E ratio has

relative value A stock's pricey-ness measured relative to other stocks.

price-earnings (P/E) ratio Current stock price divided by four quarters of earnings per share.

trailing P/E ratio The P/E ratio computed using the *past* four quarters of earnings per share.

▼**FIGURE 8.8** Historical P/E Ratio of the DJIA, Coca-Cola, and McDonald's

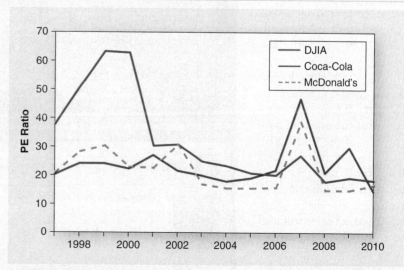

P/E ratios of large, successful companies can vary considerably over time. Here, you see that investors valued Coca-Cola over McDonald's in the late 1990s, but by the beginning of 2008 this preference had evened out.

fallen as low as single digits and climbed to over 30. The figure also shows that the P/E ratio for McDonald's has varied more than has the index's P/E ratio. The P/E ratio for Coca-Cola has experienced wild changes—as high as 63 and as low as 18. Figure 8.8 shows that investors valued Coca-Cola more than McDonald's in the late 1990s, but valued them nearly the same by the beginning of 2008.

Variations in P/E ratios between popular companies can be quite large. For example, in January of 2008, the P/E ratio for Google was 51, while the ratio for ConocoPhillips was only 13.1. Google stock is much more expensive than ConocoPhillips. But this does not mean the ConocoPhillips stock is a better deal than Google stock. Investors are willing to pay much more in relative terms for Google because they expect Google will grow much faster than ConocoPhillips. Indeed, analysts predict an annual growth rate of 34.4 percent per year for Google over the next five years, while they expect a growth rate of only 10.7 percent for ConocoPhillips. Remember that Example 8-2 shows how small changes in growth can result in large stock value changes. The large difference in expected growth between Google and ConocoPhillips causes a large difference in their relative value.

We can more directly see the impact that growth can have on the P/E ratio by modifying the constant-growth model. Begin with the model, $P_0 = D_1 \div (i - g)$. Dividing both sides by the firm's earnings results in $P_0/E_0 = (D_1/E_0) \div (i - g)$. Note that the dividend payout ratio of the firm (D/E), the discount rate (i), and the growth rate (g), taken together, determine the P/E ratio. All else held equal, larger growth rates will lead to larger P/E ratios. Also, firms that have higher payout ratios will have higher P/E ratios. Of course, if a firm pays out a high portion

> ## The value of a stock, and thus its price, relates directly to its future success.

of its earnings as dividends, then it may not have the cash to fund high growth. Thus, high dividend payout firms tend not to be priced the same as high growth firms.

The value of a stock, and thus its price, relates directly to its future success. Note that valuation models use estimates of future dividends and growth rates. Because of this focus on the future, many people prefer to use a P/E ratio that also looks forward rather than trailing. A **forward P/E ratio** uses analyst estimates of the earnings in the next 12 months instead of the past 12 months and can be denoted as P/E_1. The forward P/E ratio has the advantage over the trailing P/E ratio in that it incorporates investors' expectations of the firm's upcoming profits. A disadvantage is that expected earnings are harder to estimate and thus less accurate than past earnings. The media uses the trailing P/E ratio, while financial managers and investors use the forward P/E ratio more.

Knowledgeable investors who use the P/E ratio as a relative measure of value compare it to the firm's expected growth rate. Table 8.3 shows the forward P/E ratio and analysts' expected growth rates for the 30 Dow Jones Industrial Average firms. The firms are sorted by their forward P/E ratios. Investors consider companies with high P/E ratios and high growth rates to be appropriately priced. Companies with low P/E ratios and low growth also seem to be appropriately priced. Investors should be concerned about firms with high P/E ratios and only single-digit growth rates. As such, Coca-Cola, Procter & Gamble, Verizon, and Walt Disney, among others, may be too expensive for their expected growth rates. Many investors like to buy growth stocks. They seek companies with high growth rates. But growth stock investors are also concerned about paying too much for a stock. While examining growth stocks, they can use the P/E ratio to assess how expensive the stock is. On the other hand, investors consider companies with low P/E ratios and high expected growth to be undervalued, and they are often

What is the value of McDonalds stock?

$$P_g = \frac{\$1.50(1 + 0.392)}{1 + 0.14} + \frac{\$1.50(1 + 0.392)^2}{(1 + 0.14)^2} + \frac{\$1.50(1 + 0.392)^3}{(1 + 0.14)^3} + \frac{\frac{\$1.50(1 + 0.392)^3(1 + 0.094)}{0.14 - 0.094}}{(1 + 0.14)^3}$$

$$= \$1.83 + \$2.24 + \frac{\$46}{1.482}$$

$$= \$67.75$$

View guided examples at mhhe.com/canM2e

Since the value ($67.75 ...) e ($58), the stock is considered undervalued.

04:33 / 04:45

👍 caffeinejunkie007 and two others like this.

caffeinejunkie007 Sometimes a Big Mac is more than a Big Mac . . .
7 hours ago · Like

write a comment...

Ticker	Company Name	Stock Price	Forward P/E Ratio	Next 5 Years Growth (%)
KO	Coca-Cola Company	$58.56	15.59	8.50
MCD	McDonald's Corp	74.56	15.36	10.18
CAT	Caterpillar	78.90	14.98	20.00
HD	Home Depot	31.79	14.32	14.10
PG	Procter & Gamble	59.90	14.24	8.76
VZ	Verizon Communication	32.76	14.19	6.54
DIS	Walt Disney Company	33.25	14.05	8.81
DD	E.I. du Pont de Nemours	44.79	14.02	9.50
KFT	Kraft Foods Inc.	30.89	13.77	7.15
MMM	3M Company	87.00	13.74	12.00
UTX	United Technologies	71.46	13.44	10.36
BA	Boeing Company	66.92	13.43	9.33
GE	General Electric	16.30	12.91	13.13
JNJ	Johnson & Johnson	61.94	12.35	6.41
WMT	Walmart Stores	53.67	12.29	10.48
AA	Alcoa Inc.	12.13	12.01	15.00
AXP	American Express	42.63	11.84	9.50
T	AT&T Inc.	28.75	11.43	5.94
CSCO	Cisco Systems	22.11	11.16	12.56
IBM	International Business Machines	134.57	10.85	11.23
INTC	Intel Corporation	19.39	10.07	12.25
MRK	Merck & Company	36.79	9.80	6.01
XOM	ExxonMobil	62.03	9.76	8.40
MSFT	Microsoft Corp.	24.65	9.38	10.37
TRV	The Travelers Company	52.31	9.13	17.43
BAC	Bank of America	13.15	8.95	10.00
JPM	JP Morgan Chase	38.05	8.70	8.00
CVX	Chevron Corp.	81.28	8.28	18.00
HPQ	Hewlett-Packard	42.31	8.21	10.08
PFE	Pfizer	17.25	7.63	1.64

Source: Yahoo! Finance Screener

referred to as **value stocks.** Chevron and Travelers would qualify as value stocks. Many investors like to buy value stocks because they feel they are getting a bargain price for a stable company.

Estimating Future Stock Prices LG8-7

We can often find it useful to estimate a stock's future price. Consider equation 8-3's cash flow discount valuation model. The model requires estimates of future dividends and a future price. How can investors estimate this future price? They can use the P/E ratio model for this purpose. Upon reflection, you will see that multiplying the P/E ratio by

Chevron qualifies as a value stock.

earnings results in a stock price. So, in order to estimate a future price, simply multiply the expected P/E ratio by the expected earnings. This concept is captured in the following equation:

Future price = Future P/E ratio × Future earnings per share

$$P_n = \left(\tfrac{P}{E}\right)_n \times E_n$$
$$= \left(\tfrac{P}{E}\right)_n \times E_0 \times (1 + g)^n \qquad (8\text{-}10)$$

As the formula shows, we can use assumptions about the earnings growth rate to estimate earnings in year n. Many investors believe the firm's P/E ratio in year n is best estimated using today's P/E ratio. However, if today's P/E ratio seems unusual compared with similar firms or even compared with a stock index, then adjustments might be wise.

time out!

8-12 Consider two firms with the same P/E ratio. Explain how one could be described as expensive compared to the other.

8-13 Compute the stock price for Chevron in five years if you expect the P/E ratio to decline to 6 and the earnings per share is $8.41.

EXAMPLE 8-4

For interactive versions of this example visit www.mhhe.com/canM2e

The P/E Ratio Model for Chevron LG8-7

Look at Table 8.3 and notice that the P/E ratio for Chevron seems low at 8.28 relative to the growth (18.0 percent) that analysts expect. Chevron earned $8.41 per share and paid a $2.88 dividend last year. You decide to explore this apparent anomaly and figure out what Chevron's stock price might reach in five years.

SOLUTION:

Compute the expected future price in five years under two different scenarios. The first assumption is that Chevron's P/E ratio will be the same in five years as it is today. But since this P/E ratio seems a bit low, the second scenario allows for a rise in the P/E ratio to 11. Under these two scenarios, the future price estimates are:

$$P_5 = \left(\tfrac{P}{E}\right)_n \times E_0 \times (1 + g)^n = 8.28 \times \$8.41 \times (1 + 0.180)^5 = \$159.31$$

$$P_5 = \left(\tfrac{P}{E}\right)_n \times E_0 \times (1 + g)^n = 11 \times \$8.41 \times (1 + 0.180)^5 = \$211.64$$

Note that if the P/E ratio increases from 8.28 to 11 in five years, the future price could be more than 30 percent higher than analysts expect without the change.

Similar to Problems 8-25, 8-26, 8-35, 8-36

Get Online

mhhe.com/canM2e

for study materials including self-test problems with solutions, quizzes, research projects, minicases, and videos

Your Turn...

Questions

1. As owners, what rights and advantages do shareholders obtain? *(LG8-1)*

2. Describe how being a residual claimant can be very valuable. *(LG8-1)*

3. Obtain a current quote of McDonald's (MCD) from the Internet. Describe what has changed since the quote in Figure 8.1. *(LG8-2)*

4. Get the trading statistics for the three main U.S. stock exchanges. Compare the trading activity to that of Table 8.1. *(LG8-2)*

5. Why might the Standard & Poor's 500 Index be a better measure of stock market performance than the Dow Jones Industrial Average? Why is the DJIA more popular than the S&P 500? *(LG8-3)*

6. Explain how it is possible for the DJIA to increase one day while the NASDAQ Composite decreases during the same day. *(LG8-3)*

7. Which is higher, the ask quote or the bid quote? Why? *(LG8-4)*

8. Illustrate through examples how trading commission costs impact an investor's return. *(LG8-4)*

9. Describe the difference in the timing of trade execution and the certainty of trade price between market orders and limit orders. *(LG8-4)*

10. What are the differences between common stock and preferred stock? *(LG8-5)*

11. How important is growth to a stock's value? Illustrate with examples. *(LG8-5)*

12. Under what conditions would the constant-growth model *not* be appropriate? *(LG8-5)*

13. The expected return derived from the constant-growth-rate model relies on dividend yield and capital gain. Where do these two parts of the return come from? *(LG8-5)*

14. Describe, in words, how to use the variable-growth-rate technique to value a stock. *(LG8-6)*

15. Can the variable-growth-rate model be used to value a firm that has a negative growth rate in Stage 1 and a stable and positive growth rate in Stage 2? Explain. *(LG8-6)*

16. Explain why using the P/E relative value approach may be useful for companies that do not pay dividends. *(LG8-7)*

17. How is a firm's changing P/E ratio reflected in the stock price? Give examples. *(LG8-7)*

18. Differentiate the characteristics of growth stocks and value stocks. *(LG8-7)*

19. What's the relationship between the P/E ratio and a firm's growth rate? *(LG8-7)*

20. Describe the process for using the P/E ratio to estimate a future stock price. *(LG8-7)*

Problems

BASIC PROBLEMS

8-1 **Stock Index Performance** On October 9, 2007, the Dow Jones Industrial Average set a new high. The index closed at 14,164.53, which was up 120.80 that day. What was the return (in percent) of the stock market that day? *(LG8-3)*

8-2 **Stock Index Performance** On March 9, 2009, the Dow Jones Industrial Average reached a new low. The index closed at 6,547.05, which was down 79.89 that day. What was the return (in percent) of the stock market that day? *(LG8-3)*

8-3 **Buying Stock with Commissions** Your discount brokerage firm charges $8.95 per stock trade. How much money do you need to buy 200 shares of Pfizer Inc. (PFE), which trades at $27.22? *(LG8-4)*

8-4 **Buying Stock with Commissions** Your discount brokerage firm charges $9.50 per stock trade. How much money do you need to buy 300 shares of Time Warner Inc. (TWX), which trades at $22.62? *(LG8-4)*

8-5 **Selling Stock with Commissions** Your full-service brokerage firm charges $120 per stock trade. How much money do you receive after selling 150 shares of Nokia Corporation (NOK), which trades at $20.13? *(LG8-4)*

8-6 **Selling Stock with Commissions** Your full-service brokerage firm charges $135 per stock trade. How much money do you receive after selling 250 shares of International Business Machines (IBM), which trades at $96.17? *(LG8-4)*

8-7 **Buying Stock with a Market Order** You would like to buy shares of Sirius Satellite Radio (SIRI). The current ask and bid quotes are $3.96 and $3.93, respectively. You place a market buy order for 500 shares that executes at these quoted prices. How much money did it cost to buy these shares? *(LG8-4)*

8-8 **Buying Stock with a Market Order** You would like to buy shares of Coldwater Creek Inc. (CWTR). The current ask and bid quotes are $20.70 and $20.66, respectively. You place a market buy order for 200 shares that executes at these quoted prices. How much money did it cost to buy these shares? *(LG8-4)*

8-9 **Selling Stock with a Limit Order** You would like to sell 200 shares of Xenith Bankshares Inc. (XBKS). The current ask and bid quotes are $4.66 and $4.62, respectively. You place a limit sell order at $4.65. If the trade executes, how much money do you receive from the buyer? *(LG8-4)*

8-10 **Selling Stock with a Limit Order** You would like to sell 100 shares of Echo Global Logistics Inc. (ECHO). The current ask and bid quotes are $15.33 and $15.28, respectively. You place a limit sell order at $15.31. If the trade executes, how much money do you receive from the buyer? *(LG8-4)*

8-11 **Value of a Preferred Stock** A preferred stock from Duquesne Light Company (DQUPRA) pays $2.10 in annual dividends. If the required return on the preferred stock is 5.4 percent, what's the value of the stock? *(LG8-5)*

8-12 **Value of a Preferred Stock** A preferred stock from Hecla Mining Co. (HLPRB) pays $3.50 in annual dividends. If the required return on the preferred stock is 6.8 percent, what is the value of the stock? *(LG8-5)*

8-13 **P/E Ratio and Stock Price** Ultra Petroleum (UPL) has earnings per share of $1.56 and a P/E ratio of 32.48. What's the stock price? *(LG8-7)*

8-14 **P/E Ratio and Stock Price** JP Morgan Chase Co. (JPM) has earnings per share of $3.53 and a P/E ratio of 13.81. What is the price of the stock? *(LG8-7)*

INTERMEDIATE PROBLEMS

8-15 **Value of Dividends and Future Price** A firm is expected to pay a dividend of $1.35 next year and $1.50 the following year. Financial analysts believe the stock will be at their price target of $75 in two years. Compute the value of this stock with a required return of 11.5 percent. *(LG8-5)*

8-16 **Value of Dividends and Future Price** A firm is expected to pay a dividend of $2.05 next year and $2.35 the following year. Financial analysts believe the stock will be at their price target of $110 in two years. Compute the value of this stock with a required return of 12 percent. *(LG8-5)*

8-17 **Dividend Growth** Annual dividends of AT&T Corp (T) grew from $0.96 in 2000 to $1.33 in 2006. What was the annual growth rate? *(LG8-5)*

8-18 **Dividend Growth** Annual dividends of General Electric (GE) grew from $0.66 in 2001 to $1.03 in 2006. What was the annual growth rate? *(LG8-5)*

8-19 **Value a Constant Growth Stock** Financial analysts forecast Safeco Corp.'s (SAF) growth rate for the future to be 10 percent. Safeco's recent dividend was $1.20. What is the value of Safeco stock when the required return is 12 percent? *(LG8-5)*

8-20 **Value a Constant Growth Stock** Financial analysts forecast Limited Brands (LTD) growth rate for the future to be 12.5 percent. LTD's recent dividend was $0.60. What is the value of Limited Brands stock when the required return is 14.5 percent? *(LG8-5)*

8-21 **Expected Return** Ecolap Inc. (ECL) recently paid a $0.46 dividend. The dividend is expected to grow at a 14.5 percent rate. At a current stock price of $44.12, what is the return shareholders are expecting? *(LG8-5)*

8-22 **Expected Return** Paychex Inc. (PAYX) recently paid an $0.84 dividend. The dividend is expected to grow at a 15 percent rate. At a current stock price of $40.11, what is the return shareholders are expecting? *(LG8-5)*

8-23 **Dividend Initiation and Stock Value** A firm does not pay a dividend. It is expected to pay its first dividend of $0.20 per share in three years. This dividend will grow at 11 percent indefinitely. Using a 12 percent discount rate, compute the value of this stock. *(LG8-6)*

8-24 **Dividend Initiation and Stock Value** A firm does not pay a dividend. It is expected to pay its first dividend of $0.25 per share in two years. This dividend will grow at 10 percent indefinitely. Using an 11.5 percent discount rate, compute the value of this stock. *(LG8-6)*

8-25 **P/E Ratio Model and Future Price** Kellogg Co. (K) recently earned a profit of $2.52 earnings per share and has a P/E ratio of 19.86. The dividend has been growing at a 5 percent rate over the past few years. If this growth rate continues, what would be the stock price in five years if the P/E ratio remained unchanged? What would the price be if the P/E ratio declined to 15 in five years? *(LG8-7)*

8-26 **P/E Ratio Model and Future Price** New York Times Co. (NYT) recently earned a profit of $1.21 per share and has a P/E ratio of 19.59. The dividend has been growing at a 7.25 percent rate over the past six years. If this growth rate continues, what would be the stock price in five years if the P/E ratio remained unchanged? What would the price be if the P/E ratio increased to 22 in five years? *(LG8-7)*

8-27 **Value of Future Cash Flows** A firm recently paid a $0.45 annual dividend. The dividend is expected to increase by 10 percent in each of the next four years. In the fourth year, the stock price is expected to be $80. If the required return for this stock is 13.5 percent, what is its value? *(LG8-5)*

8-28 **Value of Future Cash Flows** A firm recently paid a $0.60 annual dividend. The dividend is expected to increase by 12 percent in each of the next four years. In the fourth year, the stock price is expected to be $110. If the required return for this stock is 14.5 percent, what is its value? *(LG8-5)*

8-29 **Constant Growth Stock Valuation** Walgreen Co. (WAG) paid a $0.137 dividend per share in 2000, which grew to $0.286 in 2006. This growth is expected to continue. What is the value of this stock at the beginning of 2007 when the required return is 13.7 percent? *(LG8-5)*

8-30 **Constant Growth Stock Valuation** Campbell Soup Co. (CPB) paid a $0.632 dividend per share in 2003, which grew to $0.76 in 2006. This growth is expected to continue. What is the value of this stock at the beginning of 2007 when the required return is 8.7 percent? *(LG8-5)*

8-31 **Changes in Growth and Stock Valuation** Consider a firm that had been priced using a 10 percent growth rate and a 12 percent required return. The firm recently paid a $1.20 dividend. The firm just announced that because of a new joint venture, it will likely grow at a 10.5 percent rate. How much should the stock price change (in dollars and percentage)? *(LG8-5)*

8-32 **Changes in Growth and Stock Valuation** Consider a firm that had been priced using an 11.5 percent growth rate and a 13.5 percent required return. The firm recently paid a $1.50 dividend. The firm has just announced that because of a new joint venture, it will likely grow at a 12 percent rate. How much should the stock price change (in dollars and percentage)? *(LG8-5)*

8-33 **Variable Growth** A fast-growing firm recently paid a dividend of $0.35 per share. The dividend is expected to increase at a 20 percent rate for the next three years. Afterwards, a more stable 12 percent growth rate can be assumed. If a 13 percent discount rate is appropriate for this stock, what is its value? *(LG8-6)*

8-34 **Variable Growth** A fast-growing firm recently paid a dividend of $0.40 per share. The dividend is expected to increase at a 25 percent rate for the next four years. Afterwards, a more stable 11 percent growth rate can be assumed. If a 12.5 percent discount rate is appropriate for this stock, what is its value? *(LG8-6)*

8-35 **P/E Model and Cash Flow Valuation** Suppose that a firm's recent earnings per share and dividend per share are $2.50 and $1.30, respectively. Both are expected to grow at 8 percent. However, the firm's current P/E ratio of 22 seems high for this growth rate. The P/E ratio is expected to fall to 18 within five years. Compute a value for this stock by first estimating the dividends over the next five years and the stock price in five years. Then discount these cash flows using a 10 percent required rate. *(LG8-5, LG8-7)*

8-36 **P/E Model and Cash Flow Valuation** Suppose that a firm's recent earnings per share and dividend per share are $2.75 and $1.60, respectively. Both are expected to grow at 9 percent. However, the firm's current P/E ratio of 23 seems high for this growth rate. The P/E ratio is expected to fall to 19 within five years. Compute a value for this stock by first estimating the dividends over the next five years and the stock price in five years. Then discount these cash flows using an 11 percent required rate. *(LG8-5, LG8-7)*

8-37 Spreadsheet Problem Spreadsheets are especially useful for computing stock value under different assumptions. Consider a firm that is expected to pay the following dividends:

Year 1	2	3	4	5	6	
$1.20	$1.20	$1.50	$1.50	$1.75	$1.90	and grow at 5% thereafter

a. Using an 11 percent discount rate, what would be the value of this stock?

b. What is the value of the stock using a 10 percent discount rate? A 12 percent discount rate?

c. What would the value be using a 6 percent growth rate after year 6 instead of the 5 percent rate using each of these three discount rates?

d. What do you conclude about stock valuation and its assumptions?

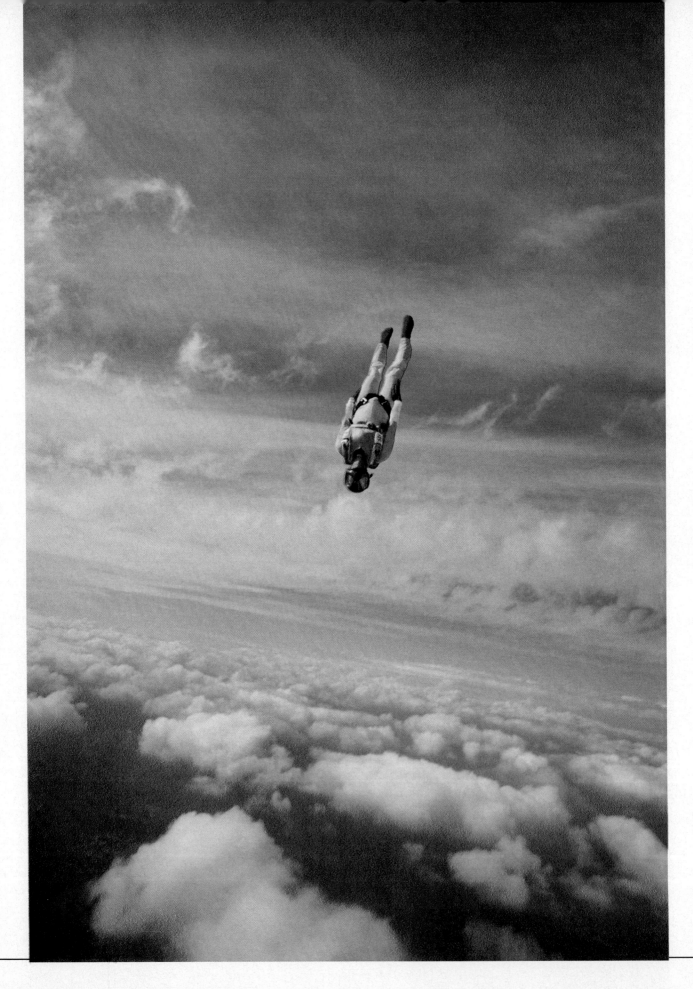

characterizing
risk + return

You can invest your money very safely by opening a savings account at a bank or by buying Treasury bills. So why would you invest your money on risky stocks and bonds if you can take advantage of low-risk opportunities? The answer: Very low risk investments also provide a very low return. Investors take on higher risk investments in expectation of earning higher returns. Likewise, businesses also take on risky capital investments only if they expect to earn higher returns that at least cover their costs, including investors' required return. Both investor and business sentiments create a positive relationship between risk and expected return. Of course, taking risk means that you get no guarantee that you will recoup your investment. In the

continued on p. 210

LEARNING GOALS

LG9-1 Compute an investment's dollar and percentage return.

LG9-2 Find information about the historical returns and volatility for the stock, bond, and cash markets.

LG9-3 Measure and evaluate the total risk of an investment using several methods.

LG9-4 Recognize the risk-return relationship and its implications.

LG9-5 Plan investments that take advantage of diversification and its impact on total risk.

LG9-6 Find efficient and optimal portfolios.

LG9-7 Compute a portfolio's return.

continued from p. 209

short run, higher risk investments often significantly underperform lower risk investments. Companies and investors should expect higher risk investments to earn higher returns only over the long term (many years). In addition, not all forms of risk are rewarded. In this chapter, you'll see how the risk-return relationship fundamentally affects finance theory. We focus on using historical information to characterize past returns and risks. We show how you can diversify to eliminate some risk and expect the highest return possible for your desired risk level. In Chapter 10, we'll turn to estimating the risks and returns you should expect in the future. ■

HISTORICAL RETURNS LG9-1

Let's begin our discussion of risk and return by characterizing the concept of return. First, we need a method for calculating returns. After computing a return, investors need to assess whether it was a good, average, or bad investment return. Examining returns from the past gives us a general idea of what we might expect to see in the future. We should think in terms of return for the long run because a return for any one year can be quite different from the average returns from the past couple of decades.

Computing Returns

How much have you earned on each of your investments? Two ways to determine this are to compute the actual dollar return or compute the dollar return as a percentage of the money invested.

Dollar Return The **dollar return** earned includes any capital gain (or loss) that occurred as well as any income that you received over the period. Equation 9-1 illustrates the dollar return calculation:

$$\text{Dollar return} = \text{Capital gain or loss} + \text{Income}$$
$$= (\text{Ending value} - \text{Beginning value}) + \text{Income} \tag{9-1}$$

For example, say you held 200 shares of RadioShack Corp's (RSH) stock. The consumer electronic goods retailer had a market price of $11.94 per share at the end of 2008. RadioShack also paid $0.25 in dividends per share during 2009. At the end of 2009, RadioShack's stock price was $19.50. For the whole of 2009, you earned a capital gain of ($19.50 − $11.94) × 200 shares, or $1,512, and received a dividend payment of 200 shares × $0.25, or $50. So the total dollar return on your investment was $1,562 (= $1,512 + $50) for 2009.

In RadioShack's case, the stock price increased a lot, so you experienced a capital gain. On the other hand, the stock price of toy and game producer Mattel Inc. (MAT) started the year at $16.00 per share, paid a $0.75 dividend, and ended 2009 at $19.98. If you owned 200 shares of Mattel, you would have experienced a capital gain of only $796. This gain would have been partially offset by the $150 of dividends received. However, the total dollar return would still have been only $946. Stock prices can fluctuate substantially and cause large positive or negative dollar returns.

Does your dollar return depend on whether you continue to hold the Mattel and RadioShack stock or sell it? No. In general, finance deals with *market* values. RadioShack stock was worth $19.50 at the end of 2009 regardless of whether you held the stock or sold it. If you sell it, then we refer to your gains as "realized" gains. If you continue to hold the stock, the gains are "unrealized" gains.

Percentage Return We usually find it more useful to characterize investment earnings as **percentage returns** so that we can easily compare one investment's return to other alternatives' returns. We calculate percentage return by dividing the dollar return by the investment's value at the beginning of the time period.

$$\text{Percentage return} = \frac{\left(\begin{array}{c}\text{Ending value} - \text{Beginning value} \\ + \text{Income}\end{array}\right)}{\text{Beginning value}} \times 100\% \tag{9-2}$$

Because it's standardized, we can use percentage returns for almost any type of investment. We can use beginning and ending values for stock positions, bond prices, real estate values, and so on. Investment income may be stock dividends, bond interest payments, or other receipts. The percentage return for holding the RadioShack stock during calendar year 2009 was a whopping 65.41 percent, computed as:

$$\text{RadioShack percentage return} = \frac{\left[\begin{array}{c}(\$19.50 \times 200) - (\$11.94 \times 200) \\ + (\$0.25 \times 200)\end{array}\right]}{\$11.94 \times 200}$$

$$= 0.6541, \text{ or } 65.41\%$$

The return for the Mattel position during the same period was 29.56 percent:

$$\text{Mattel percentage return} = \frac{\left[\begin{array}{c}(\$19.98 \times 200) - (\$16.00 \times 200) \\ + (\$0.75 \times 200)\end{array}\right]}{\$16.00 \times 200}$$

$$= 0.2956, \text{ or } 29.56\%$$

The 2009 return of 29.6 percent is still quite good for Mattel. Both firms belong to the S&P 500 Index, which earned 23.45 percent in 2009.

Are the 2009 returns for Mattel and RadioShack typical? We look to **average returns** to examine performance over time. The arithmetic average return provides an estimate for how the investment has performed over longer periods of time. The formula for the average return is:

Average return = Sum of all returns ÷ Number of returns

$$= \frac{\sum_{t=1}^{N} \text{Return}_t}{N} \tag{9-3}$$

where the return for each subperiod is summed up and divided by the number of subperiods. You can state the returns in either percentage or decimal format. Table 9.1 shows the annual returns for Mattel and RadioShack during 1985 to 2009. First, notice that over time, the returns are quite varied for both firms. The stock return for Mattel has ranged from a low of −42.2 percent in 1999 to a high of 108.8 percent in 1991. RadioShack's stock return varied between −37.1 percent (2002) to 140.1 percent (1999). Also note that the returns appear unpredictable or random.

Computing Returns LG9-1

You are evaluating a stock's short-term performance. On August 16, 2010, technology firm 3PAR saw its stock price surge on news of a takeover battle between Dell and Hewlett-Packard. 3PAR stock had closed the previous trading day at $9.65 and was up to $18.00 by the end of the day. 3PAR had ended 2009 at $11.85 and does not pay a dividend. What is the dollar return and percentage return of 300 shares of 3PAR for the day and year to date?

SOLUTION:

For the day, realize that no income is paid. Therefore, the dollar return is $2,505 = 300 × ($18.00 − $9.65) + 0 and the percent return is 86.53% = $2,505 ÷ (300 × $9.65). The year to date (YTD) return also does not include dividend income. So the dollar YTD return is $1,845 = 300 × ($18.00 − $11.85). The 3PAR YTD percentage return is:

$$\text{3PAR YTD return} = \frac{(\$18.00 \times 300) - (\$11.85 \times 300) + (\$0)}{\$11.85 \times 300} = 0.5190, \text{ or } 51.90\%$$

Hewlett-Packard eventually won the bidding war and purchased 3PAR for $33 per share!

Similar to Problems 9-1, 9-2, 9-3, 9-4

dollar return The amount of profit or loss from an investment denoted in dollars.

percentage return The dollar return characterized as a percentage of money invested.

average returns A measure summarizing the past performance of an investment.

geometric mean return The mean return computed by finding the equivalent return that is compounded for N periods.

Sometimes a large negative return is followed by another bad year, like Mattel's returns in 2007 and 2008. Other times, a poor year is followed by a very good year, like 2008 and 2009 for RadioShack. The table also reports average annual returns for Mattel and RadioShack of 15.6 percent and 13.0 percent, respectively. Over the years, these stocks have earned investors a good average rate of return.

The average returns shown in this chapter are more precisely called arithmetic average returns. These average returns are appropriate for statistical analysis. However, they do not accurately illustrate the historical performance of a stock or portfolio. To see this, consider the $100 stock that earned a 50 percent return one year (to $150) and then earned a −50 percent return the next year (to $75). The arithmetic average return is therefore (50% + −50%) ÷ 2 = 0%. Do you believe the average return was zero percent per year? If you started with a $100 stock and ended with a $75 stock, did you earn zero percent? No, you lost money. A measure of that performance should illustrate a negative return. The accurate measure to be used in performance analysis is called the **geometric mean return,** or the mean return computed by finding the equivalent return that is compounded for N periods. In this example, the mean return is $[(1 + 0.50) \times (1 + -0.50)]^{1/2} - 1 = -0.134$, or −13.4 percent.[1]

Mattel's stock returns have ranged from −42.2 percent to 108.8 percent.

Given the loss of $25 over two years, this −13.4 percent per year mean return seems more reasonable than the zero percent average return.

Performance of Asset Classes LG9-2

During any given year, the stock market may perform better than the bond market, or it may perform worse. Over longer time periods, how do stocks, bonds, or cash securities perform? Historically, stocks have performed better than either bonds or cash. Table 9.2 shows the average returns for these three asset classes over the period 1950 to 2009, as well as over various subperiods. Over the entire period, stocks (as measured by the S&P 500 Index) earned an average 12.5 percent return per year. This is double the 6.4 percent return earned by long-term Treasury bonds. Cash securities, measured by U.S. Treasury bills, earned an average 4.8 percent return.

The table also shows each asset class's average return for each decade since 1950. The best decade for the stock market was the 1950s, when stocks earned an average 20.9 percent per year. The 1990s ran a close second with a 19 percent per year return. The best decade for the bond market was the 1980s, when it earned an average 13.5 percent per year return due to capital gains as interest rates fell. Stocks have outperformed bonds in

▼ **TABLE 9.1** Annual and Average Returns for Mattel and RadioShack

	Mattel	RadioShack		Mattel	RadioShack
1985	20.0%	68.0%	1998	−35.8%	7.7
1986	−32.9	4.3	1999	−42.2	140.1
1987	−16.8	−21.2	2000	13.9	−12.6
1988	38.8	26.0	2001	20.0	−29.3
1989	107.5	−3.2	2002	11.6	−37.1
1990	2.9	−23.7	2003	2.8	65.1
1991	108.8	0.8	2004	3.6	8.0
1992	16.9	5.3	2005	−16.3	−35.3
1993	11.0	69.3	2006	47.3	−19.0
1994	15.8	2.6	2007	−12.7	2.0
1995	55.8	−15.7	2008	−12.0	−27.7
1996	14.8	7.9	2009	29.6	65.4
1997	36.6	77.5%	**Average =**	**15.6**	**13.0**

Note the range of returns. Few annual returns are close to the average return.
Data Source: Yahoo! Finance

[1]The general formula for the geometric mean return is

$$\text{Geometric mean return} = \left[\prod_{t=1}^{N}\left(1 + \frac{\text{Return}_t}{100}\right) \right]^{\frac{1}{N}} - 1$$

standard deviation A measure of past return volatility, or risk, of an investment.

total risk The volatility of an investment, which includes current portions of firm-specific risk and market risk.

▼ **TABLE 9.2** Annual and Average Returns for Stocks, Bonds, and T-Bills, 1950 to 2009

		Stocks (S&P 500)	Long-Term Treasury Bonds	T-Bills
1950 to 2009	Average	12.5%	6.4%	4.8%
1950 to 1959	Average	20.9	0.0	2.0
1960 to 1969	Average	8.7	1.6	4.0
1970 to 1979	Average	7.5	5.7	6.3
1980 to 1989	Average	18.2	13.5	8.9
1990 to 1999	Average	19.0	9.5	4.9
2000	Annual return	−9.1	20.1	5.9
2001	Annual return	−11.9	4.6	3.5
2002	Annual return	−22.1	17.2	1.6
2003	Annual return	28.7	2.1	1.0
2004	Annual return	10.9	7.7	1.4
2005	Annual return	4.9	6.5	3.1
2006	Annual return	15.8	1.9	4.7
2007	Annual return	3.5	9.8	4.4
2008	Annual return	−35.5	22.7	1.5
2009	Annual return	23.5	−12.2	0.2
2000 to 2009	Average	0.9	8.0	2.7

Returns have been very different among decades.

every decade since 1950 except the recent 2000s. Notice that the average return in the stock and bond markets has not been negative during any decade since 1950. But average stock returns do not really paint a very accurate picture of annual returns. Individual annual returns from 2000 to 2009 show that returns can vary strongly and be quite negative in any particular year. Indeed, this annual variability defines risk. The stock market return in 2008 was particularly poor because of the financial crisis. However, not all stocks fell the same amount. Notice that Mattel and RadioShack declined by only 12.0 and 27.7 percent while the stock market in general declined 35.5 percent. Financial company stocks fell the most during the crisis.

HISTORICAL RISKS

When you purchase a U.S. Treasury bill, you know exactly what your dollar and percentage return are going to be. Many people find comfort in the certainty from this safe investment. On the other hand, when you purchase a stock, you do not know what your return is going to be—either in the short term or in the long run. This uncertainty is precisely what makes stock investing risky. It's useful to evaluate this uncertainty quantitatively so that we can compare risk among different stocks and asset classes.

Computing Volatility LG9-3

Financial theory suggests that investors should look at an investment's historical returns to assess how much uncertainty to expect in the future. If you see high variability in historical returns, you should expect a high degree of future uncertainty. Table 9.2 shows that between 2000 and 2009, the stock market experienced a range of −35.5 percent return in 2008 to a 28.7 percent return in 2003. Bonds experienced a smaller variability: −12.2 percent return in 2009 to 22.7 percent return in 2008. Examining the range of historical returns provides just one way to express the return volatility that we can expect. In practical terms, the finance industry uses a statistical return volatility measure known as the **standard deviation** of percentage returns. We calculate standard deviation as the square root of the variance, and this figure represents the security's or portfolio's **total risk.** We'll discuss other risk measurements in the next chapter.

Our process of computing standard deviation starts with the average return over the period. The average annual return for the stock market since 1950 is 12.5 percent. How much can the return in any given year deviate from this average? We compute the actual annual deviation by subtracting the return each year from this average return: $\text{Return}_{(1950)}$ − Average return; $\text{Return}_{(1951)}$ − Average return; $\text{Return}_{(1952)}$ − Average return, and so on. Note that many of these deviations will be negative

time out!

9-1 How important were dividend payments to the total returns that Mattel and RadioShack offered investors?

9-2 Using the average returns shown in Table 9.2, compute how much a $10,000 investment made in each asset class at the beginning of each decade would become at the end of each decade.

(from a lower-than-average return that year) and others will be positive (from a higher-than-average return). If we computed the *average* of these return deviations, our result would be zero. Large positive deviations cancel out large negative deviations and hide the variability. To really see the size of the variations without the distractions that come with including a positive or negative sign, we square each deviation before adding them up. Dividing by the number of returns in the sample minus one provides the return *variance*.[2] The square root of the return variance is the standard deviation:

$$\text{Standard deviation} = \frac{\text{Square root of the average}}{\text{deviation of returns}}$$

$$= \sqrt{\frac{\sum_{t=1}^{N}(\text{Return}_t - \text{Average return})^2}{n-1}} \quad (9\text{-}4)$$

A large standard deviation indicates greater return volatility—or high risk. Table 9.3 shows the standard deviations of Mattel stock returns over 25 years. The Deviation column shows the annual return minus Mattel's average return of 15.6 percent. The last column squares each deviation. Then we sum up these squared deviations and divide the result by the number of observations less one (24) to compute the return variance. If we want to use a measure that makes sense in the real world (how would you interpret a squared percentage, anyway?), we take the square root of the variance to get the standard deviation. Mattel's standard deviation of returns during this sample period comes to 37.3 percent. In comparison, the standard deviation of RadioShack stock returns for this same period is

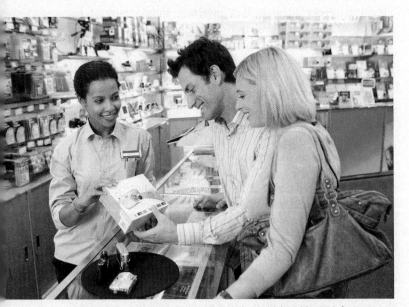

Because RadioShack's standard deviation is higher, it's stock features more total risk.

[2]We use the denominator of $N - 1$ to compute a sample's standard deviation, which is the most common for finance applications. We would divide the standard deviation of a population simply by N.

▼ **TABLE 9.3** Computation of Mattel Stock Return Standard Deviation

	Mattel Return	Deviation	Squared Deviation
1985	20.0%	4.4%	0.2
1986	−32.9	−48.5	23.5
1987	−16.8	−32.4	10.5
1988	38.8	23.2	5.4
1989	107.5	91.9	84.5
1990	2.9	−12.7	1.6
1991	108.8	93.2	86.9
1992	16.9	1.3	0.0
1993	11.0	−4.6	0.2
1994	15.8	0.2	0.0
1995	55.8	40.2	16.2
1996	14.8	−0.8	0.0
1997	36.6	21.0	4.4
1998	−35.8	−51.4	26.4
1999	−42.2	−57.8	33.4
2000	13.9	−1.7	0.0
2001	20.0	4.4	0.2
2002	11.6	−4.0	0.2
2003	2.8	−12.8	1.6
2004	3.6	−12.0	1.4
2005	−16.3	−31.9	10.1
2006	47.3	31.7	10.1
2007	−12.7	−28.2	8.0
2008	−12.0	−27.6	7.6
2009	29.6	14.0	2.0
Average =	**15.6%**	**Sum =**	**334.4**
		Variance =	**13.9**
		Std dev =	**37.3%**

Investors use standard deviation as a measure of risk; the higher the standard deviation, the riskier the asset.

Data Source: Yahoo! Finance

43.9 percent. Since RadioShack's standard deviation is higher, its stock features more total risk than Mattel's stock does.

Although analysts and investors use a stock return's standard deviation as an important and common measure of risk, it's laborious to compute by hand. Most people use a spreadsheet or statistical software to calculate stock return standard deviations.

Risk of Asset Classes LG9-2

We report the standard deviations of return for stocks, bonds, and T-bills in Table 9.4 for 1950 to 2009 and for each decade since 1950. Over the entire sample, the stock market returns' standard deviation is 17.9 percent. As we would expect,

EXAMPLE 9-2

Risk and Return LG9-1 LG9-3

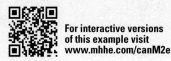

For interactive versions of this example visit www.mhhe.com/canM2e

Find the average return and risk (as measured by standard deviation) for Mattel since 2000. Table 9.3 shows the annual returns for years 2000 to 2009.

SOLUTION:

First, *compute the average annual return* for the period. Using equation 9-3:

$$\frac{13.9\% + 20.0\% + 11.6\% + 2.8\% + 3.6\% - 16.3\% + 47.3\% - 12.7\% - 12.0\% + 29.6\%}{10} = \frac{87.8\%}{10}$$

$$= 8.78\%$$

Mattel has averaged an 8.8 percent return per year since 2000. To *compute the risk*, use the standard deviation equation 9-4. First, find the deviations of return for each year:

Year 2000	2001	2002	2003	2004	2005	2006	2007	2008	2009
13.9%−8.8%	20.0%−8.8%	11.6%−8.8%	2.8%−8.8%	3.6%−8.8%	−16.3%−8.8%	47.3%−8.8%	−12.7%−8.8%	−12.0%−8.8%	29.6%−8.8%

Square those deviations:

Year 2000	2001	2002	2003	2004	2005	2006	2007	2008	2009
$(13.9\%-8.8\%)^2$	$(20.0\%-8.8\%)^2$	$(11.6\%-8.8\%)^2$	$(2.8\%-8.8\%)^2$	$(3.6\%-8.8\%)^2$	$(-16.3\%-8.8\%)^2$	$(47.3\%-8.8\%)^2$	$(-12.7\%-8.8\%)^2$	$(-12.0\%-8.8\%)^2$	$(29.6\%-8.8\%)^2$

Then add them up, divide by $N - 1$, and take the square root:

$$\sqrt{\frac{\begin{array}{c}(13.9\% - 8.8\%)^2 + (20.0\% - 8.8\%)^2 + (11.6\% - 8.8\%)^2 \\ + (2.8\% - 8.8\%)^2 + (3.6\% - 8.8\%)^2 + (-16.3\% - 8.8\%)^2 \\ + (47.3\% - 8.8\%)^2 + (-12.7\% - 8.8\%)^2 + (-12.0\% - 8.8\%)^2 + (29.6\% - 8.8\%)^2\end{array}}{10 - 1}}$$

$$= \sqrt{\frac{26.01 + 125.44 + 7.84 + 36.00 + 27.04 + 630.01 + 1{,}482.25 + 462.25 + 432.64 + 432.64}{9}}$$

$$= \sqrt{406.903} = 20.17\%$$

Mattel stock has averaged an 8.78 percent return with a standard deviation of 20.17 percent for the period 2000 to 2009.

Similar to Problems 9-15, 9-16, 9-17, 9-18, 9-33, 9-34

▼**TABLE 9.4** Annual Standard Deviation of Returns for Stocks, Bonds, and T-Bills, 1950 to 2009

	Stocks	Long-Term Treasury Bonds	T-Bills
1950 to 2009	17.9%	10.7%	2.8%
1950 to 1959	19.8	4.9	0.8
1960 to 1969	14.4	6.2	1.3
1970 to 1979	19.2	6.8	1.8
1980 to 1989	12.7	15.1	2.6
1990 to 1999	14.2	12.8	1.2
2000 to 2009	20.4	10.3	1.9

Some decades experience higher risk then others in each asset class.

stock market volatility is higher than bond market volatility (10.7 percent) or for T-bills (2.8 percent). These volatility estimates are consistent with our previously stated position that the stock market carries more risk than the bond or cash markets do. Every decade since 1950 has seen a lot of stock market volatility. The bond market experienced the most volatility in the 1980s and 1990s as interest rates varied.

You will recall from Chapter 7 that since any bond's par value and coupon rate are fixed, bond prices must fluctuate to adjust for changes in interest rates. Bond prices respond inversely to interest rate changes: As interest rates rise, bond prices fall, and if interest rates fall, bond prices rise. T-bill returns have experienced very low volatility over each decade. Indeed, T-bills are commonly considered to be one of the only risk-free assets.

> ## "Market volatility can cause investors to make emotionally based decisions—selling at low prices."

Higher-risk investments offer higher returns over time. But short-term fluctuations in the value of higher risk investments can be substantial. The stock market is risky—while it has offered a good annual return of 12.5 percent, that return comes with volatility of 17.9 percent standard deviation. Many investors may intellectually understand that this high risk means that they may receive very poor returns in the short term. Investors really felt the full force of this risk when the stock market declined three years in a row (2000 to 2002). Some investors even decided that this was too much risk for them and they sold out of the stock market before the 2003 rally. Other investors got out of the stock market after it plunged to lows in March 2009. Market volatility can cause investors to make emotionally based decisions—selling at low prices.

The stock market returns' standard deviations that appear in Table 9.4 are all considerably lower than the standard deviations of Mattel and of RadioShack stocks (37.3 percent and 43.9 percent, respectively). In this case, we measure stock market return and standard deviation using the S&P 500 Index. Mattel and RadioShack are both included in the S&P 500 Index. Why do these two large firms have measures of total risk—standard deviations—that are at least twice as large as the standard deviations on the stock market returns? Are Mattel and RadioShack just two of the most risky firms in the Index? Actually, no. The differences in standard deviations between these individual companies and the entire market have much more to do with *diversification*. Owning 500 companies, such as all of those included in the S&P 500 Index, generates much less risk than owning just one company. This phenomenon appears in the standard deviation measure. We'll discuss the effects of diversification in detail later in this chapter.

Risk versus Return LG9-4

Investors can buy very safe T-bills. Or they can take some risk to seek higher returns. How much extra return can you expect for taking more risk? This is known as the *trade-off between risk and return*. The **coefficient of variation** (CoV) is a common *relative* measure of this risk-vs-reward relationship. The equation for the coefficient of variation is simply the standard deviation divided by average return. It is interpreted as the amount of risk (measured by volatility) per unit of return:

$$\text{Coefficient of variation} = \text{Amount of risk} \div \text{Return}$$

$$= \frac{\text{Standard deviation}}{\text{Average return}} \qquad (9\text{-}5)$$

As an investor, you would want to receive a very high return (the denominator in the equation) with a very low risk (the

---

EXAMPLE 9-3

For interactive versions of this example visit www.mhhe.com/canM2e

Risk versus Return LG9-4

You are interested in the risk-return relationship of stocks in each decade since 1950. Obtain the average returns and risks in Tables 9.2 and 9.4.

SOLUTION:

Using the coefficient of variation, the average returns, and standard deviation of return, compute the following risk-return relationships:

$$CoV_{1950s} = \frac{19.8\%}{20.9\%} = 0.95 \qquad CoV_{1960s} = \frac{14.4\%}{8.7\%} = 1.66$$

$$CoV_{1970s} = \frac{19.2\%}{7.5\%} = 2.56 \qquad CoV_{1980s} = \frac{12.7\%}{18.2\%} = 0.70$$

$$CoV_{1990s} = \frac{14.2\%}{19.0\%} = 0.75 \qquad CoV_{2000s} = \frac{20.4\%}{0.9\%} = 22.67$$

Note that over short time periods, the stock risk-return relationship varies significantly.

Similar to Problems 9-7, 9-8, 9-19, 9-20, 9-33, 9-34

numerator). So, a smaller CoV indicates a better risk-reward relationship. Since the average return and standard deviation for Mattel stock are 15.6 percent and 37.3 percent, its CoV is 2.39 (= 37.3 ÷ 15.6). This is better than RadioShack's CoV of 3.38 (= 43.9 ÷ 13.0). For all asset classes for the period 1950 to 2009, the stock market earned a higher return than bonds and was also riskier. But which one had a better risk-return relationship? The CoV for common stock is 1.43 (= 17.9 ÷ 12.5). For Treasury bonds, the coefficient of a variation is 1.67 (= 10.7 ÷ 6.4). Even though stocks are riskier than bonds, they involve a somewhat better risk-reward trade-off.

time out!

9-3 What volatility measure can we use to evaluate and compare risk among different investment alternatives?

9-4 Explain why the coefficients of variation for Mattel and RadioShack are so much higher than the CoV for the stock market as a whole.

FORMING PORTFOLIOS

As we noted previously, Mattel and RadioShack stocks' risk as measured by their standard deviations appear quite high compared to the standard deviation of the S&P 500 Index. This is by no means a coincidence. Combining stocks into **portfolios** can reduce many sources of stock risk. **Diversification** reduces risk. The S&P 500 Index, for

Diversification reduces risk.

example, tracks 500 companies, which allows for a great deal of diversification.

Diversifying to Reduce Risk LG9-5

Think about a stock's total risk as having two components. The first component includes risks that are both specific to that company and common to other companies in the same industry. We call this risk **firm-specific risk.** The stock's other risk component is general risk that all firms—and all individuals, for that matter—face based upon economic strength both domestically and globally. We call this type of risk **market risk.** These risks appear in the equation

$$\frac{\text{Total}}{\text{risk}} = \frac{\text{Firm-specific}}{\text{risk}} + \frac{\text{Market}}{\text{risk}} \quad (9\text{-}6)$$

Standard deviations measure total risk. Individual stocks are subject to many firm-specific risks. We can reduce firm-specific risk by combining stocks into a portfolio. Since we can reduce firm-specific risk by diversifying, this risk is sometimes referred to as **diversifiable risk.** If RadioShack announces lower-than-expected profits, its stock price will decline. However, since this news is *specific* to RadioShack, the news should not affect Mattel stock's price. On the other hand, if the government announces a change in unemployment, both stocks' prices will change to some degree. Macroeconomic events represent market risks because such events—unemployment claims, interest rate changes, national budget deficits or surpluses—affect all companies.

Suppose that you own only RadioShack stock and have earned the annual returns shown in Table 9.5. Then someone suggests that you add Mattel to your RadioShack stock to form a two-stock portfolio. Both Mattel and RadioShack stocks carry a lot of total risk. But look at the risk and return characteristics of a portfolio consisting of 50 percent RadioShack stock and 50 percent Mattel stock. You start with RadioShack stock, which provided an average return of 13.0 percent with a risk of 43.9 percent. The two-stock portfolio earns an average 14.3 percent return with a standard deviation of only 26.9 percent. You added a high-risk stock to a high-risk stock and you ended up with a portfolio with much lower risk! This is a hallmark of most portfolios, which pool market risk but often provide offsetting, reduced firm-specific risks overall.

coefficient of variation A measure of risk to reward (standard deviation divided by average return) earned by an investment over a specific period of time.

portfolio A combination of investment assets held by an investor.

diversification The process of putting money in different types of investments for the purpose of reducing the overall risk of the portfolio.

firm-specific risk The portion of total risk that is attributable to firm or industry factors. Firm-specific risk can be reduced through diversification.

market risk The portion of total risk that is attributable to overall economic factors.

diversifiable risk Another term for firm-specific risk.

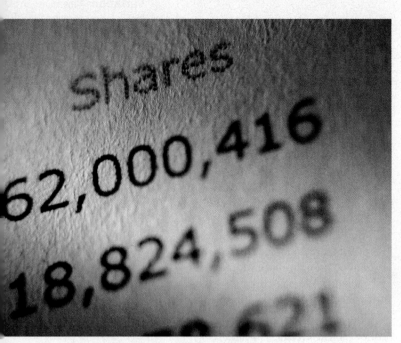

Adding IBM to the portfolio reduces total risk.

Next, add IBM stock to your Mattel and RadioShack stock portfolio. Figure 9.1 shows that the total risk of this three-stock portfolio declines to 20.8 percent. Note that adding Newmont Mining, Disney, and General Electric also reduces the total risk of the stock portfolio. As you add more stocks, the firm-specific risk portion of the total portfolio risk declines. The total risk falls rapidly as we add the first few stocks. Diversification's power to reduce firm-specific risk weakens for the later stocks added to the portfolio, because we have already eliminated much of the firm-specific risk. We could continue to add stocks until the portfolio comprises all S&P 500 Index firms, in which case the standard deviation of the portfolio would be 17.9 percent. At this point, virtually all of the firm-specific risk has been purged and the portfolio carries only market risk, which is sometimes called **nondiversifiable risk.**

Modern Portfolio Theory LG9-6

The concept that diversification reduces risk was formalized in the early 1950s by Harry Markowitz, who eventually won the Nobel Prize in Economics for his work. Markowitz's **modern portfolio theory** shows how risk reduction occurs when securities are combined. The theory also describes how to combine stocks to achieve the lowest total risk possible for a given expected return. Or, said differently, it describes how to achieve the highest expected return for the desired risk level. The combination of securities that achieves the highest expected return for a given risk level is called the investor's **optimal portfolio.**

In our Mattel and RadioShack portfolio example, we allocated 50 percent of the portfolio to Mattel and 50 percent to RadioShack. Is this the best allocation for the portfolio? Consider the different allocations shown in Figure 9.2 for the two stocks. The

▼**TABLE 9.5** Combining Stocks Can Greatly Reduce Risk

	Radioshack	Mattel	Portfolio of Radioshack and Mattel
1985	68.0%	20.0%	44.0%
1986	4.3	−32.9	−14.3
1987	−21.2	−16.8	−19.0
1988	26.0	38.8	32.4
1989	−3.2	107.5	52.2
1990	−23.7	2.9	−10.4
1991	0.8	108.8	54.8
1992	5.3	16.9	11.1
1993	69.3	11.0	40.2
1994	2.6	15.8	9.2
1995	−15.7	55.8	20.1
1996	7.9	14.8	11.4
1997	77.5	36.6	57.1
1998	7.7	−35.8	−14.1
1999	140.1	−42.2	49.0
2000	−12.6	13.9	0.7
2001	−29.3	20.0	−4.7
2002	−37.1	11.6	−12.8
2003	65.1	2.8	34.0
2004	8.0	3.6	5.8
2005	−35.3	−16.3	−25.8
2006	−19.0	47.3	14.2
2007	2.0	−12.7	−5.3
2008	−27.7	−12.0	−19.9
2009	65.4	29.6	47.5
Average =	**13.0**	**15.6**	**14.3**
Std Dev =	**43.9**	**37.3**	**26.9**

The risk-reducing power of diversification! Note that the risk of the portfolio is lower than the risk of the two stocks individually.

Data Source: Yahoo! Finance

graph shows the expected return (computed as average return) and risk (computed as standard deviation) of various portfolios. It would be terrific if you could find a portfolio located in the upper left-hand corner. That is, investors would like a high expected return with low risk. One large dot shows the risk-return point for owning only Mattel. The other large dot shows owning only RadioShack. The smaller diamonds show 10/90, 25/75, 40/60, 50/50, 60/40, 75/25, and 90/10 allocations of Mattel/RadioShack stocks.

While all these portfolios are possible, not all are desirable. For example, the portfolio of 25 percent Mattel and 75 percent RadioShack is not desirable. Other portfolios provide *both* higher return and lower risk. We say that one portfolio dominates the other if it has higher expected return for the same

▼FIGURE 9.1   Adding Stocks to a Portfolio Reduces Risk

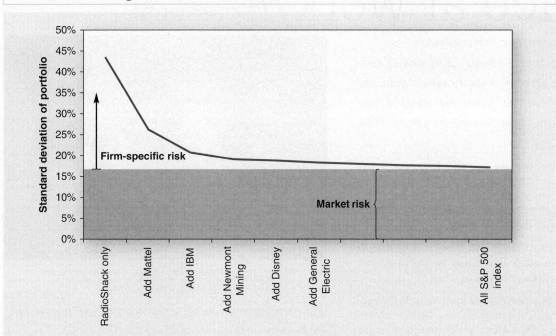

The total portfolio risk is greatly reduced by adding the first few stocks to a portfolio.

▼FIGURE 9.2   Risk and Return Ramifications of Portfolio Allocations to Mattel and RadioShack

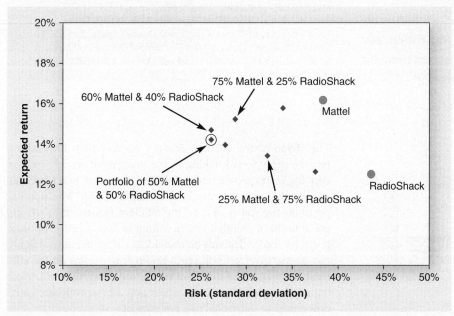

Investors only value the portfolios at the top of the graph because they offer the same risk as the lower portfolios but with higher expected return!

However, the 50/50 portfolio isn't desirable because a portfolio with slightly higher return and slightly lower risk appears above of the 50/50 portfolio: the 60/40 portfolio. Portfolios with the highest return possible for each risk level are called **efficient portfolios.** Notice that if you drew a line connecting the dots, the figure would appear like the end of a bullet. The portfolios on the top of the bullet dominate the portfolios on the bottom; the top portfolio dots show the efficient portfolios for these two stocks.

Figure 9.3 shows efficient portfolios for combining the four stocks: RadioShack, Mattel, IBM, and Newmont Mining. We used this portfolio to demonstrate how diversification reduces risk in Figure 9.1. These portfolios appear as diamonds in the figure with each diamond representing a different allocation of the four stocks. The single square represents the portfolio that consists of 25 percent in each of the four stocks. Notice that other, efficient portfolios dominate this portfolio.

(or less) risk, or the same (or higher) expected return with lower risk. The dominating portfolios appear higher and to the left in the figure. One such portfolio consists of 75 percent Mattel stock and 25 percent RadioShack stock. The 50/50 portfolio (circled in the figure) is also better than the 25/75 portfolio.

If we showed all efficient portfolios, they would appear as a line that connects the upper side of the bullet shape. If we added all available securities to the graph, then all of the efficient portfolios of those securities form the **efficient frontier.** Efficient frontier portfolios dominate all other possible stock portfolios.

finance at work //: personal

Investor Diversification Problems

Experts have examined investor behavior using detailed data-sets of stock brokerage accounts, employee pension plans, and the Survey of Consumer Finances. Studies have identified many investor behaviors that are inconsistent with the principle of full diversification:

- Many households own relatively few individual stocks—they held a median number of two stocks until 2001, when it rose to three. Of course, many households own equity indirectly, through mutual funds or retirement accounts, and these indirect holdings tend to be much better diversified.

- Ten to 15 percent of households with between $100,000 and $1 million in financial asset wealth own no stocks (neither directly nor indirectly through funds).

- Investors seem to prefer securities of local firms. Many geographic regions feature companies that are heavily concentrated in few industries. Thus, a local preference could reduce diversification opportunities.

- Many employees hold mostly their employers' stocks (more than 50 percent of employee holdings), particularly within their 401(k) retirement savings accounts. Holding a lot of a single stock creates a "portfolio" with high total risk.

Finance professionals and the investment industry have established diversification concepts for many decades and can help investors maximize their returns with appropriate risk levels. But

Ten to fifteen percent of households with between $100,000 and $1 million in financial asset wealth own no stocks.

many investors do not consult professionals; they fail to diversify and thus take unnecessary diversifiable risk.

Want to know more?

Key Words to Search for Updates: **diversification, pension plan choices, asset allocation**

Sources: John Y. Campbell, "Household Finance," *Journal of Finance* 61 (2006): 1553–1604; Valery Polkovichenko, "Household Portfolio Diversification: A Case for Rank-Dependent Preferences," *Review of Financial Studies* 18 (2005): 1467–1500; and Shlomo Benartzi, Richard Thaler, Stephen Utkus, and Cass Sunstein, "The Law and Economics of Company Stock in 401(k) Plans," *Journal of Law and Economics* 50 (2007):45–79.

▼**FIGURE 9.3** Efficient Portfolios from Four Stocks

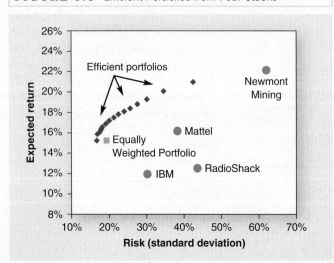

The efficient portfolios dominate all of the individual stocks.

The shape of the efficient frontier implies that diminishing returns apply to risk-taking in the investment world. To gain ever-higher expected rates of return, investors must be willing to take on ever-increasing amounts of risk. The optimal portfolio for you is one on the efficient frontier that reflects the amount of risk that you're willing to take. Clearly, optimal portfolio choice depends on individual risk preferences. Highly risk-averse investors will select low-risk portfolios on the efficient frontier, while more adventuresome investors will select higher-risk portfolios. Any choice may be appropriate, given differences in individual risk preferences.

Investors can further diversify by adding foreign stocks and commodities to their portfolio. For example, a U.S. investor can lower total risk by adding stocks from emerging market countries and gold.

How Does Diversification Work? LG9-5 Will combining any two stocks greatly reduce total risk as much as combining RadioShack and Mattel did? The answer is no. If two stocks are subject to exactly the same kinds of events such that their returns always behave the same way over time, then we have no need to own both stocks—simply pick the one that performs better. Diversification comes when two stocks are subject to different kinds of events such that their returns differ over time.

by its price volatility over time. You would like to reduce the risk by combining your position in Stock A with an equal position in Stock B. In this case, the alternative stock, Stock B, moves the same way over time as Stock A does. When Stock A goes up, so

"The shape of the efficient frontier implies that diminishing returns apply to risk-taking in the investment world."

Consider the illustration in Figure 9.4. You own Stock A in Panel A of the figure. The stock features risk, as demonstrated

does Stock B. They also decline together. A portfolio of both stocks is illustrated. Notice how the portfolio has the same volatility of Stocks A and B separately. Combining these two stocks did not reduce volatility, or total risk.

Now consider Stock C, shown in Panel B. Stock C has the same volatility as Stock A, but its price moves in different directions than does the price of Stock A. When Stock A's price increases, Stock C's price increases sometimes and decreases sometimes. As shown, a portfolio of Stock A and Stock C features much lower volatility than either Stock A or Stock C alone. Combining Stocks A and C reduces risk because their price movements often counteract one another. In short, combining stocks with similar characteristics does not provide much diversification and thus risk reduction. Combining stocks with many differences does provide diversification and thus lowers risk.

The ways that stocks co-move over time determines how much diversification and thus risk reduction we can achieve by combining them. So what we need is some measure of co-movement to help investors form diversified portfolios. That measure, called **correlation,** is denoted by the Greek letter ρ (rho). Correlation is a statistical measure with some very useful characteristics that makes it easy to interpret. Its value is bounded between −1 and +1. A correlation value of +1 means that returns from two different securities move perfectly in sync. They change lock-step up and down together. A value of −1 means that returns from two securities are perfectly inversely correlated—they move exactly opposite. A value of 0 means that the movements of the two returns over time are unrelated to one another. Investors seeking diversification look for stocks where the returns have low or negative correlations with each other.

What return correlations are common between stocks? Panel A of Table 9.6 shows the correlations between many companies. One high correlation shown is the 0.649 correlation between Citigroup and the Bank of New York. This shouldn't be surprising, because these are two similar firms

▼**FIGURE 9.4** Efficient Portfolios from Four Stocks

Panel A: Two stocks that move together over time

Panel B: Two stocks that move differently over time

Combining stocks that move together over time does not offer much risk reduction. Combining stocks that do not move together provides a lot of risk reduction.

▼ **TABLE 9.6** Correlation Between Various Stocks and Asset Classes

Panel A: Company Annual Returns, 1985 to 2009							
	RadioShack	Mattel	IBM	Newmont Mining	Disney	General Electric	Citigroup
RadioShack	1						
Mattel	−0.129	1					
IBM	0.338	−0.125	1				
Newmont Mining	−0.029	−0.130	−0.199	1			
Disney	0.325	0.352	0.004	0.228	1		
General Electric	0.565	0.238	0.337	0.002	0.542	1	
Citigroup	0.400	0.348	0.042	−0.126	0.321	0.784	1
Bank of New York	0.269	0.472	0.071	−0.306	0.438	0.644	0.649

Panel B: Asset Class Annual Returns, 1950 to 2009		
	Stocks	Long-Term Treasury Bonds	T-Bills
Stocks	1		
Long-term Treasury bonds	0.007	1	
T-bills	−0.063	0.207	1

Correlation shows that some stocks move together and some do not.

in the same industry. Combining these two stocks wouldn't reduce risk very much in a portfolio. The largest negative correlation is the correlation of −0.306 between Newmont Mining and the Bank of New York. These firms practice in very different industries and provide large risk reduction possibilities. Note that the correlation between RadioShack and Mattel is −0.129. This negative correlation gives us an answer to the question of why total risk (in the form of standard deviations) fell so much when we combined the two stocks relative to their individual standard deviations as shown in Figure 9.2. Most of the correlations in Table 9.6 are positive. Because most stocks are positively correlated, we typically add many stocks together to fully eliminate all the firm-specific risk in the portfolio, as we showed in Figure 9.1.

JustRon and four others like this.

JustRon Cool vids. The "Choose your own adventure" decision points are fun.
2 hours ago · Like

write a comment...

Panel B of Table 9.6 shows correlations between stocks, bonds, and T-bills. At 0.007, the correlation between stocks and bonds is small. The small correlation allows for the possibility of good risk reduction by adding bonds to a stock portfolio. Therefore, a well-diversified portfolio will contain both stocks and bonds.

Portfolio Return LG9-7

A portfolio's return calculation is straightforward. A portfolio's return comes directly from the returns of the portfolio securities and the proportion of the portfolio invested in each security. For example, General Electric stock earned −1.9 percent in 2009. The Newmont Mining earned 17.3 percent over the same period. If you had invested a quarter of your money in General Electric stock and three quarters of it in Newmont Mining stock, then your portfolio return would be:

finance at work //: markets

International Opportunities for Diversification

The U.S. stock market represents nearly 47 percent of all stock value worldwide. Japanese and U.K. stock markets represent 11 percent and 8 percent of the worldwide stock market value, respectively. Many investment and diversification opportunities present themselves internationally. However, most people allocate very little or none of their portfolios to international securities. If worldwide opportunities can create greater diversification, then those who don't invest in international stocks miss out on an important opportunity to reduce risk in their portfolios.

MSCI Barra is the leading provider of global stock market indexes. Some MSCI Barra indexes follow individual countries. In addition, MSCI Barra compiles composite indexes for groups of companies in developed markets, emerging markets, frontier markets, and by geographic regions. Investment managers use the MSCI World Index, the MSCI EAFE (Europe, Australasia, Far East) Index, and the MSCI Emerging Markets Index as premier benchmarks to measure global stock market performance.

The table to the right shows the average annual returns and standard deviations for the U.S. stock market, Treasury bonds, and the MSCI EAFE and MSCI Emerging Markets indexes for the period 1988 to 2009. Note that both the EAFE and the Emerging Markets indexes feature higher risk than the S&P 500 Index. The Emerging

Markets return has been high, but the EAFE return has been low compared to the U.S. stock and bond markets.

	S&P 500	Bonds	EAFE	Emerging Markets
Average	11.2%	9.2%	6.8%	17.0%
Std. deviation	19.1	10.9	21.2	36.5

The correlations among these markets appear below:

Correlation	S&P 500	Bonds	EAFE
S&P 500	1		
Treasury bonds	−0.08	1	
EAFE	0.75	−0.32	1
Emerging Markets	0.51	−0.36	0.75

The correlation between the S&P 500 Index and the MSCI EAFE is 0.75 and between the Emerging Markets is 0.51. These correlations indicate that diversification might work. Even better diversification appears to be possible between the U.S. Treasury Bond Market and the EAFE and Emerging Markets indexes—look at the negative correlations!

Want to know more?

Key Words to Search for Updates: **international diversification, global asset allocation**

Source: www.mscibarra.com

Return contribution from GE + Contribution from NEM
= $(0.25 \times -1.9\%) + (0.75 \times 17.3\%) = 12.50\%$

To calculate the return on a three-stock portfolio, you will need the proportion of each stock in the portfolio and each stock's return. We typically call these proportions *weights,* signified by *w.* So, a portfolio with *n* securities will have a return of

$$R_p = \left(\begin{array}{c} \text{Proportion of portfolio} \\ \text{in first stock} \end{array} \times \begin{array}{c} \text{That stock's} \\ \text{return} \end{array} \right)$$
$$+ \left(\begin{array}{c} \text{Second stock} \\ \text{portion} \end{array} \times \begin{array}{c} \text{Second stock} \\ \text{return} \end{array} \right)$$
$$+ \cdots$$
$$= (w_1 \times R_1) + (w_2 \times R_2) + (w_3 \times R_3)$$
$$+ \cdots + (w_n \times R_n) = \sum_{i=1}^{n} w_i R_i \qquad (9\text{-}7)$$

the Math Coach on...
Portfolio Returns

" When computing portfolio returns, use the decimal format for the portfolio weights and the percentage format for the security returns. The result of equation 9-7 will then be in percentage format. *"*

where the sum of the weights, *w*, must equal one. The portfolio's rate of return is a simple weighted sum of the returns of each stock in the portfolio. Investors choose portfolio weights by determining how much of each stock they want in their portfolios. Ideally, investors will choose weights for their portfolios located on the efficient frontier (shown in Figure 9.3).

time **out!**

9-5 Describe characteristics of companies that would be good to combine into a portfolio.

9-6 Explain why one portfolio made up of the same companies (but not in the same proportions) as another portfolio can be undesirable in comparison.

9-7 Combining which two companies in Table 9.6 would reduce risk the most? Combining which two would create the least diversification?

EXAMPLE 9-4

Computing Portfolio Returns LG9-7

For interactive versions of this example visit www.mhhe.com/canM2e

At the beginning of the year, you owned $5,000 of Disney stock, $10,000 of Bank of New York stock, and $15,000 of IBM stock. During the year, Disney, Bank of New York, and IBM returned −4.8 percent, 19.4 percent, and 12.8 percent, respectively. What is your portfolio's return?

SOLUTION:

First determine your portfolio weights. The three stocks make up a $30,000 portfolio. Disney makes up a 16.67 percent (= $5,000 ÷ $30,000) portion of the portfolio. Bank of New York stock makes up a 33.33 percent (=$10,000 ÷ $30,000) portion, and IBM a 50.0 percent (=$15,000 ÷ $30,000) portion. The portfolio return can now be computed as:

$$R_P = (0.1667 \times -4.8\%) + (0.3333 \times 19.4\%) + (0.50 \times 12.8\%) = -0.80\% + 6.47\% + 6.40\%$$
$$= 12.07\%$$

Similar to Problems: 9-11, 9-12, 9-13, 9-14, 9-23, 9-24, 9-25, 9-26, 9-29, 9-30, 9-31, 9-32

Get Online

mhhe.com/canM2e

for study materials including self-test problems with solutions, quizzes, research projects, minicases, and videos

Your Turn...

Questions

1. Why is the percentage return a more useful measure than the dollar return? *(LG9-1)*

2. Characterize the historical return, risk, and risk-return relationship of the stock, bond, and cash markets. *(LG9-2)*

3. How do we define risk in this chapter and how do we measure it? *(LG9-3)*

4. What are the two components of total risk? Which component is part of the risk-return relationship? Why? *(LG9-3)*

5. What's the source of firm-specific risk? What's the source of market risk? *(LG9-3)*

6. Which company is likely to have lower total risk, General Electric or Coca-Cola? Why? *(LG9-3)*

7. Can a company change its total risk level over time? How? *(LG9-3)*

8. What does the coefficient of variation measure? Why is a lower value better for the investor? *(LG9-4)*

9. You receive an investment newsletter advertisement in the mail. The letter claims that you should invest in a stock that has doubled the return of the S&P 500 Index over the last three months. It also claims that this stock is a surefire safe bet for the future. Explain how these two claims are inconsistent with finance theory. *(LG9-4)*

10. What does diversification do to the risk and return characteristics of a portfolio? *(LG9-5)*

11. Describe the diversification potential of two assets with a −0.8 correlation. What's the potential if the correlation is +0.8? *(LG9-5)*

12. You are a risk-averse investor with a low-risk portfolio of bonds. How is it possible that adding some stocks (which are riskier than bonds) to the portfolio can lower the total risk of the portfolio? *(LG9-5)*

13. You own only two stocks in your portfolio but want to add more. When you add a third stock, the total risk of your portfolio declines. When you add a tenth stock to the portfolio, the total risk declines. Adding which stock, the third or the tenth, likely reduced the total risk more? Why? *(LG9-5)*

14. Many employees believe that their employer's stock is less likely to lose half of its value than a well-diversified portfolio of stocks. Explain why this belief is erroneous. *(LG9-5)*

15. Explain what we mean when we say that one portfolio dominates another portfolio. *(LG9-6)*

16. Explain what the efficient frontier is and why it is important to investors. *(LG9-6)*

17. If an investor's desired risk level changes over time, should the investor change the composition of his or her portfolio? How? *(LG9-6)*

18. Say you own 200 shares of Mattel and 100 shares of RadioShack. Would your portfolio return be different if you instead owned 100 shares of Mattel and 200 shares of RadioShack? Why? *(LG9-7)*

Problems

BASIC PROBLEMS

9-1 **Investment Return** FedEx Corp. stock ended the previous year at $103.39 per share. It paid a $0.35 per share dividend last year. It ended last year at $106.69. If you owned 300 shares of FedEx, what was your dollar return and percent return? *(LG9-1)*

9-2 **Investment Return** Sprint Nextel Corp. stock ended the previous year at $23.36 per share. It paid a $2.37 per share dividend last year. It ended last year at $18.89. If you owned 500 shares of Sprint, what was your dollar return and percent return? *(LG9-1)*

9-3 **Investment Return** A corporate bond that you own at the beginning of the year is worth $975. During the year, it pays $45 in interest payments and ends the year valued at $965. What was your dollar return and percent return? *(LG9-1)*

9-4 **Investment Return** A Treasury bond that you own at the beginning of the year is worth $1,055. During the year, it pays $35 in interest payments and ends the year valued at $1,065. What was your dollar return and percent return? *(LG9-1)*

9-5 **Total Risk** Rank the following three stocks by their level of total risk, highest to lowest. Rail Haul has an average return of 12 percent and standard deviation of 25 percent. The average return and standard deviation of Idol Staff are 15 percent and 35 percent; and of Poker-R-Us are 9 percent and 20 percent. *(LG9-3)*

9-6 **Total Risk** Rank the following three stocks by their total risk level, highest to lowest. Night Ryder has an average return of 12 percent and standard deviation of 32 percent. The average return and standard deviation of WholeMart are 11 percent and 25 percent; and of Fruit Fly are 16 percent and 40 percent. *(LG9-3)*

9-7 **Risk versus Return** Rank the following three stocks by their risk-return relationship, best to worst. Rail Haul has an average return of 12 percent and standard deviation of 25 percent. The average return and standard deviation of Idol Staff are 15 percent and 35 percent; and of Poker-R-Us are 9 percent and 20 percent. *(LG9-4)*

9-8 **Risk versus Return** Rank the following three stocks by their risk-return relationship, best to worst. Night Ryder has an average return of 13 percent and standard deviation of 29 percent. The average return and standard deviation of WholeMart are 11 percent and 25 percent; and of Fruit Fly are 16 percent and 40 percent. *(LG9-4)*

9-9 **Dominant Portfolios** Determine which one of these three portfolios dominates another. Name the dominated portfolio and the portfolio that dominates it. Portfolio Blue has an expected return of 12 percent and risk of 18 percent. The expected return and risk of portfolio Yellow are 15 percent and 17 percent, and for the Purple portfolio are 14 percent and 21 percent. *(LG9-6)*

9-10 **Dominant Portfolios** Determine which one of the three portfolios dominates another. Name the dominated portfolio and the portfolio that dominates it. Portfolio Green has an expected return of 15 percent and risk of 21 percent. The expected return and risk of portfolio Red are 13 percent and 17 percent, and for the Orange portfolio are 13 percent and 16 percent. *(LG9-6)*

9-11 **Portfolio Weights** An investor owns $4,000 of Adobe Systems stock, $5,000 of Dow Chemical, and $5,000 of Office Depot. What are the portfolio weights of each stock? *(LG9-7)*

9-12 **Portfolio Weights** An investor owns $3,000 of Adobe Systems stock, $6,000 of Dow Chemical, and $7,000 of Office Depot. What are the portfolio weights of each stock? *(LG9-7)*

9-13 **Portfolio Return** Year-to-date, Oracle had earned a −1.34 percent return. During the same time period, Valero Energy earned 7.96 percent and McDonald's earned 0.88 percent. If you have a portfolio made up of 30 percent Oracle, 25 percent Valero Energy, and 45 percent McDonald's, what is your portfolio return? *(LG9-7)*

9-14 **Portfolio Return** Year-to-date, Yum Brands had earned a 3.80 percent return. During the same time period, Raytheon earned 4.26 percent and Coca-Cola earned −0.46 percent. If you have a portfolio made up of 30 percent Yum Brands, 30 percent Raytheon, and 40 percent Coca-Cola, what is your portfolio return? *(LG9-7)*

INTERMEDIATE PROBLEMS

9-15 **Average Return** The past five monthly returns for Kohls are 3.54 percent, 3.62 percent, −1.68 percent, 9.25 percent, and −2.56 percent. What is the average monthly return? *(LG9-1)*

9-16 **Average Return** The past five monthly returns for PG&E are −3.17 percent, 3.88 percent, 3.77 percent, 6.47 percent, and 3.58 percent. What is the average monthly return? *(LG9-1)*

9-17 **Standard Deviation** Compute the standard deviation of Kohls' monthly returns shown in problem 9-15. *(LG9-3)*

9-18 **Standard Deviation** Compute the standard deviation of PG&E's monthly returns shown in problem 9-16. *(LG9-3)*

9-19 **Risk versus Return in Bonds** Assess the risk-return relationship of the bond market (see Tables 9.2 and 9.4) during each decade since 1950. *(LG9-2, LG9-4)*

9-20 **Risk versus Return in T-bills** Assess the risk-return relationship in T-bills (see Tables 9.2 and 9.4) during each decade since 1950. *(LG9-2, LG9-4)*

9-21 **Diversifying** Consider the characteristics of the following three stocks:

	Expected Return	Standard Deviation
Thumb Devices	13%	23%
Air Comfort	10	19
Sport Garb	10	17

The correlation between Thumb Devices and Air Comfort is −0.12. The correlation between Thumb Devices and Sport Garb is −0.21. The correlation between Air Comfort and Sport Garb is 0.77. If you can pick only two stocks for your portfolio, which would you pick? Why? *(LG9-4, LG9-5)*

9-22 **Diversifying** Consider the characteristics of the following three stocks:

	Expected Return	Standard Deviation
Pic Image	11%	19%
Tax Help	9	19
Warm Wear	14	25

The correlation between Pic Image and Tax Help is 0.88. The correlation between Pic Image and Warm Wear is −0.21. The correlation between Tax Help and Warm Wear is −0.19. If you can pick only two stocks for your portfolio, which would you pick? Why? *(LG9-4, LG9-5)*

9-23 **Portfolio Weights** If you own 300 shares of Alaska Air at $42.88, 350 shares of Best Buy at $51.32, and 250 shares of Ford Motor at $8.51, what are the portfolio weights of each stock? *(LG9-7)*

9-24 **Portfolio Weights** If you own 400 shares of Xerox at $17.34, 500 shares of Qwest at $8.15, and 350 shares of Liz Claiborne at $44.73, what are the portfolio weights of each stock? *(LG9-7)*

9-25 Portfolio Return At the beginning of the month, you owned $5,500 of General Dynamics, $7,500 of Starbucks, and $8,000 of Nike. The monthly returns for General Dynamics, Starbucks, and Nike were 6.80 percent, −1.36 percent, and −0.54 percent. What is your portfolio return? *(LG9-7)*

9-26 Portfolio Return At the beginning of the month, you owned $6,000 of News Corp, $5,000 of First Data, and $8,500 of Whirlpool. The monthly returns for News Corp, First Data, and Whirlpool were 8.24 percent, −2.59 percent, and 10.13 percent. What's your portfolio return? *(LG9-7)*

ADVANCED PROBLEMS

9-27 Asset Allocation You have a portfolio with an asset allocation of 50 percent stocks, 40 percent long-term Treasury bonds, and 10 percent T-bills. Use these weights and the returns in Table 9.2 to compute the return of the portfolio in the year 2000 and each year since. Then compute the average annual return and standard deviation of the portfolio and compare them with the risk and return profile of each individual asset class. *(LG9-2, LG9-5)*

9-28 Asset Allocation You have a portfolio with an asset allocation of 35 percent stocks, 55 percent long-term Treasury bonds, and 10 percent T-bills. Use these weights and the returns in Table 9.2 to compute the return of the portfolio in the year 2000 and each year since. Then compute the average annual return and standard deviation of the portfolio and compare them with the risk and return profile of each individual asset class. *(LG9-2, LG9-5)*

9-29 Portfolio Weights You have $15,000 to invest. You want to purchase shares of Alaska Air at $42.88, Best Buy at $51.32, and Ford Motor at $8.51. How many shares of each company should you purchase so that your portfolio consists of 30 percent Alaska Air, 40 percent Best Buy, and 30 percent Ford Motor? Report only whole stock shares. *(LG9-7)*

9-30 Portfolio Weights You have $20,000 to invest. You want to purchase shares of Xerox at $17.34, Qwest at $8.15, and Liz Claiborne at $44.73. How many shares of each company should you purchase so that your portfolio consists of 25 percent Xerox, 40 percent Qwest, and 35 percent Liz Claiborne? Report only whole stock shares. *(LG9-7)*

9-31 Portfolio Return The table below shows your stock positions at the beginning of the year, the dividends that each stock paid during the year, and the stock prices at the end of the year. What is your portfolio dollar return and percentage return? *(LG9-7)*

Company	Shares	Beginning of Year Price	Dividend Per Share	End of Year Price
US Bank	300	$43.50	$2.06	$43.43
PepsiCo	200	59.08	1.16	62.55
JDS Uniphase	500	18.88		16.66
Duke Energy	250	27.45	1.26	33.21

9-32 Portfolio Return The table below shows your stock positions at the beginning of the year, the dividends that each stock paid during the year, and the stock prices at the end of the year. What is your portfolio dollar return and percentage return? *(LG9-7)*

Company	Shares	Beginning of Year Price	Dividend Per Share	End of Year Price
Johnson Controls	350	$72.91	$1.17	$85.92
Medtronic	200	57.57	0.41	53.51
Direct TV	500	24.94		24.39
Qualcomm	250	43.08	0.45	38.92

9-33 Risk, Return, and Their Relationship Consider the following annual returns of Estee Lauder and Lowe's Companies:

	Estee Lauder	Lowe's Companies
Year 1	23.4%	−6.0%
Year 2	−26.0	16.1
Year 3	17.6	4.2
Year 4	49.9	48.0
Year 5	−16.8	−19.0

Compute each stock's average return, standard deviation, and coefficient of variation. Which stock appears better? Why? *(LG9-3, LG9-4)*

9-34 Risk, Return, and Their Relationship Consider the following annual returns of Molson Coors and International Paper:

	Molson Coors	International Paper
Year 1	16.3%	4.5%
Year 2	−9.7	−17.5
Year 3	36.5	−0.2
Year 4	−6.9	26.6
Year 5	16.2	−11.1

Compute each stock's average return, standard deviation, and coefficient of variation. Which stock appears better? Why? *(LG9-3, LG9-4)*

9-35 Spreadsheet Problem Below are the monthly returns for May 2005 to October 2010 of three international stock indices: All Ordinaries of Australia, Nikkei 225 of Japan, and FTSE 100 of England.

Date	All Ordinaries (Australia)	Nikkei 225 (Japan)	FTSE 100 (England)
Oct. 10	2.08%	−1.78%	2.28%
Sep. 10	4.46	6.18	6.19
Aug. 10	−1.52	−7.48	−0.62
Jul. 10	4.22	1.65	6.94
Jun. 10	−2.89	−3.95	−5.23
May 10	−7.87	−11.65	−6.57
Apr. 10	−1.21	−0.29	−2.22
Mar. 10	5.20	9.52	6.07
Feb. 10	1.18	−0.71	3.20
Jan. 10	−5.85	−3.30	−4.15
Dec. 09	3.55	12.85	4.28
Nov. 09	1.48	−6.87	2.90
Oct. 09	−1.95	−0.97	−1.74
Sep. 09	5.69	−3.42	4.58
Aug. 09	5.52	1.31	6.52
Jul. 09	7.64	4.00	8.45
Jun. 09	3.53	4.58	−3.82
May 09	1.83	7.86	4.10
Apr. 09	6.01	8.86	8.09

(continued)

Date	All Ordinaries (Australia)	Nikkei 225 (Japan)	FTSE 100 (England)
Mar. 09	7.14	7.15	2.51
Feb. 09	−5.21	−5.32	−7.70
Jan. 09	−4.95	−9.77	−6.42
Dec. 08	−0.36	4.08	3.41
Nov. 08	−7.78	−0.75	−2.04
Oct. 08	−14.00	−23.83	−10.71
Sep. 08	−11.20	−13.87	−13.02
Aug. 08	3.22	−2.27	4.15
Jul. 08	−5.26	−0.78	−3.80
Jun. 08	−7.64	−5.98	−7.06
May 08	2.07	3.53	−0.56
Apr. 08	4.57	10.57	6.76
Mar. 08	−4.67	−7.92	−3.10
Feb. 08	−0.39	0.08	0.08
Jan. 08	−11.28	−11.21	−8.94
Dec. 07	−2.62	−2.38	0.38
Nov. 07	−2.74	−6.31	−4.30
Oct. 07	3.01	−0.29	3.94
Sep. 07	5.32	1.31	2.59
Aug. 07	0.98	−3.94	−0.89
Jul. 07	−1.95	−4.90	−3.75
Jun. 07	−0.49	1.47	−0.20
May 07	2.98	2.73	2.67
Apr. 07	3.00	0.65	2.24
Mar. 07	2.79	−1.80	2.21
Feb. 07	1.02	1.27	−0.51
Jan. 07	2.01	0.91	−0.28
Dec. 06	3.35	5.85	2.84
Nov. 06	2.03	−0.76	−1.31
Oct. 06	4.69	1.69	2.83
Sep. 06	0.65	−0.08	0.93
Aug. 06	2.48	4.42	−0.37
Jul. 06	−1.53	−0.31	1.63
Jun. 06	1.24	0.24	1.91
May 06	−4.51	−8.51	−4.97
Apr. 06	2.35	−0.90	0.98
Mar. 06	4.28	5.27	2.99
Feb. 06	−0.04	−2.67	0.54
Jan. 06	3.64	3.34	2.52
Dec. 05	2.73	8.33	3.61
Nov. 05	3.87	9.30	1.99
Oct. 05	−3.92	0.24	−2.93
Sep. 05	4.06	9.35	3.41
Aug. 05	1.54	4.32	0.28
Jul. 05	2.76	2.72	3.31
Jun. 05	3.92	2.73	3.01
May 05	3.23	2.43	3.38

a. Compute and compare each index's monthly average return and standard deviation.

b. Compute the correlation between *(1)* All Ordinaries and Nikkei 225, (2) All Ordinaries and FTSE 100, and (3) Nikkei 225 and FTSE 100, and compare them.

c. Form a portfolio consisting of one-third of each of the indexes and show the portfolio return each year, and the portfolio's return and standard deviation.

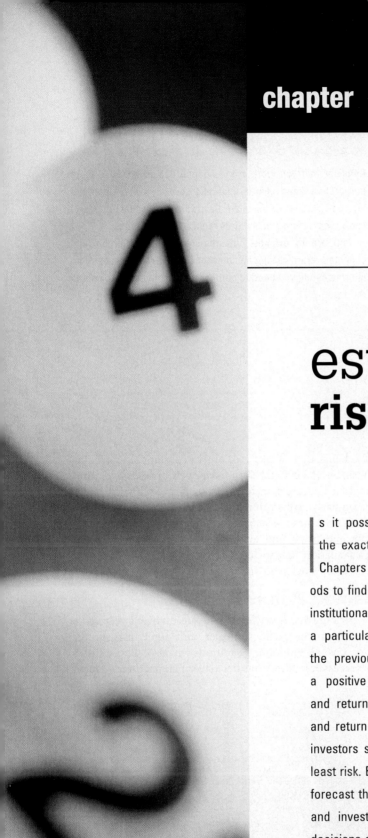

chapter ten

estimating
risk + return

I s it possible for investors to know the exact risk they have to take? In Chapters 9 and 10, we explore methods to find the return that individual or institutional investors require to make a particular investment attractive. In the previous chapter, we established a positive relationship between risk and return using historical data. Risk and return play an undeniable role as investors seek the best return for the least risk. But until there's some way to forecast the future, financial managers and investors must make investment decisions armed only with their *expectations* about future risk and return. We need an exact specification that shows directly the amount of reward required for investors to take the level of risk in a

given firm's stock or portfolio of securities. In this chapter we will also see how investors get the information they need to make risk-reward decisions.

continued on p. 234

LEARNING GOALS

LG10-1 Compute forward-looking expected return and risk.

LG10-2 Understand risk premiums.

LG10-3 Know and apply the capital asset pricing model (CAPM).

LG10-4 Calculate and apply beta, a measure of market risk.

LG10-5 Differentiate among the different levels of market efficiency and their implications.

LG10-6 Calculate and explain investors' required return and risk.

LG10-7 Use the constant-growth model to compute required return.

continued from p. 233

Investors need to know how much risk they have to take to confidently expect a 10 percent return. Managers also want to know what return shareholders require, so that they can decide how to meet those expectations. In Chapter 11, we'll explore how managers conduct financial analysis to find the shareholders' required return. If we want to specify the exact risk-return relationship, we need to develop a better measure of *risk* for individuals and institutional investors. As we saw in Chapter 9, any firm's total risk is specific to that particular firm. But the market doesn't reward firm-specific risk, because investors can easily diversify away any single firm's specific risks by owning other offsetting firms' stocks to create a portfolio subject only to market or undiversifiable risk. So, we need to find just the market risk portion of total risk for investors. The theory to find the market risk portion of stock ownership extends modern portfolio theory. Our search to find market risk will lead us to the capital asset pricing model (CAPM), which utilizes a measure of market risk called beta. CAPM's risk-return specification provides us a powerful tool to make better investment decisions.

Corporate finance managers and investment professionals commonly use the beta measure. But like any theory, CAPM has its limitations. We'll discuss the CAPM's limitations and concerns about beta and propose an alternate required return measure. Whether beta or any other risk-return specification is useful relies in part on whether a stock's price represents a fair estimate of the true company value. Stock price validity and reliability—their general correctness—is vitally important both to investors and corporate managers. ■

possibly change their stocks' risk level by substantially changing their business. If a firm takes on riskier new projects over time, or changes the nature of its business, the firm itself will become riskier. Similarly, firms can reduce their risk level—and hence, their stock's riskiness—by choosing low-risk new projects. Both investors and firms find *expected return,* a forward-looking return calculation that includes risk measures, very useful to estimate future stock performance.

Expected Return and Risk

We can attribute a company's business success over a year partly to its management talent, strategies, and other firm-specific activities. Overall economic conditions will also affect a firm's level of success or failure. Consider a steel manufacturer—Nucor

A company's success depends partly on management talent, strategies, and other activities.

EXPECTED RETURNS LG10-1

In the previous chapter, we characterized risk and return in historical terms. We defined a stock's return as the actual profit realized while holding the stock or the average return over a longer period. We described risk simply as the standard deviation of those returns—a term already familiar to you from your statistics classes. So, we did a good job describing the risk and return that the stock experienced *in the past.* But do those risk and return figures hold into the future? Firms can quite

You have just started your first job in the corporate world and need to make some retirement plan decisions. The company's 401(k) retirement plan offers three investment choices: a stock portfolio, a bond portfolio, and a money market account. For your allocation, you decide to contribute $200 per month to the stock portfolio, $100 to the bond portfolio, and $50 to the money market account.

What risk level are you taking in your retirement portfolio and what return should you expect over the long run?

Investing mainly in my own company's stock is safer, right? Mabye not . . . Scan the QR code for an extended look. Turn to the back of the book for solutions to these applications.

probability The likelihood of occurrence.

expected return The average of the possible returns weighted by the likelihood of those returns occurring.

probability distribution The set of probabilities for all possible occurrences.

in an economy with only two states: good and recession. In this scenario, Nucor's expected return would be 11 percent [=(0.7 × 20%) + (0.3 × −10%)]. Of course, nothing is quite that simple. Economists seldom predict simple two-state views of the economy as in the above example. Rather, economists give much more detailed forecasts (such as three states: red-hot economy, average expansion, and recession). So our general equation for a stock's expected return with S different conditions of the economy is

$$\begin{array}{l} \dfrac{\text{Expected}}{\text{return}} = \dfrac{\text{Sum of}}{\text{each return}} \times \dfrac{\text{Probability of}}{\text{that return}} \qquad (10\text{-}1) \\[2mm] = (p_1 \times \text{Return}_1) + (p_2 \times \text{Return}_2) \\[1mm] \quad + (p_3 \times \text{Return}_3) + \cdots + (p_s \times \text{Return}_s) \\[1mm] = \displaystyle\sum_{j=1}^{s} p_j \times \text{Return}_j \end{array}$$

The result of this expected return calculation has some interesting properties. First, the expected return figure expresses what the average return would be over time if the probabilistic states of the economy occur as predicted. For example, the 70/30 **probability distribution** for good-recession economic states suggests that the economy will be good in 7 of the next 10 years, earning Nucor shareholders a 20 percent return in each of those years. Shareholders would lose 10 percent in each of the three recession years. So the *average return* over those 10 years would be 11 percent, the same as the expected return. The second interesting property: The expected return itself will not likely occur during any one year. Remember that Nucor will earn either a return of 20 percent or −10 percent. Yet its expected return is 11 percent, a value that it cannot earn because we have no economic condition for which the return is 11 percent.

Corp. The steel business closely follows economic trends. In a good economy, demand for steel is strong as builders and manufacturers step up building and production. During economic recessions, demand for steel falls off quickly. So, if we want to assess Nucor's probabilities for success next year, we know that we must look partly at Nucor's managerial ability and partly at the economic outlook.

Unfortunately, we cannot accurately predict what the economy will be like next year. Predicting economic activity is like predicting the weather—forecasts give the **probability** of rain or sunshine. Economists cannot say for sure whether the economy will be good or bad next year. Instead, they may forecast a 70 percent chance that the economy will be good and a

> # "Economists cannot say for sure whether the economy will be good or bad next year."

30 percent chance of a recession. Similarly, analysts might say that given Nucor's managerial talent, if the economy is good, Nucor will perform well and the stock will increase 20 percent. If the economy goes into a recession, then Nucor's stock will fall 10 percent. So what return do you expect from Nucor? The return still depends on the state of the economy.

This leads us directly to a key concept: **expected return.** We compute expected return by multiplying each possible return by the probability, p, of that return occurring. We then sum them (recall that all probabilities must add to one). Let's place Nucor

Again, this illustration seems extreme because we used only two economic states. Any real economic forecast would instead include a probability distribution of many potential economic conditions.

We can also characterize risk via this expected return figure. The expected return procedure shows potential return possibilities, but we don't know which one will actually occur, so we face uncertainty. In the last chapter, we measured risk using the standard deviation of returns over time. We can use the same principle to measure risk for expected returns. What range of different expected

required return The level of total return needed to be compensated for the risk taken. It is made up of a risk-free rate and a risk premium.

risk premium The portion of the required return that represents the reward for taking risk.

market risk premium The return on the market portfolio minus the risk-free rate. Risk premiums for specific firms are based on the market risk premium.

the
Math Coach on...

Expected Return and Standard Deviation

" When you compute expected return and standard deviation, you'll find it helpful to use the decimal format for the probability of the economic state and percentages to state the return in each state. "

returns will Nucor exhibit from the expected return of 11 percent? In our two-state description of the economy, the deviation could be either 9 percent (= 20% − 11%) or −21 percent (= −10% − 11%). We compute the standard deviation of expected returns the same way we did for historical returns. We square the deviations, then multiply by the probability of that deviation occurring, and then sum them all up. So Nucor's return variance is 189.0 [=(0.7 × 9²) + (0.3 × −21²)]. As a final step, we take the square root of our result to put the figure back into sensible terms. The standard deviation for Nucor is 13.75 percent (= $\sqrt{189}$). The general equation for the standard deviation of S different economic states is:

$$\text{Standard deviation} = \begin{array}{c}\text{Square root of the sum}\\ \text{of each return's squared}\\ \text{deviation from the average}\end{array} \times \begin{array}{c}\text{Probability of}\\ \text{that return}\end{array}$$

$$= \sqrt{\begin{array}{c} p_1 \times (\text{Return}_1 - \text{Expected return})^2 + p_2 \\ \times (\text{Return}_2 - \text{Expected return})^2 + \cdots \end{array}}$$

$$= \sqrt{\sum_{j=1}^{s} p_j \times (\text{Return}_j - \text{Expected return})^2} \quad (10\text{-}2)$$

Risk Premiums LG10-2

Throughout the book, we have mentioned the positive relationship between expected return and risk. Consider this key question: You have a riskless investment available to you. The short-term government debt security, the T-bill, offers

of course, is that some investors want a higher return and are willing to take some risk to raise their returns. Investors who take on a little risk should expect a slightly higher return than the T-bill rate. People who take on higher risk levels should expect higher returns. Indeed, it's only logical that investors require this extra return to willingly take the added risk.

The expected return of an investment is often expressed in two parts, a risk-free return and a risky contribution. The return investors require for the risk level they take is called the **required return:**

Required return = Risk-free rate + Risk premium   (10-3)

The *risk-free rate* is typically considered the return on U.S. government bonds and bills and equals the real interest rate and the expected inflation premium that we discussed in Chapter 6. The **risk premium** is the reward investors require for taking risk. How large are the rewards for taking risk? As we discussed in the previous chapter, the market doesn't reward all risks. The firm-specific portion of total risk for any stock can be diversified away, and since the investor takes on such risk out of ignorance or by mistake, an efficient market will not reward anyone for taking on this "superfluous" risk. So as we examine historical risk premiums, we do so with a diversified portfolio that contains no firm-specific risk.

Table 10.1 shows the average annual return on the S&P 500 Index minus the T-bill rate for different time periods. The

> ## "The expected return of an investment is often expressed in two parts, a risk-free return and a risky contribution."

you a low return with no risk. Why would you invest in anything risky, when you could simply buy T-bills? The answer,

remainder after we subtract the T-bill rate is the risk premium; in this case, it's the **market risk premium**—the

EXAMPLE 10-1

Expected Return and Risk LG10-1

Bailey has a probability distribution for four possible states of the economy, as shown below. She has also calculated the return that Motor Music stock would earn in each state. Given this information, what's Motor Music's expected return and risk?

Economic State	Probability	Return
Fast growth	0.15	25%
Slow growth	0.60	15%
Recession	0.20	−5%
Depression	0.05	−20%

SOLUTION:

Bailey can compute the expected return using equation 10-1:

Expected return = $(0.15 \times 25\%) + (0.60 \times 15\%) + (0.20 \times -5\%) + (0.05 \times -20\%) = 10.75\%$

Then Bailey can compute the expected return by computing the standard deviation using equation 10-2:

$$\text{Standard deviation} = \sqrt{\begin{array}{l} 0.15 \times (25\% - 10.75\%)^2 + 0.60 \times (15\% - 10.75\%)^2 + 0.20 \\ \times (-5\% - 10.75\%)^2 + 0.05 \times (-20\% - 10.75\%)^2 \end{array}}$$

$$= \sqrt{30.46 + 10.84 + 49.61 + 47.28} = 11.76\%$$

The expected return and standard deviation are 10.75 percent and 11.76 percent, respectively. We could also show these equations in a table, such as:

Economic State	Probability	Return	$p \times$ Return	Deviation	Squared Dev.	$\times p$
Fast growth	0.15	25%	3.75%	14.25%	203.06	30.46
Slow growth	0.60	15	9.00	4.25	18.06	10.84
Recession	0.20	−5	−1.00	−15.75	248.06	49.61
Depression	0.05	−20	−1.00	−30.75	945.56	47.28
Sum=	1.0		10.75%			138.19
					Square root =	11.76%

Similar to Problems 10-1, 10-2, 10-17, 10-18, 10-23, 10-24

---

reward for taking general (systematic) stock market risk. Since 1950, the average market risk premium has been 7.7 percent per year. Over the long run, this is the reward for taking stock market risk. The actual, realized risk premium during particular decades has varied. The average risk premium has been as high as 18.8 percent for the 1950s and

as low as −1.8 percent during the 2000s. The performance in the 2000s is unusual; the stock market return has been so poor that it has not beaten the risk-free rate. Investors require a risk premium for taking on market risk. But taking that risk also means that they will periodically experience poor returns.

▼ **TABLE 10.1** The Realized Average Annual Risk Premium for Stocks

	1950 to 2009	1950 to 1959	1960 to 1969	1970 to 1979	1980 to 1989	1990 to 1999	2000 to 2009
Risk premium	7.7%	18.8%	4.7%	1.2%	9.3%	14.1%	−1.8%

Realized risk premiums were very different in each decade. The recent decade even had a negative risk premium!
Source: S&P 500 Index and T-bill rate data.

time out!

10-1 Describe the similarities between computing average return and expected return. Also, describe the similarities between expected return risk and historical risk.

10-2 Why would people take risks by investing their hard-earned money?

MARKET RISK

How much risk should you take to achieve the return you want over time? In the previous chapter, we demonstrated that individual stocks and different portfolios exhibit different levels of total risk. Recall that the rewards for carrying risk apply only to the market risk (or undiversifiable) portion of total risk. But how do investors know how much of the 37.3 percent standard deviation of returns for Mattel Inc. is firm-specific risk and how much of that deviation is market risk? The answer to this important question will determine how much of a risk premium investors should require for Mattel. The attempt to specify an equation that relates a stock's required return to an appropriate risk premium is known as **asset pricing.**

corporate finance professionals use CAPM widely. In developing the CAPM, Lintner and Sharpe sought to emphasize the individual investor's best strategy to maximize returns for a given amount of market risk.

CAPM starts with modern portfolio theory. Remember from the previous chapter that when you combine securities into a portfolio, you can find a set of portfolios that dominate all others. The best combinations possible use all the risky securities available (but not the risk-free asset) to create efficient frontier portfolios, as shown by the curved line in Figure 10.1, panel A. These portfolios represent combinations of various risky securities that give the highest expected return for each potential level of risk.

The idea of a risk premium in equation 10-3 implies a risk-free investment, like T-bills. Panel B shows where the risk-free asset would appear on the **capital market line (CML).** The risk-free asset must lie on the y-axis precisely because it carries no risk. Now we draw a line from the risk-free security to a point tangent to the efficient frontier. The CML relationship appears as a line because investments show a direct risk-reward relationship. You may recall from your economics classes that only one tangency point will be possible between this kind of curve and a straight line. The spot where the tangency occurs is called the **market portfolio,** which has a special significance. The market portfolio represents ownership in all traded assets in the economy, so this portfolio provides maximum diversification. You can locate your optimal portfolio on this line by owning various combinations of the risk-free security and the market portfolio. If most of your money is invested in the market portfolio, then you will have a portfolio on the line that lies just to the left of the market portfolio dot in the graph. If you own just a little of the market portfolio and hold mostly risk-free securities, then your portfolio will lie on the line near the risk-free security dot. For your investments to lie on the line

> "Borrowing money to invest is known as using financial leverage. Using financial leverage increases the overall risk of the portfolio."

The Market Portfolio LG10-3

The best-known asset pricing equation is the **capital asset pricing model,** typically referred to as **CAPM.** Though many theorists formulated theories that, in the end, supported the CAPM's effectiveness, credit for the model goes to William Sharpe and John Lintner. Sharpe eventually won a Nobel Prize for his work in 1990. (Lintner died in 1983, and Nobel Prizes are not awarded posthumously.) Today, both investors and

to the right of the market portfolio, you would have to invest all your money in the market portfolio, then borrow more money and invest these additional funds in the market portfolio. Borrowing money to invest is known as using **financial leverage.** Using financial leverage increases the overall risk of the portfolio.

Notice that if you had a portfolio on the efficient frontier (labeled "old portfolio"), you could do better. Instead of owning the old portfolio, you can put some of your money in the

Panel A: The Efficient Frontier

Panel B: Add a Risk-Free Asset and Do Even Better

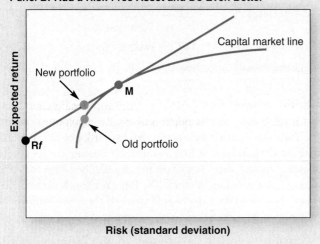

In MPT, investors want to be on the efficient frontier (Panel A) because it gives them the highest expected return for each level of risk. However, after adding a riskless asset (Panel B), investors can then get portfolios on the straight line (shown), which offers a higher expected return for each level of risk than the efficient frontier.

market portfolio and some in the risk-free security to obtain the "new portfolio." See how the new portfolio dominates that old one? It carries the same risk level, but offers a higher return. In fact, notice that the line drawn between the risk-free investment and the market portfolio dominates all of the efficient frontier portfolios (except the market portfolio itself). All portfolio allocations between the risk-free security and the market portfolio constitute the capital market line. All investors should want to locate their portfolios on the CML, rather than the efficient frontier. Portfolios on the CML offer the highest expected return for any level of desired risk, which the investor controls by deciding how much of the market portfolio and how much of the risk-free asset to hold. Risk-averse investors can put more of their money in T-bills and less into

the market portfolio. Investors willing to take on higher risk for larger returns can put more of their money in the market portfolio.

Beta, a Measure of Market Risk LG10-4

The CML demonstrates that the market portfolio is crucial. Indeed, its return less the risk-free rate represents the expected average market risk premium. The market portfolio features no firm-specific risk; all such risk is diversified away. So the market portfolio carries only market risk. So the market portfolio's risk factor allows us to compute a measure of firm-specific risk for any individual stock or portfolio. We can now examine the question posed at the beginning of this section: "How much of Mattel's total risk is attributable to market risk?" The standard deviation of returns includes all of Mattel stock's risk—it quantifies how much the stock price rises and falls. The market risk portion will rise and fall along with the market portfolio. If we subtract the market risk portion from the total risk measure, we're left with firm-specific risk. This part of risk rises and falls in ways unrelated to market changes.

Remember that portfolio theory describes a measure—correlation—that measures how two stocks move together through time. Instead of measuring how any two stocks or portfolios move together, we now want to know how a stock or portfolio moves relative to market portfolio movements. This measure is known as **beta (β).** Beta measures the comovement between a stock and the market portfolio.

If Mattel's total risk level is measured by its standard deviation, σ_{Mattel}, then we can find the risk contribution attributable to the market in general by multiplying Mattel's total risk by its correlation with the market portfolio, $\sigma_{\text{Mattel}} \times \rho_{\text{Mattel, Market}}$. The beta computation is scaled so that the market portfolio itself has a beta of one. The scaling is done by dividing by standard deviation of the market portfolio: $\sigma_{\text{Mattel}} \times \rho_{\text{Mattel,Market}} \div \sigma_{\text{Market}}$.[1] Stocks with betas larger than one are considered riskier than the market portfolio, while betas of less than one

[1] A mathematically equivalent equation for beta is $\beta = \text{cov}(R_s, R_M)/\text{var}(R_M)$, where cov() is the covariance between the stock and market portfolio returns, and var() is the variance of the market portfolio.

indicate lower risk. RadioShack has a beta of 1.84, meaning that RadioShack stock is very sensitive to market risk. When the market portfolio moves, you can expect RadioShack stock to move in the same direction. Technically, you should expect RadioShack's realized risk premium to be 84 percent more than the realized market risk premium.

Table 10.2 shows the beta for each of the 30 companies in the Dow Jones Industrial Average. Investors consider many of these companies high risk, like Bank of America ($\beta = 2.31$) and Alcoa (2.12). These firms' stocks carry high market risk because the demand for their products is very sensitive to the overall economy's strength. The financial crisis and its aftermath have put Bank of America in a risky position. Investors consider other companies safe bets with low risk, like Walmart (0.35) ExxonMobil (0.41), and McDonalds (0.47). Many lower-beta firms sell consumer goods that we consider the necessities of life, which we will buy whether the economy is in recession or expansion. The demand for these products is price inelastic and not sensitive to economic conditions. Some companies have nearly the same risk as the market portfolio, like Microsoft (1.01) and Hewlett-Packard (1.02).

The Security Market Line LG10-3

Beta indicates the market risk that each stock represents to investors. So the higher the beta, the higher the risk premium investors will demand to undertake that security's market risk. Since beta sums up precisely what investors want to know about risk, we often replace the standard deviation risk measure shown in Figure 10.1 with beta. Figure 10.2 shows required return versus beta risk. We call the line in this figure the

▼ **TABLE 10.2** Dow Jones Industrial Average Stock Betas

Company	Beta	Company	Beta
3M Company	0.84	Home Depot	0.79
Alcoa	2.12	Intel	1.15
American Express	2.08	International Business Machines	0.71
AT&T	0.62	Johnson & Johnson	0.60
Bank of America	2.31	JP Morgan	1.12
Boeing	1.32	Kraft Foods	0.55
Caterpillar	1.85	McDonald's	0.47
Chevron	0.70	Merck	0.64
Cisco	1.25	Microsoft	1.01
Coca-Cola	0.58	Pfizer	0.66
Disney	1.18	Procter & Gamble	0.48
Du Pont de Nemours	1.46	Travelers	0.59
ExxonMobil	0.41	United Technologies	1.05
General Electric	1.69	Verizon Communications	0.61
Hewlett-Packard	1.02	Walmart Stores	0.35

Data Source: Yahoo! Finance, November 4, 2010.

security market line (SML), which illustrates how required return relates to risk at any particular time, all else held equal. The SML also shows the market portfolio's risk premium or any stock's risk premium. When a stock like Boeing carries a beta greater than one, then its risk premium must be larger than the market risk premium. A stock like Johnson & Johnson carries a lower beta than does the overall market; therefore Johnson & Johnson would offer a lower risk premium to investors.

We can use the SML to show the relationship between risk and return for any stock or portfolio. To precisely quantify this relationship, we need the equation for the SML. The equation of any line can be defined as $y = b + m\,x$, where b is the intercept and m is the slope. In this case, the y axis is required return and the x axis is beta. The intercept is R_f. You may remember that the slope is the "rise over run" between two points on the line. The rise between the risk-free security and the market portfolio is $R_M - R_f$ and the run is $1 - 0$. Substituting into the line equation results in the CAPM:

$$\frac{\text{Expected}}{\text{return}} = \frac{\text{Risk-free}}{\text{rate}} + \text{Beta} \times \frac{\text{Market risk}}{\text{premium}}$$

$$= R_f + \beta(R_M - R_f) \qquad (10\text{-}4)$$

So, we have determined a way to estimate any stock's required return once we have determined its beta. Consider this: We expect the market portfolio to earn 12 percent and T-bill yields are 5 percent. Then Boeing's required return, with a $\beta = 1.32$, is 5% + 1.32 × (12% − 5%) = 14.24 percent. Table 10.3 shows the 30 Dow Jones Industrial Average stocks' required return, using these same market and risk-free rate assumptions.

Boeing's beta is 1.32, which makes it a higher risk to investors.

Higher-risk companies have higher betas, and thus require higher returns.

Portfolio Beta As you might expect, a stock **portfolio's beta** is the weighted average of the portfolio stocks' betas. The portfolio beta equation resembles equation 9-7, which gives the return of a portfolio:

$$\beta_p = \text{Sum of the beta of each stock} \times \text{Its weight in the portfolio}$$
$$= (w_1 \times \beta_1) + (w_2 \times \beta_2) + (w_3 \times \beta_3) + \cdots$$
$$+ (w_n \times \beta_n) = \sum_{j=1}^{n} w_j \beta_j \qquad (10\text{-}5)$$

With this equation, you can easily determine whether adding a particular stock to the portfolio will increase or decrease the portfolio's total market risk. If you add a stock with a higher beta than the existing portfolio, then the new portfolio will carry higher market risk than the old one did. Although we can find the effects on total portfolio risk of adding particular stocks using beta, the same is not necessarily true if we use standard deviations as our risk measure. The new stock, however risky, might have low correlations with the other stocks in the portfolio—offsetting (negative) correlations would reduce total risk.

Finding Beta LG10-4

The CAPM is an elegant explanation that relates the return you should require for taking on various levels of market risk. Although CAPM provides many practical applications, you need a company's beta to use those applications. Where or how can you obtain a beta? You have two ways. First, given the returns of the company and the market portfolio, you can compute the beta yourself. Second, you can find the beta that others have computed through financial information data providers.

Many financial outlets publish company betas. One publication that your library may have been subscribing to for decades is the *Value Line Investment Survey*. Value Line prints a terrific one-page summary of each company that includes beta. Value Line is now also online (www.value-line.com), but you need to subscribe to access this information. Nevertheless, many websites provide company betas for free: MSN Money, Yahoo! Finance, and Zacks, to name just a few. For example, in August 2012, the beta these websites listed for AT&T were: MSN Money (0.56), Yahoo! Finance (0.44), and Zacks (0.58). Note that these reported betas have some differences. To know why

▼**FIGURE 10.2** The Security Market Line Uses Beta as the Risk Measure

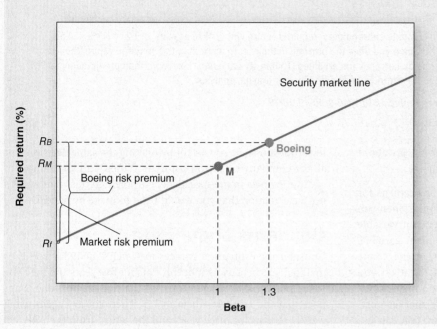

Boeing has higher risk than the overall stock market, so it should require a higher return.

▼**TABLE 10.3** Required Returns for DJIA Stocks

Company	Required Return	Company	Required Return
3M Company	10.88%	Home Depot	10.53%
Alcoa	19.84	Intel	13.05
American Express	19.56	International Business Machines	9.97
AT&T	9.34	Johnson & Johnson	9.2
Bank of America	21.17	JP Morgan	12.84
Boeing	14.24	Kraft Foods	8.85
Caterpillar	17.95	McDonald's	8.29
Chevron	9.9	Merck	9.48
Cisco	13.75	Microsoft	12.07
Coca-Cola	9.06	Pfizer	9.62
Disney	13.26	Procter & Gamble	8.36
Du Pont de Nemours	15.22	Travelers	9.13
ExxonMobil	7.87	United Technologies	12.35
General Electric	16.83	Verizon Communications	9.27
Hewlett-Packard	12.14	Walmart Stores	7.45

Higher beta stocks require higher expected returns.

Assumptions: Market return = 12% and risk-free rate = 5%.

EXAMPLE 10-2

For interactive versions of this example visit www.mhhe.com/canM2e

CAPM and Under- or Overvalued Stock LG10-3

Say that you are a corporate CFO. You know that the risk-free rate is currently 4.5 percent and you expect the market to earn 11 percent this year. Through your own analysis of the firm, you think it will earn a 13.5 percent return this year. If the beta of the company is 1.2, should you consider the firm undervalued or overvalued?

SOLUTION:

You can compute shareholders' required return with CAPM as $4.5\% + 1.2 \times (11\% - 4.5\%)$ = 12.3%. Since you think the firm will actually earn more than this required return, the firm appears to be currently undervalued. That is, its price must rise more then predicted by CAPM to obtain the return you estimated in your original analysis.

Similar to Problems 10-7, 10-8, 10-19, 10-20

---

differences might arise, consider how you would go about gathering information and computing beta yourself.

To compute your own beta, first obtain historical returns for the company of interest and of the market portfolio. Then run a regression of the company return as the dependent variable and the market portfolio return as the independent variable. The resulting market portfolio return coefficient is beta. Many important questions may come to mind. First, what do you use as the market portfolio? People typically use a major stock index like the S&P 500 Index to proxy for the market portfolio. Second, what time frame should you use? You can use daily, weekly, monthly, or even annual returns. Using monthly returns is the most common. How long a time series is needed? As you will recall, statistical estimates become more reliable and valid as more data are used. But you will have to weigh those statistical advantages against the fact that companies change their business enterprises and thus their risk levels over time. Using data from too long ago reflects risks that may no longer apply. Generally speaking, using time series data of three to five years is common. Whatever decisions you make to address

these questions, be consistent by making the same decisions for all the company betas you compute. You'll find an example of computing beta in the spreadsheet problem to this chapter. (It's not a calculation that you would want to make by hand!)

Concerns about Beta

Consider the estimation choices just mentioned. Say you estimate a firm's beta using monthly data for five years and the Dow Jones Industrial Average return as the market portfolio. Suppose that the result is a beta of 1.3. Then you try again using weekly returns for three years and the return from the S&P 500 Index as the market portfolio's yield, resulting in a beta of 0.9. These estimates are quite different and would create a large variation in required return if you plugged them into the CAPM. So, which is the more accurate estimate? Unfortunately, we may not be able to determine which is most representative, or "true." In general, you may estimate a little different beta using different market portfolio proxies, different return intervals (like monthly returns versus annual returns), and different time periods. A problem at the end of this chapter explores these differences.

EXAMPLE 10-3

For interactive versions of this example visit www.mhhe.com/canM2e

Portfolio Beta LG10-4

You have a portfolio consisting of 20 percent Boeing stock ($\beta = 1.32$), 40 percent Hewlett-Packard stock ($\beta = 1.02$), and 40 percent McDonald's stock ($\beta = 0.47$). How much market risk does the portfolio have?

SOLUTION:

Compute a beta for the portfolio. Using equation 10-5, the portfolio beta is $(0.2 \times 1.32) + (0.4 \times 1.02) + (0.4 \times 0.47) = 0.86$. Note that this portfolio carries 14 percent less market risk than the general market does.

Similar to Problems 10-11, 10-12, 10-21, 10-22, 10-27, 10-28

finance at work // : markets

One of the basic financial theories tells us how we should view the relationship between risk and expected returns. In a nutshell, risk and expected return are positively related. A high-risk investment needs to have a high expected return, or no one would want to buy that investment. With this lack of demand, the investment's price would drop until it offers new buyers a high expected return for the future. The higher return is the reward for taking the extra risk. Similarly, low-risk investments offer low expected returns.

To quantify risk, the finance industry tends to use two measures; volatility of returns and beta. The volatility, measured by variance or standard deviation, tells us how much a return can deviate from the average return. Beta tells us how much market risk an investment has. These measures are very useful in assessing the risk of an investment or portfolio and what return premium should be expected for taking risk.

However, people do not naturally think of risk within this financial theory framework. First, investors care less about how an investment's return deviates from expectations and more about how the return may be lower than expected. In other words, a higher return than expected is not considered risky, only a lower return, or even, gulp, a loss, is viewed as risk.

Also, real people do not think in terms of the high risk/return versus the low risk/return scale. Instead, people think in terms of better or worse. For example, three financial economists ran an experiment in which they asked high net worth individuals for either their expected return predictions or their risk assessment (both on a 0 to 10 scale) of over 200 of the Fortune 500 companies. When they compiled all the responses, they found the relationship in this figure. Notice anything odd? This shows that firms with low risk are expected to earn a high return. People act as if expected return and

Beliefs about Performance and Risk of Fortune 500 Firms

risk are negatively related! This is the opposite of financial theory. Instead of evaluating firms within the framework that high expected return goes with high risk and low return goes with low risk, people seem to think in terms of good versus bad stocks. What are the characteristics of a "good" stock? Characteristics that seem good are high expected return and low risk. When an investor feels a stock is good, then it is attributed with high return and low risk. When an investor feels the stock is bad, then it is attributed with low return and high risk. Psychologists call this perception or belief an "affect."

Unfortunately, thinking about risk and return from the affect framework causes investors to misunderstand the underlying dynamics of actual expected return and risk. Thus, they may make poor decisions regarding risk and return.

Want to know more?

Key Words to Search for Updates: **affect, measuring investment risk, risk and behavioral finance**

Source: Meir Statman, Kenneth Fisher, and Deniz Anginer, "Affect in a Behavioral Asset-Pricing Model," Copyright 2008, CFA Institute, Reproduced and republished from *Financial Analysts Journal*, April–March 2008, Figure 3, with permission from the CFA Institute. All rights reserved.

In addition to these estimation problems, a company can change its risk level, and thus its beta, by changing the way it operates within its business, by expanding into new businesses, and/or by changing its debt load. So even if beta is an accurate measure of what the firm's risk level was in the past, does it apply to the future? Beta's applicability will depend on the firm's future plans.

Both financial managers and investors share these concerns about beta. In the end, beta's usefulness depends on its reliability. Unfortunately, beta's empirical record is not as good as we would like. We should expect that companies with high betas

yield higher returns than companies with low betas. On average, though, this does not turn out to be the case. A company's beta does not appear to predict its future return very well. Since characterizing the risk-return relationship is so important, finance researchers have introduced other asset pricing models. One promising model adds more risk factors to the predictive relationship other than just market risk. Firm size and book-to-market ratio have had some success predicting returns, so new models often include factors derived from these characteristics along with beta as a measure of market risk.

time out!

10-3 Explain why portfolios that lie on the capital market line offer better risk-return trade-offs than those that lie on the efficient frontier.

10-4 Examine the betas in Table 10.2. Which seem about right to you and which seem to indicate too much or too little risk for that firm?

CAPITAL MARKET EFFICIENCY LG10-5

The risk and return relationship rests on an underlying assumption that stock prices are generally "correct"—they are not predictably too high or too low. Imagine having a system that identified undervalued stocks with low risks (i.e., relatively high returns with a low beta). Because those stocks are undervalued, they will earn you a high return, on average, as their stock prices rise to their correct value. Note that the CAPM's risk-return relationship would be incorrect. You would be consistently getting high returns with low risk. On the other hand, if you consistently picked overvalued stocks, you wouldn't be earning enough return to compensate you for the risks you are taking. Investors move their money to the best alternatives by selling overvalued stocks and buying undervalued stocks. This causes the prices of the overvalued stocks to drop and the prices of the undervalued stocks to rise until both stocks' returns stand more in line with their riskiness. Thus, the risk-return relationship relies on the idea that prices are generally accurate.

What conditions are necessary for an **efficient market?** Efficient, or perfectly competitive, markets feature:

- Many buyers and sellers.
- No prohibitively high barriers to entry.
- Free and readily available information available to all participants.
- Low trading or transaction costs.

Are these conditions met for the U.S. stock market? Certainly millions of stock investors trade every day, buying and selling securities. With discount brokers and online traders, the costs to trade are fairly minimal and present no real barriers to enter the market. Information is increasingly accessible from many sources and trading philosophies, and commission costs and bid-ask spreads have steadily declined. With millions of the larger companies' shares (say the S&P 500) of stock trading every day, the U.S. stock exchanges appear to meet efficiency conditions. But other segments of the market, like those exchanges that trade in **penny stocks,** feature very thin trading. The prices of these very small companies' stock may not be fair and these equities may be manipulated in fraudulent scams. In the 1970s and 1980s, penny stock king Meyer Blinder and his firm Blinder-Robinson was known as "blind 'em and rob' em" as they practiced penny stock price manipulation to rob many small investors of their entire investments in these small markets. These days, penny stock price manipulation is typically conducted through e-mail and Web posting scams.

Efficient Market Hypothesis

Our concept of market efficiency provides a good framework for understanding how stock prices change over time. This theory is described in the **efficient market hypothesis (EMH),** which states that *security prices fully reflect all available information.* At any point in time, the price for any stock or bond reflects the collective wisdom of market participants about the company's future prospects. Security prices change as new information becomes available. Since we cannot predict whether new information about a company will be good news or bad news, we cannot predict whether its stock price will go up or go down. This makes short-term stock-price movements unpredictable. But in the longer run, stock prices will adjust to their proper level as market participants gather and digest all available information.

The EMH brings us to the question of what type of information is embedded within current stock prices. Segmenting information into three categories leads to the three basic levels of market efficiency, described as:

1. Weak-form efficiency—current prices reflect all information derived from trading. This stock market information generally includes current and past stock prices and trading volume.

2. Semistrong-form efficiency—current prices reflect all **public information.** This includes all information that has already been revealed to the public, like financial statements, news, analyst opinions, and so on.

3. Strong-form efficiency—current prices reflect *all* information. In addition to public information, prices reflect the **privately held information** that has not yet been released to the public but may be known to some people, like managers, accountants, auditors, and so on.

Each of the EMH's three forms rests on different assumptions regarding the extent of information that is incorporated into stock prices at any point in time. A fourth possibility—that markets may not be efficient and prices may not reflect all the information known about a company—also arises.

The *weak-form* efficiency level involves the lowest information hurdle, stating that stock prices reflect all past price and trading volume activity. If true, this level of efficiency would have important ramifications. A segment of the investment industry uses price and volume charts to make investment timing decisions. Technical analysis has a large following and its own vocabulary of patterns and trends (resistance, support, breakout, momentum, etc.). If the market is at least weak-form efficient, then prices already reflect this information and these activities would not result in useful predictions about future price changes, and thus would be a waste of time. Indeed, the people who make the most money from price charting services are the people who sell the services, not the investors who buy and use those services.

The *semistrong-form* efficiency level assumes that stock prices include all public information. Notice that past stock prices and volumes are publicly available information, so this level includes the weak form as a subset. Important investment implications arise if markets are efficient to public information. Many investors conduct security analysis in which they obtain financial data and other public information to assess whether a company's stock is undervalued or overvalued. But in a semistrong-form efficient market, stock prices already reflect this information and are thus "correct." Using only public

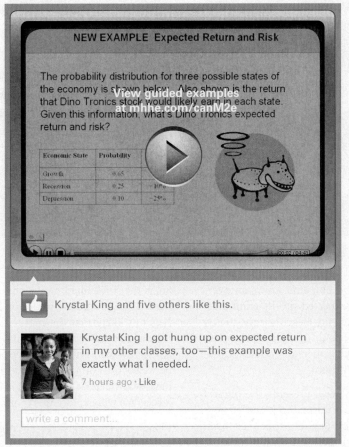

NEW EXAMPLE Expected Return and Risk

The probability distribution for three possible states of the economy is shown below. Also shown is the return that Dino Tronics stock would likely earn in each state. Given this information, what's Dino Tronics expected return and risk?

Economic State	Probability
Growth	0.65
Recession	0.25
Depression	0.10

Krystal King and five others like this.

Krystal King I got hung up on expected return in my other classes, too—this example was exactly what I needed.

7 hours ago · Like

write a comment...

information, you would not be able to determine whether a stock is misvalued because that information is already reflected in the price.

If prices reflect all public information, then those prices will react as traders hear new (or private) information. Consider a company that announces surprisingly good quarterly profits. Traders and investors will have factored the old profit expectations into the stock price. As they incorporate the new information, the stock price will quickly rise to a new and accurate price as shown in the solid black line in Figure 10.3. Note that the stock price was $35 before the announcement and $40 immediately following. If you tried to buy the stock after hearing the news, then you would have bought at $40 and not received any benefit of the good quarterly profit news. On the other hand, if the market is not semistrong-form efficient, then the price might react quickly, but not accurately. The dashed green line shows a reaction in a non-semistrong efficient market where the price continues to drift up well after the announcement. This gradual drift to the "correct" price indicates that the market initially underreacted to the news. In this case, you could have bought the stock after the announcement

▼ **FIGURE 10.3** Potential Price Reaction to a Good News Announcement

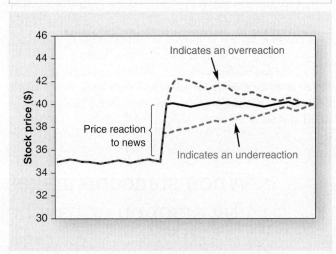

Stock prices react quickly to news, but do they react accurately?

The technology sector fell victim to a stock market bubble in 2000.

and still earned a profit. The dotted blue line shows an overreaction to the firm's better-than-expected profits announcement. If markets either consistently underreact or consistently overreact to announcements that would change stock prices (earnings, stock split, dividend, etc.), then we would believe that the market is not semistrong efficient.

The *strong-form* market efficiency level presents the highest hurdle to test market reaction to information. The strong-form level includes information considered by the weak-form, the semistrong-form, as well as privately known information. People within firms, like CEOs and CFOs, know information that has not yet been released to the public. They may trade on this privately held, or insider, information and their trading may cause stock prices to change as it reflects that private information. In this way, stock prices could reflect even privately known information. Note that the firm managers, accountants, and auditors know several days in advance that a firm has earned unexpectedly high quarterly profits. If the stock price already incorporated this closely held private knowledge, then the big price reaction shown in Figure 10.3 would not occur.

So, is the stock market efficient? If it is, at what level? This has been a hotly debated topic for decades and continues to be. It is not likely that the market is strong-form efficient. Since insider trading is punished, insider information must be valuable. However, much evidence suggests that the market could be weak-form or semistrong-form efficient. Of course, we also have evidence that the market is not efficient at any of the three levels. We will explore this more in the following section.

Behavioral Finance LG10-5

The argument for the market being efficient works as follows: Many individual and professional investors constantly look for mispriced stocks. If they find a stock that is undervalued, they will buy it and drive up its price until it's correctly priced. Likewise, investors would sell an overpriced stock, driving down its price until it's correctly valued. With so many investors looking for market "mistakes," it's unlikely that any mispriced stock opportunities will be left in the market.

The argument against the market being efficient is equally convincing. The market comprises many people transacting with one another. When someone makes trading decisions

> "When someone makes trading decisions influenced by emotion or psychological bias, those decisions may not seem rational."

influenced by emotion or psychological bias, those decisions may not seem rational. When many people fall under such influences, their trading decisions may actually drive stock prices away from the correct price as emotion carries the traders away from rationality. For example, many people believe that investors were "irrationally exuberant" about technology stocks in the late 1990s—and that their buying excitement drove prices to an artificially high level. In 2000, the excitement wore off and tech stock prices plummeted. Whenever a set of stock prices go unnaturally high and subsequently crash down, the market experiences what we call a **stock market bubble.**

In the past couple of decades, finance researchers have studied **behavioral finance** and found that people often behave in ways that are very likely "irrational." At times, investors appear to be too optimistic, as though they are looking through rose-colored glasses. At other times they appear to be too pessimistic. Common investment decisions aren't necessarily optimal ones, which flies in the face of the economist's

finance at work //: markets

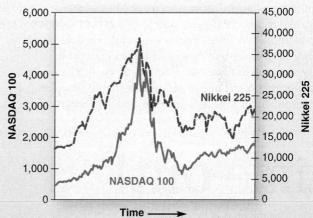

Bubble Trouble

Many professionals criticize the EMH because the overall market sometimes seems too high or too low. A very dramatic example of the market level being artificially high is the market bubble. During a market bubble, the market quickly inflates on rampant speculation and subsequently crashes. Investors who buy near the peak of the bubble risk losing nearly all their investment.

One of the United States' earliest stock market bubbles was the bubble and crash of 1929. Note from the figure that the DJIA started in 1927 at around 160. By October 1929, the DJIA had reached nearly 400 and then crashed. By mid-1932, the DJIA had fallen to the 40s. The sustained fall coincided with an economic depression. Panel A of the figure also shows a price bubble in gold. The price of gold was $230 per ounce in January 1979. The late 1970s and early 1980s saw double-digit inflation throughout the economy, and many investors felt that gold represented a safe and inflation-proof investment. Just one year later, the price had skyrocketed to $870. It then fell below $300 in less than two and a half years. Could gold

be in another bubble? In late 2008, gold's price was $750; it shot to $1,900 in 2011, and hovered around $1,600 in 2012.

See the spectacular tech bubble during the 1990s? The NASDAQ 100, which started in 1985 at 250, soared to a peak of 4,816.35 on March 24, 2000. It then fell to less than 1,000 in two and a half years. The rise and fall of the NASDAQ 100 seems much more pronounced than the Japanese stock bubble of the 1980s. From a January 2, 1985, start at 11,543, the Nikkei 225 soared to a closing high of 38,916 on December 29, 1989. The bubble then burst and the Japanese stock market plummeted. The Nikkei has yet to fully recover, trading today at around the 16,500 level.

EMH critics do not believe that the entire stock market, or a substantial segment of it, can be correctly valued before, during, or after a bubble. It certainly appears to be overvalued during the time the bubble is inflating.

Want to know more?

Key Words to Search For Updates: **stock bubble, irrational exuberance** expectation of rational economic actors. Perhaps, then, capital markets don't represent perfectly competitive or efficient markets if buyers and sellers do not always make rational choices.

It may take many biased investors to move a stock's price enough that it would be considered a pricing mistake. However, the important decisions in a company are typically made by just one CEO or a management team. Thus, their biases can have a direct impact on decisions involving hundreds of millions, or even billions of dollars. In other words, the contribution of behavioral finance to economic decision making is likely to be even more important in corporate behavior than market behavior. For example, consider the psychological concept of **overconfidence.** One of the most pervasive biases, overconfidence describes a tendency for people to overestimate the accuracy of their knowledge and underestimate the risks of a decision. These problems can adversely affect important investment (i.e., acquiring other firms) and financing (i.e., issuing new stock or bonds decisions).

research and development programs all entail risk and potential rewards. Being able to understand and characterize these decisions within a risk and return framework can help managers make better decisions. In addition, managers must understand what return their stockholders require at various times of firm operations. After all, a firm must receive enough revenue from its variously risky activities to pay its business and debt costs and reward the owners (the stockholders). Managers must thus include the return to shareholders when they analyze new business opportunities.

Firms and capital markets also interact directly. For example, a good understanding of market efficiency helps managers understand how their stock prices will react to different types of decisions (like dividend changes) and news announcements (like unexpectedly high or low profitability). In fact, many managers own company stock and are thus compensated through programs that rely on the stock price, like **restricted stock** and **executive stock options.** Companies also periodically issue (sell) additional shares of stock to raise more capital, and these sales depend upon market efficiency assumptions. The firm would not want to sell additional shares if the stock price is too low (i.e., undervalued). They *would* want to sell more shares at any time that they thought their shares are overvalued. Other times, firms repurchase (buy back) shares of stock. The firm might want to do this if its shares were undervalued, but not if its shares were overvalued. Of course, valuation is not an issue if security markets are efficient.

time out!

10-5 Can the market be semistrong-form efficient but not weak-form efficient? Explain.

10-6 If the market usually overreacts to bad news announcements, what would your return be like if you bought after you heard the bad news?

IMPLICATIONS FOR FINANCIAL MANAGERS LG10-6

Financial managers must understand the crucial relationship between risk and return for several reasons. First, while the relationship between risk and return is demonstrated here using the capital markets, it equally applies to many business decisions. A firm's product mix, marketing campaign combination, and

Using the Constant-Growth Model for Required Return LG10-7

For decades, financial managers have used the CAPM to compute shareholders' required return. Given recent concerns about beta's limitations, many see the CAPM as a less useful model for calculating appropriate returns. Some have turned instead to another model useful for computing required return—the constant-growth model discussed in Chapter 8. We can arrange the terms of that model as:

$$i = \text{Dividend yield} + \text{Constant growth}$$

$$= \frac{D_1}{P_0} + g \qquad (10\text{-}6)$$

Of course, this model assumes that the stock is efficiently priced. This model holds an advantage in that it uses current firm data (dividend, D_1, and price, P_0) and a simple forward estimate (growth, g) to assess what investors currently expect the stock to return, i. For example, Table 10.2 shows Walmart's beta as 0.35. Using this beta, Table 10.3 shows that shareholders require only 7.45 percent return to hold Walmart stock, given its low risk profile. You may find it hard to believe that Walmart's owners (the shareholders) expect such a low return from one of the world's most profitable firms. So perhaps this is a case in which the CAPM result isn't very useful. Applying the constant-growth model looks something like this: Walmart is expected to pay a $1.35 dividend this year and say the stock price currently stands at $55 per share. Financial analysts believe Walmart will grow at

time out!

10-7 Why is the shareholders' required return important to corporate managers?

10 percent per year for the next five years. The constant growth rate model suggests that Walmart shareholders expect a 12.45 percent [=($1.35 ÷ $55) + 0.10] return. So, which required return seems more likely, the 7.45 percent computed from CAPM or the 12.45 percent suggested by the constant-growth model? It is likely that Walmart investors are expecting closer to the 12 percent return than the 7 percent estimate.

Financial managers need an estimate of their shareholders' required return in order to make appropriate decisions about their companies' future growth. Good financial managers will compute shareholders' required return using as many methods as they can to determine the most realistic value possible.

EXAMPLE 10-4

Required Return LG10-6

For interactive versions of this example visit www.mhhe.com/canM2e

Note from Table 10.3 that the required returns for 3M, Home Depot, and Intel are 10.9 percent, 10.5 percent, and 13.1 percent, respectively. These expectations may seem quite far apart, considering that all three firms are in the DJIA and are leaders in their market sectors. Use the following information to compute the constant-growth model estimate of the required return:

	Expected Dividend	Current Price	Analyst Growth Estimate
3M Company	$2.16	$85.30	12.0%
Home Depot	0.98	31.50	13.3
Intel	0.70	21.20	12.3

SOLUTION:

You can now use equation 10-6 to find each company's required return as:

$$\text{3M required return} = (\$2.16 \div \$85.30) + 0.120 = 14.5\%$$

$$\text{Home Depot Required return} = (\$0.98 \div \$31.50) + 0.133 = 16.4\%$$

$$\text{Intel Required return} = (\$0.70 \div \$21.20) + 0.123 = 15.6\%$$

Note that the constant-growth model estimates are 2 to 5 percent higher than the CAPM estimates. When the CAPM estimate seems too high or too low, it's a good idea to check the constant-growth model estimate.

Similar to Problems 10-15, 10-16, 10-29, 10-30

Get Online

Your Turn...

Questions

1. Consider an asset that provides the same return no matter what economic state occurs. What would be the standard deviation (or risk) of this asset? Explain. *(LG10-1)*

2. Why is expected return considered "forward-looking"? What are the challenges for practitioners to utilize expected return? *(LG10-1)*

3. In 2000, the S&P 500 Index earned −9.1 percent while the T-bill yield was 5.9 percent. Does this mean the market risk premium was negative? Explain. *(LG10-2)*

4. How might the magnitude of the market risk premium impact people's desire to buy stocks? *(LG10-2)*

5. Describe how adding a risk-free security to modern portfolio theory allows investors to do better than the efficient frontier. *(LG10-3)*

6. Show on a graph like Figure 10.2 where a stock with a beta of 1.3 would be located on the security market line. Then show where that stock would be located if it is undervalued. *(LG10-3)*

7. Consider that you have three stocks in your portfolio and wish to add a fourth. You want to know if the fourth stock will make the portfolio riskier or less risky. Compare and contrast how this would be assessed using standard deviation versus market risk (beta) as the measure of risk. *(LG10-3)*

8. Describe how different allocations between the risk-free security and the market portfolio can achieve any level of market risk desired. Give examples of a portfolio from a person who is very risk averse and a portfolio for someone who is not so averse to taking risk. *(LG10-3)*

9. Cisco Systems has a beta of 1.25. Does this mean that you should expect Cisco to earn a return 25 percent higher than the S&P 500 Index return? Explain. *(LG10-4)*

10. Note from Table 10.2 that some technology-oriented firms (Intel) in the Dow Jones Industrial Average have high market risk while others (AT&T and Verizon) have low market risk. How do you explain this? *(LG10-4)*

11. Find a beta estimate from three different sources for General Electric (GE). Compare these three values. Why might they be different? *(LG10-4)*

12. If you were to compute beta yourself, what choices would you make regarding the market portfolio, the holding period for the returns (daily, weekly, etc.), and the number of returns? Justify your choices. *(LG10-4)*

13. Explain how the concept of a positive risk-return relationship breaks down if you can systematically find stocks that are overvalued and undervalued. *(LG10-5)*

14. Determine what level of market efficiency each event is consistent with the following:

    a. Immediately after an earnings announcement the stock price jumps and then stays at the new level. *(LG10-5)*

    b. The CEO buys 50,000 shares of his company and the stock price does not change. *(LG10-5)*

    c. The stock price immediately jumps when a stock split is announced, but then retraces half of the gain over the next day. *(LG10-5)*

    d. An investor analyzes company quarterly and annual balance sheets and income statements looking for undervalued stocks. The investor earns about the same return as the S&P 500 Index. *(LG10-5)*

15. Why do most investment scams conducted over the Internet and e-mail involve penny stocks instead of S&P 500 Index stocks? *(LG10-5)*

16. Describe a stock market bubble. Can a bubble occur in a single stock? *(LG10-5)*

17. If stock prices are not strong-form efficient, then what might be the price reaction to a firm announcing a stock buyback? Explain. *(LG10-6)*

18. Compare and contrast the assumptions that need to be made to compute a required return using CAPM and the constant-growth model. *(LG10-7)*

19. How should you handle a case where required return computations from CAPM and the constant-growth model are very different? *(LG10-7)*

Problems

10-1 Expected Return Compute the expected return given these three economic states, their likelihoods, and the potential returns: *(LG10-1)*

Economic State	Probability	Return
Fast growth	0.2	40%
Slow growth	0.4	10
Recession	0.4	−25

10-2 Expected Return Compute the expected return given these three economic states, their likelihoods, and the potential returns: *(LG10-1)*

Economic State	Probability	Return
Fast growth	0.2	35%
Slow growth	0.6	10
Recession	0.2	−30

10-3 Required Return If the risk-free rate is 6 percent and the risk premium is 5 percent, what is the required return? *(LG10-2)*

10-4 Required Return If the risk-free rate is 4 percent and the risk premium is 6 percent, what is the required return? *(LG10-2)*

10-5 Risk Premium The average annual return on the S&P 500 Index from 1986 to 1995 was 15.8 percent. The average annual T-bill yield during the same period was 5.6 percent. What was the market risk premium during these ten years? *(LG10-2)*

10-6 Risk Premium The average annual return on the S&P 500 Index from 1996 to 2005 was 10.8 percent. The average annual T-bill yield during the same period was 3.6 percent. What was the market risk premium during these ten years? *(LG10-2)*

10-7 CAPM Required Return Hastings Entertainment has a beta of 0.24. If the market return is expected to be 11 percent and the risk-free rate is 4 percent, what is Hastings' required return? *(LG10-3)*

10-8 **CAPM Required Return** Nanometrics Inc. has a beta of 3.15. If the market return is expected to be 10 percent and the risk-free rate is 3.5 percent, what is Nanometrics' required return? *(LG10-3)*

10-9 **Company Risk Premium** Netflix Inc. has a beta of 3.61. If the market return is expected to be 13 percent and the risk-free rate is 6 percent, what is Netflix' risk premium? *(LG10-3)*

10-10 **Company Risk Premium** Paycheck Inc. has a beta of 0.94. If the market return is expected to be 11 percent and the risk-free rate is 3 percent, what is Paycheck's risk premium? *(LG10-3)*

10-11 **Portfolio Beta** You have a portfolio with a beta of 1.35. What will be the new portfolio beta if you keep 95 percent of your money in the old portfolio and 5 percent in a stock with a beta of 0.78? *(LG10-3)*

10-12 **Portfolio Beta** You have a portfolio with a beta of 1.1. What will be the new portfolio beta if you keep 85 percent of your money in the old portfolio and 15 percent in a stock with a beta of 0.5? *(LG10-3)*

10-13 **Stock Market Bubble** The NASDAQ stock market bubble peaked at 4,816 in 2000. Two and a half years later it had fallen to 1,000. What was the percentage decline? *(LG10-5)*

10-14 **Stock Market Bubble** The Japanese stock market bubble peaked at 38,916 in 1989. Two and a half years later it had fallen to 15,900. What was the percentage decline? *(LG10-5)*

10-15 **Required Return** Paccar's current stock price is $73.10 and it is likely to pay a $2.69 dividend next year. Since analysts estimate Paccar will have an 11.2 percent growth rate, what is its required return? *(LG10-7)*

10-16 **Required Return** Universal Forest's current stock price is $57.50 and it is likely to pay a $0.26 dividend next year. Since analysts estimate Universal Forest will have a 9.5 percent growth rate, what is its required return? *(LG10-7)*

INTERMEDIATE PROBLEMS

10-17 **Expected Return Risk** For the same economic state probability distribution in problem 10-1, determine the standard deviation of the expected return. *(LG10-1)*

Economic State	Probability	Return
Fast growth	0.2	40%
Slow growth	0.4	10
Recession	0.4	−25

10-18 **Expected Return Risk** For the same economic state probability distribution in problem 10-2, determine the standard deviation of the expected return. *(LG10-1)*

Economic State	Probability	Return
Fast growth	0.2	35%
Slow growth	0.6	10
Recession	0.2	−30

10-19 **Under-/Overvalued Stock** A manager believes his firm will earn a 14 percent return next year. His firm has a beta of 1.5, the expected return on the market is 12 percent, and the risk-free rate is 4 percent. Compute the return the firm should earn given its level of risk and determine whether the manager is saying the firm is undervalued or overvalued. *(LG10-3)*

10-20 **Under-/Overvalued Stock** A manager believes his firm will earn a 14 percent return next year. His firm has a beta of 1.2, the expected return on the market is 11 percent, and the risk-free rate is 5 percent. Compute the return the firm should earn given its level of risk and determine whether the manager is saying the firm is undervalued or overvalued. (*LG10-3*)

10-21 **Portfolio Beta** You own $10,000 of Olympic Steel stock that has a beta of 2.7. You also own $7,000 of Rent-a-Center (beta = 1.5) and $8,000 of Lincoln Educational (beta = 0.5). What is the beta of your portfolio? (*LG10-3*)

10-22 **Portfolio Beta** You own $7,000 of Human Genome stock that has a beta of 3.5. You also own $8,000 of Frozen Food Express (beta = 1.6) and $10,000 of Molecular Devices (beta = 0.4). What is the beta of your portfolio? (*LG10-3*)

ADVANCED PROBLEMS

10-23 **Expected Return and Risk** Compute the expected return and standard deviation given these four economic states, their likelihoods, and the potential returns: (*LG10-1*)

Economic State	Probability	Return
Fast growth	0.30	60%
Slow growth	0.50	13
Recession	0.15	−15
Depression	0.05	−45

10-24 **Expected Return and Risk** Compute the expected return and standard deviation given these four economic states, their likelihoods, and the potential returns: (*LG10-1*)

Economic State	Probability	Return
Fast growth	0.25	50%
Slow growth	0.55	11
Recession	0.15	−15
Depression	0.05	−50

10-25 **Risk Premiums** You own $10,000 of Denny's Corp stock that has a beta of 2.9. You also own $15,000 of Qwest Communications (beta = 1.5) and $5,000 of Southwest Airlines (beta = 0.7). Assume that the market return will be 11.5 percent and the risk-free rate is 4.5 percent. What is the market risk premium? What is the risk premium of each stock? What is the risk premium of the portfolio? (*LG10-3*)

10-26 **Risk Premiums** You own $15,000 of Opsware Inc. stock that has a beta of 3.8. You also own $10,000 of Lowe's Companies (beta = 1.6) and $10,000 of New York Times (beta = 0.8). Assume that the market return will be 12 percent and the risk-free rate is 6 percent. What is the market risk premium? What is the risk premium of each stock? What is the risk premium of the portfolio? (*LG10-3*)

10-27 **Portfolio Beta and Required Return** You hold the positions in the table below. What is the beta of your portfolio? If you expect the market to earn 12 percent and the risk-free rate is 3.5 percent, what is the required return of the portfolio? (*LG10-3*)

	Price	Shares	Beta
Amazon.com	$40.80	100	3.8
Family Dollar Stores	30.10	150	1.2
McKesson Corp	57.40	75	0.4
Schering-Plough Corp	23.80	200	0.5

10-28 Portfolio Beta and Required Return You hold the positions in the table below. What is the beta of your portfolio? If you expect the market to earn 12 percent and the risk-free rate is 3.5 percent, what is the required return of the portfolio? *(LG10-3)*

	Price	Shares	Beta
Advanced Micro Devices	$ 14.70	300	4.2
FedEx Corp	120.00	50	1.1
Microsoft	28.90	100	0.7
Sara Lee Corp	17.25	150	0.5

10-29 Required Return Using the information in the table, compute the required return for each company using both CAPM and the constant-growth model. Compare and discuss the results. Assume that the market portfolio will earn 12 percent and the risk-free rate is 3.5 percent. *(LG10-3, LG10-7)*

	Price	Upcoming Dividend	Growth	Beta
US Bancorp	$36.55	$1.60	10.0%	1.8
Praxair	64.75	1.12	11.0	2.4
Eastman Kodak	24.95	1.00	4.5	0.5

10-30 Required Return Using the information in the table, compute the required return for each company using both CAPM and the constant-growth model. Compare and discuss the results. Assume that the market portfolio will earn 11 percent and the risk-free rate is 4 percent. *(LG10-3, LG10-7)*

	Price	Upcoming Dividend	Growth	Beta
Estee Lauder	$47.40	$0.60	11.7%	0.75
Kimco Realty	52.10	1.54	8.0	1.3
Nordstrom	5.25	0.50	14.6	2.2

 10-31 Spreadsheet Problem As discussed in the text, beta estimates for one firm will vary depending on various factors such as the time over which the estimation is conducted, the market portfolio proxy, and the return intervals. You will demonstrate this variation using returns for Microsoft.

a. Using all 45 monthly returns for Microsoft and the three stock market indexes, compute Microsoft's beta using the S&P 500 Index as the market proxy. Then compute the beta using the DJIA and the NASDAQ indexes as the market portfolio proxy. Compare the three beta estimates.

b. Now estimate the beta using only the most recent 30 monthly returns and the S&P 500 Index. Compare the beta estimate to the estimate in part (a) when using the S&P 500 Index and all 45 monthly returns.

Date	MSFT	S&P500	DJIA	NASDAQ
Oct 2010	0.52%	3.38%	2.59%	2.90
Sep 2010	8.90	3.69	3.06	5.86
Aug 2010	4.35	8.76	7.72	12.04
Jul 2010	−8.57	−4.74	−4.31	−6.24
Jun 2010	12.15	6.88	7.08	6.90
May 2010	−10.80	−5.39	−3.58	−6.55

Date	MSFT	S&P500	DJIA	NASDAQ
Apr 2010	−15.15%	−8.20%	−7.92%	−8.29%
Mar 2010	4.28	1.48	1.40	2.64
Feb 2010	2.15	5.88	5.15	7.14
Jan 2010	2.23	2.85	2.56	4.23
Dec 2009	−7.56	−3.70	−3.46	−5.37
Nov 2009	3.62	1.78	0.80	5.81
Oct 2009	6.54	5.74	6.51	4.86
Sep 2009	7.81	−1.98	0.00	−3.64
Aug 2009	4.34	3.57	2.27	5.64
Jul 2009	5.40	3.36	3.54	1.54
Jun 2009	−1.03	7.41	8.58	7.82
May 2009	13.79	0.02	−0.63	3.42
Apr 2009	3.77	5.31	4.07	3.32
Mar 2009	10.28	9.39	7.35	12.35
Feb 2009	13.73	8.54	7.73	10.94
Jan 2009	−4.92	−10.99	−11.72	−6.68
Dec 2008	−12.02	−8.57	−8.84	−6.38
Nov 2008	−3.85	0.78	−0.60	2.70
Oct 2008	−8.85	−7.48	−5.32	−10.77
Sep 2008	−16.33	−16.94	−14.06	−17.73
Aug 2008	−2.18	−9.08	−6.00	−11.64
Jul 2008	6.53	1.22	1.45	1.80
Jun 2008	−6.52	−0.99	0.25	1.42
May 2008	−2.85	−8.60	−10.19	−9.10
Apr 2008	−0.33	1.07	−1.42	4.55
Mar 2008	0.48	4.75	4.54	5.87
Feb 2008	4.34	−0.60	−0.03	0.34
Jan 2008	−16.25	−3.48	−3.04	−4.95
Dec 2007	−8.41	−6.12	−4.63	−9.89
Nov 2007	5.95	−0.86	−0.80	−0.33
Oct 2007	−8.42	−4.40	−4.01	−6.93
Sep 2007	24.92	1.48	0.25	5.83
Aug 2007	2.55	3.58	4.03	4.05
Jul 2007	−0.55	1.29	1.10	1.97
Jun 2007	−1.63	−3.20	−1.47	−2.19
May 2007	−3.96	−1.78	−1.61	−0.05
Apr 2007	2.82	3.25	4.32	3.15
Mar 2007	7.44	4.33	5.74	4.27
Feb 2007	−1.06	1.00	0.70	0.23

c. Estimate Microsoft's beta using the quarterly returns below. Compare the estimate to the ones from parts (a) and (b).

Date	Msft	S&P 500
Q3 2010	3.90%	7.41%
Q2 2010	−15.11	−7.17
Q1 2010	8.89	10.51
Q4 2009	2.06	3.64
Q3 2009	18.56	4.93
Q2 2009	16.85	13.14
Q1 2009	19.25	5.68
Q4 2008	−22.89	−14.75
Q3 2008	−12.82	−23.56
Q2 2008	−9.49	−8.53
Q1 2008	−12.20	0.51
Q4 2007	−11.13	−11.03
Q3 2007	27.40	6.47
Q2 2007	−2.85	−1.83
Q1 2007	−2.64	3.07

chapter eleven

calculating the cost of capital

In the previous two chapters, we discussed investors' required return given a particular risk profile. In this chapter, we examine the question from the firm's point of view: How much must the firm pay to finance its operations and expansions using debt and equity sources? Firms use a combination of debt and equity sources to fund their operations, projects, and any expansions they may undertake. In Chapter 14, we'll explore the factors that managers consider as they choose the optimal capital structure mix. For now, we'll assume that management has chosen the optimal mix for us, and that it's our job to implement it.

As we've seen in previous chapters, investors face different kinds of risks associated with debt, preferred stock, and equity. As a result, their required rates of return for each debt or equity source differ as well. So, as the firm uses a combination of different financing sources, we must calculate the investors' *average* required rate of return. Since firms seldom use equal amounts of debt and equity capital sources, we will need to calculate a *weighted* average, with weights based on the proportion of debt and equity capital used.

One important point about the **component costs** to be used in the firm's computation of the average required rate of return is that dividends paid to either common or preferred stockholders are not tax deductible. Thus paying a certain rate of return to either costs the firm that same rate. On the other hand, interest paid to debtholders *is* tax deductible so that the firm's effective after-tax interest cost will be equal to the interest rate paid on debt multiplied by one minus the firm's relevant tax rate.

continued on p. 260

continued from p. 259

For example, if a firm pays a 10 percent coupon on $1 million in debt while it is subject to a 35 percent tax rate, then each coupon payment will be equal to $0.10 \times \$1,000,000 = \$100,000$, but that $100,000 in interest, being tax deductible, will reduce the firm's tax bill by $0.35 \times \$100,000 = \$35,000$. So paying $100,000 in interest saves the firm $35,000 in taxes, making the effective after-tax cost of debt equal to $\$100,000 - \$35,000 = \$65,000$ and the effective after-tax interest rate equal to $10\% \times (1 - 0.35) = 6.5\%$. ■

THE WACC
FORMULA LG11-1, LG11-2

The average cost per dollar of capital raised is called the **weighted-average cost of capital (WACC).** We calculate WACC using equation 11-1:

WACC = Percentage of equity × Cost of equity
      + Percentage of preferred stock
      × Cost of preferred stock
      + Percentage of debt × After-tax cost of debt

$$= \frac{E}{E+P+D} i_E + \frac{P}{E+P+D} i_P$$

$$+ \frac{D}{E+P+D} i_D \times (1 - T_C) \qquad (11\text{-}1)$$

where

E = Market value of equity used in financing the relevant project or firm.

P = Market value of preferred stock used.

D = Market value of debt used.

$\dfrac{E}{E+P+D}$ = Percentage of financing that is equity.

$\dfrac{P}{E+P+D}$ = Percentage of financing that is preferred stock.

$\dfrac{D}{E+P+D}$ = Percentage of financing that is debt.

i_E = Cost of equity.

i_P = Cost of preferred stock.

i_D = Before-tax cost of debt.

T_C = Appropriate corporate tax rate.

Notice that we use weights based on market values rather than book values because market values reflect investors' assessment

»viewpoints

business APPLICATION

MP3 Devices Inc. is about to launch a new project to create and market a combination MP3 player-video projector. MP3 Devices currently uses a particular mixture of debt, common stock, and preferred shares in its capital structure, but the firm is thinking of using the launch of the new project as an opportunity to change that capital structure.

    The new project will be funded with 40 percent debt, 10 percent preferred stock, and 50 percent common stock. MP3 Devices currently has 10 million shares of common stock outstanding, selling at $18.75 per share, and expects to pay an annual dividend of $1.35 one year from now, after which future dividends are expected to grow at a constant 6 percent rate. MP3's debt consists of 20-year, 10-percent annual coupon bonds with a face value of $150 million and a market value of $165 million and the company's capital mix also includes 100,000 shares of 10 percent preferred stock selling at par.

    If MP3 Devices faces a marginal tax rate of 34 percent, what weighted average cost of capital should it use as it evaluates this project?

of what they would be willing to pay for the various types of securities.

Calculating the Component Cost of Equity

We could calculate i_E using the capital asset pricing model:

$$i_E = R_f + \beta(R_M - R_f) \qquad (11\text{-}2)$$

Or, we can assume that the equity in question is a constant-growth stock such as the ones we modeled in Chapter 8. Under this assumption, we can solve the constant-growth model for i_E:

$$i_E = \frac{D_1}{P_0} + g \qquad (11\text{-}3)$$

Which way is better? Well, theoretically, both should give us the same answer, but depending on the situation, some pragmatic reasons may dictate your choice.

1. In situations where you do not have sufficient historic observations to estimate β (i.e., when the stock is fairly new), or when you suspect that the past level of the stock's systematic (or market) risk might not be a good indicator of the future, you do not want to use the CAPM, where β_E estimates *future* systematic risk, calculated based on *historic* systematic risk.

2. In situations where you can expect constant dividend growth, the constant-growth model is appropriate. But although you can try to adjust the model for stocks without constant

personal APPLICATION

Mackenzie is currently finishing up her B.S. degree and is considering going back to grad school for a master's. She currently has $17,125 in student loans carrying an 8 percent interest rate from her B.S. and estimates that she will need to take out an additional $29,000 in student loans (at the same interest rate) to make it through the master's program she'd like to attend. The IRS allows taxpayers with student loans to deduct the interest on those loans, but only up to a maximum amount of $2,500 per year. Assuming that Mackenzie will face a marginal personal tax rate of 25 percent when she graduates, what will be the average after-tax interest rate that she will be paying on the student loans immediately after she graduates with her master's?

How else can Mackenzie finance her graduate degree? What will happen to her after-tax interest rate?
Scan the QR code for an extended look. Turn to the back of the book for solutions to these applications.

---

dividend growth, doing so may introduce potentially sizable errors, so it is not the best choice for stocks that increase their dividends irregularly.

Overall, we should expect that the CAPM approach to estimating i_E will apply more accurately in most cases. However, if you do encounter a situation in which the constant-growth model applies, then you can certainly use it. If we are really fortunate and happen to have enough information to use both approaches, then we should probably *use* both, taking an average of the resulting estimates of i_E.[1]

Calculating the Component Cost of Preferred Stock

As we discussed in Chapter 8, preferred stock represents a special case of the constant-growth model, wherein g equals zero. So we can estimate preferred stocks' component cost using a simplified version of equation 11-3:

$$i_P = \frac{D_1}{P_0} \qquad (11\text{-}4)$$

[1]Think of taking such an average as being intuitively the same as diversifying our "portfolio" of data across the two different estimation techniques, thereby reducing the average amount of estimation error. Taking this average is intuitively the same as diversifying your "portfolio" of data across two different estimation techniques. These options allow you to reduce your average amount of estimation error.

Calculating the Component Cost of Debt

Because of the tax deductibility of debt for the firm, computing the component cost of debt actually has two parts. We must estimate the before-tax cost of debt, i_D, and then adjust this figure to convert it to the after-tax rate of return.

To estimate i_D, we need to solve for the yield to maturity (YTM) on the firm's existing debt:

$$\text{Solve} \left\{ PV = PMT \times \left[\frac{1 - \dfrac{1}{(1+i_D)^N}}{i_D} \right] + \frac{FV}{(1+i_D)^N} \right\} \text{ for } i_D$$

(11-5)

Solve for the interest rate that makes the price equal to the sum of the present values of the coupons and the face value of the bond.

Then we adjust this result by multiplying by $(1 - T_C)$.

Choosing Tax Rates

The interest paid on debt is tax deductible, but the benefit of that tax deductibility will vary based on the firm's marginal tax rate. The appropriate tax rate to be used in the WACC will be the weighted average of the marginal tax rates that would have been paid on the taxable income shielded by the interest deduction.

For example, if a firm had earnings before interest and taxes (EBIT) of $400,000, taxable interest deductions of $100,000, and faced the corporate tax schedule shown in Table 11.1, then the appropriate tax rate would equal a weighted average of the marginal tax rates from the fourth (i.e., 39%) and fifth (34%)

component costs The individual costs of each type of capital—bonds, preferred stock, and common stock.

weighted-average cost of capital (WACC) The weighted-average after-tax cost of the capital used by a firm, with weights set equal to the relative percentage of each type of capital used.

▼**TABLE 11.1** Corporate Tax Rates

Taxable Income			Tax Rate
$0	—	$50,000	15%
50,001	—	75,000	25
75,001	—	100,000	34
100,001	—	335,000	39
335,001	—	10,000,000	34
10,000,001	—	15,000,000	35
15,000,001	—	18,333,333	38
18,333,334	+		35

EXAMPLE 11-1

Cost of Equity LG11-2

ADK Industries' common shares sell for $32.75 per share. ADK expects to set its next annual dividend at $1.54 per share. If ADK expects future dividends to grow by 6 percent per year, indefinitely, the current risk-free rate is 3 percent, the expected return on the market is 9 percent, and the stock has a beta of 1.3, what should be firm's cost of equity?

SOLUTION:

The cost of equity using the CAPM will be:

$$i_E = R_f + \beta(R_M - R_f)$$

$$= 0.03 + 1.3[0.09 - 0.03]$$

$$= 0.1080, \text{ or } 10.80\%$$

The cost of equity using the constant-growth model will be:

$$i_E = \frac{D_1}{P_0} + g$$

$$= \frac{\$1.54}{\$32.75} + .06$$

$$= 0.1070, \text{ or } 10.70\%$$

Our best estimate of ADK's equity would therefore be: $\dfrac{10.70\% + 10.80\%}{2} = 10.75\%$.

Similar to Problems 11-1, 11-2

EXAMPLE 11-2

Cost of Preferred Stock LG11-3

Suppose that ADK also has one million shares of 7 percent preferred stock outstanding, trading at $72 per share. What is ADK's component cost for preferred equity?

SOLUTION:

The cost of the preferred stock will equal:

$$i_P = \frac{D_1}{P_0}$$

$$= \frac{\$7}{\$72}$$

$$= 0.0972, \text{ or } 9.72\%$$

Similar to Problems 11-7, 11-8

---

tax brackets. The weights would be determined by the relative impacts of the brackets in the computation of the post-interest tax bill:

$$\frac{\$35,000}{\$100,000} \times 0.39 + \frac{\$65,000}{\$100,000} \times 0.34 = 0.3575, \text{ or } 35.75\%$$

Calculating the Weights LG11-4

Calculating the weights to be used in the WACC formula is mathematically very simple: We just calculate the percentages of the funding that come from equity, preferred stock, and debt, respectively.

Sounds easy, right? Well, the tricky part to this lies in determining what we mean by "the funding": If we are calculating WACC for a firm, then "the funding" encompasses all the capital in the firm, and E, P, and D will be determined by computing the total market value of the firm's common stock, preferred stock, and debt, respectively. However, if we are computing WACC for a project, then "the funding" will only include the financing for the project, and E, P, and D will be equal to the amount of each used in the financing of that project.[2]

[2]We'll discuss more about calculating WACC for a project later in the chapter.

the
Math Coach on...
Preferred Stock Dividends

❝ The assumed par value of preferred stock is $100. So, a 7 percent preferred stock pays $7 a year in dividends. ❞

EXAMPLE 11-3

For interactive versions of this example visit www.mhhe.com/canM2e

CALCULATOR HINTS

N = 20
PV = −975
PMT = 80
FV = 1000
CPT I = 8.26

Cost of Debt LG11-3

ADK has 30,000 20-year, 8 percent annual coupon bonds outstanding. If the bonds currently sell for 97.5 percent of par and the firm pays an average tax rate of 35.92 percent, what will be the before-tax and after-tax component cost for debt?

SOLUTION:

The before-tax cost of debt will be the solution to:

$$\text{Solve} \left\{ \$975 = \$80 \times \left[\frac{1 - \frac{1}{(1 + i_D)^{20}}}{i_D} \right] + \frac{\$1,000}{(1 + i_D)^{20}} \right\} \text{ for } i_D$$

which will equal 8.26 percent. Multiplying this by one minus the tax rate will yield the after-tax cost of debt: $0.0826 \times (1 - 0.3592) = 0.0529$, or 5.29%.

Similar to Problems 11-3, 11-4

EXAMPLE 11-4

For interactive versions of this example visit www.mhhe.com/canM2e

Tax Rate LG11-3

Suppose that ADK expects EBIT to be approximately $20 million per year for the foreseeable future. Given the 30,000, 20-year, 8 percent annual coupon bonds discussed in the previous example, what would the appropriate tax rate be for use in the calculation of the debt component of ADK's WACC?

SOLUTION:

The interest payments on the bonds would total $30,000 \times \$1,000 \times 0.08 = \$2,400,000$ per year, resulting in earnings before tax (EBT) of $\$20,000,000 - \$2,400,000 = \$17,600,000$.

As taxable income falls from $20,000,000 to $17,600,000 after the firm pays the interest on the bonds, $1,666,667, or 69.44 percent, of the $2,400,000 reduction would fall in the highest 35 percent bracket, while the remaining $733,333, or 30.56 percent ($733,333/$2,400,000), would occur in the 38 percent tax bracket, making the weighted average applicable tax rate equal to:

$$T_C = (0.6944 \times 0.35) + (0.3056 \times 0.38)$$

$$= 0.3592, \text{ or } 35.92\%$$

Similar to Problems 11-5, 11-6

EXAMPLE 11-5

Capital Structure Weights and WACC LG11-4

Let us continue the previous examples. Suppose that ADK has issued 3 million shares of common stock, 1 million shares of preferred stock, and the previously mentioned 30,000 bonds outstanding. What will ADK's WACC be, considering ADK as a firm?

SOLUTION:

Using the securities' prices given in previous examples, ADK's equity, preferred stock, and debt will have the following total market values:

- Equity: 3m × $32.75 = $98.25m
- Preferred stock: 1m × $72 = $72m
- Debt: 30,000 × $975 = $29.25m

The total combined market value for all three capital sources is $199.5 million. The applicable weights for each capital source will therefore be

$$\text{For common equity: } \frac{E}{E+P+D} = \frac{\$98.25m}{\$199.5m} = 0.4925, \text{ or } 49.25\%$$

$$\text{For preferred stock: } \frac{P}{E+P+D} = \frac{\$72m}{\$199.5m} = 0.3609, \text{ or } 36.09\%$$

$$\text{For debt: } \frac{D}{E+P+D} = \frac{\$29.25m}{\$199.5m} = 0.1466, \text{ or } 14.66\%$$

Tying this all in together with the answers from the previous examples, ADK will have a WACC of:

$$\text{WACC} = \frac{E}{E+P+D}\,i_E + \frac{P}{E+P+D}\,i_P + \frac{D}{E+P+D}\,i_D \times (1 - T_C)$$

$$= (0.4925 \times 0.1075) + (0.3609 \times 0.0972) + (0.1466 \times 0.0826 \times [1 - 0.3592])$$

$$= 0.0958, \text{ or } 9.58\%$$

Similar to Problems 11-9 to 11-14, 11-21, 11-22

time out!

11-1 Explain why we multiply the component cost of debt by the marginal tax rate, T_D, but don't do so for the component costs of equity or preferred stock.

11-2 How would we compute i_D if a company had multiple bond issues outstanding?

If you think about this for a second, you will realize that this means that projects can wind up having different WACCs than their firm. That is not just OK, it is also exactly right because, as we will see in a later chapter, the firm is like a diversified portfolio of different projects, all with different risks and returns. And one of the things that can contribute to the risk of a project is the choice of how much common stock, preferred stock, and debt is used to finance it.

FIRM WACC VERSUS PROJECT WACC LG11-5

So far, we have been defining the WACC as a weighted-average cost across the firm's different financing sources. If we think of the firm as a portfolio of different projects and products, we see that the WACC will be a weighted-average cost of capital across the items in that portfolio, too. This way it represents the cost of capital for the "typical" project that the firm is currently undertaking. However, firms grow by taking on new projects. So now the question is: can managers use our firmwide WACC, calculated above, to evaluate the firm's newly proposed projects?

The answer is: *it depends.* If a new project is similar enough to existing projects, then yes, managers can use the firm's WACC as the new project's cost of capital. But say that your firm is contemplating undertaking a significantly different project—one far different from any project that the firm is already engaged in. What then? Then we cannot expect the firm's overall WACC to appropriately measure the new project's cost of capital. Let your intuition work on this: If the new project is riskier than the firm's existing projects, then it should be "charged" a higher cost of capital. If it's safer, then the firm should assign the new project a lower cost of capital.

Consider a U.S. firm—let's call it GassUp—that currently owns a chain of gas stations. Firm management is considering a new project: opening up a series of gourmet coffee shops. Given the demand for upscale coffee in the United States, as well as the historically volatile oil markets, it's probably difficult to say exactly whether the coffee shops will be *more* or *less* risky than gas stations. We can probably say, though, that the two enterprises will face *different* risks. For example, if the coffee shops are located within the busiest and most stable gas stations—say the ones that lie along freeways—then the firm faces remodeling of existing buildings rather than starting from scratch. Locating the coffee shops within existing structures would likely mean that the risks will be lower than building new stations or new coffee shops.

So, does this mean that GassUp should calculate a heterogeneous WACC for each new project using purely project-specific numbers? Well, not exactly. As we'll discuss below, some inputs to WACC should be project-specific, but others should be consistent with the firmwide values used in calculating a firmwide WACC.

Project Cost Numbers to Take from the Firm

It is tempting to argue that all component inputs for a project-specific WACC should be based on the specific project attributes, but if we created all project-specific numbers, what fundamental issue related to bonds and preferred stock would we be ignoring? That both bonds and preferred stocks create claims on the *firm,* not on any particular group of projects within that firm. Furthermore, debt claims are superior to those of common stockholders. So if the new project *does* significantly increase the firm's overall risk, the increased risk will be borne disproportionately by common stockholders. Debtholders and preferred stockholders will likely face minimal impact on the risk and return that their investments give them, no matter what new project the firm undertakes—even if those claimants own bonds or preferred shares that the firm issued to fund the new project.

For example, suppose GassUp decides to build entirely separate facilities for its coffee shops, which it will name "Bottoms Up." GassUp partially finances its expansion into coffee shops with debt, and the project turns out to be more like "Bottoms Down"— far less successful than the firm had hoped. Though this would be an unfortunate turn of events for GassUp's common shareholders, the firm's creditors and preferred shareholders would likely still collect their usual interest and dividend payments from GassUp's gross revenues from gas station operations.

Creditors understand that their repayment probably comes from continuing operations and take current cash flows into account

Even if GassUp's coffee venture fails, the firm's creditors would likely still collect payments from gas station operations.

business risk The risk of a project arising from the line of business it is in; the variability of a firm's or division's cash flows.

proxy beta The beta (a measure of the riskiness) of a firm in a similar line of business as a proposed new project.

financial risk The risk of a project to equity holders stemming from the use of debt in the financial structure of the firm; refers to the issue of how a firm decides to distribute the business risk between debt and equity holders.

when a firm comes seeking funds. For example, if a small firm approaches a bank for a loan to finance an expansion, the bank will normally spend more time analyzing *current* cash flows to determine the probability that they will recoup their loan than it will analyzing the potential new cash flows from the proposed expansion.

Note that this situation holds true only as long as the new projects represent fairly small investments compared to ongoing operations. As new projects become *large* relative to ongoing cash-flow producing activities, creditors will have to examine the likelihood of being repaid from the new projects much more closely. New projects, however great their potential, inherently carry more risk than do established current operations. Changes in the proportion of new projects relative to ongoing operations will thus translate into increased risk for the creditor, who will ask for a higher rate of return to offset the risk.

Since most firms tend to grow incrementally, we will assume (unless otherwise indicated) that we're examining situations in which the number of new projects is small relative to ongoing

Obviously, no proposed new project will have a history of previous returns. Without such data, neither analysts nor investors can calculate a project-specific beta. So what data can we use? To the extent that we can find other firms engaged in the proposed new line of business, we can use their betas as proxies to estimate the project's risk. Ideally, the other firms would be engaged *only* in the proposed new line of business; such monothemed firms are usually referred to as *pure plays,* with this term also in turn being applied to this approach to estimating a project's beta.

An average of *n* such **proxy betas** will give us a fairly accurate estimate of what the new project's beta will be.[4]

$$i_E = r_f + \beta_{Avg}[E(r_M) - r_f]$$

where

$$\beta_{Avg} = \frac{\sum_{j=1}^{N} \beta_j}{n} \tag{11-6}$$

This average will be an estimate, in the strictest statistical sense of the word. You might recall from your statistics classes that we will need to be careful to get as large a sample as possible if we want to get as much statistical power for our estimate as possible. Ideally, we would like to find at least three or four companies from which to draw proxy betas, called *pure-play proxies,* to ensure that we have a large enough sample size to safely make meaningful inferences. In reality, however, two proxies (or even one) might

> ## "The firm's risk changes when it takes on a project that is noticeably different from its existing lines of business."

operations. We can therefore assume that using the firm's existing WACC for both debt and preferred stock is appropriate.

Project Cost Numbers to Find Elsewhere: The Pure-Play Approach

Since we have decided not to adjust the firmwide costs of debt or preferred stock for the risk of a project, where *should* we account for the new project risk brought to the firm overall? As with several other questions associated with risk- and profit-sharing, the answer lies with *equity*.

The firm's risk changes when it takes on a project that is noticeably different from its existing lines of business. Since debtholders and preferred stockholders will not notice this change in risk, the firm spreads the risks that it takes with new projects by transferring most of the risk to the common stockholders.

In response to such a change in the firm's risk profile, stockholders adjust their required rate of return to adjust for the new risk level. Absent any alteration to the firm's capital structure,[3] changes in the firm's risk profile are due to differences in the firm's **business risks** based on the mix of the new and existing product lines. The firm's beta reflects those differences in each product line.

represent a suitable sample if their business line resembles the proposed new project closely enough. In particular, we may want to use betas from industry front-runners, and rely less on betas of any firms that the company really doesn't want to emulate.

What shall we do if we cannot find *any* pure-play proxies? Well, in that case, we may want to use firms that, while not *solely* in the same business as the proposed project's venture, have a sizable proportion of revenues from that line. We may then be able to "back out" the impact of their other lines of business from their firm's beta to leave us with a good enough estimate of what the new project's beta might be.

Be sure to use weights based on the *project's* sources of capital, and not necessarily the *firm's* capital structure. If the new project is going to use more or less debt than the firm's existing projects

---

[3]In reality, new projects are often financed with different proportions of equity, debt, and preferred stock than were used to fund the firm's existing operations. Such a change in capital structure will result in a change in **financial risk,** with increased leverage magnifying β.

[4]We will be able to take a straight average of the proxy firm's betas as the estimate of our beta only if the capital structures of all the proxies are identical to each other and to that of our proposed new project. If not, we will need to adjust the proxies' estimated betas for differences in capital structures before averaging them. Then we will need to readjust the average beta for our project's capital structure before using the estimate.

do, then the risk- and reward-sharing are going to vary across the different types of capital, and we will want to recognize this in our WACC computation.

Finally, we need to consider the appropriate corporate tax rate to use in calculating the WACC for a project. That marginal corporate tax rate will be the average marginal tax rate to which the project's cash flows will be subject. Assume a firm with $400,000 of EBIT from current operations is considering a new project that will increase EBIT by $200,000. Since this $200,000 increase will keep the firm's marginal tax in the fifth bracket of Table 11.1, the appropriate tax rate to compute the project's WACC will simply be 34 percent.

To summarize, the component costs and weights to compute a project-specific WACC should be as shown in equation 11-7, with the source of each part indicated by the appropriate subscript:

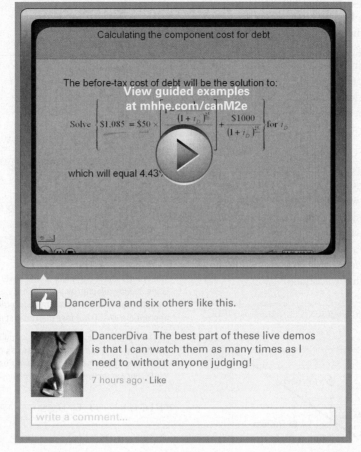

Calculating the component cost for debt

The before-tax cost of debt will be the solution to:

View guided examples at mhhe.com/canM2e

Solve $\left\{ \$1.085 = \$50 \times \dfrac{\left(1 + i_D\right)^{yr}}{} + \dfrac{\$1000}{\left(1 + i_D\right)^{yr}} \right\}$ for i_D

which will equal 4.43%

👍 DancerDiva and six others like this.

DancerDiva The best part of these live demos is that I can watch them as many times as I need to without anyone judging!

7 hours ago · Like

write a comment...

$$
\begin{aligned}
\text{WACC}_{\text{Project}} = {} & \frac{E_{\text{Project}}}{E_{\text{Project}} + P_{\text{Project}} + D_{\text{Project}}} i_{E,\,\text{Project}} \\
& + \frac{P_{\text{Project}}}{E_{\text{Project}} + P_{\text{Project}} + D_{\text{Project}}} i_{P,\,\text{Firm}} \\
& + \frac{D_{\text{Project}}}{E_{\text{Project}} + P_{\text{Project}} + D_{\text{Project}}} i_{D,\,\text{Firm}} \\
& \times \left(1 - T_{C,\,\text{Project}}\right)
\end{aligned}
\tag{11-7}
$$

DIVISIONAL WACC LG11-6

Do firms calculate risk-appropriate WACC for every new project they consider? While this would be ideal, pragmatically it just is not always feasible. In large corporations, managers evaluate dozens or even hundreds of proposed new projects each year. The costs in terms of time and effort of estimating project-specific WACCs individually for each project are simply prohibitive. Instead, large firms often take a middle-of-the-road approach that can achieve many of the of project-specific WACC calculations with much less time and resources. The key to this approach is to calculate a **divisional WACC.**

Pros and Cons of a Divisional WACC

As with most choices in life as well as finance, there are pros and cons to the divisional WACC. Let's first consider the disadvantage of using a firm's WACC to evaluate new, risk-heterogeneous projects. To make things simple, let's assume that we are looking at a firm that uses only equity finance, so that WACC is simply equal to i_E.

Take a look at Figure 11.1. Similar to our discussion of the security market line in Chapter 10, required rates of return for projects with varying degrees of risk would lie along the sloped line shown

time **out!**

11-3 For computing a project WACC, why do we take some component costs from the firm but compute others that are specific for the project being considered?

11-4 It is usually much easier to find proxy firms that are engaged in multiple lines of business than it is to find pure-play proxies. Explain how such firms can be used to estimate the beta for a new project.

▼**FIGURE 11.1** Risk-Appropriate WACCs

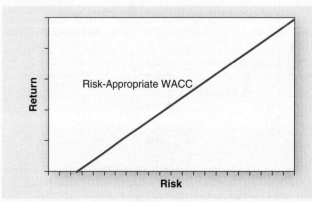

Risk-Appropriate WACC

Return

Risk

In an all-equity firm, WACC is theoretically equal to i_E for each proposed project, which will increase as the risk (i.e., β) of the project increases.

in the figure. We could then evaluate projects with various degrees of risk based on the relationship between their expected rate of return and the required rate of return for that risk level. Turning to Figure 11.2, you can see that using risk-appropriate WACCs, projects A and B would be accepted, since their *expected* rates of return would be higher than their respective *required* rates of return. Projects C and D would be rejected because our simple scheme shows that these projects are not expected to return enough to cover market-required returns, given the projects' riskiness.

However, using a firmwide WACC would result in a comparison of the project's expected rates of return to a single, flat, firmwide cost of capital as Figure 11.3 shows. Using a simple firmwide WACC to evaluate new projects would give an unfair advantage to projects that present more risk than the firm's average beta. Using a firmwide WACC would also work against projects that involved less risk than the firm's average beta. Looking at the same sample projects as before, we see that Project A would now be rejected, while Project C would be accepted.

▼**FIGURE 11.2** Sample Projects versus Risk-Sensitive WACC

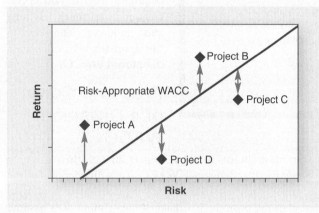

Projects A and B have expected returns *greater than* their risk-appropriate WACCs. Projects C and D have expected returns *less than* their risk-appropriate WACCs.

▼**FIGURE 11.3** Sample Project versus Firmwide WACC

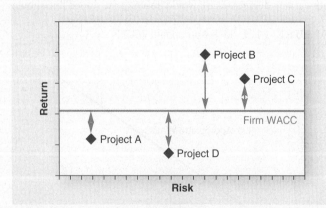

If we were to mistakenly compare projects bearing different risks to this single firmwide WACC, we would conclude that projects A and D have expected rates of return *less than* the firmwide WACC and Projects B and C have expected returns *greater than* the firmwide WACC.

▼**FIGURE 11.4** Incorrect Decisions Caused by Inappropriate Use of Firmwide WACC

The orange-shaded triangle on the lower left represents Project A, which is *incorrectly rejected* by a firm. It has risk *less than* the average risk of the firm. Its expected rate of return is *greater than* its correctly calculated risk-appropriate WACC but *less than* an inappropriately calculated firmwide WACC.

The pink-shaded triangle on the upper right represents Project C, which is *incorrectly accepted* by a firm. It has risk *greater than* the average risk of the firm. Its expected rate of return is *less than* a correctly calculated risk-appropriate WACC but *greater than* an inappropriately calculated firmwide WACC.

▼**FIGURE 11.5** Divisional WACCs

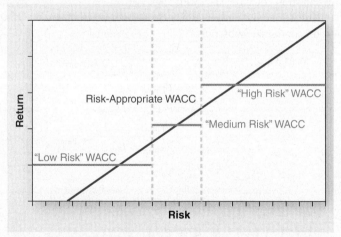

Instead of calculating a single firmwide WACC based on the average risk of all projects in the firm, assume that the firm calculates division-specific WACCs based on the average risk of the projects in each respective division.

Using a firmwide WACC in this way, as an inappropriate benchmark for projects of differing risk from the firm's current operations, will result in quite a few incorrect decisions. In fact, the use of a firmwide WACC to evaluate *any* projects with risk-return coordinates lying in the two shaded triangles shown in Figure 11.4 will result in an incorrect accept/reject decision.

A divisional WACC can be a solution. It means dividing the firm's existing projects into divisions, where the different divisions proxy for systematically different average project risk levels. Calculating WACCs for each division separately, as Figure 11.5

EXAMPLE 11-6 # Calculation of Project WACC LG11-5

Suppose that Evita's Subs, a local shipyard, is considering opening up a chain of sandwich shops. Evita's capital structure currently consists of 2 million outstanding shares of common stock, selling for $83 per share, and a $50 million bond issue, selling at 103 percent of par. Evita's stock has a beta of 0.72, the expected market risk premium is 7 percent, and the current risk-free rate is 4.5 percent. The bonds pay a 9 percent annual coupon and mature in 20 years. The current operations of the firm produce EBIT of $100 million per year, and the new sandwich operations would add only an expected $12 million per year to that. Also, suppose that Evita's management has done some research on the sandwich shop industry, and discovered that such firms have an average beta of 1.23. If the new project will be funded with 50 percent debt and 50 percent equity, what should be the WACC for this new project?

SOLUTION:

First, note that Evita's doesn't currently have any outstanding preferred stock and doesn't plan on using any to finance the new project, so that makes our job a little simpler. Also note that, though we are given enough information to calculate the firm's current capital structure weights and component cost of equity, we won't need those figures, as this new project differs from the firmwide WACC weights. We already know the capital structure weights for the new project (50 percent debt and 50 percent equity), so we just need to calculate the appropriate component costs.

For equity, the appropriate cost will be based upon the average risk of sandwich shops:

$$i_E = R_f + \beta, \text{Project } (R_M - R_f)$$

$$= 0.045 + 1.23[0.07]$$

$$= 0.1311, \text{ or } 13.11\%$$

The YTM on the new bonds issued to finance this project will be the same as the YTM on the existing bonds:

$$\text{Solve } \left\{ \$1,030 = \$90 \times \left[\frac{1 - \dfrac{1}{(1 + i_D)^{20}}}{i_D} \right] + \frac{\$1,000}{(1 + i_D)^{20}} \right\} \text{ for } i_D$$

which gives us an i_D of 8.68 percent.

Finally, the current EBIT already puts the firm in the top 35 percent tax bracket, so the additional EBIT generated by the project will also be taxed at this same marginal 35 percent tax rate. Therefore, the WACC of the new project will be:

$$\text{WACC}_{\text{Project}} = \frac{E_{\text{Project}}}{E_{\text{Project}} + P_{\text{Project}} + D_{\text{Project}}} i_{E, \text{Project}} + \frac{D_{\text{Project}}}{E_{\text{Project}} + P_{\text{Project}} + D_{\text{Project}}} i_{D, \text{Firm}} \times (1 - T_{C, \text{Project}})$$

$$= 0.5 \times 0.1311 + 0.5 \times 0.0868 \times (1 - 0.35)$$

$$= 0.0938, \text{ or } 9.38\%$$

Similar to Problems 11-16 to 11-21

CALCULATOR HINTS

$\boxed{N} = 20$
$\boxed{PV} = -1030$
$\boxed{PMT} = 90$
$\boxed{FV} = 1000$
$\boxed{CPT \, I} = 8.68$

---

shows, greatly reduces the problem of basing decisions on inaccurate results from using firmwide WACC for all projects.

Using divisional WACCs like this will not *eliminate* problems of incorrect acceptance and incorrect rejection, but it will greatly reduce their frequency. Instead of making errors corresponding to the two large triangular areas indicated in Figure 11.4, we

will instead have six smaller areas of error shown in Figure 11.6. More acceptance/rejection regions will result in fewer errors.

For example, let's consider our four sample projects from before. We now evaluate them using divisional WACCs as shown in Figure 11.7. We would correctly accept both projects A and B and correctly reject projects C and D.

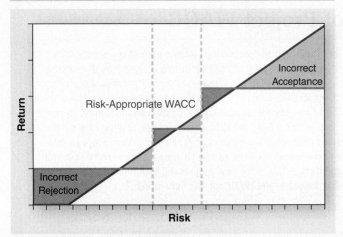

Total incorrect acceptances/rejections turn out to be less when divisional WACCs are used.

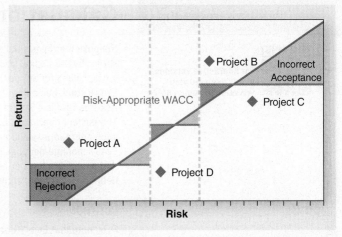

Projects A and B here are *correctly accepted,* while projects C and D are *correctly rejected.*

Subjective versus Objective Approaches

We can form divisional WACCs subjectively by simply considering the project's risk relative to the firm's existing lines of business. If the project is riskier (safer) than the firm average, adjust the firm WACC upward (downward) to account for our subjective opinion of project riskiness. The biggest disadvantage to this approach is that the adjustments are pretty much picked out of thin air and created just for the project at hand. For example, consider the sample subjective divisional WACCs in Table 11.2. Both the project assignments to the divisions and then the WACC adjustments for the very low risk, low risk, high risk, and very high risk are fairly arbitrary.

An objective approach would be to compute the average beta per division, use these figures in the CAPM formula to calculate i_E for each division, and then, in turn, use divisional estimates of i_E to construct divisional WACCs. Though the

objective approach would usually be more precise, resulting in fewer incorrect accept/reject decisions, the subjective approach is more frequently used because it is easier to implement.

time out!

11-5 Divisions of a corporation are not usually formed based explicitly on differences in risk between the projects in different divisions. Rather, they are normally formed along product-type or geographic differences. Explain how this division scheme may still result in divisions that *do* differ among themselves by average risk. Also explain why calculating divisional WACCs in such a situation will still improve decision making over simply using a firmwide WACC for project acceptance or rejection.

11-6 Explain why, in Example 11-7, using objectively computed divisional WACCS still resulted in an incorrect accept/reject decision for project D.

▼ **TABLE 11.2** Subjective Divisional WACCs

Risk Level	Discount Rate
Very low risk	Firm WACC − 5%
Low risk	Firm WACC − 2%
Same risk as firm	Firm WACC
High risk	Firm WACC + 3%
Very high risk	Firm WACC + 7%

For interactive versions
of this example visit
www.mhhe.com/canM2e

EXAMPLE 11-7 | Divisional Costs of Capital LG11-7

Assume that BF Inc. an all-equity firm, has a firmwide WACC of 10 percent, and that the firm is broken into three divisions: Textiles, Accessories, and Miscellaneous. The average Textiles project has a beta of 0.7; the average Accessories project has a beta of 1.3; and the average Miscellaneous project has a beta of 1.1.

The firm is currently considering the projects shown in the table below. The current approach is to use the firm's WACC to evaluate all projects, but management sees the wisdom in adopting a subjective divisional cost of capital approach. Firm management is thus considering a divisional cost of capital scheme in which they will use the firm's WACC for Miscellaneous projects, the firm's WACC minus 1 percent for Textiles projects, and the firm's WACC plus 3 percent for Accessories projects. The current expected return to the market is 12 percent, and the current risk-free rate is 5.75 percent.

Project	Division	Expected i_E	Beta
A	$\beta_{Accessories}$	17.00%	1.3
B	$\beta_{Accessories}$	15.00	1.2
C	$\beta_{Miscellaneous}$	13.00	1.3
D	$\beta_{Miscellaneous}$	11.00	0.7
E	$\beta_{Textiles}$	9.00	0.8
F	$\beta_{Textiles}$	7.00	0.5

For this group of projects, how much better would their accept/reject decisions be if they used this approach rather than if they continued to use the firm's WACC to evaluate all projects? Would switching to an objective divisional cost of capital approach, where the WACC for each division is based on that division's average beta, improve their accept/reject criteria any further?

SOLUTION:

Determine the required rates of return for each project assuming that the firm uses the firm-wide WACC and adds the subjective adjustments to construct divisional WACCs. The objective computation of divisional WACCs using each division's average beta and the i_E computed using each project's specific beta is indicated in the table below. In each case, project acceptances appear in blue print, and project rejections appear in red print.

Project	Division	Expected i_E	Beta	Firm WACC	Subjective i_E	Objective i_E	Specific i_E
A	$\beta_{Accessories}$	17.00%	1.3	10.00%	13.00%	13.88%	13.88%
B	$\beta_{Accessories}$	15.00	1.2	10.00	13.00	13.88	13.25
C	$\beta_{Miscellaneous}$	13.00	1.3	10.00	10.00	12.63	13.88
D	$\beta_{Miscellaneous}$	11.00	0.7	10.00	10.00	12.63	10.13
E	$\beta_{Textiles}$	9.00	0.8	10.00	9.00	10.13	10.75
F	$\beta_{Textiles}$	7.00	0.5	10.00	9.00	10.13	8.88

Using the "Specific i_E" yields the "correct" accept/reject decision; that is, these accept/reject decisions would be generated exactly the same if the firm had the time and resources to compute the i_E on a project-by-project basis. In this particular situation, using the firm WACC as a benchmark for all the projects would result in projects E and F being rejected, since they both will return expected rates less than the firm's 10 percent required rate of return. By comparison to the results using the Specific i_E, both of these rejections are appropriate. We would prefer that the accept/reject criteria took account of risk; that is, both projects would be rejected because their expected returns (9 percent and 7 percent, respectively) are less than the required returns (10.75 and 8.88 percent, respectively) based on their specific levels of project risk rather than assuming that both projects carry the same risk as the firm's overall risk. However, using the firm's WACC incorrectly accepts project C.

Using the subjectively adjusted approach to calculating i_E results in required rates of return of 13 percent for Accessories projects, 10 percent for Miscellaneous projects, and 9 percent for Textiles projects. The associated accept/reject decisions actually incorrectly accepts projects C and E, making the subjectively adjusted WACC approach worse (in this specific example) than simply using the firmwide WACC.

Finally, using the objective approach to constructing divisional costs of capital, along with the three divisions' average betas given above, results in required rates of return for the three divisions of:

$$i_E = R_f + \beta(R_M - R_f)$$

$$i_{E,\,Accessories} = 0.0575 + 1.3[0.12 - 0.0575] = 0.1388, \text{ or } 13.88\%$$

$$i_{E,\,Miscellaneous} = 0.0575 + 1.1[0.12 - 0.0575] = 0.1263, \text{ or } 12.63\%$$

$$i_{E,\,Textiles} = 0.0575 + 0.7[0.12 - 0.0575] = 0.1013, \text{ or } 10.13\%$$

As the solutions above show, using these divisional cost of capital figures as required rates of return for each project results in correct rejections of projects E and F, but also results in an incorrect rejection of project D and an incorrect acceptance of project C relative to computing i_E on a project-by-project basis.

Overall, using either the objective or subjective approaches to calculating divisional costs of capital will not be as precise as using project-specific WACCs: We will wind up incorrectly accepting and/or rejecting some projects. Making incorrect decisions on some of our project choices may be worth it if the projects in question aren't large enough for project-specific calculations to be cost-effective.

Similar to Problems 11-25 to 11-28

FLOTATION COSTS LG11-8

We know that firms use varied sources of funding. Up to now, our calculations have use of retained earnings to fund projects What if a firm funds a project by issuing externally generated new capital—additional stock, bonds, and so on? Then the firm has to pay commissions to the underwriting firm that floats the issue. So to figure project WACCs, we must integrate these **flotation costs** into our component costs as well.

We can approach the commission costs in two basic ways. We can either increase the project's WACC to incorporate the flotation costs' impact as a percentage of WACC, or we can leave the WACC alone and adjust the project's initial investment upward to reflect the "true" cost of the project. Both approaches have advantages and disadvantages. The first approach tends to understate the component cost of new equity, and the latter approach violates the **separation principle** of capital budgeting, which states that the calculations of cash flows should remain independent of financing. We will discuss the separation principle and the second approach in the next chapter.

Adjusting the WACC

The first approach to adjusting for flotation costs is to adjust the issue price of new securities by subtracting flotation cost, *F*, to reflect the net security price. Then use this net price to calculate the component cost of capital. For equity, this approach is most commonly applied to the constant-growth model:

$$i_E = \frac{D_1}{P_0 - F} + g \qquad (11\text{-}8)$$

If we instead want to apply this approach to the cost of equity obtained from the CAPM formula, we would adjust it upward by an equivalent amount.

time out!

11-7 Why should we expect the flotation costs for debt to be significantly lower than those for equity?

11-8 Explain how we should go about computing the WACC for a project which uses both retained earnings and a new equity issue.

EXAMPLE 11-8   Flotation-Adjusted Cost of Equity LG11-8

**For interactive versions
of this example visit
www.mhhe.com/canM2e**

Suppose that, as in Example 11-1, ADK Industries' common shares are selling for $32.75 per share, and the company expects to set its next annual dividend at $1.54 per share. All future dividends are expected to grow by 6 percent per year indefinitely. In addition, let us suppose that ADK faces a flotation cost of 20 percent on new equity issues. Calculate the flotation-adjusted cost of equity.

SOLUTION:

Twenty percent of $32.75 will be $6.55, so the flotation-adjusted cost of equity will be:

$$i_E = \frac{D_1}{P_0 - F} + g$$

$$= \frac{\$1.54}{\$32.75 - \$6.55} + 0.06$$

$$= 0.1188, \text{ or } 11.88\%$$

Notice that the result is 1.18 percent above the non-flotation-adjusted cost of equity, 10.70 percent, computed using the constant-growth model in Example 11-1. If we instead wanted to use the CAPM estimate, we would take the non-flotation-adjusted CAPM estimate from the same example, 10.80 percent, and add the same differential of 1.18 percent to it to get the flotation-adjusted value:

$$i_E = 0.1080 + 0.0118 = 0.1198 \text{ or } 11.98\%$$

The adjustments for the component costs of preferred stock and debt will be similar:

$$i_P = \frac{D_1}{P_0 - F} \tag{11-9}$$

$$\text{Solve} \left\{ PV - F = PMT \times \left[\frac{1 - \frac{1}{(1 + i_D)^N}}{i_D} \right] + \frac{FV}{(1 + i_D)^N} \right\} \text{ for } i_D \tag{11-10}$$

Similar to Problems 11-23, 11-24

Get Online

mhhe.com/canM2e

for study materials including self-test problems with solutions, quizzes, research projects, minicases, and videos

Your Turn...

Questions

1. How would you handle calculating the cost of capital if a firm were planning to issue two different classes of common stock? *(LG11-1)*

2. Why don't we multiply the cost of preferred stock by 1 minus the tax rate, as we do for debt? *(LG11-2)*

3. Expressing WACC in terms of i_E, i_P, and i_D, what is the theoretical minimum for the WACC? *(LG11-2)*

4. Under what situations would you want to use the CAPM approach for estimating the component cost of equity? The constant-growth model? *(LG11-3)*

5. Could you calculate the component cost of equity for a stock with nonconstant expected growth rates in dividends if you didn't have the information necessary to compute the component cost using the CAPM? Why or why not? *(LG11-3)*

6. Why do we use market-based weights instead of book-value-based weights when computing the WACC? *(LG11-4)*

7. Suppose your firm wanted to expand into a new line of business quickly, and that management anticipated that the new line of business would constitute over 80 percent of your firm's operations within three years. If the expansion was going to be financed partially with debt, would it still make sense to use the firm's existing cost of debt, or should you compute a new rate of return for debt based on the new line of business? *(LG11-5)*

8. Explain why the divisional cost of capital approach may cause problems if new projects are assigned to the wrong division. *(LG11-6)*

9. When will the subjective approach to forming divisional WACCs be better than using the firmwide WACC to evaluate all projects? *(LG11-7)*

10. Suppose a new project was going to be financed partially with retained earnings. What flotation costs should you use for retained earnings? *(LG11-8)*

Problems

11-1 Cost of Equity Diddy Corp. stock has a beta of 1.2, the current risk-free rate is 5 percent, and the expected return on the market is 13.5 percent. What is Diddy's cost of equity? *(LG11-3)*

11-2 Cost of Equity JaiLai Co.'s stock has a beta of 0.9, the current risk-free rate is 6.2 percent, and the expected return on the market is 12 percent. What is JaiLai's cost of equity? *(LG11-3)*

11-3 Cost of Debt Oberon Inc. has a $20 million (face value) 10-year bond issue selling for 97 percent of par that pays an annual coupon of 8.25 percent. What would be Oberon's before-tax component cost of debt? *(LG11-3)*

11-4 Cost of Debt KatyDid Clothes has a $150 million (face value) 30-year bond issue selling for 104 percent of par that carries a coupon rate of 11 percent, paid semiannually. What would be KatyDid's before-tax component cost of debt? *(LG11-3)*

11-5 Tax Rate Suppose that LilyMac Photography expects EBIT to be approximately $200,000 per year for the foreseeable future, and that it has 1,000 10-year, 9 percent annual coupon bonds outstanding. What would the appropriate tax rate be for use in the calculation of the debt component of LilyMac's WACC? *(LG11-3)*

11-6 Tax Rate PDQ Inc. expects EBIT to be approximately $11 million per year for the foreseeable future, and that it has 25,000 20-year, 8 percent annual coupon bonds outstanding. What would the appropriate tax rate be for use in the calculation of the debt component of PDQ's WACC? *(LG11-3)*

11-7 Cost of Preferred Stock ILK has preferred stock selling for 97 percent of par that pays an 8 percent annual coupon. What would be ILK's component cost of preferred stock? *(LG11-3)*

11-8 Cost of Preferred Stock Marme Inc. has preferred stock selling for 96 percent of par that pays an 11 percent annual coupon. What would be Marme's component cost of preferred stock? *(LG11-3)*

11-9 Weight of Equity FarCry Industries, a maker of telecommunications equipment, has 2 million shares of common stock outstanding, 1 million shares of preferred stock outstanding, and 10,000 bonds. If the common shares are selling for $27 per share, the preferred shares are selling for $14.50 per share, and the bonds are selling for 98 percent of par, what would be the weight used for equity in the computation of FarCry's WACC? *(LG11-4)*

11-10 Weight of Equity OMG Inc. has 4 million shares of common stock outstanding, 3 million shares of preferred stock outstanding, and 5,000 bonds. If the common shares are selling for $17 per share, the preferred shares are selling for $26 per share, and the bonds are selling for 108 percent of par, what would be the weight used for equity in the computation of OMG's WACC? *(LG11-4)*

11-11 Weight of Debt FarCry Industries, a maker of telecommunications equipment, has 2 million shares of common stock outstanding, 1 million shares of preferred stock outstanding, and 10,000 bonds. If the common shares are selling for $27 per share, the preferred shares are selling for $14.50 per share, and the bonds are selling for 98 percent of par, what weight should you use for debt in the computation of FarCry's WACC? *(LG11-4)*

11-12 Weight of Debt OMG Inc. has 4 million shares of common stock outstanding, 3 million shares of preferred stock outstanding, and 5,000 bonds. If the common shares are selling for $27 per share, the preferred shares are selling for $26 per share, and the bonds are selling for 108 percent of par, what weight should you use for debt in the computation of OMG's WACC? *(LG11-4)*

11-13 Weight of Preferred Stock FarCry Industries, a maker of telecommunications equipment, has 2 million shares of common stock outstanding, 1 million shares of preferred stock outstanding, and 10,000 bonds. If the common shares sell for $27 per share, the preferred shares sell for $14.50 per share, and the bonds sell for 98 percent of par, what weight should you use for preferred stock in the computation of FarCry's WACC? *(LG11-4)*

11-14 Weight of Preferred Stock OMG Inc. has 4 million shares of common stock outstanding, 3 million shares of preferred stock outstanding, and 5,000 bonds. If the common shares sell for $17 per share, the preferred shares sell for $16 per share, and the bonds sell for 108 percent of par, what weight should you use for preferred stock in the computation of OMG's WACC? *(LG11-4)*

INTERMEDIATE PROBLEMS

11-15 WACC Suppose that TapDance Inc.'s capital structure features 65 percent equity, 35 percent debt, and that its before-tax cost of debt is 8 percent, while its cost of equity is 13 percent. If the appropriate weighted average tax rate is 34 percent, what will be TapDance's WACC? *(LG11-2)*

11-16 WACC Suppose that JB Cos. has a capital structure of 78 percent equity, 22 percent debt, and that its before-tax cost of debt is 11 percent while its cost of equity is 15 percent. If the appropriate weighted-average tax rate is 25 percent, what will be JB's WACC? *(LG11-2)*

11-17 WACC Suppose that B2B Inc. has a capital structure of 37 percent equity, 17 percent preferred stock, and 46 percent debt. If the before-tax component costs of equity, preferred stock, and debt are 14.5 percent, 11 percent, and 9.5 percent, respectively, what is B2B's WACC if the firm faces an average tax rate of 30 percent? *(LG11-2)*

11-18 WACC Suppose that MNINK Industries' capital structure features 63 percent equity, 7 percent preferred stock, and 30 percent debt. If the before-tax component costs of equity, preferred stock, and debt are 11.60 percent, 9.5 percent, and 9 percent, respectively, what is MNINK's WACC if the firm faces an average tax rate of 34 percent? *(LG11-2)*

11-19 WACC TAFKAP Industries has 3 million shares of stock outstanding selling at $17 per share, and an issue of $20 million in 7.5 percent annual coupon bonds with a maturity of 15 years, selling at 106 percent of par. If TAFKAP's weighted average tax rate is 34 percent and its cost of equity is 14.5 percent, what is TAFKAP's WACC? *(LG11-3)*

11-20 WACC Johnny Cake Ltd. has 10 million shares of stock outstanding selling at $23 per share and an issue of $50 million in 9 percent annual coupon bonds with a maturity of 17 years, selling at 93.5 percent of par. If Johnny Cake's weighted-average tax rate is 34 percent, its next dividend is expected to be $3 per share, and all future dividends are expected to grow at 6 percent per year, indefinitely, what is its WACC? *(LG11-3)*

11-21 WACC Weights BetterPie Industries has 3 million shares of common stock outstanding, 2 million shares of preferred stock outstanding, and 10,000 bonds. If the common shares are selling for $47 per share, the preferred shares are selling for $24.50 per share, and the bonds are selling for 99 percent of par, what would be the weights used in the calculation of BetterPie's WACC? *(LG11-4)*

11-22 WACC Weights WhackAmOle has 2 million shares of common stock outstanding, 1.5 million shares of preferred stock outstanding, and 50,000 bonds. If the common shares are selling for $63 per share, the preferred shares are selling for $52 per share, and the bonds are selling for 103 percent of par, what would be the weights used in the calculation of WhackAmOle's WACC? *(LG11-4)*

11-23 Flotation Cost Suppose that Brown-Murphies' common shares sell for $19.50 per share, that the firm is expected to set their next annual dividend at $0.57 per share, and that all future dividends are expected to grow by 4 percent per year, indefinitely. If Brown-Murphies faces a flotation cost of 13 percent on new equity issues, what will be the flotation-adjusted cost of equity? *(LG11-8)*

11-24 Flotation Cost A firm is considering a project that will generate perpetual after-tax cash flows of $15,000 per year beginning next year. The project has the same risk as the firm's overall operations and must be financed externally. Equity flotation costs 14 percent and debt issues cost 4 percent on an after-tax basis. The firm's D/E ratio is 0.8. What is the most the firm can pay for the project and still earn its required return? *(LG11-2)*

11-25 Firmwide vs. Project-Specific WACCs An all-equity firm is considering the projects shown below. The T-bill rate is 4 percent and the market risk premium is 7 percent. If the firm uses its current WACC of 12 percent to evaluate these projects, which project(s), if any, will be incorrectly rejected? *(LG11-6)*

Project	Expected Return	Beta
A	8.0%	0.2
B	19.0	1.4
C	13.0	0.8
D	17.0	1.3

11-26 Firmwide vs. Project-Specific WACCs An all-equity firm is considering the projects shown below. The T-bill rate is 4 percent and the market risk premium is 7 percent. If the firm uses its current WACC of 12 percent to evaluate these projects, which project(s), if any, will be incorrectly accepted? *(LG11-6)*

Project	Expected Return	Beta
A	8.0%	0.5
B	19.0	1.2
C	13.0	1.4
D	17.0	1.6

11-27 Divisional WACCs Suppose your firm has decided to use a divisional WACC approach to analyze projects. The firm currently has four divisions, A through D, with average betas for each division of 0.6, 1.0, 1.3, and 1.6, respectively. If all current and future projects will be financed with half debt and half equity, and if the current cost of equity (based on an average firm beta of 1.0 and a current risk-free rate of 7 percent) is 13 percent and the after-tax yield on the company's bonds is 8 percent, what will the WACCs be for each division? *(LG11-7)*

11-28 Divisional WACCs Suppose your firm has decided to use a divisional WACC approach to analyze projects. The firm currently has four divisions, A through D, with average betas for each division of 0.9, 1.1, 1.3, and 1.5, respectively. If all current and future projects will be financed with 25 percent debt and 75 percent equity, and if the current cost of equity (based on an average firm beta of 1.2 and a current risk-free rate of 4 percent) is 12 percent and the after-tax yield on the company's bonds is 9 percent, what will the WACCs be for each division? *(LG11-7)*

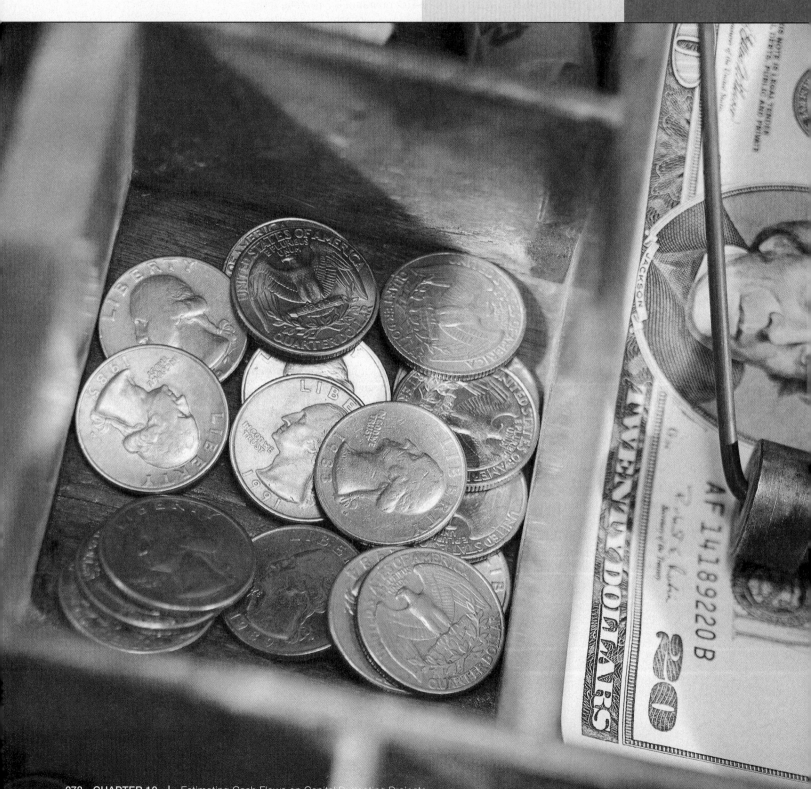

chapter twelve

estimating cash flows on capital budgeting projects

To evaluate capital budgeting projects, we have to estimate how much cash outflow each project will need and how much cash inflow it will generate, as well as exactly when such outflows and inflows will occur. Estimating these cash flows isn't difficult, but it is *complicated,* as there are lots of little details to keep track of. Accordingly, as you look through this chapter's examples, questions, and problems, you'll notice that these types of problems involve a lot more information than those you've seen elsewhere in the text, such as:

- The particular new product or service's costs and revenues.
- The likely impact that the new service or product will have on the firm's existing products' costs and revenues.
- The impact of using existing assets or employees already employed elsewhere in the firm.
- How to handle charges such as the research and development costs incurred to develop the new product.

One of the keys to this chapter will be making sure that we have a systematic approach to handling and arranging details. In the next few sections, we're going to construct a process which, if we follow it faithfully, will guide us in considering factors such as those listed above.

LEARNING GOALS

LG12-1 Explain why we use pro forma statements to analyze project cash flows.

LG12-2 Identify which cash flows we can incrementally apply to a project and which ones we cannot.

LG12-3 Calculate a project's expected cash flows using the free cash flow approach.

LG12-4 Explain how accelerated depreciation affects project cash flows.

LG12-5 Calculate free cash flows for replacement equipment.

LG12-6 Calculate cash flows associated with cost-cutting proposals.

LG12-7 Demonstrate the EAC approach to choosing among alternative cash streams for recurring projects.

LG12-8 Adjust initial project investments to account for flotation costs.

The exact process that we're going to use is more formally referred to as **pro forma analysis.** In particular, we will use a form of *pro forma analysis* that will estimate expected future cash flows of a project using only the necessary parts of the balance sheet and income statements: if a part of either financial statement doesn't change because of the new project, we'll ignore it. This approach will allow us to focus on the question, "What will be this project's impact on the firm's total cash flows if we go forward?"

SAMPLE PROJECT DESCRIPTION LG12-1

Let's suppose that we are working for a game development company, First Strike Software (FSS). FSS is considering leasing a new plant in Gatlinburg, Tennessee, which it will use to produce copies of its new game "FinProf," a role-playing game where the player battles aliens invading a local college's finance department.

FSS will price this game at $39.99, and the firm estimates sales for each of the next three years as shown in Table 12.1. Given buyers' rapidly changing tastes in computer games, FSS does not expect to be able to sell any more copies after year 3.

Variable costs per game are low ($4.25), and FSS expects fixed costs to total $150,000 per year, including rent. Start-up costs include $75,000 for a software-duplicating machine, plus an additional $2,000 in shipping and installation costs. For our first stab at analyzing this project, we will assume that the duplicating machine will be straight-line depreciated to $5,000 over the life of the project. We'll expect that machine to bring only $2,000 on the market after we're done using it.

FinProf is an updated version of an older game sold by FSS, Mkt-Prof. FSS intends to keep selling MktProf but anticipates that FinProf will decrease sales of MktProf by 2,000 units per year throughout the life of the new game. MktProf sells for $19.99 and has variable costs

»viewpoints

business APPLICATION

Suppose that McDonald's is considering introducing the McTurkey Dinner (MTD). The company anticipates that the MTD will have unit sales, prices, and cost figures as shown below for the next five years, after which the firm will retire the MTD. Introducing the MTD will require $7 million in new assets, which will fall into the MACRS five-year class life. McDonald's expects the necessary assets to be worth $2 million in market value at the end of the project life. In addition, the company expects that NWC requirements at the beginning of each year will be approximately 13 percent of the projected sales throughout the coming year and fixed costs will be $2 million per year. McDonald's uses an 11 percent cost of capital for similar projects and is subject to a 35 percent marginal tax rate. What will be this project's expected cash flows?

McTurkey Dinner Projections

Year	Estimated Unit Sales	Estimated Selling Price Per Unit	Estimated Variable Cost Per Unit
1	400,000	$7.00	$3.35
2	1,000,000	7.21	3.52
3	1,000,000	7.43	3.70
4	1,000,000	7.65	3.89
5	500,000	7.88	4.08

of $3.50 per unit. The decrease in MktProf sales will not affect either NWC or fixed assets.

Development costs totaled $150,000 throughout development of the game, and First Strike estimates its NWC requirements at the beginning of each year will be approximately 10 percent of the projected sales during the coming year. First Strike is in the 34 percent tax bracket and uses a discount rate of 15 percent on projects with risk profiles such as this. The relevant question: Should FSS put FinProf into production or not?

▼**TABLE 12.1** Sample Project Projected Unit Sales

Year	Unit Sales
1	15,000
2	27,000
3	5,000

Achmed contemplates going back to school part-time to get an MBA. He anticipates that it would take him four years to get his MBA, and the program would cost $15,000 per year in books and tuition (payable at the beginning of each year). He also thinks that he would need to get a new laptop (which he was going to buy anyway as a portable gaming system) for $2,500 when he starts the program, and he just paid $250 to take the GMAT. After graduation, Achmed anticipates that he will be able to earn approximately $10,000 more per year with the MBA, and he thinks he'll work for about another 20 years after getting the MBA. What total cash flows should Achmed consider in his decision?

Thinking about an MBA? What returns can you expect from the investment? Scan the QR code for an extended look. Turn to the back of the book for solutions to these applications.

GUIDING PRINCIPLES FOR CASH FLOW ESTIMATION LG12-2

When we calculate a project's expected cash flows, we must ensure that we cover all **incremental cash flows,** that is, the cash flow changes that we would expect throughout the entire firm as the new project comes on board. Some incremental cash flow effects are fairly obvious. For example, suppose a firm has to buy a new asset to support a new project but would not be buying the asset if the project were not adopted. Clearly, the cash associated with buying the asset is due to the project, and we should therefore count it when we calculate the cash flows associated with that project. But we can hardly expect *all* incremental cash flows to be so obvious. Other incremental cash flows, as discussed below, are more subtle, and we'll have to watch for them very carefully.

Opportunity Costs

As you likely remember from your microeconomics classes, an **opportunity cost** exists whenever a firm has to choose how to allocate scarce resources. If those resources go into project A, the firm must forgo using them in any other way. Those forgone choices represent lost opportunities, and we have to account for them when calculating cash flows attributable to project A.

For example, suppose that FSS already owned the piece of software-duplicating machinery discussed above. If the machinery was already being fully utilized by another project within the company, then obviously switching it over to the FinProf game would require that other project to find another source of software duplication. Therefore, to be fair, the FinProf project should be charged for the use of the machinery.

Even if the machinery was not currently being used in any other projects, it could still possibly have an opportunity cost associated with using it in the FinProf project. If FSS could potentially sell the machinery on the open market for $75,000, the company would have to give up receiving that $75,000 in order to use the piece of machinery for the FinProf game. In the end, it would not really matter whether the firm had to buy the asset from outside sources or not: either way, the project will be tying up $75,000 worth of capital, and it should be charged for doing so.

The underlying concept behind charging the project for the opportunity cost of using an asset also has broader implications: overall, we should charge any new project for any assets used by that project as well as any wages and benefits paid to employees working on it. Even if the firm was already employing those people prior to starting work on the new project, they are no longer available to work on any existing projects; and if the firm did not have any new projects, it could have laid those employees off, saving their wages and benefits.

Sunk Costs

If a firm has already paid an expense or is obligated to pay one in the future, regardless of whether a particular project is undertaken, that expense is a **sunk cost.** A firm should *never* count sunk costs in project cash flows.

opportunity cost The dollar cost or forgone opportunity of using an asset already owned by the firm, or a person already employed by the firm, in a new project.

sunk cost A cost that has already been incurred and cannot be recovered.

> "A firm should *never* count sunk costs in project cash flows."

For example, FSS incurred $150,000 in development costs in the example above. Development costs would presumably include items such as the salaries of the game's programmers, market research costs, and so forth. Since we are not told otherwise, we can sensibly assume that the money is gone, and that FSS will never recoup its development money, even if it decides not to go ahead with publishing the game. Thus those costs are sunk, and FSS should not even consider them as part of its decision about whether to move forward with putting the FinProf game into production.

Substitutionary and Complementary Effects

If a new product or service will either reduce or increase sales, costs, or necessary assets for existing products or services, then those changes are incremental to the project and should rightfully be included in the project cash flows. For example, consider how FSS's FinProf game may affect the existing MktProf game. The gross sales and variable cost figures for the new game might be as shown in Table 12.2.

However, FSS also expects the MktProf game to lose yearly sales of 2,000 × $19.99 = $39,980 when FinProf comes aboard. Further, the decrease in sales of MktProf will also result in a decrease in yearly variable costs of 2,000 × $3.50 = $7,000 per year. So the net incremental sales and variable cost figures for the project will be as shown in Table 12.3.

We see a reduction in both sales and variable costs because FinProf is a partial **substitute** for MktProf. If the new game had been a **complement,** then both sales and variable costs of the existing product would have increased instead.

▼**TABLE 12.2** Gross Sales and Variable Costs for FinProf

Year	Sales	Variable Costs
1	15,000 × $39.99 = $599,850	15,000 × $4.25 = $63,750
2	27,000 × $39.99 = $1,079,730	27,000 × $4.25 = $114,750
3	5,000 × $39.99 = $199,950	5,000 × $4.25 = $21,250

▼**TABLE 12.3** Net Incremental and Variable Costs for FinProf

Year	Sales	Variable Costs
1	$599,850 − $39,980 = $559,870	$63,750 − $7,000 = $56,750
2	$1,079,730 − $39,980 = $1,039,750	$114,750 − $7,000 = $107,750
3	$199,950 − $39,980 = $159,970	$21,250 − $7,000 = $14,250

Stock Dividends and Bond Interest

One final, important note concerning incremental project cash flows: We will never count any **financing costs,** including dividends paid on stock or interest paid on debt, as expenses of the project. The costs of capital are already included as component costs in the weighted average cost of capital (WACC) that we will be using to discount these cash flows in the next chapter. If we were to include them in the cash flow figures as well, we would be double-counting them.

time out!

12-1 Suppose that your manager will be devoting half of her time to a new project, with the other half devoted to currently existing projects. How would you reflect this in your calculation of the incremental cash flows of the project?

12-2 Could a new product have both substitutionary and complementary effects on existing products?

TOTAL PROJECT CASH FLOW LG12-3

In Chapter 2, we discussed the concept of free cash flow (FCF), which we defined as

$$FCF = \frac{Operating}{cash\ flow} - \frac{Investment\ in}{operating\ capital} \qquad (12\text{-}1)$$

$$= [EBIT\,(1 - Tax\ rate) + Depreciation]$$

$$- \left[\begin{array}{c} \Delta\ Gross\ fixed \\ assets \end{array} + \begin{array}{c} \Delta\ Net\ operating \\ working\ capital \end{array} \right]$$

In this chapter, we are going to use this variable again as a measure of the total amount of available cash flow from a project. However, we will observe two important differences from how we used it in Chapter 2. First, since we will be considering potential projects rather than a particular firm's actual, historic activities, the FCF numbers we calculate will be, frankly, guesses—informed guesses, surely, but guesses nonetheless. Since we will be "calculating" guesses, we will introduce possible estimation error into our capital budgeting decision statistics, which we will discuss in the next chapter.

Second, we will now calculate FCF on potential projects individually, rather than across the firm as a whole as we did in Chapter 2. In some ways, calculating FCF on individual projects will make our job much easier, since we need not worry about estimating an entire set of balance sheets for the firm. Instead, we will only have to be concerned with the limited subset of pro forma statements necessary to keep track of the assets, expense categories, and so on that a new project will affect. Unfortunately, the elements of that limited set will vary from situation to situation, and the hard part will be identifying which parts of the balance sheets are necessary and which are not.

Calculating Depreciation

Expected depreciation on equipment used during the life of the project will affect both the operating cash flows and the change in gross fixed assets that will occur at the end of the project, so let's start our organizing there.

For First Strike's proposed FinProf project, the firm will depreciate capital assets such as the software-duplicating machine using the straight-line method to an ending book value of $5,000. To calculate the annual depreciation amount, First Strike will first need to compute the machinery's **depreciable basis.** According to the Internal Revenue Service's (IRS) Publication 946, the depreciable basis for real property is:

- Its cost.
- Amounts paid for items such as sales tax.
- Freight charges.
- Installation and testing fees.

So the depreciable basis for the new project's software-duplicating machine will be the $75,000 purchase price plus the $2,000 shipping and installation cost, for a total depreciable basis of $77,000.

Under straight-line depreciation, the annual depreciation for each year will be equal to the depreciable basis minus the

The depreciable basis for real property includes freight charges.

projected ending book value, all over the number of years in the life of the asset:

$$\text{Depreciation} = \frac{\text{Depreciable basis} - \text{Ending book value}}{\text{Life of asset}} \quad (12\text{-}2)$$

We'll discuss later in the chapter why this depreciation assumption is far too simple, and why other, more complicated depreciation methods can be much more advantageous to the company. For now, though, this straight-line depreciation approach will suffice for our initial go at calculating the project's cash flows.

Calculating Operating Cash Flow

We defined operating cash flow (OCF) in Chapter 2 as *EBIT* (1 − *Tax rate*) + *Depreciation*. We will still calculate OCF as being mathematically equal to *EBIT* (1 − *Tax rate*) + *Depreciation*. But remember that we will be constructing the FCF components ourselves instead of taking them off an income statement that someone else has already produced. So we will usually find it most helpful to conduct this calculation by using what we will call a "quasi-income statement" that leaves out some components like interest deductions. (Note that the process of leaving out any interest deduction is exactly in line with our discussion above of not counting interest on debt as an expense of the project, but the resulting financial statement would *not* make an accountant happy).

Such a statement is shown in Table 12.4 for First Strike's proposed project. The primary benefit of calculating OCF this way instead of as an algebraic formula is that with this format, we have space to expand subcalculations, such as the impact of FinProf being a partial substitute for the MktProf product.

Before we move on, notice that not only is EBIT negative in year 3 of OCF calculations, but we also assume that this negative EBIT, in turn, generates a "negative tax bill" (i.e., a tax credit, when we subtract the negative tax amount of −$9,615 from the negative EBIT). Why do we make this assumption?

Well, the rule for handling negative EBIT is that when calculating the cash flows for a single project for a firm, we assume that any loss by the project in a particular period can be applied against assumed before-tax profits made by the *rest* of the firm in that period. So, while our project is expected to have a loss of $28,280 before taxes during year 3, the assumed ability of the firm to use that loss to shelter $28,280 in before-tax profits *elsewhere* in the firm means that the incremental after-tax net income for this project during year 3 is expected to be −$28,280 − (−$9,615) = −$18,665. Still negative, but less negative than the EBIT because of this tax-sheltering effect.

What would we do if we expected a negative EBIT during a particular year and this was the only project the firm was undertaking, or if this project was so big that a negative EBIT would overshadow any potential profits elsewhere in the firm? Long

	Year 1		Year 2		Year 3
Sales of FinProf	$599,850		$1,079,730		$199,950
Less: Reduced sales of MktProf	39,980		39,980		39,980
Net incremental sales		$559,870		$1,039,750	$159,970
Variable costs of FinProf	$ 63,750		$ 114,750		$ 21,250
Less: Reduced costs of MktProf	7,000		7,000		7,000
Less: Incremental variable costs		56,750		107,750	14,250
Less: Fixed costs		150,000		150,000	150,000
Less: Depreciation		24,000		24,000	24,000
Earnings before interest and taxes		$329,120		$ 758,000	−$28,280
Less: Taxes		111,901		257,720	−9,615
Net income		$217,219		$ 500,280	−$18,665
Plus: Depreciation		24,000		24,000	24,000
Operating cash flow		$241,219		$ 524,280	$ 5,335

story short, we would not get to take the tax credit during that year . . . but we will leave the discussion of just exactly when we *would* get to take it to a more advanced text.

Calculating Changes in Gross Fixed Assets

Gross fixed assets will change in almost every project at both the beginning (when assets are usually purchased) and at the end (when assets are usually sold). First Strike's proposed project is no exception.

Calculating the change in gross fixed assets at the beginning of the project is fairly straightforward—it will simply equal the

is the same appropriate corporate tax rate discussed in the previous chapter.

$$\text{ATCF} = \frac{\text{Book}}{\text{value}} + \left(\frac{\text{Market}}{\text{value}} - \frac{\text{Book}}{\text{value}}\right) \times (1 - T_C) \qquad (12\text{-}3)$$

Since the machinery for FSS's project will be depreciated down to $5,000 but is expected to sell for only $2,000, the ATCF for that asset's sale will equal:

$$\text{ATCF} = \$5,000 + (\$2,000 - \$5,000) \times (1 - 0.34)$$
$$= \$3,020$$

Note that this formula would work equally well on an asset sold at a gain.

> GROSS FIXED ASSETS WILL CHANGE IN ALMOST EVERY PROJECT AT BOTH THE BEGINNING (WHEN ASSETS ARE USUALLY PURCHASED) AND AT THE END (WHEN ASSETS ARE USUALLY SOLD).

asset's depreciable basis. So, for FSS's project, we will increase gross fixed assets by $77,000 at time zero.

At the end of a project, the change in gross fixed assets is a little more complicated, because whenever a firm sells any asset, it has to consider the tax consequences of that sale. The IRS treats any sale of assets for more than depreciated book value as taxable gains and any sale for less than book value as taxable losses. In either event, we can calculate the after-tax cash flow (ATCF) from the sale of an asset using the following formula, where T_C

Calculating Changes in Net Working Capital

We can make several different assumptions concerning the NWC level necessary to support a project. The most straightforward of these would be to simply assume that we add NWC at the beginning of the project and subtract it at the end. This assumption would be valid if the project is expected to have steady sales throughout its life, or if variations in NWC do not affect the project much.

EXAMPLE 12-1

ATCF for an Asset Sold at a Gain LG12-3

For interactive versions of this example visit www.mhhe.com/canM2e

Suppose that a firm facing a marginal tax rate of 25 percent sells an asset for $4,000 when its depreciated book value is $2,000. What will be the ATCF from the sale of this asset?

SOLUTION:

The ATCF will equal:

$$\text{ATCF} = \$2,000 + (\$4,000 - \$2,000) \times (1 - 0.25)$$

$$= \$3,500$$

Similar to Problems 12-1, 12-8.

FSS's proposed project, however, features a more typical product life cycle. Its unit sales will follow an approximate bell-shaped curve. When sales are timed in this way, FSS needs to give a little more thought to exactly when the firm needs to set aside net working capital to support high sales volumes and when it can reduce NWC as sales drop off.

The assumption that First Strike's NWC at any particular time will be a function of the *next* year's sales might seem odd at first glance. But a little thought about how we measure balance sheet numbers (such as NWC) and income statement items (such as sales) will show that, really, this assumption makes a lot of sense. Since income statements (and our quasi-income statement discussed above) measure what happens *during* a period, the sales show up on the statement at the end of the year, even though they actually start accumulating at the *beginning* of the year. The balance sheet "snapshots," on the other hand, capture how much capital sits in NWC accounts *at a particular point in time*. Therefore, for example, the sales figures that appear in the time 1 OCF calculation must be supported when they start occurring, at time zero. The time zero NWC changes need to reflect that activity. Of course, the same argument holds true in general, too: Any sales figure that appears in a time *N* OCF calculation needs NWC support at the *beginning* of year *N*, which is actually time *N* − 1. So NWC at time *N* − 1 should vary with time *N* sales.

Also, note that it is just the *changes* in the level of NWC, not the levels themselves, that will affect our cash flows. To explain why, we need to throw a little more intuition into the pot here.

First, we have to admit that we do not really care about the changes in NWC, either, at least not for their own sake; instead, what we are actually measuring is the *investment* in capital necessary to make those changes happen. (And that's why there is a negative sign in front of NWC in our formula for free cash flow: It *costs* us money to make NWC bigger, and vice versa).

Second, we need to think a little about exactly what we are measuring when we talk about using NWC to support sales. Since NWC equals current assets minus current liabilities, it's probably easier to think of it as being composed of cash, accounts receivable, and

inventory, net of current liabilities. Do these types of assets get used up? Sure, when cash is used to make change, or when someone pays off an account receivable, or when we sell finished goods out of inventory, the respective account will go down. But those accounts go down *because we are bringing in money,* and some of that money can be used to "restock the shelves," so to speak; that is, when someone buys one of our products out of inventory, we assume that part of the purchase price goes toward replenishing the inventory we just sold, and when someone pays off an account receivable, we assume that allows us to turn around and lend that money to someone else; and so forth.

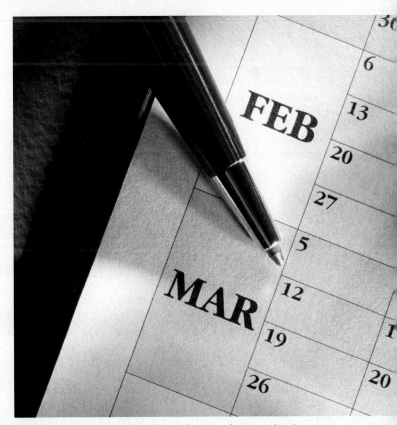

First Strike's NWC at any time will be a function of next year's sales.

The basic point here is that cash, once invested in NWC, pretty much replenishes itself until we manually take it back out. So when we are looking at the levels of NWC throughout the life of a project, it is the *changes* in those levels that we have to finance, not the levels themselves. Once we put a million dollars into inventory, it sort of stays there because of this idea of replenishment, even when we sell some of the inventory. And if we are keeping track of the amount of money that we have to invest in inventory or some other type of NWC account, we will find investment necessary only when we need to *grow* NWC by adding to that million dollars (or when we decide to take some of it back out).

So, we can use the given information for the First Strike project to compute the NWC necessary to support sales throughout the project's life, and then in turn use NWC levels to compute the necessary changes in NWC, as shown in Table 12.5. Notice that the NWC level at each time is simply 10 percent of the following year's sales figures from Table 12.4.

This method for computing changes in NWC levels has several appealing features:

- The changes in NWC at the beginning of a project will always equal the level at time 0, as NWC will be going from a presumed zero level before the project starts up to that new, non-zero level.

- Allowing NWC to vary as a percentage of coming sales like this allows FSS to add NWC during periods when it expects sales to increase (e.g., years 0 and 1 in this example) and to decrease NWC when it expects sales to fall off (e.g., years 2 and 3 in this example). NWC levels fall off the last two years of this project precisely because FSS expects sales to fall off and is adjusting NWC to compensate.

- Finally, one especially nice feature of this approach is that it will always automatically bring NWC back down to a zero level when the project ends. Since sales in the year *after* the project ends are always zero, 10 percent of zero will also be zero. This corresponds to what we would expect to see in the real world: when a project ends, the firm sells off inventory, collects from customers, pays off accounts receivable, and so forth.

Bringing It All Together

Using the numbers that we calculated for OCF, change in gross fixed assets, and change in NWC, First Strike's expected total cash flows from the new project would be as shown in Table 12.6.

Note, in particular, that correct use of the after-tax cash flow from selling the machinery at the end of the project requires that we change the cash flows' sign to negative when we enter it for year 3. Why? Because the ATCF formula shown in equation 12-3 does a little *too* much work for us. It computes cash flow effects of selling the asset, while the formula we are using for FCF wants us to enter the change in fixed assets. Or, to put it another way, cash flow at the end of the project should go up *because* fixed assets decrease. We subtract that decrease in our FCF = OCF − (ΔFA + ΔNWC) calculation, which has the effect of "subtracting a minus." Eventually, then, we increase the final year's FCF above that which we would have generated by just combining OCF with the cash freed up from decreasing NWC.

time out!

12-3 Explain why an increase in NWC is treated as a cash outflow rather than as an inflow.

12-4 Will OCF typically be larger or smaller than net income? Why?

▼ **TABLE 12.5** Change in NWC

Year:	0	1	2	3
Level of NWC	$59,985	$107,973	$19,995	$0
$NWC_t − NWC_{t-1} = \Delta NWC_t$	$59,985 − $0 = $59,985	$107,973 − $59,985 = $47,988	$19,995 − $107,973 = −$87,978	$0 − $19,995 = −$19,995

▼ **TABLE 12.6** Total Cash Flows

Year:	0		1	2		3
OCF		$ 0	$241,219		$524,280	$ 5,335
FA	$77,000	$ 0	$ 0		−$3,020	
NWC	59,985		47,988		−87,978	−19,995
Less: IOC		136,985	47,988		−87,978	−23,015
FCF		−$136,985	$193,231		$612,258	$28,350

ACCELERATED DEPRECIATION AND THE HALF-YEAR CONVENTION LG12-4

Our FCF calculation in the previous section was complete, but we used a rather simplistic assumption concerning depreciation in the calculations. In reality, the IRS requires that depreciation must be calculated using the *half-year convention*. The IRS thus requires that all property placed in service during a given period is assumed to be placed in service at the midpoint of that period.[1] By implication, three years of asset life, such as the machinery in the First Strike example, will extend over *four* calendar years of the firm. Table 12.7 shows an excerpt from the IRS depreciation table for straight-line depreciation using the half-year convention.

The percentage figures denote how much of the asset's depreciable basis may be deducted in each respective firm calendar year. For example, an asset with a depreciable basis of $100,000 falling into the 3-year class life would be depreciated $100,000 × 0.1667 = $16,670 during the first calendar year the firm owned it, $33,330 during the second and third years of ownership, and another $16,670 during the fourth year of ownership.

▼ **TABLE 12.7** Excerpt of Straight-Line Depreciation Table with Half-Year Convention

	Normal Recovery Period				
Year	2.5	3	3.5	4	5
1	20.00%	16.67%	14.29%	12.50%	10.00%
2	40.00	33.33	28.57	25.00	20.00
3	40.00	33.33	28.57	25.00	20.00
4	0.00	16.67	28.57	25.00	20.00
5	0.00	0.00	0.00	12.50	20.00
6	0.00	0.00	0.00	0.00	10.00

MACRS Depreciation Calculation

Though the IRS allows firms to use the straight-line method with the half-year convention to depreciate assets, most businesses probably benefit from using some form of *accelerated depreciation*. Accelerated depreciation allows firms to expense more of an asset's cost earlier in the asset's life. An example of this is the double-declining-balance (DDB or 200 percent declining balance) depreciation method, under which the depreciation rate is double that used in the straight-line method. The IRS also uses the half-year convention with DDB depreciation. MACRS

> "Accelerated depreciation allows firms to expense more of an asset's cost earlier in the asset's life."

The IRS provides guidance on which categories various assets fall into, so it's usually pretty easy to figure out which column to use. For this text, we will assume that we are always told which column to use.

Note that the IRS's interpretation of the half-year convention is not as direct as simply taking one-half of the first year's depreciation and moving it to the end of the asset's life. For example, the column for 3.5-year depreciation shows that such an asset would have 14.29 percent of its value depreciated during the first year and 28.57 percent during each of the second, third, and fourth years. So, rather than using a formula to compute the depreciation percentage, it's preferable to look the percentages up from the appropriate IRS table. A copy of the entire table for straight-line depreciation using the half-year convention appears in the Appendix at the end of this chapter.

(Modified Accelerated Cost Recovery System) uses DDB for 3- to 10-year property. For 15- to 20-year property, MACRS uses the 150 percent declining balance method. Both of these methods switch to straight-line (SL) depreciation whenever SL becomes more advantageous to the taxpayer. For real estate, MACRS uses straight-line depreciation and the mid-month convention. The good news is that the applicable depreciation percentages are provided for you in the MACRS depreciation tables compiled by the IRS. We have provided this for you in Appendix 12. An excerpt of the DDB section of the MACRS table appears as Table 12.8. MACRS is generally the depreciation method of choice for firms since it provides the most advantageous method of depreciation.

Section 179 Deductions

We can accelerate asset expensing even further by expensing assets immediately in the year of purchase. The IRS allows most businesses to immediately expense up to $500,000 of property placed in service each year under what is referred

---

[1]There are also midmonth and midquarter conventions, which apply in special circumstances. Please refer to IRS Publication 946 for details.

to as a **Section 179 deduction.** The Section 179 deduction is obviously targeted at helping small businesses, so it places an annual limit on the amount of deductible property. If the cost of qualifying Section 179 property you put into service in a single tax year exceeds the current statutory base of $2 million (year 2010), then you cannot take the full deduction. The maximum deduction is also limited to the annual taxable income from the active conduct of the business.

For example, consider a manufacturer who completely re-equips his facility in 2010, at a cost of $2.1 million. This is $100,000 more than allowed, so he must reduce his eligible deductible limit to $400,000, which is the current $500,000 expensing limit minus the $100,000 excess over the current statutory base limit. To take this deduction, the firm must have at least $400,000 of taxable income for the year. A company that spent $2.5 million (= $2 million + $500,000) or more on qualifying Section 179 property would not be able to take the deduction at all, regardless of its taxable income. Property that does not qualify for a Section 179 deduction can be depreciated using MACRS.

Property eligible for a Section 179 deduction includes:

- Machinery and equipment.

- Furniture and fixtures.

- Most storage facilities.

- Single-purpose agricultural or horticultural structures.

- Off-the-shelf computer software.

- Certain qualified real property (limited to $250,000 of the $500,000 expensing limit).

Ineligible property includes:

- Buildings and their structural components (unless specifically qualified).

- Income-producing property (investment or rental property).

- Property held by an estate or trust.

- Property acquired by gift or inheritance.

- Property used in a passive activity.

- Property purchased from related parties.

- Property used outside of the United States.

▼ **TABLE 12.8** DDB Depreciation with Half-Year Convention

	Normal Recovery Period			
Year	3	5	7	10
1	33.33%	20.00%	14.29%	10.00
2	44.45	32.00	24.49	18.00
3	14.81	19.20	17.49	14.40
4	7.41	11.52	12.49	11.52
5	0.00	11.52	8.93	9.22
6	0.00	5.76	8.92	7.37
7	0.00	0.00	8.93	6.55
8	0.00	0.00	4.46	6.55
9	0.00	0.00	0.00	6.56
10	0.00	0.00	0.00	6.55
11	0.00	0.00	0.00	3.28
12	0.00	0.00	0.00	0.00
13	0.00	0.00	0.00	0.00
14	0.00	0.00	0.00	0.00
15	0.00	0.00	0.00	0.00
16	0.00	0.00	0.00	0.00
17	0.00	0.00	0.00	0.00
18	0.00	0.00	0.00	0.00
19	0.00	0.00	0.00	0.00
20	0.00	0.00	0.00	0.00
21	0.00	0.00	0.00	0.00

Like many IRS deductions, there are several terms and conditions that apply, so be sure to get all the facts if you intend to use this method of depreciation.

Impact of Accelerated Depreciation

So, let's return to our FSS example and FinProf. Remember that our initial, simplistic view of depreciation had us taking $24,000 per year for each of the three years of the project's life. If the software reproduction machinery fell into the 3-year life class, we could instead have taken the depreciation amounts in Table 12.9 by using either the straight-line or DDB approaches.

If First Strike could take advantage of the Section 179 deduction that would probably be the most advantageous way to deduct the cost of the new machinery—it could deduct the entire $77,000 in year 1. If FSS could not use a Section 179 deduction,

▼ **TABLE 12.9** FSS's Yearly Depreciation and Ending Book Values under Alternative Depreciation

	Year 1	Year 2	Year 3	Ending Bv
Straight-line	$77,000 × 16.67% = $12,835.90	$77,000 × 33.33% = $25,664.10	$77,000 × 33.33% = $25,664.10	$12,835.90
DDB	$77,000 × 33.33% = $25,664.10	$77,000 × 44.45% = $34,226.50	$77,000 × 14.81% = $11,403.70	$5,705.70

Machinery is eligible for a Section 179 deduction.

time out!

12-5 Explain why, under MACRS, "5-year" depreciation is actually spread over six years, 6-year depreciation spreads into seven years, and so forth.

12-6 If the IRS wanted to encourage businesses to invest in certain types of assets, would it put them into shorter or longer MACRS life-class categories?

the DDB depreciation available under MACRS would result in the next quickest recovery of the tax breaks associated with the machinery purchase.

"SPECIAL" CASES AREN'T REALLY THAT SPECIAL LG12-5

As long as we are consistent in using incremental FCF to calculate total project cash flows, we can handle many project types that are habitually viewed as "special" cases requiring extraordinary treatment with some relatively simple revisions to the methods we used for valuing First Strike's proposed new project.

EXAMPLE 12-2

Replacement Problem LG12-5

Suppose that Just-in-Time Donuts is considering replacing one of its existing ovens. The original oven cost $100,000 when purchased five years ago and has been depreciated by $9,000 per year since then. Just-in-Time thinks that it can sell the old machine for $65,000 if it sells today, and for $10,000 by waiting another five years until the oven's anticipated life is over. Just-in-Time is considering replacing this oven with a new one, which costs $150,000, partly because the new oven will save $50,000 in costs per year relative to the old oven. The new oven will be subject to 3-year class life DDB depreciation under MACRS, with an anticipated useful life of five years. At the end of the five years, Just-In-Time will abandon the oven as worthless. If Just-in-Time faces a marginal tax rate of 35 percent, what will be the total project cash flows if it replaces the oven?

SOLUTION:

If Just-in-Time Sells the old oven today for $65,000 when it has a remaining book value of $55,000 ($100,000 purchase price − 5 years of $9,000 per year depreciation), then the ATCF from its sale will equal:

$$\text{ATCF} = \text{Book value} + (\text{Market value} - \text{Book value}) \times (1 - T_C)$$

$$= \$55,000 + (\$65,000 - \$55,000) \times (1 - 0.35)$$

$$= \$61,500$$

In return for selling the old oven today, however, JIT will have to forgo both the yearly depreciation that the company would have received for it over the next five years and the $10,000 that it could get for selling it at the end of the five years. We must reflect both of these factors in our calculation of incremental FCFs so that we are reckoning the true costs of the project. In addition, switching from the old oven to the new one would apparently alter neither sales nor NWC requirements across the 5-year life of the new oven:

Year	Time 0	Year 1	Year 2	Year 3	Year 4	Year 5
Net incremental sales		$ 0	$ 0	$ 0	$ 0	$ 0
Less: Net incremental variable costs		−50,000	−50,000	−50,000	−50,000	−50,000
Depreciation on new oven	$49,995	$66,675	$22,215	$11,115		$0
Forgone depreciation on old oven	−9,000	−9,000	−9,000	−9,000	−9,000	
Less: Incremental depreciation		40,995	57,675	13,215	2,115	−9,000
EBIT		$ 9,005	−$7,675	$36,785	$ 47,885	$ 59,000
Less: Taxes		3,152	−2,686	12,875	16,760	20,650
"Net income"		$ 5,853	−$4,989	$23,910	$ 31,125	$ 38,350
Plus: Depreciation		40,995	57,675	13,215	2,115	−9,000
OCF		$46,848	$52,686	$37,125	$33,240	$29,350
ΔFA for new oven	$150,000					$ 0
ΔFA for old oven	−61,500					10,000
ΔFA	$ 88,500					$10,000
ΔNWC	0					0
Less: Investment in operating capital	$88,500	0	0	0	0	10,000
FCF = OCF − IOC	−$88,500	$46,848	$52,686	$37,125	$33,240	$19,350

We usually think that a positive value for ΔFA is associated with the purchase of FA. But note that in this circumstance, the $10,000 for the forgone sale of the old oven at time 5 is *not* an investment in fixed assets, but rather the opportunity cost of not getting to sell the old oven at that time.

Similar to Problem 12-13.

EXAMPLE 12-3

Cost-Cutting Problem LG12-6

For interactive versions of this example visit www.mhhe.com/canM2e

Your company is considering a new computer system that will initially cost $1 million. It will save your firm $300,000 a year in inventory and receivables management costs. The system is expected to last for five years and will be depreciated using three-year MACRS. The firm expects that the system will have a salvage value of $50,000 at the end of year 5. This purchase does not affect net working capital; the marginal tax rate is 34 percent, and the required return is 8 percent. What will be the total project cash flows if this cost-cutting proposal is implemented?

SOLUTION:

Since the new computer falls into the 3-year MACRS category, it will be fully depreciated when the project ends five years from now. As a result, the ATCF from the sale of the computer will be:

$$ATCF = BV + (MV - BV) \times (1 - T_c)$$
$$= \$0 + (\$50,000 - \$0) \times (1 - 0.34)$$
$$= \$33,000$$

And the FCFs for the cost-cutting proposal will be equal to:

Year	Time 0	Year 1	Year 2	Year 3	Year 4	Year 5
Net incremental sales		$ 0	$ 0	$ 0	$ 0	$ 0
Less: Incremental variable costs		−300,000	−300,000	−300,000	−300,000	−300,000
Less: Incremental depreciation		333,300	444,500	148,100	74,100	0
EBIT		−$33,300	−$144,500	$ 151,900	$225,900	$300,000
Less: Taxes		−11,322	−49,130	51,646	76,806	102,000
"Net income"		−$21,978	−$95,370	$ 100,254	$ 149,094	$198,000
Plus: Depreciation		333,300	444,500	148,100	74,100	0
OCF		$311,322	$349,130	$248,354	$223,194	$198,000
ΔFA	$1,000,000				−$33,000	
ΔNWC	0				0	
Less: Investment in operating capital	$1,000,000	0	0	0	0	−33,000
FCF = OCF − IOC	−$1,000,000	$311,322	$349,130	$248,354	$223,194	$231,000

Similar to problem 12-9.

time out!

12-7 Explain why, in Example 12-2, the investment in operating capital in the last year of the project was positive instead of negative.

12-8 Would it ever be possible to have a project that generated net positive cash flows across all years of a project's life just by buying and depreciating assets?

CHOOSING BETWEEN ALTERNATIVE ASSETS WITH DIFFERING LIVES: EAC LG12-7

One type of problem that also deserves special mention involves situations where we're asked to choose between two different assets that can be used for the same purpose. Such a problem does not usually require the computation of incremental FCF, but instead will require you to take the two alternatives sets of incremental cash flows associated with the two assets and restructure them so that they can be compared to each other.

For example, suppose a company has decided to go ahead with a project but needs to choose between two alternative assets, wherein:

- Both assets will result in the same sales.

- Both assets may have different costs and recurring expenses.

- Assets will last different lengths of time.

- When the chosen asset wears out, it will be replaced with an identical machine.

In such a situation, the firm can not really compare one iteration of each machine to the other, since they last different lengths of time. The key here is to use the fact that, since the firm will replace each machine with another identical machine when it wears out, it is really

View guided examples at mhhe.com/canM2e

Example 12-5: ADJUSTING CF₀ FOR FLOTATION

Eric Martinez and five others like this.

Eric Martinez The Excel run-throughs were really helpful when I was doing my homework.
2 hours ago · Like

write a comment...

To compute and use the EACs of two or more alternative assets:

1. Find the sum of the present values of the cash flows (the net present value, or NPV, which we will cover in great detail in the next chapter) for one iteration of A and one iteration of B.

2. Treat each sum as the present value of an annuity with life equal to the life of the respective asset, and solve for each asset's payment.

3. Choose the asset with the highest (i.e., least negative) EAC.

It may seem that we have just done exactly what we said we should not do: compare the cash flows from one machine A to those from one machine B. In fact, the comparison we just did is actually much broader than that, though it will take a little explanation to see.

being asked to choose between two sets of infinite, but systematically varying, sets of cash flows. To handle such a situation, "smooth out" the variation in each set of cash flows so that each becomes a perpetuity. Then the company can choose between the two machines based on which will generate the highest present value of cash flows.

Since the decision will involve only a subset of a project's cash flows—the purchase of one of a choice of assets—that present value will probably be negative. If the firm were to look at all the benefits deriving from the choice of which asset to use, including expected sales and so forth, the present value of all cash flows would need to be positive for the entire project to be attractive. We will discuss this in much greater depth in the next chapter when we cover the net present value (NPV) rule for capital budgeting decisions.

The basic concept behind the EAC approach is to use TVM to turn each iteration of each project into an annuity. Once we have done that, then we can think of the stream of iterations of doing that project again and again as a stream of annuities, all with equal payments—or, to put it another way, as a perpetuity.

Visualize the cash flows to the infinitely repeated purchases of machine B (chosen simply because it has a short life, so it will be easier to see multiple iterations on a time line in the following discussion) as shown in Figure 12.1.

Notice that, after the initial purchase of the first machine B, the cash flows exhibit a systematic cycle: −$3,500 for two years, followed by −$15,500 for one year (when the next machine B is purchased), repeating this way forever. This systematic cycle, which we don't have a formula for valuing, makes it necessary to convert these cash flows into a perpetuity, which we *can* value.

When we computed the NPV of one iteration of machine B, we basically "squished" that machine's cash flows down to a single lump sum, and when we treated that as the present

FIGURE 12.1 Cash Flows of Repeated Purchases of Machine B

Year	0	1	2	3	4	5	6
B	−$12,000	−$3,500	−$3,500	−$ 3,500			
				−$12,000	−$3,500	−$3,500	−$ 3,500
							−$12,000
B Total	−$12,000	−$3,500	−$3,500	−$15,500	−$3,500	−$3,500	−$15,500

For interactive versions
of this example visit
www.mhhe.com/canM2e

EXAMPLE 12-4

EAC Approach LG12-7

Suppose that your company has won a bid for a new project—painting highway signs for the local highway department. Based on past experience, you are pretty sure that your company will have the contract for the foreseeable future, and now you have to decide whether to use machine A or machine B to paint the signs: Machine A costs $20,000, lasts five years, and will generate annual after-tax net expenses of $2,500. Machine B costs $12,000, lasts three years, and will have after-tax net expenses of $3,500 per year. Assume that, in either case, each machine will simply be junked at the end of its useful life, and the firm faces a cost of capital of 12 percent. Which machine should you choose?

SOLUTION:

One iteration of each machine will consist of the sets of cash flows shown below:

Year	0	1	2	3	4	5
Machine A CFs	−$20,000	−$2,500	−$2,500	−$2,500	−$2,500	−$2,500
Machine B CFs	−12,000	−3,500	−3,500	−3,500		

The sum of the present values of machine A's cash flows will be

$$\sum_{t=0}^{5}\frac{CF_t}{(1+i)^t} = \frac{CF_0}{(1+i)^0} + \frac{CF_1}{(1+i)^1} + \frac{CF_2}{(1+i)^2} + \frac{CF_3}{(1+i)^3} + \frac{CF_4}{(1+i)^4} + \frac{CF_5}{(1+i)^5}$$

$$= \frac{-\$20,000}{(1.12)^0} + \frac{-\$2,500}{(1.12)^1} + \frac{-\$2,500}{(1.12)^2} + \frac{-\$2,500}{(1.12)^3} + \frac{-\$2,500}{(1.12)^4} + \frac{-\$2,500}{(1.12)^5}$$

$$= -\$29,012$$

Treating this as the present value of a 5-period annuity, setting i to 12 percent, and solving for payment will yield a payment of −$8,048, which is machine A's EAC.

The sum of the present values of machine B's cash flows will be:

$$\sum_{t=0}^{3}\frac{CF_t}{(1+i)^t} = \frac{CF_0}{(1+i)^0} + \frac{CF_1}{(1+i)^1} + \frac{CF_2}{(1+i)^2} + \frac{CF_3}{(1+i)^3}$$

$$= \frac{-\$12,000}{(1.12)^0} + \frac{-\$3,500}{(1.12)^1} + \frac{-\$3,500}{(1.12)^2} + \frac{-\$3,500}{(1.12)^3}$$

$$= -\$20,406$$

Treating this as the present value of a 3-period annuity, setting i to 12 percent, and solving for payment will yield a payment of −$8,496, which is machine B's EAC.

Since machine A's EAC is less negative than machine B's, your firm should choose machine A.

Similar to Problems 12-3 to 12-5.

CALCULATOR HINTS

N = 5
I = 12
PV = 29,012
FV = 0
CPT PMT = −8,048

CALCULATOR HINTS

N = 3
I = 12
PV = 20,406
FV = 0
CPT PMT = 8,496

value of an annuity and solved for the payments we were effectively taking that same value and spreading it evenly across the life of the first machine B. Furthermore, since subsequent machine B purchases will be identical to this first one, we can visualize doing the exact same thing to *every* machine B's cash flow. Turning each machine B's cash flow into an annuity in this manner has the net effect of turning all the machine B's cash flows into a perpetuity, as shown in Figure 12.2.

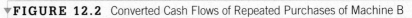

▼ **FIGURE 12.2** Converted Cash Flows of Repeated Purchases of Machine B

Year	0	1	2	3	4	5	6
New B	$0	−$8,496	−$8,496	−$8,496 $0	−$8,496	−$8,496	−$8,496 $0
New B Total	$0	−$8,496	−$8,496	−$8,496	−$8,496	−$8,496	−$8,496

In the process, we also turn the repeated purchase of machine A into a perpetuity. We *could* calculate the present values of these two perpetuities and then compare them, which is what we're really interested in doing:

$$PV_{\text{Perpetuity of Infinitely Repeated As}} \text{ vs. } PV_{\text{Perpetuity of Infinitely Repeated Bs}}$$

$$\frac{-\$8,048}{0.12} \text{ vs. } \frac{-\$8,496}{0.12}$$

But do we really need to? No. The relationship between these two present values of the respective perpetuities is really the same as the relationship between their payment amounts[2]—each machine's respective EAC.

FLOTATION COSTS REVISITED LG12-8

In the previous chapter, we talked about how to take flotation costs into account by adjusting the WACC upwards, incorporating flotation costs directly into the issue prices of the securities used to fund projects. Another way that we can account for

time out!

12-9 Explain how the EAC approach turns uneven cash flows for infinitely repeated asset purchases into perpetuities.

12-10 What if two alternative assets lasted the same length of time? Would the EAC approach still work?

[2]Because the two perpetuities have the same interest rate and the same periodicity (i.e., length between payments), the only possible source of difference in their present values would be the respective payment amounts.

EXAMPLE 12-5

[For interactive versions of this example visit www.mhhe.com/canM2e]

Adjusting CF_0 for Flotation Cost LG12-8

Your company is considering a project that will cost $1 million. The project will generate after-tax cash flows of $375,000 per year for five years. The WACC is 15 percent and the firm's target D/A ratio is 0.375. The flotation cost for equity is 5 percent, the flotation cost for debt is 3 percent, and your firm does not plan on issuing any preferred stock within its capital structure. If your firm follows the practice of incorporating flotation costs into the project's initial investment, what will the flotation-adjusted cash flows for this project be?

SOLUTION:

Since the D/A is 0.375, the E/A ratio will be equal to $1 - 0.375 = 0.625$, and the weighted-average flotation cost for the firm will be:

$$f_A = \frac{E}{E + P + D} f_E + \frac{P}{E + P + D} f_P + \frac{D}{E + P + D} f_D$$
$$= (0.625 \times 0.05) + (0.375 \times 0.03)$$
$$= 0.0425, \text{ or } 4.25\%$$

Using this, the adjusted CF_0 for the project will be:

$$\text{Adjusted } CF_0 = \frac{CF_0}{1 - f_A}$$
$$= \frac{-\$1,000,000}{1 - 0.0425}$$
$$= -\$1,044,386$$

So the flotation-adjusted cash flows for the project will be:

Year	0	1	2	3	4	5
Cash Flow	−$1,044,386	$375,000	$375,000	$375,000	$375,000	$375,000

flotation costs is to adjust the project's initial cash flow so that it will reflect the flotation costs of raising capital for the project as well as the necessary investment in assets.

In this approach, we will:

1. Compute the weighted average flotation cost, f_A, using the firm's target capital weights (because the firm will issue securities in these percentages over the long term):

$$f_A = \frac{E}{E + P + D} f_E + \frac{P}{E + P + D} f_P + \frac{D}{E + P + D} f_D \qquad (12\text{-}4)$$

where f_F, f_P, and f_D are the percentage flotation costs for new equity, preferred stock, and debt, respectively.

2. Compute the flotation-adjusted initial investment, CF_0, using:

$$\text{Adjusted } CF_0 = \frac{CF_0}{1 - f_A} \qquad (12\text{-}5)$$

Your Turn...

Questions

1. How is the pro forma statement we used in this chapter for computing OCF different from an accountant's income statement? *(LG12-1)*

2. Suppose you paid your old college finance professor to evaluate a project for you. If you would pay him regardless of your decision concerning whether to proceed with the project, should his fee for evaluating the project be included in the project's incremental cash flows? *(LG12-2)*

3. Why does a decrease in NWC result in a cash inflow to the firm? *(LG12-3)*

4. Everything else held constant, would you rather depreciate a project with straight-line depreciation or with DDB? *(LG12-4)*

5. Everything else held constant, would you rather depreciate a project with DDB depreciation or deduct it under a Section 179 deduction? *(LG12-4)*

6. In a replacement problem, would we ever see changes in NWC? *(LG12-5)*

7. In a replacement problem, will incremental net depreciation always be less than the gross depreciation on the new piece of equipment? *(LG12-5)*

8. In a cost-cutting proposal, what might cause you to sometimes have negative EBIT? *(LG12-6)*

9. How many TVM formulas do you use every time you calculate EAC for a project? *(LG12-7)*

10. Will an increase in flotation costs increase or decrease the initial cash flow for a project? *(LG12-8)*

Problems

BASIC PROBLEMS

12-1 **After-Tax Cash Flow from Sale of Assets** Suppose you sell a fixed asset for $109,000 when its book value is $129,000. If your company's marginal tax rate is 39 percent, what will be the effect on cash flows of this sale (i.e., what will be the after-tax cash flow of this sale)? *(LG12-3)*

12-2 **PV of Depreciation Tax Benefits** Your company is considering a new project that will require $1 million of new equipment at the start of the project. The equipment will have a depreciable life of 10 years and will be depreciated to a book value of $150,000 using straight-line depreciation. The cost of capital is 13 percent, and the firm's tax rate is 34 percent. Estimate the present value of the tax benefits from depreciation. *(LG12-4)*

12-3 **EAC Approach** You are trying to pick the least-expensive car for your new delivery service. You have two choices: the Scion xA, which will cost $14,000 to purchase and which will have OCF of −$1,200 annually throughout the vehicle's expected life of three years as a delivery vehicle; and the Toyota Prius, which will cost $20,000 to purchase and which will have OCF of −$650 annually throughout that vehicle's expected 4-year life. Both cars will be worthless at the end of their life. If you intend to replace whichever type of car you choose with the same thing when its life runs out, again and again out into the foreseeable future, and if your business has a cost of capital of 12 percent, which one should you choose? *(LG12-7)*

12-4 **EAC Approach** You are evaluating two different cookie-baking ovens. The Pillsbury 707 costs $57,000, has a 5-year life, and has an annual OCF (after tax) of −$10,000 per year. The Keebler CookieMunster costs $90,000, has a 7-year life, and has an annual OCF (after tax) of −$8,000 per year. If your discount rate is 12 percent, what is each machine's EAC? *(LG12-8)*

12-5 **EAC Approach** You are considering the purchase of one of two machines used in your manufacturing plant. Machine A has a life of two years, costs $80 initially, and then $125 per year in maintenance costs. Machine B costs $150 initially, has a life of three years, and requires $100 in annual maintenance costs. Either machine must be replaced at the end of its life with an equivalent machine. Which is the better machine for the firm? The discount rate is 12 percent and the tax rate is zero. *(LG12-8)*

INTERMEDIATE PROBLEMS

12-6 **Project Cash Flows** KADS Inc. has spent $400,000 on research to develop a new computer game. The firm is planning to spend $200,000 on a machine to produce the new game.

Shipping and installation costs of the machine will be capitalized and depreciated; they total $50,000. The machine has an expected life of three years, a $75,000 estimated resale value, and falls under the MACRS 7-year class life. Revenue from the new game is expected to be $600,000 per year, with costs of $250,000 per year. The firm has a tax rate of 35 percent, an opportunity cost of capital of 15 percent, and it expects net working capital to increase by $100,000 at the beginning of the project. What will the cash flows for this project be? *(LG12-3)*

12-7 Depreciation Tax Shield Your firm needs a computerized machine tool lathe which costs $50,000 and requires $12,000 in maintenance for each year of its 3-year life. After three years, this machine will be replaced. The machine falls into the MACRS 3-year class life category. Assume a tax rate of 35 percent and a discount rate of 12 percent. Calculate the depreciation tax shield for this project in year 3. *(LG12-4)*

12-8 After-Tax Cash Flow from Sale of Assets If the lathe in the previous problem can be sold for $5,000 at the end of year 3, what is the after-tax salvage value? *(LG12-4)*

12-9 Project Cash Flows You have been asked by the president of your company to evaluate the proposed acquisition of a new special-purpose truck for $60,000. The truck falls into the MACRS 3-year class, and it will be sold after three years for $20,000. Use of the truck will require an increase in NWC (spare parts inventory) of $2,000. The truck will have no effect on revenues, but it is expected to save the firm $20,000 per year in before-tax operating costs, mainly labor. The firm's marginal tax rate is 40 percent. What will the cash flows for this project be? *(LG12-6)*

ADVANCED PROBLEMS

12-10 Change in NWC You are evaluating a project for The Tiff-any golf club, guaranteed to correct that nasty slice. You estimate the sales price of The Tiff-any to be $400 per unit and sales volume to be 1,000 units in year 1; 1,500 units in year 2; and 1,325 units in year 3. The project has a 3-year life. Variable costs amount to $225 per unit and fixed costs are $100,000 per year. The project requires an initial investment of $165,000 in assets, which will be depreciated straight-line to zero over the 3-year project life. The actual market value of these assets at the end of year 3 is expected to be $35,000. NWC requirements at the beginning of each year will be approximately 20 percent of the projected sales during the coming year. The tax rate is 34 percent and the required return on the project is 10 percent. What change in NWC occurs at the end of year 1? *(LG12-3)*

12-11 Operating Cash Flow Continuing the previous problem, what is the operating cash flow for the project in year 2? *(LG3)*

12-12 Project Cash Flows You are evaluating a project for The Ultimate recreational tennis racket, guaranteed to correct that wimpy backhand. You estimate the sales price of The Ultimate to be $400 per unit and sales volume to be 1,000 units in year 1; 1,250 units in year 2; and 1,325 units in year 3. The project has a 3-year life. Variable costs amount to $225 per unit and fixed costs are $100,000 per year. The project requires an initial investment of $165,000 in assets, which will be depreciated straight-line to zero over the 3-year project life. The actual market value of these assets at the end of year 3 is expected to be $35,000. NWC requirements at the beginning of each year will be approximately 20 percent of the projected sales during the coming year. The tax rate is 34 percent and the required return on the project is 10 percent. What will the cash flows for this project be? *(LG12-3)*

12-13 Project Cash Flows Mom's Cookies Inc. is considering the purchase of a new cookie oven. The original cost of the old oven was $30,000; it is now five years old, and it has a current market value of $13,333.33. The old oven is being depreciated over a 10-year life toward a zero estimated salvage value on a straight-line basis, resulting in a current book value of $15,000 and an annual depreciation expense of $3,000. The old oven can be used for six more years but has no market value after its depreciable life is over. Management is contemplating the purchase of a new oven whose cost is $25,000 and whose estimated salvage value is zero. Expected before-tax cash savings from the new oven are $4,000 a year over its full MACRS depreciable life. Depreciation is computed using MACRS over a 5-year life, and the cost of capital is 10 percent. Assume a 40 percent tax rate. What will the cash flows for this project be? *(LG12-5)*

MACRS depreciation tables

▼ **MACRS DEPRECIATION**

			Normal Recovery Period				Real Estate Residential	Real Estate Nonresidential	
Year	3	5	7	10	15	20	27.5	31.5	39
1	33.33%	20.00%	14.29%	10.00%	5.00%	3.750%	3.485%	3.042%	2.461%
2	44.45	32.00	24.49	18.00	9.50	7.219	3.636	3.175	2.564
3	14.81	19.20	17.49	14.40	8.55	6.677	3.636	3.175	2.564
4	7.41	11.52	12.49	11.52	7.70	6.177	3.636	3.175	2.564
5	0.00	11.52	8.93	9.22	6.93	5.713	3.636	3.175	2.564
6	0.00	5.76	8.92	7.37	6.23	5.285	3.636	3.175	2.564
7	0.00	0.00	8.93	6.55	5.90	4.888	3.636	3.175	2.564
8	0.00	0.00	4.46	6.55	5.90	4.522	3.636	3.175	2.564
9	0.00	0.00	0.00	6.56	5.91	4.462	3.636	3.174	2.564
10	0.00	0.00	0.00	6.55	5.90	4.461	3.637	3.175	2.564
11	0.00	0.00	0.00	3.28	5.91	4.462	3.636	3.174	2.564
12	0.00	0.00	0.00	0.00	5.90	4.461	3.637	3.175	2.564
13	0.00	0.00	0.00	0.00	5.91	4.462	3.636	3.174	2.564
14	0.00	0.00	0.00	0.00	5.90	4.461	3.637	3.175	2.564
15	0.00	0.00	0.00	0.00	5.91	4.462	3.636	3.174	2.564
16	0.00	0.00	0.00	0.00	2.95	4.461	3.637	3.175	2.564
17	0.00	0.00	0.00	0.00	0.00	4.462	3.636	3.174	2.564
18	0.00	0.00	0.00	0.00	0.00	4.461	3.637	3.175	2.564
19	0.00	0.00	0.00	0.00	0.00	4.462	3.636	3.174	2.564
20	0.00	0.00	0.00	0.00	0.00	4.461	3.637	3.175	2.564
21	0.00	0.00	0.00	0.00	0.00	2.231	3.636	3.174	2.564
22	0.00	0.00	0.00	0.00	0.00	0.00	3.637	3.175	2.564
23	0.00	0.00	0.00	0.00	0.00	0.00	3.636	3.174	2.564
24	0.00	0.00	0.00	0.00	0.00	0.00	3.637	3.175	2.564
25	0.00	0.00	0.00	0.00	0.00	0.00	3.636	3.174	2.564
26	0.00	0.00	0.00	0.00	0.00	0.00	3.637	3.175	2.564
27	0.00	0.00	0.00	0.00	0.00	0.00	3.636	3.174	2.564
28	0.00	0.00	0.00	0.00	0.00	0.00	1.970	3.175	2.564
29	0.00	0.00	0.00	0.00	0.00	0.00	0.00	3.174	2.564
30	0.00	0.00	0.00	0.00	0.00	0.00	0.00	3.175	2.564
31	0.00	0.00	0.00	0.00	0.00	0.00	0.00	3.174	2.564
32	0.00	0.00	0.00	0.00	0.00	0.00	0.00	1.720	2.564
33	0.00	0.00	0.00	0.00	0.00	0.00	0.00	0.00	2.564
34	0.00	0.00	0.00	0.00	0.00	0.00	0.00	0.00	2.564
35	0.00	0.00	0.00	0.00	0.00	0.00	0.00	0.00	2.564
36	0.00	0.00	0.00	0.00	0.00	0.00	0.00	0.00	2.564
37	0.00	0.00	0.00	0.00	0.00	0.00	0.00	0.00	2.564
38	0.00	0.00	0.00	0.00	0.00	0.00	0.00	0.00	2.564
39	0.00	0.00	0.00	0.00	0.00	0.00	0.00	0.00	2.564
40	0.00	0.00	0.00	0.00	0.00	0.00	0.00	0.00	0.107
41	0.00	0.00	0.00	0.00	0.00	0.00	0.00	0.00	0.000

▼ SL DEPRECIATION

Year						Normal Recovery Period						
	2.5	3	3.5	4	5	6	6.5	7	7.5	8	8.5	9
1	20.00%	16.67%	14.29%	12.50%	10.00%	8.33%	7.69%	7.14%	6.67%	6.25%	5.88%	5.56%
2	40.00	33.33	28.57	25.00	20.00	16.67	15.39	14.29	13.33	12.50	11.77	11.11
3	40.00	33.33	28.57	25.00	20.00	16.67	15.38	14.29	13.33	12.50	11.76	11.11
4	0.00	16.67	28.57	25.00	20.00	16.67	15.39	14.28	13.33	12.50	11.77	11.11
5	0.00	0.00	0.00	12.50	20.00	16.66	15.38	14.29	13.34	12.50	11.76	11.11
6	0.00	0.00	0.00	0.00	10.00	16.67	15.39	14.28	13.33	12.50	11.77	11.11
7	0.00	0.00	0.00	0.00	0.00	8.33	15.38	14.29	13.34	12.50	11.76	11.11
8	0.00	0.00	0.00	0.00	0.00	0.00	0.00	7.14	13.33	12.50	11.77	11.11
9	0.00	0.00	0.00	0.00	0.00	0.00	0.00	0.00	0.00	6.25	11.76	11.11
10	0.00	0.00	0.00	0.00	0.00	0.00	0.00	0.00	0.00	0.00	0.00	5.56
11	0.00	0.00	0.00	0.00	0.00	0.00	0.00	0.00	0.00	0.00	0.00	0.00
12	0.00	0.00	0.00	0.00	0.00	0.00	0.00	0.00	0.00	0.00	0.00	0.00
13	0.00	0.00	0.00	0.00	0.00	0.00	0.00	0.00	0.00	0.00	0.00	0.00
14	0.00	0.00	0.00	0.00	0.00	0.00	0.00	0.00	0.00	0.00	0.00	0.00
15	0.00	0.00	0.00	0.00	0.00	0.00	0.00	0.00	0.00	0.00	0.00	0.00
16	0.00	0.00	0.00	0.00	0.00	0.00	0.00	0.00	0.00	0.00	0.00	0.00
17	0.00	0.00	0.00	0.00	0.00	0.00	0.00	0.00	0.00	0.00	0.00	0.00
18	0.00	0.00	0.00	0.00	0.00	0.00	0.00	0.00	0.00	0.00	0.00	0.00
19	0.00	0.00	0.00	0.00	0.00	0.00	0.00	0.00	0.00	0.00	0.00	0.00
20	0.00	0.00	0.00	0.00	0.00	0.00	0.00	0.00	0.00	0.00	0.00	0.00
21	0.00	0.00	0.00	0.00	0.00	0.00	0.00	0.00	0.00	0.00	0.00	0.00
22	0.00	0.00	0.00	0.00	0.00	0.00	0.00	0.00	0.00	0.00	0.00	0.00
23	0.00	0.00	0.00	0.00	0.00	0.00	0.00	0.00	0.00	0.00	0.00	0.00
24	0.00	0.00	0.00	0.00	0.00	0.00	0.00	0.00	0.00	0.00	0.00	0.00
25	0.00	0.00	0.00	0.00	0.00	0.00	0.00	0.00	0.00	0.00	0.00	0.00
26	0.00	0.00	0.00	0.00	0.00	0.00	0.00	0.00	0.00	0.00	0.00	0.00
27	0.00	0.00	0.00	0.00	0.00	0.00	0.00	0.00	0.00	0.00	0.00	0.00
28	0.00	0.00	0.00	0.00	0.00	0.00	0.00	0.00	0.00	0.00	0.00	0.00
29	0.00	0.00	0.00	0.00	0.00	0.00	0.00	0.00	0.00	0.00	0.00	0.00
30	0.00	0.00	0.00	0.00	0.00	0.00	0.00	0.00	0.00	0.00	0.00	0.00
31	0.00	0.00	0.00	0.00	0.00	0.00	0.00	0.00	0.00	0.00	0.00	0.00
32	0.00	0.00	0.00	0.00	0.00	0.00	0.00	0.00	0.00	0.00	0.00	0.00
33	0.00	0.00	0.00	0.00	0.00	0.00	0.00	0.00	0.00	0.00	0.00	0.00
34	0.00	0.00	0.00	0.00	0.00	0.00	0.00	0.00	0.00	0.00	0.00	0.00
35	0.00	0.00	0.00	0.00	0.00	0.00	0.00	0.00	0.00	0.00	0.00	0.00
36	0.00	0.00	0.00	0.00	0.00	0.00	0.00	0.00	0.00	0.00	0.00	0.00
37	20.00	16.67	14.29	12.50	10.00	8.33	7.69	7.14	6.67	6.25	5.88	5.56
38	0.00	33.33	28.57	25.00	20.00	16.67	15.39	14.29	13.33	12.50	0.00	11.11
39	0.00	0.00	0.00	0.00	0.00	0.00	0.00	0.00	0.00	0.00	0.00	0.00
40	0.00	0.00	0.00	0.00	0.00	0.00	0.00	0.00	0.00	0.00	0.00	0.00
41	0.00	0.00	0.00	0.00	0.00	0.00	0.00	0.00	0.00	0.00	0.00	0.00
42	0.00	0.00	0.00	0.00	0.00	0.00	15.39	14.28	0.00	0.00	0.00	0.00
43	0.00	0.00	0.00	0.00	0.00	0.00	0.00	0.00	0.00	0.00	0.00	0.00
44	0.00	0.00	0.00	0.00	0.00	0.00	0.00	0.00	0.00	0.00	0.00	11.11
45	0.00	0.00	0.00	0.00	0.00	0.00	0.00	0.00	0.00	0.00	0.00	11.11
46	0.00	0.00	0.00	0.00	0.00	0.00	0.00	0.00	0.00	0.00	0.00	0.00
47	0.00	0.00	0.00	0.00	0.00	0.00	0.00	0.00	0.00	0.00	0.00	0.00
48	0.00	0.00	0.00	0.00	0.00	0.00	0.00	0.00	0.00	0.00	0.00	0.00
49	0.00	0.00	0.00	0.00	0.00	0.00	0.00	0.00	0.00	0.00	0.00	0.00
50	0.00	0.00	0.00	0.00	0.00	0.00	0.00	0.00	0.00	0.00	0.00	0.00
51	0.00	0.00	0.00	0.00	0.00	0.00	0.00	0.00	0.00	0.00	0.00	0.00
52	0.00	0.00	0.00	0.00	0.00	0.00	0.00	0.00	0.00	0.00	0.00	0.00

	Normal Recovery Period												
Year	9.5	10	10.5	11	11.5	12	12.5	13	13.5	14	15	16	16.5
1	5.26%	5.00%	4.76%	4.55%	4.35%	4.17%	4.00%	3.85%	3.70%	3.57%	3.33%	3.13%	3.03%
2	10.53	10.00	9.52	9.09	8.70	8.33	8.00	7.69	7.41	7.14	6.67	6.25	6.06
3	10.53	10.00	9.52	9.09	8.70	8.33	8.00	7.69	7.41	7.14	6.67	6.25	6.06
4	10.53	10.00	9.53	9.09	8.69	8.33	8.00	7.69	7.41	7.14	6.67	6.25	6.06
5	10.52	10.00	9.52	9.09	8.70	8.33	8.00	7.69	7.41	7.14	6.67	6.25	6.06
6	10.53	10.00	9.53	9.09	8.69	8.33	8.00	7.69	7.41	7.14	6.67	6.25	6.06
7	10.52	10.00	9.52	9.09	8.70	8.34	8.00	7.69	7.41	7.14	6.67	6.25	6.06
8	10.53	10.00	9.53	9.09	8.69	8.33	8.00	7.69	7.41	7.15	6.66	6.25	6.06
9	10.52	10.00	9.52	9.09	8.70	8.34	8.00	7.69	7.41	7.14	6.67	6.25	6.06
10	10.53	10.00	9.53	9.09	8.69	8.33	8.00	7.70	7.40	7.15	6.66	6.25	6.06
11	0.00	5.00	9.52	9.09	8.70	8.34	8.00	7.69	7.41	7.14	6.67	6.25	6.06
12	0.00	0.00	0.00	4.55	8.69	8.33	8.00	7.70	7.40	7.15	6.66	6.25	6.06
13	0.00	0.00	0.00	0.00	0.00	4.17	8.00	7.69	7.41	7.14	6.67	6.25	6.06
14	0.00	0.00	0.00	0.00	0.00	0.00	0.00	3.85	7.40	7.15	6.66	6.25	6.06
15	0.00	0.00	0.00	0.00	0.00	0.00	0.00	0.00	0.00	3.57	6.67	6.25	6.06
16	0.00	0.00	0.00	0.00	0.00	0.00	0.00	0.00	0.00	0.00	3.33	6.25	6.06
17	0.00	0.00	0.00	0.00	0.00	0.00	0.00	0.00	0.00	0.00	0.00	3.12	6.07
18	0.00	0.00	0.00	0.00	0.00	0.00	0.00	0.00	0.00	0.00	0.00	0.00	0.00
19	0.00	0.00	0.00	0.00	0.00	0.00	0.00	0.00	0.00	0.00	0.00	0.00	0.00
20	0.00	0.00	0.00	0.00	0.00	0.00	0.00	0.00	0.00	0.00	0.00	0.00	0.00
21	0.00	0.00	0.00	0.00	0.00	0.00	0.00	0.00	0.00	0.00	0.00	0.00	0.00
22	0.00	0.00	0.00	0.00	0.00	0.00	0.00	0.00	0.00	0.00	0.00	0.00	0.00
23	0.00	0.00	0.00	0.00	0.00	0.00	0.00	0.00	0.00	0.00	0.00	0.00	0.00
24	0.00	0.00	0.00	0.00	0.00	0.00	0.00	0.00	0.00	0.00	0.00	0.00	0.00
25	0.00	0.00	0.00	0.00	0.00	0.00	0.00	0.00	0.00	0.00	0.00	0.00	0.00
26	0.00	0.00	0.00	0.00	0.00	0.00	0.00	0.00	0.00	0.00	0.00	0.00	0.00
27	0.00	0.00	0.00	0.00	0.00	0.00	0.00	0.00	0.00	0.00	0.00	0.00	0.00
28	0.00	0.00	0.00	0.00	0.00	0.00	0.00	0.00	0.00	0.00	0.00	0.00	0.00
29	0.00	0.00	0.00	0.00	0.00	0.00	0.00	0.00	0.00	0.00	0.00	0.00	0.00
30	0.00	0.00	0.00	0.00	0.00	0.00	0.00	0.00	0.00	0.00	0.00	0.00	0.00
31	0.00	0.00	0.00	0.00	0.00	0.00	0.00	0.00	0.00	0.00	0.00	0.00	0.00
32	0.00	0.00	0.00	0.00	0.00	0.00	0.00	0.00	0.00	0.00	0.00	0.00	0.00
33	0.00	0.00	0.00	0.00	0.00	0.00	0.00	0.00	0.00	0.00	0.00	0.00	0.00
34	0.00	0.00	0.00	0.00	0.00	0.00	0.00	0.00	0.00	0.00	0.00	0.00	0.00
35	0.00	0.00	0.00	0.00	0.00	0.00	0.00	0.00	0.00	0.00	0.00	0.00	0.00
36	0.00	0.00	0.00	0.00	0.00	0.00	0.00	0.00	0.00	0.00	0.00	0.00	0.00
37	0.00	0.00	0.00	0.00	0.00	0.00	0.00	0.00	0.00	0.00	0.00	0.00	0.00
38	0.00	0.00	0.00	0.00	0.00	0.00	0.00	0.00	0.00	0.00	0.00	0.00	0.00
39	0.00	0.00	0.00	0.00	0.00	0.00	0.00	0.00	0.00	0.00	0.00	0.00	0.00
40	0.00	0.00	0.00	0.00	0.00	0.00	0.00	0.00	0.00	0.00	0.00	0.00	0.00
41	0.00	0.00	0.00	0.00	0.00	0.00	0.00	0.00	0.00	0.00	0.00	0.00	0.00
42	0.00	0.00	0.00	0.00	0.00	0.00	0.00	0.00	0.00	0.00	0.00	0.00	0.00
43	0.00	0.00	0.00	0.00	0.00	0.00	0.00	0.00	0.00	0.00	0.00	0.00	0.00
44	0.00	0.00	0.00	0.00	0.00	0.00	0.00	0.00	0.00	0.00	0.00	0.00	0.00
45	0.00	0.00	0.00	0.00	0.00	0.00	0.00	0.00	0.00	0.00	0.00	0.00	0.00
46	0.00	0.00	0.00	0.00	0.00	0.00	0.00	0.00	0.00	0.00	0.00	0.00	0.00
47	0.00	0.00	0.00	0.00	0.00	0.00	0.00	0.00	0.00	0.00	0.00	0.00	0.00
48	0.00	0.00	0.00	0.00	0.00	0.00	0.00	0.00	0.00	0.00	0.00	0.00	0.00
49	0.00	0.00	0.00	0.00	0.00	0.00	0.00	0.00	0.00	0.00	0.00	0.00	0.00
50	0.00	0.00	0.00	0.00	0.00	0.00	0.00	0.00	0.00	0.00	0.00	0.00	0.00
51	0.00	0.00	0.00	0.00	0.00	0.00	0.00	0.00	0.00	0.00	0.00	0.00	0.00
52	0.00	0.00	0.00	0.00	0.00	0.00	0.00	0.00	0.00	0.00	0.00	0.00	0.00

▼ SL DEPRECIATION

					Normal Recovery Period									
Year	17	18	19	20	22	24	25	26.5	28	30	35	40	45	50
1	2.94%	2.78%	2.63%	2.50%	2.273%	2.083%	2.00%	1.887%	1.786%	1.667%	1.429%	1.25%	1.111%	1.00%
2	5.88	5.56	5.26	5.00	4.545	4.167	4.00	3.774	3.571	3.333	2.857	2.50	2.222	2.00
3	5.88	5.56	5.26	5.00	4.545	4.167	4.00	3.774	3.571	3.333	2.857	2.50	2.222	2.00
4	5.88	5.55	5.26	5.00	4.545	4.167	4.00	3.774	3.571	3.333	2.857	2.50	2.222	2.00
5	5.88	5.56	5.26	5.00	4.546	4.167	4.00	3.774	3.571	3.333	2.857	2.50	2.222	2.00
6	5.88	5.55	5.26	5.00	4.545	4.167	4.00	3.774	3.571	3.333	2.857	2.50	2.222	2.00
7	5.88	5.56	5.26	5.00	4.546	4.167	4.00	3.773	3.572	3.333	2.857	2.50	2.222	2.00
8	5.88	5.55	5.26	5.00	4.545	4.167	4.00	3.774	3.571	3.333	2.857	2.50	2.222	2.00
9	5.88	5.56	5.27	5.00	4.546	4.167	4.00	3.773	3.572	3.333	2.857	2.50	2.222	2.00
10	5.88	5.55	5.26	5.00	4.545	4.167	4.00	3.774	3.571	3.333	2.857	2.50	2.222	2.00
11	5.89	5.56	5.27	5.00	4.546	4.166	4.00	3.773	3.572	3.333	2.857	2.50	2.222	2.00
12	5.88	5.55	5.26	5.00	4.545	4.167	4.00	3.774	3.571	3.333	2.857	2.50	2.222	2.00
13	5.89	5.56	5.27	5.00	4.546	4.166	4.00	3.773	3.572	3.334	2.857	2.50	2.222	2.00
14	5.88	5.55	5.26	5.00	4.545	4.167	4.00	3.773	3.571	3.333	2.857	2.50	2.222	2.00
15	5.89	5.56	5.27	5.00	4.546	4.166	4.00	3.774	3.572	3.334	2.857	2.50	2.222	2.00
16	5.88	5.55	5.26	5.00	4.545	4.167	4.00	3.773	3.571	3.333	2.857	2.50	2.222	2.00
17	5.89	5.56	5.27	5.00	4.546	4.166	4.00	3.774	3.572	3.334	2.857	2.50	2.222	2.00
18	2.94	5.55	5.26	5.00	4.545	4.167	4.00	3.773	3.571	3.333	2.857	2.50	2.222	2.00
19	0.00	2.78	5.27	5.00	4.546	4.166	4.00	3.774	3.572	3.334	2.857	2.50	2.222	2.00
20	0.00	0.00	2.63	5.00	4.545	4.167	4.00	3.773	3.571	3.333	2.857	2.50	2.222	2.00
21	0.00	0.00	0.00	2.50	4.546	4.166	4.00	3.774	3.572	3.334	2.857	2.50	2.222	2.00
22	0.00	0.00	0.00	0.00	4.545	4.167	4.00	3.773	3.571	3.333	2.857	2.50	2.222	2.00
23	0.00	0.00	0.00	0.00	2.273	4.166	4.00	3.774	3.572	3.334	2.857	2.50	2.222	2.00
24	0.00	0.00	0.00	0.00	0.000	4.167	4.00	3.773	3.571	3.333	2.857	2.50	2.222	2.00
25	0.00	0.00	0.00	0.00	0.000	2.083	4.00	3.774	3.572	3.334	2.857	2.50	2.222	2.00
26	0.00	0.00	0.00	0.00	0.000	0.000	2.00	3.773	3.571	3.333	2.857	2.50	2.222	2.00
27	0.00	0.00	0.00	0.00	0.000	0.000	0.00	3.774	3.572	3.334	2.857	2.50	2.223	2.00
28	0.00	0.00	0.00	0.00	0.000	0.000	0.00	0.000	3.571	3.333	2.858	2.50	2.222	2.00
29	0.00	0.00	0.00	0.00	0.000	0.000	0.00	0.000	1.786	3.334	2.857	2.50	2.223	2.00
30	0.00	0.00	0.00	0.00	0.000	0.000	0.00	0.000	0.000	3.333	2.858	2.50	2.222	2.00
31	0.00	0.00	0.00	0.00	0.000	0.000	0.00	0.000	0.000	1.667	2.857	2.50	2.223	2.00
32	0.00	0.00	0.00	0.00	0.000	0.000	0.00	0.000	0.000	0.000	2.858	2.50	2.222	2.00
33	0.00	0.00	0.00	0.00	0.000	0.000	0.00	0.000	0.000	0.000	2.857	2.50	2.223	2.00
34	0.00	0.00	0.00	0.00	0.000	0.000	0.00	0.000	0.000	0.000	2.858	2.50	2.222	2.00
35	0.00	0.00	0.00	0.00	0.000	0.000	0.00	0.000	0.000	0.000	2.857	2.50	2.223	2.00
36	0.00	0.00	0.00	0.00	0.000	0.000	0.00	0.000	0.000	0.000	1.429	2.50	2.222	2.00
37	0.00	0.00	0.00	0.00	0.000	0.000	0.00	0.000	0.000	0.000	0.000	2.50	2.223	2.00
38	0.00	0.00	0.00	0.00	0.000	0.000	0.00	0.000	0.000	0.000	0.000	2.50	2.222	2.00
39	0.00	0.00	0.00	0.00	0.000	0.000	0.00	0.000	0.000	0.000	0.000	2.50	2.223	2.00
40	0.00	0.00	0.00	0.00	0.000	0.000	0.00	0.000	0.000	0.000	0.000	2.50	2.222	2.00
41	0.00	0.00	0.00	0.00	0.000	0.000	0.00	0.000	0.000	0.000	0.000	1.25	2.223	2.00
42	0.00	0.00	0.00	0.00	0.000	0.000	0.00	0.000	0.000	0.000	0.000	0.00	2.222	2.00
43	0.00	0.00	0.00	0.00	0.000	0.000	0.00	0.000	0.000	0.000	0.000	0.00	2.223	2.00
44	0.00	0.00	0.00	0.00	0.000	0.000	0.00	0.000	0.000	0.000	0.000	0.00	2.222	2.00
45	0.00	0.00	0.00	0.00	0.000	0.000	0.00	0.000	0.000	0.000	0.000	0.00	2.223	2.00
46	0.00	0.00	0.00	0.00	0.000	0.000	0.00	0.000	0.000	0.000	0.000	0.00	1.111	2.00
47	0.00	0.00	0.00	0.00	0.000	0.000	0.00	0.000	0.000	0.000	0.000	0.00	0.000	2.00
48	0.00	0.00	0.00	0.00	0.000	0.000	0.00	0.000	0.000	0.000	0.000	0.00	0.000	2.00
49	0.00	0.00	0.00	0.00	0.000	0.000	0.00	0.000	0.000	0.000	0.000	0.00	0.000	2.00
50	0.00	0.00	0.00	0.00	0.000	0.000	0.00	0.000	0.000	0.000	0.000	0.00	0.000	2.00
51	0.00	0.00	0.00	0.00	0.000	0.000	0.00	0.000	0.000	0.000	0.000	0.00	0.000	1.00
52	0.00	0.00	0.00	0.00	0.000	0.000	0.00	0.000	0.000	0.000	0.000	0.00	0.000	0.00

chapter thirteen

weighing net present value +
other capital budgeting criteria

Once you have calculated the cost of capital for a project and estimated its cash flows, deciding whether to invest in that project basically boils down to asking the question "Is the project worth its projected present value?" To answer this question, we will, not surprisingly, turn once again to the time value of money (TVM) formulas we used to value stocks, bonds, loans, and other marketable securities in Chapters 7 and 8. But first, a caveat: Though the *mechanics* of using the TVM formulas will be the same, the *intuition* underlying our analysis of investment criteria is very different. You will recall that we used the pricing equations for stocks, bonds, and other instruments with an emphasis on equations that had "=" signs. We

continued on p. 304

LEARNING GOALS

LG13-1 Analyze the logic underlying capital budgeting decision techniques.

LG13-2 Calculate and use the payback (PB) and discounted payback (DPB) methods for valuing capital investment opportunities.

LG13-3 Calculate and use the net present value (NPV) method for evaluating capital investment opportunities.

LG13-4 Calculate and use the internal rate of return (IRR) and the modified internal rate of return (MIRR) methods for evaluating capital investment opportunities.

LG13-5 Use NPV profiles to reconcile sources of conflict between NPV and IRR methods.

LG13-6 Compute and use the profitability index (PI).

continued from p. 303

will see here that most capital budgeting decision rules that we will encounter will have ">" or "<" signs. This difference arises because marketable securities are *financial* assets that trade in competitive financial markets, while capital budgeting projects usually involve the purchase of *real* assets, which typically trade in much less competitive markets. Real assets are considerably less liquid than are financial assets, and firms purchase real assets in the form of capital equipment to create value for their customers. As a result, projects and purchases that involve capital equipment typically convey at least some monopoly power (and the associated monopolistic profits) to the firm purchasing them and adopting them for long-term use. In fact, the reason for the inequality signs in the capital budgeting decision rules we will be examining is that, rather than looking for projects that are worth "enough," we seek projects that are worth "more than enough." That is, capital budgeting equations seek projects that offer more return than they should (sometimes called *economic profits*), even after taking into account their associated risk. ■

THE SET OF CAPITAL BUDGETING TECHNIQUES LG13-1

So, now we are going to apply what we have learned in the preceding two chapters about the cost of capital and cash flows that result from capital budgeting decisions to choose the projects that most deserve the scarce capital—that is, to determine which projects promise the best returns to the company. No one can predict the future, so these techniques are accompanied by uncertainty. That said, commonly used capital budgeting techniques include:

- NPV (net present value).
- IRR (internal rate of return).
- PB (payback).
- DPB (discounted payback).
- MIRR (modified internal rate of return).
- PI (profitability index).

As we discuss each of these techniques in this chapter, you will find that, while the net present value (NPV) technique is

the preferred one for most project evaluations, in some cases using one of the other decision rules, either in lieu of NPV or in conjunction with it, makes sense. For example, a company or person faced with a time constraint to repay the initial capital for a project may be more worried about a project's payback (PB) statistic, while a firm facing capital constraints might prefer to use one of the interest-rate-based decision statistics, such as the profitability index (PI), to prioritize its project choices. How you choose a capital budgeting technique or techniques is affected by five subchoices:

1. The statistical format you choose.

2. The benchmark you compare it to.

3. Whether you compute it with TVM.

4. Whether non-normal cash flows are a factor.

5. What other projects you may or may not have to decide among.

Table 13.1 organizes these capital budgeting factors in the decision process.

THE CHOICE OF DECISION STATISTIC FORMAT

Managers tend to focus on three general measurement units for financial decisions: currency, time, and rate of return. Of these three types, rate-based statistics can potentially be the trickiest to use. Computing these statistics usually involves summarizing the relationship between cash inflows and cash outflows across

Letitia Tyler is considering some improvements to her house. The work will take six months to complete, and the contractor has asked for payments of $5,000 at the start, $5,000 after three months, and another $10,000 upon completion. Letitia plans to sell the house in approximately three years and estimates that the work will increase the selling price of her house by approximately $30,000 from its current estimated market price of $124,000. If she must borrow money to pay for the improvements from the bank at an APR (based upon monthly compounding) of 9 percent, should she have the improvements done?

How do interest rates impact Letitia's decision? What does that have to do with the economy? Scan the QR code for an extended look. Turn to the back of the book for solutions to these applications.

the project's lifetime through the use of a ratio. Any time we use a ratio to create a summary statistic like this, some (crucial) information is lost along the way.

In particular, although rate-based decision statistics tell us the rate of return *per dollar* invested, they don't reflect the *amount* of the investment on which that return is based. To see why this can be a problem, particularly when choosing between two or more projects, ask yourself this question: Would you rather earn a 10 percent rate of return on $100 or a 9 percent rate of return on $1,000?

Despite this tendency to focus on the return per dollar invested while ignoring the number of dollars in question, rate-based decision statistics are actually very popular. Managers appreciate being able to easily compare the expected "earned" rate of return constructed by these decision rules with the "borrowing" rates that potential lenders and the capital markets are quoting to them.

PROCESSING CAPITAL BUDGETING DECISIONS

For all of our decision techniques, we need to identify how to calculate a *decision statistic*; decide on an appropriate *benchmark* for comparing the calculated statistic; and define what relationship between the two will dictate project acceptance.

▼**TABLE 13.1** Capital Budgeting Technique Attributes

Technique	Unit of Measurement	Benchmark	Uses TVM	Works Well with Non-Normal Cash Flows	Works Well for Choosing Among Projects
PB (payback)	Time	Varies	No	No	No
DPB (discounted payback)	Time	Varies	Yes	No	No
NPV (net present value)	Dollars	$0	Yes	Yes	Yes
IRR (internal rate of return)	Rate	Cost of capital	Yes	No	No
MIRR (modified internal rate of return)	Rate	Cost of capital	Yes	Yes	No
PI (profitability index)	Rate	0%	Yes	Yes	No

Among currency, time, and rate of return, managers usually prefer rate-based statistics.

When we consider one project at a time, or when we examine each of a group of independent projects, capital budgeting techniques involve two-step decision processes:

1. Compute the statistic.

2. Compare the computed statistic with the benchmark to decide whether to accept or reject the project.

However, when we deal with mutually exclusive projects, we will need to add a new step in the middle of the process:

1. Compute the statistic for each project.

2. *Have a "runoff" between the mutually exclusive projects, choosing the one with the best statistic.*

3. Compare the computed statistic from the runoff winner with the benchmark to decide whether to accept or reject.

As we will see, the presence of this runoff step for mutually exclusive projects, as well as its placement, will create problems when we use decision statistics that either ignore or summarize critical information in the first step.

PAYBACK AND DISCOUNTED PAYBACK

Both the payback and discounted payback rules carry great emotional appeal: If we assume that we are borrowing money to finance a new project, both techniques answer slightly different versions of the question, "How long is it going to take us to recoup our costs?"

So it would seem that these techniques use the same reasoning that banks and other lenders employ when they examine a potential borrower's finances to determine the probability of repayment. While at first this seems like a fairly simple question, it can actually lead to some rather sophisticated insight concerning a project's potential. For example, a project that lasts seven years but is slated to repay its initial investment within the first two years is obviously a stronger candidate than a project that also repays in two years but is slated to last only three years, assuming that the two projects are expected to have the same yearly cash flows once payback is achieved.

Payback Statistic LG13-2

The **payback (PB)** statistic remains very popular because it is easy to compute. All we have to do is keep a running subtotal of the cumulative sum of the cash flows up to the point that this sum exactly offsets the initial investment. That is, PB is determined by using this formula:

$$0 = \sum_{n=0}^{PB} CF_n \qquad (13\text{-}1)$$

Notice that this computation demands a couple of strong assumptions:

1. The concept of payback rests on the assumption that cash flows are **normal,** with all outflows occurring at the beginning of the project's life, so that we can think of the PB statistic as a type of recovery period for that initial investment. This implies that payback would be meaningless for a set of non-normal cash flows. If, for example, a project required an infusion of cash after it started, such as the cash outflows shown at times 1 and 2 in Table 13.7 later in this chapter, we could not calculate a payback statistic.

2. Note that PB will not be very likely to occur in an exact, round number of periods, so we will need to make another assumption concerning how cash inflows occur *during* the course of a year. The usual approach to handling this condition is to assume that cash flows arrive smoothly throughout each period, allowing us to count out the months and days to estimate the exact payback statistic.

Payback Benchmark

The payback method shows an additional weakness in that its benchmark must be exogenously specified: In other words, it is not always the same value, nor is it determined by the required rate of return or any other input variable. Ideally, the maximum allowable PB for a project should be set based on some relevant external constraint, such as the number of periods until capital providers need their money back, or the time available until a project would violate a bond issue's protective covenants. As you might suspect, in real life managers often indicate the maximum allowable payback—that is, set the exogenous specification—arbitrarily.

Let us assume that we have been told that the maximum allowable payback for this project is three years. With this decision rule, we want to accept projects that show a calculated statistic less than the benchmark of three years:

$$\begin{array}{ccc} \text{Accept project if} & \leq & \text{Maximum} \\ \text{calculated payback} & & \text{allowable payback} \end{array}$$

$$\begin{array}{ccc} \text{Reject project if} & > & \text{Maximum} \\ \text{calculated payback} & & \text{allowable payback} \end{array} \qquad (13\text{-}2)$$

"Yet another problem that arises when we use the payback technique is that it does not recognize or incorporate the time value of money."

Discounted Payback Statistic

Yet another problem that arises when we use the payback technique is that it does not recognize or incorporate the time value of money. To compensate for this exclusion, we often calculate the **discounted payback (DPB)** statistic instead, using the following formula:

$$0 = \sum_{n=0}^{DPB} \frac{CF_n}{(1+i)^n} \qquad (13\text{-}3)$$

Notice that all we are doing here is summing the *present values* of the cash flows until we get a cumulative sum of zero, instead of summing the cash flows themselves as we did for the PB statistic. Other than that, we follow all the steps in the computation of DPB just as we did for the PB statistic.

Discounted Payback Benchmark

We may be tempted to assume that we should simply use the same maximum allowable payback benchmark for DPB that we used for PB. If we did so, then we would obviously have to reject this project, since its calculated DPB is 3.56 years

(Example 13-2) versus a stated maximum allowable time of only three years. However, we should be very cautious about applying the same benchmark to DPB that we did to PB. To see why, recall that payback calculations only make sense when applied to normal cash flows, so we would assume that we will be dealing with normal cash flows here. But think about *which* cash flows are affected when we switch from calculating payback to discounted payback: Only the ones in the future will fall to lower values, because the present value of the time 0 cash flow will always be the same as its nominal value. And, if the future cash flows are all positive and the initial cash flow is negative, then it is only the positive cash flows that will be affected by switching to cumulative present value for DPB.

In other words, we would expect the calculated DPB statistic to always be larger than the "regular" PB statistic because DPB incorporates the interest you must pay

---

EXAMPLE 13-1

For interactive versions of this example visit www.mhhe.com/canM2e

CALCULATOR HINTS

[CF0] =	−10000
[CF1] =	2500
[CF2] =	3500
[CF3] =	5000
[CF4] =	4000
[CF5] =	2000
[NPV]	
[I] =	12
CPT [PB] =	2.80

Payback Calculation LG13-2

Consider the sample project with the cash flows shown in Table 13.2. Should this project be accepted based on payback if the maximum allowable payback period is three years?

▼ **TABLE 13.2** Payback Calculation on Sample Project with Normal Cash Flows

Year:	0	1	2	3	4	5
Cash flow	−$10,000	$2,500	$3,500	$5,000	$4,000	$2,000
Cumulative cash flow	−10,000	−7,500	−4,000	1,000		

SOLUTION:

To calculate this project's payback, we would first calculate the cumulative cash flows until they went from negative to positive. From this first step, we know that payback occurs somewhere between periods 2 and 3. To determine the exact statistic, we note that if the magnitude of the last negative cumulative cash flow represents how much cash flow we *need* during year 3 to achieve payback, then the marginal cash flow for year 3 represents how much we will *get* over the course of the entire third year. By linear interpolation, our exact statistic is therefore where we start (year 2) plus what we need (the absolute value of the last negative cumulative cash flow, −$4,000) over what we are going to get during that year:

$$PB = 2 + \frac{\$4,000}{\$5,000} = 2.8 \text{ years}$$

Since our calculated payback is 2.8 years and the maximum allowable payback period is three years, we should accept the project based on the payback rule.

Similar to Problems 13-5, 13-6, 13-17, 13-23

EXAMPLE 13-2

Discounted Payback Calculation LG13-2

For interactive versions
of this example visit
www.mhhe.com/canM2e

Consider the same project from Example 13-1. To calculate this project's discounted payback, we would first need to calculate the PV of each cash flow separately. Assuming a 12 percent interest rate, we would calculate these values as shown in Table 13.3.

▼ **TABLE 13.3** Discounted Payback Calculation: Present Values of Cash Flows

Year:	0	1	2	3	4	5
Cash flow	−$10,000.00	$2,500.00	$3,500.00	$5,000.00	$4,000.00	$2,000.00
Cash flow present value	−10,000.00	2,232.14	2,790.18	3,558.90	2,542.07	1,134.85

In Table 13.4 we calculate the cumulative present value of the cash flows until they switch from negative to positive:

▼ **TABLE 13.4** Discounted Payback Calculation on Sample Project with Normal Cash Flows

Year:	0	1	2	3	4	5
Cash flow	−$10,000.00	$2,500.00	$3,500.00	$5,000.00	$4,000.00	$2,000.00
Cash flow present value	−10,000.00	2,232.14	2,790.18	3,558.90	2,542.07	1,134.85
Cumulative cash flow PV	−10,000.00	−7,767.86	−4,977.68	−1,418.78	1,123.29	

CALCULATOR HINTS

$[CF0] = -10000$
$[CF1] = 2500$
$[CF2] = 3500$
$[CF3] = 5000$
$[CF4] = 4000$
$[CF5] = 2000$
[NPV]
$[I] = 12$
$CPT\ [DPB] = 3.56$

SOLUTION:

As before, we can stop once the cumulative values go from negative to positive. In this case, linear interpolation will give us a DPB statistic of:

$$DPB = 3 + \frac{\$1,418.78}{\$2,542.07} = 3.56 \text{ years}$$

Similar to Problems 13-7, 13-8, 13-18, 13-24

the Math Coach on...

Payback and Discounted Payback Using Financial Calculators and Spreadsheet Programs

" Most financial calculators and spreadsheet programs (with the notable exception of Texas Instrument's BA II Plus Professional) will not compute PB or DPB for you. Instead, you have to go through the process of cumulating cash flows or the PV of cash flows noted in Examples 13-1, 13-2, and 13-3. "

until you reach the benchmark. Said another way, DPB will always take longer to achieve payback if you are "chipping away" at the same-sized initial cash outflow with the present values of a bunch of positive cash inflows rather than their simple nominal values. Therefore, it probably is not fair to hold the DPB statistic up to the same benchmark we use for the PB statistic.

What benchmark should we use? Well, as with PB, management will set the DPB maximum allowable payback exogenously and, once again,

EXAMPLE 13-3

Payback Calculation for Alternative Project LG13-2

Consider once again the sample project shown in Table 13.2. As we calculated in Example 13-1, that project has a PB statistic of 2.8 years. Now, compare that project to the one shown in Table 13.5:

▼ **TABLE 13.5** Payback Calculation on Alternative Sample Project with Normal Cash Flows

Year:	0	1	2	3	4	5
Cash flow	−$10,000	$2,500	$3,500	$4,000	$104,000	$102,000
Cash flow present value	−10,000	−7,500	−4,000	0	0	0

SOLUTION:

This project would have a slightly higher PB statistic of 3.0. Given that it still achieves payback in exactly the maximum allowable three years, it should be highly favored over the first project due to the large positive cash flows that will accrue in the later years. But managers who ignore this aspect of the PB rule and who focus only on the PB statistics of these two projects will likely incorrectly choose the first project due to its lower PB statistic.

Note that NPV will *not* suffer from this problem. Since the NPV statistic takes all of a project's cash flows into account, there aren't "remaining" cash flows to get left out of the statistic as there are with PB and DPB.

Similar to Problems 13-5, 13-6, 13-17, 13-23

often arbitrarily. Let us assume that we are told that senior management has set the maximum allowable payback for DPB as 3.5 years.

$$\text{Accept project if} \atop \text{calculated DPB} \leq \text{Maximum allowable} \atop \text{discounted payback}$$

$$\text{Reject project if} \atop \text{calculated DPB} > \text{Maximum allowable} \atop \text{discounted payback} \quad (13\text{-}4)$$

Since our calculated DPB is 3.56 years and the maximum allowable amount is 3.5 years, we should reject the project.

Payback and Discounted Payback Strengths and Weaknesses LG13-1

A common criticism of PB is that it does not account for the time value of money; the use of PV formulas in computing DPB compensates for TVM. But DPB is not intended to really replace PB, but rather to complement it, providing additional information to analyze capital budgeting decisions.

For example, if we consider a typical, normal payback statistic based on a set of cash flows as a loan problem in which the company borrows the money for the initial investment and then pays it off over time, then PB will intuitively equal the

amount of time necessary to repay just principal on the loan, and DPB will indicate the time necessary to repay principal plus interest.

Both PB and DPB have yet another serious flaw. Both decision statistics completely ignore any cash flows that accrue *after* the

time out!

13-1 Which should we expect to be larger: a project's payback statistic, or its discounted payback statistic?

13-2 If the discount rate is increased, will a project's discounted payback period increase or decrease?

net present value (NPV) A technique that generates a decision rule and associated metric for choosing projects based on the total discounted value of their cash flows.

project reaches its respective payback benchmark. Ignoring this vital information can have serious implications when managers choose between two mutually exclusive projects that have very similar paybacks but very different cash flows after payback is achieved.

NET PRESENT VALUE LG13-1

At its heart, **net present value (NPV)** represents the "purest" of capital budgeting rules, measuring exactly the value we are interested in: the amount of wealth increase we expect from accepting a project. As we cover in more detail below, the NPV

NPV Statistic LG13-3

We actually already know how to calculate the NPV statistic. In fact, we use a very similar approach in developing bond and stock pricing equations. The NPV statistic is simply the sum of all the cash flows' present values:

$$NPV = \frac{CF_0}{(1+i)^0} + \frac{CF_1}{(1+i)^1} + \cdots + \frac{CF_N}{(1+i)^N}$$

$$= \sum_{n=0}^{N} \frac{CF_n}{(1+i)^n} \tag{13-5}$$

NPV Benchmark

NPV analysis includes all of the cash flows—both inflows and outflows. This inclusion implies that any required investment in

> AT ITS HEART, NET PRESENT VALUE (NPV) REPRESENTS THE "PUREST" OF CAPITAL BUDGETING RULES, MEASURING EXACTLY THE VALUE WE ARE INTERESTED IN: THE AMOUNT OF WEALTH INCREASE WE EXPECT FROM ACCEPTING A PROJECT.

method measures this expected wealth increase by computing the difference between the present values of a project's cash inflows and outflows. Since this calculation includes the necessary capital expenditures and other startup costs of the project as cash outflows, a positive value indicates that the project is desirable—that it more than covers all of the necessary resource costs to do the project.

the project is already factored in, so any NPV greater than zero represents value *above and beyond* that investment. Accordingly, the NPV decision rule is:

Accept project if NPV ≥ 0

Reject project if NPV < 0 (13-6)

NPV Strengths and Weaknesses

One strength of the NPV rule is that the statistic is *not* a ratio as with the rate-based decision statistics. It works equally well for independent projects and for choosing among mutually exclusive projects. In the latter case, the mutually exclusive project with the highest NPV should add the most wealth to the firm, and so management should accept it over any competing projects.

Unfortunately, this ability to choose among projects stems from exactly

the
Math Coach on...

Financial Calculators versus Spreadsheet Programs

" While financial calculators expect to be told CF0 when being asked to compute NPV, the NPV functions in spreadsheet programs such as Microsoft Excel usually *don't* want to be told CF0. Instead, they expect you to handle the inclusion of CF0 in the calculation of the NPV statistic outside the NPV function. For example, if you wanted to find the NPV of the cash flows in Example 13-4 using Excel, the function would look like "=NPV(.12,2500,3500,5000, 4000,2000) − 10000". "

the
Math Coach on...

Using a Financial Calculator—Part 2 (Revisited)

The TVM worksheet present in most financial calculators has been fine, so far, for the types of TVM problems we've been solving. Sometimes we had to use the worksheet two or three times for a single problem, but that was usually because we needed an intermediate calculation to input into another TVM equation.

In this chapter, we will generally be using simpler TVM equations (i.e., PV and FV), but we'll find ourselves having to use them repeatedly, making only small variations in inputs over and over again within the same problem. We're also going to run up against the problem of cash flow inconsistencies in most projects. If you thought the cash flows of stocks jumped around a lot, wait until you see what project cash flows do! If we stick with the TVM worksheet, these inconsistent cash flows will be a problem for us. If we want to solve for a "common" *i* or *N* value, the TVM worksheet won't let us enter multiple cash flows unless we're solving an annuity problem. (The one notable exception to this has been when we used the TVM worksheet to simultaneously solve the annuity/lump sum problems that arise with bonds. If you recall, those problems require agreement between the inputs to the annuity and the lump sum problems. This kind of agreement is highly unlikely to occur in other circumstances.)

Remember that most financial calculators also have built-in worksheets specifically designed for computing NPV in problems with multiple nonconstant cash flows. In many cases, they will also calculate most of the other decision rule statistics that we're going to be discussing.

Here is what we already know: To make calculator worksheets as flexible as possible, they are usually divided into two parts: One for input, which we'll refer to as the CF (cash flow) worksheet, and one or more for calculating decision statistics. The CF worksheet is usually designed to handle inputting sets of multiple cash flows as quickly as possible. As a result, it normally consists of two sets of variables or cells—one for the cash flows and one to hold a set of frequency counts for the cash flows, so that we can tell it we have seven $1,500 cash flows in a row instead of having to enter $1,500 seven times.

Using the frequency counts to reduce the number of inputs is handy, but you must take care. Frequency counts are only good for embedded annuities of identical cash flows. You have to ensure that you don't mistake another kind of cash flow for an annuity.

Also, using frequency counts will usually affect the way that the calculator counts time periods. As an example, let's talk about how we would put the set of cash flows shown here into a CF worksheet:

Period	0	1	2	3	4	5	6	7	8
	10%								
Cash flow	−$800	$150	$200		$150	$150	$150	$75	$75

To designate which particular value we'll place into each particular cash flow cell in this worksheet, we'll note the value and the cell identifier, such as CF0, CF1, and so forth. We'll do the same for the frequency cells, using F1, F2, etc., to identify which CF cell the frequency cell goes with. (Note that in most calculators, CF0 is treated as a unique value with an unalterable frequency of 1; we're going to make the same assumption here so you'll never see a listing for F0. For this sample timeline, our inputs would be:

−$800	[CF0]		
$150	[CF1]	1	[F1]
$200	[CF2]	1	[F2]
$0	[CF3]	1	[F3]
$150	[CF4]	3	[F4]
$75	[CF5]	2	[F5]

Then, on the NPV worksheet, you would simply need to enter the interest rate and solve for the NPV:

Note a few important things about this example:

10%	[I]	
[CPT]	[NPV] =	−$144.61

1. We had to manually enter a value of $0 for CF3: If we hadn't, the calculator wouldn't have known about it and would have implicitly assumed that CF4 came one period after CF2.

2. Once we use a frequency cell for one cash flow, all numbering on any subsequent cash flows that we enter into the calculator is going to be messed up, at least from our point of view. For instance, the first $75 isn't what we would call "CF5," is it? We'd call it "CF7" because it comes at time period 7; but calculators usually treat CF5 as "the fifth set of cash flows," so we'll just have to try to do the same to be consistent.

3. If we really don't need to use frequency cells, we will usually just leave them out of the guidance instructions in this chapter to save space.

EXAMPLE 13-4

For interactive versions of this example visit www.mhhe.com/canM2e

CALCULATOR HINTS

[CF0] = −10000
[CF1] = 2500
[CF2] = 3500
[CF3] = 5000
[CF4] = 4000
[CF5] = 2000
[NPV]
[I] = 12
CPT [NPV] = 2,258.15

NPV for a Normal Set of Cash Flows LG13-3

A company is evaluating a project with a set of normal cash flows using a risk-appropriate discount rate of 12 percent as shown in Table 13.6. Compute the NPV to determine whether the company should undertake the project.

▼**TABLE 13.6** Sample Project with Normal Cash Flows

Year:	0	1	2	3	4	5
Cash flow	−$10,000	$2,500	$3,500	$5,000	$4,000	$2,000

SOLUTION:

The NPV statistic for this project will be:

$$NPV = \frac{-\$10,000}{(1.12)^0} + \frac{\$2,500}{(1.12)^1} + \frac{\$3,500}{(1.12)^2} + \frac{\$5,000}{(1.12)^3} + \frac{\$4,000}{(12.1)^4} + \frac{\$2,000}{(1.12)^5}$$

$$= \$2,258.15 > 0$$

The NPV decision will be to *accept* the project.

When you first start calculating NPV, it is easy to miss its deeper meaning. A relatively small NPV, such as the $2,258.15 figure in this example, raises the question of whether $2,258.15 is "worth it," in this sense: Will the project cover the opportunity cost of using the $10,000 of necessary capital? The point, of course, is that the $2,258.15 is above and beyond the recovery of that opportunity cost, so, *yes, it's worth it.*

Similar to Problems 13-1, 13-2, 13-21, 13-27

EXAMPLE 13-5

For interactive versions of this example visit www.mhhe.com/canM2e

CALCULATOR HINTS

[CF0] = 5000
[CF1] = −10000
[CF2] = −3000
[CF3] = 5000
[CF4] = 4000
[CF5] = 2000
[NPV]
[I] = 12
CPT [NPV] = 915.67

NPV for a Non-Normal Set of Cash Flows LG13-3

Note that the NPV rule works equally well with non-normal cash flows, such as those for the project shown in Table 13.7. Compute the NPV for this project to determine whether it should be accepted. Use a 12 percent discount rate.

▼**TABLE 13.7** Sample Project with Normal Cash Flows

Year:	0	1	2	3	4	5
Cash flow	$5,000	−$10,000	−$3,000	$5,000	$4,000	$2,000

SOLUTION:

The NPV statistic will be:

$$NPV = \frac{\$5,000}{(1.12)^0} + \frac{-\$10,000}{(1.12)^1} + \frac{-\$3,000}{(1.12)^2} + \frac{\$5,000}{(1.12)^3} + \frac{\$4,000}{(12.1)^4} + \frac{\$2,000}{(1.12)^5}$$

$$= \$915.67 > 0$$

Based on this NPV, the project should be accepted.

Similar to Problems 13-3, 13-4

what gives it its greatest weakness: the format of the statistic. Since the NPV statistic is a dollar figure, it accurately reflects the net effect of any differences in timing or scale of two projects' expected cash flows. It thus allows comparisons of two projects' NPV statistics to fully incorporate those differences. However, this same currency format often results in confusion for uninformed decision makers: managers not completely familiar with how the NPV statistic works often insist on comparing the NPV to the *cost* of the project, not understanding that the cost is already incorporated into the NPV.

time out!

13-3 Why is a project's cost *not* an appropriate benchmark for its NPV?

13-4 Assuming that it is fairly priced, what should be the NPV of a purchase decision on a corporate bond?

INTERNAL RATE OF RETURN AND MODIFIED INTERNAL RATE OF RETURN LG13-1

The **internal rate of return (IRR)** technique is, by far, the most popular rate-based capital budgeting technique. The main reason for its popularity is that, if you are considering a project with normal cash flows that is independent of other projects, the IRR statistic will give exactly the same accept/reject decision as the NPV rule does. This is due to the fact that NPV and IRR are very closely related. NPV is the sum of the present values of the cash flows at a particular interest rate (usually the firm's cost of capital), whereas IRR is the interest rate that will cause the NPV to be equal to zero.

Solve for NPV:

$$NPV = \sum_{n=0}^{N} \frac{CF_n}{(1+i)^n}$$ versus

Solve for IRR:

$$0 = \sum_{n=0}^{N} \frac{CF_n}{(1+IRR)^n}$$ (13-7)

> *IRR runs into a lot of problems if project cash flows are not normal or if you are using this statistic to decide among mutually exclusive projects.*

As long as the cash flows of a project are normal, the NPV calculated in the equation on the left will be greater than zero if and only if the IRR calculated in the equation on the right is greater than i.

However, IRR runs into a lot of problems if project cash flows are not normal or if you are using this statistic to decide among mutually exclusive projects. As we will show below, we can correct for the non-normal cash flows, but all of the rate-based decision statistics will exhibit the problem of choosing between multiple projects that we discussed above.

Internal Rate of Return Statistic LG13-4

To solve for the IRR statistic, we simply solve the NPV formula for the interest rate that will make NPV equal zero:

$$0 = \sum_{n=0}^{N} \frac{CF_n}{(1 + IRR)^n}$$ (13-8)

Unfortunately, we cannot solve directly for the interest rate that will set NPV equal to zero. We either have to use trial-and-error to determine the appropriate rate, or we have to rely on a calculator or computer, both of which use much the same approach.

Internal Rate of Return Benchmark

Once we calculate the IRR, we must then compare the decision statistic to the relevant cost of capital for the project—the average rate of return necessary to pay back the project's capital providers, given the risk that the project represents:

Accept project if IRR $\geq$ Cost of capital

Reject project if IRR $<$ Cost of capital (13-9)

At this point, you may find yourself getting a little confused about which rate is *the* interest rate. The IRR statistic will equal the expected rate of return, which incorporates risk (as probabilities). We will compare that expected rate of return to the cost of capital, which is often called the *required rate of return*. Up until this chapter, we have been using all of these phrases interchangeably for "*the*" interest rate. We have been able to get away with doing so up until now because stocks, bonds, and all other types of financial assets trade in relatively liquid, competitive financial markets. In liquid markets, the rate of return you expect to earn is pretty much equal to the

internal rate of return (IRR)
A capital budgeting technique that generates decision rules and associated metrics for choosing projects based on the implicit expected geometric average of a project's rate of return.

EXAMPLE 13-6   IRR Calculation LG13-4

For interactive versions of this example visit www.mhhe.com/canM2e

Looking once again at our sample set of normal cash flows from Table 13.6, IRR will be the solution to:

$$0 = \frac{-\$10{,}000}{(1 + IRR)^0} + \frac{\$2{,}500}{(1 + IRR)^1} + \frac{\$3{,}500}{(1 + IRR)^2} + \frac{\$5{,}000}{(1 + IRR)^3} + \frac{\$4{,}000}{(1 + IRR)^4} + \frac{\$2{,}000}{(1 + IRR)^5}$$

$IRR = 0.2062$, or 20.62%

CALCULATOR HINTS

[CF0] =	−10000
[CF1] =	2500
[CF2] =	3500
[CF3] =	5000
[CF4] =	4000
[CF5] =	2000
[IRR]	
[CPT] [IRR] =	20.61

Similar to Problems 13-9, 13-10, 13-19, 13-25

rate of return you require for taking on that particular security's risk. In such an environment, it makes sense to assume that we are not going to be able to earn any "extra" return or economic profit above and beyond what is appropriate for the amount of risk we are bearing.

Remember, though, that in this chapter, we are no longer talking about *financial* assets, but *real* assets such as land, factories with inventories, and production lines. These types of assets do not generally trade in perfectly competitive markets. Instead, they trade in quite illiquid markets in which an individual or a firm can gain at least some amount of market or monopoly power by virtue of technological, legal, or marketing expertise.

We noted this difference at the beginning of this chapter when we differentiated between formulas for financial assets such as stocks and bonds and the equations we are using in this chapter to value projects. The formulas we used to value stocks and bonds use "=" signs because those assets trade in nearly perfectly competitive markets, where what you get is (approximately, at least) equal to what you paid for it. Here, on the other hand, we examine situations in which companies seek to choose projects that are worth *more* than what they pay for them—leaving room for economic profit. That is why all of these capital budgeting rules use ">" and "<" signs.

So, when we deal with physical asset projects, we have to expect that two different rates of return will arise. The best way to think of these two rates is as the *expected* rate of return (IRR), and the *required* rate of return (*i*). We only want to invest in projects where the rate we expect to get (IRR) is larger than the rate investors require (*i*) based on the project's expected return, including risk.[1]

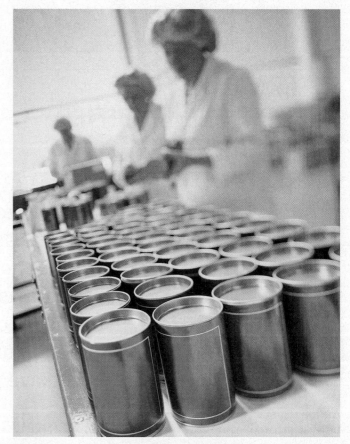

Real assets like production lines don't trade in perfectly, competitive markets.

[1] As explained in earlier chapters, by definition the expected rate of return incorporates risk.

Problems with Internal Rate of Return LG13-4, LG13-5

As we mentioned above, IRR will give the same accept/reject decision as NPV if two conditions hold true:

1. The project has normal cash flows.

2. We are evaluating the project independently of other projects—that is, we are not considering mutually exclusive projects.

To see the problems that arise if these conditions do *not* hold, we will make use of a tool called the **NPV profile.** This is simply a graph of a project's NPV as a function of possible capital costs. The NPV profile for our sample project with normal cash flows from Table 13.6. appears as Figure 13.1.

As you can see, the NPV profile for this normal set of cash flows slopes downward. As we noted above concerning the

relationship between the PB and DPB statistics, increasing values of i with a normal set of cash flows affect the present value of positive cash flows, but not that of negative cash flows. All sets of normal cash flows will therefore share this general, downward-sloping shape.

Note that IRR appears on this graph as the intersection of the NPV profile with the x-axis (horizontal)—the intersection will represent the interest rate where NPV equals exactly zero. With normal cash flows such as these, the constant downward slope of the NPV profile dictates that only one such intersection will exist for each project.

IRR and NPV Profiles with Non-Normal Cash Flows LG13-5

But let us revisit what happens to the NPV profile if cash flows are *not* normal. The NPV profile will not necessarily slope continually downward and thus may cross over the x-axis at more than one interest rate. In this case we may find more than one valid IRR for which NPV equals zero. An example of such an NPV profile, constructed from the cash flows in Table 13.7, appears in Figure 13.2.

In this instance, the project shows two valid IRRs: one at 23.62 percent and another at 88.62 percent. Which of these two should we use as "the" statistic? Well, it depends on what the firm pays as the actual cost of capital. If the firm pays 12 percent for capital, then using either of these two IRR values would generate a correct "accept" decision, as the project *does* have a positive NPV at $i = 12$ percent. But what if the firm paid a relatively high cost of capital, for example, 30 percent? Then the IRR rule would have us accept the project if we used the higher value (88.62 percent) as the project's statistic, but reject it if we

time out!

13-5 Is it possible for the NPV profile of a finite set of normal cash flows to never cross the *x*-axis?

13-6 Suppose a normal set of cash flows has an IRR equal to zero. Would NPV accept or reject such a project?

▼**FIGURE 13.1** NPV Profile for Sample Normal Cash Flows

This graph presents our sample project's NPV profile, using the normal cash flows listed in Table 13.6.

used the lower IRR (23.62 percent). Of course, since the project generates a negative NPV if *i* is 30 percent, we would actually want to reject the project.

Using the IRR technique requires a bit more complicated analysis if we come across more than one valid IRR like this. Perhaps the best thing to do in such a situation is to simply use a decision statistic other than IRR on projects with non-normal cash flows.

If you (or, more likely, upper management) insist on using IRR with non-normal cash flows, you are going to need to use some trial and error to find all the possible IRRs. It will help to know how many there might possibly be. According to the Rule of Signs,[2] we can end up with no more different positive IRRs than the number of sign changes in the cash flows—that is, inflows to outflows or outflows to inflows. Since our non-normal cash flow set shows two sign changes (one change from positive to negative and one change from negative to positive), we know that the two IRRs we have found constitute the entire possible set.

Luckily we can solve IRR's problems associated with non-normal cash flows by using the modified internal rate of return (MIRR), which also accounts for another problem associated with IRR, that of an unrealistic reinvestment rate assumption.

Differing Reinvestment Rate Assumptions of NPV and IRR

In addition to the problems associated with non-normal cash flows and handling mutually exclusive projects discussed above, IRR also has a different assumption than NPV concerning what we do with the cash inflows once we get them back. IRR assumes that any cash inflows will be

reinvested in another project with the same earning power as the first project, while NPV assumes that cash inflows will be reinvested at the cost of capital, *i*.

Which assumption is more reasonable? NPV's is, because one way to effectively "earn" the cost of capital is to pay back your capital investors, and all companies have this option. One the other hand, IRR's assumption seems a little far-fetched: If we assume that this project beat out a bunch of other projects at step 2 of the decision process, it must have had the highest possible IRR among all the alternatives, right? But now that the cash flows are rolling in, we find another project with *the same "highest"* possible rate of return? Seems like a little too much to expect, doesn't it?

Modified Internal Rate of Return Statistic LG13-4

The name **modified internal rate of return** is a little misleading. We are going to calculate IRR the same way we did before, but we are going

▼ **FIGURE 13.2** NPV Profile for Sample Non-Normal Cash Flows

Notice how the graph shows two valid IRRs. Which one should you use?

[2]First described by René Descartes in his 1637 manuscript *La Geometrie.*

the
Math Coach on...
MIRR Using Financial Calculators and Spreadsheet Programs

" Notice that we have assumed that both the positive and negative cash flows get moved using the same interest rate. In many situations, practitioners want to move the negative cash flows using one interest rate and the positive cash flows using another. Because of this, both spreadsheet programs and more advanced financial calculators allow for the use of two interest rates in exactly that way. For now, if you are using a calculator or spreadsheet program that requires two interest rates, just use the cost of capital for both rates. "

modified internal rate of return (MIRR) A capital budgeting method that converts a project's cash flows using a more consistent reinvestment rate prior to applying the IRR decision rule.

to *modify* the set of cash flows to account for the cost of capital before we calculate IRR. We first use the cost of capital to "move" all the negative cash flows to the initial project start date (i.e., time 0) and all the positive cash inflows to the project termination date—and only *then* will we use the regular steps to calculate IRR.

EXAMPLE 13-7

MIRR Calculation LG13-4

For interactive versions of this example visit www.mhhe.com/canM2e

Turning once again to the sample non-normal project cash flows in Table 13.7, and assuming that the firm still faces a cost of capital of 12 percent, we convert the cash flows as shown in Table 13.8.

▼ **TABLE 13.8** MIRR Cash Flow Adjustments for Sample Project with Non-Normal Cash Flows

Year:	0	1	2	3	4	5
Cash flow	$5,000.00	−$10,000.00	−$3,000.00	$5,000.00	$4,000.00	$2,000.00
Present value (if negative)		−8,928.57	−2,391.58			
Sum of PVs	−11,320.15					
Future value (if positive)	8,811.71			6,272.00	4,480.00	2,000.00
Sum of FVs						21,563.71
Modified CFs	−11,320.15					21,563.71

CALCULATOR HINTS

[CF0] = 5000
[CF1] = −10000
[CF2] = −3000
[CF3] = 5000
[CF4] = 4000
[CF5] = 2000
[IRR]
[I] = 12
[RI] = 12
[CPT] [MOD] = 13.76

SOLUTION:

With this new set of modified cash flows, the (M)IRR is:

$$0 = \frac{-\$11,320.15}{(1 + IRR)^0} + \frac{\$21,563.71}{(1 + IRR)^5}$$

IRR = 0.1376, or 13.76%

Since our (M)IRR decision statistic exceeds the 12 percent cost of capital, we would accept the project under the MIRR method, which uses the same benchmark as the IRR rule. Notice that, regardless of how many possible IRRs a project may have, it will only ever have *one* possible MIRR. When you take a bunch of cash flows and convert them into two cash flows, one negative and one positive, you will only ever see one change in sign.

Similar to Problems 13-11, 13-12, 13-20, 13-26

CHAPTER 13 | Weighing Net Present Value and Other Capital Budgeting Criteria **317**

IRRs, MIRRs, and NPV Profiles with Mutually Exclusive Projects LG13-5

Even if we use the MIRR method for a project with non-normal cash flows, we can still run into problems if we try to use either IRR or MIRR to choose between mutually exclusive projects.

Two (or more) projects are **mutually exclusive** if management can accept one, the other, or neither, but not both, projects. As discussed below, if we compare two mutually exclusive projects using a rate-based decision statistic, problems can arise if the projects' cash flows exhibit differences in *scale* or *timing* (i.e., the size of the initial investment in each project). Over time, a "large" project that earns a slightly lower rate of return may be a better choice for the firm than a "small" project that earns a higher rate, but we will see that the rate-based decision techniques do not do well in choosing between these types of alternative projects.

What makes two or more projects mutually exclusive? Generally, mutually exclusive projects either share a common asset or target a common market, but the firm can only spare resources for one of them, or the market may only accept one product. Consider the prototypical example of mutually exclusive projects: A landowner owns two plots of land on either side of a river that people want to cross, and she is considering either building a bridge or operating a ferry for that purpose.

First, let us assume there is enough land on each lot to provide space for bridge footings or for pier pilings, but not for both. In this case, the two plots of land represent assets that the two projects can not share, which is the first factor making the bridge and the ferry mutually exclusive projects.

Second, even if the land provided enough room to build both ferry landing piers and bridge footings, it stands to reason that no one would take the ferry if they could simply drive across the bridge—so the two projects' inability to share a potential target market provides a second reason why the projects are mutually exclusive.

▼ **TABLE 13.9** Sample Mutually Exclusive Projects

Year:	0	1	2	3	4	5
Project A cash flows	−$800	$600	$500	$ 40	$ 0	$200
Project B cash flows	−400	250	200	250	50	100

To see the problems associated with choosing between two mutually exclusive projects using a rate-based decision statistic, let us suppose that we face a choice between two mutually exclusive projects with the cash flows shown in Table 13.9.

Calculating the NPVs for these two projects across a range of possible rates as shown in Table 13.10 will yield the NPV profiles shown in Figure 13.3.

As you can see approximately (and calculate precisely), A's IRR equals 32.88 percent and B's equals 40.59 percent. You will also notice that the two NPV profiles cross each other in the first quadrant, and that intersection is exactly what is going to cause problems for us as we try to apply an IRR decision rule.

To see why, recall our discussion of the three-step decision process necessary for mutually exclusive projects, and go through that process for both NPV and IRR using a couple of not-so-arbitrary interest rates.

▼ **TABLE 13.10** NPV Profiles

i	NPV A	NPV B
0%	$540.00	$450.00
2	487.66	409.68
4	439.15	372.48
6	394.07	338.08
8	352.09	306.22
10	312.91	276.63
12	276.27	249.12
14	241.92	223.48
16	209.67	199.54
18	179.33	177.16
20	150.75	156.20
22	123.76	136.54
24	98.25	118.07
26	74.10	100.69
28	51.21	84.32
30	29.47	68.88
32	8.80	54.30
34	−10.86	40.51
36	−29.61	27.45
38	−47.49	15.07
40	−64.56	3.33

▼FIGURE 13.3 NPV Profiles for Sample Mutually Exclusive Projects

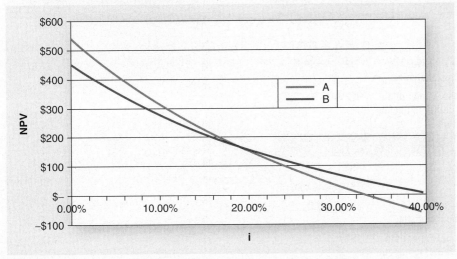

Notice how the two profiles cross each other in the first quadrant. How will this intersection affect how we apply an IRR decision?

First, let us suppose that the project would be subject to a 30 percent cost of capital. In that case, as per Table 13.11, the NPV for project A would be $29.47 and the NPV for project B would be $68.88. This means that project B would win the runoff. Since its NPV is greater than zero, the NPV decision rule would have us also accept project B.

Likewise, if we were using IRR in the same situation, project B's IRR of 40.59 percent would win the runoff over project A's IRR of 32.88 percent. But since 40.59 percent is greater than the 30 percent cost of capital, IRR would also have us accept project B. These results appear in Table 13.11.

mutually exclusive projects Groups or pairs of projects where you can accept one but not all.

interest-rate cognizant A decision-making process that includes the cost of capital calculation.

Now let's see what happens if the cost of capital is, say, 10 percent. In that case, as per Table 13.10, the NPV for project A would be $312.91 and the NPV for project B would be $276.63. This means that project A would now win the runoff and, ultimately, would be accepted under the NPV statistic as well.

However, if we were using IRR in the same situation, project B's IRR of 40.59 percent would *still* win the runoff over project A's IRR of 32.88 percent, and, since 40.59 percent is greater than the 30 percent cost of capital, IRR would continue to have us accept project B. These results are summarized in Table 13.12.

Why is IRR still choosing project B, despite the 30 percent cost of capital? Well, IRR's refusal to "change its mind"[3] arises from a combination of how we calculate the statistic and how we use it in the three-step decision process. Think about it this way: The NPV statistic includes the cost of capital in its calculation, so when we get to the runoff, NPV is able to make an **interest-rate-cognizant** decision. IRR does not incorporate the cost of capital in calculating its statistic. Therefore, when it reaches step 2 it will always be comparing the same two IRRs for two particular projects, no matter what the cost of capital is.

The implication here is that for any interest rate to the right of where the two NPV profiles cross, NPV and IRR will make the same accept/reject decision. For rates to the left of the crossover point, NPV will choose the right project but IRR will chose the wrong project. So, since it is sort of important, how do we calculate the rate at which the two NPV profiles cross? Well, we mathematically manipulate each NPV profile until one comes as close to the x-axis as possible, and then figure out the rate at which they cross each other as the IRR of the other project.

It sounds complicated, but it really is not. All we have to do is subtract one project's cash flows from those of the other, period by period, to get a new set of cash flows that show the differences between the original two projects' cash

▼TABLE 13.11 Decision Process for Projects A and B at *i* = 30%

NPV	
1. Compute the statistic for each project.	NPV$_A$ = $29.47
	NPV$_B$ = $68.88
2. Have a runoff between the mutually exclusive projects, choosing the one with the best statistic.	NPV$_B$ > NPV$_A$
3. Compare the computed statistic for the winner of the runoff to the benchmark to decide whether to accept or reject.	**NPV$_B$ > 0**

IRR	
1. Compute the statistic for each project.	IRR$_A$ = 32.88%
	IRR$_B$ = 40.59%
2. Have a runoff between the mutually exclusive projects, choosing the one with the best statistic.	IRR$_B$ > IRR$_A$
3. Compare the computed statistic for the winner of the runoff to the benchmark to decide whether to accept or reject.	**IRR$_B$ > 30%**

[3]You will sometimes hear this phenomenon referred to as IRR being "myopic," which is the technical name for nearsightedness.

NPV		
1. Compute the statistic for each project.	NPV_A = $312.91	
	NPV_B = $276.63	
2. Have a runoff between the mutually exclusive projects, choosing the one with the best statistic.	$NPV_A > NPV_B$	
3. Compare the computed statistic for the winner of the runoff to the benchmark to decide whether to accept or reject.	**$NPV_A > 0$**	

IRR		
1. Compute the statistic for each project.	IRR_A = 32.88%	
	IRR_B = 40.59%	
2. Have a runoff between the mutually exclusive projects, choosing the one with the best statistic.	$IRR_B > IRR_A$	
3. Compare the computed statistic for the winner of the runoff to the benchmark to decide whether to accept or reject.	**$IRR_B > 10\%$**	

▼ **TABLE 13.13** Difference in Cash Flows—Sample Mutually Exclusive Projects

Year:	0	1	2	3	4	5
Project A cash flows	−$800	$600	$500	$ 40	$ 0	$200
Project B cash flows	−400	250	200	250	50	100
A-B	−400	350	300	−210	−50	100

▼ **TABLE 13.14** NPV Profile, A-B

i	NPV, A-B
0%	$ 90.00
2	77.98
4	66.67
6	55.99
8	45.88
10	36.28
12	27.15
14	18.45
16	10.13
18	2.17
20	−5.45
22	−12.77
24	− 19.81
26	−26.59
28	−33.12
30	−39.41
32	−45.49
34	−51.37
36	−57.06
38	−62.56
40	−67.89

flows, and then find the IRR of these differences. The values for the cash flows of "A-B," the calculated values for the NPV profile of these differences, and the resulting translated NPV profiles appear in Table 13.13, Table 13.14, and Figure 13.4. Note that A' will be equal to "A-B," while B' will be the new, translated, x-axis.

The crossover rate will be equal to the IRR of the "A-B" cash flows:

$$0 = \frac{-\$400}{(1 + IRR)^0} + \frac{\$350}{(1 + IRR)^1} + \frac{\$300}{(1 + IRR)^2} + \frac{-\$210}{(1 + IRR)^3}$$
$$+ \frac{-\$50}{(1 + IRR)^4} + \frac{\$100}{(1 + IRR)^5}$$

$IRR = 0.1856$, or 18.56%

So now, IRR will give us the correct answer for these two projects if i is greater than 18.56 percent, and will choose exactly the wrong project if i is less than 18.56 percent.

You may have noticed that the set of "A-B" cash flows is *not* normal. How, then, can we feel comfortable using IRR to calculate "the" crossover rate given that we have previously decided not to use IRR with non-normal cash flows? Well, this is a special case: We knew that the two original projects' cash flows *were*

CALCULATOR HINTS

[CF0] = −$400
[CF1] = $350
[CF2] = $300
[CF3] = −$210
[CF4] = −$ 50
[CF5] = $100
[IRR]
[CPT] [IRR] = 18.56

normal. So we intuitively understood that their NPV profiles, while not exactly straight lines, at least sloped downward continually. So, if two "almost straight" lines do cross, they are probably only going to cross once. That is, we expect only one solution to the IRR problem for the "A-B" differences in cash flows.

Also notice that we have to worry about IRR giving incorrect decisions only if the NPV profiles cross in the so-called first quadrant of the graph. If they cross outside this quadrant at a rate higher than both projects' IRRs, then we do not have to worry about problems with IRR choosing the wrong project. Any cost of capital high enough for IRR to reject the project at the third step of the IRR decision process will also result in a negative NPV.[4]

---

[4]Actually, in such cases the IRR rule will still choose the wrong project at step 2 of the decision process, the runoff, but the last step of the decision process, the comparison with the benchmark, will save us. The wrong project may be chosen at the runoff, but if they are both bad projects, they will be rejected anyway.

▼FIGURE 13.4 Translated NPV Profiles

two sample mutually exclusive projects of Table 13.9 and compute each project's MIRR (using a 12 percent rate to move the cash flows), we will still see that the MIRR of project B (23.39 percent) will *always* be greater than the MIRR of project A (18.85 percent), causing the MIRR to also choose the incorrect project to the left of the crossover rate.

There is an old joke in computer programming that gets reused every time a major software product is revised: "That's not a bug, it's a feature!" Well, this "problem" we are experiencing with IRR and MIRR, as well as NPV, truly *is* a feature. It's a feature of all rate-based decision statistics: They tend to focus on the rate of return *per dollar invested* at the expense of ignoring *how many* dollars are getting invested in each project. IRR and MIRR chose project B all the time because, even though it sometimes had a lower NPV, it was always earning a higher rate of return *per dollar invested*.

What causes this confusion? The two cash flows differ in timing and scale. Looking back at the cash flows associated with our two mutually exclusive projects again (shown again in Table 13.15) we see that project B costs only half as much as project A. Also, project B has a "flatter," less steeply sloped, indifference curve.

time **out!**

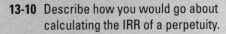

13-7 Suppose two projects with normal cash flows, X and Y, have exactly the same required initial investment, but X has a longer payback. Can we say anything about X's IRR versus that of Y?

13-8 Assume you are evaluating a project that requires an initial investment of $5,000 at time zero, then another investment of $4,000 in one year, after which it will have cash inflows of $3,000 per year for five years. How many IRRs could this project possibly have?

time **out!**

13-9 For a project with normal cash flows, what would you expect the relationship to be between its IRR and its MIRR?

13-10 Describe how you would go about calculating the IRR of a perpetuity.

MIRR Strengths and Weaknesses

As we have constructed it, the MIRR statistic explicitly corrects IRR's faulty and unreasonable reinvestment rate assumption, implicitly fixing any problems with non-normal cash flows along the way. However, it does not correct the problem of IRR choosing the wrong mutually exclusive project for a particular range of rates. For example, even if we go back to the

PROFITABILITY
INDEX LG13-6

Another popular rate-based decision technique is the **profitability index (PI).** PI is based upon NPV, so its results will more closely resemble NPV than will those of IRR or PB/DPB. PI takes a project's NPV and standardizes it by simply dividing by the project's initial investment. The result: We get a

▼TABLE 13.15 Sample Mutually Exclusive Projects

Year:	0	1	2	3	4	5
Project A cash flows	−$800	$600	$500	$ 40	$ 0	$200
Project B cash flows	−400	250	200	250	50	100

EXAMPLE 13-8 Calculation of Profitability Index LG13-6

Turning yet again to the sample project cash flows in Table 13.6, the PI for that project will be:

$$PI = \frac{\$2,258.15}{\$10,000} = 22.58\%$$

Similar to Problems 13-13, 13-14, 13-22, 13-28

> "Remember that the NPV already includes the necessary investment, so any PI above zero is "found money" or the present value of expected economic profits."

decision statistic that measures "bang per buck invested." Such a measure comes in handy when the firm faces resource constraints concerning how much capital is available for new projects.

Profitability Index Statistic

The mathematics of computing the PI are straightforward:

$$PI = \frac{NPV}{CF_0} \qquad (13\text{-}10)$$

Profitability Index Benchmark LG13-6

Because of its close linkage to the NPV statistic, PI's benchmark is, not surprisingly, identical to that of NPV:

$$\text{Accept project if } PI \geq 0$$

$$\text{Reject project if } PI < 0 \qquad (13\text{-}11)$$

Though we might be tempted to assume that, like IRR and MIRR, we should compare the PI to the cost of capital, this is not the case. Remember that the NPV already includes the necessary investment, so any PI above zero is "found money" or the present value of expected economic profits. In this case, the PI of 22.58 percent is telling us that the project will, roughly

speaking, earn the equivalent of a 22.58 percent return on the initial investment of $10,000 above and beyond the return necessary to repay the initial cost.

time out!

13-11 There is another version of the PI that uses the present value of just the future cash flows as its numerator instead of the NPV. How would you expect that version's benchmark to change from the version of PI we initially discussed?

13-12 Suppose you have a project whose discounted payback is equal to its termination date. What can you say for sure about its PI? (*Hint:* What will the project's NPV be?)

Get Online

mhhe.com/canM2e

for study materials including self-test
problems with solutions, quizzes,
research projects, minicases, and videos

Your Turn...

Questions

1. Is the set of cash flows depicted below normal or non-normal? Explain. *(LG13-1)*

Time:	0	1	2	3	4	5
Cash flow	−$100	−$50	−$80	$0	$100	$100

2. Derive an accept/reject rule for IRR similar to equation 13-8 that would make the correct decision on cash flows that are non-normal, but which always have one large positive cash flow at time zero followed by a series of negative cash flows. *(LG13-1)*

Time:	0	1	2	3	4	5
Cash flow	+	−	−	−	−	−

3. Is it possible for a company to initiate two products that target the same market that are *not* mutually exclusive? *(LG13-1)*

4. Suppose that your company used "APV," or "All-the-Present Value-Except-CF$_0$," to analyze capital budgeting projects. What would this rule's benchmark value be? *(LG13-3)*

5. Under what circumstances could payback and discounted payback be equal? *(LG13-2)*

6. Could a project's MIRR ever *exceed* its IRR? *(LG13-4)*

7. If you had two mutually exclusive, normal-cash-flow projects whose NPV profiles crossed at all points, for which range of interest rates would IRR give the right accept/reject answer? *(LG13-5)*

8. Suppose a company wanted to double the firm's value with the next round of capital budgeting project decisions. To what would it set the PI benchmark to make this goal? *(LG13-6)*

9. Suppose a company faced different borrowing and lending rates. How would this range change the way that you would compute the MIRR statistic? *(LG13-4)*

Problems

13-1 NPV with Normal Cash Flows Compute the NPV for Project M and accept or reject the project with the cash flows shown below if the appropriate cost of capital is 8 percent. *(LG13-3)*

Project M						
Time:	0	1	2	3	4	5
Cash flow	−$1,000	$350	$480	$520	$600	$100

13-2 NPV with Normal Cash Flows Compute the NPV statistic for Project Y and indicate whether the firm should accept or reject the project with the cash flows shown below if the appropriate cost of capital is 12 percent. *(LG13-3)*

Project Y					
Time:	0	1	2	3	4
Cash flow	−$8,000	$3,350	$4,180	$1,520	$300

13-3 NPV with Non-Normal Cash Flows Compute the NPV statistic for Project U and recommend whether the firm should accept or reject the project with the cash flows shown below if the appropriate cost of capital is 10 percent. *(LG13-3)*

Project U						
Time:	0	1	2	3	4	5
Cash flow	−$1,000	$350	$1,480	$520	$300	−$100

13-4 NPV with Non-Normal Cash Flows Compute the NPV statistic for Project K and recommend whether the firm should accept or reject the project with the cash flows shown below if the appropriate cost of capital is 6 percent. *(LG13-3)*

Project K						
Time:	0	1	2	3	4	5
Cash flow	−$10,000	$5,000	$6,000	$6,000	$5,000	−$10,000

13-5 Payback Compute the payback statistic for Project B and decide whether the firm should accept or reject the project with the cash flows shown below if the appropriate cost of capital is 12 percent and the maximum allowable payback is three years. *(LG13-2)*

Project B						
Time:	0	1	2	3	4	5
Cash flow	−$11,000	$3,350	$4,180	$1,520	$0	$1,000

13-6 Payback Compute the payback statistic for Project A and recommend whether the firm should accept or reject the project with the cash flows shown below if the appropriate cost of capital is 8 percent and the maximum allowable payback is four years. *(LG13-2)*

Project A						
Time:	0	1	2	3	4	5
Cash flow	−$1,000	$350	$480	$520	$300	$100

13-7 Discounted Payback Compute the discounted payback statistic for Project C and recommend whether the firm should accept or reject the project with the cash flows shown below if the appropriate cost of capital is 8 percent and the maximum allowable discounted payback is three years. *(LG13-2)*

Project C						
Time:	0	1	2	3	4	5
Cash flow	−$1,000	$480	$480	$520	$300	$100

13-8 Discounted Payback Compute the discounted payback statistic for Project D and recommend whether the firm should accept or reject the project with the cash flows shown below if the appropriate cost of capital is 12 percent and the maximum allowable discounted payback is four years. *(LG13-2)*

Project D						
Time:	0	1	2	3	4	5
Cash flow	−$11,000	$3,350	$4,180	$1,520	$0	$1,000

13-9 IRR Compute the IRR statistic for Project E and note whether the firm should accept or reject the project with the cash flows shown below if the appropriate cost of capital is 8 percent. *(LG13-4)*

Project E						
Time:	0	1	2	3	4	5
Cash flow	−$1,000	$350	$480	$520	$300	$100

13-10 IRR Compute the IRR statistic for project F and note whether the firm should accept or reject the project with the cash flows shown below if the appropriate cost of capital is 12 percent. *(LG13-4)*

Project F					
Time:	0	1	2	3	4
Cash flow	−$11,000	$3,350	$4,180	$1,520	$2,000

13-11 MIRR Compute the MIRR statistic for Project I and indicate whether to accept or reject the project with the cash flows shown below if the appropriate cost of capital is 12 percent. *(LG13-4)*

Project I					
Time:	0	1	2	3	4
Cash flow	−$11,000	$5,330	$4,180	$1,520	$2,000

13-12 MIRR Compute the MIRR statistic for Project J and advise whether to accept or reject the project with the cash flows shown below if the appropriate cost of capital is 10 percent. *(LG13-4)*

Project J						
Time:	0	1	2	3	4	5
Cash flow	−$1,000	$350	$1,480	−$520	$300	−$100

13-13 PI Compute the PI statistic for Project Z and advise the firm whether to accept or reject the project with the cash flows shown below if the appropriate cost of capital is 8 percent. *(LG13-6)*

Project Z						
Time:	0	1	2	3	4	5
Cash flow	−$1,000	$350	$480	$650	$300	$100

13-14 PI Compute the PI statistic for Project Q and indicate whether you would accept or reject the project with the cash flows shown below if the appropriate cost of capital is 12 percent. *(LG13-6)*

Project Q					
Time:	0	1	2	3	4
Cash flow	−$11,000	$3,350	$4,180	$1,520	$2,000

13-15 Multiple IRRs How many possible IRRs could you find for the following set of cash flows? *(LG13-1)*

Time:	0	1	2	3	4
Cash flow	−$11,000	$3,350	$4,180	$1,520	$2,000

13-16 Multiple IRRs How many possible IRRs could you find for the following set of cash flows? *(LG13-1)*

Time:	0	1	2	3	4
Cash flow	−$211,000	−$39,350	$440,180	$217,520	−$2,000

INTERMEDIATE PROBLEMS

Use this information to answer the next six questions. If a particular decision method should not be used, indicate why.

Suppose your firm is considering investing in a project with the cash flows shown below, that the required rate of return on projects of this risk class is 8 percent, and that the maximum allowable payback and discounted payback statistics for the project are 3.5 and 4.5 years, respectively.

Time:	0	1	2	3	4	5	6
Cash flow	−$5,000	$1,200	$2,400	$1,600	$1,600	$1,400	$1,200

13-17 Payback Use the payback decision rule to evaluate this project; should it be accepted or rejected? *(LG13-2)*

13-18 Discounted Payback Use the discounted payback decision rule to evaluate this project; should it be accepted or rejected? *(LG13-2)*

13-19 IRR Use the IRR decision rule to evaluate this project; should it be accepted or rejected? *(LG13-4)*

13-20 MIRR Use the MIRR decision rule to evaluate this project; should it be accepted or rejected? *(LG13-4)*

13-21 NPV Use the NPV decision rule to evaluate this project; should it be accepted or rejected? *(LG13-3)*

13-22 PI Use the PI decision rule to evaluate this project; should it be accepted or rejected? *(LG6)*

Use this information to answer the next six questions. If you should not use a particular decision technique, indicate why.

Suppose your firm is considering investing in a project with the cash flows shown below, that the required rate of return on projects of this risk class is 11 percent, and that the maximum allowable payback and discounted payback statistics for your company are 3 and 3.5 years, respectively.

Time:	0	1	2	3	4	5
Cash flow	−$235,000	$65,800	$84,000	$141,000	$122,000	$81,200

13-23 Payback Use the payback decision rule to evaluate this project; should it be accepted or rejected? *(LG13-2)*

13-24 Discounted Payback Use the discounted payback decision rule to evaluate this project; should it be accepted or rejected? *(LG13-2)*

13-25 IRR Use the IRR decision rule to evaluate this project; should it be accepted or rejected? *(LG13-4)*

13-26 MIRR Use the MIRR decision rule to evaluate this project; should it be accepted or rejected? *(LG13-4)*

13-27 NPV Use the NPV decision rule to evaluate this project; should it be accepted or rejected? *(LG13-3)*

13-28 PI Use the PI decision rule to evaluate this project; should it be accepted or rejected? *(LG13-6)*

ADVANCED PROBLEMS

Use the project cash flows for the two mutually exclusive projects shown below to answer the following two questions.

Time:	Project A Cash Flow	Project B Cash Flow
0	−$725	−$850
1	100	200
2	250	200
3	250	200
4	200	200
5	100	200
6	100	200
7	100	200

13-29 NPV Profiles Graph the NPV profiles for both projects on a common chart, making sure that you identify all of the "crucial" points. *(LG13-5)*

13-30 IRR Applicability For what range of possible interest rates would you want to use IRR to choose between these two projects? For what range of rates would you NOT want to use IRR? *(LG13-5)*

13-31 Multiple IRRs Construct an NPV profile and determine EXACTLY how many nonnegative IRRs you can find for the following set of cash flows: *(LG13-5)*

Time:	0	1	2	3	4	5	6	7
Cash flow	−$200	$400	$150	−$100	−$100	−$300	$200	−$300

13-32 Multiple IRRs Construct an NPV profile and determine EXACTLY how many nonnegative IRRs you can find for the following set of cash flows: *(LG13-5)*

Time:	0	1	2	3	4	5	6	7
Cash flow	−$150	$275	$150	−$100	$300	−$300	$200	−$300

Working Capital
Management
and Policies

I n this chapter, we want to focus on the major trade-off implicit in funding net working capital. By and large, the trade-off involves comparing how much it costs the firm to carry an investment in current assets with the **shortage costs** associated with the firm not having enough cash, inventory, or accounts receivable.

As we'll see, the firm's ideal solution to providing net working capital would be to get someone else to foot the bill. Though this may be a valid approach to fund *some* of the firm's current assets, it's usually difficult to get someone else to cover the *entire* amount of net

continued on p. 330

LEARNING GOALS

LG14-1   Set overall objectives of a good working capital policy.

LG14-2   Discuss how net working capi- tal serves the firm.

LG14-3   Analyze the firm's operating and cash cycles to determine what funding for current assets the firm needs.

LG14-4   Model the optimal trade-off between carrying costs and shortage costs that dictates the firm's current asset investment.

LG14-5   Compare the flexible and restrictive approaches to financing current assets.

LG14-6   Differentiate among sources of short-term financing available for funding current assets.

LG14-7   Justify the firm's need to hold cash.

LG14-8   Use the Baumol and Miller-Orr models for determining cash policy.

LG14-9   Identify sources of float and show how to control float for the firm's disbursement and collection functions.

L14-10   Identify firms' choices for using excess cash.

L14-11   Connect the firm's credit terms and collection policy and the amount of capital the firm has invested in accounts receivable.

continued from p. 329

working capital necessary to run the firm efficiently. We will, however, discuss how to shift those costs elsewhere as much as possible in this chapter by covering the following topics:

1. How to determine the optimal amount of investment in current assets.

2. How to measure the portion of current assets that the firm is responsible for funding.

3. How to choose the source of funding for that portion of current assets. ■

»viewpoints

business APPLICATION

Chewbacca Manufacturing expects sales of $32 million next year. CM's cost of goods sold normally runs at 55 percent of sales; inventory requirements are usually 10 percent of annual sales; the average accounts receivable balance is one-sixth of annual sales; and the average accounts payable balance is 5 percent of sales. If all sales are on credit, what will Chewbacca's level of net working capital and its cash cycle be?

REVISITING THE BALANCE-SHEET MODEL OF THE FIRM LG14-1, LG14-2

Remember our discussion of the balance sheet in Chapter 2. At a glance, the balance sheet brings together the firm's assets or sources of financing and its liabilities, or investments, as Table 14.1 shows. Net working capital reflects the need for the firm to generate funds to stay in business and maximize profit.

Earlier in the book, we discussed the fact that the current assets, while the most liquid, are also usually less profitable than fixed assets. This explains why some managers like to think of net working capital as *"the net amount of current assets that the firm has to fund, above and beyond those that someone else funds for us."*

To put it bluntly, net working capital is a necessary evil: Most firms can't sell finished goods without inventory to display, or without offering to sell to customers on credit, and so forth. Firms incur costs associated with keeping inventory on hand and with selling to customers on credit.

But just because a firm has to fund *some* net working capital does not mean that it should fund all of it or even a large portion of it. Instead, the firm should, to the best of its ability, ensure that the marginal benefit of each dollar tied up in net working capital equals the marginal **opportunity cost** of not having that dollar invested in fixed assets with positive net present value (NVP).

time out!

14-1 Why might a firm's creditors *not* think of net working capital as a necessary evil, but rather as a good thing?

14-2 If demand for a firm's products suddenly slows down so that inventory increases while sales decrease, how will the firm's needs for net working capital react?

▼ **TABLE 14.1** The Basic Balance Sheet

Total Assets		Total Liabilities and Equity
Current assets:	Net working capital	Current liabilities:
Cash and marketable securities		Accrued wages and taxes
Accounts receivable		Accounts payable
Inventory		Notes payable
Fixed assets:		Long-term debt
Gross plant and equipment		Stockholders' equity:
Less: Depreciation		Preferred stock
Net plant and equipment		Common stock and paid-in surplus
Other long-term assets		Retained earnings

TRACING CASH AND NET WORKING CAPITAL LG14-3

To trace cash flows through the firm's operations, we must measure the **operating cycle**—the time necessary to acquire raw materials, turn them into finished goods, sell them, and receive payment for them—as well as the firm's **cash cycle.**

Let's think of net working capital as the portion of current assets that the firm must fund (above and beyond those assets funded by current liabilities). Then we can similarly think of the firm's cash cycle as the portion of the operating cycle that the firm must finance.

The Operating Cycle

To measure the firm's operating cycle, we need to turn to some of the ratios that we discussed in Chapter 3:

$$\text{Operating cycle} = \frac{\text{Days' sales in inventory}} {} + \frac{\text{Average collection period}} {} \qquad (14\text{-}1)$$

$$= \frac{\text{Inventory} \times 365}{\text{Cost of goods sold}}$$

$$+ \frac{\text{Accounts receivable} \times 365}{\text{Credit sales}}$$

The Cash Cycle

The firm's cash cycle will simply be the operating cycle minus the average payment period as shown in Figure 14.1:

$$\frac{\text{Cash}}{\text{cycle}} = \frac{\text{Operating}}{\text{cycle}} - \frac{\text{Average payment}}{\text{period}} \qquad (14\text{-}2)$$

$$= \frac{\text{Operating}}{\text{cycle}} - \frac{\text{Accounts payable} \times 365}{\text{Cost of goods sold}}$$

shortage costs Costs associated with not having sufficient cash, inventory, or accounts receivable.

opportunity cost The cost or forgone opportunity of using an asset already in use by the firm, or a person already employed by the firm, in a new project.

operating cycle The time required to acquire raw materials and to produce, sell, and receive payment for the finished goods.

cash cycle The operating cycle minus the average payment period.

EXAMPLE 14-1 — Calculation of Operating Cycle LG14-3

For interactive versions of this example visit www.mhhe.com/canM2e

Suppose that MMK Industries has annual sales of $1 million, cost of goods sold of $650,000, average inventories of $116,000, and average accounts receivable of $150,000. Assuming that all MMK's sales are on credit, what will be the firm's operating cycle?

SOLUTION:
The operating cycle will be equal to:

$$\text{Operating cycle} = \frac{\text{Inventory} \times 365}{\text{Cost of goods sold}} + \frac{\text{Accounts receivable} \times 365}{\text{Credit sales}}$$

$$= \frac{\$116,000 \times 365}{\$650,000} + \frac{\$150,000 \times 365}{\$1,000,000}$$

$$= 65.14 \text{ days} + 54.75 \text{ days}$$

$$= 119.89 \text{ days}$$

So it will take MMK almost 120 days from the time it receives raw materials to produce, market, sell, and collect the cash for the finished goods.

Similar to Problems 14-13, 14-14

carrying costs
The opportunity costs associated with having capital tied up in current assets instead of more productive fixed assets and explicit costs necessary to maintain the value of the current assets.

Note that even though it will take MMK almost 120 days to turn the raw materials into cash, the cash cycle indicates that the firm will have to foot the bill for its production cycle for only 52.50 days of that time. This is the crux of managing the firm's operating and cash cycles: Minimize the number of days that the firm has to pay for its production cycle.

▼**FIGURE 14.1** Relationship between Operating and Cash Cycles

Days' Sales in Inventory ⟵⟶ Average Collection Period

Operating Cycle

Average Payment Period ⟵⟶ Cash Cycle

The firm's cash cycle will simply be the operating cycle minus the average payment period.

time out!

14-3 How will a firm affect its operating cycle if it can reduce inventory on hand?

14-4 When we compare two firms, will the one with the longer cash cycle tend to have more or less net working capital requirements than the one with a shorter cash cycle, everything held equal? Why?

SOME ASPECTS OF SHORT-TERM FINANCIAL POLICY LG14-4

In the last section, we derived the cash cycle by first determining the operating cycle and then subtracting the payment cycle. This derivation suggests two obvious ways that firms can reduce their net working capital needs.

1. They can manage their need for current assets.

2. They can seek to obtain as many current liabilities as economically feasible to fund the current assets that they do need.

The Size of the Current Assets Investment

Choosing the optimal level of investment in each current asset type involves a trade-off between carrying costs and shortage costs.

EXAMPLE 14-2

For interactive versions of this example visit www.mhhe.com/canM2e

Calculation of Cash Cycle LG14-3

Extending the previous example, assume that MMK's average accounts payable balance is $120,000. What will be the firm's cash cycle?

SOLUTION:

The cash cycle will be equal to:

$$\text{Cash cycle} = \text{Operating cycle} - \frac{\text{Accounts payable} \times 365}{\text{Cost of goods sold}}$$

$$= 119.89 \text{ days} - \frac{\$120,000 \times 365}{\$650,000}$$

$$= 119.89 \text{ days} - 67.38 \text{ days}$$

$$= 52.50 \text{ days}$$

Similar to Problems 14-15, 14-16

finance at work // : global

Carrying costs are associated with having current assets and fall into two general categories:

1. The opportunity costs associated with having capital tied up in current assets instead of more productive fixed assets.
2. Explicit costs necessary to maintain the value of the current assets.

For example, a car dealer who purchases used vehicles and keeps them in inventory would incur the opportunity cost of not being able to invest the money paid for the used vehicles in a more lucrative opportunity, such as new hybrid vehicles. Our car dealer will also have to pay rental or lease payments on the piece of property where the used cars are on display and any maintenance costs necessary to keep the cars ready to sell.

Shortage costs are the costs associated with not having enough current assets and can include opportunity costs such as sales lost due to not having enough inventory on hand, as well as any explicit transaction fees paid to replenish the particular type of current asset. For example, consider a camera shop that has a reorder policy to reorder particular lenses from its supplier only if a customer comes in asking for them, and even then to order only one at a time. In today's business environment, most customers who are seeking an item want it *now*. If that item is out of stock at one store, the customer will probably buy it either at another store or online, resulting in lost sales to the store. If, in addition, we assume that stores pays a shipping fee for every order placed—or if they get quantity discounts if they order in bulk—then their policy will probably result in higher shipping fees. Stores may also face higher costs of goods sold than they would if they ordered in quantity.

Carrying costs will increase, and shortage costs will decrease, as a firm buys more of any particular asset. Therefore, firms should ideally try to choose the point of an asset's lowest total cost, which occurs where marginal carrying and shortage costs are equal. This level is identified as CA* in Figure 14.2.

▼ **FIGURE 14.2** Carrying and Shortage Costs

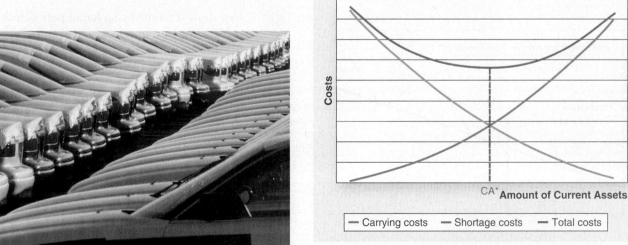

CA* **Amount of Current Assets**

— Carrying costs   — Shortage costs   — Total costs

The point at which marginal carrying and shortage costs are equal (CA) is the optimal level of investment for each current asset category.

Vehicles kept in inventory incur an opportunity cost.

Alternative Financing Policies for Current Assets LG14-5

In a perfect world, a firm would use long-term debt and equity to finance long-term (i.e., fixed) assets and short-term debt to finance current assets. Such an approach would allow the firm to maturity-match assets with their corresponding liabilities, resulting in a low or nonexistent level for net working capital. As we have previously discussed, in the real world, net working capital is usually positive for most firms. The implication: At least some portion of current assets must be financed with long-term debt, equity, or a mixture of both.

Assuming that most firms can expect to have some steady, stable need for current assets throughout their calendar year and additional demand for current assets that fluctuates on some seasonal cycle, a growing firm's total demand for assets would resemble that shown in Figure 14.3.

So, a firm in such a situation faces the basic question of whether it should finance the peaks or the valleys of total asset demand (or somewhere in between) using long-term financing. Figure 14.4, Figure 14.5, and Figure 14.6 illustrate some of these choices.

We usually refer to the decision to finance the peaks of asset demand with long-term debt and equity, shown in Figure 14.4, as a *flexible financing policy*. It provides the firm with a surplus of cash and marketable securities most of the time—except during peak asset demand.

On the opposite side of the continuum, we refer to a decision to finance the troughs or valleys of asset demand with long-term debt and equity, shown in Figure 14.5, as a *restrictive financing policy*. Under this policy, the firm will have to

Flexible financing policy reflects the decision to finance the peaks of asset demand with long-term debt and equity.

▼ **FIGURE 14.5** Restrictive Financing of CA

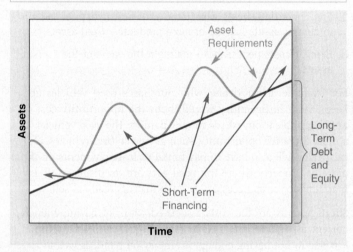

Restrictive financing policy reflects the decision to finance the troughs of asset demand with long-term debt and equity.

▼ **FIGURE 14.3** Components of Current Assets

A firm makes long- or short-term financing decisions by examining the peaks and valleys of total asset demand.

seek short-term financing for all peak demand fluctuations for current assets, as well as for in-between demand situations. In some ways, this policy is the most "conservative"; on the other hand, it's also the least convenient for the firm, as it involves seeking some level of short-term financing almost all of the time.

A third choice is to follow a *compromise financing policy,* wherein the firm finances the seasonally adjusted average level of asset demand with long-term debt and equity. The firm uses both short-term financing and short-term investing as needed. Figure 14.6 illustrates such a policy. Which approach works best? As is the case with almost all working capital decisions, it depends on several factors:

compensating balance Amount of money required to be kept in a firm's deposit accounts with a lender according to a lending arrangement.

asset-based loans Short-term loans secured by a company's assets.

FIGURE 14.6 Compromise Financing of CA

Compromise financing policy reflects the decision to finance the seasonally adjusted average level of asset demand with long-term debt and equity.

- Current and future expected interest rate levels. If we expect rates to rise in the future, the firm may want to lock in fixed rates for a longer time by shifting toward a flexible financing policy. With falling rates, the opposite would of course hold true.

- The spread between short- and long-term rates. Long-term borrowing usually costs more than short-term financing, but the "gap" (called the *spread*) between the two terms may be historically small or large, encouraging firms to shift to a more flexible or restrictive policy, respectively.

- Alternative financing availability and costs, discussed below. Firms with easy and sustained access to alternative sources will want to shift toward more restrictive policies.

time out!

14-5 Suppose that the gap between short-term rates and long-term rates increases. Would firms tend to shift more toward flexible current asset financing policies or toward more restrictive policies?

14-6 If a firm offers longer credit terms to its customers, what will happen to its carrying costs?

THE SHORT-TERM FINANCIAL PLAN LG14-6

Firms that follow any financing policy other than a flexible financing plan will find themselves forced to seek short-term financing at times. Depending on their industry, they may find themselves using unsecured loans, secured loans, or other sources of short-term financing.

Unsecured Loans

For most businesses—particularly smaller ones—the most common way to cover a short-term financing need is to apply at a bank for a commercial loan. The company may expect to need such short-term loans repeatedly in the future—perhaps because it is following a restrictive financing policy but faces seasonal fluctuations in asset demand, as discussed above. If the bank deems the firm creditworthy enough, the bank will usually grant the firm a *line of credit,* upon which the firm can draw and then pay off repeatedly as the firm goes through those seasonal fluctuations.

Fees for lines of credit can be both explicit (usually taking the form of an interest rate equal to the bank's prime lending rate plus a small premium) and implicit (as a compensating balance requirement and/or a bank's up-front commitment fee). A **compensating balance** is a percentage of the borrowed money (usually 5 to 10 percent) that the bank requires the firm to keep on deposit in the firm's bank accounts. In return, the bank agrees to lend money to the firm.[1]

Commitment fees, if charged, are usually calculated as a flat percentage of the credit line. But banks also charge commitment fees based on the portion of the line of credit "taken down" (i.e., used by the firm) or even of the portion *not* taken down. The amount of fees the bank charges for a line of credit and their type will depend on whether the bank is trying to encourage the use of the line of credit or not.

Secured Loans

Asset-based loans are short-term loans secured by a company's assets. Secured loans carry lower interest rates than unsecured loans, so it is usually in the firm's best interest to provide security (or collateral) when it can. Though real estate, accounts receivable, inventory, and equipment are all sometimes used

[1]If you are sitting there wondering why the bank doesn't just lend only 95 percent or 90 percent of the money, instead of lending it all and then asking for part of it back, the answer has to do with bank regulations. Though it's too complicated to go into great detail, the simple answer is that bank regulators see a difference between a $900,000 loan and a $1,000,000 loan with a 10 percent compensating balance requirement, though they may sound the same to us.

factor An entity that will buy accounts receivable from a firm before they are due on a discounted basis.

assignment A process whereby the firm borrows money from another entity, providing in return both a lien on the accounts receivable and the right of recourse.

recourse The legal right to hold a firm responsible for payment of a debt if the debtors do not repay as promised.

commercial paper A money-market security, issued by large banks and medium-to-large corporations, that matures in nine months or less.

banker's acceptance (B.A.) A short-term promissory note issued by a corporation, bearing the unconditional guarantee (*acceptance*) of a major bank.

to back asset-based loans, most firms seeking such a loan to finance seasonal fluctuations in current assets will typically prefer to use inventory or accounts receivable as security for the loan, as they won't wish to encumber long-term assets such as real estate or equipment.

Accounts receivable can either be sold outright to a factor or assigned. A **factor** is an entity who will buy accounts receivable on a discounted basis before they are due, with the spread between the discounted price and the receivable's face value providing the factor with expected compensation for both the time value of money and the expected level of defaults among the accounts receivable. **Assignment** is a process whereby the firm borrows money from another entity, providing in return a lien on the accounts receivable as well as the right of **recourse** (i.e., the legal right to hold the firm responsible for payment of the debt if the accounts receivable debtors do not repay as promised).

Firms can also use their inventory as collateral for an inventory loan, a secured short-term loan used to purchase that inventory. Inventory loans include blanket inventory liens, trust receipts, and field warehousing financing. The major difference between the three lies with the question of who owns and keeps the inventory in question:

- Under a blanket inventory lien, the lender gets a lien against all the firm's inventory, but the firm retains ownership and possession.

- When the borrower holds the inventory in trust for the lender, with any proceed from the sale of the inventory being the property of that lender, the document acknowledging this loan commitment is referred to as the *trust receipt.*

- In field warehousing financing, a public warehouse company takes possession and supervises the inventory for the lender.

Other Sources

Two other primary sources of short-term financing are commercial paper issues and financing through banker's acceptances. **Commercial paper** is a money-market security, issued by large banks and medium-to-large corporations, that matures in nine months or less. Since these issues have such short durations, and since firms use the proceeds only for current transactions, commercial paper (or simply *paper*) is exempt from registering as a security with the SEC. The corresponding lack of paperwork and regulations to issue short-term debt, along with the fact that commercial paper is usually issued only by firms with very high credit rankings, makes commercial paper cheaper than using a bank line of credit.

A **banker's acceptance (B.A.)** is a short-term promissory note issued by a corporation, bearing the unconditional guarantee (*acceptance*) of a major bank. The bank guarantee makes them very safe, and the rates are usually roughly equivalent to those charged on commercial paper.

time out!

14-7 If its bank started charging fees to a firm based upon the portion of a line of credit not taken down, how would the firm's financing policy for current assets likely change? Why would a bank take such a stance?

14-8 If a firm starts selling its accounts receivable to a factor, how will the firm's cash cycle change?

Firms can also use their inventory as collateral for an inventory loan.

CASH MANAGEMENT LG14-7

One confusing distinction in this class is the difference between a *cash flow* and a *cash account*. Cash flows, which we have discussed in a number of contexts within this book, such as estimating cash flows for proposed new projects in Chapter 12, are a good thing. A cash account, on the other hand, is a current asset account just like all the other current asset accounts we have been discussing, and it has exactly the same attributes of high liquidity and low profitability that inventory and accounts receivable accounts have. Sure, cash may be a bit more liquid than inventory or money tied up in accounts receivable, but it's not really any more profitable.[2]

Reasons for Holding Cash

A firm may keep part of its capital tied up in cash for three primary reasons:

1. **Transaction facilitation:** Firms need cash to pay employees' wages, taxes, suppliers' bills, interest on debts, and stock dividends. Though the firm will have cash coming in from

[2]Most students realize that cash held in the form of currency does not earn any interest, but they are usually surprised to learn that, by law, corporate checking accounts at commercial banks are not allowed to earn interest, either. Though firms find legal ways around that restriction, we'll leave that discussion to a more advanced text on financial institutions.

transaction facilitation The use of cash to pay employees' wages, taxes, suppliers' bills, interest on debts, and dividends on stock.

day-to-day operations and any financing activities, the inflows and outflows are not usually perfectly synchronized, so the firm will need to keep enough cash on hand to meet reasonable transaction demands.

2. Compensating balances: As we previously discussed, firms must often keep a certain percentage of borrowed funds in their checking accounts with their lending institution. Since lenders are exempt from paying interest on corporate checking accounts, compensating balances become a cheap source of funds for the lender and represent opportunity costs for borrowing firms.

3. Investment opportunities: In some industries, investment opportunities come and go very quickly. Sometimes, this happens even too quickly for the firm to arrange a loan or seek other financing, so having excess cash on hand may allow the firm to take advantage of investment opportunities that would otherwise be impossible to transact.

To determine how much cash to keep on hand, firms must trade off the opportunity costs associated with holding too much cash against the shortage costs of not holding enough. The two standard models for calculating the trade-offs are the Baumol Model and the Miller-Orr Model.

time out!

14-9 In what types of industries would firms need more cash on hand for transaction facilitation? In what industries might firms need less?

14-10 If a firm is going to take a loan with a bank that has a compensating balance requirement, how does that affect the amount of money the firm must borrow?

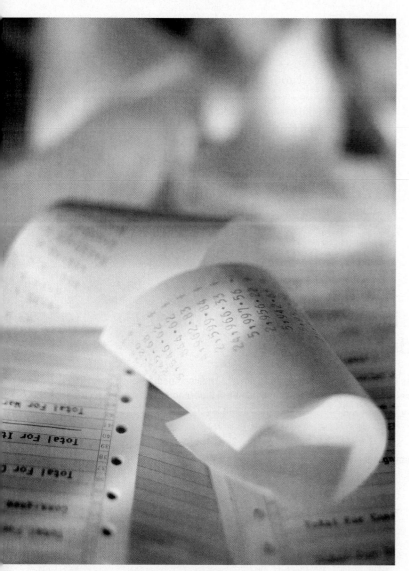

Firms need cash to pay employees' wages and payroll taxes among other things.

Determining the Target Cash Balance: The Baumol Model LG14-8

An economist named William Baumol developed the first model designed to minimize the sum of the opportunity costs associated with holding cash and the trading costs associated with converting other assets to cash.[3] Baumol's model is intuitively appealing,

[3]See W. S. Baumol, "The Transactions Demand for Cash: An Inventory Theoretic Approach," *Quarterly Journal of Economics* 66, no. 4 (November 1952), pp. 545–556.

safety stock Excess amounts of a current asset kept on hand to meet unexpected shocks in demand.

replenishment level The level to which the cash account is "refilled" when marketable securities are sold to recapitalize it.

and analysts still use it in industries for which cash outflows are fairly predictable. For other industries, its use is more problematic due to the model's rather unrealistic assumptions:

• The model assumes that the firm has a constant, perfectly predictable disbursement rate for cash. In reality, disbursement rates are much more variable and unpredictable.

• The model assumes that no cash will come in during the period in question. Since most firms hope to make more money than they pay out, and usually have cash inflows at all times, this assumption is obviously at odds with what we usually see.

• The model does not allow for any **safety stock** of extra cash to buffer the firm against an unexpectedly high demand for cash.

In Baumol's model, cash is assumed to start from a **replenishment level,** C, and then decline smoothly to a value of zero. When cash declines to zero, it can be immediately replenished by selling another C worth of marketable securities, for which the firm has to pay a trading cost of F.

Thus the model implies that cash levels will follow a cyclical pattern throughout the year. For example, if a firm sells $20,000 worth of marketable securities each time it needs to replenish cash and disburses $5,000 in cash each week, then the cash balance would cycle every four weeks, as shown in Figure 14.7.

Notice another implication of the cash being disbursed at a constant rate. The average cash level should equal one-half of the replenishment level, C/2. If the firm can earn an interest rate

FIGURE 14.7 Cash Flow Patterns of the Baumol Model

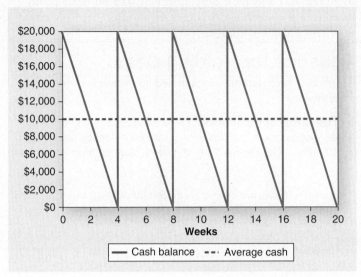

In this model, when cash declines to zero, it can be immediately replenished by selling marketable securities.

i on marketable securities, then keeping an average cash balance of C/2 will impose an opportunity cost on the firm of:

$$\text{Opportunity cost} = \frac{C}{2} \times i \qquad (14\text{-}3)$$

If we also assume that a particular firm faces an annual demand for cash of T, then the firm will need to sell marketable securities T/C times during the year, incurring in the process annual trading costs of:

$$\text{Trading cost} = \frac{T}{C} \times F \qquad (14\text{-}4)$$

EXAMPLE 14-3

Optimal Cash Replenishment under Baumol Model LG14-8

For interactive versions of this example visit www.mhhe.com/canM2e

Suppose that AFS Industries faces an annual demand for cash of $2 million, incurs transaction costs of $150 every time it sells marketable securities, and can earn 6 percent on its marketable securities. What will be the firm's optimal cash replenishment level?

SOLUTION:

The optimal cash replenishment level will be:

$$C^* = \sqrt{2TF/i}$$
$$= \sqrt{2(\$2,000,000)(\$150)/0.06}$$
$$= \$100,000$$

Similar to Problems 14-19, 14-20

| EXAMPLE 14-4 | **Calculation of Optimal Return Point and Upper Limit for the Miller-Orr Model** LG14-8 |

For interactive versions of this example visit www.mhhe.com/canM2e

Suppose that Dandy Candy Inc. would like to maintain its cash account at a minimum level of $100,000 but expects the standard deviation in net daily cash flows to be $5,000; the effective annual rate on marketable securities will be 8 percent per year, and the trading cost per sale or purchase of marketable securities will be $200 per transaction. What will be Dandy Candy's optimal cash return point and upper limit?

SOLUTION:

The daily interest rate on marketable securities will equal:

$$i_{day} = \sqrt[365]{1.08} - 1 = 0.000211$$

And the optimal cash return point and upper limit will equal:

$$Z^* = \sqrt[3]{3F\sigma^2/4i_{day}} + L$$
$$= \sqrt[3]{3(\$200)(\$5,000)^2/(4 \times 0.000211)} + \$100,000$$
$$= \$126,101.72$$

$$H^* = 3Z^* - 2L$$
$$= \$178,305.16$$

Similar to Problems 14-21, 14-22, 14-23, 14-24

The firm's total annual costs associated with its cash management policy will therefore be:

$$\text{Total cost} = \frac{C}{2} \times i + \frac{T}{C} \times F \qquad (14\text{-}5)$$

Solving this for the value of C that minimizes annual costs, C^*, yields:

$$C^* = \sqrt{2TF/i} \qquad (14\text{-}6)$$

Determining the Target Cash Balance: The Miller-Orr Model

The Miller-Orr model takes a different approach to calculating the optimal cash management strategy.[4] It assumes that daily net cash flows are normally distributed and allows for both cash inflows and outflows. This model bases its computations on information about:

- The lower control limit, L.

- The trading cost for marketable securities per transaction, F.

- The standard deviation in net daily cash flows, σ.

[4]See M.H. Miller and D. Orr, "A Model of the Demand for Money by Firms," *Quarterly Journal of Economics* 80, no. 3 (August 1966), pp. 413–435.

- The daily interest rate on marketable securities, i_{day}.

Using their model, Miller and Orr show that the optimal cash return point, Z^*, and upper limit for cash balances, H^*, are equal to:

$$Z^* = \sqrt[3]{3F\sigma^2/4i_{day}} + L \qquad (14\text{-}7)$$
$$H^* = 3Z^* - 2L \qquad (14\text{-}8)$$

Note that the firm determines L, and that the firm can set it to a non-zero number to recognize the use of safety stock.

The optimal cash return point, Z^*, is analogous to the replenishment level, C^*, in Baumol's model, but with one key difference. Since Baumol's model only allowed for cash disbursements, C^* was always "replenished to" from a level of zero. In the Miller-Orr model, Z^* will be the replenishment level to which cash is replenished when the cash level hits L, but it will also be the return level that cash is brought back *down* to when cash hits H^*.

As Figure 14.8 shows, the firm will reduce cash to $126,101.72 by buying marketable securities when the cash balance gets up to $178,305.16, and it will increase cash to $126,101.72 by selling marketable securities when the cash balance gets down to $100,000.

▼ FIGURE 14.8 Cash Flow Patterns of the Miller-Orr Model

The model assumes that the distribution of daily net cash flows is normally distributed and allows for both cash inflows and outflows.

Other Factors Influencing the Target Cash Balance

Even the Miller-Orr model, the more realistic of the two models because it deals with both cash inflows and outflows, still ignores fundamental factors that influence firms' cash management practices. First, firms also have the option of borrowing short-term to meet unexpected demands for cash. Though the short-term borrowing rate faced by the firm is likely to be more expensive than the opportunity cost incurred by selling marketable securities,[5] this isn't necessarily the comparison that matters. If the probability of an unexpected demand for cash causing a firm to borrow in the short term is low enough, or if the amount of interest to be earned by investing in longer-term securities is sufficiently higher than that to be earned on marketable securities, then it might be worth it for the firm to risk occasionally paying a relatively high interest rate on short-term borrowing if it can earn a substantially higher return by investing the funds that would have been tied up in marketable securities in something more lucrative.

Second, the authors of both models developed their ideas when buying and selling marketable securities was a relatively expensive and time-consuming proposition. The costs and delays of trading securities have fallen dramatically since the advent of the Internet. The cost has fallen so much that many large firms habitually use all or the majority of their available cash to purchase overnight securities. If trading costs are low enough that it makes sense for the firm to incur at least two sets of trading costs each day—one for selling enough marketable securities in the morning to make it through the day, and another for purchasing marketable securities at the end of the business day—then it's also probable that any unforeseen demand for cash *during* the day can probably be met fairly cheaply by selling marketable securities as needed. Or, put another way, the transactions costs associated with trading securities have fallen so dramatically relative to the opportunity costs of not having cash invested in marketable securities that keeping any "extra" money idle in cash just doesn't make sense.

Finally, both models ignore the fact that many firms must keep compensating balances in their deposit accounts as part of borrowing agreements with their banks. If the compensating balance requirement was a constant amount or percentage, then we could adjust the Miller-Orr model so that L included the compensating balance, but many firms must only keep a certain minimum compensating balance *on*

> ## "The costs and delays of trading securities have fallen dramatically since the advent of the Internet."

[5]To see why, go down to your local bank or savings and loan and see which is higher: the rate it pays on savings accounts or the rate it charges on short-term borrowing.

time out!

14-11 What effect does increasing the standard deviation in daily cash flows have on the cash return point in the Miller-Orr model?

14-12 If you were asked to adjust the Baumol model to reflect the need to keep a minimum cash balance, how would you go about doing so?

average. This implies that an unforeseen demand for cash that causes a firm's deposit account to temporarily dip below the minimum compensating balance can be offset by keeping a corresponding amount of excess cash in the account in a later period. Even the more modern Miller-Orr model does not allow for that.

FLOAT CONTROL: MANAGING THE COLLECTION AND DISBURSEMENT OF CASH LG14-9

The economic definition of cash includes undeposited checks, but as we all know, an undeposited check is not as liquid as the same amount of cash sitting inside your checking account. So another component of a good cash management policy involves making sure that checks clear in a timely manner.

Accelerating Collections

The period of time between when a check is written and when it clears and the funds are available for use is referred to as **float.** As illustrated in Figure 14.9, the checks sent to a firm experience three different types of collection float:

1. Mail float is the length of time that checks are en route to the firm, either through the postal system or through some sort of electronic transfer.

2. In-house processing float is the length of time needed for the firm to process and deposit check payments from its customers once they have been received.

3. Availability float is the length of time necessary for a check to clear through the banking system once it has been deposited.

Together, these three types of float span the entire length of time between the customer sending a payment and the firm receiving cash in its account.

Several different techniques can help firms reduce collection float:

• A lockbox system is a collection of geographically dispersed post office boxes, each maintained for the firm by a local bank to the respective box. For firms with hundreds or thousands of customers spread across a large region, the ideal situation is to have enough locations so that no customer is more than a couple of hundred miles from one of the firm's post office boxes. By having customers send their payments to the closest post office box, and then having the local bank pick

up and handle the payment processing several times a day, the firm can reduce both mail float and in-house processing float.

• Concentration banking accelerates cash collections from customers by having funds sent to several geographically situated regional banks and then transferred to a main concentration account in another bank. The funds can be transferred through depository transfer checks and electronic transfers.

• Wire transfers are the fastest way of transmitting money from a local bank into the concentration bank. Banks within the United States utilize the Society for Worldwide Interbank Financial Telecommunication (SWIFT) system to make payments to banks in countries outside of the United States. Bank-to-bank transfers conducted within the United States take place over the Fedwire system, which uses the Federal Reserve System and its assignment of bank routing numbers.

Delaying Disbursements

Disbursement float is the delay between the firm sending out a payment and the money being taken out of the firm's bank

float The period of time between when a payment is sent out and when the money is actually received by the collecting firm.

FIGURE 14.9 Components of Collection Float

Mail Float	In-House Processing Float	Availability Float
	Collection Float	

Cash is not always liquid due to collection float.

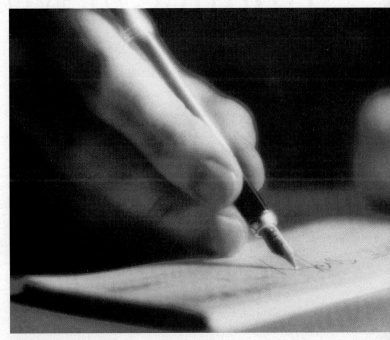

The period of time between when a check is written and when it clears is referred to as float.

zero-balance account A corporate checking account which keeps a zero balance, automatically transferring in just enough funds to cover any checks received on the account from another interest-bearing account.

draft Similar to a check, but payable by the issuing firm rather than by its bank.

account. Two legal ways to increase disbursement float involve keeping the cash available to the firm until the very last moment:

- A **zero-balance account** is a checking account that the firm sets up so that the bank agrees to automatically transfer funds from an interest-bearing account to pay off any checks presented. Since zero-balance accounts never contain excess cash, they represent one way that firms can get around regulations against corporations having interest-bearing checking accounts.

- **Drafts** resemble checks, but differ in that they are payable by the firm issuing them rather than payable by a bank. When a draft is sent to the firm's bank for payment, the bank must present the draft to the firm *before* disbursing the funds.

Ethical and Legal Questions

Using collected cash before actually receiving it, or continuing to use disbursed cash after you have sent a check out, can earn your firm higher returns, but this practice is illegal. The most extreme form of taking illegal advantage of disbursement float is a practice called *check kiting*, which is any sort of fraud that involves drawing out money from a bank account with insufficient funds to cover the check.

The Check Clearing for the 21st Century Act, which allows for transmitting electronic images of checks rather than the physical paper checks themselves, has greatly reduced the incidence of check kiting by substantially shortening the time required for a check to be cleared from one bank to another.

time out!

14-13 In Japan, many consumers pay their bills by electronic deduction from their checking accounts instead of using paper checks. What effect do you think this has on the collection float of Japanese firms versus that of American firms?

14-14 What's the difference between a lockbox system and concentration banking?

finance at work // : global

Cultural Differences in Preferences for Paying Bills

Japan's Postal Savings Bank, the world's largest bank, has long been used as an example of the efficiencies available to both individuals and businesses of electronic transactions. Electronic transactions are instantaneous transactions that use security authentication rather than conventional check-clearing processes to transfer funds from a buyer to the seller.

However, in 2006, one of the Nikkei trade papers summarized the results of a survey among Japanese women regarding payment methods used for Internet shopping. Not surprisingly, the vast majority (56 percent) of respondents purchasing goods over the Internet reported that they used credit cards for their transactions. However, the distribution of the rest of the responses illustrates a vast difference between alternative payment pipelines that American and Japanese consumers use.

For example, 17.6 percent of Japanese respondents ordered online, then paid in cash at their local convenience store; 13.1 percent paid COD when the mailman delivered the goods; and 4.3 percent paid using electronic transfers from their post office savings accounts.

What implications does this have for the money management policies of firms doing business in Japan? Well, given that a far larger percentage of Americans probably pay for their online purchases with credit cards, and that the alternative methods of payment listed above could be expected to have different clearing times than do payments received through a merchant's credit card account, it's something that firms seeking to do business in Japan should consider.

Want to know more?

Key Words to Search for Updates: **"Marketing Tip: Payment Methods"** (see the Japan Marketing News blog at www.japanmarketingnews.com/consumer_industry_data/index.html)

credit terms A listing
of the credit period, the
cash discount, and the
type of credit instrument to
be used.

INVESTING IDLE CASH LG14-10

As both the Baumol and Miller-Orr models imply, firms habitually move cash into and out of marketable securities in order to partially offset the opportunity costs of having capital tied up in current assets. Most large firms will manage their marketable securities investments themselves. Smaller firms will typically invest through an independently managed money-market fund or by letting their bank transfer all available excess funds at the end of each business day into a sweep account, which will then be invested on their behalf.

Why Firms Have Surplus Cash

Firms tend to have surplus cash available either due to seasonal fluctuations in their cash flow patterns, or in preparation for planned expenditures. Seasonal fluctuations in the amount of cash on hand can occur as a result of either cyclical sales or cyclical purchases of raw materials. For example, a firm that produces swimming pool accessories will obviously experience higher sales from spring through late fall, and a firm that distributes fresh vegetables purchased on the

The cash cycle will be equal to:

Cash Cycle = Operating Cycle - Average Payment Period

Operating Cycle − Accounts Payable · 365 / Cost of Good Sold

= 119.89 days − [($120,000 x 365)/$650,000]
= 119.89 days − 67.38 days
= 52.50 days

Even though it will take about 120 days to turn their raw materials into cash, the cash cycle indicates that they will only have to foot the bill for their production cycle for 52.50 days of that time.
Minimize the number of days that the firm has to pay for its production cycle.

View guided examples
at mhhe.com/canM2e

01:56 / 01:58

👍 Caitlin Wysocki and four others like this.

Caitlin Wysocki The TI-83 walkthrough saved me SO much time on my assignment!
10 hours ago · Like

write a comment...

spot market will have higher cash outflows during the harvest season.

Firms' cash balances may also temporarily increase immediately prior to a planned expenditure, either because they have been "saving up" for the expenditure, or because they issued stocks or bonds in advance of the expenditure but need someplace to "park" the funds until they are needed.

What to Do with Surplus Cash

As mentioned, firms usually put surplus cash into money-market securities. These include Treasury bills, federal funds and repurchase agreements, commercial paper, negotiable certificates of deposit, and banker's acceptances.

CREDIT MANAGEMENT LG14-11

As is the case with the firm's cash management policy, the firm's optimal credit policy will trade off the opportunity cost of lost sales (if the firm does not grant credit or is too conservative in terms of the credit it does grant) against the carrying costs associated with funding the accounts receivable plus the expected costs of default on the accounts receivable.

Credit Policy: Terms of the Sale

As a minimum, the **credit terms** of sale usually contain at least the credit period, the cash discount, and a description of the type of credit instrument. The credit period is the maturity of the credit that the firm is willing to extend, which varies based on attributes of the goods being sold and the customer purchasing the goods. For example, perishable goods will usually carry a lower credit period, regardless of who is purchasing them. Creditworthy, established customers will probably be given better credit terms than customers the firm has not dealt with before.

time out!

14-15 Should a firm with nonseasonal cash flows that lacks any good prospective investments keep excess cash on hand? Why or why not?

14-16 Suppose a firm has a temporary surplus of cash meant to fund an upcoming expansion project. Why might it not wish to invest these funds in capital-market (as opposed to money-market) securities?

To encourage early repayment, firms will often offer a percentage discount if the bill is paid within a certain time period. For example, a firm that quotes customers terms of "2/10, net 30" is offering them the choice between paying the entire bill within 30 days or taking a 2 percent discount off the invoiced price if they pay within 10 days.

For most trade credit, the invoice is the only type of credit instrument involved. When the customer signs a copy upon receipt of the goods, the customer makes an implicit promise to pay under the terms listed on the invoice. If a firm wishes for a customer to make a more explicit acknowledgment of its ability and obligation to pay, a firm can ask the customer to sign a promissory note upon delivery of the goods or to furnish a commercial draft or banker's acceptance in advance of the delivery of the goods.

Credit Analysis

Before granting a customer credit, the firm may wish to engage in **credit analysis.** Such analysis involves a systematic determination of the potential borrower's ability and willingness to pay for the goods being provided on credit. A thorough credit analysis will look at the potential borrower's past record and its present and forecasted future financial condition, which generally involves examining the "five C's":

1. *Capacity:* Does the borrower have the legal and economic ability to pay?

2. *Character:* Does the borrower's reputation indicate a willingness to settle debt obligations?

3. *Capital:* Having assets at risk makes it more likely that the borrower will repay as promised.

4. *Collateral:* Goods that can be seized and sold, with the proceeds being used to pay the firm in the event of bankruptcy by the borrower, also makes it more likely that the customer will repay as promised.

5. *Conditions:* Any economic conditions that may affect the borrower's ability to repay the loan should also be taken into account.

Collection Policy

The firm's collection policy is aimed at collecting past-due debts from customers. The usual procedure for collecting follows a typical path of:

1. Sending one or more delinquency letters informing the customer of the past-due status of the account, asking the customer to contact the firm to discuss alternative means of repayment and pointing out what legal recourse the firm has.

2. Initiating telephone calls conveying the same information as above.

▼ **TABLE 14.2** Sample Aging Schedule

Age Bracket	Percentage of AR in Bracket
0–10 DAYS	10%
11–30 DAYS	35
31–60 DAYS	45
61–90 DAYS	7
OVER 90 DAYS	3
	100

3. Employing a collection agency.

4. Taking legal action against the customer if all else fails.

To monitor and control this process, firms use a tool called an *aging schedule,* which stratifies a firm's accounts receivable by the age of each account. For example, a firm that offers terms of 2/10, net 60 to its customers might want to measure the age of accounts receivable using the categories shown in Table 14.2.

Such an aging schedule would allow the firm to see what percentage of its customers are still eligible to take the discount (i.e., those in the "0–10 days" category), how many are past due by less than 30 days (i.e., those in the "61–90 days" category), and how many are over 30 days past due (i.e., those in the "Over 90 days" category).

Firms often link their collection policies to their aging schedules. For example, the customers in Table 14.2 that fall into the "61–90 days" category might be sent a delinquency letter, while those in the "Over 90 days" category might be phoned.

time out!

14-17 Why do firms offer customers discounts for paying early?

14-18 Should a firm always turn far-overdue bills from customers over to a collection agency or sue the customers? Why or why not?

Get Online

mhhe.com/canM2e

for study materials including self-test problems with solutions, quizzes, research projects, minicases, and videos

Your Turn...

Questions

1. Is it possible for a firm to have negative net working capital? How? *(LG14-1)*

2. Would it be possible for a decision to deny credit to your customers to be value maximizing? How? *(LG14-1)*

3. Which of the following will result in an increase in net working capital? *(LG14-2)*
   a. An increase in cash.
   b. A decrease in accounts payable.
   c. An increase in notes payable.
   d. A decrease in accounts receivable.
   e. An increase in inventory.

4. Would it be possible for a firm to have a negative cash cycle? How? *(LG14-3)*

5. If a firm's inventory turnover ratio increases, what will happen to the firm's operating cycle? *(LG14-3)*

6. If a firm's inventory turnover ratio increases, what will happen to the firm's cash cycle? *(LG14-3)*

7. Everything else held constant, will an increase in the amount of inventory on hand increase or decrease the firm's profitability? *(LG14-4)*

8. Would a firm ever use short-term debt to finance permanent current assets? Why or why not? *(LG14-5)*

9. Suppose that short-term borrowing actually becomes more expensive than long-term borrowing: How would this affect the firm's choice between a flexible financing policy and a restrictive policy? *(LG14-5)*

10. If asset-backed loans are cheaper than unsecured loans, what is the disadvantage to the firm in using an asset-backed loan? *(LG14-6)*

11. Is an increase in the cash account a source of funds or a use of funds? *(LG14-7)*

12. What will be the carrying cost associated with a compensating balance requirement? *(LG14-7)*

13. What will be the shortage cost associated with a compensating balance requirement? *(LG14-7)*

14. What would be the shortage costs associated with a restaurant not having enough cash on hand to make change? *(LG14-7)*

15. If a firm needs to keep a minimum cash balance on hand and faces both cash inflows and outflows, which of the cash management models discussed in this chapter would be more appropriate for the firm to use? *(LG14-8)*

16. What effect will increasing the trading costs associated with selling marketable securities have on the optimal replenishment level in the Baumol Model? Why? *(LG14-8)*

17. What effect will an increase in the standard deviation of daily cash flows have on the return point in the Miller-Orr model? Why? *(LG14-8)*

18. Could a firm ever have negative collection float? Why or why not? *(LG14-9)*

19. Could a firm ever have negative disbursement float? Why or why not? *(LG14-9)*

20. Would a draft have availability float? Why or why not? *(LG14-9)*

21. From our discussion of capital markets elsewhere in this book, why would you expect a firm to have a time delay between raising funds to finance a project and the expenditure of those funds on that project? *(LG14-9)*

22. What purpose does a discount on credit terms serve? What is the cost of such a discount to the offering firm? *(LG14-9)*

Problems

BASIC PROBLEMS

14-1 **Net Working Capital Requirements** JohnBoy Industries has a cash balance of $45,000, accounts payable of $125,000, inventory of $175,000, accounts receivable of $210,000, notes payable of $120,000, and accrued wages and taxes of $37,000. How much net working capital does the firm need to fund? *(LG14-2)*

14-2 **Net Working Capital Requirements** Dandee Lions Inc. has a cash balance of $105,000, accounts payable of $220,000, inventory of $203,000, accounts receivable of $319,000, notes payable of $65,000, and accrued wages and taxes of $75,000. How much net working capital does the firm need to fund? *(LG14-2)*

14-3 **Days' Sales in Inventory** Dabble Inc. has sales of $980,000 and cost of goods sold of $640,000. The firm had a beginning inventory of $36,000 and an ending inventory of $46,000. What is the length of the days' sales in inventory? *(LG14-3)*

14-4 **Days' Sales in Inventory** Sow Tire Inc. has sales of $1,450,000 and cost of goods sold of $980,000. The firm had a beginning inventory of $97,000 and an ending inventory of $82,000. What is the length of the days' sales in inventory? *(LG14-3)*

14-5 **Average Payment Period** If a firm has a cash cycle of 67 days and an operating cycle of 104 days, what is its average payment period? *(LG14-3)*

14-6 **Average Payment Period** If a firm has a cash cycle of 45 days and an operating cycle of 77 days, what is its average payment period? *(LG14-3)*

14-7 **Payables Turnover** If a firm has a cash cycle of 73 days and an operating cycle of 127 days, what is its payables turnover? *(LG14-3)*

14-8 **Payables Turnover** If a firm has a cash cycle of 54 days and an operating cycle of 77 days, what is its payables turnover? *(LG14-3)*

14-9 **Compensating Balance** Would it be worthwhile to incur a compensating balance of $10,000 in order to get a 1 percent lower interest rate on a 1-year, pure discount loan of $225,000? *(LG14-7)*

14-10 **Compensating Balance** Would it be worthwhile to incur a compensating balance of $7,500 in order to get a 0.65 percent lower interest rate on a two-year, pure discount loan of $150,000? *(LG14-7)*

14-11 **Collection Float** CM Enterprises estimates that it takes, on average, three days for customers' payments to arrive, one day for the payments to be processed and deposited by the bookkeeping department, and two more days for the checks to clear once they are deposited. What is CM's collection float? *(LG14-9)*

14-12 **Collection Float** Smelpank Inc. estimates that it takes, on average, four days for customers' payments to arrive, three days for the payments to be processed and deposited by the bookkeeping department, and three more days for the checks to clear once they are deposited. What is the firm's collection float? *(LG14-9)*

14-13 Operating Cycle Suppose that Dunn Industries has annual sales of $2.3 million, cost of goods sold of $1,650,000, average inventories of $1,116,000, and average accounts receivable of $750,000. Assuming that all of Dunn's sales are on credit, what will be the firm's operating cycle? *(LG14-3)*

14-14 Operating Cycle Suppose that LilyMac Photography has annual sales of $230,000, cost of goods sold of $165,000, average inventories of $4,500, and average accounts receivable of $25,000. Assuming that all of LilyMac's sales are on credit, what will be the firm's operating cycle? *(LG14-3)*

14-15 Cash Cycle Suppose that LilyMac Photography has annual sales of $230,000, cost of goods sold of $165,000, average inventories of $4,500, average accounts receivable of $25,000, and an average accounts payable balance of $7,000. Assuming that all of LilyMac's sales are on credit, what will be the firm's cash cycle? *(LG14-3)*

14-16 Cash Cycle Suppose that Ken-Z Art Gallery has annual sales of $870,000, cost of goods sold of $560,000, average inventories of $244,500, average accounts receivable of $265,000, and an average accounts payable balance of $79,000. Assuming that all of Ken-Z's sales are on credit, what will be the firm's cash cycle? *(LG14-3)*

14-17 Compensating Balance Interest Rate Suppose your firm is seeking an eight-year, amortizing $800,000 loan with annual payments, and your bank is offering you the choice between an $850,000 loan with a $50,000 compensating balance and an $800,000 loan without a compensating balance. If the interest rate on the $800,000 loan is 8.5 percent, how low would the interest rate on the loan with the compensating balance have to be for you to choose it? *(LG14-4)*

14-18 Compensating Balance Interest Rate Suppose your firm is seeking a four-year, amortizing $200,000 loan with annual payments and your bank is offering you the choice between a $205,000 loan with a $5,000 compensating balance and a $200,000 loan without a compensating balance. If the interest rate on the $200,000 loan is 9.8 percent, how low would the interest rate on the loan with the compensating balance have to be for you to choose it? *(LG14-4)*

14-19 Optimal Cash Replenishment Level Rose Axels faces a smooth annual demand for cash of $5 million, incurs transaction costs of $275 every time the company sells marketable securities, and can earn 4.3 percent on its marketable securities. What will be its optimal cash replenishment level? *(LG14-8)*

14-20 Optimal Cash Replenishment Level Watkins Resources faces a smooth annual demand for cash of $1.5 million, incurs transaction costs of $75 every time the firm sells marketable securities, and can earn 3.7 percent on its marketable securities. What will be its optimal cash replenishment level? *(LG14-8)*

14-21 Optimal Cash Return Point HotFoot Shoes would like to maintain its cash account at a minimum level of $25,000, but expects the standard deviation in net daily cash flows to be $4,000, the effective annual rate on marketable securities to be 6.5 percent per year, and the trading cost per sale or purchase of marketable securities to be $200 per transaction. What will be its optimal cash return point? *(LG14-8)*

14-22 Optimal Cash Return Point Veggie Burgers Inc. would like to maintain its cash account at a minimum level of $245,000 but expects the standard deviation in net daily cash flows to be $12,000, the effective annual rate on marketable securities to be 4.7 percent per year, and the trading cost per sale or purchase of marketable securities to be $27.50 per transaction. What will be its optimal cash return point? *(LG14-8)*

14-23 Optimal Upper Cash Limit Veggie Burgers Inc. would like to maintain its cash account at a minimum level of $245,000 but expects the standard deviation in net daily cash flows to be $12,000, the effective annual rate on marketable securities to be 3.7 percent per year, and the trading cost per sale or purchase of marketable securities to be $27.50 per transaction. What will be its optimal upper cash limit? *(LG14-8)*

14-24 Optimal Upper Cash Limit HotFoot Shoes would like to maintain its cash account at a minimum level of $25,000 but expects the standard deviation in net daily cash flows to be $2,000, the effective annual rate on marketable securities to be 3.5 percent per year, and the trading cost per sale or purchase of marketable securities to be $200 per transaction. What will be its optimal upper cash limit? *(LG14-8)*

cash budget
A calculation of the estimated cash flow from receipts and disbursements over a specific time period.

the cash budget

THE CASH BUDGET LG14-12

LEARNING GOALS

L14-12 Be able to create and interpret a cash budget.

The production and sales in many firms vary over the year. For example, a toy retailer will have many more sales in November and December than in March and April. On the other hand, consider the manufacturer of toys. That company would have to manufacture most of the toys it will sell to the retail stores before November. For the most part, all businesses have some seasonality in their sales and/or production cycle. This seasonality creates periods during the year in which the firm will generate large cash surpluses and other periods in which it will generate large cash deficits. Financial managers must plan ahead for such times so that the firm always has adequate cash to pay its liabilities. The **cash budget** is the instrument they use.

Consider the example of Yellow Jacket Inc. a manufacturer of coats and jackets that has decided to operate its factory at a constant pace all year. Thus, inventory builds up until early fall, when it ships large amounts of its product to retailers. The coats are mostly sold in the fall, depleting inventory. This strategy allows the company to keep a few full-time workers instead of hiring many seasonal employees and then laying them off during the slow times of the year. However, incurring costs during most of the year with few sales and then selling the coats in the fall creates a serious cash flow problem that the financial manager is responsible for resolving.

Cash budgets can be created for daily, monthly, or quarterly time periods. Given the severe seasonality of Yellow Jacket's sales, its cash budget is done monthly. The cash budget begins with a projection of sales for the year. In this case, Yellow Jacket is projecting a 10 percent increase in sales each month from the same month of the previous year. The top of Table 14A.1 shows these monthly projected sales, which are quite seasonal. Many companies have sales terms like 2/10 net 45, which means that customers must pay within 45 days of the sale—but if they pay within

▼ **TABLE 14A.1** Cash Collection

	A	B	C	D	E	F	G	H	I	J	K	L	M
1	($ millions)	**Jan**	**Feb**	**Mar**	**Apr**	**May**	**Jun**	**Jul**	**Aug**	**Sep**	**Oct**	**Nov**	**Dec**
2													
3	Sales	10	10	5	2	1	1	1	5	20	30	25	15
4													
5	Cash Collection	14.3	10.7	8.5	5.1	2.3	1.2	1.0	2.2	8.6	19.8	26.4	22.9
6													
7													
8	_Assumptions_												
9	Collection:												
10	Month 0, 30% pay with 2% discount												
11	Month 1, 50% pay												
12	Month 2, 20% pay												
13													
14	10% increase in sales from previous year												
15													

October cash collection comes from:

30% × October sales after 2% discount = 0.3 × 0.98 × $30
plus   50% × September sales = 0.5 × $20
plus   20% × August sales = 0.2 × $5

Total = $19.8

▼ **TABLE 14A.2** Cash Disbursement

($ millions)	Jan	Feb	Mar	Apr	May	Jun	Jul	Aug	Sep	Oct	Nov	Dec
	Jan	**Feb**	**Mar**	**Apr**	**May**	**Jun**	**Jul**	**Aug**	**Sep**	**Oct**	**Nov**	**Dec**
Sales	10	10	5	2	1	1	1	5	20	30	25	15
Cash Collection	14.3	10.7	8.5	5.1	2.3	1.2	1.0	2.2	8.6	19.8	26.4	22.9
Disbursements												
Materials	5.2	5.2	5.2	5.2	5.2	5.2	5.2	5.2	5.2	5.2	5.2	5.2
Wages, Salaries & Other	1.6	1.6	1.6	1.6	1.6	1.6	1.6	1.6	1.6	1.6	1.6	1.6
Taxes	0	0	2.7	0	0	2.7	0	0	2.7	0	0	2.7
Capital Projects	0	0	0	0	0	15.0	0	0	0	0	0	0
Long-Term Financing (interest & dividends)	0	1.0	5.0	0	1.0	0	0	1.0	5.0	0	1.0	0
Total Cash Disbursement	6.8	7.8	14.5	6.8	7.8	24.5	6.8	7.8	14.5	6.8	7.8	9.5

Assumptions
Disbursement:
Material is 50% of sales
Wages, etc. are 15% of sales
$15 million factory upgrade in June
$5 million in interest, twice per year
$1 million in dividends, quarterly
$2.7 million in taxes, quarterly

November cash disbursement comes from:

$5.2 million in materials purchased
+ $1.6 million in wages
+ $2.7 million in quarterly taxes paid
+ $5.0 million in semiannual interest payment on debt

$14.5 million

▼ **TABLE 14A.3** Cash Budget

($ millions)	Jan	Feb	Mar	Apr	May	Jun	Jul	Aug	Sep	Oct	Nov	Dec
	Jan	**Feb**	**Mar**	**Apr**	**May**	**Jun**	**Jul**	**Aug**	**Sep**	**Oct**	**Nov**	**Dec**
Sales	10	10	5	2	1	1	1	5	20	30	25	15
Cash Collection	14.3	10.7	8.5	5.1	2.3	1.2	1.0	2.2	8.6	19.8	26.4	22.9
Disbursements												
Materials	5.2	5.2	5.2	5.2	5.2	5.2	5.2	5.2	5.2	5.2	5.2	5.2
Wages, Salaries & Other	1.6	1.6	1.6	1.6	1.6	1.6	1.6	1.6	1.6	1.6	1.6	1.6
Taxes	0	0	2.7	0	0	2.7	0	0	2.7	0	0	2.7
Capital Projects	0	0	0	0	0	15.0	0	0	0	0	0	0
Long-Term Financing (interest & dividends)	0	1.0	5.0	0	1.0	0	0	1.0	5.0	0	1.0	0
Total Cash Disbursement	6.8	7.8	14.5	6.8	7.8	24.5	6.8	7.8	14.5	6.8	7.8	9.5
Net Cash Flow	7.5	2.9	−6.0	−1.7	−5.5	−23.3	−5.8	−5.6	−5.9	13.0	18.6	13.4
Cumulative Net Cash Flow	7.5	10.4	4.4	2.7	−2.8	−26.1	−31.9	−37.5	−43.4	−30.4	−11.8	1.6
Minimum Cash Balance	2.0	2.0	2.0	2.0	2.0	2.0	2.0	2.0	2.0	2.0	2.0	2.0
Cash Surplus or Deficit	5.5	8.4	2.4	0.7	−4.8	−28.1	−33.9	−39.5	−45.4	−32.4	−13.8	−0.4

Assumptions
Minimum cash balance of $2 million

Cumulative net cash flow =
Last month's cumulative cash flow +
This month's net cash flow

Net cash flow =
Cash collection - Total cash disbursement

Cash surplus or deficit =
Cumulative net cash flow -
Minimum cash balance

10 days they can take a 2 percent discount. Even with terms like this, Yellow Jacket has found that its customers take the 2 percent discount if they pay in the same month of the sale, which 30 percent do. Then 50 percent pay in the month after the sale, leaving the final 20 percent to pay in the following month. This is illustrated in the cash collection row of the table. Note that the firm collects only $1 million in cash payments in July while it collects as much as $26.4 million in November.

The total sales for the year are $125 million. If the company pursues the level production strategy, then it needs to produce the coats at a sale value rate of $10.42 million per month (= $125 million ÷ 12). Table 14A.2 shows the cash disbursements per month. The manufacturing costs are assumed to be materials at 50 percent of sales, while wages are 15 percent of sales. Thus, material cost payments are $5.2 million per month (= $10.42 million × 50%) and wage payments are $1.6 million per month (= $10.42 million × 15%). Other payments predicted throughout the year are those for capital investments, interest payments, and dividend payments. Yellow Jacket plans to invest in some factory upgrades for which it will pay $15 million in June. Interest payments on its bonds are semiannual (March and September), while quarterly dividends are paid in February, May, August, and November. Notice that the total cash disbursements have a high degree of variability over time. In addition, the payments do not align well with the cash collection. For example in June, the firm receives only $1.2 million in cash and expects to pay $24.5 million. On the other hand, it expects to collect $26.4 million in November and pay only $7.8 million.

The cash budget can now be completed. Table 14A.3 shows that the next step is to compute the net cash flow generated each month. This is simply the cash collection for that month minus that month's disbursement. Note that Yellow Jacket has seven months in a row (March through September) in which it generates a negative cash flow. The cumulative net cash flow row shows that the surplus of cash generated in January and February helps with the deficits from March and April.

However, by May, Yellow Jacket enters a cash deficit situation that lasts the rest of the year. The deficit is increased by the fact that the firm likes to have a cash balance minimum of $2 million at all times. Finally, the cash budget shows the cash account surplus or deficit during the year. It is apparent that Yellow Jacket will need to obtain a bank loan or line of revolving credit that can handle a maximum of $45.4 million (September's deficit is the highest).

Note that Yellow Jacket is a profitable firm. Yet, the seasonality in the sales of coats and jackets causes severe cash deficit problems during the year. If financial managers do not plan ahead for this situation, then the firm will experience significant financial stresses that can damage its reputation and relationship with suppliers and customers. The value of building the cash budget on a spreadsheet (as shown in these tables) is that sensitivity analysis and what-if scenarios can easily be implemented.

time out!

14A-1 Should all cash payments and receipts made by the firm be included in the cash budget?

14A-2 Due to the nature of Yellow Jacket's business, they are likely to experience significant cash deficits each year. How is their bank likely to view this situation?

Problems

BASIC PROBLEMS

14A-1 Cumulative Net Cash Flow The net cash flow for a firm in January, February, and March is $−2.5 million, $−3.0 million, and $2.4 million, respectively. What is the cumulative net cash flow for March? *(LG14-12)*

14A-2 Cumulative Net Cash Flow The net cash flow for a firm in January, February, and March is $3.5 million, $−1.0 million, and $1.4 million, respectively. What is the cumulative net cash flow for March? *(LG14-12)*

14A-3 Cash Disbursement The Hug-a-Bear company makes its teddy bears the month before they are sold and pays for all materials in the month of purchase. If sales of $2.5 million are expected in November and the firm pays 50 percent of sales in material costs, then what is the materials cash disbursement in October? *(LG14-12)*

14A-4 Cash Disbursement The Snow Adventures company makes its snowboards the month before they are sold and pays for all materials in the month of purchase. If sales of $7.8 million are expected in November and the firm pays 65 percent of sales in material costs, then what is the materials cash disbursement in October? *(LG14-12)*

14A-5 Cash Collection Consider a company that has sales in May, June, and July of $10 million, $12 million, and $9 million, respectively. The firm is paid by 35 percent of its customers in the month of the sale, 40 percent in the following month, and 22 percent in the next month (3 percent are bad sales and never pay). What is the cash collected in July? *(LG14-12)*

14A-6 Cash Collection Consider a company that has sales in May, June, and July of $11 million, $10 million, and $12 million, respectively. The firm is paid by 25 percent of its customers in the month of the sale, 50 percent in the following month, and 23 percent in the next month (2 percent are bad sales and never pay). What is the cash collected in July? *(LG14-12)*

14A-7 Cash Surplus or Deficit A firm has estimated the 2-month cash budget below. What is the cash surplus or deficit for these two months? *(LG14-12)*

($ in millions)	MAR	APR
Sales	120.0	130.0
Cash collection	84.0	90.0
Total cash disbursement	90.0	85.0
Net cash flow	26.0	5.0
Cumulative net cash flow	215.0	?
Minimum cash balance	10.0	10.0
Cash surplus or deficit	?	?

14A-8 Cash Surplus or Deficit A firm has estimated the two-month cash budget below. What is the cash surplus or deficit for these two months? *(LG14-12)*

($ in millions)	MAR	APR
Sales	75.0	68.0
Cash collection	63.0	65.0
Total cash disbursement	60.0	57.0
Net cash flow	3.0	8.0
Cumulative net cash flow	11.0	?
Minimum cash balance	3.0	3.0
Cash surplus or deficit	?	?

14A-9 Cash Budget Spreadsheet Problem The company from the text, Yellow Jacket, has decided to change its production strategy. Instead of a steady production throughout the year, they will produce the coats they estimate to sell in the month prior. This will impact the materials and wage disbursements of the cash budget. (For the December computation, assume that the following January sales will increase by 10 percent from the prior year.) Build this cash budget. How does this impact the cash surplus/deficit of the firm? *(LG14-12)*

chapter one

BUSINESS APPLICATION SOLUTION

Because Caleb is a sole proprietor of a small business, he will have trouble getting loans for large amounts of money if he wants to expand. Caleb should consider the following options.

First, Caleb can expand slowly. He can get a small loan or self-fund an expansion into one other mall. Once the new juice stand is making a profit, he can expand again. The advantage of this slow expansion is that he retains full ownership and control of his business. One significant risk is that others may copy his idea and open their own stands, thus taking the prime spots in malls before he gets there.

In order to obtain the capital to expand more quickly, Caleb may have to take on a partner. Forming a partnership with an angel investor or a venture capitalist who can provide business expertise and substantial amounts of capital would allow for much faster expansion. The disadvantage of this option is that Caleb will have to give up some ownership of his business.

PERSONAL APPLICATION SOLUTION

Dagmar should know that the market gives no guarantees against losing money investing in company stocks. These companies failed for different reasons. Lehman Brothers failed because it adopted too-risky business practices, the Chrysler bankruptcy has been blamed on speculation by a small group of investors, and Six Flags' bankruptcy was caused by commitments to pay dividends that it couldn't honor.

Dagmar should also know that the collapse of these firms, and others, has led to a strengthened corporate governance system for monitoring managerial actions. We all hope that this new governance system will reduce the number of company failures due to managerial malfeasance. Nevertheless, she can minimize her loss from a corporate bankruptcy by not putting all her "eggs in one basket." Diversification is a finance principle discussed in detail later in this book.

chapter two

BUSINESS APPLICATION SOLUTION

If the managers of DPH Tree Farm increase the firm's fixed assets by $27 million and net working capital by $8 million in 2013, the balance sheet would look like the one below. That is, gross fixed assets increase by $27 million, to $395 million; cash, accounts receivable, and inventory would increase by $1 million, $5 million, and $6 million, respectively. DPH Tree Farm's total assets will thus grow by $39 million to $609 million by year-end 2013. This growth in assets would be financed with $4 million in accounts payable, and the remaining $35 million will be financed with 40 percent long-term debt ($0.4 \times \$35m = \$14m$) and 60 percent with common stock ($0.6 \times \$35m = \$21m$).

PERSONAL APPLICATION SOLUTION

As Chris Ryan examines the 2012 financial statements for DPH Tree Farm Inc. she needs to remember that the balance sheet reports a firm's assets, liabilities, and equity at a particular point in time, the income statement reports the total revenues and expenses over a specific period of time, the statement of cash flows shows the firm's cash flows over a period of time, and the statement of retained earnings reconciles net income earned during

DPH TREE FARM INC. Balance Sheet as of December 31, 2013 (in millions of dollars)					
Assets	2013		**Liabilities and Equity**	2013	
Current assets:			Current liabilities:		
Cash	$ 25	($24 + $1)	Accrued wages and taxes	$ 20	
Accounts receivable	75	($70 + $5)	Accounts payable	59	($55 + $4)
Inventory	117	($111 + $6)	Notes payable	45	
Total	$217		Total	$124	
Fixed assets:					
Gross plant and equipment	$395	($368 + $27)	Long-term debt:	$209	($195 + 0.4($39 − $4))
Less: Depreciation	53		Stockholders' equity:		
Net plant and equipment	$342		Preferred stock (5 million shares)	$ 5	
Other long-term assets	50		Common stock and paid-in surplus (20 million shares)	61	($40 + 0.6($39 − $4))
			Retained earnings	210	
Total	$392		Total	$276	
Total assets	$609	($570 + $39)	Total liabilities and equity	$609	($570 + $39)

a given period and any cash dividends paid with the change in retained earnings over the period.

GAAP procedures dictate how each financial statement is prepared. GAAP requires that the firm recognizes revenue when the firm sells the product, which is not necessarily when the firm receives the cash. Likewise, under GAAP, expenses appear on the income statement as they match sales. That is, the income statement recognizes production and other expenses associated with sales when the firm sells the product. Again, the actual cash outflow associated with producing the goods may actually occur at a very different time than that reported.

In addition, the income statement contains several noncash items, the largest of which is depreciation. As a result, figures shown on an income statement may not be representative of the actual cash inflows and outflows for a firm during any particular period.

For investors like Chris Ryan, the actual cash flows are often more important than the accounting profit listed on the income statement. Cash, not accounting profit, is needed to pay the firm's obligations as they come due to fund the firm's operations and growth and to compensate the firm's owners. So Chris is more likely to find the answers she seeks in the statement of cash flows, which shows the firm's cash flows over a given period of time. The statement of cash flows reports the amounts of cash generated and cash distributed by a firm during the time period analyzed.

Finally, Chris must remember that firms are required to prepare their financial statements according to GAAP. GAAP allows managers to have significant discretion over their reported earnings, in other words, to *manage earnings*. Indeed, managers can report their results in a way that indicates to investors that the firm's assets are growing more steadily than may really be the case. Similarly, the choice of depreciation method—straight-line or MACRS—for fixed assets may make two firms with identical fixed assets appear to have very different results. Thus, Chris may need to delve more deeply into research about this firm's—or any firm's—financial condition before she makes any final investment decision.

chapter three
BUSINESS APPLICATION SOLUTION

The managers of DPH Tree Farm Inc. have stated that its performance surpasses that of other firms in the industry. Particularly strong are the firm's liquidity and asset management positions. The superior performance in these areas has resulted in superior overall returns for the stockholders of DPH Tree Farm Inc. according to DPH management. Having analyzed the financial statements using ratio analysis, we could conclude that these statements are partially true. All three liquidity ratios show that DPH Tree Farm holds more liquidity on its balance sheet than the industry average. Thus, DPH Tree Farm has more cash and other liquid assets (or current assets) available to pay its bills (or current liabilities) as they come due than the average firm in the tree farm industry. In all cases, the asset management ratios show that DPH Tree Farm Inc. is outperforming the industry average in its asset management. The firm is turning over its inventory faster than the average firm in the tree farm industry, thus producing more dollars of sales per dollar

of inventory. It is also collecting its accounts receivable faster and paying its accounts payable slower than the average firm. Further, DPH Tree Farm is producing more sales per dollar of fixed assets, working capital, and total assets than the average firm in the industry. The profitability ratios show that DPH Tree Farm Inc. is more profitable than the average firm in the tree farm industry. The profit margin, BEP, and ROA are all higher than the industry. Despite this, the ROE for DPH Tree Farm is much lower than the average for the industry.

What the managers do not state is that the debt management ratios show that DPH Tree Farm Inc. holds less debt on its balance sheet than the average firm in the tree farm industry. This is a good sign in that this lack of financial leverage decreases the firm's potential for financial distress and even failure. If the firm has a bad year, it has promised relatively few payments to debt holders. Thus, the risk of bankruptcy is small. Further, the firm has more dollars of operating earnings and cash available to meet each dollar of interest obligations on the firm's debt.

However, when DPH Tree Farm Inc. does well, the low level of financial leverage dilutes the return to the stockholders of the firm. This profit dilution will likely upset the firm's common stockholders. Indeed, the market value ratios show that DPH Tree Farm's investors will not pay as much for a share of the firm's stock per dollar of book value and earnings as the average for the industry. The low debt level and high equity level used by DPH Tree Farm relative to the industry is likely a main reason for this unenthusiastic response by DPH investors.

PERSONAL APPLICATION SOLUTION

To evaluate DPH Tree Farm Inc.'s financial statements, Chris Ryan would want to perform ratio analysis in which she uses the financial statements to calculate the most commonly used ratios. These include liquidity ratios, asset management ratios, debt management ratios, profitability ratios, and market value ratios. The value of these ratios for DPH Tree Farms and the tree farming industry are presented in Table 3.1. Chris might also want to spread the financial statements. These calculations yield common-size, easily compared financial statements that can be used to identify changes in corporate performance as well as how DPH Tree Farm compares to other firms in the industry. Having calculated these ratios, Chris can identify any interrelationships in the ratios by performing a detailed analysis of ROA and ROE using the DuPont system of analysis. A critical part of performance analysis lies in the interpretation of these numbers against some benchmark. To interpret the financial ratios, Chris will also want to evaluate the performance of the firm over time (time series analysis) and the performance of the firm against one or more companies in the same industry (cross-sectional analysis). Finally, Chris needs to exercise some cautions when reviewing data from financial statements. For example, the financial statement data are historical and may not be representative of future performance. Further, she needs to know what accounting rules DPH Tree Farm uses before making any comparisons or conclusions about its performance from ratio analysis. Finally, DPH Tree Farm's managers may have window dressed their financial statements to make them look better.

chapter four

BUSINESS APPLICATION SOLUTION

You must compare the cash flows of buying the wire now at a discount, or waiting one year. The cost of the wire should include both the supplier's bill and the storage cost, for a total of $452,000. What interest rate is implied by a $452,000 cash flow today versus $500,000 in one year? Using equation 4-2:

$$FV_N = PV \times (1 + i)^N$$

$$\$500,000 = \$452,000 \times (1 + i)^1$$

$$i = \$500,000/\$452,000 - 1 = 0.1062 \text{ or } 10.62\%$$

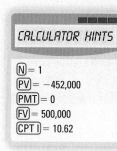

Whether your company should purchase the wire today depends on the cost of the firm's capital (discussed in Chapter 11). If it costs the firm less than 10.6 percent to obtain cash, then you should purchase the wire today. Otherwise, you should not.

PERSONAL APPLICATION SOLUTION

Since Anthony's loan of $300 requires an immediate $50 payment, the actual cash flow is $250 (= $300 − $50). He then must repay the full $300. Use equation 4-2 to compute the interest rate you pay for the period:

$$FV_N = PV \times (1 + i)^N$$

$$\$300 = \$250 \times (1 + i)^1$$

$$i = \$300/\$250 - 1 = 0.20 \text{ or } 20\%$$

Anthony is paying 20 percent for a loan of only two weeks! This is equivalent to paying 11,348 percent per year (this is shown in Chapter 5). He will never be able to build wealth if he continues to pay interest rates like this. Indeed, many people get trapped in a continuing cycle, obtaining one payday loan after another.

WARNING: Payday loans are almost always terrible deals for the borrower!

chapter five

BUSINESS APPLICATION SOLUTION

Walkabout Music Inc. pays $700,000 (= $20 million × 0.07 ÷ 2) in interest every six months on its existing debt. The new debt would require payments of $600,000 (= $20 million × 0.06 ÷ 2) every six months, which represents a $100,000 savings semiannually.

The present value of these savings over the next 20 years is computed using 40 semiannual periods and a 3 percent interest rate per period:

$$PVA_N = \$100,000 \times \left[\frac{1 - \frac{1}{(1 + 0.03)^{40}}}{0.03}\right] = \$2,311,477.20$$

Since this savings is less than the $2.6 million cost of refinancing, the CFO should not refinance the old debt at this time. The company should wait until it can find more favorable terms.

PERSONAL APPLICATION SOLUTION

Should you switch to a new home mortgage with a lower interest rate? To answer this question, first find the monthly savings with the new mortgage. Then compare the present value of the savings to the cost of getting the new mortgage.

The current monthly mortgage payments are:

$$PMT_N = \$150,000 \times \left[\frac{0.00667}{1 - \frac{1}{(1 + 0.00667)^{360}}}\right] = \$1,100.65$$

The new mortgage payments would be:

$$PMT_N = \$145,920.10 \times \left[\frac{0.00583}{1 - \frac{1}{(1 + 0.00583)^{324}}}\right] = \$1,003.66$$

The new mortgage would save you $96.99 per month for the next 27 years. The present value of these savings at the current 7 percent interest rate is:

$$PVA_N = \$96.99 \times \left[\frac{1 - \frac{1}{(1 + 0.00583)^{324}}}{0.00583}\right] = \$14,101.18$$

Since the present value of the monthly savings is greater than the $1,000 broker fee, you should refinance the mortgage.

chapter six

BUSINESS APPLICATION SOLUTION

In deciding when to issue new debt, DPH Corporation needs to consider two main factors. First, what might happen to specific factors that affect interest rates on any debt the firm may issue? Such specific factors include changes in the firm's default risk, liquidity risk, any special provisions regarding the use of funds raised by the firm's security issuance, and the debt's term to maturity. An increase (decrease) in any of these risks over the next two years would increase (decrease) the rate of interest DPH Corp. would be required to pay to holders of the new debt and would potentially make the debt issue in two years less (more) attractive. Second, what might happen to the general level of interest rates in the U.S. economy over the next two years? This involves an analysis of any changes in inflation or the "real" interest rate. DPH can estimate how interest rates may change by examining the term structure of interest rates or the current yield curve. In addition to any internal analysis of these factors, DPH Corp. can get expert advice about the timing of its debt issue and get the new debt to the capital market with help from an investment bank. These financial institutions underwrite securities and engage in related activities, such as making a market in which securities can trade.

PERSONAL APPLICATION SOLUTION

In deciding which corporate bond to buy, John Adams needs to consider specific factors that affect differences in interest rates on debt. These specific factors include the general level of inflation and the "real" interest rate in the U.S. economy, as well as the default risk, liquidity risk, any special provisions regarding the use of funds raised by a security issuance, and the term to maturity of the two debt issues. While one bond earns more (10.00 percent) than the other (8.00 percent), it may be that the higher-yielding bond has more default, liquidity, or other risk than the lower-yielding bond. Thus, the higher yield brings with it more risk. John Adams must consider whether he is willing to incur higher risk to get higher returns. In addition to his own analysis of these factors, John Adams can get expert advice about which bond to buy and then buy the bond with a securities firm's help. These financial institutions engage in activities such as securities brokerage, securities trading, and making markets in which securities can trade.

chapter seven

BUSINESS APPLICATION SOLUTION

To raise $150 million, Beach Sand Resorts would need to issue 150,000 bonds at the customary $1,000 par value (= $150 million ÷ $1,000). The bonds will have to offer a 7 percent coupon. This means that Beach Sand Resorts will pay $35 in interest every six months for each bond issued (= 0.07 × $1,000 ÷ 2). So for all 150,000 bonds, they will pay $5.25 million semiannually (= $35 × 150,000).

PERSONAL APPLICATION SOLUTION

You can calculate that buying 10 of the Trust Media bonds at the quoted price of 96.21 will cost $9,621 (= 0.9621 × $1,000 × 10) and would generate $285 (= 0.057 × $1,000 × 10 ÷ 2) in interest payments every six months. Buying the bond in 2012, it is priced to offer a 6.47 percent yield to maturity. Ten of the Abalon bonds would cost $10,194

(= 1.0194 × $1,000 × 10) and pay $268.75 (= 0.05375 × $1,000 × 10 ÷ 2) in interest payments every six months. This bond is priced to offer a 5.0 percent yield to maturity. The Trust bonds cost less to purchase, pay more in interest, and offer a higher return than the Abalon bonds. This is because the Trust bonds have higher credit risk. You must decide if the higher return of the Trust bonds is worth taking the extra risk.

chapter eight

BUSINESS APPLICATION SOLUTION

You can compute the expected return using equation 8-7 as,

$$i = \frac{\$2 \times (1 + 0.08)}{\$65} + 0.08 = 0.0332 + 0.08 = 0.1132$$

Investors expect an 11.32 percent return.

The P/E ratio of 16.25 and the stock price of $65 indicates that earnings were $4.00 per share (= $65 ÷ 16.25). If the P/E ratio of 16.25 continues, then the price of the stock in three years may be $81.88 [= 16.25 × $4 × (1.08)^3]. However, a P/E ratio of 16.25 may seem a little high for a firm with an 8 percent growth rate. So the P/E ratio might decline a bit to 15. If so, the stock price in three years would be $75.58. On the other hand, P/E ratios in the stock market may increase in general, thereby inflating this firm's ratio to 17. In this case, the price would be $85.66.

You should report an expected stock price range of $75.58 to $85.66 with a target of $81.88.

PERSONAL APPLICATION SOLUTION

The information provided allows for two growth rate estimates for stock valuation. The dividend growth from $1.25 to $1.68 in three years implies a 10.36 percent historical growth rate (N = 3, PV = −1.25, PMT = 0, FV = 1.68, CPT I = 10.36). Since analysts' mean growth estimate is 10.1 percent, you can use either, or both, rates in the constant-growth-rate model using a 13.5 percent discount rate:

$$P_0 = \frac{\$1.68 \times (1 + 0.1036)}{0.135 - 0.1036} = \$59.05$$

$$P_0 = \frac{\$1.68 \times (1 + 0.101)}{0.135 - 0.101} = \$54.40$$

Both valuation estimates exceed the current price of $54. The current stock price does not appear overvalued, so you can consider the purchase.

chapter nine

BUSINESS APPLICATION SOLUTION

We can apply diversification concepts and modern portfolio theory to many more applications than just investment portfolios. For example, a manufacturing facility can be more efficient by producing different products during the year as demand dictates the need for one product over another. Salespeople can reduce the volatility of their commission incomes by having many different products to sell.

Although new project ideas have more risk, they could actually reduce the firm's overall risk if the projects diversify the firm's current business operations. You could evaluate this possibility by determining the correlation between the expected cash flows from each project idea with the expected cash flows of the firm's current business operations. A low or negative correlation would mean that the new projects could actually reduce risk for the firm. Note that some firms may find that their position is too conservative and that they wish to increase their risk to increase the possibility of earning a higher return.

PERSONAL APPLICATION SOLUTION

Since 1950, Tables 9.2 and 9.4 show that the bond market experienced an average return and standard deviation of 6.4 percent and 10.7 percent, respectively. Stocks earned a 12.5 percent return with a 17.9 percent standard deviation. The investor is correct in the belief that the stock market is riskier than the bond market.

However, Table 9.6 shows that the correlation between the stock and bond market is very low, at 0.007. This result allows some diversification opportunity. Indeed, a portfolio of 10 percent stocks and 90 percent bonds would have experienced an average annual return of 7.0 percent with a standard deviation of 9.8 percent since 1950. The broker is correct; adding a small portion of stocks to a bond portfolio actually reduces total risk!

chapter ten

BUSINESS APPLICATION SOLUTION

You need to determine the firm's level of market risk. If you can obtain a beta, then you can make a required return estimate using CAPM. To assess the result, you can use the constant-growth model to check the CAPM estimated required return for comparison's sake.

If you find the beta of the firm to be 1.8, assume a market return of 11 percent, and note a 5 percent T-bill rate, the CAPM computations would be:

$$5\% + 1.8 \times (11\% - 5\%) = 15.8 \text{ percent}$$

The firm will pay a $0.50 dividend next year and the current stock price is $32. Managers believe the company will grow at 13 percent per year for the foreseeable future. The constant-growth model computation gives:

$$\$0.50 \div \$32 + 0.13 = 0.1456, \text{ or } 14.56 \text{ percent}$$

You can now take these estimates to the team.

PERSONAL APPLICATION SOLUTION

You are investing 57.1 percent (= $200 ÷ $350) of your monthly contribution in stocks. You are also contributing 28.6 percent in bonds and 14.3 percent into a money market account. The diversified stock portfolio has a beta of 1. The long-term bond portfolio has a beta of 0.18. By definition, the money market account is risk-free and thus has a beta of zero.

The beta of this portfolio is therefore:

$$0.571 \times (1) + 0.286 \times (0.18) + 0.143 \times (0) = 0.62$$

With a portfolio beta of 0.62, a market return of 11 percent, and a risk-free rate of 5 percent, you can expect a return of:

$$5\% + 0.62 \times (11\% - 5\%) = 8.72 \text{ percent}$$

If you want a higher expected return, you will have to take more risk. You can do that by contributing a higher proportion of your funds to the stock portfolio.

chapter eleven

BUSINESS APPLICATION SOLUTION

MP3 Devices Inc. faces current component costs of capital equal to:

$$i_E = \frac{D_1}{P_0} + g \qquad\qquad i_P = \frac{D_1}{P_0}$$

$$= \frac{\$1.35}{\$18.75} + 0.06 \qquad = \frac{\$10}{\$100}$$

$$= 0.1320, \text{ or } 13.20\% \qquad = 0.1000, \text{ or } 10.00\%$$

$$\text{Solve} \left\{ \$1,100 = \$100 \times \left[\frac{1 - \dfrac{1}{(1 + i_D)^{20}}}{i_D} \right] + \frac{\$1,000}{(1 + i_D)^{20}} \right\} \text{ for } i_D$$

gives $i_D = 0.0891$, *or* 8.91%

CALCULATOR HINTS

N = 20
PV = −1,100
PMT = 100
FV = 1000
CPT I = 8.91%

Using the target capital structure weights, MP3's WACC equals:

$$\text{WACC} = 0.5 \times 0.1320 + 0.1 \times 0.10 + 0.4 \times 0.0891 \times (1 - 0.34)$$

$$= 0.0995, \text{ or } 9.95\%$$

PERSONAL APPLICATION SOLUTION

Mackenzie can expect a total of $17,125 + $29,000 = $46,125 in student loans when she graduates from her master's program. At an 8 percent rate of interest, the yearly interest charges will be $3,690 immediately after she graduates (though they will go down once she starts paying off some of the principal). Since the yearly interest will be more than the allowable $2,500 deduction, we can express her after-tax interest rate as the following weighted average:

$$\text{WACC} = \frac{D_{Nondeductible}}{D_{Nondeductible} + D_{Deductible}} i_D$$

$$+ \frac{D_{Deductible}}{D_{Nondeductible} + D_{Deductible}} i_D \times (1 - T_P)$$

$$= \frac{\$3,690 - \$2,500}{\$3,690} \times 0.08 + \frac{\$2,500}{\$3,690} \times 0.08 \times (1 - 0.25)$$

$$= 0.3225 \times 0.08 + 0.6775 \times 0.08 \times 0.75$$

$$= 0.0664, \text{ or } 6.64\%$$

chapter twelve

BUSINESS APPLICATION SOLUTION

Based on the given information, the yearly sales, levels of NWC and resulting changes in NWC for McDonald's will be:

Year	Yearly Sales	Yearly Levels of NWC	Changes in NWC
0	$ 0	$364,000	$364,000
1	2,800,000	937,300	573,300
2	7,210,000	965,900	28,600
3	7,430,000	994,500	28,600
4	7,650,000	512,200	−482,300
5	3,940,000	0	−512,200

OCF calculations, ΔNWC, and ΔFA for each year are shown below:

(in millions)	Time 0	Year 1	Year 2	Year 3	Year 4	Year 5
Sales		$2.8000	$7.2100	$7.4300	$7.6500	$3.9400
Less: Variable costs		1.3400	3.5200	3.7000	3.8900	2.0400
Less: Fixed costs		0.0000	0.0000	0.0000	0.0000	0.0000
Less: Depreciation		0.0000	0.0000	0.0000	0.0000	0.0000
Earnings before interest and taxes		$1.4600	$3.6900	$3.7300	$3.7600	$1.9000
Less: Taxes		0.0000	0.0000	0.0000	0.0000	0.0000
Net income		$1.4600	$3.6900	$3.7300	$3.7600	$1.9000
Plus: Depreciation		0.0000	0.0000	0.0000	0.0000	0.0000
Operating cash flow		$1.4600	$3.6900	$3.7300	$3.7600	$1.9000
Δ Fixed assets	$7.0000	$0.0000	$0.0000	$0.0000	$0.0000	$0.0000
Δ Net working capital	0.0000	0.0000	0.0000	0.0000	0.0000	0.0000
Less: Investment in operating capital	$7.0000	0.0000	0.0000	0.0000	0.0000	0.0000
Free cash flow	−$7.0000	$1.4600	$3.6900	$3.7300	$3.7600	$1.9000

PERSONAL APPLICATION SOLUTION

Achmed's purchase of a new computer should not be counted as an incremental cash flow to getting an MBA, as he has indicated that he would be getting one anyway. Likewise, the $250 that he paid to take the GMAT is a sunk cost, and should not be counted, either. His tuition payments constitute an annuity due, so his incremental cash flows will equal:

Years	0–3	4–23
FCF	−$15,000	$10,000

chapter thirteen

BUSINESS APPLICATION SOLUTION

ADK's project will have an NPV of:

$$NPV = \frac{-\$5m}{(1.14)^0} + \frac{\$1.2m}{(1.14)^1} + \frac{\$1.6m}{(1.14)^2}$$

$$+ \frac{\$2.3m}{(1.14)^3} + \frac{\$2.8m}{(1.14)^4}$$

$$= \$494,038.89 > 0$$

and an IRR of:

$$NPV = \frac{-\$5m}{(1 + IRR)^0} + \frac{\$1.2m}{(1 + IRR)^1} + \frac{\$1.6m}{(1 + IRR)^2}$$

$$+ \frac{\$2.3m}{(1 + IRR)^3} + \frac{\$2.8m}{(1 + IRR)^4}$$

$$IRR = 18.09\% > 14\%$$

Both the NPV and IRR support accepting the project.

We could also calculate MIRR (16.72%) and PI (9.88%), and these would provide additional support for accepting the project.

Finally, though we are not given maximum allowable payback or discounted payback, values of 2.96 and 3.70, respectively, would seem to be in an acceptable range, too.

PERSONAL APPLICATION SOLUTION

First, we should note that, since cash flows occur every three months, we need to convert the APR of 9 percent to a quarterly rate:

$$i_{qtr} = \left(1 + \frac{0.09}{12}\right)^3 - 1 = 0.0227$$

With these types of cash flows, our choice of decision rules is limited to NPV, MIRR, or PI; we cannot use either the payback rule or IRR because of the non-normality.

The NPV of this project will be:

$$NPV = \frac{-\$5,000}{(1.0227)^0} + \frac{-\$5,000}{(1.0227)^1}$$

$$+ \frac{-\$10,000}{(1.0227)^2} + \frac{\$30,000}{(1.0227)^{12}}$$

$$= -\$3,473.72 > 0$$

This NPV indicates that the project should be accepted.

chapter fourteen

BUSINESS APPLICATION SOLUTION

Chewbacca's operating cycle will be equal to:

$$\text{Operating cycle} = \frac{0.1 \times 365}{0.55} + \frac{0.1667 \times 365}{1}$$

$$= 127.20 \text{ days}$$

Their cash cycle will be equal to:

$$\text{Cash cycle} = 127.20 - \frac{0.05 \times 365}{0.55}$$

$$= 94.02 \text{ days}$$

Absent any other information about current assets or current liabilities, Chewbacca's net working capital will be:

$$(0.10 + 0.1667 - 0.05) \times \$32 \text{ million} = \$6.93 \text{ million}$$

PERSONAL APPLICATION SOLUTION

Since Wanda will be drawing out the money smoothly from the account, she can use the Baumol model to determine the optimal replenishment level for her personal stock of cash:

$$C^\star = \sqrt{2(\$25,000)(\$9.95)/0.035}$$

$$= \$3,770.18$$

photo credits

CHAPTER 1

Page 2: Stockbyte/Getty Images RF; p. 8: Purestock/Superstock RF; p. 11: © The McGraw-Hill Companies, Inc./John Flournoy, photographer; p. 13: Chris Ratcliffe/Bloomberg via Getty Images; p. 15: Digital Vision/Getty Images RF; p. 18: © The McGraw-Hill Companies, Inc./Christopher Kerrigan, photographer.

CHAPTER 2

Page 22: Photographer's Choice/Getty Images RF; p. 27: Royalty-Free/Corbis RF; p. 34: Photo courtesy of USDA Natural Resources Conservation Service; p. 38: Royalty-Free/Corbis RF.

CHAPTER 3

Page 48: Royalty-Free/Corbis RF; p. 52: Ryan McVay/Getty Images RF; p. 57: Photodisc/Getty Images RF.

CHAPTER 4

Page 74: Royalty-Free/Corbis RF; p. 83: Ryan McVay/Getty Images RF; p. 88: © Trevor Lush/Blend Images LLC RF.

CHAPTER 5

Page 96: Royalty-Free/Corbis RF; p. 103: Chris Ryan/Getty Images RF; p. 106: © Akihiro Sugimoto/age fotostock RF; p. 109: © Paul King/Alamy RF; p. 114: Phillip Spears/Getty Images RF.

CHAPTER 6

Page 124: Brand X Pictures/Punchstock RF; p.130: Jack Star/PhotoLink/Getty Images RF; p. 134: © The McGraw-Hill Companies, Inc./Andrew Resek, photographer; p. 135: Stockbyte/Punchstock RF; p. 138: © Eyewire/Photodisc/Punchstock RF.

CHAPTER 7

Page 154: Stockbyte/Getty Images RF; p.160: Comstock Images/Jupiter Images RF; p. 172: Royalty-Free/Corbis RF; p. 175: Digital Vision/Punchstock RF.

CHAPTER 8

Page 182: © The McGraw-Hill Companies, Inc./Jill Braaten, photographer; p. 185: Image Source/Corbis RF; p. 188: © TongRo Image Stock/Alamy RF; p. 189: Brand X Pictures RF; p. 191: © The McGraw-Hill Companies, Inc./Jill Braaten, photographer; p. 192: © The McGraw-Hill Companies, Inc./John Flournoy, photographer; p. 201: David Paul Morris/Bloomberg via Getty Images.

CHAPTER 9

Page 208: Brand X Pictures/Jupiter Images RF; p. 212: Mark Steinmetz RF; p. 214: Juice Images/Corbis RF; p. 217: Dimitri Vervitsiotis/Getty Images RF; p. 218: Brand X Pictures RF; p. 220: Photodisc/Punchstock RF.

CHAPTER 10

Page 232: Royalty-Free/Corbis RF; p. 234: Getty Images RF; p. 240: Ingram Publishing RF; p. 246: Janis Christie/Getty Images RF.

CHAPTER 11

Page 258: Royalty-Free/Corbis RF; p. 265(left): Ingram Publishing/Superstock RF; p. 265(right): Tetra Images/Alamy RF.

CHAPTER 12

Page 278: Royalty-Free/Corbis RF; p. 280: Stockbyte/Punchstock RF; p. 283: Stockdisc RF; p. 285: Brand X Pictures RF; p. 289: Brand X Pictures/Punchstock RF.

CHAPTER 13

Page 302: Stockbyte/Getty Images RF; p. 305(left): Stockbyte/Getty Images RF; p. 305(center): P. Ughetto/PhotoAlto RF; p. 305(right): imageshop/Punchstock RF; p. 314: Digital Vision/Punchstock RF; p.318: Stockbyte RF.

CHAPTER 14

Page 328: Stockbyte/Getty Images RF; p. 333: Comstock Images/Jupiter Images RF; p.336: Brand X Pictures/Punchstock RF; p. 337: Stockbyte/Punchstock RF; p. 341: Digital Vision/Getty Images RF.

TIME OUT BOXES (VARIOUS PAGES)

© Ryan McVay/Getty Images; © Stockbyte/Getty Images; © Thomas Vogel/iStockphoto; © Viorika Prikhodko/iStockphoto; © Irina Tischenko/iStockphoto; © Thomas Vogel/iStockphoto

THE MATH COACH ON BOXES (VARIOUS PAGES)

© Royalty-Free/CORBIS

GET ONLINE BOXES (VARIOUS PAGES)

© artparadigm/Getty Images

index

A page number followed by an *e* indicates an example; *f,* a figure; *n,* a note; *t,* a table.

2-1 Assets = Liabilities + Equity

2-2 Net working capital = Current assets − Current liabilities

2-3 $\text{Earnings per share (EPS)} = \dfrac{\text{Net income available to common stockholders}}{\text{Total shares of common stock outstanding}}$

2-4 $\text{Dividends per share (DPS)} = \dfrac{\text{Common stock dividends paid}}{\text{Number of shares of common stock outstanding}}$

2-5 $\text{Book value per share (BVPS)} = \dfrac{\text{Common stock + Paid-in surplus + Retained earnings}}{\text{Numbers of shares of common stock outstanding}}$

2-6 Market value per share (MVPS) = Market price of the firm's common stock

2-7 $\text{Average tax rate} = \dfrac{\text{Tax liability}}{\text{Taxable income}}$

2-8 $\text{FCF} = [\text{EBIT}(1 - \text{Tax rate}) + \text{Depreciation}] - [\Delta \text{ Gross fixed assets}$
$+ \Delta\text{Net operating working capital}]$
$= \text{Operating cash flow} - \text{Investment in operating capital}$

3-1 $\text{Current ratio} = \dfrac{\text{Current assets}}{\text{Current liabilities}}$

3-2 $\text{Quick ratio (acid-test ratio)} = \dfrac{\text{Current assets} - \text{Inventory}}{\text{Current liabilities}}$

3-3 $\text{Cash ratio} = \dfrac{\text{Cash and marketable securities}}{\text{Current liabilities}}$

3-4 $\text{Inventory turnover} = \dfrac{\text{Sales or cost of goods sold}}{\text{Inventory}}$

3-5 $\text{Days' sales in inventory} = \dfrac{\text{Inventory} \times 365 \text{ days}}{\text{Sales or cost of goods sold}}$

3-6 $\text{Average collection period (ACP)} = \dfrac{\text{Accounts receivable} \times 365 \text{ days}}{\text{Credit sales}}$

3-7 $\text{Accounts receivable turnover} = \dfrac{\text{Credit sales}}{\text{Accounts receivable}}$

3-8 $\text{Average payment period (APP)} = \dfrac{\text{Accounts payable} \times 365 \text{ days}}{\text{Cost of goods sold}}$

3-9 $\text{Accounts payable turnover} = \dfrac{\text{Cost of goods sold}}{\text{Accounts payable}}$

3-10 $\text{Fixed asset turnover ratio} = \dfrac{\text{Sales}}{\text{Fixed assets}}$

3-11 $\text{Sales to working capital} = \dfrac{\text{Sales}}{\text{Working capital}}$

3-12 $\text{Total assets turnover ratio} = \dfrac{\text{Sales}}{\text{Total assets}}$

3-13 $\text{Capital intensity} = \dfrac{\text{Total assets}}{\text{Sales}}$

3-14 $\text{Debt ratio} = \dfrac{\text{Total debt}}{\text{Total assets}}$

3-15 $\text{Debt-to-equity} = \dfrac{\text{Total debt}}{\text{Total equity}}$

3-16 $\text{Equity multiplier} = \dfrac{\text{Total assets}}{\text{Total equity}} \text{ or } \dfrac{\text{Total assets}}{\text{Common stockholders' equity}}$

3-17 $\text{Times interest earned} = \dfrac{\text{EBIT}}{\text{Interest}}$

3-18 $\text{Fixed-charge coverage ratio} = \dfrac{\text{Earnings available to meet fixed charges}}{\text{Fixed charges}}$

3-19 $\text{Cash coverage ratio} = \dfrac{\text{EBIT} + \text{Depreciation}}{\text{Fixed charges}}$

3-20 $\text{Profit margin} = \dfrac{\text{Net income available to common stockholders}}{\text{Sales}}$

3-21 $\text{Basic earnings power (BEP)} = \dfrac{\text{EBIT}}{\text{Total assets}}$

3-22 $\text{Return on assets (ROA)} = \dfrac{\text{Net income available to common stockholders}}{\text{Total assets}}$

3-23 $\text{Return on equity (ROE)} = \dfrac{\text{Net income available to common stockholders}}{\text{Common stockholders' equity}}$

3-24 $\text{Dividend payout ratio} = \dfrac{\text{Common stock dividends}}{\text{Net income available to common stockholders}}$

3-25 $\text{Market-to-book ratio} = \dfrac{\text{Market price per share}}{\text{Book value per share}}$

3-26 $\text{Price-earning (PE) ratio} = \dfrac{\text{Market price per share}}{\text{Earnings per share}}$

3-27 $\text{ROA} = \text{Profit margin} \times \text{Total asset turnover}$
$\dfrac{\text{Net income available to common stockholders}}{\text{Total assets}} = \dfrac{\text{Net income available to common stockholders}}{\text{Sales}} \times \dfrac{\text{Sales}}{\text{Total assets}}$

3-28 $\text{ROE} = \text{ROA} \times \text{Equity multiplier}$
$\dfrac{\text{Net income available to common stockholders}}{\text{Common stockholders' equity}} = \text{ROA} \times \dfrac{\text{Total assets}}{\text{Common stockholders' equity}}$

3-29 $\text{ROE} = \text{Profit margin} \times \text{Total asset turnover} \times \text{Equity multiplier}$
$\dfrac{\text{Net income available to common stockholders}}{\text{Common stockholders' equity}} = \dfrac{\text{Net income available to common stockholders}}{\text{Sales}} \times \dfrac{\text{Sales}}{\text{Total assets}}$
$\times \dfrac{\text{Total assets}}{\text{Common stockholders' equity}}$

3-30 $\text{Internal growth rate} = \dfrac{\text{ROA} \times \text{RR}}{1 - (\text{ROA} \times \text{RR})}$

3-31 $\text{Retention ratio (RR)} = \dfrac{\text{Addition to retained earnings}}{\text{Net income available to common stockholders}}$

3-32 $\text{Retention ratio} = 1 - \text{Dividend payout ratio}$

3-33 $\text{Sustainable growth rate} = \dfrac{\text{ROE} \times \text{RR}}{1 - (\text{ROE} \times \text{RR})}$

4-1 Future value in 1 year $= FV_1 = PV \times (1 + i)$

4-2 Future value in N years $= FV_N = PV \times (1 + i)^N$

4-3 Future value in N periods $= FV_N = PV \times (1 + i_{\text{period 1}}) \times (1 + i_{\text{period 2}})$

$$\times (1 + i_{\text{period 3}}) \times \cdots \times (1 + i_{\text{period N}})$$

4-4 Present value of next period's cash flow $= PV = \dfrac{FV_1}{(1 + i)}$

4-5 Present value of cash flow made in N years $= PV = \dfrac{FV_N}{(1 + i)^N}$

4-6 Present value with different discount rates

$$= PV = \dfrac{FV_N}{(1 + i_{\text{Period 1}}) \times (1 + i_{\text{Period 2}}) \times (1 + i_{\text{Period 3}}) \times \cdots \times (1 + i_{\text{Period N}})}$$

4-7 Approximate number of years to double an investment $= \dfrac{72}{\text{Interest rate}}$

5-1 $FV_N =$ Future value of first cash flow
$+$ Future value of second cash flow
$+ \cdots +$ Future value of last cash flow

$$= PMT_m \times (1 + i)^{N-m} + PMT_n \times (1 + i)^{N-n} + \cdots + PMT_p \times (1 + i)^{N-p}$$

5-2 $FVA_N = PMT \times \dfrac{(1 + i)^N - 1}{i}$

5-3 $PV =$ Present value of first cash flow $+$ Present value of second cash flow
$+ \cdots +$ Present value of last cash flow

$$= \dfrac{PMT_m}{(1 + i)^{N-m}} + \dfrac{PMT_n}{(1 + i)^{N-n}} + \cdots + \dfrac{PMT_p}{(1 + i)^{N-p}}$$

5-4 $PVA_N = PMT \times \left[\dfrac{1 - \dfrac{1}{(1 + i)^N}}{i} \right]$

5-5 PV of a perpetuity $= \dfrac{PMT}{i}$

5-6 FVA_N due $= FVA_N \times (1 + i)$

5-7 PVA_N due $= PVA_N \times (1 + i)$

5-8 $EAR = \left(1 + \dfrac{APR}{m}\right)^m - 1$

5-9 $PMT_N = PV \times \left[\dfrac{i}{1 - \dfrac{1}{(1 + i)^N}} \right]$

6-1 $IP = \dfrac{CPI_{t+1} - CPI_t}{CPI_t} \times 100$

6-2 $i = $ Expected $IP + RIR$

6-3 $RIR = i - $ Expected IP

6-4 $DRP_j = i_{jt} - i_{Tt}$

6-5 $i_j^* = f(IP, RIR, DRP_j, LRP_j, SCP_j, MP_j)$

6-6 $(1 + {}_1R_N)^N = (1 + {}_1R_1)[1 + E({}_2r_1)] \ldots [1 + E({}_Nr_1)]$

6-7 ${}_1R_N = \{[1 + {}_1R_1][1 + E({}_2r_1)] \ldots [1 + E({}_Nr_1)]\}^{1/N} - 1$

6-8 ${}_1R_N = \{[1 + {}_1R_1][1 + E({}_2r_1) + L_2] \ldots [1 + E({}_Nr_1) + L_N]\}^{1/N} - 1$

6-9 ${}_1R_2 = \{[1 + {}_1R_1][1 + ({}_2f_1)]\}^{1/2} - 1$

6-10 ${}_2f_1 = [(1 + {}_1R_2)^2/(1 + {}_1R_1)] - 1$

6-11 ${}_Nf_1 = [(1 + {}_1R_N)^N/(1 + {}_1R_{N-1})^{N-1}] - 1$

7-1 Present value of bond $=$ Present value of interest payments
$+$ Present value of par value

$$= PMT \times \left[\dfrac{1 - \dfrac{1}{(1 + i)^N}}{i} \right] + \dfrac{\$1{,}000}{(1 + i)^N}$$

7-2 Bond price $= PV$ of annuity $(PMT, i, N) + PV (FV, i, N)$

7-3 Price of a callable bond $=$ Present value of interest payments to call date
$+$ Present value of call price

$$= PMT \times \left[\dfrac{1 - \dfrac{1}{(1 + i)^N}}{i} \right] + \dfrac{\text{Call price}}{(1 + i)^N}$$

7-4 Equivalent taxable yield $= \dfrac{\text{Muni yield}}{1 - \text{Tax rate}}$

8-1 $P_0 = \dfrac{D_1 + P_1}{1 + i}$

8-2 $P_0 = \dfrac{D_1}{1 + i} + \dfrac{D_2 + P_2}{(1 + i)^2}$

8-3 $P_0 = \dfrac{D_1}{1 + i} + \dfrac{D_2}{(1 + i)^2} + \cdots + \dfrac{D_n + P_n}{(1 + i)^n}$

8-4 $P_0 = \dfrac{D_1}{1 + i} + \dfrac{D_2}{(1 + i)^2} + \dfrac{D_3}{(1 + i)^3} + \cdots$

8-5 $P_0 = \dfrac{D_0(1 + g)}{1 + i} + \dfrac{D_0(1 + g)^2}{(1 + i)^2} + \dfrac{D_0(1 + g)^3}{(1 + i)^3} + \cdots$

8-6 Constant-growth model $= P_0 = \dfrac{D_0(1 + g)}{i - g} = \dfrac{D_1}{i - g}$

8-7 Expected return $= i = \dfrac{D_1}{P_0} + g =$ Dividend yield $+$ Capital gain

8-8 $P_0 = \dfrac{D_0(1 + g_1)}{1 + i} + \dfrac{D_0(1 + g_1)^2}{(1 + i)^2} + \dfrac{D_0(1 + g_1)^3}{(1 + i)^3}$

$+ \cdots + \dfrac{D_0(1 + g_1)^n + \dfrac{D_0(1 + g_1)^n(1 + g_2)}{i - g_2}}{(1 + i)^n}$

8-9 $\text{P/E} = \dfrac{\text{Current stock price}}{\text{Per-share earnings for last 12 months}}$

8-10 $P_n = (^P/_E)_n \times E_n = (^P/_E)_n \times E_0 \times (1 + g)^n$

9-1 Dollar return $=$ (Capital gain or loss) $+$ Income

$\qquad\qquad = $ (Ending value $-$ Beginning value) $+$ Income

9-2 Percentage return $= \dfrac{\text{Ending value} - \text{Beginning value} + \text{Income}}{\text{Beginning value}} \times 100\%$

9-3 Average return $= \dfrac{\displaystyle\sum_{t=1}^{N} \text{Return}_t}{N}$

9-4 Standard deviation $= \sqrt{\dfrac{\displaystyle\sum_{t=1}^{N} (\text{Return}_t - \text{Average return})^2}{N - 1}}$

9-5 Coefficient of variation $= \dfrac{\text{Standard deviation}}{\text{Average return}}$

9-6 Total risk $=$ Firm-specific risk $+$ Market risk

9-7 $R_p = (w_1 \times R_1) + (w_2 \times R_2) + (w_3 \times R_3) + \cdots + (w_n \times R_n) = \displaystyle\sum_{i=1}^{n} w_i R_i$

10-1 Expected return $= (p_1 \times \text{Return}_1) + (p_2 \times \text{Return}_2) + (p_3 \times \text{Return}_3)$

$+ \cdots + (p_s \times \text{Return}_s) = \displaystyle\sum_{j=1}^{s} p_j \times \text{Return}_j$

10-2 Standard deviation $= \sqrt{\begin{array}{l} p_1 \times (\text{Return}_1 - \text{Expected return})^2 + p_2 \\ \times (\text{Return}_2 - \text{Expected return})^2 + \cdots \end{array}}$

$= \sqrt{\displaystyle\sum_{j=1}^{s} p_j \times (\text{Return}_j - \text{Expected return})^2}$

10-3 Required return $=$ Risk-free rate $+$ Risk premium

10-4 Expected return $= R_f + \beta(R_M - R_f)$

10-5 $\beta_p = (w_1 \times \beta_1) + (w_2 \times \beta_2) + (w_3 \times \beta_3) + \cdots + (w_n \times \beta_n) = \displaystyle\sum_{j=1}^{n} w_j \beta_j$

10-6 $i =$ Dividend yield $+$ Constant growth $= \dfrac{D_1}{P_0} + g$

11-1 $\text{WACC} = \dfrac{E}{E + P + D} i_E + \dfrac{P}{E + P + D} i_P$

$+ \dfrac{D}{E + P + D} i_D \times (1 - T_C)$

11-2 $i_E = R_f + \beta(R_M - R_f)$

11-3 $i_E = \dfrac{D_1}{P_0} + g$

11-4 $i_p = \dfrac{D_1}{P_0}$

11-5 Solve $\left\{ PV = PMT \times \left[\dfrac{1 - \dfrac{1}{(1 + i_D)^N}}{i_D} \right] + \dfrac{FV}{(1 + i_D)^N} \right\}$ for i_D

11-6 $i_E = r_f + \beta_{Avg}[E(r_M) - r_f]$

where

$\beta_{Avg} = \dfrac{\displaystyle\sum_{j=1}^{N} \beta_j}{n}$

11-7 $WACC_{Project} = \dfrac{E_{Project}}{E_{Project} + P_{Project} + D_{Project}} i_{E,\,Project}$

$+ \dfrac{P_{Project}}{E_{Project} + P_{Project} + D_{Project}} i_{P,\,Firm}$

$+ \dfrac{D_{Project}}{E_{Project} + P_{Project} + D_{Project}} i_{D,\,Firm}$

$\times (1 - T_{C,\,Project})$

11-8 $i_E = \dfrac{D_1}{P_0 - F} + g$

11-9 $i_P = \dfrac{D_1}{P_0 - F}$

11-10 Solve $\left\{ PV - F = PMT \times \left[\dfrac{1 - \dfrac{1}{(1 + i_D)^N}}{i_D} \right] + \dfrac{FV}{(1 + i_D)^N} \right\}$ for i_D

12-1 FCF = Operating cash flow − Investment in operating capital

$= [\text{EBIT}(1 - \text{Tax rate}) + \text{Depreciation}]$

$- [\Delta\text{Gross fixed assets} + \Delta\text{Net operating working capital}]$

12-2 $\text{Depreciation} = \dfrac{\text{Depreciable basis} - \text{Ending book value}}{\text{Life of asset}}$

12-3 $\text{ATCF} = \text{Book value} + (\text{Market value} - \text{Book value}) \times (1 - T_C)$

12-4 $f_A = \dfrac{E}{E + P + D} f_E + \dfrac{P}{E + P + D} f_P + \dfrac{D}{E + P + D} f_D$

12-5 $\text{Adjusted } CF_0 = \dfrac{CF_0}{1 - f_A}$

13-1 **Payback Statistic**

$0 = \displaystyle\sum_{n=0}^{PB} CF_n$

13-2 **Payback Decision Rule**

Accept project if calculated payback ≤ Maximum allowable payback
Reject project if calculated payback > Maximum allowable payback

13-3 **Discounted Payback Statistic**

$0 = \displaystyle\sum_{n=0}^{DPB} \dfrac{CF_n}{(1 + i)^n}$

13-4 **Discounted Payback Decision Rule**

Accept project if calculated DPB ≤ Maximum allowable discounted payback
Reject project if calculated DPB > Maximum allowable discounted payback

13-5 **NPV Statistic**

$NPV = \dfrac{CF_0}{(1 + i)^0} + \dfrac{CF_1}{(1 + i)^1} + \cdots + \dfrac{CF_N}{(1 + i)^N}$

$= \displaystyle\sum_{n=0}^{N} \dfrac{CF_n}{(1 + i)^n}$

13-6 **NPV Decision Rule**

Accept project if NPV ≥ 0
Reject project if NPV < 0

13-7 **Formula Comparison (13-5 to 13-8)**

Solve for NPV

$NPV = \displaystyle\sum_{n=0}^{N} \dfrac{CF_n}{(1 + i)^n}$ versus

Solve for IRR

$0 = \displaystyle\sum_{n=0}^{N} \dfrac{CF_n}{(1 + IRR)^n}$

13-8 **IRR Statistic**

$0 = \displaystyle\sum_{n=0}^{N} \dfrac{CF_n}{(1 + IRR)^n}$

13-9 **IRR Decision Rule**

Accept project if IRR ≥ Cost of capital
Reject project if IRR < Cost of capital

13-10 **Profitability Index Statistic**

$PI = \dfrac{NPV}{CF_0}$

13-11 **Profitability Index Decision Rule**

Accept project if PI ≥ 0
Reject project if PI < 0

14-1 Operating cycle = Days' sales in inventory + Average collection period

$$= \frac{\text{Inventory} \times 365}{\text{Cost of goods sold}} + \frac{\text{Accounts receivable} \times 365}{\text{Credit sales}}$$

14-2 Cash cycle = Operating cycle − Average payment period

$$= \text{Operating cycle} - \frac{\text{Accounts payable} \times 365}{\text{Cost of goods sold}}$$

14-3 Opportunity cost $= \dfrac{C}{2} \times i$

14-4 Trading cost $= \dfrac{T}{C} \times F$

14-5 Total cost $= \dfrac{C}{2} \times i + \dfrac{T}{C} \times F$

14-6 $C^{*} = \sqrt{2TF/i}$

14-7 $Z^{*} = \sqrt[3]{3F\sigma^{2}/4i_{day}} + L$

14-8 $H^{*} = 3Z^{*} - 2L$